Hubert Harrison

The John Hope Franklin Series in African American History and Culture
Waldo E. Martin Jr. and Patricia Sullivan, editors

The best scholarship in African American history and culture compels us to expand our sense of who we are as a nation and forces us to engage seriously the experiences of all Americans who have shaped the development of this country. By publishing pathbreaking books informed by several disciplines, the John Hope Franklin Series in African American History and Culture seeks to illuminate America's multicultural past and the ways in which it has informed the nation's democratic experiment.

A complete list of books published in the John Hope Franklin Series in African American History and Culture is available at https://uncpress.org/series/john-hope-franklin-series-african-american-history-culture.

Hubert Harrison

Forbidden Genius of Black Radicalism

BRIAN KWOBA

The University of North Carolina Press
Chapel Hill

This book was published with the assistance of the Authors Fund of the University of North Carolina Press.

© 2025 Brian Kwoba
All rights reserved

Set in Minion Pro by Westchester Publishing Services
Manufactured in the United States of America

Library of Congress Cataloging-in-Publication Data
Names: Kwoba, Brian, 1982– author.
Title: Hubert Harrison : forbidden genius of Black radicalism / Brian Kwoba.
Other titles: John Hope Franklin series in African American history and culture.
Description: Chapel Hill : The University of North Carolina Press, [2025] |
  Series: John Hope Franklin series in African American history and culture |
  Includes bibliographical references and index.
Identifiers: LCCN 2025001989 | ISBN 9781469675343 (cloth ; alk. paper) |
  ISBN 9781469675350 (pbk. ; alk. paper) | ISBN 9781469675367 (ebook) |
  ISBN 9781469687513 (pdf)
Subjects: LCSH: Harrison, Hubert H. | African American political activists—
  Biography. | African American journalists—Biography. | African American
  radicals—Biography. | Socialists—United States—Biography. | Harlem
  Renaissance. | BISAC: BIOGRAPHY & AUTOBIOGRAPHY / Cultural, Ethnic &
  Regional / African American & Black | POLITICAL SCIENCE / Political Ideologies
  / Radicalism | LCGFT: Biographies.
Classification: LCC E185.97.H367 K96 2025 | DDC 323.1196/0730092 [B]—dc23/
  eng/20250324
LC record available at https://lccn.loc.gov/2025001989

Cover artwork designed by Teddy Bechman.

Chapter 7 is a modified version of an article entitled "Pebbles and Ripples: Hubert Harrison and the Rise of the Garvey Movement," originally published in the *Journal of African American History* (Summer 2020) © ASALH. 1548-1867/2020/10503-0002. All Rights reserved. DOI: 10.1086/709374.

The map in chapter 5 was first published in Eltis & Richardson, *Atlas of the Transatlantic Slave Trade* (New Haven, CT: Yale University Press, 2010).
© Yale University Press. All rights reserved.

For product safety concerns under the European Union's General Product Safety Regulation (EU GPSR), please contact mailto:gpsr@mare-nostrum.co.uk or write to the University of North Carolina Press and Mare Nostrum Group B.V., Mauritskade 21D, 1091 GC Amsterdam, The Netherlands.

*Dedicated to the young people
into whose hands
this world
will eventually pass
and all of those
young and old
who still have the power
to change it*

Figure 0.1 Portrait of Hubert Harrison. Hubert H. Harrison Papers, flat box 740, Rare Book and Manuscript Library, Columbia University, New York.

Contents

List of Illustrations, ix
Preface, xi
Acknowledgments, xvii
Author's Note on Typography and Violence, xxiii

Introduction: The Crystallization of a Touchstone, 1

Chapter 1 Socialism or Southernism?, 28

Chapter 2 New Negro Politics: *The Voice*, the League, and the Liberals, 58

Chapter 3 Black Socrates in the Outdoor Grioversity, 90

Chapter 4 The White War and the Colored International, 120

Chapter 5 The Untamed, Untamable African, 156

Chapter 6 Black Free Love Politics and the Queer New Negro, 190

Chapter 7 Hubert Harrison: Global Mass Movement Catalyst, 226

Chapter 8 A Garvey Critic like No Other, 254

Chapter 9 The Renaissance School of Negro History, 282

Conclusion: The Forbidden Legacy of Hubert Harrison, 310

Notes, 329
Bibliography, 363
Index, 387

Illustrations

Figures

0.1 Hubert Harrison portrait photo, vi
I.1 Picture of a lynching, 17
1.1 John D. Rockefeller with the tiny little government, 29
1.2 "The Bosses of the Senate," 30
1.3 "The Hand That Will Rule the World" cartoon, 41
1.4 "At the Parting of the Ways" cartoon, 42
1.5 Hubert Harrison with Paterson Silk Strike leaders, 55
2.1 Frances Reynolds Keyser and the White Rose Home, 62
2.2 Liberty League poster, 1917, 66
2.3 Silent Protest Parade of July 1917, 70
2.4 Vladimir Lenin and Leon Trotsky in Teatralnaya Square, Moscow, 83
3.1 Harlem Street speaker in a large crowd, 92
3.2 Orator on a stepladder, 98
3.3 Hubert Harrison teaching a class on "World Problems of Race," 116
4.1 Cartoon of J. P. Morgan rowing Uncle Sam, 122
4.2 The Liberty Congress delegates, 141
5.1 Egyptian pyramids, 172
6.1 Hubert Harrison's sex lectures in 1917, 193
6.2 "Six Lectures on Sex and Sex Problems," 194
7.1 Liberty League membership card, 237
9.1 Ella Fitzgerald at the Savoy Ballroom in Harlem, 283
c.1 Hubert Harrison with a cane, 312

Maps

I.1 Lynchings in the United States, 18
5.1 Europeans' trans-Atlantic enslavement of Africans, 158–59

Preface

> Sure
> I may teach it *now*
> but
> believe it or not
> I never liked history

Not in elementary school, nor middle school, nor high school. I just never had a history teacher who made history relevant. In fact, I never even took a single history course as an undergraduate at Cornell University.

But after my junior year, I traveled to Cuba for academic research for the Cornell Undergraduate Research Scholars program, a trip that would change my life. The Cuban adventure set in motion a series of events that would lead me to Hubert Henry Harrison and to the dozen or so years I have spent working on this book about him.

In the summer of 2003, I went to Cuba as a plucky young jazz pianist in order to study *son*, salsa, Latin jazz, and the Spanish language. As fate would have it, the music conservatories were all closed for summer holiday break, so I ended up studying the music I heard in the streets: Afro-Cuban folkloric and ceremonial traditions like *Rumba* and *Batá*. It proved a formative experience because it planted the seeds of decolonization, reindigenization, and African spirituality in me that would begin to blossom many years later.

At the same time, the contrast between life on the ground in Cuba versus my USA-default Cold War view of the tiny Caribbean island nation was glaring. More importantly, it raised political, historical, and economic questions that my twenty-year-old self was not equipped to answer. Back then, I lacked the political consciousness to even have an opinion for or against the Iraq War when George W. Bush and Tony Blair launched the US-UK invasion of Iraq just a few months before my trip to Cuba.

While moving around Havana, the police repeatedly stopped me and asked for my ID, particularly when I visited touristy areas. However, when I showed them my US passport, they immediately backed down and apologized for bothering me.

Experiences like these and others raise a number of questions that I did not have the political awareness to answer. Why did the United States still relentlessly pursue a policy of blockade, embargo, and hostility to Cuba more than a decade after the Cold War had ended? Why did the Cuban police keep stopping me to ask for identification, as if performing a racial profiling operation on a suspicious, young Afro-Cuban, and then back off with embarrassed apologies when I showed them a foreign passport? (Sample answer: Cuba relied on tourism for economic support, so they were not keen on harassing international visitors.) Why doesn't the United States celebrate the achievements of the Cuban Revolution in areas like health care, literacy, and agriculture? Why was there such a large distance in political perspective between that of the elite European-descended Cuban family that I rented a room from (on the top floor of a posh high-rise apartment building in Vedado) and that of the Black working-class Cubans that I met in the streets of Havana? How in the world could the United States and Cuba—two governments administering what were clearly class-divided and racially stratified societies—represent the opposite ends of a spectrum of alternatives between "capitalism" and "communism"?

Upon my return to Cornell, I saw an offering in the fall 2003 course catalog titled "Masks of Power and Strategies of Resistance and Subversion." Taught by a Marxist Iranian anthropologist, Jakob Rigi, Dr. Rigi had a fascinating story, having been tortured as a political dissident under the US-backed Shah of Iran in the 1970s. Meanwhile, in that course I met amazing classmates like Malav Kanuga and Mark Olynciw. We engaged with books by figures like Noam Chomsky, Karl Marx, Vladimir Lenin, Subcomandante Marcos and the Zapatista movement, and anarchist books like *Days of War and Nights of Love: Crimethink for Beginners*.

In the following (spring 2004) semester of my senior year at Cornell, I joined the now-defunct International Socialist Organization (ISO). I started listening to Amy Goodman's radio and TV program *Democracy Now!* I also joined Cornell for Peace and Justice in order to activate my newfound political opposition to the US war on Iraq. My very first protest march took place in March of 2004, on the one-year anniversary of the "Shock and Awe" of the US invasion. I remember being right in front of a contingent of Bronx high schoolers who chanted, in a charmingly Ludacris fashion, "Move, Bush! Get out the way! Get out the way, Bush! Get out the way!" Thanks to books like Howard Zinn's *A People's History of the United States*, I began to develop an appreciation of history for the way it explains how we arrived at a situation in which the United States could and would kill a million Iraqis for oil right in front of our eyes.

In other words, not until I tried to change the world did I realize how important history is for explaining *how* we got the world that we now have. As a result of my discovery of radical political traditions like anarchism, Socialism, Communism, and Marxism, I began to piece together some powerful answers to my growing thirst for global economic, social, and political transformation.

I share these bits of my own story in order to contextualize my approach to Hubert Henry Harrison and to shed light on how and why I interpret his significance in the ways that I do. I found that studying Harrison and his world helped me to understand myself and my place in the world.

As the academics' joke goes, "research is *me*-search."

As someone born in the United States who has also lived in the UK and Kenya, I can relate to Hubert Henry Harrison's status as an immigrant with more than one national identity. As the child of a Black Kenyan father and a white British-descended mother, I have been fascinated by questions of racial Blackness and African ethnicity and national identity my whole adult life, much like Harrison. He once, tongue in cheek, signed a letter to the editor "A St. Croix Creole."

I first learned of Hubert Harrison in the summer of 2009, from a review by Brian Jones in *Socialist Worker* of the freshly published first volume of Jeff Perry's Harrison biography. Ever since my first encounter with his unique "voice of Harlem radicalism," I felt a spiritual kinship of sorts with Harrison, which would grow, deepen, and evolve the more I studied his ideas in the ensuing years.

Another reason for my interest in Harrison has to do with various life experiences we share. For example, I can relate to his experience as a young activist in—and then out—of the Socialist Party of America because I too spent some years in a Socialist organization during my twenties. Like Harrison, I became deeply inspired about building a Socialist party and dove into the branch work of selling newspapers, learning Marxist theory, studying radical labor and revolutions in history, and doing what we called "movement work." This usually meant single-issue political campaigns from which we could make progress toward immediate, concrete, and practical reforms (like marching for universal health care or doing blockades to prevent police from evicting poor people from their homes) while also recruiting more Socialists for the long-term struggle against the system.

Without realizing it initially, I had in fact joined an organization that descended from the same Socialist Party of America that Hubert Harrison once called his political home. Throughout my six years in the organization, I studied deeply the same Russian Revolution that Harrison witnessed from afar in real time. This explains in part why the Russian revolution serves as a recurring pedal point in this book.

In addition to the historical study and theoretical training, I got direct experience working on issues like Haiti solidarity, social justice trade unionism, immigrants' and workers' rights, Palestine solidarity, Green Party, and independent electoral political campaigns. So I've been to countless political marches, rallies, organizing meetings, and protests over the years. Just like Harrison.

And, like Harrison, I too eventually chafed at the bureaucratic, authoritarian, and top-down structure of the "revolutionary" Socialist organization supposedly committed to the emancipation of the working class "from below." Like Harrison, I started recruiting a group of young and promising new members and eventually developed and presented a sophisticated plan to grow and transform the organization from some of its old and stagnant ways. As in Harrison's case, the bureaucratic "leaders" of the organization were not inspired by my efforts to reach new constituencies. Instead, they apparently decided I posed a threat and launched a campaign of persecution against me. They created an intimidating atmosphere in which any idea that wasn't in line with theirs was relentlessly attacked by a barrage of more experienced members. This practice stifled new perspectives, induced passivity in the rank and file, and generated fear on the part of newer activists about speaking up or even asking questions.

Like Harrison, I eventually had to part ways with the Socialist organization I once held so near and dear. I then had decided to apply the lessons learned—both positive and negative—from the experience to a new phase of struggles, most immediately the Occupy Wall Street and Occupy Boston movements.

My time in the ISO left a bad taste in my mouth regarding white radicals and, like his own did for Harrison, the experience would lead me to put a much higher premium on racial consciousness as I began to turn my focus more intentionally toward questions of Black and pan-African liberation. For example, I recall with wistful nostalgia my work to help facilitate the founding of the People of Color Working Group within Occupy Boston, as well as Occupy the Hood in Roxbury and Ocupemos El Barrio in East Boston.

Long before I got to Hubert Harrison, I had begun to grapple with questions of Black history and African identity. But by now I had some basic familiarity with civil rights and Black Power, Malcolm X, Martin Luther King Jr., SNCC, the Black Panther Party, the anti-apartheid struggle in South Africa, and the story of the Haitian revolution as recounted in a life-changing book by CLR James called *The Black Jacobins*.

I can relate to Hubert Harrison's experience of losing his job as a postal clerk for his politics, having also been fired from a job for my politics. From

2007 to 2010, I taught high school history at the Cambridge Rindge and Latin School, a public high school in Cambridge, Massachusetts. I enjoyed teaching US and world history to the diverse range of students there, and I began to organize various extracurricular activities with them.

In 2008, I took students on a trip overseas to help build an elementary school in Tanzania. I revived the dormant Peace and Justice Club and organized an in-school assembly with guest speakers from Iraq Veterans Against the War. In January 2009, I sent an email to all staff announcing a meeting to address Israel's massive attack on the Gaza Strip ("Operation Cast Lead"). The administration lambasted me for having the audacity to "take a side" (as faculty advisor to the Peace Club, mind you). After this incident, the administration put up resistance to the posting of our club's flyers in the school and censored any mention of US foreign policy from our mission statement. I tried to bring the Palestinian hip-hop group DAM to the school, which the administration initially green-lighted then suddenly forbade a couple of days later. I cochaperoned a busload of our LGBTQ students and allies to the National Equality March in Washington, DC, in 2009. After the devastating 2010 earthquake in Haiti, we tried to organize a rally for Haiti with the Haitian Students Club, which they also prohibited.

In the last semester before I was due to achieve tenure, I suddenly got a negative work evaluation (even though all my previous evaluations had been positive), which became the excuse for them to not renew my contract. To make a longer story short, I secured a meeting with the superintendent, and I brought with me the affirmative action officer for the school district, the teacher's union vice president, a parent who had put up a petition online to retain me (which garnered a signature from Noam Chomsky!), and questions like, How can the school district retain its precious few Black teachers if they keep getting rid of us? The superintendent listened politely and then a few weeks later upheld my school principal's decision to get rid of me. Like Hubert Harrison's firing from his postal job for criticizing Booker T. Washington, my sudden job loss did not cause me to moderate my politics. Instead, it opened my eyes wider to the injustice of the system and fueled my fire for broader political awakening and transformation.

In order to speak freely to the public outdoors, Harrison got arrested multiple times as part of a larger fight for free speech alongside other Socialists, Wobblies, and freethinkers who defied prohibitions on outdoor public speechmaking in the early twentieth century. Like Harrison, I too have been arrested on more than one occasion for doing political activism.

I can relate to Harrison's enormous heart and the expansive love he had for the people. I can also relate to Harrison's freethinking and agnosticism as someone who considered myself an atheist during my years as a card-carrying Socialist. I can relate to his eclecticism, because I too am fascinated by a wide range of subjects and bodies of knowledge. I can relate to Harrison's experience with multiple and overlapping (and sometimes contradictory or even counterproductive) efforts at liberation. I've learned new things from studying his attempts to integrate various ideas to reach even more forward-thinking perspectives. Far more than just a serious scholarly study, this book for me contains many hard-won lessons from my own life's journey as a truth seeker. A huge part of my heart-mind resides in these pages. It is my testament.

I can relate to Harrison speaking multiple languages, having struggled to learn Spanish, then Japanese, then Russian, then KiSwahili. My mother had a decades-long career as a public school teacher of French, Spanish, and Japanese language, and it's thanks to her that I became a teacher myself. Harrison was nothing if not a teacher, especially when perched on a stepladder addressing large crowds outdoors on street corners. As a teacher and an activist, I can relate to the drive to teach so freely and wi(l)dely. Before teaching high school, I had worked in an elementary school. After my firing from Rindge, I taught middle school. So as a teacher writing about another teacher, I try throughout the book to teach not only about Harrison but also about what the many radical and liberatory traditions in which he stood still have to teach us.

Acknowledgments

I must first thank my mother Susan Jean Goddard for her tireless help with editing my work—and for birthing and raising me! Like Harrison, I developed a great love for teaching and learning, and it all began with my mother, who planted the seeds of the teacher's ethos in me at a young age. I simply would not be the person I am without her wellspring of warmth, encouragement, and unconditional love. A poem expressing my gratitude for her would take a million epic verses. Same goes for my grandmother, Jean Southard Goddard, who in another plane remains a beacon of light and love from which all her descendants are continuously warmed. I give thanks to my grandfather Douglas, who I never got to meet in person, and my great-grandparents Myra and Robert Woodruff "Bopi" Southard, and Bertin and Clara Goddard. I give thanks to my maternal uncles Dale and Rob, who chose to play a pragmatic, loving role as my father figures when I was growing up. Over time, that has come to mean more to me than I can put into words. Thanks to all my English ancestors!

I give thanks to my biological father, Frederick Walidadi Kwoba. I'll always cherish the memories of his role in my introduction to *Sarafina!*, Paul Simon, Ladysmith Black Mambazo, Tracy Chapman, and rafting on the Charles River. I also give thanks to the grandparents I never got to meet in person, Kwoba and Selina, without whom I would not be here and who surely have contributed to my life in countless unseen ways. I give thanks to my great grandfather Musolongwa and to all my Kenyan ancestors.

I give thanks to the whole family of my late adopted father, the Harlem Hospital–born revolutionary Kwame Ajamu Montsho Somburu (1934–2016), for his unforgettable influence and inspiration.

I give thanks to all the people, including Rev. Ethelred Brown, John G. Jackson, John Henrik Clarke, Philip Foner, Portia James, Robert Hill, Winston James, Joyce Moore Turner, Ernest Allen, Richard B. Moore, Harold Cruse, J. A. Rogers, Irma Watkins-Owens, Thabiti Asukile, Herb Boyd, Jared Ball, Wilfred Samuels, and Irwin Marcus, who have helped preserve the memory of Hubert Henry Harrison.

The most influential scholar in my decision and ability to undertake this research remains the late Jeffrey B. Perry. I can hardly imagine having decided to make Harrison the focus of my doctoral research if not for Perry's decades of scholarly work and decisive initial encouragement of my interest in studying Harrison. Perry's tireless effort set the bar for writing about Harrison at a level one could only hope to reach by the better part of a lifetime of dedication. I caught the spark from Perry's infectious enthusiasm for the "father of Harlem radicalism."

I give thanks for my doctoral program supervisor at Oxford, Stephen Tuck, for his patience with me and especially for the free rein he gave me ideologically, intellectually, and politically. He provided me with valuable and consistent guidance, helping me hone and refine my thinking. He wisely—and regularly—pushed me to situate Harrison in his wider world. From agreeing to supervise me as a doctoral student, to encouraging me to go after what inspired me, to the countless meetings in which he shared his feedback and suggestions, to letting me teach his undergraduates about Harrison, to establishing the "Race and Resistance" seminar at TORCH (The Oxford Research Centre in the Humanities), to hosting the Callaloo conference and fiftieth anniversary of Malcolm X at Oxford and other events, there are so many things for which I can only thank Stephen. I cannot imagine what my academic experience at Oxford would have been like without his unwavering and enthusiastic support.

I give thanks for my scholarly mentors and supporters: Robin D. G. Kelley, Minkah Makalani, Claudrena Harold, Russell Rickford, Gerald Horne, Keisha Blain, and J. T. Roane. Carole Boyce Davies has offered me exceptional encouragement, including an invitation to a Caribbean studies conference in St. Croix, generative feedback on my manuscript, and so many other forms of support, for which I'm eternally grateful. I'm also grateful for the generous feedback from Josh Myers and Tommy Curry on the draft of my manuscript.

I give thanks for scholars of my generation who not only gave feedback on my work but stimulated my growth in multiple ways, including Ben Woods, J. T. Roane, Charisse Burden-Stelly, Ashley Farmer, Randi Gill-Sadler, Adom Getachew, Sandy Placido, Jarvis Givens, Takiyah Harper-Shipman, Shamara Wyllie Hassan, the Masterminds group, Ben Weber, the Caribbean Studies Association, and the Association for the Study of African American Life and History (ASALH).

I have a special place in my heart for all the activists, scholars, and social justice advocates who inspired or supported me in the course of my doctoral program, including Steve Cohen, Abdi Ali, Victor Yang, Tyler Alabanza-Behard, Mbongeni Ndlovu, Adam Elliot-Cooper, Shakina Chinedu, Patricia Daley, Dalumuzi Mhlanga, Simukai Chigudu, Anu Henriques, Lina Ahmed Abushouk, Kofi Klu, Esther Stanford-Xosei, Nathaniel Adam Tobias Coleman, Hope Levy-Shepherd, and Hassan Mwakimako. I give thanks for the

Oxford Pan-Afrikan Forum, "I, Too, Am Oxford," Skin Deep, the Oxford Black Students Union, the Oxford African-Caribbean Society, the Oxford Africa Society, and the Campaign for Racial Awareness and Equality. Y'all taught me so much!

I also have a special place in my heart for my Rhodes Must Fall comrades, particularly Sizwe Mpofu-Walsh, Tadiwa Madenga, Ntokozo Qwabe, Athinangamso Esther Nkopo, Rose Chantiluke, Marc Shi, Ndjodi Ndeunyema, Roné McFarlane, Arthur Eirich, Max Harris, Zakir Gul, Oluwafemi Nylander, Miriam Kilimo, Rachel Harmon, Claudio Sopranzetti, and Julian Brave NoiseCat, for helping to humanize Oxford as we attempted to decolonize it too. I give thanks also to the many Oxford community activists outside the university—Junie James, Sister Pat Green, Chaka Artwell, Dan Glazebrook, and Angelique Bayley—for keeping me grounded.

I give thanks for the many lessons in Marxist political theory, global revolutionary history, and community organizing that I gained while in the International Socialist Organization. In the years following my days as a card-carrying Socialist, I've been involved in other movements, including Occupy Wall Street, Palestine solidarity, and Black Lives Matter. I'm grateful for all that I've learned from campaigns like these and the wide array of self-sacrificing activists I've met along the way.

I thank my various readers, including Michael Kebede, Claudio Sopranzetti, Imaobong Umoren, Musab Younis, Lloyd Pratt, Pekka Hämäläinen, Mara Keire, Kristin Hoganson, Michael O. West, David Thurston, Kevin Cobham, V. P. Franklin, K. T. Ewing, Derefe Chevannes, and the American History Graduate Seminar at the Rothermere American Institute, who all gave valuable feedback on individual chapters. I'm grateful for the help of Aidan Majewski's research assistance.

I give a special shout-out and thanks to the cohort of scholars-in-residence I joined in 2021–22 at the Schomburg Center for Research in Black Culture, including Gail Dottin, Sean Smith, Abosede George, Naomi Jackson, Jessica Larson, Nina Mercer, Alexis Callendar, Petra Richterova, Stephane Robolin, Laila Amine, Marina Bilbija, and Arlene Keizer. And, of course, a huge thank-you and shout-out to the incomparable Brent Hayes Edwards, who gave so generously of his time and knowledge to all of us. Without the Schomburg residency, I would not have had the means to write the chapter on Black free love politics (chapter 6), the most challenging to write, but also perhaps the most stimulating in this book!

I thank my Boricua atheist Communist padrino Ricardo Ortiz-Pérez for teaching me so much about revolutionary, anti-imperialist, and working-class politics, theory, and history on so many different levels. Muchas gracias padrino! A big thanks to my love gurus: Kenya, Rakhem, Malika, and Evita.

Speaking of Kenyans, I must give thanks to my day-ones, Kiama, Mwaura, and Ngotho Kaara, and to Mama Wahu and the extended Kikuyu family. I also give thanks to Martin, mzee Lusaka, mama Anne, Manase Wanjala, Pamela, Vincent, and my blood relatives on the Luhya side. I'm also grateful for Waluhya Watano Maprofesa wa Memphis: Shadrack Nasong'o, Bernadette Ombayo, Selina Makana, and Samson Ndanyi. Shout-out to ndugu zangu wa Tanzania pia: Yusuph, Seth, and Leo. And, of course, to all those who have offered their love, support, friendship, and hard-learned lessons on the ground in the Motherland. Y'all have made me so much stronger and more grounded. Hakuna mahali kama nyumbani! I love y'all! Asanteni sana!

I give thanks to Beverly Bond, Dennis Laumann, Aram Goudsouzian, Cookie Woolner, Andrew Daily, Amanda Lee Savage, Michael Monahan, and all my University of Memphis colleagues for welcoming me to be a part of their world. I give thanks to the many other comrades, scholars, grad students, and friends I have met in Memphis too, including Akil Mensah, Danyel Clark, Evelyn Jackson, Jasper St. Bernard, Corey Reed, John Torrey, Luvell Anderson, Shirletta Kinchen, James Conway, Terrence Tucker, Andre E. Johnson, Shelby Crosby, Ladrica Menson-Furr, Earnestine Jenkins, Alexandrea Golden, Kalemba Kizito, Cam Mtenzi, Kairys Slayer, Paola Cavallari, Aniya Gold, Damarius Harris, the Graduate Association of African American History, all the students who have taken my history courses over the years, and so many others. I give a special shout-out to my student interns: Zurich McGhee for his help with the bibliography and Brianna Harrison for her gracious help with editing the draft chapters of the manuscript and copyediting the endnotes. I also give thanks for my editors at The University of North Carolina Press, Brandon Proia and Andrew Winters. Thanks to Mary Ann Lieser for the index and production editor Michelle Scott.

Big thanks to Yvette N. Richardson-Hudson, a great-granddaughter of Hubert Harrison, who gave me her blessing for this book. I also give thanks to those who offered insight and perspective on Harrison's relationship to St. Croix: Chenzira Kahina, Russell Christopher, and George Tyson.

I give thanks for the years of encouragement from my ex-wife, Anasstassia Baichorova. Her idea that I apply for doctoral study at Oxford was one of the ways her influence pushed me to grow and evolve during our time together.

I give thanks to my best man, Wadson Michel, who not only makes me smile every time I think of him but also inspires me to live life to the fullest and always make time for joy and fun.

I give thanks to my spiritual teachers and kinfolk, including George Keith, Art Lande, Thomas, Naiima, los niños santos, Wayne Snellgrove, Christian "Dessalines" Guerrier, Malidoma and Sobonfu Somé, Sherri Mitchell, and Hadithi, for holding space for me to heal, decolonize, and reindigenize. And

I give a hearty, long-distance, and interstellar thanks to John William Coltrane, one of my greatest spiritual teachers of all and truly a love supreme.

I also give a big and hearty thanks to the wondrous young Zambian pencil artist Teddy Bechman for his masterful pencil drawing (not photo!) that graces the book cover.

Author's Note on Typography and Violence

In the early twentieth century, a range of figures including W. E. B. Du Bois, Hubert Harrison, Ida B. Wells-Barnett, and Robert R. Moton fought for the capitalization of the *n* in the printed word *Negro*. They felt that because the group that is today most commonly referred to as "African American" formed a distinct ethnoracial minority in the United States, it deserved to have its name capitalized, much like Jewish American, Italian American, or Irish American people did. As a term of racial classification, *Negro* in many ways corresponded to *Caucasian*, whose capitalization did not generate controversy. Although most newspapers did not capitalize the *n* in the word *negro* in 1900, by the 1930s many mainstream publications and newspapers had changed their editorial policy. The *New York Times*, for example, began to capitalize the *n* in *Negro* on the grounds that "it is an act in recognition of racial self-respect for those who have been for generations in 'the lower case'" (March 7, 1930).

In the modern period, the Spanish-derived word *Negro* is no longer used, having been replaced with its English equivalent. For the same reasons stated above, I choose to capitalize the *b* in *Black* when referring to this group. I do this not only to pay respect to the previous struggle for typographical dignity but also as an analogous contemporary assertion of dignity as against the status of inferiority that continues today in new forms for people of African descent in the United States and beyond.

This book also contains an image (in the introduction) of a lynching, the horrific method of maniacal mob murder that was widespread grew into a national epidemic in Harrison's time.

Hubert Harrison

Introduction: The Crystallization of a Touchstone

> Hubert Henry Harrison
> broke his foot off
> in everybody's *ass*
>
> It wasn't personal
> but political
>
> He lived
> in troubled and turbulent
> times

He saw staggering luxury for the few alongside misery and poverty for the many. A world in which the terrorism of white supremacy brought daily headlines of racial horrors. Where imperial conquest and world war wrought destruction upon entire countries and nations of people. A world where a global pandemic threatened an already precarious human condition all across the planet. A world in which the capitalist "robber barons"—those who paid off politicians to enact laws oppressing women, immigrants, racial minorities, and other scapegoats—got rich through their relentless exploitation of working people and children.

Hubert Henry Harrison's significance—as a journalist, thinker, activist, and community educator in the early twentieth century—lies in his crystallization of radical answers to radical problems that continue to haunt humanity right into the twenty-first century.

A Messenger of the Grassroots

Hubert Harrison celebrated the great potential he saw in the youth. Speaking of the old guard African American leaders, he noted in 1924 that "whether in their day they called themselves radicals or subservients is nothing to the point.... Having done what little they could do for progress, their control of the line of march is now a bar to further progress. They must make way for Youth—gladly or sadly, but they must make way."[1]

His faith in young people dovetailed with his belief in the power and dignity of the Black masses more generally:

> When I hear great masses of my fellow-men referred to as "rats" . . . I recall how in the great Washington and Chicago race-riots it was the "rats" who upheld the honor of the race and fought to maintain its safety from murderous assaults. I feel that we owe them a vast debt of gratitude, even though they belong to the lowest levels of those whom we call the Common People. Much golden eloquence has been squandered upon the successful and the good; much stern condemnation has been vented upon the wicked and unclad. I venture now to plead for those of our poor brothers and sisters who are despised and rejected of men. For after all they are the real tests of our theories of brotherhood and racial solidarity.[2]

Harrison did not look to an elite "talented tenth" of African Americans for the salvation or leadership of Black people. "By and large, the Common People are the real race," he wrote. "They may not have much to give, but, such as it is, they give it without stint; loyalty, respect, friendliness and help in the hour of need. . . . They are a perpetual reservoir of healthy enthusiasm and their rough but genuine appreciation is like a tonic to the soul that is sick of the shams and insincerities of those who call themselves 'cultured.' They are the dependable back-bone of every good cause and the making of many." Harrison's love for the people helped him to alchemize a multiplicity of Black radical politics of, by, and for the grassroots.[3]

A Kaleidoscope of Radical Gemstones

> It was [Harrison's newspaper] *The Voice* that really crystallized the radicalism of the Negro in New York and its environs.
>
> —Harlem activist Hodge Kirnon

What does it mean to be "radical"? The powers that be would have us associate this word with irrational or violent extremism. But civil rights movement mother and Harlem-trained grassroots organizer Ella Baker spoke eloquently to the true definition of what it means to be radical: "In order for us as poor and oppressed people to become a part of a society that is meaningful, the system under which we now exist has to be radically changed. This means that we are going to have to learn to think in radical terms. I use the term radical in its original meaning—getting down to and understanding the root cause. It means facing a system that does not lend itself to your needs and devising means by which you change that system."[4]

Hubert Harrison was radical in this sense—getting to the root of the systems that created the world-historical injustices that he witnessed in real time. Given the continuities between his day and ours, his multidimensional political vision presents many ways of seeing possibilities for social transformation in the present. His story offers radical inspiration for what we can aspire to think, feel, dream, and achieve.

What does it mean to be a crystallizer? A crystal is a solid form with component atoms or molecules highly organized into a distinctive structure. A crystal gemstone is one that can have a more amorphous or unpredictable arrangement. Chemists who want to synthesize new compounds often have difficulty getting them to crystallize, but once the first breakthrough takes place, it can become the seed form for a rapid and widespread proliferation of a new structure, which often supersedes the crystalline forms that preceded it.[5] Hubert Harrison crystallized an array of groundbreaking political radicalisms for a traumatized and traumatizing world.

In the face of the superexploitation of working people by the likes of John D. Rockefeller, Andrew Carnegie, and J. P. Morgan—the capitalist robber barons of the Gilded Age—Harrison crystallized a secular Black revolutionary Socialist politics. In so doing, he theorized the role of anti-Black racial oppression in preventing the emancipation of the working class from the wage slavery of industrial capitalism.

In contrast to the Eurocentric mass media and education systems, Harrison's spellbinding street-corner speaking, commitment to grassroots empowerment, fearless journalism, and encyclopedic knowledge allowed him to crystallize a new and revolutionary model—what some called the "Outdoor University"—for free urban Black emancipatory education. It stood in stark contrast to both the industrial education symbolized by Booker T. and Margaret Murray Washington's Tuskegee Institute *and* the "higher" elite education of the colleges and universities that were inaccessible to the masses of Black people. Perched atop a sidewalk stepladder at 135th Street and Seventh Avenue and addressing audiences large enough to block traffic, Harrison spoke on subject matter ranging across such topics as African American art and popular culture, sociology, scientific racism, English literature, evolutionary biology, theological criticism, African history, macroeconomics, and global geopolitics. A. Philip Randolph aptly described this model of education as "one of the great intellectual forums in America."[6]

In the face of rampant racism in white society and President Woodrow Wilson's decision to take the United States of America into World War I, Harrison helped crystallize Harlem's political "New Negro" movement. Calling for voting rights for Black men and Black women, federal antilynching legislation, armed self-defense, and an end to Jim Crow racial oppression, Harrison's Liberty League of Negro-Americans cohered a pan-African and people-centered movement for Black self-empowerment. By recruiting and training an unknown Jamaican immigrant by the name of Marcus Garvey,

Harrison's Liberty League catalyzed the emergence of the largest international organization of Black people in modern history.

Harrison spoke out about injustices taking place all over the globe. Standing against European colonialism and the predatory imperial powers of the world, Harrison crystallized a new form of radical internationalism in his groundbreaking theorization of the "Colored International." As a revolutionary political alliance of colonized peoples in the Islamic world, India, the Caribbean, Latin America, Africa, Europe, and Asia, the Colored International he envisioned would smash the giant triplets of capitalism, imperialism, and white racial domination.

In a city where white people put a Congolese man named Ota Benga on display in the Bronx Zoo, Harrison self-identified as an "untamed, untamable African" and crystallized a model of African consciousness for the Black diaspora based on his deep study of African history, culture, and politics.[7]

After a childhood upbringing steeped in the Anglican Church, Harrison broke with Christianity and religion more generally. He would later emerge as the most prominent Black freethinker of his generation. As against the conservative dogmas of the church, Harrison crystallized—for a new generation—a Black agnosticism grounded in modern science, empirical evidence, and rational explanation over religious dogma. As a militant "truth seeker," he demanded the taxation of church properties, an end to prayers in school and courtroom Bible oaths, and a complete separation of church and state.

In the face of federal government censorship, repression, and criminalization of sexuality—and widespread policing of sexual morality by the church—Harrison crystallized a Black free love politics. In that respect, he emerged among the earliest of Black voices advocating for legalizing access to contraception, offering public-facing courses in sex education, and explicitly advancing a conception of love based on variety and freedom from compulsory monogamy and the Puritanical sex-negativity of US culture and society.

As a result of crystallizing so many political breakthroughs, Harrison developed a kaleidoscopic radicalism that connected multiple worlds of counter-hegemonic knowledge. As Kirnon put it, "Harrison was the first Negro who boldly preached racialism and all forms of radicalism in New York. He preached them continuously and consistently. He was the first Negro whose radicalism was comprehensive enough to include racialism, science, politics, sociology and education in a thorough-going, scientific manner."[8]

By integrating Harrison's broad array of radical perspectives—and applying his intellectually eclectic way of remixing them—we can generate new angles of vision that connect forces like capital, the state, racial oppression, colonialism, gender and sexuality repression, religion, science, corporate media, fossil fuel domination, and the education system. Harrison's life also shows how the social movements against these forces held the power to transform political horizons and open up profound and revolutionary possibilities.

Harrison's legacy defies easy categorization and cannot be pigeonholed into any single political framework. His propensity for shattering orthodox categories and taking radical thought beyond a boundary requires one to study many different traditions in order to fully understand and appreciate his ideas and actions. Because he integrated Socialist, Black (inter)nationalist, freethinking, sexually liberated, *and* African-centered valences of political radicalism, people familiar with any one (or none) of these frameworks who study Harrison have an opportunity to rethink the relationship of each of these formulations *in light of each other.*

Said differently, Harrison offers a unique point of departure for a kind of "unified field theory" of radical politics that reveals revolutionary possibilities inherent in the integration of liberatory traditions that are too often compartmentalized from one another. Engaging the many dimensions of Harrison's politics, therefore, presents a singularity through which multiple streams of radical thought can illuminate and expand each other, as the interconnected pieces of a larger puzzle.

Harlemites like Kirnon eulogized Harrison's brilliant mind with a twinge of humor: "I think it was Thomas Carlyle who defined genius as the infinite capacity for taking pains, but another able thinker conceived it as the ability to do without effort what others have to labor to perform. Hubert Harrison's great ability took the middle ground between these two opposing views."[9] To his friend and brilliant self-taught historian from Jamaica J. A. Rogers, Harrison "was not only perhaps the foremost Afro-American intellect of his time, but one of America's greatest minds."[10]

Harrison, of course, was not the only learned mind in Harlem. Writing from his home neighborhood, Harrison himself noted how "I can walk a mile from the place where this is written and converse with the ablest economist of our race. A few blocks north I can shake hands with our best biologist (barring Ernest Just). I am acquainted with a journalist who slings niftier prose than anyone else whom I know, and a scholar whose book reveals a wider historic knowledge of racial contacts than any other scholar, white or Black. Their names? Well you would not recognize them if I gave them here. For Harlem doesn't 'boost' Harlem."[11] Harrison here touched on one of the intellectual consequences of racial segregation: the singular brains that do exist in Black communities often go unrecognized (and therefore unknown) by the dominant white society.

The famous New York City–born evolutionary biologist Stephen Jay Gould spoke to this problem when he mentioned that he "[was], somehow, less interested in the weight and convolutions of Einstein's brain than in the near certainty that people of equal talent have lived and died in cotton fields and sweatshops."[12] Unfortunately, "genius" is coded white and male and math/sci, as in Einstein's case. But the genius (which shares a root with generative force) of Blackness is always a collectivity. *Ubuntu* and *umoja*. Far from the only underappreciated mind in Harlem, he naturally worked out his ideas in collaboration and contestation with the larger communities to which he belonged.

Wisdom can come from any direction, and Harrison's insights came from many. His multidimensionality presents a proverbial kaleidoscope of visionary politics. By bringing together many different radical traditions in one place, any serious engagement with Harrison inevitably requires us to reflect critically on our own assumptions and to look in the mirror in ways that might make us uncomfortable. This book invites us to lean into that discomfort. Deeper intellectual understanding and political growth can emerge more readily from sitting with uncomfortable feelings and listening to what they have to teach us, rather than running away from them.

I set the stage this way because examining the world through Harrison's eyes often presents a challenging encounter with some of our most cherished myths and deeply internalized beliefs. Whenever I reread them, I'm often nearly as startled by the force of his ideas as I was when I first encountered them. He challenges us to think outside the box.

So why had I not heard about Hubert Henry Harrison sooner?

Erasing Writing Hubert Harrison from Out of History

> There are those who will consider it their duty, as "friends of the Negro people," to tell us to revile him, to flee, even from the presence of his memory, to save ourselves by writing him out of the history of our turbulent times.
>
> —Ossie Davis, "Eulogy for Malcolm X"

On the chilly morning of Saturday, February 27, 1965, Ossie Davis gave his famous eulogy at the funeral of Malcolm X (El Hajj Malik El-Shabazz) in Harlem. Davis's comment above offers a commentary not just on Malcolm's legacy but perhaps even more poignantly on Harrison's. While everyone knows of Malcolm X, most people alive today have never even heard of Hubert Henry Harrison. And herein lies the problem. Harrison's ideas—groundbreaking and profoundly influential in his own time—have been speaking to the present ever since he walked the streets of Harlem. However, his impact and legacy have been largely erased from scholarly history and popular memory. For example, the University of Oxford's five-volume *Encyclopedia of African American History* mentions his name only four times, always just in passing.[13]

Most Black history books have likewise omitted any mention of Harrison, as have the high school history textbooks.

Only twenty years after Harrison's death, J. A. Rogers could already make the exact same observation. Rogers spoke of how "no one worked more seriously and indefatigably to enlighten his fellow men . . . but others, unquestionably his inferiors, received the recognition that was his due. Even today [only] a very small proportion of the Negro intelligentsia has ever heard of him."[14] Since at least 1947, Harrison has remained largely unknown to most of the public.

How has he been so thoroughly forgotten?

Of course, Harrison had a number of flaws, contradictions, and limitations. He did a terrible job as a manager of his finances, for instance. He was also humble to a fault, making it easier for others to take credit for his accomplishments. He spoke with a bluntness and candor that many of his interlocutors did not appreciate. Moreover, as Harrison's biographer Jeffrey Perry has argued, "though he worked with many organizations and played important roles in several key ones, he had no long term, sustaining, and identifying relationship with any [single] organization or institution, and so lacked the recognition and support that would have come with such a tie."[15] Yet even the most well-known historical figures all had their spots and their wrinkles too. Why didn't that stop *them* from being celebrated and memorialized down through the ages?

The Crystallizer as Touchstone

To understand Harrison's historical erasure, we can riff on a metaphor that he himself employed: the touchstone. "Politically," Harrison observed, "the Negro is the touchstone of the modern democratic idea. The presence of the Negro puts our democracy to the proof and reveals the falsity of it." A touchstone is a hard, dark stone that is used to test the purity of precious metals by seeing what kinds of streaks they leave behind when rubbed against it. To illustrate his point about the Negro as the touchstone of democracy, he gave the example of the Declaration of Independence (a founding document of the United States), which seemed to articulate a "splendid truth" by declaring that "all men are created equal." However, he noted, "the Black man merely touched it and it became a splendid lie."[16] After all, the enslavement of Africans (not to mention the oppression of Indigenous peoples, women, and poor European Americans) gave lie to the Declaration's claim about equality.

Harrison's restoration to the historiographies of political formations that he helped crystallize reveals him to be a proverbial "touchstone" that puts them to the test and reveals their limitations. In particular, when we restore

Harrison's example to the history of the Socialist/Communist parties, the Garvey movement, or the "Harlem Renaissance," they quickly lose some of their most defining claims. For example, how does the Socialist Party's claim—that they represented the political party for the emancipation of working people—look in the face of the rampant attitudes of indifference, neglect, and even outright endorsement of relentless racial violence against African Americans, who comprised the most ruthlessly exploited section of the US working class, as Harrison attempted to show them? How do Marcus Garvey's claims of having 20,000 delegates at the Universal Negro Improvement Association's first international convention and 4 million members in the organization hold up in the face of Harrison's authoritative firsthand observation that Garvey had "plastered the air with lies" to achieve these astronomically inflated figures? What happens to the standard narrative about the "Negro Renaissance" in light of Harrison's claim that "the matter of a Negro literary renaissance is like that of the snakes of Ireland—there isn't any"?[17]

In other words, Harrison's example makes hallowed myths into hollow creeds, like a touchstone revealing the impurities of the metal that it touches. After all, he criticized the Socialists, the Garvey movement, and the so-called Harlem Renaissance *from within* and in ways that revealed an embarrassing gap between what they practiced and what they preached. For some, his very existence created too much cognitive dissonance, a phenomenon that journalist Pam Atherton described so perfectly: "Sometimes people hold a core belief that is very strong. When they are presented with evidence that works against that belief, the new evidence cannot be accepted. It would create a feeling that is extremely uncomfortable called cognitive dissonance. And because it is so important to protect the core belief, they will rationalize, ignore and even deny anything that doesn't fit in with the core belief."[18] Much of the erasure and marginalization of Harrison in the history books flows from the way his example creates cognitive dissonance for so many orthodoxies of political thought.

When Harrison felt that the organization he joined no longer respected him (or he no longer respected it), he left and often made some very sharp criticisms of them. These critiques stung not only those organizations but also their historians, who tend to replicate their research subjects' disinterest in remembering Harrison. For example, the white ignorance of the Socialist Party loves to reappear in its historians. Harrison's historic marginalization thus speaks to a very human problem: the difficulty of receiving criticism. "As a people," wrote the late great John Henrik Clarke, "we have not carefully listened to our greatest messengers. Harrison was one of them."[19] Part of the reason we haven't listened to Harrison is that too often we would rather take serious criticism personally than politically so that we can ignore the cognitive dissonance or uncomfortable truth in the criticism.

Harrison understood the dangers of challenging figures and institutions that people hold near and dear. By his own admission, "I know the tremendous weight of the social proscription which it is possible to bring to bear upon those who dare defy the idols of our tribe. For those who live by the people must... be careful of the people's gods." And yet, he refused to relinquish his commitment to telling the truth, however inconvenient or disturbing it may be. In this way, Harrison functions as a touchstone of Black kryptonite to many different people's "gods."[20] So buckle up and get ready.

While his fearlessness in voicing candid criticisms surely stung those who otherwise might have kept his memory alive, Harrison didn't make it a personal matter. In fact, he took issue with those who did not make a distinction between personal relationships and political ideas. Regarding people like this, he regretted how "if you oppose them in politics they make a personal matter of it: either you must always hold the same political views as they, or you must become their personal enemies. The only other alternative is to keep your mouth shut as a point of politeness, so far as these real differences are concerned." This latter point speaks to the still common practice of keeping politics away from the dinner table and from "polite" and "respectable" conversations. By contrast, "we ourselves developed under quite different conditions," recalled Harrison. "In the days of our apprenticeship at old St. Benedict's [Catholic] and St. Mark's [AME Church] lyceums, the fiercest opposition in debate could not take from the cordiality of personal friendship... and this manner we propose to take with us into public life."[21] (And into this book!)

Political disagreement need not—and did not, for Harrison—entail personal enmity. But the targets of his criticism, especially the most prominent and egotistical of them, did not operate this way. "He died... for his convictions," noted Harlem resident Edgar Grey in his eulogy of Harrison. "He died at 44, starved, underpaid, abused, hated by jealous men who feared the force of his mind and the immensity of his information."[22] (And into this book!)

Scholars of a particular figure or organization are often ideologically partisan toward it and therefore less comfortable remembering—let alone actually engaging with—forceful internal critics like Harrison. As Harrison once observed, "Even savants are prone to forget that they do most of their thinking with their desires, beliefs, prejudices and subconscious urges, which they then proceed to rationalize."[23] This explains, in part, why those who are partial to one or another ideological framework that Harrison criticized have so often run from him—whether consciously or subconsciously—like a rich person avoiding a beggar. His legacy has been forbidden precisely because it forces us to rethink fundamentally what we think we know—about everything from poverty, war, and racism, to love, sex, and religion.

And this is precisely why it is so revealing to study Hubert Henry Harrison.

On the one hand, the most relevant historiographies—of Black Marxism, Black freethinkers, Garveyism, Black sexual liberation, and the New Negro "Renaissance"—have either marginalized or omitted him entirely. On the other hand, Harrison played a groundbreaking role in the crystallization of each of these formations. Therefore, putting him back into the picture opens multiple highly revealing angles of vision on the conjunctures both within and between them.

Recovering Harrison's legacy requires us to: reexamine the history of Black people in relation to the Socialist and Communist Parties; recover a forgotten strand of Black class-conscious, anti-imperialist, "colored" internationalism; reframe the spatial and intellectual possibilities for Black liberatory education in light of Harlem's "Outdoor University"; rethink the genealogy of the Black secular and freethinking traditions; reappraise the origins and pitfalls of the global Garvey movement; reinterrogate the mythology of the "Harlem Renaissance"; excavate an onyx crystalline layer in the historical geology of free love politics.

In short, to reimagine the horizons of the Black radical tradition.

The long-standing exclusion of Harrison from historiography and memory, alongside his crystallography of influential ideas and radical breakthroughs, also forces us to reckon with the politics of historical narratives—and the eerie silences we have erected in relation to our past. That such an innovative mover and shaker as Harrison could remain obscure for so long speaks to the power and resilience of the many factors and forces that converged to erase him from history, a theme which we will revisit in greater depth in the book's conclusion.

Not Biography but Intellectual History

In my efforts to interpret Harrison's significance and restore him to the recognition he deserves, I have built on the work of individuals and communities that precede me. Harrison's church offers a startling and ironic example. In the 1930s, following Harrison's death, the Jamaica-born Reverend Egbert Ethelred Brown, a Unitarian Universalist, renamed his Harlem Unitarian Church the Hubert Harrison Memorial Church. For an agnostic freethinker to be given a status tantamount to sainthood by a Black church gives a sense of the immense *spiritual* power Harrison carried in his home neighborhood of

Harlem. It is one of the only churches in history explicitly named for a Black citizen of the United States and almost certainly the only one named for a vociferous agnostic who maintained that the Christian church worked hand in glove with the capitalist class to dupe and exploit the workers of the world!

The Hubert Harrison Memorial Church recalls Harriet Tubman's honorary biblical nickname "Moses," which she earned for leading so many enslaved people out of bondage. It evokes the "love supreme" of the St. John Coltrane Church in San Francisco. In another ripple of Blackened spacetime, it conjures the spirit of Jean-Jacques Dessalines, the only Haitian revolutionary figure to ascend to the status of *Lwa* or venerated spirit in the cosmology of Haitian Vodou.[24]

In the decades following World War II, a number of scholars wrote articles or book chapters that sought to rescue Harrison from obscurity.[25] More recently, a growing wave of interest in Harrison's life and legacy has emerged thanks to the tireless efforts of the late great independent scholar, postal worker, and activist Jeffrey Babcock Perry.[26]

In the early 1980s, Perry wrote a PhD dissertation on Harrison and cultivated a close relationship with Harrison's descendants. They eventually gave him the vast trove of Harrison's diaries, scrapbooks, letters of correspondence, and hundreds of writings, many of them unpublished. In 2001, Perry edited and published a book of Harrison's writings (*A Hubert Harrison Reader*). Then Perry sorted, organized, cataloged, and donated a large trove of Harrison's archive to Columbia University, much of which is now accessible online as the Hubert H. Harrison Papers. In addition, Perry published the only book-length studies of Harrison to date. His two-volume biography, totaling nearly 1,200 pages (not including endnotes), is detailed and meticulous like a reference work, bearing a scholarly rigor that only his forty-something years of dedication could produce.[27]

By the same token, the long length and obsessive attention to detail in Perry's tomes make for a very high bar of entry, which threatens to deter some readers from getting acquainted with Hubert Harrison. This book, as the first single-volume analytical interpretation of Harrison's political significance, advances its scholarly arguments and contributions with an eye toward reaching a broader audience beyond just the academy. To social justice activists, for example, Harrison's legacy represents a very "usable past" because of the broad range of his experiences and insights—regarding things like capitalism, racial oppression, US national and international geopolitics, pan-African liberation, gender and sexuality, emerging technology, state censorship, and public education—that remain painfully relevant to the political landscape of the twenty-first century.

To be clear: I am eternally grateful to Perry for his many decades of work on Harrison because without it I would never have found out about Harrison's existence, let alone started down this intellectual journey of my own. Perry had a formative influence on my appreciation of Harrison's importance, especially as a Black theoretician and organizer in the Socialist Party of America. And Perry's work remains the gold standard for scholarly studies of Harrison. As a result, ever since I started this project as a graduate student, the perennial question I have encountered is, "What are you doing with Harrison that is different from Perry?"

Harrison had an intellectual breadth that defies easy categorization, and he left behind a rich documentary archive. As a result, his political depth has yet to be fully appreciated. Therefore, as with other notable historical figures of the era like W. E. B. Du Bois and Ida B. Wells-Barnett, there is room for multiple different book-length treatments of Hubert Harrison.

As only the second scholar after Perry to produce such a treatment, I have delved into numerous areas of Harrison's intellectual life and politics that Perry—along with those who wrote about Harrison before him—simply have not adequately addressed. One obvious example concerns the contours and profound implications of Harrison's free love politics. Another example concerns Harrison's Africa-centered knowledge and identity. A third example is Harrison's decisive role in catalyzing the rise of Marcus Garvey and the largest multinational organization of Black people in modern history.

It is not merely a contribution of subject matter, however, but also one of perspective. In his remarks on the struggle for Irish freedom, Harrison noted that "no Irishman would be inclined to dispute the fact that other men, even Englishmen like John Stuart Mill ... could feel the woes of Ireland as profoundly as any Irishman."[28] Likewise, African people would not be inclined to dispute the fact that other people, even white radicals, could feel the woes of Africa as profoundly as any African. As the African proverb says, "until lions write their own history, the tales of the hunt will always glorify the hunter."

My work thus builds upon Perry's momentous restoration of Harrison at the same time as it differs from it. My view of Harrison is grounded in my self-consciously Black and African angles of vision on him. Perry's primary interest in Harrison reflected that of an Irish American socialist and labor union organizer seeking to recover Harrison's race and class radicalism on behalf of the working-class struggle against capitalism and white supremacy. While honoring these indispensable aspects of Harrison's significance, I view other dimensions—his contributions to Marcus Garvey's movement, pan-African consciousness, and sexual liberation—as equally (if not *more* compelling) elements of his intellectual and political legacy.

So rather than attempt to recount his life story comprehensively from start to finish, which Perry has already done with such painstaking attention to detail, I instead focus on drawing out the major themes of Harrison's political and intellectual radicalism and their most stimulating and enduring implications.

While this book is an intellectual history rather than a biography, I do occasionally recount certain parts of Harrison's life story for two reasons: first, because the basic facts of his biography are not widely known, and second, because it helps to explain the trajectory of his political evolution.

In writing a book that attempts to interpret and analyze various dimensions of a highly unorthodox, complex, and many-sided figure, I strive to honor his voice and the generative power of his own words and ideas. At the same time, one cannot fully grasp Harrison's radical ideas without understanding their context. If we liken Harrison to a tree, Perry's biography is primarily focused on recreating all the detailed minutiae of the tree itself, whereas this book paints a picture of the tree within its forest and the larger national and global ecosystems in which it took root.

My interpretations of Harrison's significance have been driven by a number of questions: What can we learn from the various cutting-edge social movements that he joined? What hidden corners and connections does his field of vision expose? How do Harrison's ideas and political projects relate to those of other important figures before, during, and after his time? What larger local, national, or international forces did he amplify or resist? What lessons from his life experience can we apply today?

In order to present more robust answers to these questions, I have taken great care in this book to illustrate the intellectual climate zones and discursive backdrops of Harrison's world in order to illustrate the political context within which he worked: the ascendance of the capitalist robber barons; the enormous strength and appeal of the labor and Socialist movements; the myriad monstrosities of white terrorism and anti-Black violence; the vast expansion of the American empire abroad; the global anticolonial and race-conscious political awakening detonated by the First World War and the Russian Revolution; the rise of the New Negro movement and the "Harlem Renaissance"; and so on. The deep and lasting significance of historical developments like these has been too often marginalized (where not omitted entirely) in high school history classes. Therefore, I render detailed historical backdrops like these in order to tell a "people's history" of Harrison's world because that too, in and of itself, offers new and luminous angles of vision on the present. I also do this because one simply cannot fully grasp a complicated iconoclast like Harrison without a broader picture of the world to which his many radicalisms responded. A perfect example concerns the status of Black life in the early twentieth-century United States.

African American Life in Harrison's Day

Hubert Henry Harrison was born on April 27, 1883, on Estate Concordia by the Salt River, which bisects the northern side of the Caribbean island of St. Croix. Both of his parents worked on plantations to survive and also lived through the great Fireburn rebellion and uprising of Crucian plantation workers in 1878.

By his own account, Harrison seems to have generally enjoyed his childhood. He obtained a ninth-grade education in the Danish colony as well as some religious training in the Anglican Church.[29] As a teen, he taught young pupils in the largest rural school in Friedensfeld.[30] After his mother died in 1899, Harrison sought to better his educational and life prospects in the United States. In so doing, he became part of a wave of tens of thousands of US-bound Caribbean immigrants who moved to the US in the early twentieth century as a result of adverse economic conditions on their islands of origin. Thanks to the assistance of his sister Mary, he managed to relocate to New York City as a bright seventeen-year-old in 1900.

While the economic conditions of Black life in the late nineteenth-century Caribbean were harsh, St. Croix (like the rest of the Caribbean) lacked the pervasive phenomenon of anti-Black terrorism and violent white racism that characterized the United States.[31] For that reason, the encounter of Caribbean migrants like Harrison with the strict US regime of racial oppression constituted a major factor in their political radicalization.[32] In his efforts to explain and make legible this racial oppression to white people, Harrison chronicled a number of examples that reveal the world he saw and also what weighed most heavily on his heart and mind.

British writer Rudyard Kipling popularized the notion of the so-called white man's burden of having to rule over people of color in faraway lands. In response, Harrison made a case for the shoe on the other foot, arguing white colonizers were actually "the Black man's burden." Chief among Harrison's examples of this burden was the Southern economic practice of debt peonage, which he described as "slavery unsanctioned by law." In Harrison's words, "One of the forms of this second slavery is the proprietary system, according to which the Negro laborer or tenant farmer must get his supply at the proprietor's store—and he gets it on credit. The accounts are 'cooked' so that the Negro is always in debt to the modern slave-holder. Some of them spend a life-time working out an original debt of five or ten dollars." In Harrison's view, not only had this peonage system in the South reduced many

Black families to a new slavery, but Black workers in Northern cities from Cincinnati to New York were systematically excluded from the labor unions and even physically attacked when attempting to enter trades that white people viewed as their own racially exclusive domain for jobs and promotions.[33]

Political disenfranchisement formed another pillar of racial oppression for Harrison as Southern states created new laws that were used to roll back the right of Black men to vote, which had been won during the Reconstruction period following the Civil War. How was this disenfranchisement done? "By fraud and force," wrote Harrison. "[Senator] Tillman of South Carolina has told in the United States Senate how the ballot was taken from Negroes by shooting them—that is, by murder." Not only that, but "in certain southern states in order to vote a man must have had a grandfather who voted before Negroes were freed. In others, he must be able to interpret and understand any clause in the Constitution—and a white registration official decides whether he does understand."[34] In other cases, poll taxes, which required payment to vote, were made high enough to discourage voting by poor people, both Black and white. These measures excluded the vast majority of Black men in the South from voting. And the Southern states had never granted Black women the right to vote.

The infamous 1896 *Plessy* decision of the Supreme Court, which established the nefarious legal doctrine of "separate but equal," symbolized the culmination of a series of legal decisions that obliterated the formal and legal equality established by the Fourteenth Amendment to the Constitution, which had supposedly enshrined equality before the law for all US citizens. Such legal decisions opened the door for Southern states to prohibit Black people and white people from inhabiting the same social spaces. "And so we find," lamented Harrison, "that in 'the home of the free and the land of the brave' Negroes must not ride in the same cars in a train as white people. On street-cars, certain sections are set apart for them. They may not eat in public places where white people eat nor drink at the same bar. They may not go to the same church (although they are foolish enough to worship the same god) as white people; they may not die in the same hospital nor be buried in the same grave-yard."[35]

Harrison, like so many other frustrated Black people in the North and South, watched the unfolding of the Jim Crow laws with exasperation. "But why is segregation necessary?" he asked rhetorically. "Because white Americans are afraid that their 'inherent' superiority may not, after all, be so very evident either to the Negro or to other people. They, therefore, find it necessary to enact it into law." The system of spatial and physical separation by race came to be called "Jim Crow," named after a popular nineteenth-century minstrel show character that demeaned Black people.[36]

The grisly terrorism of lynching—the extrajudicial killing of individual people by lawless white mobs—formed another key mechanism of anti-Black oppression that would become a chief concern of Harrison's as he developed his political consciousness. In his first book, *The Negro and the Nation*, Harrison recounted how

> at Honeapath, S.C., a Negro was lynched. . . . The howling mob which did him to death was composed of "prominent citizens" who made up automobile parties to ride to the affair. Among those prominently present was the dishonorable Joshua Ashley, a member of the state legislature. He and his friends cut off the man's fingers as souvenirs and were proud of their work. Why shouldn't they? You see, it help to keep "niggers" in their place. . . . Governor Blease of South Carolina was also proud of the event and said that instead of stopping the horrible work of the mob he would have resigned his office to lead it. . . .
>
> In Okemeah, Oklahoma, last June a band of white gentlemen raped a Negro woman and then lynched her and her fourteen-year-old son. Nothing has been done to them.
>
> At Durant, Okla., and elsewhere, the savages have posed around their victims to have their pictures taken. One man, from Alabama, sent to the Rev. John Haynes Holmes, of Brooklyn, New York, a post-card (by mail) bearing a photography of such a group. "This is the way we treat them down here," he writes, and, after promising to put Mr. Holmes' name on his mailing list, declares that they will have one, at least, each month. . . .
>
> When President Roosevelt discussed lynching some years ago, he severely reprobated *the colored people* for their tendency to shield their "criminals" and ordered them to go out and help hunt them down. So was insult added to injury. (italics in the original)[37]

As historian Darius Young puts it, "White vigilantes often targeted black businessmen, doctors, lawyers, and other professionals for the crime of merely exceeding their white counterparts in wealth, education, and prominence." Lynching thus formed a key mechanism of resubjugating Black people by providing the ultimate means of neutralizing the threat of Black advancement. Between 1880 and 1930, white mobs lynched an average of some 101 people per year—mostly Black men, though white people also lynched each other people from other racial groups, and Black women too.[38]

Alongside the injustice of lynching, the period witnessed widespread rape and sexual assault of Black women. During and after the South's postwar Reconstruction, many Black women earned a living as domestic workers in white people's homes, making them vulnerable to rape, violence, and various forms of abuse at the hands of their employers—not to mention sexual

Figure I.1 Three African American circus workers, Elias Clayton, Elmer Jackson, and Isaac McGhie, lynched on June 15, 1920, in Duluth, Minnesota.

violence outside the workplace. As Angela Y. Davis has argued, "Group rape, perpetrated by the Ku Klux Klan and other terrorist organizations of the post-Civil War period, became an un-camouflaged political weapon in the drive to thwart the movement for Black equality."[39] We will never know how many Black women (and men) were raped and sexually traumatized, but as an endemic feature of Southern African American life, it left deep scars.

The South was not the only place seething with white mob violence against Black people. In the North, historians have uncovered a shocking, albeit long-hidden history of white supremacist municipal racial "cleansing" between 1890 and 1940 and the creation of thousands of all-white "sundown towns."[40] Many of these towns emerged from the nationwide epidemic of anti-Black pogroms in which white mobs perpetrated horrific attacks, property destruction, and full-scale pogroms and massacres against Black communities.[41]

In order to control the thoughts and aspirations of Black people in the South, Northern industrialists with economic interests in the South sponsored industrial education as a means of racial resubjugation, as historians like Donald Spivey have argued.[42] Harrison emerged as a staunch critic of industrial

Introduction 17

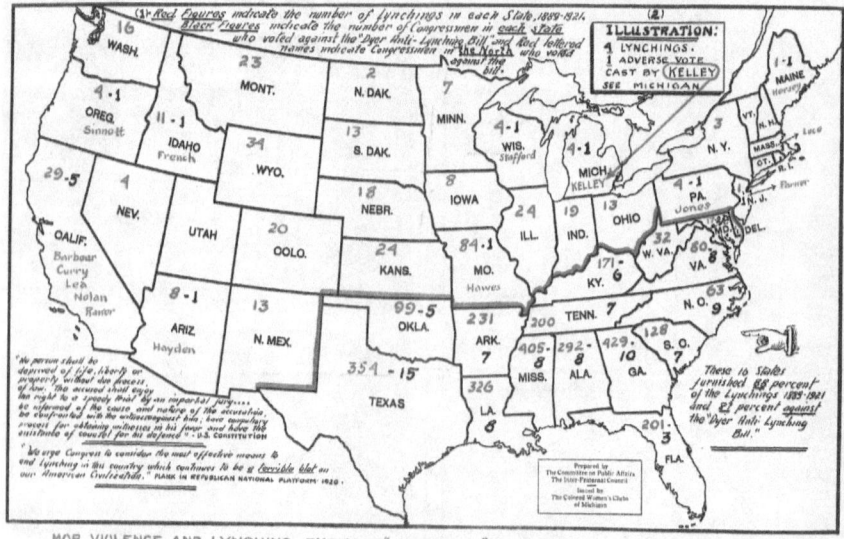

Map I.1 This map was created by the groundbreaking antilynching crusader Ida B. Wells-Barnett and was submitted to Congress in 1922 in support of antilynching legislation sponsored by Republican Leonidas Dyer of Missouri. The primary number in each state is the number of lynchings; the secondary number in each state, if there is one, is the number of Congress members who voted against the Dyer antilynching bill. "Red Record of Lynching Map," 1922, Papers Accompanying Specific Bills and Resolutions of the Committee on the Judiciary from the 67th Congress (HR67A-D18), Bill Files, 1903–1968, Records of the US House of Representatives, Record Group 233, National Archives Building, Washington, DC.

education for Black people, arguing that it formed a mechanism for keeping Black people in the position of docile laborers. "The General Education Board which disburses millions of dollars annually in the South for education has, so far, given to forty-one Negro schools the sum of $464,015," observed Harrison in 1912. Although touted as a philanthropic agency empowering Southern Black people with an education they wouldn't otherwise possess, the General Education Board was founded and sustained by money from the Rockefellers and other white monopoly capitalists who profited from the exploitation of cheap Black Southern labor.

"Only in two instances has any money been given to a real college," wrote Harrison. "Practically all of it went to the labor-caste schools. Why? Because the dark degradation of the Negro must be lightened by no ray of learning. That would never do. We need them as 'hewers of wood and drawers of water.'

And in the meanwhile, this is what the richest country on earth offers to ruthlessly exploited people as a training for life." Harrison decried how in the Southern states Black people made up 40.1 percent of the population but received only 14.8 percent of the state funds allocated for education. Citing numerous other similar inequities, Harrison concluded, "Thus does America keep knowledge from her Negroes. She is afraid of the educated black man. Of such are the people who taunt Negroes with ignorance."[43]

Industrial education symbolized a model that contributed in particular ways to the cultural assimilation and mental colonization of Black people, which fit hand in glove with the political disenfranchisement they faced from the state governments. Harrison spoke out against the folly of Booker T. Washington's philosophy of acquiescence: "Now if education of any sort is training for life, is it not evident here that Black children are being robbed of their chance in life? Why? Is it to be supposed that their fathers are so stupid as to allow this if they could vote their own needs? Yet Mr. Washington decries the agitation for the ballot as unwise and never loses an opportunity of sneering at those who see something of value in it."[44]

As Donald Spivey has argued, "Blacks faced a neo-slave system when the Civil War ended. Cotton still had to be picked, tobacco fields needed to be tended, and menial labor was required for the industries of the New South. It has been documented that sharecropping, debt peonage, and convict lease were means used to resubjugate Black labor and that the South sought through Jim Crow, night riders, and lynch law to nullify the civil and political rights guaranteed to Blacks under the thirteenth, fourteenth, and fifteenth amendments. But another tool was used against Blacks: industrial education."[45]

If there's one constant in human history, it is that oppression breeds resistance.

Therefore, alongside unremitting racial oppression and anti-Black violence, the late nineteenth and early twentieth centuries also saw the emergence of a new, post-Reconstruction generation for the resistance and defiance. In 1880, for example, Mary Ann Shadd Cary organized the Colored Women's Progressive Franchise Association to promote uplift and empowerment of Black women. In 1890, T. Thomas Fortune founded the National Afro-American League to fight for civil rights through agitation and protest as a strategy to challenge the horrendous treatment of African Americans.[46] In the 1890s, Ida B. Wells spearheaded an international movement against lynching. By inspiring Black women to challenge the mainstream racist depictions of Black men and women, Wells's campaign gave a decisive stimulus to the rise of the Black women's club movement.[47] In 1896, Black women's clubs came together to form the National Association of Colored Women, which by 1914 had "a membership of fifty thousand, far surpassing the membership of every other protest organization of the time, including the National Association for the Advancement of Colored People and the National Urban League," according to pioneering Black women's historian Darlene Clark Hine.[48]

With the founding of the *Guardian* in 1900, William Monroe and Geraldine Trotter blazed a trail for the generation of "protestants" of Booker T. Washington's political hegemony. In 1905, the Trotters and W. E. B. Du Bois and others founded the Niagara Movement, which advanced a politics of protest that built on the legacy of Fortune's Afro-American League.[49] Meanwhile, working-class Black men and women developed social networks, built community institutions, joined labor unions, went on strike, and deployed an arsenal of tactics to resist their racial, economic, and gendered subjugation.[50] All across the country, Black people exercised their agency in resisting oppression in large and small, collective and individual ways.

This period of African American history took place alongside large-scale industrial, technological, and cultural transformations in the United States. By 1915, there had arisen explicit and millenarian talk of the "New Politics" that would broaden the boundaries of American democracy, a "New Woman" who would be free to work outside the home and determine her own life and sexuality, and a "New Psychology" that would free the human personality through Sigmund Freud's novel method of psychoanalysis. The creative spirit of the age found expression in a "New Art" that took the form of cubism, expressionism, surrealism, and other modernist impulses and a "New Theatre" that addressed serious political and social issues rather than the sentimental and romantic dramas of the Victorian era.[51] President Theodore Roosevelt spoke of a "New Nationalism" in 1910, and his successor Woodrow Wilson spoke of a "New Freedom" in a book by the same name that he published in 1913 during his first year in office.[52]

It is in this context that Harrison would give voice to a new valence of "New Negro" politics as a leading voice for the people who began to manifest an uncompromising racial pride and awakened political consciousness, a historic break with the moderate "Old Crowd" Black leaders of the previous era.[53] In this way, Harrison's turn-of-the-century transition from the tiny agricultural island of St. Croix to the vast megalopolis of Manhattan was not only a geographical move but also a kind of diachronic historical leap from a traditional, rural, and agrarian world to a modern, urban, and industrial one.[54]

Upon his arrival in New York City in 1900, Harrison took up residence with his sister Mary in the majority-Black San Juan Hill area on West Sixty-Second Street. Residents lived in dilapidated and overcrowded housing conditions. Educational opportunities for Black people were extremely limited, as the first evening high school in the "Negro district" would not be established until 1905.[55] Harrison's sister greatly aided in getting him settled, a common experience for migrants from the Caribbean. As literary scholar Louis Parascandola has pointed out, Caribbean women made critical contributions to the social network of the immigrant community, especially when they were the first members of their families to arrive in the United States. Caribbean-born people like Cyril Briggs, W. A. Domingo, and Richard B. Moore, who would become important Harlem-based activists, all joined and were supported by women family members when they first got to the United States.[56]

After seven years in Manhattan's West Side San Juan Hill neighborhood, in 1907 Harrison moved to Harlem, which would become the largest and most concentrated Black neighborhood in New York City between 1900 and 1930.[57] In addition to family support networks, benevolent associations like the American West Indian Association, New York Colored Mission, and the White Rose Home for Colored Girls played key roles in finding jobs and housing for so many newly arrived Black migrants to the city. Real estate firms like Philip Payton's Afro-American Realty Company laid the groundwork for some $2 million in Black property ownership in Harlem by 1928. Various Black churches like the African Orthodox Church, African Methodist Episcopal "Mother Zion," Abyssinian Baptist, Bethel African Methodist Episcopal, the Harlem Community Church, and St. Mark's Methodist Episcopal, among others, all cultivated their congregations uptown.[58]

Because Black people had to work throughout the city but were de facto barred from access to housing in most neighborhoods, Harlem became the epicenter of New York City's Black community. This led to an economic life based on, as historian Joyce Moore Turner has put it, "two Harlems: one of the day and one of the night." During the day, white business owners and clerks, public school teachers, policemen, doctors for the Harlem hospital, restaurateurs, salesmen, and truck drivers came uptown. Black Harlem residents who weren't working on railroads or steamships went downtown by day to work as elevator operators, bellhops, domestics, seamstresses, and other service workers. During the night, white New Yorkers from downtown came up to hop from cabaret to cabaret, listen to blues and jazz, and engage in more salacious forms of entertainment. Black Harlemites in the entertainment industry worked as musicians, actors, dancers, bartenders, and waiters.[59] Not to mention those who labored in the underground economy as sex workers, psychics, and numbers runners, as LaShawn Harris has shown.[60]

Thanks to the influx of African American migrants from the South and African Caribbean migrants from the Antilles, Harlem became its own hub of economic, cultural, and international exchange. Fraternal orders like the Prince Hall Masons, the Odd Fellows, and the Elks grew in Harlem and fostered mutual economic protection societies as they helped to forge Black class and gender identities and solidarities through their rituals of brotherhood.[61] Meanwhile, ethnic voluntary associations for national groups like Virgin Islanders, Jamaicans, Bermudians, and Barbadians sprang up. In addition, numerous formations coalesced to give political expression to Black Harlem's aspirations through organizations like the Socialist Party of America, the Independent Political Council, the Radical Forum, the Liberty League of Negro-Americans, the suffragist Negro Women's Campaign Committee, the Universal Negro Improvement Association, the Women's Political Association, the African Blood Brotherhood, the Communist Party, and the Harlem Tenants League. By 1930, Harlemites had built and cultivated such a rich tapestry of social and community institutions that writer, diplomat, and National Association for the Advancement of Colored People (NAACP) field organizer James Weldon Johnson could write that "throughout colored America, Harlem is the recognized Negro capital. Indeed, it is Mecca for the sightseer, the pleasure-seeker, the curious, the adventurous, the enterprising, the ambitious, and the talented of the entire Negro world."[62]

Hubert Harrison both taught and learned from this confluence of various currents of transnational migration, intellectual vibrancy, and multiethnic Afro-descended cultures. Thanks to New York City's size, technological development, and cosmopolitan character, Harrison would cultivate and engage with all of the cutting-edge ideas and trends within a key node of global economic, cultural, and political cross fertilization.

Chapter Outline

In this day and age it feels like books have become an endangered species. As a result, it may seem odd to publish such a heavy-duty book as this one, with essentially nine different minibooks inside. But I believe in the staying power of good books, even if their competition with more bite-sized media morsels feels like an uphill battle. And I have written this book as a series of thematic interpretations so as to make the chapters serviceable in a stand-alone fashion.

Chapter 1 establishes Harrison's crystallization of a Black Socialist politics as an organizer in the Socialist Party of America. Harrison made the case that the party had a duty to champion the cause of Black workers and reject racism, or else it could never reach its stated objective of uniting the working class in a struggle for Socialism and against capitalism. Ultimately, Harrison failed to convince the party to take him seriously and instead faced persecution and hostility for posing before the party so sharply the question "Socialism or Southernism?"—that is, whether the party would choose genuine solidarity for the whole working class or instead pander to the white supremacist mindset of

Southern white workers. By cataloging and assessing Harrison's theoretical and practical contributions to the Socialist cause, the chapter locates him in a larger context of Black Socialist praxis before and after his tenure in the party.

Chapter 2 explores the formative influence of women's suffrage and Black women's activism on Harrison's development. On this note, we see a range of influences and interlocutors in his relationships to figures like Frances Reynolds Keyser, Ida B. Wells-Barnett, Eslanda Cardozo Goode, and Grace P. Campbell. The chapter then engages Harrison's crystallization of the World War I–era New Negro movement in Harlem through his Liberty League of Negro-Americans organization and *The Voice* newspaper. It explores how and why Harrison saw the need for a more radical organization than what the NAACP represented as the most prominent national organization advocating for African Americans during this period. As against that white-founded association, Harrison founded the Liberty League on the basis that Black people in the Western world had to pledge their allegiance to a leadership funded and selected by Black people themselves. Harrison's Liberty League marked the crystallization of a new organizational model by bringing African Americans and African Caribbeans of various national backgrounds together for the first time into a single political organization and mass movement for Black self-help, political protest, and race-conscious internationalism. The chapter closes by placing these developments within a larger frame of the postwar global political awakening that detonated the Russian Revolution and a similar fervor for revolution in the United States.

Chapter 3 explores Harrison's role in crystallizing a social infrastructure I call the "Outdoor Grioversity." Harrison helped inaugurate a new educational institution that synthesized the Western style of knowledge production through engaging university-based European scholarship with a modern version of the storyteller-historian role played by the griot in West African cultures. The chapter paints a picture of Harrison's encyclopedic knowledge and his emergence as the most prominent Black agnostic freethinker of his generation. Both of these things informed his work to establish a grassroots and community-based intellectual culture in Harlem based on street-corner speaking.[63] It also elaborates the outlines of his philosophy of education, which constituted a distinctively Black and radical model of free education of, by, and for the common people.

Chapter 4 investigates the New Negro politics of what Harrison called the "white world war." It chronicles Harrison's crystallization of a new form of radical internationalism, the political theory of the "Colored International," which envisioned a global alliance of the "darker races" of the world against capitalism, white racial domination, and imperialism. We unpack the way in which Harrison skillfully managed to continue giving voice to the myriad grievances of African Americans while simultaneously avoiding wartime state repression and censorship. This would prove decisive during his chairmanship of the Liberty Congress of Negro-Americans, a national gathering of wartime dissidents in Washington, DC, which the US government attempted to forestall through its own pro-war conference for Black editors across the country. The chapter also engages Harrison's dramatic public exposition of the attempt by W. E. B. Du Bois to become a captain in US military intelligence in order to spy on Black radicals to police expressions of Black dissent during the war.

Chapter 5 analyzes Harrison's African politics and his contribution to African consciousness in Harlem. The chapter focuses on the meaning of Harrison's early self-identification as an "untamed, untamable African" and his proud identification with the African continent and its peoples, which formed a paradigm shift from the paternalistic mindset of nineteenth-century Black nationalist tradition. Harrison's insistence that the task of Black people in the diaspora was *not to teach but to learn* from continental Africans demonstrated a radical embrace of African identity that stood in stark contrast to the predominant civilizationist views of both his white and Black contemporaries. Under the mentorship of John E. Bruce and Arturo Schomburg, this outlook positioned Harrison to serve as a node and conduit for the spread of African consciousness and what we now call Black or Africana studies, in conjunction with a larger community of African-centered scholars both within and outside of formal academic institutions.

Chapter 6 unearths the contours Harrison's sexual radicalism and his crystallization of what I call a "Black free love politics." It is not easy to imagine a time when the ritualized public mob murder of Black men often included their castration, or when not just abortion was illegal but also birth control, sex toys, anal sex, oral sex, publications with anatomical and sex-related information, and erotic literature of even the mildest kind. Yet at precisely such a time, Harrison emerged as one of the first Black voices to speak publicly in favor of access to contraception, to give public sex education lectures, and to argue that human beings are not sexually monogamists by nature, but as a result of coercive social pressures from the church, the state, and white monopoly capital. The chapter demonstrates how Harrison's sex radicalism connected to his other political commitments like building momentum for Socialism, Pan-Africanism, and women's liberation. It also explores the ways in which his arguments in the 1910s about the historically contingent and socially constructed nature of sexuality received a spectacular confirmation in the blossoming of a wide range of casual, colorful, and queer New Negro sexualities in the Harlem of the 1920s.

Chapters 7 and 8 take a dive deep into Harrison's relationship to the Garvey movement. Marcus Garvey remains the namesake of the movement that built not just a large business empire and pan-African nationality, but the largest international organization of Black people in modern history. And it was Hubert Harrison's Liberty League that catalyzed it. Yet Harrison's role in stimulating the rise of Marcus Garvey has been all but forgotten. Recovering Harrison's decisive role in the emergence of a global mass movement reveals a range of new insights about both Garvey and Garveyism.

The Garvey movement has often been vastly overestimated in numerical size and strength by its supporters and greatly underestimated in historical and political importance by its critics. Restoring Harrison to the story offers a touchstone-like test—and interpretive paradigm shift—for both of these camps. Chapter 7 explores the decisive impact Harrison had on the rise of Marcus Garvey and Garveyism. It shows how Harrison's Liberty League laid the foundational elements without which the rise of a Garvey *movement* would not have been possible: the "race first" ideology; the mass movement orientation; and the bringing together of African Americans and African Caribbeans in a single organization behind a global pan-African vision of Black collective self-help. Chapter 8 traverses Harrison's criticisms of Garvey and the various steps Harrison took to push the Garvey movement in a more class-conscious, anti-imperialist, and political-party-building direction.

Chapter 9 interrogates Harrison's removal from historical memory by the invention of the so-called Harlem Renaissance. It examines how Alain Locke's reinterpretation of the New Negro movement as a cultural "renaissance" of high art deliberately sought to overshadow and replace the postwar radical New Negro movement with its pesky politics of protest and Black radicalism. Although Locke would very quickly relinquish his own investment in the "renaissance" fad, the narrative that he helped set in motion would only grow larger and more entrenched in the ensuing decades. This chapter shows how Harrison's critical assessment of the "renaissance" phenomenon invites a critical cross-examination of what I call the "Harlem Renaissance Industry," which has dominated both popular and scholarly understandings of early twentieth-century Harlem—and helped erase Hubert Henry Harrison from history.

The conclusion reflects on Harrison's erasure, legacy, and significance. It also explores a key implication of his historical restoration, namely the importance of studying other touchstone-type figures like Harrison. The technological genius of Nikola Tesla offers a case in point, especially in light of Harrison's radical critique of white science under capitalism. What emerges from putting Harrison and Tesla in conversation illuminates an incalculably revolutionary solution to the heartrending, impending, and mind-bending crisis of global warming and climate catastrophe. After all, radical problems require radical solutions. Tesla created extraordinary clean energy alternatives to oil, gas, coal, and the internal combustion engine, only to be suppressed and banished from popular memory, much like Hubert Harrison. And, like so many of Harrison's ideas, recovering Tesla's incalculably revolutionary vision of clean energy appears increasingly urgent for the future of all humanity and our relationship to Mother Earth.

A Great Man against the "Great Man" Theory of History

Although this study focuses on the masculine figure of Hubert Harrison, I do not subscribe to the "Great Man" theory of history, according to which the agency and decision-making of exceptional individual males constitutes the motive force of history. Social change over time—which may or may not become recorded, conceived, or accessed in some way as *history* or *herstory* or *ourstory* after the fact—is shaped by a confluence of larger forces. The struggles between contending social classes, racial/national/ethnic groups, political formations, and mass protest movements are all, by definition, forged collectively. They cannot be reduced to the individuals associated with them, who are too often misleadingly cast as "The Leader." For example, Black women often form the backbone and bedrock of Black social movements—and of the most visible male leaders. More generally and universally, women have made decisive contributions, offered unique forms of leadership, and exerted an indispensable agency of their own. This has always been part of the process of social change, even when they do not receive any credit or mainstream visibility.

At the same time, there *are* great (with a small *g*) men and women and nonbinary people who have shaped the course of history through their charismatic leadership. Unfortunately, the most courageously radical and forward-thinking figures of all genders are often written out of the mainstream historical narrative because of the dominant culture's hostility towards views and ideas that challenge those who benefit from the status quo. Therefore, in this study I have sought to make space for various notable contemporaries of Harrison who have also been marginalized in history to one degree or another because of the political threat they pose to the standard historical narratives.

Hubert Henry Harrison lived as a working-class orphan, teacher, lynch mob survivor, immigrant, husband, sex educator, father, journalist, lover, intellectual, brother, bookseller, griot, and prophet, and he played the harmonica. Like any other human being, Harrison had many flaws and contradictions. His story speaks of a man struggling to find and keep his voice (and his life) intact through the traumatic dislocations of a hostile world.

Harrison is worthy of study not just because of the ideas generated by his brilliant mind but also because he worked so hard to offer his encyclopedic and liberatory knowledge to the people in ways that can uncover new possibilities for the future in the present. As one of his obituaries noted, Harrison's achievements "should prove an inspiration to many young Negroes, for, despite the handicap of poverty, he became one of the most learned men of his day and was able to teach the wide masses of his race how to appreciate and enjoy all of the finer things of life, to glance back over the whole history of mankind, and to look forward 'as far as thought can reach.'"[64]

Though difficult at times to digest, Harrison's ideas and example ultimately offer us a desperately needed approach to living, understanding, and being in the modern world: how to get the *kind* of knowledge that is power, particularly for the youth of the next generation. In his words, the task of young people was to get education "not only in school and college, but in books and newspapers, in market-places, institutions, and movement. Prepare by knowing; and never think you know until you have listened to ten others who know differently—and have survived the shock."[65]

To that end, may the spirit of Harrison's multifaceted onyx crystalline touchstone "shock" us all into a wider knowledge, deeper empowerment, and a brighter future.

Chapter 1

Socialism or Southernism?

> Southernism or Socialism—which? Is it to be the white half of the working class against the black half, or all the working class?
>
> —Hubert Harrison, "Socialism and the Negro"

Hubert Henry Harrison witnessed an explosion of world-historic economic advances for global capitalism. He also witnessed the rise of militant labor and Socialist movements, which have been all but forgotten in popular memory. By offering a Black angle of vision on socialism and a Socialist angle of vision on Black people, he emerged as one of the first Black figures in the Socialist Party of America to articulate a systematic analysis of the so-called Negro problem that theorized the relationship between capitalism and racism through the historical development of the material conditions in society. Harrison founded the party's first official Black-led organization, the Colored Socialist Club in Harlem, in order to develop a special outreach program to recruit Black workers for Socialism. Hubert Harrison's distinctive contributions both in theory and practice to the Socialist cause have only become more relevant over time. Over a century after birth, they still offer multiple lessons in the struggle for liberation from the exploitation of working people under capitalism.

A World for the Robber Barons

GOD TO HUNGRY CHILD

By Langston Hughes

Hungry child,
I didn't make this world for you.
You didn't buy any stock in my railroad.
You didn't invest in my corporation.
Where are your shares in standard oil?
I made the world for the rich
And the will-be-rich
And the have-always-been-rich.
Not for you,
Hungry child.

Figure 1.1 John D. Rockefeller depicted in the political cartoon "The Trust Giant's Point of View" by Horace Taylor in "The Verdict," 1900. The original caption read, "The Trust Giant's Point of View. What a funny little government." Everett Collection Historical/Alamy Stock Photo.

As in Europe, capitalist economic development in the United States had made great strides by the end of the nineteenth century, in part due to the rise of corporate monopolies. Figures like Jay Gould and Cornelius Vanderbilt created huge railroad enterprises, in part by offering hundreds of thousands of dollars in bribes and stock shares to politicians in exchange for millions of dollars' worth of free land and federal bonds, which they then resold for millions of dollars in profit. Before expanding into industries like iron, copper, coal, shipping, and banking, John D. Rockefeller founded Standard Oil in 1870 and built it into a fossil fuel monopoly through bribing railroad operators for reduced transportation rates to undercut his competitors.

Andrew Carnegie built a steel monopoly by paying his steelworkers a pittance, crushing all attempts at worker unionization, and then undercutting and buying out his competitors in the market. J. P. Morgan built a banking monopoly and, through his control of finance capital, spearheaded the formation of large-scale and monopolistic corporations like US Steel (steel), International Harvester (agriculture), General Electric (industrial manufacturing), Aetna (insurance), Western Union (communication), and the Pullman Car

Figure 1.2 "The Bosses of the Senate," a political cartoon by Joseph Keppler, published in *Puck* magazine in 1889. This cartoon has been a staple of US history textbooks and depicts corporate interests like steel, copper, oil, iron, sugar, tin, and coal and their domination of the US Senate. The door to the upper-level gallery, the "people's entrance," is closed and locked while the special interests have free rein to enter. The sign behind them reads, "This is the Senate of the Monopolists by the Monopolists and for the Monopolists!"

Company (railroads). Fighting against antitrust legislation and other regulatory mechanisms, the key figures of the American ruling class entrenched their power by spending large sums bribing local, state, and national-level lawmakers to make government policies in their own interest.

In short, capital—both as physical means of production and financial capacity for investment—underwent massive expansion around the turn of the century. The interdependence of different industries on each other, amid a competitive market, led inexorably to the centralization and concentration of capital through vertical integration of huge conglomerates, syndicates, and trusts. Industrial-scale commerce required industrial-scale transportation of the kind that railroad development afforded. Railroad construction required lumber and steel. Steel production required raw materials like iron and coal. Meanwhile, the expansion of each of these industrial concerns required investment from the finance capital of the banks. According to an early study of Wall Street, in the quarter century between 1890 and 1915 the total capitalization in the form of corporate stocks and bonds in the United States expanded a hundredfold, from less than 200 million to nearly 20 billion dollars![1]

Hubert Harrison denounced the absurdity of abject poverty and starvation in such a world of plenty. "We raise in this country food enough to feed the world," said Harrison in a 1912 speech in upstate New York. "Our food is here in plenty all the time, and still in the midst of plenty people here in the ciliated United States die of starvation, and countless number of men, women and children are at the point of starvation during the entire course of their natural lives. That's what the capitalistic system does for us." He went on to joke with his audience about how "they tell us that the best people, the cultured, intelligent classes support this system. What do you think of a system which makes it possible for the son of George Westinghouse to fall heir to $50,000,000 without ever doing a stroke of work? What do you think of a system under which it is possible for seven women to give a dinner costing $8,000 in the Hotel Vanderbilt to seven dogs—and they were not American dogs at that—they were Japanese poodles? [much laughter]." For Socialists like Harrison, the vast sums of wealth hoarded by capitalist robber barons symbolized the obscene greed and inequality of the system.[2]

Uncle Sam's Violent Hidden Labor History

RISING WATERS

By Langston Hughes

To you
Who are the
Foam on the sea
And not the sea—
What of the jagged rocks,
And the waves themselves,
And the force of the mounting waters? You are
But foam on the sea,
You rich ones—
Not the sea.

Labor creates all wealth. Why? Because, as Hubert Harrison put it, "I have seen labor functioning without capital, but never capital without labor." The wealth of the robber barons was created by the labor they ruthlessly exploited: coal miners, steelworkers, timber workers, sharecroppers, and penniless immigrants from Europe, Asia, and the Caribbean. The number of child laborers under the age of sixteen grew to 1.6 million by 1900. In the late nineteenth century, the capitalist class even developed a system for leasing convicted prisoners—mostly Southern African American men—to private industry as cheap labor. By tradition, women undertook untold millions of dollars' worth of yearly reproductive labor like cooking and cleaning in the home with a compensatory wage only granted when employed in homes other than their own—as in the case of African American women who labored as domestic workers for white households in the Jim Crow South. Meanwhile, from 1881 to 1900 some 35,000 workers *per year* lost their lives in industrial accidents on the job. Not to mention the history of "Manifest Destiny," or the large-scale conquest and genocide of countless Indigenous peoples of Turtle Island (North America) by the US military, so that the colonial-unsettler economy could gain access to continent-spanning lands rich in raw materials like coal, timber, iron, copper, and oil.[3]

If there is one constant in history, it is that oppression breeds resistance. The economic atrocities that fueled the rise of industrial capitalism explain why US capitalism has such a dramatic and violent labor history, despite its marginalization in high school history textbooks. Witness, for example, the massacre of some thirty African Americans after a sugar workers' strike at Thibodaux, Louisiana, in 1873. Or the Pennsylvania coal wars of the 1870s. Or the violent railroad strike of 1877. The year 1886 witnessed the May Day strike and subsequent execution of the Haymarket Square martyrs in Chicago. 1892 witnessed insurrections against the system of convict leasing, a miners' strike in Tennessee, a violent copper miners' strike in Coeur d'Alene, Idaho, the bloody Homestead Strike against Carnegie Steel, and the New Orleans general strike of Black and white workers for a shorter working day and better pay. The months-long violent Pullman Strike of the American Railway Workers Union in 1894 propelled strike leader Eugene V. Debs into national prominence and radicalized him. Miners faced down the Lattimer massacre in Pennsylvania (1897), the Ludlow massacre in Colorado (1914), the Matewan massacre in West Virginia (1920), and the Herrin massacre in Illinois (1922). And these are but a mere sampling. According to one estimate, between 1881 and 1905, "7.5 million workers took part in a total of 38,303 strikes across the United States. In that same time period, 198 strikers or sympathizers were killed, 1,966 were wounded, and 6,114 arrested."[4]

Socialist historian Sidney Lens summarized the good that came from the militancy of the US working class. In his words, "The labor wars, after torturous decades and innumerable picket line murders, secured for the workingman a right which he had been previously denied, totally or partially: the right to collective action. Without that right much of what we consider progressive today in the American way of life would have been impossible—the abolition of child labor, workmen's compensation for accidents, safety standards, protection of women and immigrants, unemployment compensation, social security, low-cost housing (inadequate as it is), Medicare, and many other reforms." Not to mention the eight-hour work day and the weekend! Without the labor movement, Lens observed, "tens of millions of proletarians would be chained to their machines without benefit of shorter hours, seniority rights, grievance machinery, paid vacations and holidays, sick pay, supplemental unemployment compensation, and health insurance. All of these benefits had to be won through bitter contention."[5]

African Americans also responded to the violent rise of monopoly capital with significant efforts to organize in defense of their lives and dignity. Black workers, particularly in the South, created wealth for corporations that exploited them for their cheap labor as timber workers, coal miners, sharecroppers, and railroad workers. They were also used as scabs by the employing class to break the strikes of white workers. Sometimes, where unions did not exist, wildcat strikes broke out, as in the case of the Black women's laundry workers' strike in Atlanta in 1888. Black workers joined multiracial labor unions like the Brotherhood of Timber Workers—affiliated with the Industrial Workers of the World (IWW)—which led strikes of thousands of Black and white workers. The United Mine Workers also led thousands of Black and white workers into battle for union recognition, higher wages, and better working conditions. Black IWW organizer Ben Fletcher's Local 8 organized a radical multiracial longshoreman's union on the docks of Philadelphia. Black and white miners fought dramatic battles against their employers in the Alabama coal fields. This labor upsurge culminated in the formation of organizations like the Brotherhood Workers of America, a radical Southern Black industrial union in the Tidewater region of Virginia.[6]

Although the growth of the Black industrial working class offered new opportunities for multiracial and even Black-led union organizing along industrial lines, in the first two decades of the twentieth century it often prompted white workers to cling ever more tightly to their white skin privileges. For example, the American Federation of Labor (AFL), the largest federation of organized labor, generally abided by the exclusion of Black workers from its affiliates. In the first two decades of the twentieth century, labor organizations open to Black workers were few and far between. While the IWW, the United Mine Workers, the Brotherhood of Timber Workers in Louisiana, and the International Longshoremen's Association in New Orleans were notable for their multiracialism, they were also exceptions to the rule.

Moreover, according to labor historian Eric Arnesen, most of these "integrated" unions failed to challenge the racially discriminatory divisions of labor within their industries.[7] As historian Philip Foner has argued, "despite its advanced position against race prejudice and its opposition to segregation in the labor movement, the failure of the I.W.W. to concern itself with the Negro's demand and struggle for civil and political rights restricted its appeal to the Negro masses." Meanwhile, white workers in small towns across the country engaged in hysterical mob attacks and pogroms against Black communities, culminating in the formation of thousands of all-white "sundown towns."[8] One can only wonder how many more Black workers could have been recruited to organizations like the IWW had more white workers recognized the lynching, rape, and disenfranchisement, which terrorized so many Black people during the Jim Crow era, as attacks on their fellow workers.

Hubert Harrison in the Black Working Class

Upon his arrival in New York, Harrison followed a path trod by most West Indian migrants in the city: working various service jobs to eke out a living. At different times, he earned a living as a messenger, a bellhop, an elevator operator, and a stock clerk in a Japanese fan company.[9] After some years of initially struggling to find steady work and pay rent, Harrison eventually secured a job as a clerk at the post office in 1907, which at last afforded him a more consistent and salaried employment. As a postal worker, Harrison chafed under the twelve-hour days, six-to-seven-day workweeks, poor ventilation, and abusive managers. He also witnessed the labor organizing competition between the pro-management United National Association of Post Office Clerks (Local No. 1) and the pro-worker National Federation of Post Office Clerks (Local No. 10), which was affiliated with the AFL.[10]

Despite the oppressive working conditions, Harrison proved fortunate on some level to secure employment as a postal worker because the apartheid-like racial regime of the United States labor market meant most Black workers could only find employment at the bottom rung of the ladder. Charles S. Johnson of the National Urban League pointed out in 1925 that the Black worker "may be a porter in charge of a sleeping car without a conductor, but never a conductor; he may be a policeman but not a fireman; a linotyper but not a motion picture operator; a glass annealer, but not a glass blower; a deck hand, but not a sailor." Within New York City, some urban Black people could find work in the entertainment industry as musicians, actors, sex workers, or dancers. But Black communities had no equivalent economic avenues comparable to "the Jews in the garment industry, Italians in grocery stores and contracting, the Chinese in laundries," or the political patronage jobs of the Irish. Postal work made for one of the better-paying jobs that a Black immigrant could hope for as the first decade of the twentieth century drew to a close, and Harrison consistently earned promotions for his diligent work ethic each of his first four years until he would become a target of the repressive machinery of the most powerful Black man in the country, Booker T. Washington.[11]

Born enslaved in 1856, Washington worked his way "up from slavery" to emerge first as the star student of Samuel Chapman Armstrong's Hampton Institute. A child of white Christian missionaries, Armstrong "believed that Blacks should be taught to remain in their place, stay out of politics, keep quiet about their rights, and work. The educational theme that he emphasized was the need for Blacks to be good, subservient laborers." His star student at Hampton emerged in the young Booker T. Washington, whom Armstrong would recommend as head of the Tuskegee Institute along the same model and ideological framework of industrial education. As Washington acknowledged in his autobiography *Up From Slavery*, Armstrong "made the greatest and most lasting impression upon me" and "was a great man—the noblest, rarest human being that it has ever been my privilege to meet."[12]

After Washington's famous 1895 speech at the Atlanta Cotton Expo, in which he advocated a strategy of accommodation to racial segregation, Washington was anointed and hailed by the white press as the new "leader" of Black America. For his accommodationist approach to Jim Crow and for promoting a model of industrial education that emphasized the need for Black people to avoid fighting for their rights and just be good and quiet laborers, Washington garnered financial support for his school from rich white donors like Carnegie, Rockefeller, and Morgan, who all happened to have financial investments in the industries of the "New South" that squeezed profits from the cheapened labor of Southern Black workers. With the financial support of the capitalist robber barons, Washington bought controlling shares in Black newspapers, planted spies in Black organizations advocating agitation and protest, and paid Black newspaper editors to attack his ideological competitors who advocated political strategies that rejected any accommodation to Jim Crow segregation. For his much-appreciated services, Washington was granted access to the White House and influence over federal job appointments for Black people, a power which he used to reward his acolytes and punish his critics.

As a prime example, Hubert Harrison wrote a pair of op-ed pieces in the *New York Sun* in December of 1910 that defended those, including William Monroe Trotter and W. E. B. Du Bois, who advocated an active political fight to secure full citizenship for African Americans and had voiced criticisms of Washington's accommodationist stance. Washington had claimed, while traveling in London earlier that year, that the South offered better opportunities for Black people "than almost any other country in the world."[13] This idea would have been news to the thousands of Black victims of white lynch mobs. Harrison's response used numerous facts and simple logic to argue that insisting on the real grievances of the race and fighting against them presented a more effective course of action than the willful denial-based approach that Washington had articulated.¹⁴ In retaliation, Charles Anderson, a New York Republican Party functionary and close friend of Washington's, arranged for Harrison to be fired from his job at the post office.¹⁵

Harrison's firing demonstrated a concrete example of the consequences of criticizing Booker T. Washington, whose powerful "Tuskegee Machine" of political patronage formed a nationwide mechanism for policing the boundaries of acceptable Black thought and political speech.¹⁶ Given Harrison's exemplary workplace performance record, the firing constituted an underhanded and vindictive act of Washington's repressive political machinery.¹⁷ But far from silencing Harrison, the termination only further fueled his political radicalization, leading him to join the Socialist Party as a full-time speaker and organizer.

The Case against Capitalism

One of the intellectual weapons that Harrison honed and sharpened during his time in the Socialist Party was the same one all Socialists had to deploy against defenders of capitalism, who often advance arguments based on lofty generalities that simply do not hold up to scrutiny. For example, they claim that capitalism fosters creativity and innovation. Yet creativity and innovation are acceptable only within the bounds of what is profitable to the masters of capital. Inevitably, they move to crush all creativity and innovation—from individual workers like Hubert Harrison all the way up to the general strike—that threaten their real or perceived interests.

Defenders of capitalism claimed that the so-called free market exemplified the liberty and dynamism of the system. Yet long before the massive infusion of taxpayer money into the military industrial complex by way of the Pentagon, the market had ceased being "free." From the very beginning, US industrial development depended heavily on government interventions such as protective tariffs, business subsidies, land grants, economic crisis-moment bailouts, the use of slave patrols to crush slave resistance and rebellion, police and National Guard troops to crush organized labor, and the use of the US Army to conquer new territories from Indigenous peoples and defend capital invested abroad, to name just a few of the nonmarket forces that paved the way for US capitalist development. Hence John Dewey's contention that "politics is the shadow cast on society by big business."¹⁸

But even on purely economic terms, the rise of monopolies—and other large-scale concentrations of capital that inevitably sought to suppress competition, fix prices, and dominate the market in their own interest—obliterates the claim that capitalism promotes free competition. Similarly, advocates for the supposed "efficiency" of capitalism in producing and distributing cheaper products conveniently overlook the innumerable inbuilt *inefficiencies* of the system: the redundancy of widespread product duplication, permanent and systemic unemployment, cyclical overproduction and waste of unsold goods, planned obsolescence, price gouging, the creation of false desires by the advertising industry, the proliferation of socially unnecessary and nonproductive "jobs" like that of stock market speculators, and so on.[19]

Once all other arguments fail, we are told that the emphasis on individual self-interest fostered by capitalism supposedly accords with our inborn "human nature." However, even a cursory glance across space and time reveals a wide range of possibilities for human nature. What appears as "natural" human behavior is in fact dependent upon specific social and material conditions, which vary drastically. On one end of the spectrum, we can find examples of poverty and economic scarcity that lead even "good" and generous people toward depraved behavior. On the other end, we can find examples of abundance (e.g., at the family holiday dinner feast) where even "bad" or greedy people are somehow able to relate on the basis of sharing and cooperation.

If you put two selfish and greedy people on a desert island, their behavior will tend to shift toward cooperation and sharing. This is not the result of a sudden change in their "human nature" but of a change in their specific and contingent material conditions: suddenly they must collaborate—whether they like it or not—in order to survive. As Karl Marx put it in his *Theses on Feuerbach*, "The human essence is no abstraction inherent in each single individual. In its reality it is the ensemble of the social relations."[20] Human nature clearly changes from one set of conditions to another. Therefore, the individualistic behaviors stoked by capitalism's inequalities and scarcity-inducing material conditions must not be mistaken for an ahistorical or universal expression of "human nature."

Apart from falling flat on their face upon interrogation, the arguments for capitalism are meant to mask the blood, sweat, and world-historic traumas inherent in its actual sociohistorical development: the colonization and genociding of countless Indigenous peoples; the monstrosity of slavery with its ongoing legacy of white terrorism and supremacy; the rampant exploitation of women, children, and working people; the despoliation of flora, fauna, and mycelia by profit-driven raw material extraction and fossil fuels; the endless wars for imperial expansion and world domination; and relentless state repression against all manner of freedom-seeking visionaries. Other than that, it's a beautiful system!

The Heyday of American Socialism

While in the Socialist Party, Hubert Harrison studied Karl Marx and Friedrich Engels very closely because they pioneered some of the most influential and revolutionary analyses and critiques of industrial capitalism. Engels summarized his friend and collaborator Marx's key theoretical contributions to their message in the *Communist Manifesto*.

> The basic thought running through the Manifesto—that economic production, and the structure of society of every historical epoch necessarily arising therefrom, constitute the foundation for the political and intellectual history of that epoch; that consequently . . . all history has been a history of class struggles, of struggles between exploited and exploiting, between dominated and dominating classes at various stages of social evolution; that this struggle, however, has now reached a stage where the exploited and oppressed class (the proletariat) can no longer emancipate itself from the class which exploits and oppresses it (the bourgeoisie), without at the same time forever freeing the whole of society from exploitation, oppression, [and] class struggles—this basic thought belongs solely and exclusively to Marx.[21]

In other words, the material conditions of any given age establish the framework of that age's politics and ideas, and the class struggle ultimately determines which politics and ideas become dominant. The class struggle under industrial capitalism had established the productive economic capacity to provide for everyone and thus put an end to material scarcity and class-based society itself. Capitalism also created the class with the means and interest to overthrow the system, namely the proletariat or modern working class. According to Marx and Engels, those "who live only so long as they find work, and who find work only so long as their labor increases capital" faced a struggle against the bourgeoisie or capitalist class (those who owned the means of economic production in the form of land, factories, mines, and office buildings and employed wage labor to work in them). As a movement of the immense majority in the interest of the immense majority, the proletarian revolution had the potential to take political power collectively into its own hands, overthrow the capitalist class, and establish a collective socialization of the economy that would function in the interest of all. Subsequent developments would show these basic ideas of Marxism to be easier to imagine than to actualize, a lesson that Hubert Harrison would learn the hard way in the Socialist Party of America.

Given the naked, pompous, and visceral brutalities of US capitalism at the turn of the century, the Socialist Party grew massively in the first decade of its existence to become the largest Socialist Party in US history. Formed in 1901 out of a merger between the Social Democratic Party and the Socialist Labor Party, by 1912 it boasted over 100,000 members, with over 1,000 of them holding elected offices throughout the country. The Socialist Party had 323 newspapers, including the *Appeal to Reason*, which boasted a circulation of 761,000. The Socialist Party featured a Women's National Committee and commanded the allegiance of such trailblazing women as Helen Keller, Kate O'Hare, Margaret Sanger, and Mary Harris "Mother" Jones. It attracted radical muckraking journalists like Upton Sinclair, John Reed, and Gustavus Myers, as well as race-conscious liberal reformers like Charles Edward Russell, William English Walling, and Mary White Ovington. With moderate reformists and radical revolutionaries, Northerners and Southerners, immigrant and native-born workers, the party that Hubert Harrison would join existed as a "seething complex of diverse, often antipathetic, groups, persons, and political tendencies."[22]

Hubert Harrison joined the Socialist Party at a time when Eugene V. Debs had established himself as the party's perennial presidential candidate. Becoming politically radicalized as leader of the American Railway Union during the Pullman strike of 1894, Debs became one of the best-known popularizers of the case for Socialism as the party's perennial presidential candidate. "The Socialist Party," he declared, "as the party of the exploited workers in the mills and mines, on the railways and on the farms, the workers of both sexes and all races and colors, the working class in a word, constituting a great majority of the people and in fact THE PEOPLE, demands that the nation's industries shall be taken over by the nation and that the nation's workers shall operate them for the benefit of the whole people."[23]

In his campaign speeches, Debs made clear the Socialist demands of the party:

> We demand the machinery of production in the name of the workers and the control of society in the name of the people. We demand the abolition of capitalism and wage-slavery and the surrender of the capitalist class. We demand the complete enfranchisement of women and the equal rights of all the people regardless of race, color, creed or nationality. We demand that child labor shall cease once and forever and that all children born into the world shall have equal opportunity to grow up, to be educated, to have healthy bodies and trained minds, and to develop and freely express the best there is in them in mental, moral and physical achievement. We demand complete control of industry by the workers; we demand all the wealth they produce for their own enjoyment, and we demand the earth for all the people.[24]

Inspired by nineteenth-century masters of oratory like Robert Ingersoll, Debs ranked among the party's most compelling and accessible public speakers. "Political parties are responsive to the interests of those who finance them," Debs declaimed. "This is the infallible test of their character and applied to the Republican, Democratic and Progressive Parties, these parties stand forth as the several political expressions of the several divisions of the capitalist class. The funds of all these parties are furnished by the capitalist class for the reason, and only for the reason, that they represent the interests of that class." Moreover, "the Republican, Democratic and Progressive Parties all stand for private ownership and competition. The Socialist Party alone stands for social ownership and co-operation.... The Republican, Democratic and Progressive Parties uphold the wage system; the Socialist Party demands its overthrow."[25]

Harrison endorsed Debs's run for president and campaigned for the Socialist ticket in local and state elections. In 1917, Harrison argued that "the Socialist Party in power would mean the absolute cessation of police brutality and the conscienceless evictions by conscienceless landlords; would mean bathhouses and playgrounds, municipal markets to cut down the high cost of living, municipal ownership of ice and milk.... Now for the first time in year, they have a chance to win.... If the Negroes of this great city want and need the things for which they stand, let them vote for the Socialist candidates ... in this [upcoming] election."

Harrison also made arguments at the beginning of the twentieth century that also remain eerily relevant at the beginning of the twenty-first. "The New Negro in America will never amount to anything politically until he enfranchises himself from the Grand Old Party, which has made a political joke of him," he wrote.[26] Here it becomes hard not to notice that Harrison could easily have said a similar thing about the party of liberalism today: African Americans will never amount to anything politically until we enfranchise ourselves—that is, declare our independence—from the Democratic Party, which has made a political joke of us.[27]

Like Socialist, Communist, Green Party, and other independent progressive electoral candidates today, the Socialists faced the argument that a vote for a third party would act as a spoiler on the ability of the "lesser evil" to get elected. Echoing Eugene Debs, Harrison responded unequivocally, arguing that "the talk of 'throwing away your vote' is sheer humbug. For, even if it came to the worst, it is better to vote for what you want and not get it, than to vote for what you don't want—and get it." In particular, it was better that working people vote for the Socialist candidates they wanted and not get them than to vote for the "lesser" of two capitalist evils and get more evil as a result.[28]

Figure 1.3 Ralph Chaplin's cartoon "The Hand That Will Rule the World" (published June 30, 1917, in *Solidarity*) symbolized the collective working-class power that the IWW sought to build by organizing all the workers into "one big union."

Overlapping with Socialist Party goals in many ways, the IWW, colloquially known as the "Wobblies," emerged in 1905 as the first organization to attempt to organize the entire industrial working class into "One Big Union." Like the Socialist Party, the Wobblies saw capitalism as the root problem and the organization of workers as the solution. However, the IWW focused on the economic struggle that would build workers' power at the point of production through industrial organization for direct action, sabotage, and mass strikes rather than the project of building a workers' political party that could run for office, take power in government, and enact progressive legislation. The IWW counted among its ranks and supporters some of the most consistent and radical labor organizers in the country, such as Lucy Parsons, Ben Fletcher, Elizabeth Gurley Flynn, William "Big Bill" Haywood, and Mary Harris "Mother" Jones. The Wobblies organized workers who had been left out of AFL unions, such as the so-called unskilled workers, as well as Black workers in industries like lumber and mining. For this reason, when push came to shove between Socialists and Wobblies, Harrison sided with the Wobblies.

Figure 1.4 This IWW cartoon "At the Parting of Ways," from the May 1919 issue of the periodical *One Big Union*, shows the working class facing a choice between reform, where the path marked "craft unionism" leads, versus revolution, where the path marked industrial unionism leads. It was highlighted in the Lusk Committee report, an organization formed by the New York State Legislature in 1919 to investigate radical and "seditious" activity in the state.

Socialist Party Race Politics before Harrison

Although ethnolinguistic associations of Italians, Hungarians, Jews, Germans, Poles, and Finns comprised nearly a sixth of total party membership, the Socialist Party's overwhelmingly white American leadership embodied a markedly nativist politics. In one of the first book-length histories of the party, historian Ira Kipnis wrote that "the only official statement on the rights of the foreign-born was one passed by the party's national committee in 1907. It urged Socialists to stand for equal civil and political rights for all residents regardless of race or nativity." On the face of it, this resolution appeared quite progressive for its time, but in reality, "nothing was ever done to implement this resolution. And the immigration controversy which developed in 1907 . . . indicated that a good proportion of the party, anxious to win the support of [American Federation of Labor] leaders, had no desire for immigrants in the country, much less in the party."[29] To be more specific, the party apparently had no desire for *nonwhite* immigrants, since Finns, Italians, Germans, Jews,

Poles, Russians, and other Socialists of European descent each had autonomous ethnolinguistic federations, newspapers, and even community centers of their own within the party. By contrast, the Socialist Party generally wanted nothing to do with Asian immigrants, who *Appeal to Reason* called the "Mongolian hordes" and the "yellow peril."[30] What about African Americans?

Harrison built upon the Black Socialist tradition in the United States. Figures like Peter Clark, Rev. George and Annie Woodbey, and Rev. George Slater forged a path before him by their efforts to make a special case for Socialism to African Americans.[31] To its credit, the Socialist Party even passed an antiracist resolution at its founding 1903 convention. There was a report, though unconfirmed, of an all-Black Socialist Party local in the tiny town of Lutcher, Louisiana, in 1905. Another report surfaced regarding a clandestine Black organization in Muskogee, Oklahoma, called the "United Socialists" that fought a gun battle with police and federal officers in 1907 and claimed the right to expropriate private property because "their authority was higher than that of the United States." The official Oklahoma Socialist Party fought state laws designed to disenfranchise African American voters—and won some degree of respect and interest from African Americans in the state as a result. Cases like these, though fascinating, constitute exceptions that prove the general rule of the party's more general failure to devote significant attention to recruiting Black members in its early years.[32]

Ida M. Raymond, the state secretary of the Socialist Party of Mississippi, provides a prime example of Socialist "Southernism." According to her, Northerners could not understand the "Negro question" in the South because Northern Black people represented mostly "the better class of colored people," who "know their position and do not presume to step outside of that line." Black people in the South, by contrast, were "worse than the 'Uncle Tom' of slavery days" because they were "always scheming whereby they may get the advantage of the white man." She went even further. The South, she pleaded, "has had a taste of what the negroes would do if they were to be allowed full political rights accorded them by the Constitution, and can you blame them if they, remembering those awful days [of Reconstruction], should fear a repetition of the time when the Ku Klux Klan had to take matters in their own hands and save their women, their homes, and their country from the terrible outrages that were perpetrated by the Negroes as long as they were allowed the constitutional rights without limitation?"[33] Raymond here gave voice to the typical white racist narrative about Reconstruction, one she shared with far less "progressive" white Southerners than her. That a sitting state secretary of the party could so publicly and unapologetically praise the Ku Klux Klan provides yet another example of why so few Black workers identified with the Socialist cause.[34]

According to Philip Foner, "apart from the question of the farmers' role in the Socialist Party, the Negro question was the most widely debated issue in American socialist circles during the opening years of the twentieth century." However, he also pointed out that it was almost entirely white people doing the debating.[35] Like their Southern counterparts, some Northern-based parties' leaders held openly racist views about Black people. One wing of the party "declared that the whites disliked the Negroes because Negroes were inferior, depraved degenerates who went 'around raping women [and] children.'" Victor Berger, a German-speaking Jewish immigrant in Wisconsin and the first Socialist Party representative elected to the United States Congress, declared "that the free contact with the whites has led to the further degeneration of the negroes" and that white women "who were 'depraved' enough to associate with Negroes only did so because capitalism prevented them from earning a living 'in a natural way.'"[36]

Some party members contested such anti-Black positions in the party. For example, a Russian Jewish Socialist in New York City named Isaac Rubinow wrote a series of sixteen articles in the *International Socialist Review*, some of the only such articles written on Black people and Socialism from 1905 until Harrison's writings in 1911.[37] Rubinow argued against anti-Black racism and for greater attention to the so-called Negro problem, concluding his series with a challenge to the party about whether it would be wise enough to address the issue of race prejudice.[38] Apparently, the only positive response came from Local New York, even though "prior to 1911 . . . local New York never once discussed the recruiting of Negroes, nor did it raise any specific demands of interest to blacks." According to Foner, only two branches—Branches 5 and 7 in New York City—had more than one or two Black members at the time.[39]

Eugene V. Debs emerged as the most famous left-wing leader and perennial Socialist Party candidate for president. He also had a serious weakness in his race politics. On the one hand, Debs opposed discrimination and called on Black workers "to reject the false doctrines of 'meekness and humility.'" Debs also refused to speak to segregated audiences in the South and welcomed African Americans to the labor and Socialist movements. Yet, on the other hand, Debs also insisted that "there is no Negro question outside of the labor question—the working class struggle," that the Socialists had "nothing special to offer the Negro," and that "we cannot make separate appeals to all the races," because ultimately "the class struggle is colorless."[40] What about separate train cars, bathrooms, and water fountains, denial of the right to vote, rampant sexual violence against Black women, weekly lynchings of Black men, and entire African American towns like Oscarville (Georgia) and Kowaliga (Alabama) deliberately and permanently submerged under water? For the "radical" Debs, the party had nothing special to offer about all of that!

"In capitalism the Negro question is a grave one and will grow more threatening as the contradictions and complications of capitalist society multiply," Debs allowed. "But this need not worry us. Let them settle the Negro question in their way, if they can. We have nothing to do with it, for that is their fight." Debs here exemplified the way in which even radical white people who called for a working-class revolution against capitalism could simultaneously distance themselves from the specific challenges facing most oppressed segment of the working class.[41]

Hubert Harrison's Black Socialist Politics

Harrison's work on the Negro and Socialism can be boiled down to two main contributions to the Socialist movement. He offered one of the first historical materialist (or economic development-based) analyses of the relationship between race and class in US history and also one of the first systematic challenges to the Socialist Party's internal racism by a Black party member. In this regard he extended the work of white Socialists like Isaac Rubinow, who had articulated Socialist arguments about the relationship between class consciousness and anti-Black racism and challenged the party to do right by Black workers. By making a historical argument linking slavery and racism to capitalism through a Black worker's angle of vision, Harrison crystallized a secular Black Socialist politics that would be elaborated in subsequent decades by a long line of Black socialist and communist thinkers that came after him.

In 1911 and 1912, Harrison wrote a five-part series of articles on "The Negro and Socialism" for Local New York's newspaper (the *New York Call*) and a three-part series for the nationally distributed and Chicago-based *International Socialist Review*, which articulated the key elements of his case for building the Socialist movement in Black communities and formed one of the earliest—if not *the* earliest—series-length exposition on this subject by a Black party member.[42]

Harrison articulated the case for Socialism based on arguments about capitalism's systemic exploitation of working people. He observed how in 1905 the average annual wealth produced per capita reached $2,450, while the average annual wage was $437. "Or in other words for every $6 produced the producer got only one dollar, the other five dollars having been filched from him."

Because the Socialist Party conceived of itself as "the political expression of the economic interests of the workers," Harrison emphasized the class position of African Americans.[43] In his words, "the ten million Negroes of America form a group that is more essentially proletarian than any other American group." In addition, he pointed out that Black workers were generally paid less than other workers for their labor and often worked longer hours under worse conditions. In short, the system exploited Black workers more fully and intensely than any other group of workers.[44] "In the good old days the chattel slave would be fastened with a chain if they thought that he might escape. Today no chain is necessary to bind us to the tools. We are free as air. Of course. We are free to starve. And that chain of the fear of starvation binds us to the tools owned by the capitalist as firmly as any iron chain ever did."[45]

As for how Black workers got into their acutely proletarian position, he recounted the brutality of Christopher Columbus, the European conquest of the Indigenous people of the Americas, and how the Europeans enslaved Africans as a fresh supply of labor to produce wealth for them. "Since the Negroes were brought here as chattels," he argued, "their social status was fixed by that fact." The notion of Black people as subhuman arose from the need of Europeans to justify the enslavement of African labor.[46] Therefore, race prejudice emerged as a product of economic subjection, a problem with "roots in slavery past and present."[47]

Harrison argued that race prejudice benefited the ruling class and ultimately harmed both Black and white workers. He maintained that race prejudice harmed Black workers because they could get no protection from the courts, the ballot, and public opinion. Meanwhile, even white workers who enjoyed these protections could not demand higher wages, better conditions, or strike action without the employers threatening to replace them with Black workers. Therefore, white workers also suffered materially in the long run from the system of race prejudice. The capitalist class sustained race prejudice in order to keep wages low, strikes infrequent, and workers divided.

Indeed, the ruling class deliberately fostered race prejudice by its control of the mass media: "The newspapers, owned by the capitalist class of the South, with their brother barons in the North, have entered upon a campaign of deprecation, vilification, calumny and lies in an endeavor to use the ignorance and superstition of the workers against workers." He described how they did this by such tactics as playing up crimes allegedly committed by Black people while remaining silent about examples of Black ingenuity and achievement and telling various pernicious and racist lies about African Americans.[48]

Harrison had to contend with the argument of those, including some Socialists, who defended the racial hierarchy on the grounds that racial inequality followed naturally from biological differences between racial groups. For example, the December 1913 issue of the Socialist monthly *New Review* published an article titled "The Inferior Races from an Anthropologist's Point of View" by the associate editor of *American Anthropologist*, Robert Lowie. Lowie argued that "biologically, it seems obvious that non-Caucasian races resemble more closely the non-human ancestors of man than do the Caucasians. Psychologically, the high civilization achieved by the white race seems to prove even more clearly its superiority over other varieties of *Homo sapiens*." He went on to posit a fundamental difference between "the European and the darker races" on the grounds that Caucasians had larger brains than Pacific Islanders, who in turn had larger brains than "African Negroes."[49] Naturally, if racial differences were a matter of biology, then the "race prejudice is innate" argument would make sense.

In response, Harrison pointed to the Southern aristocrat, the "ablest defender" of the idea that race prejudice was natural for humans. He questioned why the Southern aristocrat with his inborn racial hatred preferred to have Black people nursing his children and serving him. Harrison further suggested that there appeared no innate repulsion between white men and Black women, or else there would not exist so many racially mixed people. Therefore, there was nothing natural about race prejudice. After all, if it were innate, then it "would not be necessary to teach it to children by separate schools or to adults by separate cars." Referring to Jim Crow laws separating white people and Black people, he reasoned that "every single fabric in the great wall of segregation which America is so laboriously building is an eloquent argument against the belief that race prejudice is innate. If it were innate it would never be necessary to bolster it up by legislative enactments." Harrison adamantly rejected the idea that race prejudice was innate, insisting that race prejudice could not be justified "on scientific, social, or ethical grounds."[50]

Harrison placed the arguments supporting race prejudice into their social context. Echoing Marx and Engels's argument that the ruling ideas of any epoch are the ideas of the ruling class, Harrison argued that the ideas and opinions dominant at any stage of human history are created and shaped by the material conditions of society. He then cleverly took a simple argument about socioeconomic class interests and extended its logic to the domain of race: "Whenever large groups of men find profit in injustice to other men, they will evolve a system of ethics to reconcile their minds to that injustice. They cannot continue to do wrong without calling that wrong right. That is why the capitalist class cannot even think justice so far as the workers are concerned. And that is why men who think that they can see a social or economic advantage for themselves in the degradation of the Negro will continue to think that degradation right."[51] The white American ruling class could not even "think justice" for white workers, let alone African Americans. In a similar fashion, white workers who perceived an advantage for themselves in the degraded status of Black people would inevitably create a psychological and intellectual justification for it.

Harrison explained how Black economic subjection went hand in hand with political disenfranchisement. "Politically," he wrote, "the Negro is the touchstone of the modern democratic idea" because "the presence of the Negro puts our democracy to the proof and reveals the falsity of it." He gave the example of the United States Declaration of Independence, which seemed to articulate a "splendid truth." "But," he noted, "the black man merely touched it and it became a splendid lie." After all, he reasoned, if Black people were to get political freedom, they would free themselves from economic exploitation and contempt, implying "a revolution ... startling even to think of." In short, they would get free from both racial oppression as Black people and from class exploitation as workers.[52]

From this, Harrison concluded that because "the mission of the Socialist Party is to free the working class from exploitation" and since "the Negro is the most ruthlessly exploited working class group in America, the duty of the party to champion his cause is as clear as day." This formed the capstone of Harrison's whole line of argument: the party had to extend the message of Socialism to African Americans. Not only that, but the party needed to organize African Americans, teach them the tenets of Socialism, and inspire them by their solidarity with the hope of a new republic founded on the "brotherhood of man." Referencing Karl Marx explicitly, Harrison claimed this possibility on the grounds that "the working class united, and conscious of its proletaria[n] aims, can, against the world, achieve anything."[53]

Alongside his hope in the power of working-class unity, Harrison remained sober about the difficulties of changing racial attitudes: "I do not expect that the advent of Socialism will at once remove race prejudice—unless it remove[s] ignorance at the same time. . . . But . . . I do expect that it will take the white man from off the black man's back" because ultimately "socialism is here to put an end to the exploitation of one group by another, whether that group be social, economic, or racial." Harrison argued that this egalitarian ethos drove the thinking of Marx, Engels, Karl Kautsky, "and every great leader of the Socialist movement" because egalitarianism was "embedded in the very fabric of the Socialist philosophy."

Harrison posed for the party a question not only pertinent but ominous: "Does the Socialist Party feel that it needs the Negroes as much as the Negro needs Socialism?" He then publicly challenged the party to match its actions with its rhetoric. "If we feel that we can advance to the conquest of capitalism with one part of the proletariat against us, let us say so. But I haven't the slightest doubt that our program requires all the proletariat." He felt that if the party were to take organizing Black workers seriously, it would only "add to the strength of the organized, all-inclusive class conscious working class movement."[54]

If the party ignored Black workers, then Black workers would inevitably be used against the labor movement, "as the [racially exclusionary AFL-affiliated] craft unions have begun to find out." In Harrison's words, "the capitalists of America are not waiting. Already they have subsidized Negro leaders, Negro editors, preachers and politicians to build up in the breasts of black people those sentiments which will make them subservient to their will." As a result, "we find that the prevailing social philosophy among Negroes—that which white capitalism will pay to have them taught—is one of submission and acquiescence in political servitude." Here he implied that the Tuskegee Institute garnered the financial support of rich white people thanks to Booker T. Washington's advocacy of Black accommodation of the status quo. Therefore, if the party did not recruit Black workers for Socialism, then capitalist society would continue recruiting them for capitalism. Thus the issue had been "squarely presented: Southernism or Socialism—which? Is it to be the white half of the working class against the black half, or all the working class?"[55]

Harrison made a reasonable case that Socialists needed to recruit Black workers. After all, how could the party object to giving special attention to African Americans, given that it had carried on special outreach work among groups like the Poles, Slovaks, Finns, Hungarians, and Lithuanians? He argued white social movements had historically broken down as soon as they crossed the color line, so African Americans were generally unaccustomed to joining or participating in them and would therefore require a unique approach if Socialists were to make inroads in Black communities. Harrison pointed to the utility of racially specific literature, such as Rev. George Slater's 1911 pamphlet *The Colored Man's Case as Socialism Sees It* and another by Eugene Debs featuring a picture of wage slavery and chattel slavery, which he found to be quite effective in outreach to Black workers.[56] He also described the special "form of address" for this task, which according to him meant making the "ABC arguments" of Socialism but to cram them full of facts drawn from African American history and experience so as to tailor the case for Socialism to Black workers' specific concerns and racial consciousness.

Speaking from his own experience with the effectiveness of this approach, Harrison maintained that Black Socialists had a special role to play in recruiting African Americans to the party. He argued that in order to recruit in the Black community, "one must know the people, their history, their manner of life, and modes of thinking and feeling." He urged his comrades to learn "the psychology of the Negro and how to address [the Socialist message] both to the 'heart' and to the 'head.'" He argued that Black comrades could do better outreach to Black communities because the aforementioned considerations would be second nature thanks to their Black racial experience and identity, which white comrades lacked.[57]

Harrison offered some suggestions about how white Socialists should relate to Black people. Observing that many Socialists often said things like

"I have always been friendly with colored people" and "I have never felt any prejudice against Negroes," Harrison suggested that if a comrade's heart were in the right place it would appear in their actions. "Treat them," he urged, "simply as human beings as if you had never looked at the color of their faces." This approach, nowadays called "color blindness," remains a problematic ideology, for a variety of reasons.[58] But in 1911, Harrison's suggestion that white comrades treat African Americans as though they had no color represented an attempt to affect a more egalitarian racial ethos among white party members, as compared with the explicitly anti-Black prejudices that so many of them demonstrated.[59]

Harrison concluded his case with a call for white Socialists to sit down and be humble: "Socialists in general need to learn a great many things about the Negro—not only of his racial psychology, but also of his history and of his present achievements in the various lines of human endeavor. If the white man of Europe knows nothing of the Negro, the white man of America knows a great deal that isn't so. And one has to unlearn much before he can begin to learn."[60] If the party wanted to recruit among African Americans, white comrades would need to acknowledge their racial ignorance about Black people and adopt a posture of respect and humility toward them.

The Colored Socialist Club: Harrison's Organizational Contribution

Overall, in terms of its scope, depth, and timing, Harrison made a groundbreaking and incisive case that the Socialist Party needed to transform its theoretical and practical approach to Black workers. Soon his argument began to bear fruit. In October of 1911, the secretary of the party's Branch 5 in Harlem, Samuel Romansky, wrote to Local New York headquarters that because Harrison understood Black life and history and was a good public speaker, the branch proposed that he be "made a paid speaker and organizer for Local New York for special work in Negro districts."[61] Branch 5 happened to also be the branch of a young Margaret Sanger, whose articles in the party's *New York Call* newspaper about sex education, women's bodies, and contraception would influence Harrison's own birth control advocacy and sexual politics, as we will see in chapter 6.

By December, secretary of the executive committee (EC) Julius Gerber admitted that "we have carried our propaganda to the Polish, Hungarian, Slavic, Lithuanian and Finnish workers; to the organized and unorganized men and women. But so far one section of the working-class in America has not even been approached. Local New York has taken this fact under advisement and has perfected plans for the work among Negroes."[62] Harrison had found a receptive ear in the New York EC, and the Harlem branch moved to make him the local's first full-time Black organizer to help the party recruit Black workers.

This newfound support from the New York leadership opened the door to a new organizational formation, the Colored Socialist Club (CSC). The CSC represented a Black-led and multiracial party formation that held meetings and distributed Socialist literature specifically oriented toward Black people. With Harrison's leadership, it held weekly meetings in Harlem and educated participants about the specific role of Black workers in the class struggle as well as what Socialism could do for African Americans. In Harrison's words, "If the overturning of the present system should elevate a new class into power; a class to which the negro belongs; a class which has nothing to gain by the degradation of any portion of itself; that class will remove the economic reason of the degradation of the negro. That is the promise of Socialism, the all-inclusive working-class movement. In the final triumph of this movement lies the only hope of salvation from this second slavery of black men and of white."[63] Guided by the notion that Socialism would abolish the economic system responsible for racial oppression, the CSC within weeks affected a "tremendous increase of Socialist sentiment among the Negroes of Harlem," according to its organizer. The club represented the first Black-led special organizational formation in the party's history.[64]

Interestingly, opposition to the formation of the club came from not only white comrades but also Black ones. In particular, W. E. B. Du Bois and Black Socialist preacher and Niagara Movement veteran Rev. George Frazier Miller of Brooklyn raised public concerns in the party's *New York Call* that the whole project smacked of segregation. They thought, mistakenly, that the project sought to create a Black-only branch. Harrison responded to their concerns by making it clear that no segregation was intended and that if it was then the EC would never have selected him as its spearhead and leading organizer. In a statement suggesting Du Bois and Miller had gone public with their concerns without first consulting him, Harrison pleaded that anyone familiar with him and his politics would have known that he was not aiming for segregation but for special outreach to Black workers on their own terms, which is why the racially inclusive CSC meetings took place in Harlem and welcomed all racial groups.[65]

Unfortunately, as a result of a sudden reversal by the EC, the CSC would be short-lived. In late February 1912, less than three months after it got off the ground, the EC abandoned the project, supposedly due to lack of available funds, poor attendance, and concerns about a party structure based on "segregation." Given that the club received funding by donations from local branches and ethnolinguistic associations, the excuse of a depleted party treasury did not hold water. As for attendance, Harrison acknowledged that it had recently been uneven but argued that attendance appeared spotty at other party meetings and in those cases did not necessarily indicate lack of interest or potential. He claimed that the party had not done its full duties yet to support the club and should give it a chance to succeed. Given Harrison's own clear and public repudiation of the notion that a separate Black-only branch was intended, the segregation charge was also spurious.[66]

What really explains the EC's sudden cancellation of the CSC? Could their accusation of "segregation" against Harrison have been a subconscious admission of their own aims? According to Foner, Harrison grew suspicious that the initial basis of EC support for the CSC flowed from its desire to insulate white Socialists from Black members.[67] It certainly did not help that Du Bois, the most prominent Black intellectual in the country, editor of the National Association for the Advancement of Colored People (NAACP) magazine *The Crisis*, and a Socialist Party member, had publicly urged the EC to oppose the Harrison-led project. Rev. Miller and Du Bois had been friends and colleagues since the Niagara Movement in 1905, and they now maintained ties to an NAACP (with a leadership dominated by white liberals) and Socialist party whose politics did not accommodate equity for Black political leadership. Given the reappearance of the "segregation" charge as an official reason for terminating the club after Harrison dispelled it, their lack of familiarity with Harlem, and their apparent failure to consult Harrison directly with their concerns about his vision for the CSC, one wonders if Miller and Du Bois were acting to assuage the white fragility of local party leaders and to highlight their political deference to them, in contrast to the threat of racial equality in organizational leadership that Harrison's CSC posed.[68] Most likely, the white party leaders were troubled by the threat of a good example whose success would have necessitated a more decisive and permanent shift in the local's balance of racial power in the direction of even more Black members and leaders in the future. As the saying goes: to those accustomed to privilege, equality feels like oppression.

The Negro as a "Crucial Test": Harrison's Break with the Socialists

1912 marked a decisive year not only in the rise and fall of Harrison's CSC in New York City but also for the national party as a whole, which would clarify its position on racial issues (among others) at its national convention. The convention did not address the "Negro question" directly, as only one delegate (IWW leader "Big Bill" Haywood) even mentioned it.[69] Yet the Majority Report of the Committee on Immigration fatefully declared that "race feeling is not so much a result of social as of biological evolution. It does not change essentially with changes of economic systems.... It exists ... as a product of biology.... We may temper this race feeling by education, but we can never hope to extinguish it altogether. Class consciousness must be learned, but race-consciousness is inborn and cannot be wholly unlearned.... Where races struggle for the means of life ... economic and political considerations lead to racial fights and to legislation restricting the invasion of the white man's domain by other races."[70] Simply put, race prejudice was biologically rather than socially determined, timeless and inborn rather than contingent and extinguishable. In taking this position, the party unequivocally rejected Harrison's preconvention arguments about the political, historical, and above all socioeconomic roots of race prejudice.

Alongside the resolution espousing an essentialist position on racial differences, the 1912 convention also made official the party's precipitous move in a more conservative direction. It passed an amendment to the party constitution that read, "Any member of the party who opposes political action or advocates crime, sabotage, or other methods of violence as a weapon of the working class shall be expelled from membership."[71] Supporters of the amendment, which Eugene Debs supported, quickly used it to attack the leftist, pro-IWW wing of the party, beginning with the recall of the radical IWW leader "Big Bill" Haywood from the national EC. The moderates, thinking that a purge of the "anarchistic" elements of the party would improve its respectability and thereby pave the way for it to grow larger, were in for a big surprise. Haywood's recall precipitated an exodus of his supporters, and party membership dropped below 80,000 from its high point of 135,000 at the time of the 1912 convention. The party executive used the fateful amendment in other reactionary ways, for example by abruptly terminating funding for the Women's National Committee on the grounds that its existence and activities were "unessential."[72]

Meanwhile, as the party lurched to the right, Harrison grew even more radical. He spoke in Elizabeth, New Jersey, in November 1912, advocating industrial unionism, syndicalism, and "direct action on the economic field," a tendency that emerged from the reaction among rank-and-file workers to the "old style craft unionism which had utterly failed to keep step with the march of industry." Harrison criticized the AFL style of unionism for representing overwhelmingly "the skilled and better paid workers, leaving the great army of unskilled men, women and children with nothing to protect their interests." He also noted, approvingly, that some workers were showing disdain for the Socialist Party's purely electoral and nonindustrial approach. Harrison's speech revealed his sympathy with the racially inclusive and industry-wide organizing strategy of the IWW. He spoke in favor of industrial sabotage, direct action, and the general strike, citing various examples of their application in recent European labor battles. These themes located their advocate on the revolutionary left wing of the party.[73]

Harrison further revealed his move away from the moderate, middle-class, elections-focused wing of the party by his support for the massive 25,000-strong Paterson (New Jersey) Silk Strike of 1913.[74] In the course of that strike, he shared speaking platforms with such national left-wing labor leaders as "Big Bill" Haywood, Elizabeth Gurley Flynn, Carlo Tresca, and Arturo Giovannitti. One can only imagine the electrifying effect that this incendiary Black orator had on the thousands of striking European-descended men, women, and child laborers who filled the strike support meeting halls:

> We consider, whether right or wrong, every blow struck by labor against capital is a blow for labor. . . . As for the Socialist Party, no one asked the Socialist Party to come into this strike. Let it stay out—if it dares! In season and out of season, we Socialists must go to the workers to hear what we must do. The revolution is not coming from above, remember, but from below, working its way up from the depths. . . . We are not here because they invaded our rights. We have none. We never had any. We are working not to get rights, but to get might, and when we have *that*, we will have right![75]

This speech highlighted Harrison's militancy (arguing not for rights but for working-class power) and also his radical humility ("we Socialists must go to the workers to hear what we must do"). It also revealed his conception of revolution coming "from below" and his criticism of (and growing distance from) the official Socialist Party leadership.

During the silk strike, Harrison supported the tactic of industrial sabotage—that is, workers deliberately undermining the efficiency of production, either in terms of quantity or quality—as a weapon in the class struggle. IWW leader Frederick Sumner Boyd had been arrested and convicted for advising the silk workers to sabotage production if the mill owners refused to meet their demands for better wages and working conditions. Elizabeth Gurley Flynn wrote an entire pamphlet on sabotage to clarify its utility, morality, and legality, as Boyd's case was the first time anyone had been arrested for advocating sabotage.[76] In defense of Boyd's radicalism, Harrison also advocated sabotage, arguing that, as workers, "it is our one great weapon" and is "feared by capitalists more than anything else." Therefore, if the Paterson silk mill capitalists "want[ed] to lose $200,000" by not accepting the workers' demands, then "let them go ahead" and see what consequences would follow.[77]

The Paterson *Evening News* found Harrison's statements "unfit to print," to which Elizabeth Gurley Flynn replied, "He tells plain facts and the bosses

Figure 1.5 Hubert Harrison with Elizabeth Gurley Flynn, William "Big Bill" Haywood, and other leaders of the Paterson Silk Strike. According to Harrison's biographer Jeffrey B. Perry, this photo was probably taken when Harrison spoke to striking silk workers in Paterson, New Jersey (April 17, 1913), or in Haledon, New Jersey (May 19, 1913), or when he spoke in New York City at a mass protest meeting of the Paterson Defense Committee (February 4, 1914). Before it was defeated, Harrison had denounced the Socialist Party's attacks on the strike and the IWW because he felt the silk workers needed all the financial, political, and moral support they could get. American Labor Museum/Botto House National Landmark, Haledon, New Jersey.

don't like them."[78] Even the Socialist Party's *New York Call*, which he had criticized for refusing to print a letter from a prominent speaker at the IWW's Paterson Defense Conference, praised one of Harrison's speeches, reporting that "he filled in the remarks of the [other] speakers as the ocean does a chain of islands."[79] Harrison embodied a major asset to the workers' movement, but his passion for industrial sabotage, the general strike, and industry-wide organizing at the point of production proved irksome not only to the capitalist press but also to the moderate and gradualist Socialist Party leaders.

In response to Harrison's outspoken independence and increasingly left-wing politics, the party's EC of Local New York began to move against him. First, they reduced his pay to one-third of that offered to white speakers. Then they removed him from the party's speakers list and forbade all branches from scheduling their own speakers. They declined a request to have him speak in favor of "industrial action" for other branches. They cast suspicion upon him

Socialism or Southernism? 55

by smearing his name in the party press for his public support of outspoken left-wingers like Alexander Scott and F. Sumner Boyd, who had both been arrested for pro-sabotage speeches. They attempted to prohibit him from speaking and from publicly debating the anti-Socialist lecturer Frank Urban, despite the fact that Harrison earned his living as a lecturer. Eventually, they suspended him for disobeying their order. For its failure to state what party laws or policies he had violated, Harrison suggested the EC's behavior represented "a most contemptible form of persecution."[80]

On account of his experience with the racism of the Socialist Party, Harrison looked with approval at the IWW as an alternative to the party. In an 1914 letter to the editors of *The New Review* that they refused to publish, Harrison pointed out that the IWW "has no scruples about affirming the full import of its revolutionary doctrine at all times and all places—even in the South" and that "it actually opposes race prejudice, with success, as in Louisiana, where it organized 14,000 black timber workers, together with 18,000 white timber workers, with 'mixed' locals, too, in spite of Southern sentiment." Because of these facts, Harrison boldly stated, "I wonder, now, whether any Socialist, Southern or other, could blame me for throwing in my lot with the I.W.W."[81] Unlike the heterogeneous Socialist Party with its radical left and moderate right wings, the IWW had a radical program for the entire working class, namely "the abolition of the wage system." Harrison left the Socialist Party just a few months after his pro-IWW letter.[82]

Harrison made numerous contributions to the Socialist movement. By 1914 he even managed to get elected to the New York City Central Committee, helping to discuss and direct the activities of thousands of white Socialists.[83] Yet the other party leaders' anti-Black behavior—aborting the CSC, cutting Harrison's pay, declaring racial difference a matter of genetics rather than political economy—rendered the party unable to retain Harrison's membership. Despite being "the leading Black organizer, orator, and theoretician of the Socialist Party," as his biographer Jeffrey Perry puts it, Harrison's attempt to "carry on special work aimed at African Americans, to agitate for revolutionary socialism and industrial unionism . . . and to be free to debate and speak publicly" without prior permission from party leaders had "touched some very sensitive nerves in the Socialist Party."[84]

Hubert Harrison's break from the Socialist Party proved a decisive moment because it forced him to drastically rethink his estimation of the capacity of white radicals to manifest real class solidarity with Black workers. Initially, he had taken the Socialists at their word, assuming that they stood for the emancipation of the whole working class, but experience demonstrated that his efforts to organize the most thoroughly proletarian population in the country hardly gained traction or support among multiethnic cosmopolitan

Socialist radicals in New York City, never mind the "Southernists" in the Deep South.[85] Ultimately, in the words of John Henrik Clarke, Harrison "was a socialist until he discovered that most socialists are not true to the teachings of socialism."[86] In short, he formed a crystalline touchstone for the white left.

Of course, defeat clarifies the mind. In the aftermath of his failure to change the Socialist Party, Harrison's race consciousness grew by leaps and bounds because he saw firsthand how the Socialists insisted on maintaining white domination above the call of solidarity with the most essentially proletarian segment of the population. The party, in Harrison's words, put "race first and class after." If this constituted the political position of white *radicals* (never mind white liberals and conservatives), then Black people needed likewise to operate from the principle of "race first"—as a self-defense mechanism against the racial superiority complex of white people of all political stripes. Harrison thus learned how large a barrier white racism poses for the project of building a working-class movement worthy of the name in the United States.

Harrison's experience of joining—and leaving—the party would not be the last of its kind. Almost the entire post-Harrison generation of Black Socialists (W. A. Domingo, Richard B. Moore, Grace P. Campbell, Chandler Owen, A. Philip Randolph) would eventually leave the Socialist Party due to its anti-Black racism. To his credit, Harrison did not get discouraged from political organizing by his failure to change the Socialists from within. Instead, he determined to place the needs and interests of Black poor and working people and their struggles against racial capitalism at the center of his worldview going forward. In 1915, the year after he left the Socialists, Harrison concluded that in order for Harlem to get "more schools and playgrounds, lower rents, higher wages, [and] better treatment at the hands of policemen," African Americans would have to unite to demand these things for themselves. In his words, "for the money, the organization, the push, we must depend upon ourselves and not upon white people."[87] This commitment to Black people would ground Harrison's political outlook for the rest of his life, starting with his role as a key crystallizer of the "New Negro" movement in Harlem. His efforts would give expression to a larger global political awakening and open entirely new vistas and opportunities in his quest for Black liberation.

Chapter 2

New Negro Politics: *The Voice*, the League, and the Liberals

> Unbeknown to the white people of this land a temper is being developed among Negroes with which the American people will have to reckon.
>
> —Hubert Harrison, "Arms and the Man"

June 12, 1917, was a warm summer day in New York City, but the weather was not the only thing heating up in town. A massive body of over 2,000 politically minded Black Harlemites had gathered in the Bethel AME church to hear fiery speeches from the young activist Chandler Owen of the Independent Political Council and Rev. Adam Clayton Powell Sr. of the Abyssinian Baptist Church, not to mention a young Jamaican by the name of Marcus Garvey, who shined before this huge Black audience according to Owen's best friend A. Philip Randolph. Though attendance records are scarce, the gathering likely included Black activist women in New York such as Eslanda Cardozo Goode, Grace P. Campbell, Madam C. J. Walker, A'Lelia Walker, Lucille Randolph, Williana Burroughs, and Irena Moorman-Blackston. The mass meeting elected Hubert Harrison president of a new organization, the Liberty League of Negro-Americans, and raised funds to produce a new newspaper that he would edit called *The Voice*. Right in the middle of a bloody world war, Hubert Harrison emerged as a leading light of the "New Negro" movement.[1]

By 1919, the federal government had developed its own view of the "new negro," which it identified in a memorandum dated August 15, 1919, for the director of US military intelligence. The memo noted that "radical propaganda had made noteworthy headway among the colored people in this country," that Black soldiers had returned from the war in France with a new racial awareness and determination, and that publications like the Socialist *Messenger* and subversive organizations like the Industrial Workers of the World were "daily winning new converts" in Black communities. The document described how "the long continued propaganda . . . urging the colored people to insist upon equality with white people and to resort to force, if necessary, in order to establish their rights, is now bearing abundant fruit. Beyond a doubt, there is a new negro to be reckoned with in our political and social life."[2]

Harrison's centrality to this New Negro movement emerges in stark terms from the reports of the Military Intelligence Bureau. Major Walter Loving, the highest-ranking African American officer in military intelligence, spent two years in plain clothes attending progressive Black meetings, speeches, and events across multiple cities and states. His work culminated in a *Final Report on Negro Subversion*, prepared for the director of US military intelligence. The director, Brigadier General Marlborough Churchill, noted that Maj. Loving had "always been regarded as one of the best types of 'white man's negro.'" In a report that included sections on Marcus Garvey, Black Socialists A. Philip Randolph and Chandler Owen, and Black activist war veterans, Maj. Loving observed that New York City formed the "fountainhead of all radical propaganda among Negroes" and that Hubert Harrison's influence proved "more far reaching than that of any other individual radical."[3] How did Harrison develop such an extraordinary level of influence in Harlem? In order to answer this, we have to rewind the tape to the Black women that shaped him.

A Black Man among Black Activist Women

Ida B. Wells-Barnett (1862–1931) was a key political foremother of Harrison's Liberty League. Born enslaved in Holly Springs, Mississippi, during the fiery trial of the American Civil War, Wells grew up during the Black political heyday of Reconstruction. Thanks to her father's political engagements and losing both her parents to yellow fever at age sixteen, Wells developed a fierce resilience and independence that would drive her political activism, including her early legal challenges to the discrimination she faced on the railroads. Thanks to her passion for justice, Wells became the first woman owner and editor of a Black newspaper in US history (the *Free Speech and Headlight*) and the first journalist, Black or white, to systematically research the grisly phenomenon of lynching.[4]

Charging Black men with raping a white woman constituted a common justification for lynching and a difficult charge to contest given the taboo on discussing sex in the Victorian culture of the nineteenth-century South.[5] However, Wells's experience as an activist and her positionality as a Black woman afforded her a unique angle of vision with which to see through the myth of the ubiquitous Black male rapist—and to call it out for what it was.[6] By openly analyzing and exposing the sexual and racial politics underlying one of the most "commonsense" justifications for lynching, this four-and-a-half-foot-tall, unmarried descendant of enslaved rural Southerners without a college degree precipitated a radical rethinking of the "Southern Horror" underlying Jim Crow and effectively broke the white supremacist and patriarchal ideology that sustained it.[7] In so doing, she effectively founded what would become a transatlantic antilynching movement.[8] Harrison would emulate the antilynching agitation and general journalistic fearlessness of Ida B. Wells in a number of ways.

Building on efforts like Wells's attempt to get the fledgling National Association for the Advancement of Colored People (NAACP) to support a federal antilynching bill in 1909,[9] Harrison's Liberty League submitted a petition to the House of Representatives on July 4, 1917, to make lynching a federal crime. It would take another year before the NAACP would begin to support such legislation, and even then it would do so only with great hesitance and political timidity initially.[10] The Liberty League also demanded that Black people in the North disclaim allegiance to all political parties and instead organize the Black vote independently to swing elections in favor of Black interests, much like the Trotters and T. Thomas Fortune had previously advocated.[11] As we will see in chapter 8, Harrison would take this political idea of "race first, then party" even further with the founding of the all-Black Liberty Party in 1920, an effort to declare independence from the white-owned Democrat and Republican Parties.

In addition to Wells, Victoria Earle Matthews represented a key foremother of Harrison's race-conscious activism. Born enslaved in Georgia on May 27, 1861, Matthews dropped out of public school to become a domestic, eventually moving to New York, where she would write articles as a journalist about everything from race politics to domestic household management. In 1892, Matthews organized the Women's Loyal Union, which raised the money to publish Ida B. Wells's first pamphlet against lynching, *Southern Horrors*.[12] Matthews served as the chairwoman of the executive board of the National Association of Colored Women (NACW) in 1896.

In 1897, Matthews made a lasting institutional contribution to the cause of racial uplift by founding the White Rose Mission and Industrial Association (later known as the White Rose Home for Colored Working Girls). The organization's charter framed its objective as follows: "to establish and maintain a Christian, industrial, nonsectarian home for Afro-American and Negro working women and girls, where they may be educated and trained in the principles of practical self-help and right living." Its program included offering shelter for young Black girls, a free temporary home for the needy, help in finding legitimate employment, training for the unskilled in becoming self-supporting, protection against "city evils," a clean and respectable home where girls could entertain their friends, and classes for mothers and children in housekeeping, cooking, sewing, laundering, child-rearing, and similar subjects. Notably, Matthews also maintained a small library of books—which Harrison would make use of—relating to African American history and literature, which included "not only the well-known authors such as Booker Washington, Charles Chesnutt and Paul Laurence Dunbar . . . but little known colored men who have contributed works of genuine interest," such as a 1773 edition of the poems of Phillis Wheatley, a volume of the *Anglo-African Magazine* published in New York in 1859, abolitionist literature, and slave narratives.

When Matthews passed away in 1907, her longtime assistant Frances Reynolds Keyser (1862–1932) took her place as superintendent of the White Rose Home. Keyser became a towering figure in the Black women's club movement. Though details about her early life are scarce, Keyser was born in Georgia and moved to New York in the 1870s to train as a teacher. She was admitted to the Normal College, later known as Hunter College, and graduated in 1880. She found work at the New York Evening School but returned to the South to teach in Maryland and Florida before Victoria Matthews convinced her to return to New York to succeed her as head of the White Rose Mission in the early 1900s. Keyser emerged as a leading Black club woman and suffragette in New York City. She also became an officer in the NACW after founding and serving as the first president of the Empire State Federation of Women's Clubs (ESFWC), which raised money to sustain the aging and legendary Black abolitionist Harriet Tubman in Auburn, New York. Keyser also served on the first executive committee of the NAACP. In 1908, she also worked with Dr. Varina Morton Jones's Equal Suffrage League in Brooklyn. She would return to Florida in 1912 to assist Mary McCleod Bethune with her Daytona Normal and Industrial Institute.

Hubert Harrison probably first encountered Keyser at St. Mark's AME church lyceum. He began volunteering at the White Rose Mission in 1907. He started a Black history class there, and Keyser also put him in charge of the boy's club and made him an advisor to the ladies' literary club. Around this time, Harrison considered himself a "Du Bois man" in the sense of supporting a "bold, aggressive agitation" strategy for racial advancement, as the Niagara Movement had done, in defiance of Booker T. Washington's disdain for protest politics.[13]

Notably, Harrison had also been working on a reconceptualization of the history of Reconstruction "from the Negro's side" and taught a specific course on that subject with his Black history students at the White Rose Mission. In 1908, Harrison even arranged for his friend Charles Burroughs to send his notes on Reconstruction "from the Negro's side" to W. E. B. Du Bois. Du Bois then gave his first address on that very subject one year later at the American Historical Association annual meeting and would later write his groundbreaking and magisterial book *Black Reconstruction* in the 1930s.[14]

Figure 2.1 Frances Reynolds Keyser and the White Rose Home, July 1909. Ms. Keyser is in the front and center, with the white dress and the black necklace. Photograph by A. A. Moore,. Hubert H. Harrison Papers, box 15, folder 2, Rare Book and Manuscript Library, Columbia University, New York.

Keyser was not just Harrison's employer and supervisor at the mission but also his maternal mentor. She was deeply religious, leading a Sunday afternoon Bible study at the White Rose Home. Harrison took explicit note in his diary of how he received "spiritual values" from Keyser. He also confided in her about his conversion from Christianity to agnosticism.[15] (We will further explore Harrison's break from Christianity—and his militant advocacy of reason over religion as a trailblazing Black voice of the freethought movement—in chapter 3.) In his reflection on all the friends he had gained through his work at the White Rose Mission, he noted how Mrs. Keyser was "*facile princeps* (easily first)" and "intellectual—and yet unassuming, tactful, kindly, meek as a martyr and good as gold."[16]

Harrison's work with Keyser drew him into the orbit of the larger Black women's club movement. For example, he heard one E. Lindsey Davis of the Phillis Wheatley (Club) Home Association of Chicago speak at the colored Young Women's Christian Association (YWCA). He also attended the sixth biennial convention of the NACW to hear Davis and other notable club women speak. When some of the NACW delegates gathered at Keyser's behest at the

White Rose Home, he was grateful to have met them. "The work in which [Davis] is engaged is a great and noble one, as is the general work of the Association," noted Harrison in his diary. "She leaves with my highest commendation and heartiest good wishes. These women of the association have been a great inspiration to me."[17]

Harrison deepened and developed his commitment to women's suffrage thanks to the Black club women of the NACW. In March 1909, for example, Harrison heard Ida B. Wells-Barnett speak on women's suffrage at St. Mark's Lyceum.[18] St. Mark's Lyceum, founded sometime in 1880, comprised a literary organization for "many of the best and most representative colored men and women in Greater New York."[19] It featured a newsletter, *St. Mark's Mirror*, which Harrison edited for a time. It also boasted a library and forum for discussion and debate of cutting-edge topics of the day. In April, Keyser spoke in favor of women's suffrage at the St. Mark's Lyceum. At this time it was still a hotly contested topic, and four other lyceum members, including three women, argued against Keyser's pro-suffrage stance.[20]

In July, Harrison spoke at the first annual convention of the ESFWC on the importance of "rescue work" such as the White Rose Home was doing. He encouraged the federation to begin making statistical data collection a feature of its activities.[21] By December 1909, Harrison had begun cultivating a working relationship with Rev. Adam Clayton Powell Sr.'s Abyssinian Baptist Church, laying the foundation for Powell's role as a speaker at Harrison's launching of the Liberty League some years later. By the end of 1910, Harrison had spoken in favor of women's suffrage before Rev. Powell's congregants in Abyssinian, alongside Irena L. Moorman-Blackston, who had a subway-entrance newsstand and became president of the Women's Business League of Greater New York and a leading figure in the Political Equality Association, and also Harriet May Mills, the white president of the Woman Suffrage League of New York State.[22]

Black suffragettes like Eslanda Cardozo Goode (mother of the Eslanda Goode who would marry Paul Robeson) spoke alongside Harrison on street corners about the "New Negro Woman." During the election season of 1917, Goode played a leading role in the struggle for Black women's political rights and against the racism of the white suffragettes. In so doing, Black suffragettes like Goode would learn a similar lesson about the racism of white "progressive" women that Harrison had learned about the white men and women in the Socialist Party.

In the elections of 1917, which included a women's suffrage amendment on the ballot in New York State, Harrison spoke at events alongside Goode. Goode wanted Black suffragists to stay organizationally independent from white women, and she "wanted Black men to withhold their vote on the amendment until the Women's Suffragist Party declared its position on the status of black women."[23] As a result, Harrison echoed this demand in his influential *Voice* newspaper, to which we will soon return, urging his readers on the eve of the election not to vote for the amendment.

It represented an attempt to impose a defeat on the racist white suffragettes for ignoring the demands of Black women for equal voting rights, which many in the white suffragist movement could not countenance. It may have seemed an unexpected late-stage change of tactics after so many years of suffragist campaigning that included "mass meetings, street meetings by the hundreds, moving picture exhibits showing women's war work and illustrating the suffrage arguments, parades, Watchers' schools, conferences, open-air rallies, hearings before clubs, the distribution of thousands of suffrage leaflets by Literature Squads operating near theatres, movie houses, synagogues, churches and clubs."[24] But it showed how exasperated and enraged some Black suffragists had become with their white counterparts. As fate would have it, the amendment passed, and as a result some 75,000 Black women became enfranchised in New York State. Not only that, the first Black representative to the New York State Assembly, Edward A. Johnson, and the first Black alderman of New York City, James C. Thomas Jr., were also elected. A "New Negro" was indeed emerging in New York.[25]

In his post-mortem *Voice* editorial, Harrison defended the Black women's campaign to kill the amendment while also celebrating the election result as a step forward for women. He spoke of the enfranchisement of women as a "great" and "outstanding" outcome, "which we had opposed in the latter part of the campaign, not on principle, but as a protest against the cowardly race-prejudice of the white women of the Woman Suffrage Party. . . . However, it is here; and it is, undoubtedly, a great step in the direction of democracy at home. From the first of January, 1918, our women will be our fellow-citizens." He then sounded a note of antisexist optimism and encouragement for Black women. "We wonder whether our Negro women will be as easy meat for the politicians (of both sexes) as our Negro men have been. We doubt it."[26]

Through his work with suffragettes and Black club women, Harrison also came into contact with the groundbreaking activist Grace Philomena Campbell. Campbell was born in Georgia in 1875 to an African American mother and a Jamaican father. She grew up with her mother's family in Washington, DC, and in 1897 Campbell graduated from the Colored Women's League Kindergarten Training School, headed by Anna Julia Cooper. She undertook further kindergarten training in the Park Temple School and also the Normal Teachers College at Howard University, establishing in 1903 a model kindergarten at the Magruder School in Washington, DC, and earning the position of principal by 1907.

Campbell's outstanding work drew the ire of Black administrators like Anna E. Murray, who managed to get her fired and blacklisted from her position in the DC school system for reasons that remain unclear. According to historian Lydia Lindsey, DC school board member and leading club woman Mary Church Terrell supported Campbell through the agonizing ordeal, while Fannie Barrier Williams helped Campbell find a job as director of a kindergarten at Lincoln Settlement in Brooklyn in 1909. By 1912, Campbell had become active in Keyser's ESFWC, at whose conference Harrison had been a speaker.[27] Campbell also worked for the National League for the Protection of Colored Women (NLPCW), which sought to aid and uplift Black women migrants to the city. Campbell would later emerge as New York's first (and only, for a time) Black woman probation officer, working to support and advocate for Black women and girls caught up in the racist criminal (in)justice system.[28] In the late 1910s, she would follow Harrison's footsteps in joining the Socialist Party. On account of the white racism of the Socialists, Campbell would in the 1920s become a leading organizer of the African Blood Brotherhood and the first generation of Black Communists.

A Mass Organization for the New Negro: Harrison's Liberty League

The lessons Harrison learned from Black women grounded his post-socialist shift towards agitating among Black working people in his home neighborhood of Harlem. Between 1915 and 1917, Harrison preached an "advanced type of radicalism with a view to impressing race-consciousness and effecting racial solidarity among Negroes," according to Caribbean-born Harlem activist Anselmo Jackson.[29] In this endeavor, he would build upon the extraordinary work of figures like William Monroe Trotter, who had logged many years as a tireless and militant advocate for Black racial dignity and equality.[30]

On December 24, 1916, Harrison gave a talk titled "When the Negro Wakes: A Lecture on 'The Manhood Movement' among the Negro People of America," which, according to Jeff Perry, "stands as the birthday of the 'New Negro Manhood Movement.'"[31] Sometimes Harrison would refer to "manhood" as a redefinition of what it meant to be a Black man—for example, no more submission or selling out to "Old Crowd" Blacks and rich white "friends of the Negro." At other times, he would refer to "manhood" more as a sense of humanity and what it meant for Black men and women to be equal to any other racial group in dignity, intelligence, historical achievement, and worthiness of respect. In his publicity for the launch of the Liberty League of Negro-Americans in 1917, Harrison explicitly appealed to those who believed in "New Negro Manhood" and also "New Negro Womanhood."

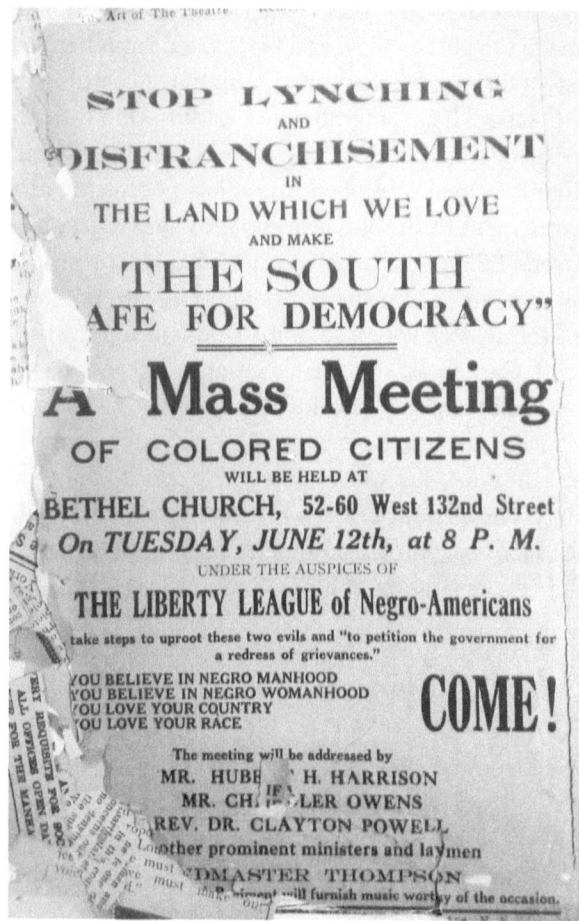

Figure 2.2
Poster advertising the launching of the Liberty League in 1917. The phrase "make the South safe for democracy" was a play on Woodrow Wilson's official war aim to "make the world safe for democracy." Hubert H. Harrison Papers, flat box 740, Rare Book and Manuscript Library, Columbia University, New York.

After over two full years of Harlem-based agitation, Harrison felt ready to create his own organization for the New Negro moment he had helped to cultivate. When the United States declared war on Germany in April 1917 with the stated aim of making the world "safe for democracy," Harrison and his co-organizers cleverly seized the opportunity to make not the world but the Jim Crow South "safe for democracy." Such was Harrison's network and influence that when they put out a call for a mass meeting on June 12 to protest against lynching and racial oppression, some 2,000 people turned up, packing the Bethel African Methodist Episcopal Church on West 123rd Street for the inauguration of Harrison's Liberty League of Negro-Americans.

The program of the Liberty League represented a "race first" message and political agenda. In its inaugural mass meeting, the league passed resolutions calling on all "true friends of democracy" to help Black people secure their democratic rights and demanded that the government acknowledge the danger to democracy of the continued violation of the Thirteenth, Fourteenth, and Fifteenth Amendments to the Constitution, which (on paper) abolished slavery, granted Black people full citizenship and equal protection of the law, and enshrined for Black men the right to vote. The league declared it would fight segregation, Jim Crowism, and peonage, and would "protest and agitate by every legal means until we win these rights from the hands of our government." The declaration called for making lynching a federal crime and for federal intervention to prevent it. It also took a clear position endorsing universal adult suffrage for Black men and women and the organization of the Black vote independent of any allegiance to the white-dominated political parties. In addition, Harrison declared that since lynching amounted to lawless murder, Black people must be the ones to maintain the law and "put down the law-breakers by organizing all over the South to defend their own lives whenever their right to live was invaded by mobs which the local authorities were too weak or unwilling to suppress."[32]

Thanks to Harrison's radical internationalism, the Liberty League declared solidarity with the struggles of oppressed peoples across the world. Its Declaration of Principles stated, "This is the era of revolutionary ferment all over the world, and we realize that we, too are living in the world." Mentioning explicitly the struggle of the Irish, the Russian revolution, and the Indian subcontinent, the Liberty League's inaugural resolutions boldly articulated an international duty to the darker races of the world and a "special sympathy" for the "250 millions of our brethren in Africa." The official resolutions passed at the founding Liberty League meeting reflected Harrison's keen grasp of global geopolitics. In particular, the league predicted—in 1917—not only that World War I would culminate in a "council of peace" whose ostensible purpose would be promoting self-determination but also that more wars in the future would follow if Africans and other colonized peoples were not granted the right to rule their own ancestral lands. This is precisely what happened with the emergence of World War II and the subsequent wars of national liberation in the colonized world.[33]

As a response, in part, to white racist popular songs like "Every Race Has a Flag But the Coon," the Liberty League raised a new flag to symbolize its worldly goal of empowering people of color. Declaring that it had a "duty" to the "seventeen hundred millions" across the globe who were "colored—black and brown and yellow," the league sought to "affiliate itself with similar organizations of the darker races in other lands; to sympathize with their just aims and afford them such aid as may be within its power." To concretize in iconographic form this political commitment to the people of the global majority, the league adopted a tricolor of black, brown, and yellow in parallel vertical stripes, which symbolized, in Harrison's words, "the dual relationship to our own and other peoples."[34]

More locally and concretely, the demographics of the Liberty League's participants show that it managed to combine African Americans and African Caribbean immigrants from various islands under the same banner in a mass movement for Black empowerment.[35] It would set the stage for even larger-scale pan-African organization in the form of the Garvey movement, as we will see in chapter 7.

Building on the strength of its program and principles, the Liberty League got off to an auspicious start. The day after the league's momentous launch in Harlem, Trotter organized a meeting for Harrison at Faneuil Hall in Boston. In his speech there, Harrison "suggested that the colored people rise against the government, just as the Irish against England, unless they get their rights." In this way, Harrison's politics of "race first" drew inspiration from the Irish and other struggles of oppressed people internationally, as those of Trotter's generation and the abolitionists before him had also done. Just a couple of weeks after these remarks at the initial meetings of the Liberty League, the nation would bear witness to another sickening outbreak of white savagery.

In the early days of July 1917, white mobs descended on the Black community of East St. Louis to perpetrate one of the most infamous orgies of anti-Black violence in US history, attacking and killing Black men, women, and children indiscriminately and setting fire to numerous Black homes and businesses. The white mobs went on an unrestrained rampage as local policemen encouraged the attacks and National Guardsmen even joined in the killing.[36] To their great and heroic credit, African American men in East St. Louis organized and coordinated a powerful armed self-defense operation. They secured the perimeter to ensure the historically Black Denverside neighborhood would remain untouched during the pogrom thanks to the use of armed guards and snipers posted on its outskirts. The African Methodist Episcopal (AME) church in the community served as a hub of resistance where the Black community gathered to plan its defense, and its church bell was used strategically as an alarm system.[37] Historian Malcolm McLaughlin has recounted how Black businessman Dr. Le Roy Bundy solicited military training from Black war veterans and coordinated drilling exercises with the Black fraternal society the Odd Fellows.[38]

Black East St. Louisians thus drew on their own resources and community institutions in order to prevent white incursions, to escape from the attackers, and to offer safety to refugees of the attacks. As McLaughlin concludes, "By holding back the white mobs, African American resistance significantly limited the scope of the race riot and the number of casualties."[39] Historian

Charles Lumpkins has summarized the outcome, writing that "white attackers had destroyed property worth three million dollars, razed several neighborhoods, injured hundreds, and forced at least seven thousand black townspeople to seek refuge across the Mississippi River.... By the official account, nine white men and thirty-nine black men, women, and children lost their lives.... Others said that more than nine white people and many more—perhaps up to five hundred—black citizens had perished."[40] Because it took place so soon after President Wilson's decision to place the United States into a war "to make the world safe for democracy," the East St. Louis pogrom seared itself into the consciousness of African Americans throughout the country.

Unfortunately, the East St. Louis massacre was no isolated incident. White mobs went on a four-day rampage against the Black community in Philadelphia in 1918. Then came the "Red Summer" of 1919, wherein white mob attacks on Black communities erupted in Knoxville (TN), Washington (DC), Chicago (IL), Charleston (SC), Longview (TX), Omaha (NE), San Francisco (CA), Bisbee (AZ), El Dorado and Elaine (AR), Bogalusa (LA), Montgomery (AL), Pickens, Vicksburg, and Ellisville (MS), Lake City (FL), Gary (IN), at least seven cities in Georgia, as well as Corbin (KY), Norfolk (VA), and New London (CT).[41] This post–World War I outbreak of racist white mob violence grew out of the vast array of prewar anti-Black massacres in places like Wilmington (NC) in 1898, New York City (NY) in 1900,[42] New Orleans (LA) and Akron (OH) in 1900,[43] Evansville (IN) in 1903,[44] Springfield (OH) in 1904 and 1906, Harrison (AR) in 1905,[45] Argenta (AR) in 1906,[46] Greensburg (IN) and Atlanta (GA) in 1906,[47] and Springfield (IL) in 1908. Then came the continuation of anti-Black pogroms *after* the Red Summer in places like Ocoee (FL) in 1920, Tulsa (OK) in 1921, and Rosewood (FL) in 1923.[48] And not to mention similar attacks on Indigenous Native American, Chinese, and Mexican-descended communities in the Southwest, West Coast, and Northwest areas of the United States.[49]

This epidemic of American pogroms—coinciding with the creation of *thousands* of all-white "sundown towns"—is one of the most underappreciated serial atrocities of the era, what journalist Elliot Jaspin calls the "hidden history of racial cleansing in America."[50] In response, untold numbers of African Americans took direct action in the form of mass evacuations from mostly Northern rural and small towns to Northern big cities, alongside—and in some ways hidden by—the so-called Great Migration from the South to Northern urban centers like Chicago, Detroit, Philadelphia, and New York.[51] In many instances besides East St. Louis, including Chicago and Washington, DC, Black people fought back courageously despite lacking any economic,

Figure 2.3 Children's contingent in the Silent Protest Parade on Fifth Avenue, New York City, July 28, 1917, in response to the East St. Louis race riot. The protest was headed by figures like James Weldon Johnson, W. E. B. Du Bois, Rev. Hutchens Chew Bishop, rector of St. Philip's Episcopal Church (Harlem), and Harlem realtor John E. Nail. Photographs of Prominent African Americans, James Weldon Johnson Collection, Yale Collection of American Literature, Beinecke Rare Book and Manuscript Library, New Haven, CT.

political, legal, racial, or numerical advantages over their white oppressors. The courageous resistance of Black working people to this epidemic sparked a fire in the young Jamaican-born revolutionary Socialist poet Claude McKay, who in 1919 penned the militant poem "If We Must Die," which became a kind of anthem for New Negro militancy. It closed with the lines

> Like men we'll face the murderous, cowardly pack,
> Pressed to the wall, dying, but fighting back!

During the East St. Louis pogrom, the Liberty League held a second mass meeting, this time on Independence Day for the United States (July 4). The meeting featured speakers like Harrison, Trotter, and the Socialist preacher Rev. George Frazier Miller of St. Augustine's Church in Brooklyn. The meeting also featured musical performances by organist Melville Charleton and African American opera singers Abbie Mitchell and Lena Sanford, who had married the stride pianist and jazz composer Charles "Luckey" Roberts. Liberty League events often had live music.

Thanks in part to their vociferous denunciation of the East St. Louis pogrom and open advocacy of armed self-defense, these early meetings of the Liberty League went so well that Black men and women across the United States and the West Indies donated money, pledged support to it, and became members of the organization. The league and its collaboration with the Trotters put Harrison in position to help issue a call to Black organizations across the country to send delegates to "a great race-congress" that would meet in Washington and coalesce New Negro dissent at a national level amid intensive wartime state surveillance and repression, a political breakthrough to which we will return in the chapter on the "white world war" (chapter 4).[52]

The Liberty League had an immediate and natural appeal not only to the younger "New Negro" but also to some of the older and more seasoned veterans of the struggle, like John E. Bruce, who Harrison described as his "father in journalism." Bruce was born enslaved in 1856 in Piscataway, Maryland. His father was sold to a Deep South plantation when he was three years old, and at age four his family got free when Union soldiers passed through Maryland. He grew up in Washington, DC, and though he received some brief training at the Free Library School and Howard University, he was a largely self-educated man. Bruce knew multiple prominent nineteenth-century abolitionists and Black nationalists such as Henry Highland Garnet, Edward Wilmot Blyden, Alexander Crummell, and J. Robert Love. A member of the AME Zion Church, he played a role alongside T. Thomas Fortune in forming the Afro-American League and the Afro-American Council, two of the key civil rights organizations of the 1890s. Bruce built a career in journalism, working for some two dozen newspapers. Bruce and Arturo Schomburg founded the Negro Society for Historical Research, which taught Harrison a great deal, as we explore in chapter 5 on Harrison's African politics.

Bruce wrote a letter to Harrison after the founding meeting of the Liberty League, calling the League's call to action "at once the most safe and practical of all that have been put forward in the past forty years. Your plan to go before Congress with your races grievances is *The plan*." Bruce suggested to Harrison that he "weed out the handkerchief heads from your privy council and surround yourself with men loyal and true" because he believed that Harrison had laid "a bigger foundation than you perhaps realize in the formation of this Liberty League."[53] These were encouraging words from a friend, elder, and mentor who represented a bridge between the post-Reconstruction generation of Black struggle and the New Negro and Garvey movement generation. William Monroe Trotter similarly lauded Harrison and thanked him for his service to the race.⁵⁴ These commendations would find further confirmation in the way Harrison's newspaper would inspire a whole new generation of New Negro papers.

In terms of ideological orientation, Harrison put out his first book, *The Negro and the Nation*, that same year, influencing members of the Liberty League and so many Harlem activists in its orbit as a kind of handbook of New Negro political education. Harrison published it just two months after the Liberty League's launch in order to "help throw into strong relief the present situation of the Negro in present day America" and also to "set forth the aims and ideals of the new Manhood movement among American Negroes" that had been sparked by President Wilson's decision to wage war for "democracy." As Harrison readily acknowledged, he compiled articles he had written for Socialist and freethought publications, thus seeding the minds of Harlem's New Negroes with Harrison's radical arguments about the systemic nature of racial oppression, the power of the working class, the conservative influence of the church, the anti-Black racism of the mainstream media, and the meaning of Socialism to Black people. With a print run of 5,000 copies, it became a political education handbook or "primer for Harlem radicals," according to historian Minkah Makalani. Meanwhile, according to Harrison's son William, Harrison gave the name "Liberty Hall" to the venue at 114 West 138th Street where Liberty League meetings would take place.⁵⁵

A New Negro *Voice* in Journalism

In the early twentieth century, the Black press underwent a transformation, especially within Northern urban African American communities. The "Great Migration" from the South and the "Great Retreat" from the epidemic of anti-Black pogroms outside of the South led to the movement of over 1 million African Americans from rural villages and towns to Northern urban centers and big cities. The concentration of African Americans in cities like Chicago and New York and their entrance into a cash economy created a whole new readership and market for Black newspapers.⁵⁶ Meanwhile, access to more and better schools opened the door to historic decreases in African American illiteracy, which went from 70 percent in 1880 down to 23 percent by 1920.⁵⁷

Politically, the rise of Jim Crow segregation heightened racial consciousness and grievances, prompting Black editors to challenge the hegemony of Booker T. Washington, whose "Tuskegee Machine" had exerted such a strong influence by the turn of the century.⁵⁸ A prime example concerned what Harrison called T. Thomas Fortune's "extrusion" from the *New York Age* in 1907, as Washington decisively took ownership over the paper. Late nineteenth-century figures like Fortune and Ida B. Wells had set an example for aspiring Black journalists in the early twentieth century. Following their lead, numerous new periodicals started to appear, including papers like the *Boston Guardian* in 1901, the *Chicago Defender* in 1905, the *Amsterdam News* in 1909, and *The Crisis* in 1910. In the New York context specifically, John E. Bruce, who Harrison considered his own "father in journalism," founded the *Weekly Standard* in Yonkers.[59]

In order to usher in a stronger representation of the radical New Negro voice in the Black press, Hubert Harrison founded the first newspaper of the militant New Negro movement in Harlem, *The Voice*. Harrison, in the very first issue, published on July 4, 1917, declared that the paper would "in all things maintain the principle of 'Africa first.'" As Harrison himself made clear, he meant Africa in a racial rather than geographical sense.[60] He explained the purpose of the new paper by way of a nautical metaphor. Likening *The Voice* to a small ship "swimming in a sea of servility," Harrison envisioned how "the breakers of race prejudice roll between it and the shore it seeks; the sharks of racial treachery abound in these waters, and overhead the lightnings of lick-spittledom and the thunders of its malice would seem to threaten its chances of getting safe to shore." This language evoked the resilience and perseverance of enslaved Africans during the so-called Middle Passage.[61] Yet, despite the dangers, *The Voice* had no fear because "it [put] itself under the protection of that Providence which is—the plain people of Negro ancestry." Harrison here articulated his commitment to the Black working class, as opposed to a "talented tenth" who already had various publications of their own.[62]

Harrison's paper grew quickly among readers in and beyond Harlem, and they sustained its production financially. A collection from the people raised an initial $200 of seed money for the paper at the historic Bethel AME Church meeting on June 12, 1917, that launched the Liberty League. In the first months of its existence, the people backed Harrison's paper "with their personal help, their pennies and their loans," which they often gave at street meetings and indoor talks that Harrison would give. During the week of August 7, one month after its founding, Harrison recorded that the initial weekly print run of *The Voice* reached 11,000 copies.[63]

Not everybody in the community supported the upstart newspaper. Despite the enthusiasm of many ordinary people for *The Voice*, "the 'Big Negroes' withheld their help—even in the matter of advertisements." Nevertheless, the paper remained fiercely independent and "would not cringe before the Exalted Ones," instead opting to place its fate in the hands of the "Negro masses." Harrison initially tried to undercut the more established newspapers with a low price, but eventually he had to raise it to their going rate of five cents. Harrison assured his readers that with a rise in price to five cents, *The Voice* would "not need to bite its tongue, to 'sell out' to white politicians, nor to hold back from 'showing up' the highly placed Judases who are selling the race and its future for a mess of pottage."[64] Although financing a newspaper so fiercely radical and independent was not easy, Harrison appealed to his readers directly for support.

Indeed, Harrison advanced a class-conscious strategy of appealing to Black workers rather than a "talented tenth," not only for financial support but as part of a people-centered production process. For example, in a September 4 editorial titled "Send Us the News," Harrison expressed the desire to offer more news than the three main competing newspapers (the *Age*, the *Amsterdam News*, and the *New York News*) combined. To successfully do this, the *Voice* editor called on the readership to join in creating stories for the paper: "This is essentially the people's paper. So bring us your news; and if it is legitimate, we will publish it."[65] Harrison wanted not only to reach the masses but to actively involve them in producing the content of the paper—another example of the radical character of his vision for the New Negro movement.

The *Voice* sought to uplift Black self-love by avoiding the degrading ads that other Black newspapers at the time featured: "All Negroes have been waiting for years for a paper which they could open in street cars and other public places without feeling ashamed at the 'Kink-No-More,' 'Kongolene Knocks Kinks,' 'Oxonized Ox Marrow,' 'Raddrizator Hair Straightening Outfits,' and the big black person turned into a white person in two ticks, which disgrace so many of our 'colored' journals."[66] As a dark-skinned person, he hated colorism and felt that papers with ads for skin bleach or hair-straightening products degraded Black self-esteem and racial pride. He also distinguished between "selling space vs. selling self," emphasizing that it wasn't ads in and of themselves that were the problem, just ads that were demeaning to Black people.[67] Thanks to his years of collaboration with activist Black women, the Liberty League and *The Voice* won their enthusiastic support. Irena Moorman-Blackston sold *The Voice* at her subway-entrance newsstand on 135th and Lenox. Eslanda Cardozo Goode organized volunteers to sell *The Voice* on the street, solicit subscriptions, and take it to churches on Sunday.[68]

The Voice's articulation of New Negro politics sparked the proliferation of a whole range of innovative papers that would define a new era of radical Black journalism. In November of 1917, a few months after the birth of *The Voice*, A. Philip Randolph and Chandler Owen started *The Messenger* as their own Socialist newspaper focused on the concerns of Black workers.[69] The year 1918 witnessed the emergence of Amy Ashwood and Marcus Garvey's *Negro World* and William Bridges's *Challenge*. The year 1919 saw Cyril Briggs's

Crusader burst onto the scene, alongside smaller papers like August Bernier's *Clarion*. The following year, 1920, saw the emergence of W. A. Domingo's *Emancipator*.

The influence and inspiration of Harrison's *Voice* seems, paradoxically, to also have been its downfall. Because it stimulated so much new radical Black journalism, including competition for a limited pool of readers and subscribers, *The Voice* eventually ran into financial troubles. By all accounts, Harrison proved himself a poor manager of financial matters. As J. A. Rogers put it, Harrison's "enthralling oratory should have paid him well, yet, like so many scholars, he was so thoroughly wrapped up in his work that this aspect of the situation quite escaped him. Whatever money he received usually drifted to him as food to a polyp attached to the piles of a pier."[70] Harrison also harbored the vice of borrowing money, a habit that followed him in life "as a curse" on account of his bad money management.[71] Harrison's financial problems limited the newspaper's lifespan, but this was not the only such factor.

Many of the other radical Black newspaper editors of the time relied upon women for their existence. Deenie Trotter worked tirelessly to keep the Boston-based *Guardian* afloat.[72] Lucille Randolph helped to fund and financially manage *The Messenger*. As the owner of her own beauty salon, Lucille Randolph was far more financially savvy than her husband, Asa Philip. She developed into a leading political figure in her own right, as demonstrated, for example, by her run for alderman in the Twenty-First Assembly district of Manhattan on the Socialist ticket in 1923.[73]

Madam C. J. Walker, the first African American woman millionaire, who built her fortune as a pioneering beauty products manufacturer, gave financial support to *The Messenger* and *Negro World*, the latter of which Amy Ashwood also played a key role in launching and distributing.[74] Bertha Florence Johnson, the wife of Cyril Briggs, took on the role of business manager for *The Crusader*. As historian Joyce Moore Turner has pointed out, too many wives and other key women have remained unknown in the historiography of Black radicalism, regardless of the extent of their assistance with financial support for their husbands.[75] Not to mention all of the clerical, ideological, political, and emotional support they often provided.

As we will see in the chapter on his love politics (chapter 6), Harrison had a difficult and strained relationship with his wife, Irene Louise "Lin" Harrison (née Horton). By the time he founded the Liberty League and *The Voice* they were no longer living together. Thus Harrison could not look to his wife for financial support of *The Voice*, unlike so many other Black male editors whose papers could not have survived without the good graces, financial and otherwise, of their wives.

Harrison's convictions also made his fundraising battle much harder. Faced with a choice between money and principles, he refused to compromise his principles. For example, whereas *The Messenger* featured ads from Madam C. J. Walker's hair-straightening products, Harrison rejected ads like this because of the way he felt they were demeaning to Black people by perpetuating white beauty standards. While maintaining the political high ground, positions like this undoubtedly made it harder to raise money for the paper given the extremely low levels of Black access to capital in the 1910s. According to Perry, Harrison once refused to accept a sum of $10,000 from a white donor, instead opting to keep the paper a Black-funded operation on principle. By contrast, organs like *The Messenger* and *The Crusader* received critical financial backing from white radicals.[76]

Despite financial difficulties, Harrison still strove to put out publications that would express a militant, uncompromising, and independent "New Negro" viewpoint. Thus after the decline of his weekly *Voice* by the spring of 1919, Harrison began editing a monthly magazine that autumn for August Bernier called *The New Negro*. Similar to *The Voice*, it represented "a magazine for the New Negro," a journal "intended as an organ of the international consciousness of the darker races—especially the Negro race."[77] The monthly emerged, in Harrison's words, from "the need and value of extending racial consciousness beyond the bounds of the white countries in which we find ourselves," the need for a common current knowledge of world events and their relevance to the "darker races" and oppressed peoples everywhere, and the need to see the Black struggle in an international context.[78] It predated Alain Locke's *New Negro* anthology by six years, a fact whose significance we will explore further in chapter 9 on Harrison's relationship to the "Harlem Renaissance."

One gets a sense of Harrison's internationalism by surveying the content covered in *The New Negro*'s pages. One of the journal's issues included articles on such topics as race and ethnicity in Harlem, labor organizing in British Guyana, the "new spirit" of labor rebellion in Trinidad, Latin America, Egypt, lynching in the South, and "poems for the people." Another issue featured pieces on African history, US military rule in the Virgin Islands, West African women, the white curriculum of the education system (including within historically Black colleges and universities), interracial marriage, "race riots" in Britain, and anticolonial revolt in India. The *New Negro* not only chronicled key world events but also interpreted them in race-conscious ways in order to maintain a critical view of "the interpretations put on these world events by the controlling culture of the white world." Harrison explained that he intended for *The New Negro* to cultivate the "international consciousness of the darker races." To do this, it maintained contact with "colored writers in Asia, South Africa, West Africa,

Egypt, Europe, America and the West Indies" so that "by this means its readers [would] receive all the different currents of ideas that flow into the sea of racial consciousness."[79] Right from its first issue in September of 1919, the *New Negro* magazine caused alarm for US and British military intelligence agents.[80]

Harrison's *Voice* and *New Negro* emerged as radical elements within a larger transnational Black print culture, including what historian Lara Putnam has called the "circum-Caribbean." As Putnam observes, "The *Pittsburgh Courier* had subscribers in Costa Rica, the *New York Age* and *Chicago Defender* were routinely quoted by the *Panama Tribune*, [and] the Barbados *Weekly Herald* was spread in hundreds of Brooklyn households. News of discrimination against people of color in Britain and France—and of anti-imperialist organizing in the same—got prominent coverage, drawing in part on reports from Europe-based, black-run periodicals like the *African Times and Orient Review* [from London] or *La Depeche Africaine* [in Paris]."[81]

Harrison's journalistic contacts speak to not only a "circum-Caribbean" but an even broader trans-Atlantic and global circuitry of print culture. His publication exchange list included *The Gold Coast Leader*, *The Liberian News*, *The Agricultural World* (Liberia), *The Saturday Magazine* (Sierra Leone), *The Guardian* (Sierra Leone), *The Echo* (Sierra Leone), *The International* (South Africa), *The Lagos Standard*, *The Lagos Weekly Record*, *The Barbados Times*, *The Daily Gleaner* (Jamaica), *The Dispatch* (Panama Canal Zone), *The Belize Independent*, and *The Oriental Economist* (Japan). Harrison not only read but also reprinted articles from these publications in *The New Negro*, thus joining the conversation within a larger "self-aware, race conscious, transnational Black press" that gave concrete informational circuitry that stoked Harrison's radical vision for the Colored International, as we see in chapter 4.[82]

New Negroes and White Liberals

When Harrison founded the Liberty League in 1917, there already existed two prominent New York City–based racial advancement organizations: the National Urban League and the NAACP. The National Urban League, originally known as the National League on Urban Conditions Among Negroes, emerged in 1910 out of a merger of two white-funded organizations: the Committee for Improving Industrial Conditions Among Negroes in New York, which sought to expand employment opportunities for Black people, and the NLPCW, for which Grace P. Campbell worked. The organization received funding from robber barons like John D. Rockefeller and wealthy advocates of industrial education for Black people like William H. Baldwin and Julius Rosenwald.[83]

Harrison described the Urban League as a "scab organization" for the way it behaved during the waiters' strike in 1912. "I saw then," noted Harrison retrospectively, "that its policy was to corral young Negroes of ability and harness them to the wagon of its social-uplift program in such a way as to keep them in the straight road of conservatism."[84] He deduced this from his assessment of the organization's director, George Haynes, and its assistant director, Eugene Kinckle Jones. Grace Campbell apparently drew similar conclusions about these men and their ethos, as Haynes and Jones played a key role in the termination of her job with the NLPCW in 1913.[85] Despite his critique of the Urban League, Harrison remained open to working with it, as he remained open to joining John M. Royall's United Civic League of Black Harlem, which also competed with Jones for Harrison's attention. Yet neither organization could quench Harrison's thirst for an organization that would unite and organize Black workers to fight against both racial oppression and economic dispossession.

By 1914, the NAACP had grown into the most prominent racial reform organization. The savage violence of an anti-Black massacre in Abraham Lincoln's birthplace of Springfield, Illinois, in 1908 shocked born-rich reformers like William English Walling, who sent out an impassioned call for a revival of "the spirit of the abolitionists," lest the Southern "race war" get transferred to the North. This generated a response from the Socialist researcher and settlement worker Mary White Ovington, who eventually met with Walling and social reformer Dr. Henry Moskowitz in New York to hatch a plan for forming a racial reform organization, reaching out to *New York Post* editor and journalist Oswald Garrison Villard, a grandson of famed white abolitionist William Lloyd Garrison. The NAACP's founding executive committee included Boston lawyer Moorfield Storey as national president, Walling as chairman of the executive committee, wealthy businessman John E. Milholland as treasurer, Villard as disbursing treasurer, sociological researcher and charity worker Frances Blascoer as executive secretary, and one Black person, Dr. William Edward Burghardt Du Bois, as director of publicity and research.[86] In short, the NAACP was not just conceived but also founded, framed, and funded by elite white liberals.

Du Bois, in "The Talented Tenth" (1903), argued that the Black masses could not be more quickly raised up than by the work of an "aristocracy of talent and character." Du Bois wondered rhetorically, "Was there ever a nation on God's fair earth civilized from the bottom upward? Never; it is, ever was and ever will be from the top downward that culture filters. The Talented Tenth rises and pulls all that are worth the saving up to their vantage ground."[87] Du Bois's advocacy of "talented tenth" Black leadership in this period is well known. But as historian Evelyn Higginbotham has argued, the notion originated not with Du Bois but with the nineteenth-century Rockefeller-funded white liberal American Baptist Home Missionary Society. The Missionary Society saw the education of a middle-class Black social stratum as a key mechanism for the racial management of Black communities, one that would complement the Hampton and Tuskegee model of industrial education, which Donald Spivey has called "schooling for the new slavery."[88] To his credit, Du Bois himself would eventually relinquish the notion that civilization comes "from the top downward" to those "that are worth the saving" as he became sympathetic to the cause of labor and Communism from the 1930s onward.

Harrison, by contrast, saw the lack of Black unity in this period as the fault of bourgeois-minded Black leaders like Du Bois, who "have generally gone at the problem from the wrong end. They have begun at the top when they should have begun at the bottom." For Harrison, the "attempt to unite the 'intellectuals' at the top is not the same thing as uniting the Negro masses. For, very often the 'intellectuals' assume the airs of superior beings who are made of finer clay and expect that the others will run to seek them out."[89] Harrison's conception of New Negro politics focused on the "common people" and collective, bottom-up unity, rather than the selection and anointment of middle-class Black leaders by white capitalist donors.[90]

In this frame, the seemingly intractable contest between the "Bookerite" advocates of industrial education and the "anti-Bookerite Protestants" had something in common. Namely, they both endorsed capitalist economic relations and the upwardly mobile aspirations of "respectable" and individualist examples of Black excellence. Du Bois himself admitted as much later in life, remarking about the relationship between his approach and Washington's that "these two theories of Negro progress were not absolutely contradictory. Neither I nor Booker Washington understood the nature of capitalistic exploitation of labor, and the necessity for a direct attack on the principle of exploitation as the beginning of labor uplift."[91] In other words, the Du Bois–Washington debate gave expression to a clash of ideas *within* the Black elite, as both factions were concerned with maintaining the hegemony of capital over labor and the hegemony of Black leaders dependent on elite white funding and approval.

To be fair, Hubert Harrison felt the NAACP had done "splendid work" in fighting lynching and segregation.[92] So why didn't he simply join the organization and try making it more effective from within? Since its formation in 1909, Harrison had been a keen and critical observer of the association. For example, Harrison attended the 1909 National Negro Conference in New York (which effectively gave shape to the NAACP) and noted with disapproval how the conference had censored from the official report of its proceedings comments made by Mrs. Celia Parker Wooley, a white racial reformer from Chicago, who claimed that in response to widespread white hatred of Black people there was a growing Black hatred of white people.[93] This exemplified his opposition to the NAACP's strategy, which he saw as overly dependent on the moral suasion of white people and the notion that certain attitudes toward them were more "fit and proper" than others. As against this politics of respectability, Harrison saw and felt, in his words, "the need for a more radical policy than that of the NAACP."[94]

Harrison's creation of an independent Black radical organization in the same New York City which housed the NAACP headquarters provoked a stiff rebuke from some of its white progressive founders. Shortly after forming the Liberty League and the *Voice* newspaper in the summer of 1917, he received a condescending letter from the acting chair of the NAACP (and Socialist Party member), Mary White Ovington.[95] It read,

> My dear Mr. Harrison,
>
> I don't see any reason for another organization, or another paper. If you printed straight socialism it might be different.
>
> Yours truly,
> MARY W. OVINGTON.

Given their different social sets, it is not clear why Ovington would have been in correspondence with Harrison at this point unless, for example, Harrison had reached out to the Socialist Party for financial support for *The Voice*. In any case, Harrison called Ovington's letter "bossy and dictatorial" and responded to her without mincing words: "These 'good white people' must really forgive us for insisting that we are not children, and that, while we want all the friends we can get, we need no benevolent dictators. It is we, and not they, who must shape Negro policies. If they want to help in carrying them out we will appreciate their help." Much like Trotter, Fortune, and the club women he learned from, Harrison felt Black people needed their own organizations and newspapers as a basic matter of self-determination, something the white-owned NAACP and Socialist Party could not provide.[96]

Harrison would talk disparagingly about the NAACP crowd as "Professional Friends of the Negro" for their paternalistic relationship to the same Black people they claimed to be helping. He criticized the way white liberals told Black people to "go slow" in seeking equality, that "Rome was not built in a day," and that "half a loaf of bread is better than no bread."[97] He gave the example of an editorial in the *New York Evening Post*, owned by the white NAACP cofounder Oswald Garrison Villard. Villard had a progressive reputation, being born into an abolitionist family and having founded the Anti-

Imperialist League during the Spanish-American War of 1898. However, in Harrison's view, Villard's *Post* exposed its true cards by going silent about lynching during the war, by calling for the "severest punishment" (i.e., the death penalty) for the Black soldiers' protest against racial oppression in Houston in 1917, and by only selectively criticizing racial segregation. For Harrison, examples like these showed the conditional and problematic nature of white liberal "friendship." To make matters worse, "many Negroes who have a wish-bone where their back-bone ought to be," and insisted upon accommodating or even parroting this white liberal political orientation.[98]

As a result, Black people had to "insist on being our own best friends." If white "friendship" meant "compulsory compromise foisted on us by kindly white people, or by cultured Negroes whose ideal is the imitation of the urbane acquiescence of these white friends, then we had better learn to look a gift horse in the mouth whenever we get the chance." Rather than submit to "Caucasian overlordship," African Americans needed an independent Black leadership. Having paid for his independence first by losing his postal job, then by losing the support of the Socialist Party, he resolved to be led by white masters and their Black parrots no longer. As Harrison declared, "We, the Negroes of the Western world, do pledge our allegiance to leaders of our own race, selected by our own group and supported financially and otherwise exclusively by us."[99] The touchstone simply would not budge.

Interestingly, Harrison's case did not rest solely on his own experience, or even that of other people of African descent. Instead, he cited how "whenever a leader of the Irish has to be selected by the Irish it is an Irishman who is selected" because "no Irishman would be inclined to dispute the fact that other men, even Englishmen like John Stuart Mill and the late [Scottish Socialist] Keir Hardie, could feel the woes of Ireland as profoundly as any Irishman." Here came an argument by analogy: those who did not have the lived experience of being Black could never completely "feel the woes" of those who themselves were Black. Therefore African Americans needed leaders selected from among those with the relevant lived experience for the job. Here he spoke to the colonial dimension of anti-Blackness.

Harrison went further and addressed the class divide in Black communities. During slavery, he wrote, "it was those whom Denmark Vesey of Charleston described as 'house niggers' who got the master's cast-off clothes, the better scraps of food and culture which fell from the white man's table, who were looked upon as the Talented Tenth of the Negro race. The opportunities of self-improvement, in so far as they lay within the hand of the white race, were accorded exclusively to this class of people who were the left-handed progeny of the white masters." Written in the context of criticizing the NAACP, Harrison's contention that white elites selected Black leaders who were closest in economic proximity and outlook to them comes across as a thinly veiled criticism of W. E. B. Du Bois, the left-handed editor of *The Crisis*.[100]

Harrison's class politics and racial militancy emerged as he took aim at the NAACP while simultaneously protesting the anti-Black discrimination of the Red Cross in not hiring Black women, even amidst the wartime labor shortage: "Up to date the American Red Cross Society, which receives government aid and cooperation to help win the war, cannot cite the name of a single Negro woman as a nurse," decried Harrison's *Voice*. He criticized how the Red Cross failed to live up to the "democracy" of the official war aim and declared that the American Red Cross must be compelled to end its racial discrimination. Moreover, he added, "if the N.A.A.C.P. were truly what it pretends instead of a National Association for the Advancement of Certain People, it would put its high-class lawyers on the job and bring the case into the United States courts . . . and if it does not . . . then it will merit the name which one of its own members gave it—the National Association for the Acceptance of Color Proscription."[101]

Backdrop for the "New Negro": A Global Political Awakening

To appreciate the broader significance of the New Negro movement of Harrison's day, it must be seen in view of the worldwide and world-historic sea change in political consciousness sparked by the destructive monstrosity of the First World War. Most dramatically in 1917, the same year Harrison founded the Liberty League and *The Voice*, the Russian people made not just one revolution but two. First, on March 8 (International Women's Day) in 1917, women workers sparked a strike wave that grew so massive that the monarch Czar Nicholas II and his regime had to step down and cede power to a provisional republican government. As in the abortive revolution of 1905, democratically elected councils of workers', peasants', and soldiers' representatives (called *soviets* in Russian) spread like wildfire. Soviet representatives were elected directly by the people and were immediately recallable, the kind of radical working-class democracy that first emerged in the Paris Commune of 1871. The spontaneous spread of these soviets created a situation of "dual power" in which the pro-capitalist and pro-war provisional government presided over a country whose toilers were developing their own collective organs of radical democracy and grassroots workers' power. In the eyes of Lenin's Bolshevik Party, soviets established the social infrastructure for the historic demand of Marxian Socialism: workers' control of the means of production.

And the Russian Revolution did not stop there. However, the rest of the story has been buried under a century-high mountain of lies. The anti-Russian and anti-Communist dogmas of Western "civilization" have construed

Figure 2.4 Vladimir Lenin and Leon Trotsky on May 5, 1920, in Teatralnaya Square (then Sverdlov Square), where a parade of the Moscow garrison troops took place.

everything from October 1917 onwards in Russia as an evil Communist plot with Joseph Stalin's degenerate regime of dictatorship emerging as the inevitable and intentional outcome of his sinister forerunner Vladimir Lenin. The historical reality that Harrison's generation witnessed unfolding in real time looks quite different. And it remains a sad fact of history that, just like Harrison, the political genius of Lenin and the phenomenal accomplishments of his people and his party have been nearly obliterated from popular memory.

Vladimir Ilyich Ulyanov (1870–1924) emerged as a brilliant and steel-willed leader of the Russian revolutionary movement in the early 1900s. Lenin, as he was known, played a key role in building the Marxist-oriented Bolshevik Party from its inception in 1903. Lenin's genius for building the party entered a crucible during the heady months between February and October of 1917. This period saw the overthrow of the czar by the Russian working class, continued Russian participation in the European war, a deepening economic crisis from recurring breakdowns in industry, incessant peasant rebellions in the countryside, a level of state repression against the Bolsheviks that drove Lenin into hiding, mutinies in the army, a right-wing military coup attempt by General Lavr Kornilov, and widespread disillusionment with the provisional government.

Thanks to the political sophistication, determination, and dynamic leadership that Lenin's generation of revolutionaries cultivated over many years in exile for the Russian Socialist movement, the Bolshevik Party would grow rapidly after the overthrow of the czar in February of 1917. By September, the Bolsheviks had won clear majorities in the election of workers', peasants', and soldiers' delegates within the soviet democracy operating as a "dual power" underneath Alexander Kerensky's provisional government. This made it clear that the revolutionary masses could tolerate sharing power with a capitalist and imperialist government no longer. In October, the Bolsheviks led an insurrection to overthrow the provisional government and take power in a second revolution at the behest of the All-Russian Congress of Soviets representing workers', peasants', and soldiers' councils all across the country.[102]

The triumphant Bolshevik-led Socialist government took the most revolutionary steps of any modern republic in world history. It abolished private ownership of land and expropriated the landowners without compensation to meet the historic demand for the granting of land to the landless peasants. It elaborated a system for coordinating workers' control over the manufacture, purchase, sale, and storage of produce and raw materials. It established workers' control over the financial activity of enterprises in all industrial, commercial, banking, agricultural, cooperative, and other sectors of the economy. The revolution gave birth to a new world.

US journalist John Reed, who wrote *10 Days That Shook the World* about his firsthand experience of the revolution, described the intellectual awakening of the people that it generated:

> All Russia was learning to read, and reading—politics, economics, history—because the people wanted to know. . . . In every city, in most towns, along the [military] Front, each political faction had its newspaper—sometimes several. Hundreds of thousands of pamphlets were distributed by thousands of organizations, and poured into the armies, the villages, the factories, the streets. The thirst for education, so long thwarted, burst with the Revolution into a frenzy of expression. From Smolny Institute alone, the first six months, went out every day tons, car-loads, train-loads of literature, saturating the land. Russia absorbed reading matter like hot sand drinks water, insatiable. And it was not fables, falsified history, diluted religion, and the cheap fiction that corrupts—but social and economic theories, philosophy, the works of Tolstoy, Gogol, and Gorky. . . .
>
> Lectures, debates, speeches—in theatres, circuses, school-houses, clubs, Soviet meeting-rooms, Union headquarters, barracks. Meetings in the trenches at the Front, in village squares, factories. What a marvelous sight to see Putilovsky Zavod (the Putilov factory) pour out its forty thousand [metal workers] to listen to Social Democrats, Socialist

Revolutionaries, Anarchists, anybody, whatever they had to say, as long as they would talk! For months in Petrograd, and all over Russia, every street-corner was a public tribune. In railway trains, street-cars, always the spurting up of impromptu debate, everywhere.[103]

In a land haunted by anti-Jewish racism and pogroms, the revolution elected the Ukraine-born Russian Jew Leon Trotsky as president of the Petrograd soviet, the political nerve center of the revolution. One of the first decrees of the Bolshevik government granted the right of self-determination to the nationalities historically oppressed by the Czarist empire (e.g., Estonians, Latvians, Lithuanians, Poles, Finns, Belarussians, Ukrainians, Muslim Tatars and Chechens, etc). The Bolsheviks extracted Russia from the world war. They created the Женотдел (*Zhenotdel* or Women's department) under the leadership of Alexandra Kollontai, which socialized the labor of houseworkers for the benefit of the working class by setting up free government-funded kindergartens, daycare nurseries, children's homes, canteens, schools, and laundry operations in cities and remote villages throughout the country.

In short, the October Revolution began to sweep away not just a decrepit dynastic monarchy into the dustbin of history but also the structures of feudalism, capitalism, imperialism, Russian national chauvinism, anti-Jewish hate, Islamophobia, and women's oppression. The revolution brought radical new creatives into being who channeled the revolution to make art and channeled art to make revolution: Wassily Kandinsky, Alexander Rodchenko, Natalia Goncharova, Kazimir Malevich, and Vladimir Tatlin. Konstantin Yuon's famous painting *New Planet* depicted the "Red October" as an event of cosmic proportions—because that is exactly what it felt like.

These facts explain why by January 1919, the top-ranking Black US military intelligence officer expressed alarm at the popularity of a radical Black speaker's declaration in a mass meeting in Washington, DC, that "Bolshevism is the salvation of America." The speaker, of course, was Hubert Henry Harrison.

The "threat of a good example" constitutes the simplest reason why Lenin's extraordinary body of revolutionary political thought (not to mention the larger Socialist and Communist corpus before, during, and since Lenin's time) has been effectively persecuted into prohibition by the ferociously anti-Communist culture of the United States. But there is another reason. Namely, the way in which the revolution that brought figures like Lenin, Trotsky, and Kollontai to state power in a country of 130 million also sent a revolutionary shock wave *all over the world*.[104]

One year after the Bolsheviks' rise to power in Russia, the workers of Vienna embarked upon a revolutionary road, rising up to overthrow the

Austro-Hungarian Empire and creating independent Austrian and Hungarian republics. In November of 1918, a revolt of German sailors in Kiel sparked a general strike that overthrew Kaiser Wilhelm II and a Prussian monarchy that had existed for centuries. A revolutionary movement began to sweep right across Germany, the military-industrial powerhouse of central Europe.

Over the next five years, Germany would witness the rise of protofascist right-wing death squads like the Freikorps, the formation of the German Communist Party, the murder of Karl Liebknecht and Rosa Luxemburg by the Freikorps under a government led by Social Democrats, the proliferation of thousands of democratically elected workers' and soldiers' councils (just like the Russian soviets), and a right-wing coup attempt led by the conservative nationalist Wolfgang Kapp. Most spectacularly, the period of 1918 to 1923 witnessed a militant German working class willing to undertake multiple general strikes that repeatedly raised the possibility of a "Bolshevik October" led by a unified German Communist Party of 400,000 members contending for political leadership of the largest working class in Europe.[105]

Europeans on opposite sides of the continent saw an unprecedented transformation taking place across the lands in between them. In the east, Russian revolutionary novelist and historian Victor Serge, for example, spoke of how the newspapers of the period were "astonishing" for their reports of "riots in Paris, riots in Lyon, revolution in Belgium, revolution in Constantinople, victory of the soviets in Bulgaria, rioting in Copenhagen. In fact the whole of Europe is in movement, clandestine or open soviets are appearing everywhere, even in the Allied armies; everything is possible, everything."[3] In the west, British prime minister Lloyd George observed that "the whole of Europe is filled with the spirit of revolution. There is a deep sense not only of discontent but of anger and revolt amongst the workmen against the pre-war conditions. The whole existing order in its political, social and economic aspects is questioned by the masses of the population from one end of Europe to the other." It marked a world-historic moment of potential transformation in the very heart of the socioeconomic organism of capitalist imperialism. The European working class appeared ready to take power and convert war into peace, capital into cooperation, and nationalist rivalry into international solidarity.

Even Uncle Sam got singed by the flames of the world revolutionary upsurge. In August of 1917, just a few months after the US entry into the inter-European war, a coalition of destitute African Americans, Seminoles, Muscogee Creeks, and European Americans launched an armed uprising against the war and the landlord class in rural Oklahoma. Thanks to the plans of the rebels to march a multiracial poor people's army all the way to Washington, DC, eating corn, they called it the Green Corn Rebellion. In short order, antiradical militias of white people assembled to put down the rebellion. Though the insurrection ended up short-lived, "three men died in the conflict, and more than four hundred others were arrested. Of those, 150 were convicted and received federal prison terms of up to ten years," according to the Oklahoma Historical Society. "After the rebellion failed, the Oklahoma Socialist Party disbanded. State and federal authorities used the failed insurrection as an excuse to suppress the IWW [Industrial Workers of the World], although neither it, nor the Socialist Party, had any official part in the uprising."[106]

Although wartime state repression temporarily kept a lid on workers' capacity for rebellion, the end of the war witnessed multiple new and dramatic explosions of it. As the year of the first antiradical "Red Scare" and the "Red Summer" of anti-Black pogroms, 1919 emerged as "one of the most militant in US labor history," according to labor historian Philip Foner. Some 3,630 strikes were called involving 4,160,000 workers in 1919, an increase of 2,933,000 over the number of workers involved in strikes in 1917.[107] Even the general strikes that Harrison advocated caught up with Uncle Sam.

Most spectacularly, the working people of Seattle launched a general strike in 1919, seizing political power and temporarily running the city themselves under workers' control. Radical journalist Anna Louise Strong, writing in the *Seattle Union Record*, gave voice to the revolutionary significance of working-class power:

> We are undertaking the most tremendous move ever made by LABOR in this country, a move which will lead—NO ONE KNOWS WHERE. . . .
>
> LABOR WILL FEED THE PEOPLE.
>
> Twelve great kitchens have been offered, and from them food will be distributed by the provision trades at low cost to all.
>
> LABOR WILL CARE FOR THE BABIES AND THE SICK.
>
> The milk-wagon drivers and the laundry drivers are arranging plans for supplying milk to babies, invalids and hospitals, and taking care of the cleaning of linen for hospitals.
>
> LABOR WILL PRESERVE ORDER.
>
> The strike committee is arranging for guards, and it is expected that the stopping of the cars will keep people at home. . . .
>
> NOT THE WITHDRAWAL OF LABOR POWER, BUT THE POWER OF THE STRIKERS TO MANAGE WILL WIN THIS STRIKE. . . .

The closing down of Seattle's industries, as a MERE SHUTDOWN, will not affect these eastern gentlemen much. They could let the whole northwest go to pieces, as far as money alone is concerned.

BUT, the closing down of the capitalistically controlled industries of Seattle, while the WORKERS ORGANIZE to feed the people, to care for the babies and the sick, to preserve order—THIS will move them, for this looks too much like the taking over of POWER by the workers.

Labor will not only SHUT DOWN the industries, but Labor will REOPEN, under the management of the appropriate trades, such activities as are needed to preserve public health and public peace. If the strike continues, Labor may feel led to avoid public suffering by reopening more and more activities,

UNDER ITS OWN MANAGEMENT.

And that is why we say that we are starting on the road that leads—NO ONE KNOWS WHERE.[108]

The working class of Seattle created a strike committee to oversee coordination of the strike with subcommittees for pickets, food, health care, and security. In so doing, they offered a concrete picture—however briefly—to the question of what a Socialist or workers' revolution in the United States could look like. It seemed the red-hot spirit of Russian revolutionary "Bolshevism" had reached the shores of America. (And much like Hubert Harrison and the Russian Revolutions, radical moments like the Seattle general strike remain all but forbidden from the grade-school US history curriculum.)

New radical organizations emerged to put teeth into the revolutionary mood of the times. The formation of the Communist-oriented Workers Party in 1919, built largely from an antiwar breakaway faction within the Socialist Party, gave concrete political and ideological organization to the kind of workers' power glimpsed in Seattle and more fully developed in the Russian and pan-European revolutionary convulsions then underway.

Harrison's Liberty League of Negro-Americans, founded the same year as the Russian Revolution and the Green Corn Rebellion, gave expression to the Harlem section of a political awakening taking place among working people all across the world. In the wake of Harrison's Liberty League (1917), numerous radical "New Negro" formations took shape, including Amy Ashwood and Marcus Garvey's reimagined Universal Negro Improvement Association and African Communities League (1918), Cyril Briggs and Grace Campbell's African Blood Brotherhood (1919), the recruitment of Black workers into the Communist party and the IWW, and the formation of the National Brotherhood Workers of America, a radical Southern Black labor union (1919). Alongside the rise of new leaders, organizations, and political possibilities, another extraordinary social experiment emerged out of Harlem's radical New Negro movement. One of the most spectacular expressions of this global political awakening emerged around the stepladders on the bustling street corners of Harlem. Like the thirst for education in the Russian revolution, the subway goers, clerks, bellhops, entertainers, migrants, messengers, and savants managed to co-create a cost-free Black intellectual awakening that would open and develop poor and working people's minds like no other educational institution had ever done before.

Chapter 3

Black Socrates in the Outdoor Grioversity

Evolution Discussed on Harlem Streets
Associated Negro Press, August 23, 1926

The Age of Pericles and Socrates in ancient Athens had nothing on the present age of Harlem in New York.

Coming out of the "movies" between 137th street and 138th street on Seventh avenue, we saw one of the biggest street-corner audiences that we have ever met in this block, which is famous for street-corner lectures. . . . This was not a selected audience, but the "run of the street," and their faces were fixed on a black man who stood on a ladder platform, with his back to the avenue and the passing buses and his face to the audience which blocked the spacious sidewalk. And what was he talking about?

Evolution!

The theory of evolution, and its illustration in different lines of material and biological development—the Darwinian science of the evolution of life, and the Marxian philosophy of the evolution of capitalism—and a possible development from capitalism to a state of communism.

I have the sorry burden of listening to so many poor lectures indoors, including those of my own, that I seldom tarry at a street-corner talk. But catching wind of the subject, I wanted to see what a random Harlem audience would do at such a lecture—with autos, two story busses and clanging fire-engines passing. Not in my life have I seen a more attentive audience at a lecture on a subject of this magnitude. How much were they "getting"? Their faces were certainly fixed on the speaker, who was Hubert H. Harrison. In half an hour none of those who were near enough to hear well left, and none seemed to lose attention. And it was not funny— they were not laughing.

The only time when there seemed to be smiles and bits of merriment was when the speaker fell to discussing certain theological dogmas and some hard-boiled religious creeds in the light of evolutionary science. I noticed that when he bore down on the fixed, immovable and unprogressive science of the pulpit, the people laughed. . . .

Now, why is it that the people will listen like this to a street talk on what is proverbially supposed to be a "dry subject," and yet are supposed to be uninclined to attend indoor sermons and lectures! I tell you, there must be something missing in those formal discourses. This street talk was virile and unconventional. Most of the indoor kind are platitudinous, artificial and lack courage. A fellow who is burdened with the weight of a church, a school . . . or some other institution is afraid to say some of the things which Harrison said boldly on this street-corner. The indoor talks are generally limited, muzzled, tongue-tied. This street talk was unchained, free, even daring. Perhaps, like Socrates, we must pursue truth on the street corners . . . and seek the Beautiful and the Good in the mob and among the outcasts.[1]

National Association for the Advancement of Colored People (NAACP) field organizer and Yale graduate William Pickens's story above captured the most common and concrete way Harlem saw Hubert Harrison. Harrison embodied a modest figure with a height of five feet and seven inches, weighing 170 pounds. Nevertheless, he exerted a profound influence as an educator by cultivating a culture of street-corner oratory in Harlem. In historian Ralph Crowder's words, Harrison represented "the only person to work effectively in the two dimensions of the Street Scholar experience, [both] self-trained historical research and street corner speaking."[2] According to historian Theodore Vincent, Harrison was "the man most responsible for building the tradition" of stepladder speaking in the community.[3]

Firsthand observers like Pickens compared the intellectual culture of the outdoor street speaking in Harlem to that of ancient Greece, with its romantic history evoked by such telling architectural survivals as the Acropolis. Harrison earned the nickname of the "Black Socrates" from his fellow Harlemites because of how "night after night he was to be found on the streets and avenues of Harlem preaching his doctrines of uplift and encouragement to the masses of his people."[4]

Yet however similar Harrison's dynamic oratory may have been to the historic lyceums of Plato and Aristotle's day, his identity and heritage as a descendant of African peoples—much like his Harlem audiences—suggests that an even better analogy might be found in the West African oral tradition of the griot. Griots served their communities as living storehouses of knowledge and ancestral wisdom. They traditionally played a key role in the shaping of thought and ideation in their communities. Different ethnolinguistic groups have different words for this role (in Wolof *guewel*, Mande *jeli*, Songhay *jeseré*, and Fulani *mabo*). According to scholar Thomas A. Hale, the key contribution of the griot and feminine griotte to the evolution of West African thought was their role as repositories of history. They could "reinterpret the past to listeners in the present" by retelling past events in a "fluid, situationally

Figure 3.1 This street speaker gives a glimpse into Harlem's outdoor oral culture, including the rapt audiences filling up the sidewalks. Photograph © Morgan and Marvin Smith, 1938.

specific synthesis of past and present values."⁵ Recounting the history, achievements, and sophistication of ancient African civilizations to demolish predominant notions of Black inferiority offered but one such example of the griot-like capacity in which Harrison served the community. As a storyteller, spokesperson, translator, poet, teacher, social interpreter, and orator, Harrison channeled the multidimensional energies of this West African tradition from his perch atop the stepladder. He was a St. Croix Creole griot in Harlem.⁶

I call Harlem's outdoor oral communication infrastructure, based on a collective culture of free education through engagement with stepladder orators, the Outdoor *Grioversity*. I do this in part to respond to a problem of language: there is no preexisting word or phrase for what Harrison and the larger community of orators and their engaged audiences created. And lack of distinctive language explains, in part, how a phenomenon can be forgotten. Community residents like Rev. Egbert Ethelred Brown referred to it as the "Outdoor University."⁷ *Outdoor* makes sense because of the various liberties that the open-air forum afforded. *University* also makes some sense in reference to the educational aspect, as does the notion of a "campus" where people congregated to learn. However, *university* conjures a specific faculty, enrolled students, a predetermined curriculum, and above all, rules set down by a top-down institutional administration. These were not exactly the elements informing Harlem's bustling street corners, which were free-flowing and dynamic, not fixed. Also, *university* doesn't adequately connote the African oral culture and tradition, like that of the griot. *Grioversity* speaks to both the African and European elements, as realized and creolized in practice, while still conjuring the university-level educational sophistication.

A Social Organism like No Other: The Outdoor Grioversity

As Harlem grew into a cosmopolitan mecca for Black people, residential "strolling" marked the vibrant outdoor culture of social life in the community. As NAACP organizer and writer James Weldon Johnson recounted,

> Strolling in Harlem does not mean merely walking along Lenox or upper Seventh Avenue or One Hundred and Thirty-Fifth Street; it means that those streets are places for socializing. One puts on one's best clothes and fares forth to pass the time pleasantly with the friends and acquaintances and, most important of all, the strangers he is sure of meeting. One saunters along, he hails this one, exchanges a word or two with that one, stops for a short chat with the other one.... The hours of a summer evening run by rapidly. This is not simply going out for a walk; it is more like going out for adventure.[8]

Another writer, Wallace Thurman, added further texture to this description, noting that while strolling in Harlem one might find "a Hindoo faker here, a loud Socialist there, a medicine doctor ballyhooing, a corn doctor, a blind musician, serious people, gay people, philanderers, and preachers. Seventh Avenue is filled with deep rhythmic laughter."[9]

As Thurman's description suggests, in addition to strolling, Harlem featured a distinctive culture of street-corner orators, who did not offer dry academic lectures but a lively, unpredictable, and entertaining form of collective address. In the 1920s, Harlem residents could not peruse their social media feeds after a hard day's work, nor could they have even watched shows on a home television set. Although radio formed an increasingly prominent mode of mass communication in the early twentieth century, most of the Black-oriented programming it featured before World War II consisted of demeaning, nineteenth-century-style blackface dialect comedy.[10] Harlem residents therefore often went out in the evening to partake of the cultural and social life of the street-corner orators. Community members knew the time and place where speakers would declaim and would congregate for this purpose "with such regularity that only foul weather or the police interrupted the message of the stepladder radicals."[11]

Street-corner speaking in Harlem constituted a distinctively Black urban spatial medium of communication, collective information processing, and knowledge creation. As historian Ira Reid puts it, "Street-corner speaking became the device through which loyalties were analyzed, interpreted, and received into group action." Street speakers like Harrison ventilated the political pulse of the community. And if frequency of engagement gave any measure, then the orators in fact may have exerted far more influence than any other social actor. In most Black communities, the church formed the key community institution, and there was no shortage of Christian congregations in Harlem.[12] However, street speakers like Harrison would hold forth on a range of themes that would not have been aired in church, including radical criticism of religion and the church itself.

More importantly, the outdoor forums occurred far more frequently than religious services. Indeed, unlike a weekly trip to church, secular outdoor gatherings formed an almost nightly event, offering spirited nodes of collective public engagement at multiple sites throughout the neighborhood. For example, according to historian Joyce Moore Turner, Black Socialists were out on some corner almost every night except Sunday in the 1920s: "On the same evening [Richard B.] Moore, Ethelred Brown, and H. Leadett would be speaking at Lenox Avenue and 128th street, while [W. A.] Domingo, John Patterson, and Frank Poree were holding forth at Lenox Avenue and 133rd street.... By 1921 the socialists were rotating their soapboxes among nine different sites."[13] One need not go into detail about the suffragists, Garveyists, preachers, Communists, and others to know that Socialists were far from the only street-corner speakers on offer.[14]

As important as newspapers and print culture were for shaping circuits of ideational exchange nationally and internationally, the oral medium of the soapbox became a central sociocultural institution for the shaping of Black thought at a local level in Harlem. And if the street speaking formed a central community institution, then "the Campus" on the northeast corner of 135th Street and Seventh Avenue constituted its main stage, thanks to the subway stop nearby at Eighth Avenue, which formed a central transit hub for neighborhood residents. Not only did small businesses naturally coalesce around that intersection but so did would-be orators who sought an audience continuously infused by mass subway exhalations of passengers who rode the 2 and 3 trains to and from their workplaces downtown. Only the best could hold forth at this site thanks to its central geographical location and the heightened expectations the community placed upon its orators.[15]

Because of this already stimulating outdoor social life, intellectually inclined street-corner orators like Hubert Harrison had to hold the rapt attention and interest of their audience in order to be effective and not dismissed as a distraction from something more interesting. Much like they would later do at the Apollo Theatre's "Amateur Night," a dissatisfied Harlem audience could at any time boo off the platform quickly and unceremoniously any prospective speechmaker who just didn't have the juice.[16] For this reason, as Crowder has pointed out, stepladder orators were "experts in utilizing the cultural dynamics of public debate in urban Black communities. Spontaneity, improvisation, call and response, and the ability to read the shifting climate of the audience were all essential skills for effective oratory."[17] Thus the art of street-corner speaking evolved as an interactive process wherein the speaker formed the focal point while working-class Harlemites vocally exhorted or heckled them, enforcing their own standards and expectations, and otherwise participating actively in a dialectical contestation, affirmation, and collective communication and knowledge-building process.[18]

One of the first Black women in the Communist Party, Hermie Dumont Huiswoud, recalled how when Harrison spoke "it was not long before the crowd swelled . . . and even children ceased romping, keeping quiet as he developed his subject. His audience was always spell-bound and attentive as his address was so simply presented that his listeners had no difficulty understanding the subject and were also amused at the subtle humor he injected."[19]

As a key crystallizer of Harlem's Outdoor Grioversity, Harrison's oratory invariably held the rapt interest of his listeners far beyond his home neighborhood. For example, in September 1912, a century before the Occupy Wall Street movement, the *New York Times* noted how Harrison "shattered all records for distance in an address on Socialism in front of the Stock Exchange building" on Wall Street, the economic heart of the American ruling class. The report noted how he was still going strong at the beginning of the third hour of his oration, but eventually his voice grew "huskier and huskier" as "his auditors drew closer and closer" until his voice faded into a hoarse whisper before the big bell announced the closing of the Exchange for the day.[20]

The freethought publication *Truth Seeker* noted how on numerous occasions, his two-and-a-half-hour talks drew 1,500 people.[21] Outdoors, Harrison often spoke without notes because of his uncanny ability to store and recall information, something akin to what reemerged decades later as "freestyling" in the hip-hop generation of Black New York's Grioversity-inflected culture. When speaking about evolution, for example, Harrison would routinely recite from memory long passages—quoted verbatim—from the works of Charles Darwin, Alfred Russell Wallace, Thomas Henry Huxley, Herbert Spencer, and Ernst Haeckel.[22]

If stories like these offer any indication, one simply cannot measure the cumulative impact Harrison had by giving talks of this kind multiple nights a week for some twenty years on any and every subject imaginable to mass audiences in and beyond Harlem. Not to mention the multiplier effect from the influence of the wider landscape of orators including women like Helen Holman, Anna Brown, Elizabeth Hendrickson, Eslanda Cardozo Goode, Grace P. Campbell, Henrietta Vinton Davis, and Lucille Randolph, who took up the stepladder alongside the men they worked with in the Socialist, suffragist, Garveyist, Communist, and other movements.

Black radical political organizations established their offices in the same area as the street speaking locations. As Richard B. Moore recalled, "It was a matter of steps between the offices of Randolph and Owen's *Messenger* at 2305 Seventh Avenue, William Bridges' *Challenge* at 2305 Seventh Avenue, Cyril V. Briggs's *Crusader* at 2299 Seventh Avenue, and Marcus Garvey's *Negro World* at 56 West 135th Street, and no more than a few blocks to the homes, soapboxer corners, and meeting halls of the African Blood Brotherhood, Universal Negro Improvement Association, the Liberty League, and other militant organizations."[23] The average listener who came into the orbit of this dynamic intellectual and political epicenter of New Negro politics in Harlem would have thus heard speakers offering an array of radical and unorthodox ideas. Moore's observation thus points to the aspect of Harlem culture whereby most Harlemites did not necessarily see competing Black activist formations as incompatible. Indeed, most folks maintained multiple (and sometimes contradictory) ideological commitments (e.g., Black/African pride vs. Eurocentric aspirations) and political affinities (e.g., social democratic, liberal integrationist, Black nationalist, communist, and capitalist) at the same time. Not to mention the influence of the larger complex of social and community institutions like the church, the salon, the lodge, the cabaret, the barbershop, or the Renaissance Casino.

Harrison fought an uphill battle in the course of establishing a mass-based open-air forum for radical intellectual exploration. He often found himself in the middle of free speech struggles of the kind made famous by the Industrial Workers of the World in defiance of harassment from the police. For example, the New York Police Department would arrest him for "obstructing" the sidewalk. Then they would fine him for his obligatory US flag display not being large enough.[24]

At other times, white mobs physically attacked Harrison for expressing his views. In August 1914, for example, a *New York World* article reported that several times over the preceding month Harrison had narrowly escaped being mobbed because of his denunciations of "the Church in general and the Catholic Church in particular."[25] One night, he gave a lecture at 181st Street and

St. Nicholas in the predominantly Irish neighborhood of Washington Heights. His talk suffered frequent hostile interruptions from the hecklers in the crowd.[26] Upon its termination, some fifty angry listeners followed him into the underground passage leading to the subway station, pursuing him with "murderous intent."[27] Then, right in front of the ticket window, "the mob which had been shouting threatening remarks after him, rushed and began to beat him." Harrison, reportedly having armed himself with a wooden table leg, parried a blow from one of the mob ringleaders, William McElroy, and then struck him on the head, inflicting a bad wound. In the end, the police took Harrison to the 177th Street station house and locked him up on a charge of felonious assault, while McElroy was taken to the Washington Heights Hospital.[28] Thanks to his use of armed self-defense, Hubert Henry Harrison ended that day as a lynch mob survivor. Experiences like these gave his repeated arguments for Black self-defense a distinctive and highly personal fire.

Although Harrison often faced heckling from those who disagreed with him, it did not dampen his fire in the slightest. Harrison protégé Richard B. Moore recalled how Harrison's "keen black eyes could almost transfix an opponent; when they opened slightly and his lips pulled up somewhat, then a withering blast was on its way. Although generally amiable and never pompous, he bore a reserved but pleasant mien, always bearing himself with conscious dignity."[29] The famous writer Henry Miller recalled how no matter what the provocation, Harrison always retained his self-possession and his dignity: "He had a way of placing the back of his hand on his hip, his trunk tilted, his ears cocked to hear every last word of the questioner, or the heckler put to him. Well he knew how to bide his time! When the tumult had subsided there would come that broad smile of his, a broad, good-natured grin, and he would answer his man—always fair and square, always full on, like a broadside. Soon everyone would be laughing, everyone but the poor imbecile who had dared to put the question."[30]

Whatever challenges came his way—and in New York City they inevitably did—he found ways to meet them, often turning them to his advantage. According to his close friend Claude McKay, when Harrison laughed, he "exploded in his large sugary black African way, which sounded like the rustling of dry bamboo leaves agitated by the wind."[31] According to the *New York Times*, Harrison's wide knowledge, jocular wit, and lyrical language eventually "disarmed all those who came to scoff and turned them into his admiring pupils."[32]

Major Walter Loving, the highest-ranking African American officer in military intelligence, spent two full years in plainclothes attending Black political meetings, speeches, and events across multiple cities and states. He offered a candid assessment of Harrison's oratorical style in his *Final Report*

Figure 3.2 An outdoor stepladder orator in Harlem. Morgan and Marvin Smith, 1938, Schomburg Center for Research in Black Culture, New York.

on Negro Subversion for the director of US military intelligence. Maj. Loving noted that Harrison

> is not affiliated with any political party and freely criticizes all of them.... He also makes frequent attacks upon the church, asserting that its influence has been inimical to the progress of humanity by enslaving the minds of the people with foolish dogmas and theories that will not bear the light of reason. He pictures the heads of the church as being in league with the master capitalists in a pact to plunder the proletariat of all nations. Thoroughly versed in history and sociology, Mr. Harrison is a very convincing speaker. I consider his influence to be more far reaching that that of any other individual radical because his subtle propaganda, delivered in such scholastic language and backed by the facts of history, carries an appeal to reason that reaches the more thoughtful and conservative class of Negroes who could not be reached by the "cyclone" methods of the more extreme radicals.

Though the Military Intelligence Bureau did not harbor any sympathies for the Black radicals it surveilled, this assessment rings true to the spirit of Harrison's influence as a street speaker.

His designation as having an influence "more far reaching" than any other radical appears even more extraordinary in light of New York's particular relationship to Black radicalism. Maj. Loving's 1919 report spoke of how "New York City is the fountainhead of all radical propaganda among Negroes. Centered in this city are the most radical Negro publications and the most radical Negro speakers. Frequent mass meetings are held to spread radical propaganda and soap box orators speak on the streets of Harlem every night arousing the masses to hostile action against present conditions.... Harlem, 'the black belt' of New York, with one hundred thousands of Negroes of various nationalities, is a hot bed of radicalism which requires continual vigilance on the part of the government." Hubert Henry Harrison thus appeared to military intelligence as the greatest tributary to the national fountainhead of Black radicalism.

US military intelligence made both quantitative and qualitative assessments of his influence. For example, Maj. Loving enclosed a list of important mass meetings held during the month of January with the names of the speakers who delivered the addresses. Out of thirty-three meetings on his list, Harrison's name is the second most common after Marcus Garvey's (Garvey had sixteen, Harrison six, Rev. R. D. Jonas (an undercover British intelligence asset) three, Rev. George F. Miller three, Chandler Owen two, A. Philip Randolph two, and William Monroe Trotter one). In his report Maj. Loving noted that

> all of the speakers named on [the] enclosed list are radicals and frequently advocate Bolshevism in their speeches. This is especially true of Mr. Hubert Harrison, who claims that "Bolshevism is the salvation of America." The conservative colored population of Washington had never been accustomed to radical addresses of this nature and when Mr. Harrison first appeared before Washington audiences the people listened at him in awed silence. Now that he has been delivering addresses there for the past six weeks, the people have not only become accustomed to his philosophy but are applauding it. During this brief period of six weeks Mr. Harrison has developed a very large following in the city of Washington, just as he did in New York.[33]

A Black Griot of the Harlem Acropolis

Harrison's Outdoor Grioversity offered free education in terms not only of cost or freedom of speech (and assembly) but also of free-ranging ideation. The spatiality of the open-air forum elegantly bypassed the ideological confines of such forces as the church, the white left, the Tuskegee Machine, public schools, the corporate media, the Tammany Hall Democratic Party machine, the liberal "race magazines," and the conservative Black press. Harrison's outdoor speaking struck listeners as "virile and unconventional," noted Pickens. "A fellow who is burdened with the weight of a church, a school . . . or some other institution is afraid to say some of the things which Harrison said boldly on this street-corner. . . . This street talk was unchained, free, even daring."[34] Harrison's method thus promoted an extremely rare space where Black thought could range freely within the public square, both figuratively and literally.

Harrison's model represented a grassroots, mass-based medium of popular education and intellectual development. In particular, those without any formal schooling (e.g., African American migrants streaming in from the Jim Crow South) could access a fount of education of, by, and for those with a similar racial and socioeconomic position to their own. For this reason, the Outdoor Grioversity of Harrison's day comprised a forerunner to Paolo Freire's concept of the "pedagogy of the oppressed."[35] As Harlem activist Hodge Kirnon put it, Harrison "taught the masses and he drew much of his inspiration from them. He became their most articulate intellectual expression."[36]

Harrison's work to create an intellectual culture in Harlem, while overwhelmingly ignored by the white world, represented something profound to the community itself. Richard B. Moore maintained that Harrison represented the figure most responsible for making Harlem "the Mecca of Negro intellectual culture."[37] Harrison protégé A. Philip Randolph, a firsthand witness and practitioner of the culture established at 135th Street and Seventh Avenue, described it as "the center of the militant consciousness of black America" where an array of soapbox-amplified intellects "shared the same platform, and took turns enlarging upon everything from the French Revolution, the history of slavery, to the rise of the working class. It was one of the great intellectual forums of America."[38]

Harlem's Outdoor Grioversity had its equivalents elsewhere, such as the "bug house square" and Washington Park Forum of Chicago's South Side, where Black radicals of various stripes would also engage in dynamic orations with mass audiences. According to eminent African American historian John H. Bracey, the people who spoke there had a "breathtaking" level of knowledge "on all matters political, economic, philosophical," and more. The same place where Harrison himself spoke multiple times during a visit to Chicago in 1924.[39]

Given the range of subjects covered and its role as a wellspring of intellectual development, the Outdoor Grioversity was one of the great intellectual forums of not just the country but the *world*. Consider, for example, a similar space that emerged in the Russian Revolution of 1917, in the modern circus building of Petrograd (now St. Petersburg) where speakers would hold forth regularly on the burning questions of land, bread, and peace—the ideational fountainhead of that revolution. One of the Russian Revolution's greatest orators offered a description that coincided with the "New Negro" awakening in Harlem's Outdoor Grioversity. In his autobiography, the Ukraine-born Russian Jewish revolutionary Leon Trotsky recounted the following:

> I usually spoke in the Circus in the evening, sometimes quite late at night. My audience was composed of workers, soldiers, hard-working mothers, street urchins—the oppressed under-dogs of the capital. Every square inch was filled, every human body compressed to its limit. Young boys sat on their fathers' shoulders; infants were at their mothers' breasts. No one smoked. The balconies threatened to fall under the excessive weight of human bodies. I made my way to the platform through a narrow human trench, sometimes I was borne overhead. The air, intense with breathing and waiting, fairly exploded with shouts and with the passionate yells peculiar to the Modern Circus. Above and around me was a press of elbows, chests, and heads. I spoke from out of a warm cavern of human bodies; whenever I stretched out my hands I would touch some one, and a grateful movement in response would give me to understand that I was not to worry about it, not to break off my speech, but keep on. No speaker, no matter how exhausted, could resist the electric tension of that impassioned human throng. They wanted to know, to understand, to find their way. At times it seemed as if I felt, with my lips, the stern inquisitiveness of this crowd that had become merged into a single whole. Then all the arguments and words thought out in advance would break and recede under the imperative pressure of sympathy, and other words, other arguments, utterly unexpected by the orator but needed by these people, would emerge in full array from my subconsciousness. On such occasions I felt as if I were listening to the speaker from the outside, trying to keep pace with his ideas, afraid that, like a somnambulist, he might fall off the edge of the roof at the sound of my conscious reasoning. Such was the Modern Circus. It had its own contours, fiery, tender, and frenzied. The infants were peacefully sucking the breasts from which approving or threatening shouts were coming. The whole crowd was like that, like infants clinging with their dry lips to the nipples of the revolution. But this infant matured quickly. Leaving the Modern Circus was even more difficult than entering it. The crowd was unwilling to break up its new-found unity; it would refuse to disperse. In a semi-consciousness of exhaustion, I had to float on countless arms above the heads of the people, to reach the exit.[40]

Trotsky's vivid description of the orator's process—from the boisterous and cantankerous heckling to spiritual merging and harmonization with his mass audience—would have sounded familiar to Harrison. The point here is not to compare Petrograd apples to Harlem oranges but to index the Outdoor Grioversity to the larger global political awakening of the World War I era, which bore a range of revolutionary fruits all over the world.

In his cultivation of the Outdoor Grioversity, Harrison helped inaugurate a new pedagogical model for community-based education that stood in stark contrast to the others on offer. For example, Harrison called *industrial education* a "humorous phrase" on the grounds that it fostered ignorance and prepared Black people to be little more than "hewers of wood and drawers of water."[41] In response to those advocating a higher education in the liberal arts, Harrison insisted that "those who have knowledge must come down from their Sinais and give it to the common people. Theirs is the great duty to simplify and make clear, to light the lamps of knowledge that the eyes of their race may see; that the feet of their people may not stumble. This is the task of the Talented Tenth."[42] Meanwhile, if Harrison Blackened the Socialist, anarchist, freethinking, and working-class curricula of the Rand and Modern Schools as liberating pedagogies, he also bemoaned the way white social movements, however "radical" they seemed, generally "broke down as soon as they crossed the color line."[43]

A New Negro Theory of Education

> To the Negro America offers Jim Crow, segregation, disfranchisement and the lynching-bee. But at the same time she also offers him free schools and colleges, free public libraries and the second-hand bookshops where he can "sit with Shakespeare," walk with [George Bernard] Shaw, commune with poets, philosophers, scientists, historians, novelists, and draw "sweetness and light" from the noblest souls of the past and present. What a blessing it would be if, while we fight against the evil in America's left hand, we should utilize the powers which she holds in her right to make our fight more effective!
>
> —Hubert Harrison, "Education in and out of School," *Boston Chronicle*, February 23, 1924

> The most that they can teach you in college is how to gather knowledge, and if you can't go to college as long as you can read you may still master that art. How to use knowledge—that no one can teach you, either in college or out of it. . . . While we chatter about "segregation" we segregate ourselves from that community of culture and knowledge that is as wide open to us as the winds of heaven and limitless as the eternal sea.
>
> —Hubert Harrison, "Education in and out of School"

Hubert Harrison's proximity to poverty influenced his conception of Black education, as he was born of field-laboring African Caribbean parents and arrived in New York as a Black working-class orphan and immigrant. Harlem resident Oscar Benson recalled that Harrison "loved children, the poor, the common folks; those who were victims of circumstances."[44] Hodge Kirnon observed that "no trace of the Brahmin spirit was to be found in Harrison. He lived with and among his people—not on the fringes of their social life."[45] These comments speak to the relationship between Harrison's working-class socioeconomic background and his focus on those of similarly humble origins.

Harrison did not harbor any shame about his humble class background. Writing in his private diary as early as 1908, a year after securing his postal job, he noted "what a damned powerful modifier of a man's philosophy of life is poverty and the pressure of hunger! If ever I forget this as a starting-point for any scheme of things that I may construct I hope I'll go hungry for three days so that I may remember it."[46] Later in life, the *Amsterdam News* quoted him sounding a similar theme: "I have often thought that this contact with the stern realities of poverty was good for me. It has kept my heart open to the call of those who are down and has kept me from giving myself such airs as might make a chasm between myself and my people."[47] Far from feeling shame for his humble class status, he recognized its positive impact for keeping him grounded and connected to his community. Similarly, Harrison avoided personal publicity and hated praise.[48]

Harrison's conception of leadership put the masses at the center of a collective and bottom-up conception of racial advancement. The community recognized him, appreciated his contributions to it, and supported him in ways that the elites never did. Harrison's belief in the ability of the grass roots to learn, think, and develop explains the consistency of his commitment to the Outdoor Grioversity, which emerged in large part from his placement of the "common people" at the center of Black life, in addition to his attitude of profound respect and humility toward them.

Moreover, Harrison knew from his own experience that a wide range of knowledge does not come from a lucky birth but from old-fashioned hard work. As Harrison's friend Oscar Benson recounted, "I once asked him to give me a proximity of the number of books he read in one day and he shocked me by saying perhaps five or six."[49] The librarian at the 135th Street public library remarked how no one checked out more books than Harrison.[50] He eventually obtained eye glasses, apparently in part because of the weakening of his vision due to his regimen of nightly reading by lamplight.[51] Yet Harrison did not read voraciously just because he enjoyed it.

Harrison saw reading as a key path to developing the kind of knowledge necessary for fighting systems oppression. Making young people into adults fit for a free world required an educational model that would "shape their souls for continued conflict with a theory and practice [with] which most of the white world that surrounds them are at one." Education had to prepare students for long-term struggle against the worldview and practical results of white supremacy. Because most sources of power were controlled by white people, Harrison felt it incumbent upon people of color to get wise—literally. He insisted that Black people must "develop to the fullest that organ whereby weakness has been able to overcome strength; namely, the intellect.... We Negroes must take to reading, study and the development of intelligence as we have never done before." He criticized the scientific racism of standardized testing, noting how "the results of the Army Intelligence Tests are generally cited as 'scientific' proofs of white superiority and Negro inferiority; since the I.Q.'s of Negroes, it is said, were lower than this of whites."[52]

Harrison also repeatedly stressed the need for Black people to take responsibility for their own learning, and he encouraged a culture of reading by selling books at his outdoor talks, starting a lecture forum at the 135th Street public library, and initiating the first regular book review column in a Black newspaper.[53] His skill as a reviewer undoubtedly grew out of consorting with some of the leading white literary figures of the day. At the Sunrise Club, for example, Harrison met and engaged with figures like H. L. Mencken, Theodore Dreiser, Ludwig Lewisohn, Heywood Broun, Charles Hanson Towne, and Burton Rascoe.[54]

He saw independent study as crucial in part because of his critique of the mainstream education system. Harrison described the system of public education as one that "poisoned the streams" of public knowledge. For example, the history curriculum taught to children consisted of little more than "official fairy tales in which men who had swindled their governments and robbed the people ... were represented as sturdy democrats, ascetics and paragons of all the virtues." Students in the system were thus indoctrinated at a tender age into a "cult of national patriotism," such that when they became adults they would be "ready to be turned into cannon-fodder whenever the knowing ones who managed public affairs wanted to have their mines and factories in other lands protected, or to secure a market for the sale of goods for lack of which their own people were starving." Normalizing and acclimating young people to glaring contradictions like this one—between grinding poverty at home and capitalist wars for profit abroad—formed a key function of the education system in Harrison's view.[55]

Harrison also criticized the way schools inculcated a white supremacist world view. Noting how the education system in the United States and the

Caribbean was "shaped by white people for white youth, and from their point of view, it fits their purpose well," he decried how "the examples of valor and virtue on which [student] minds are fed are exclusively white examples. What wonder, then, that each generation comes to maturity with the idea imbedded in its mind that only white men are valorous and fit to rule and only white women are virtuous and entitled to chivalry, respect, and protection?" He concluded that any place that claimed to be an institution of learning for Black people, especially historically Black colleges and universities, needed to counteract white domination in the curriculum by offering courses in Black history and African languages and cultures.[56] Interestingly, although the course he taught in the fall semester of 1926 at New York University (NYU) included a majority-Black reading list, Africana studies would not begin to emerge in the formal academy until street scholars like John Henrik Clarke and Black student activists built the Black studies movement of the 1960s.[57]

Harrison felt these problems in primary and secondary education originated in the narrow-mindedness of the higher educational institutions. He lamented, for example, how common it was "for the head of a college to discharge a professor who had become too radical—by which was meant a proneness to such truths as were subversive of the overlordship of those who supplied the funds for the maintenance of the college." The trustees and financial interests exerted undue influence over who and what could be taught. Moreover, because professors were dependent on the universities for their livelihood, they eventually "came to constitute a class functionally similar to that of the priesthood, a class of defenders of the existing institutions and of the ideas which buttressed them." By weeding out the truth tellers and subordinating intellectual content to the interests of donors and funders, universities perpetuated the status quo.

For all of these reasons, Harrison maintained that true learning required going beyond the confines of formal schooling. "Go to school whenever you can," he insisted, "but remember always that the best college is that on your bookshelf: the best education is that on the inside of your own head." To this end, he noted the existence of free schools and colleges, free public libraries and the secondhand bookstores where anyone could "commune with poets, philosophers, scientists, historians, novelists, and draw 'sweetness and light' from the noblest souls of the past and present." To buttress his argument he noted that Abraham Lincoln, Toussaint L'Ouverture, and Frederick Douglass were all educated, even though none of them had gone to college or even high school.[58]

In short, Harrison's educational philosophy found its base in the notion that one must strive to "read, reason, and think on all sides of all subjects." As noted, his invitation to young people was to "get education. Get it not only in school and college, but in books and newspapers, in market-places, institutions, and movements. Prepare by knowing; and never think you know until you have listened to ten others who know differently—and have survived the shock."[59] This notion that one had to test one's knowledge against ten other ways of knowing reflected Harrison's own rigorous independent studies and his experience surviving not only the shock of countless books, church lyceum sessions, and street-corner hecklers but also the fierce intellectual contestations within the freethought, Socialist, women's suffrage, and New Negro movements.

A Black Sheep among Freethinkers

> The criticism of religion is the prerequisite of all criticism. . . . *Religious* suffering is, at one and the same time, the *expression* of real suffering and a *protest* against real suffering. Religion is the sigh of the oppressed creature, the heart of a heartless world, and the soul of soulless conditions. It is the *opium* of the people. . . . The [demand for] abolition of religion as the *illusory* happiness of the people is the demand for their *real* happiness. To call on them to give up their illusions about their condition is to call on them to *give up a condition that requires illusions*. [emphasis in original]
>
> —Karl Marx, "A Contribution to the Critique of Hegel's Philosophy of Right"

Harrison's break with (and criticisms of) religion would set the stage for his rise to become the most prominent Black freethinker of his generation. It would also, as the Marx quote above suggests, form part and parcel of a larger intellectual and political awakening and his radical rejection of a traumatizing world that required the soothing "illusions" of institutionalized religion.

Harrison "divorced" himself from orthodox and institutional Christianity sometime around 1901. He then trained in debate lyceums of Catholic and AME churches. But in a letter to Frances Reynolds Keyser in 1908, Harrison described how reading Thomas Paine's *Age of Reason* showed him an attack on religious dogma so convincing that Harrison's "poor wounded soul cried out in agony" as he "saw the whole fabric of [religious] thought and feeling" that he had adhered to now suddenly "crumbling at its very foundations." Although he now identified as an agnostic, he admitted that "it is only fair to confess that Reason alone has failed to satisfy all my needs. For there are needs, not merely ethical, but spiritual, inspirational—what I would call personal dynamics; and these also must be filled. . . . I do not necessarily commit myself to [belief in] immortality or any allied doctrine when I say that the soul yearns for the support of something." In other words, as much as he could see the power of reason for explaining the world, he also could see its limitations, and he appreciated the value of beliefs which promoted spiritual development even if those beliefs' "correspondence with fact cannot be demonstrated."[60]

After a rigorous study of the historical conditions under which Christianity originated, "one of the main conclusions at which I had arrived was this: that Catholicism was the representative type of Christianity; whatever was absurd in it... was due to an absurdity inherent in the very texture of Christianity." Somewhat contradictorily in his letter to Keyser, he also mentions being attracted to Catholicism for "the beauty and solemnity of its ritual" and "the dignity, antiquity and power of that venerable institution itself." But he ultimately concludes, "Entre nous, I doubt whether I will ever be anything but an honest Agnostic because I prefer, as I once told you, to go to the grave with my eyes open." Harrison had theological problems with Christianity but he also acknowledged the spiritual striving that even an agnostic like himself could still feel so deeply.[61]

His criticism of Christianity went beyond theology or concerns about its subordination of reason to faith, because he analyzed its relationship to political and economic power in the real world. For example, his piece entitled "The Menace of Exemption," about the $400,000,000 worth of Church property in New York that managed to avoid paying any taxes, featured on the front page of the national weekly freethinking *Truth Seeker* magazine. Freethinkers represented a secular and rationalist movement from the nineteenth century that challenged church dogmas and religious authority in general. Over the years, a secular readership grew for *The Truth Seeker*, which supported free speech, a free press, and "free mails" against government censorship. Its contributors and readers also demanded taxation of church properties, discontinuance of military chaplains, an end to prayers in school and courtroom Bible oaths, and a complete separation of church and state.[62]

By 1911, at age twenty-eight, he represented the most prominent Black voices in the freethought movement.[63] For example, the *Truth Seeker*'s fiftieth-anniversary "Golden Jubilee" edition in 1923 highlighted all of the leading white freethinkers of the previous half century including Mark Twain, Robert Ingersoll, Thomas Huxley, Ernst Haeckel, Moncure D. Conway, Luther Burbank, and John E. Remsburg.[64] In a telling sign of his unusual position, the special edition featured only one Black figure within this pantheon of freethinkers: Hubert Henry Harrison.

In order to attain such a distinction and prove his salt—as a Black freethinker among the most prominent white freethinkers—Harrison had attained a higher level of mastery with religion than most. In 1914, he began teaching a course in comparative religion at the Modern School, a project founded in 1911 as part of the radical educational movement that emerged globally following the state-sponsored execution of Spanish anarchist and freethinking educator Francisco Ferrer (1859–1909).[65] Harrison's course covered Hinduism, Buddhism, Taoism, the teachings of Confucius and other religions of China, Islam, and the debt of Christianity to paganism. He gave lectures with titles like "Religion and Government," focusing on "the Adulterous Union of Church and State"; "Religion and the Proletariat," on "why all religions are reactionary"; "Two Ways to Kill Off Revolution," a comparative critique of Christian preachers Bouck White and Billy Sunday; and "Religion and Culture," which looked at the conflicts between religion and culture. In another talk, he offered "An Agnostic's Apology," conveying "The Duty of Free Thinking and Plain Speaking."[66] Harrison also lectured on subjects like "How God Grew: The Evolution of the Idea of God" and "Jesus Christ and the Working Man: A Challenge to the Christian Socialists."[67] Thanks to his command of Christian theology, he reportedly once received an offer to take a position as the president of a theological seminary.[68]

Although sometimes associated with atheism, Harrison self-identified as an agnostic. Writing to his mentor, spiritual adviser, and White Rose Home director Frances Reynolds Keyser in 1908, Harrison stated plainly, "I am an agnostic; not a dogmatic *dis*believer nor a bumptious and narrow infidel.... I am (in my mental attitude) such an Agnostic as Huxley was and my principles are the same." Retrospectively known as "Darwin's Bulldog" for his staunch support of Darwin against his critics, Thomas Huxley coined the term *agnosticism*. He defined it as "the essence of science, whether ancient or modern. It simply means that a man shall not say he knows or believes that which he has no scientific grounds for professing to know or believe." Huxley saw agnosticism not as a creed but a method, the essence of which consisted in the "rigorous application of a single principle.... Positively the principle may be expressed: In matters of the intellect, follow your reason as far as it will take you, without regard to any other consideration. And negatively: In matters of the intellect do not pretend that conclusions are certain which are not demonstrated or demonstrable."[69]

Harrison studied keenly the religion of Deism, as advocated by European Enlightenment thinkers like Jean-Jacques Rousseau, Voltaire, and Constantin-François Volney. He advised his street-corner audiences to read such classics of theological criticism as Thomas Paine's *Age of Reason*, Volney's *Ruins of Empires*, John William Draper's *Conflict between Religion and Science*, Andrew Dickson White's *Warfare of Science and Theology*, and the *Lectures of Robert Ingersoll*.[70] Volney connected the prominence of the church to the rule of wealth and advocated for the abolition of religion. He disputed the very notion of a soul continuing to live after the body's expiration, claiming heaven and hell were the carrot and stick with which the ruling class convinces ordinary people to die to protect their powerful positions. Paine's pamphlet comprised a Deist attack on organized religion, which Paine regarded as a human invention set up to terrify and enslave mankind for profit. Paine argued that the natures of revelations and prophecies change according to political climate of the times and that the church exists only to amass capital and maintain existing power structures. Harrison praised Paine as the one who brought "militant unbelief and democratic dissent" down from the clouds to the level of ordinary people.[71]

Draper's book popularized the "conflict thesis" proposing an inherent antagonism between religion and science. He argued that the structures erected by organized religion grant them enhanced political and social power to combat scientific advancement, and he attacked religious institutions as a regressive and anti-intellectual force. A. D. White, another influential advocate of the conflict thesis, saw the efforts of the church to suppress scientific advancement as ultimately harmful to science and religion both. White argued that the history of scientific advancement was a story of the conflict between two antagonistic forces: the expansive human intellect and the suppression of that force by traditional faith. White maintained that all scientific discovery is inherently beneficial to society, even if that discovery comes at the cost of religious credibility, as in the denial of the literal interpretation of Genesis and the gradual acceptance of earth's sphericity and the heliocentric model of the cosmos that saw the Earth as orbiting the sun, rather than the Church's insistence that the sun orbited the Earth. As a part of his rational agnosticism, Harrison generally believed scientific explanations like this to be the correct ones.

One of the clearest examples of Harrison's freethinking is a talk he gave in 1916 titled "Infidelity among Our Ministers." It was pitched as a "startling lecture" that would demonstrate a number of heretical views held by prominent Christian ministers like the archbishop of Canterbury and the Congregationalist clergyman Henry Ward Beecher. Harrison made five main contentions: that the Bible was not the word of God; that Moses did not write the first five books; that the Apostles did not write the Gospels; that Jesus was not the son of God; and that the Adam and Eve story was a fairy tale. A report on the lecture in *The Truth Seeker* said that Harrison in his speech "argued that the Christian church is kept by the clergy in absolute ignorance of the fact that these radical conclusions are commonplace among the educated clergy."[72]

In terms of the racial component of his freethinking, Harrison made a searing indictment of Christianity's role in the oppression of Black people. "It should seem that Negroes, of all Americans," wrote Harrison, "would be found in the Freethought fold, since they have suffered more than any other class of Americans from the dubious blessings of Christianity. . . . Yet the church among the Negroes today exerts a more powerful influence than anything else in the sphere of ideas." In Harrison's view, Christianity played a pernicious role in justifying the emergence and perpetuation of slavery on American soil. "The church saw to it that the religion taught to slaves should stress the servile virtues of subservice and content, and these things have bitten deeply into the souls of black folk."

Harrison endorsed Friedrich Nietzsche's contention that the ethics of Christianity are the slave's ethics. "Show me a population that is deeply religious," argued Harrison, "and I will show you a servile population, content with whips and chains, contumely and the gibbet, content to eat the bread of sorrow and drink the waters of affliction." He maintained that in the United States, the spirit of Black people had been transformed by three centuries of physical and mental subjection to the point that most had even glorified the fact of their own subjection and subservience. "How many Negro speakers have I not heard vaunting the fact that when in the dark days of the South the Northern armies had the Southern aristocracy by the throat, there was no Negro uprising to make their masters pay for the systematic raping of Negro women and the inhuman cruelties perpetrated on Negro men. And yet the sole reason for this 'forbearance' is to be found in the fact that their spirits had been completely crushed by the system of slavery. And to accomplish this, Christianity—the Christianity of their masters—was the most effective instrument."[73]

Much like his trailblazing crystallizations in other areas, Harrison's race-conscious freethinking helped pave the way for other Black atheist, agnostic, and church-skeptical voices of the postwar "New Negro" generation, including figures like A. Philip Randolph, Chandler Owen, Nella Larsen, George Schuyler, Zora Neale Hurston, J. A. Rogers, Walter Everette Hawkins, Richard B. Moore, and Claude McKay. Before Harrison, valences of anti-clerical thought in figures like Frederick Douglass, William Wells Brown, and W. E. B. Du Bois spoke of an even older tradition of Black freethinkers.[74]

One of Harrison's brightest of Black freethinking protégés, John G. Jackson, gestured toward the irreverent humor Harrison employed in discussing this subject with Black audiences. As Jackson recounted,

> In the Christian pantheon, god is white, and so is Jesus Christ, the Holy Ghost, and all the angels. The only Black member is the devil. [Harrison] pointed out how pathetic it is to go to a Jim Crow church on Sunday and hear Black people singing a hymn, asking god to bleach them whiter than snow, so that they might enter into the Kingdom of Heaven. . . . Harrison argued that he would rather remain Black and go to hell. After all, the devil and his imps are Black and he would feel at home among

Black people. There would be a heat problem, but in due time one would get used to it and perhaps enjoy it. Once gets a glimpse into the "ebony hard" humor with which Harrison refused to bow down to a lily-white god or worship a "Jim Crow Jesus."[75]

As a natural complement to his agnosticism, Harrison took a keen interest in science, including scientific theories of biological evolution. In particular, he studied the work of figures like Charles Darwin, Alfred Russell Wallace, Thomas Huxley, Herbert Spencer, and Ernst Haeckel.[76] Darwin had become a founding father of evolutionary biology and a controversial scientist in his own time whose theories on natural selection came to dominate and define a new paradigm of philosophical and sociological thinking. His ideas about natural selection also inspired several generations of eugenicists, race "scientists," and reactionary social engineers who elaborated elitist and Eurocentric ideas to justify the domestic and international exploits of industrial capitalism and the socioeconomic and racial inequalities it produced.

Harrison also took a keen interest in the philosophy of science. For example, speaking about sixteenth-century philosopher and scientist Francis Bacon's *The Advancement of Learning* and *The Novum Organon*, Harrison noted that "these were the first works since the era of Islamic science in which a European writer had massed all the available information about the universe into a systematic survey." Having created much of the empirical scientific method as we know it today, Bacon advocated a scientific approach that proceeds through rigorous prodding and criticism among peers as a vital part of the discovery process, bolstered by experimentation and observation, complimented the rational, explanation-seeking agnosticism of Harrison.

Harrison further noted that since Bacon's time, the creation of other systematic methodological frameworks had been done in works such as Baron D'Holbach's *System of Nature* (1770), Alexander von Humboldt's *The Cosmos* (1851), Auguste Comte's *Course of Positive Philosophy* (1830), Ludwig Buchner's *Force and Matter* (1864), Earnest Haeckel's *The Riddle of the Universe* (1895), Herbert Spencer's *First Principles* (1862), and John Fiske's *Outlines of Cosmic Philosophy* (1871).[77] Holbach's atheistic *System of Nature* posited a universe consisting only of matter and motion, so that human consciousness and agency, which most confounded materialist philosophers at the time, consisted of the expressions of the matter that a human is made of and the physical laws that govern the senses we receive and the way in which we process those sensory inputs. Humboldt envisioned his multivolume *Cosmos* as a synthesis of scientific knowledge, arguing that the natural world operated on a prescribed set of coherent and universal laws, an approach that greatly influenced Darwin and other naturalists. Comte's *Positive Philosophy* elaborated a particular school of philosophy called positivism, which argued that any rational assertion can be proven using science, logic, or mathematics. Positivism thereby rejected metaphysical and theistic approaches to the traditional sciences (e.g., physics, chemistry, biology) as well as to "social physics," which would later become sociology.

Buchner's *Force and Matter* propounded a rigorous scientific materialism based on the indestructibility of matter and the conservation of energy (force), which formed an intellectual bedrock for the German Freethinkers League, which Buchner founded. Haeckel's *Riddle of the Universe* argued for a materialistic monism similar to Buchner's view, in which the universe was unified by a set of laws governing matter and energy, completely rejecting as explanations God, divinity, and the metaphysics of consciousness, which Haeckel had explained as the mechanical work of the neuron cells. Spencer's *First Principles* advanced an evolutionary framework according to which the universe tends toward heterogeneity and increasing complexity with time due to the compulsion through the movement of energy of all things to change, which meant that there were certain basic things that were unknowable in such a way that both science and religion failed to acknowledge. Fiske's *Cosmic Philosophy* took inspiration from Spencer and Darwin to propound evolutionary theory but with a degree of sympathy for the social and cultural prominence of Christianity, positing no inherent conflict between religion and science.

Harrison at times made comments about the personal aspects of his resonance with certain philosophers. For example, though not a student of astrology, Harrison noted how he had the same birthday as Herbert Spencer (April 27) and also shared number of his personality traits.[78] In a diary entry about how poverty and hunger constituted "a damned powerful modifier of a man's philosophy of life," he noted his perplexity at how the first major German pessimists Arthur Schopenhauer and Karl Robert Eduard von Hartmann never suffered economically. He also wondered how much economic deprivation shaped the thinking of nihilist philosophers like Friedrich Nietzsche and Max Stirner.[79]

Harrison's Intellectual Pastures beyond Freethinking

According to William Pickens, Harrison could speak "more easily, effectively, and interestingly on a greater variety of subjects than any man I have ever met in the great universities."[80] This quote points toward the vastness of Harrison's knowledge far beyond his prominent stature as a freethinker and despite his economic deprivation and lack of a college degree. How did he achieve it?

As a young boy Hubert showed great mental agility long before his foray into public life. For example, the *New York World* of April 1903 ran an article about the twenty-year-old titled "Speaker's Medal to Negro Student: The Board of Education Finds a Genius in a West Indian Pupil." The story quoted one of Harrison's teachers who spoke of how he was the only one to pass the "rigid" final exams with a perfect score of 100 percent in the mostly white school. Henry Carr, an English professor at his school, noted prophetically that "he will be heard from if learning has anything to do with success."[81]

Not satiated by what he learned in his evening high school, Harrison undertook to educate himself further outside of the formal classroom. Primarily, he nurtured a ravenous appetite for reading anything and everything he could get his hands on. Also, beginning sometime around 1905, Harrison began to practice his skills in intellectual debate at the Black church lyceums of St. Mark's and St. Benedict's. These lyceums offered a lively community built around enriching guest lectures, political and philosophical debates, and friendly but fierce oratorical battles. In this setting, Harrison encountered and befriended Black bibliophiles like John E. Bruce and Arturo Schomburg and also received rigorous training in critical thinking, public speaking, editing the *St. Mark's Mirror* newsletter, and navigating the contentious internal political struggles for elected leadership positions within the lyceum.[82]

While writing, speaking, and agitating for the Socialist cause, Harrison taught a course in labor economics at the Rand School of Social Science, a Socialist Party–affiliated institution for developing workers' class and political consciousness. His course covered feudalism, capitalism, the wage system, and class struggle with a reading list that included Karl Marx's *Wage Labor and Capital*, Karl Kautsky's *The Class Struggle*, Paul Lafargue's *The Evolution of Property*, and Mary E. Marcy's *Shop Talks on Economics*.[83] He also incorporated readings from anthropologist and social theorist Lewis Henry Morgan and the founder of German Socialism, Ferdinand August Bebel.[84] In addition, Harrison studied the work of critical modern European economists like Eugen von Böhm-Bawerk and Thomas Edward Cliffe Leslie.[85]

Although he studied freethought, religion, and economics, Harrison's real forte emerged in the subject that he lived daily and therefore felt more acutely than the others: Black studies. For example, in June of 1918 Harrison delivered a lecture on "Negro History and Its Place in Negro Education." In the presentation, Harrison brought to bear his knowledge of anthropology and sociology, explaining the sacred traditions and evolutionary stages of various African societies. He interpreted African psychology, family customs, and the African notion that "maternity is a matter of fact and paternity is a matter of faith." According to Harrison, this proverbial wisdom demonstrated the great love African people have for the maternal figure and their respect for women. He also compared the temperament of West Indians with that of West Africans and contrasted different dimensions of American society with those of African societies, as we will see in chapter 5.[86]

Another of Harrison's intellectual interests included reading novels, essays, and poetry, and as the first Black staff lecturer for the New York City Board of Education he gave numerous public talks on what would eventually become canonical English literature. Between the fall of 1922 and spring of 1924, for example, he gave lecture-length meditations on the literature of Charles Dickens, Henry Wadsworth Longfellow, Rudyard Kipling, Mark Twain, Alfred Tennyson, Edgar Allan Poe, and H. G. Wells. In other series, he lectured on Sir Walter Scott, Ralph Waldo Emerson, Thomas Macaulay, Victor Hugo, Charles Reade, Bret Harte, Rider Haggard, Thomas Carlyle, James Russell Lowell, Sir Arthur Conan Doyle, John Keats, James Fenimore Cooper, William Wordsworth, Mary Johnston, Herman Melville, William Bliss Carman, Anatole France, George Bernard Shaw, "Negro Poets of Note," and "the Negro in American Literature." Once, on the birthday of Lewis Carroll, Harrison even gave a talk at the North Harlem Community Forum on *Alice in Wonderland*—for children![87]

Alongside his enthusiasm for English literature, Harrison read widely in the new social sciences like anthropology and sociology. In his writings and criticisms of thinkers in this area, Harrison cited a range of figures, including Numa Denis Fustel de Coulanges, Georges Vacher de Lapouge, Charles Jean Marie Letourneau, Herbert Spencer, John Lubbock, Edward Burnett Tylor, Ludwig Gumplowicz, Friedrich Ratzel, Lewis Henry Morgan, James George Frazer, Georg August Schweinfurth, and Oscar Peschel.[88] Harrison thus kept tabs on contemporary social scientific thought emerging from France, England, Poland, Germany, the United States, Scotland, and Latvia, among other countries. Notwithstanding whatever constructive intellectual contributions they made, almost all of these thinkers (including Darwin) held a Eurocentric view of human societies that betrayed to one or another degree the racial superiority complex typical of "educated" thought in nineteenth-century Europe.

As a race-conscious Black thinker engaging with so much European intellectual output, Harrison naturally took a keen interest in the various "scientific" justifications for racial hierarchy. In 1926, the *Amsterdam News* covered one of Harrison's talks at NYU, noting that Harrison's lecture on "Science and Race Prejudice" surprised his listeners by omitting any mention of the so-called Negro problem would mark the first time a Black lecturer at the university did not focus on that subject.[89] As the report put it, the speaker handled his subject matter "in the objective manner of the scientist" by "bringing to the bar of psychology and sociology all the proponents of race prejudice," including Count Arthur de Gobineau, James Anthony Froude, Edward Augustus Freeman, and Thomas Carlyle from the nineteenth century and Houston Chamberlain, Madison Grant, William McDougall, Lothrop Stoddard, and Albert Edward Wiggam from the twentieth.[90] All these figures propounded openly racist ideas whether in the form of opposition to racial mixing due to fear of white racial extinction or in the form of espousing some kind of Aryan, Nordic, Anglo-Saxon, or Teutonic (German) racial supremacy. Although a sharp critic of race prejudice in general, Harrison took special care to deconstruct the various scholarly ideologues of racial difference more so than the evolutionary naturalists like Darwin or Spencer. In this NYU talk, he did not apparently criticize Darwin or Spencer, whose racist views he may have seen as secondary to their biological theory of natural selection as a better explanation for species evolution than divine providence.

Following his talk on scientific racism at NYU, he proceeded to demonstrate his grasp of global geopolitics with a follow-up lecture on "Locarno, Imperialism and the League of Nations," which analyzed the geopolitics behind the post–World War I treaty that had recently been signed in Locarno, Switzerland. When his audience asked him to return a third time, Harrison modestly declined, "playfully declaring that, if such invitations were kept up he would have to apply for an adjunct professorship in the university." Nevertheless, the students persisted, and they scheduled Harrison, the "famous Negro scholar" without a university degree, to lecture yet again on the provocative question, "Is the Politician Necessary?" One can only imagine the electric excitement of a downtown NYU auditorium jam-packed for the series-culminating encore lecture from Harlem's "Black Socrates." The *Amsterdam News* noted the extreme anomaly of the lecture series, whereby "a black scholar, without even touching on the Negro problem, discusses with the authority of modern scholarship problems of science and international affairs and is warmly welcomed and sought after by white university students, the intellectual cream of the white race." Following the success of his July lecture, he ended up teaching a class in the fall semester on "the American race problem," whose ten-item reading list included seven works by Black authors, likely the first syllabus with a majority of readings by Black thinkers ever taught at the institution.[91]

The NYU experience speaks to Harrison's great interest in the global politics of race. On this score, Harrison eventually developed a whole course on the subject with lecture titles including "Race and Its Reactions in History

Figure 3.3 Hubert H. Harrison teaching a class on "World Problems of Race." Harrison's protégés Richard B. Moore and W. A. Domingo are in attendance. Hubert H. Harrison Papers, box 15, folder 3, Rare Book and Manuscript Library, Columbia University, New York.

and Science," "The White Race's Rise to Power and Prestige," "Race and Color Problems in America and the West Indies," "The Brown Bridge of Britain's Empire—From Egypt to India," "China and the Powers," "Soviet Russia: Its Bearing on White Rulership over Darker Races," and "The League of Nations and the Future of the Darker Races."[92] In 1926, he taught a "World Problems of Race" course for Willis N. Huggins's Institute for Social Study in Harlem. In that capacity, he gave talks with titles like "The Rise of the Modern Idea of Race," "The Revolt of Islam," "The Black Man's Burden in Africa," "Cultural and Religious Aspects of Race," "Japan: The Frankenstein of European Imperialism," and "The Nemesis of White Imperialism."[93] In courses like these, one glimpses the educational application of Harrison's "colored internationalism," which we will explore in chapter 4.

Harrison demonstrated various other unusual skills and intellectual faculties. For example, in April of 1921, he began a stint as an instructor at the New York School of Chiropractic in Harlem, where he delivered a twelve-lecture course on the subject of embryology, an extension of his fascination with evolutionary biology.[94] As one of the first theater critics in Harlem, he began writing a book about the sociology of the Black theater.[95] At one point,

Harrison tutored private students in grammar, composition, literature, history, Latin, English, rhetoric, and geography. Black journalist Floyd Calvin once noted that Finns and Hungarians remembered Harrison as "the man who devised a way of teaching them English without knowing a word of their language."[96] Yet Harrison was no stranger to other languages. According to his biographer Jeff Perry, Harrison spoke or read English, Danish, Latin, French, German, and Arabic.[97]

Obviously, Harrison came to master a truly staggering body of knowledge. In the words of William Pickens, Harrison embodied "a 'walking cyclopedia' of current human facts," and it made "no difference" whether he spoke about "*Alice in Wonderland* or the most extensive work of H. G. Wells; about the lightest shadows of Edgar Allan Poe or the heaviest depths of Kant; about music, or art, or science, or political history."[98] Harrison studied, wrote, and lectured on theological criticism, comparative religion, economics, Black arts and culture, sociology, anthropology, scientific racism, international geopolitics, philosophy, sexuality, English literature, African history, and evolutionary biology. Not to mention his attentiveness to political developments current events in Africa, Asia, Europe, the Caribbean, Latin America, and the Islamic world.

And while he certainly relished the street corner stepladder, Harrison did not confine himself to the open-air forum. At the very same time as he cultivated the Outdoor Grioversity, he also built some of Black Harlem's first public indoor educational spaces. Beginning in 1914 he founded the Radical Forum, a multiracial space that he described as the first work he freely undertook for exploring a range of topics of interest to forward-thinking New Yorkers. Then in 1916 he started a similar forum at the 135th Street public library, aimed more squarely at broadening the intellectual range of his home community. Before this forum, he wrote, Black Harlemites gathered "mainly to discuss only two topics: religion and politics." On account of Harrison's wide-ranging interests, his forums addressed these two topics as well as others like sociology, economics, art, Black history, and science. Crucially, according to Harrison, the library forum in particular "preached the propaganda of RACE when no one else had courage or initiative enough to do so. It was the earliest promoter of the study of Negro history in Harlem and many hundreds and thousands of Harlemites drew their earliest inspiration from it."[99]

Harrison elaborated this work of indoor community-based education with a number of cothinkers and collaborators. For example, he taught courses at Willis Huggin's Institute for Social Study.[100] Huggins, an activist in the Garvey movement, became a teacher in the New York public schools and fought to get Black history into the school curriculum. Huggins's institute counted Communist Party members like Grace P. Campbell, Richard B. Moore, and

Williana Burroughs among its officers. It also garnered participation from Harlem activists Elliot Rawlins, Mabel Byrd, Louise Jackson, Eugene Corbie, N. E. White, and Peter D. Codrington. Following in Harrison's footsteps, Huggins held community history classes at Harlem's 135th Street YMCA and founded the Blyden Bookstore and Blyden Society (originally called the Harlem History Club), named for pan-African scholar and St. Thomas–born Virgin Islander Edward Wilmot Blyden.[101] These spaces facilitated the self-education of numerous community residents, including notable street scholars like John Henrik Clarke, who among other things would emerge as a spearhead of the Black studies movement in the 1960s.[102]

John G. Jackson emerged to become another brilliant yet scandalously marginalized protégé of Harrison's. Jackson was born in 1907 in Aiken, South Carolina. He migrated to New York City sometime around 1922, attending Stuyvesant High School. Jackson began to study African history following his encounter with Harrison, who also introduced him to J. A. Rogers. Jackson learned a great deal from Harrison and Rogers and would serve alongside figures like W. A. Domingo and Frank Crosswaith as a director of Rev. Ethelred Brown's Hubert Harrison Memorial Church after Harrison's death. In the Harlem History Club at the YMCA, Jackson worked with Willis Huggins to write books and curricula on the history of African civilizations. Jackson would go on to author a number of books on this subject, including *An Introduction to African Civilizations: With Main Currents in Ethiopian History*, *Pagan Origins of the Christ Myth*, *Ethiopia and the Origin of Civilization*, and *Christianity before Christ*. These books offer a shining example of the depth of knowledge that Harrison's students and protégés developed about African history.[103]

Harrison also greatly influenced Richard B. Moore, who began collecting books in 1918, "having been led into the field by Hubert Harrison," as he put it.[104] After a stint in the Socialist Party, Moore would join the African Blood Brotherhood and by the 1930s emerged as a leading Black Communist in Harlem. As a result of his tours speaking for the Communist Party's campaign to free the Scottsboro boys in the 1930s, Moore became known as one of the top orators in Harlem, a skill he learned by observing the likes of Harrison and other stepladder speakers. Following his break with the Communists, Moore founded and ran the Frederick Douglass Book Center on West 125th Street for twenty-five years.

Harrison's educational work thus helped cultivate Harlem as a mecca of Black intellectual culture and political awakening and demonstrated Robin D. G. Kelley's observation that "collective social movements are incubators of new knowledge." This is especially true in the history of the many "freedom dreams" that have emerged from what Kelley calls the "Black radical imagination."[105] All the freedom dreams and social movements that had captured Harrison's imagination would receive a sudden and severe test when President Woodrow Wilson decided to send the United States Army onto blood-soaked battlefields of the war already raging in Europe. That turn of events forced a whole generation to confront anew the very meaning of "democracy" and would lead Harrison to confront and expose the most prominent African American leader in the nation, W. E. B. Du Bois.

Chapter 4

The White War and the Colored International

> Ten million were to die on the battlefield; 20 million were to die of hunger and disease related to the war. And no one since that day has been able to show that the war brought any gain for humanity that would be worth one human life.
>
> —Howard Zinn, *A People's History of the United States*

> The average American citizen needs some positive proof of the assertion that this war is being waged to determine who shall dictate the destinies of the darker peoples and enjoy the usufruct of their labor and their lands. For the average American citizen is blandly ignorant of the major facts of history and has to be told.
>
> —Hubert Harrison, "The White War and the Colored Races"

Much as he had done with the Colored Socialist Club, the Liberty League, the *Voice*, and the Outdoor Grioversity, Hubert Henry Harrison crystallized a unique international politics of revolution.[1] Budding first within the international program of the Liberty League in 1917, blooming through his editorship of the *New Negro* magazine in 1919, and fully blossoming on the crest of his tenure in the Garvey movement in 1920–21, Harrison advanced a radical, new, and "colored" internationalism. For the early 1920s, Harrison's vision of a "Colored International" comprised an internationalism unlike that of any other major figure or organization in the United States, white or Black. More than just a fanciful theory, Harrison would develop and apply his perspective as the chairman of the national Liberty Congress of Negro-Americans in Washington, DC, which gave unprecedented expression to the special grievances of African Americans amidst the patriotic fervor for war. And his ability to maintain a dissident editorial line in the face of wartime state repression and naked censorship of antiwar speech allowed him to avoid political capitulation on the one hand and prison or deportation on the other. As a result, Harrison's reaction to the First World War—both in theory and practice—remains supremely instructive for students of imperialism and political economy.

US Capitalism and Wilsonian ~~Idealism~~ Imperialism

One's grasp of US imperialism today can only deepen with a critical retrospection on its track record. In the era of Hubert Henry Harrison's lifetime, as historian Sidney Lens has argued, it is impossible to understand why the United States entered World War I without understanding the banking house of J. P. Morgan, which constituted the financial epicenter of US capitalism. Originally, investment bankers had simply acted as middlemen between investors and companies, without trying to assert power over the businesses for whom they collected capital. Under "Morganization," as it was called, the House of Morgan achieved dominance over the companies that came to it for financial backing. In return for access to capital, Morgan demanded and received positions on their boards of directors and wound up as the de facto master of multiple corporations.[2]

The crowning achievement of Morganization came in the formation in 1901 of the United States Steel Corporation, the first billion-dollar corporation in the nation's history. By 1912, it controlled twelve big banks; three insurance firms; eleven major railroads plus the Pullman Company; Adams Express; at least five industrial goliaths, including United States Steel, General Electric, American Telephone and Telegraph, International Harvester, and Western Union; a host of public utilities; and two corporations in Latin America. The assets of this empire of capital rose to $10.3 billion at a time when the entire US federal government took in only $700 million a year.[3]

As an inexorable result of its centralization and concentration of capital, the House of Morgan would ascend to a level where the geopolitical edges of its power began to rub against those of its rivals on the global stage, much like tectonic plates. Two enormous electrical trusts, AEG (*Allgemeine Elektricitäts-Gesellschaft* or General Electricity Company) of Germany and Morgan's General Electric in the United States, concluded an agreement in 1907 through which they effectively divided entire continents of the world between them. General Electric "got" the United States and Canada, while AEG "got" Germany, Austria, Russia, Holland, Denmark, Switzerland, Turkey, and the Balkans.[4]

By the early 1900s, the world oil market got similarly divided between two main financial groups: John D. Rockefeller's Standard Oil and the European Rothschild and Nobel families, with Royal Dutch Shell also entering the market. In commercial shipping, the tendency toward monopoly ended up in the division of the world between two powerful German companies, the Hamburg-Amerika and the Norddeutscher Lloyd, and the House of Morgan's International Mercantile Marine Company. As early as 1903, the German giants and the American-British trust concluded an agreement to divide up the world, with a consequent division of profits. The German companies agreed not to compete with Anglo-American traffic. They stipulated precisely which ports were to be "allotted" to each, set up a joint committee of control, and made provisions for nullifying the agreement in the event of war.[5]

Figure 4.1 This cartoon by Joseph Keppler, published in 1911 in *Puck* magazine, shows the enormous power of John Pierpont Morgan, the robber baron of finance capital, as compared to the lesser power of Uncle Sam, who personifies the US government. "The Helping Hand / J.K. after Renouf," United States, 1911. Photograph, Library of Congress Prints and Photographs Division, Washington, DC, https://www.loc.gov/item/98518246.

What does all of this have to do with Woodrow Wilson taking the United States into the inter-European war? War is politics by other means, and these examples point to the way in which the world had already been divided economically among capitalist associations backed by the imperial force of their respective governments. Morgan would secure a contract as the official purchasing agent of US-made war goods for the British government, at a 1 percent commission, giving Morgan a dominant role and direct financial stake in the Allied war effort. A win for the Allies would now be a win for the center of US finance capital—the lifeblood and kingmaker of the US capitalist class.

A truly stunning testimonial on the relationship between American corporate power and the imperialism of the US government emerged in the voice of one of its battle-tested military officers. Major General Smedley Darlington Butler represented the most decorated US Army soldier in history when he died in 1940 after over thirty years of active military service in the Marine Corps. He served in various commissioned ranks from second lieutenant to major general and garnered multiple military awards, including two Presidential Medals of Honor. Upon leaving the army, he started to think for himself, reflecting critically on what he had done. For example, he spoke openly about how he "helped make Mexico, especially Tampico, safe for American oil interests in 1914. I helped make Haiti and Cuba a decent place for the National City Bank boys to collect revenues in. I helped in the raping of half a dozen Central American republics for the benefits of Wall Street.... I helped purify Nicaragua for the international banking house of Brown Brothers in 1909–1912.... I brought light to the Dominican Republic for American sugar interests in 1916. In China I helped to see to it that Standard Oil went its way unmolested." Simply put, all of Butler's military operations had one thing in common: serving the interests of the American financial oligarchy. Butler remarked, jokingly, that "looking back on it, I feel that I could have given Al Capone a few hints. The best he could do was to operate his racket in three districts. I operated on three continents."[6]

Comparing his work for Uncle Sam to one of the most notorious crime bosses in history reflected a courage to admit one's own wrongdoing that remains highly unusual of for military men of his rank. Thanks to his burning conscience and deep introspection, the major general concluded that "I spent most of my time being a high class muscle-man for big business, for Wall Street and for the bankers. In short, I was a racketeer, a gangster for capitalism." Statements like these would win Butler the respect of antiwar progressives for decades to come, as did his preemptive exposure of a fascist plot to overthrow the administration of Franklin D. Roosevelt in a military coup.

If the Wilson administration had spoken as candidly as Smedley Butler, it would never have been able to sell the war to the people. This becomes crystal clear by comparing Wilson's statements before he took the United States into war versus afterwards. Before the war Wilson had acquired a reputation as a "progressive," in part because of his stated concerns about how the US government had become a tool of corporate power. In his book *The New Freedom*, published in 1913 during the first year of his presidential administration, Wilson stated bluntly that "the masters of the government of the United States are the combined capitalists and manufacturers of the United States."[7]

Though he could sound progressive on the issue of corporate power, Woodrow Wilson also proved an ardent white supremacist. For example, he loved to tell racist "darky" jokes to dignitaries, other politicians, his staff, and various friends.[8] Wilson screened the racist propaganda film *The Birth of a Nation* inside the White House for his cabinet; maintained that segregation fit with African Americans' best interests; permitted the civil service to bar African Americans; formalized segregation in the departments of the Post Office, the Treasury, the Interior, and the navy; and oversaw the introduction of some two dozen segregationist legislative attempts in the House and Senate, including the exclusion of Black immigrants, racial segregation of streetcars, and a ban on interracial marriages in the District of Columbia. Hubert Harrison sadly noted how Wilson "became famous for preaching a 'new freedom' while pregnant Black women were roasted by white savages in Wilson's section of the South."[9]

Once in office, and like every other White House occupant before and since, Wilson proved to be an arch-imperialist. In 1907, some six years before becoming president, Wilson spoke with a startling candor about how "since trade ignores national boundaries and the manufacturer insists on having the world as a market, the flag of his nation must follow him, and the doors of the nations which are closed against him must be battered down. Concessions obtained by financiers must be safeguarded by ministers of state, even if the sovereignty of unwilling nations be outraged in the process. Colonies must be obtained or planted, in order that no useful corner of the world may be overlooked or left unused." At this stage, he didn't even pretend to care about the "self-determination" of small nations that he would later trumpet at the postwar peace talks in Paris. Upon his taking the White House, Wilson disavowed his former endorsements of US imperialism (for public relations purposes) when he solemnly declared in 1913 that "the United States will never again seek one additional foot of territory by conquest."[10] It was a bold-faced lie.

The very next year, the Wilson administration targeted the first Black republic in the Western Hemisphere in a move that would become one of the most heinous of all of Wilson's imperial atrocities. In December of 1914, just five months after the outbreak of the war in Europe, US marines "landed at Port au Prince in broad daylight, marched to the vaults of the National Bank, helped themselves to a half million dollars in monies that were security for the national currency, and loaded it on the gunboat *Machias* for delivery to the National City Bank in New York." The Wilson administration then set in motion a US military occupation of Haiti that would continue for the next nineteen years. US forces overthrew the Haitian government, imposed forced labor to build infrastructure favorable to US business interests, rewrote the Haitian constitution to allow penetration by US capital, and massacred thousands of Haitians who resisted. As Maj. Smedley Butler, who oversaw the counterinsurgency campaign put it, using a derogatory term for Haitian freedom fighters, they "hunted the *Cacos* like pigs."[11] In response to the US invasion, Hubert Harrison gave talks on the virtues of the Haitian Revolution and Toussaint L'Ouverture's role in leading the only slave rebellion in history that successfully established a modern Black republic.[12]

Haitians lived on the western side of the island of Hispaniola, and their neighbors to the east would suffer a similar fate in the talons of Uncle Sam. In the spring of 1916, a military general named Desiderio Arias Álvarez initiated a revolt in the Dominican Republic. The Wilson administration sent in the marines and demanded a treaty that provided for US control of customs, the Treasury, the police, and the army. The US Army occupied the Dominican Republic and imposed a military dictatorship there from 1916 to 1924. They suspended the Dominican Congress and a rear admiral of the US Navy became governor of the country with all executive and legislative functions. Meanwhile, the cabinet posts were manned by marine and naval officers of the United States. According to a select committee of the US Congress in 1922, "Elections were prohibited; thousands of marines were spread over the country and with unlimited authority over the natives; public meetings were not permitted; ... destructive bombs were dropped from airplanes upon towns and hamlets; every home was searched for arms, weapons, and implements; homes were burned; natives were killed; tortures and cruelties committed; and [General Valeriano] 'Butcher' Weyler's horrible concentration camps were established."[13]

US imperialism intervened overseas quite extensively in this period, like an insatiable power-hungry monster. In 1917, the Wilson administration purchased the so-called Virgin Islands from Denmark, including Harrison's native island of St. Croix, and placed them under a brutal US military regime. During the Russian Civil War of 1918–22, Wilson sent US forces to aid in the White Army's counterrevolutionary war on the fledgling Socialist workers' state in Soviet Russia. The US Treasury made available to representatives of the counterrevolutionary forces $1.2 million from funds that had been marked for the pro-war and pro-capitalist Kerensky regime that the Bolshevik-led Russian workers and peasants overthrew in October of 1917. By late 1918 there were 7,000 US soldiers on Russian soil and eventually the counterrevolutionary troops of fourteen nations, including Britain and France. In addition, President Wilson sent US forces into Mexico, Cuba, Panama, Honduras, Guatemala, and China. These interventions marked a vast expansion in the reach and power of US imperialism during the First World War.[14]

Nevertheless, the Wilson administration took care to dress up its imperialist gangsterism in the rhetoric of "democracy," "progressive idealism," and "peace." In 1916, for example, President Wilson ran on a reelection campaign under the slogan "He Kept Us Out of War!" referring to the bloody conflict that had been raging in Europe. Months later, he took the United States into that very same bloody war in order to "make the world safe for democracy." Never mind that the Allies he sided with (especially Britain under prime minister David Lloyd George and France under Georges Clemenceau) ruled their own vast colonial empires, over whose gross violations of democracy the "sun never set."

Like every other US intervention overseas, the White House entered the "Great War" for the benefit of American business interests, at the expense of American workers and soldiers. On the one hand, over 116,000 US troops were killed, and the total financial cost was some $32 billion or 52 percent of gross national product at the time. On the other hand, the war created at least 21,000 new millionaires and billionaires in the United States as industries like steel, manufacturing, shipping, and banking saw skyrocketing profits and expansion during wartime.[15]

The financial aristocracy that ran the country created a system whereby the burden of war, both financially and physically, would be placed on the American working people rather than themselves. As General Butler poignantly asked in his famous book *War Is A Racket*, "How many of these war millionaires shouldered a rifle? How many of them dug a trench? How many of them knew what it meant to go hungry in a rat-infested dug-out? How many of them spent sleepless, frightened nights, ducking shells and shrapnel and machine gun bullets? How many of them parried a bayonet thrust of an enemy? How many of them were wounded or killed in battle?" In statements like these, one catches a glimpse of the deep wells of grief and rage that Butler's experience in the trenches gave him, as compared to the cushy life and lavish mansions of the war profiteers and robber barons.[16]

The White World War

The intra-European war of 1914–18 offers a prime example of the clarity of Harrison's radical thought, as well as the concision of his pen in distilling and illuminating complex processes in a language that working people could understand. Beginning in 1915, his speeches outdoors and indoors began to dissect the racial and economic politics of what he called the "white world war."[17] Harrison penned his first elaboration on this subject in a piece for *The Voice* in August 1917 titled "The White War and the Colored World." He argued that 1.2 out of the 1.7 billion people in the world were "colored—black, brown, and yellow" and were at relative peace until the eruption of war amongst the European imperial powers. Therefore, he argued, it represented "a war of the white race wherein the stakes of the conflict are the titles to possession of the lands and destinies of [the] colored majority in Asia, Africa, and the islands of the sea." The white race appeared superior "not because it [had] better morals[,] more religion, or higher culture" but because it had the guns, soldiers, and financial power to dominate other peoples.

Harrison began his case by putting forward the keystone of his theory of international relations: people of color suffered the most in the world because, in addition to the economic exploitation that all people suffered, they had to endure the oppression that issued from the "degrading dogma of the color line; that dogma which has been set up by the Anglo-Saxon peoples and adopted in varying degrees by other white peoples who have followed their footsteps in the path of capitalistic imperialism; that dogma which declares that the lands and labors of the colored races everywhere shall be the legitimate prey of white peoples." In short, white supremacy constituted a structuring reality of the global political system, part and parcel of capitalist imperialism.

With this framework, Harrison contested the official justification for the war: it was not about the good democracy of the Allies versus the evil monarchy of Germany but a war of clashing European empires. More specifically, the struggle represented a conflict of interests that would determine "whose will shall be accepted as the collective will of the white race." Although he lamented the loss of life that the war entailed, he found consolation in the hope that the white world's blood-soaked bout of massive internecine violence would inevitably weaken its ability to oppress and dominate the nonwhite peoples of the world. As a result, Harrison looked forward to the darker peoples of the world getting independence, because the "majority races" would not be coerced into accepting white domination forever.[18]

The following year, while the war still raged, Harrison articulated an even more expansive and rigorous analysis of the war. He argued that "democracy" could not have been the reason for war given that millions of Black people in the United States were disenfranchised and terrorized by lynching and Jim Crow. Similarly, the claim that the Allies fought to defend "small nationalities" was disproved by the realities of British imperialism, given its domination over various smaller nations from Ireland to India and beyond.

To bolster his case, Harrison cited the writings of Sir Harry Johnston. Johnston represented the foremost British authority on Africa, having received a knighthood-level honorific title for his successes in securing treaties and land on behalf of British claims in the colonial "scramble for Africa."[19] Johnston had predicted that if the British were victorious, Africa would repay Britain and her allies the cost of the war. "The war, deny it who may, was really fought over African questions," he wrote, because "the Germans wished, as the chief gain of victory, to wrest rich Morocco from French control, to take the French Congo from France, and the Portuguese Congo from Portugal, to secure from Belgium the richest and most extensive tract of alluvial goldfields as yet discovered." He argued that Africa would "eventually show itself to be the most richly endowed of all the continents in valuable vegetable and mineral substances." Johnston's analysis spoke volumes due to his expertise and brutal honesty about European interests on the African continent. Usually, noted Harrison, the real aims of the war were not so "frankly avowed."[20]

Harrison analyzed the economic backdrop of the war, using a class-conscious perspective he developed in the Socialist movement. He argued that, at its root, the world war comprised "a natural and inevitable effect of the capitalist system" because that system was based upon the wage relationship between those who owned the "gigantic forces of land and machinery" and those who worked them: "Under this system no capitalist employs a worker for two dollars a day unless that worker creates more than two dollars' worth of wealth for him. Only out of this surplus can profits come. If ten million workers should thus create one-hundred-million dollars' worth of wealth each day and get twenty five or fifty million in wages, it is obvious that they can expend only what they have received."

The working class created more wealth than the wages it received as compensation, and therefore workers could never buy all the commodities they collectively produced. Likewise, at a global level the economy of every capitalist country produced a surplus of commodities over and above that which its workers could collectively afford to buy. But, as Harrison put it, "before these [excess] products can return to their owners as profits they must be sold somewhere. Hence the need for foreign markets, for fields of exploitation and 'spheres of influence' in 'undeveloped' countries." The surplus products of any given country would have to be sold outside of that country, and so too would surplus capital have to be invested outside the originating country.

"These markets change their character under the impact of international trade," Harrison continued, "and are no longer simply markets for the absorption of finished products, but become fields for the investment of accumulated surplus profits, in which process they are transformed into original sources for the production of surplus profits by the opening up of mines, railroads and other large-scale capitalist enterprises. It becomes necessary to take over the government of selected areas in order that the profits may be effectually guaranteed, and 'spheres of influence,' 'protectorates,' and 'mandates' are set up." Harrison's analysis echoed that of Marx and Engels, who described how the European bourgeoisie (or capitalist class) "compels all nations, on pain of extinction, to adopt the bourgeois mode of production ... i.e., to become bourgeois themselves. In one word, it creates a world after its own image."[21]

Of course this economic imposition on colonized lands would be masked as a "civilizing mission" for the benefit of the native. Harrison saw through that lie too: "The real civilization meant by most whites who talk of civilizing Africa is the system which produces profits by taking the land from under the feet of the workers, producing a propertyless, landless proletarian class which must either work (for wages) or starve. Such a class doesn't exist anywhere among black Africans except where white peoples have robbed them of their lands by force." He concluded that the "civilizing" of Africa meant "the establishment of the European system, of 'concessions' for rubber, railroads, factories and mines, whereby the labor of the native population and the new tastes developed in their minds yield enormous revenues to the white people who rule these lands."[22] "Civilization" thus served as a euphemism for penetration and exploitation by white capital.

"But," noted Harrison, "since every industrial nation is seeking the same outlet for its products, clashes are inevitable" in the form of competition for markets, "and in these clashes beaks and claws—armies and navies—must come into play. Hence beaks and claws must be provided beforehand against the day of conflict, and hence the exploitation of white men in Europe and America becomes the reason for the exploitation of black and brown and yellow men in Africa and Asia."[23]

In short, capitalism's drive for endless expansion lay at the root of the world war.

Harrison's clarity on the capitalist roots of the war positioned him to criticize white liberals who failed to expose this underlying reality. In his review of the veteran war journalist Frederick Palmer's book *The Folly of Nations*, Harrison appreciated that Palmer reported on the dirt, cruelty, and lies of war, as well as the "cynical indifference of statesmen drunk with power to the miseries they invoke." Yet he also lamented that Palmer saw them "through a haze of pathetic optimism and futile sentimentality" and that a basic grasp of underlying causes of the war seemed to escape him altogether. In Harrison's words, "Imperialism, which puts the war-making powers of the modern state in the hands of those who own the earth and its products, and sends its millions of men to die abroad for markets when they lack meat at home—to this the old war reporter remains blind to the last." Palmer demonstrated a humanitarian anguish regarding the effects of the war but lacked "the insight of the seer, the probing power of the physician, who diagnoses the disease and points to its hidden causes before prescribing the remedy." Harrison felt that as long as those who wrote about the war shirked their duty to explain its cause, so long would such writers "fail to exert any appreciable influence on the recovery of a sick world." Finishing off his critique of the well-meaning white liberal, Harrison quoted William Shakespeare's dictum that "diseases desperate in their nature grown require desperate remedies," pointing to the simple fact that radical problems demand radical solutions.[24]

Harrison argued that because economic competition lay at the root of the war, it was "hypocritical and absurd to pretend that the capitalist nations can ever intend to abolish wars." Moreover, "economic motives have always their social side," and in this case European exploitation of the "lands and labor of colored folk expresses itself in the social theory of white domination." Harrison highlighted how when people of color, "who make up the overwhelming majority of this world," demanded decent treatment, white supremacists accused them of impudence or of seeking social equality, but when white people insisted on the right to manage their ancestral lands free from domination, they called it "democracy" or "self-determination." He then predicted that wars would be more widespread and more terrible as long as the theory of white domination sought to suppress the global majority under the "iron heel of racial repression."[25]

Harrison developed a hopeful and uncannily accurate prognosis about the outcomes and consequences of the "white world war." Noting how the very basis of white world domination—superior guns, money, and resources—was being destroyed in the war, he underscored that white war-making nations would be less able to force their will upon the darker races of the world. Harrison predicted that as the darker races felt the weakening of white rule, they would "first ask, then demand, and finally secure" the right of self-determination. This would lead to independence for such nations as Egypt and India and eventually to "independent African states as large as Germany and France—and larger," necessitating a shifting of the whole basis of global politics, business, and international control. This is precisely what happened following World War II, as the destruction of European economies and the rise of third world nationalism led to formal independence in most of the colonized world. Although it would take another half century and a second worldwide war for Harrison's predictions about African and Asian independence to come true, his prognosis in 1918 appears startlingly prophetic.[26]

Harrison arrived at his far-reaching geopolitical forecast by drawing on multiple influences that were emerging in African American political thinking about the "Great War" in Europe. According to historian Jeffrey Stewart, Alain Locke was the first African American to argue that imperialism caused World War I in his lecture "The Great Disillusionment," which he gave at the Negro Society for Historical Research (NSHR) on September 26, 1914.[27] In that lecture, Locke argued that the war was fundamentally a contest between the British and German empires for control of the "unconquered" domains of Africa and Asia, a "war of race" that would break the "pretentions of European civilization to world-dominance and eternal superiority."[28] It is likely that Harrison attended this lecture, as he was a member and secretary of the NSHR from its founding in 1911.[29] A similarly race-conscious position emerged from the pen of Benjamin Brawley, the dean of Morehouse College, who argued that "the Civil War in the United States was fought to decide the destiny of the Negro in America. The great war of our own day is to determine the future of the Negro in the world." Harrison built on these arguments from Locke and Brawley, which spoke to the broader skepticism of New Negro political thinking on the war.[30]

W. E. B. Du Bois formed another key influence on Harrison's thinking. In 1915, Du Bois wrote his famous *Atlantic Monthly* piece "The African Roots of War," whose themes can be seen throughout Harrison's analysis. Du Bois, for example, denounced the methods of European colonialism in Africa and argued that "Africa is a prime cause of this terrible overturning of civilization." Du Bois spoke to the way economic exploitation of the poor and weak at home created the "dream" of exploitation abroad and posited that it was both capital and labor that united in the new democratic Western nations on the basis of "white hegemony" to "share the spoil of exploiting 'chinks and niggers'" who populated the "darker nations of the world."[31]

A. Philip Randolph and Chandler Owen represented another example of Harrison's political kindred spirits during the war, especially the views they expressed in their 1917 pamphlet titled *Terms of Peace and the Darker Races*. On the eve of joining the Socialist Party and founding the Black Socialist *Messenger* magazine, Randolph and Owen honed their analytical and debating skills in a student organization called the Independent Political Council. The organization convened students from schools like Columbia, City College, and New York University for weekend discussions of Socialist politics and discussion of subjects like the "war to end all wars" raging in Europe. In their pamphlet, Randolph and Owen spoke to the capitalist roots of the war and also the racial dynamics of white capitalists fighting over the labor and lands of the darker peoples of the world. Randolph and Owen were arrested and temporarily imprisoned in 1918 for speaking publicly against the war. Perhaps fearing their own potential imprisonment for sedition, Du Bois and the National Association for the Advancement of Colored People (NAACP) kept silent about their case, but eventually a racist judge ended up exonerating Randolph and Owen because he didn't think "Negroes" could have produced the antiwar views and utterances attributed to them. Harrison called their pamphlet "unique" and commented that the two "brilliant young leaders" had knowledge and opinions "well worth the getting."[32]

In addition to other Black thinkers like these, Harrison's perspective shared common ground with white antiwar Socialists. Eugene Debs, for example, in a 1918 speech in Canton, Ohio, eloquently argued that the rich declared wars while the poor fought and died in them. In response to this speech, the United States imprisoned Debs under the Sedition Act. And yet he still won nearly

1 million votes or 3.4 percent of the electorate—from his prison cell—as the Socialist Party candidate for president.[33]

As Anthony Arnove and Howard Zinn have argued, "One of the most important—and earliest—voices against the war was Helen Keller." US public schools often teach about Helen Keller as a deaf and blind woman who became a famous author, but rarely do they mention her Socialist politics. Keller gave an antiwar speech at Carnegie Hall in New York City at an event sponsored by the Women's Peace Party and the Labor Forum. She argued that every modern war was rooted in exploitation and that workers themselves had the power to end wars and the system of exploitation that causes them. "Strike against all ordinances and laws and institutions that continue the slaughter of peace and the butcheries of war!" she encouraged. "Strike against war, for without you no battles can be fought! Strike against manufacturing shrapnel and gas bombs and all other tools of murder! Strike against preparedness that means death and misery to millions of human beings!" Keller argued that by withholding their labor power, workers themselves could end the war and transform society. "Be not dumb, obedient slaves in an army of destruction," urged Keller. "Be heroes in an army of construction!"[34] This speech of Keller's would have landed her in prison if not for the fact that she delivered it in January of 1916, before the US government had officially entered the war and passed the Espionage and Sedition Acts that criminalized antiwar speech.

European Socialists and Marxists often had some of the most advanced theorizations of imperialism and world economy. V.I. Lenin, for example, in his "popular outline" of 1916, famously theorized imperialism as the "highest stage of capitalism."[35] Lenin argued that the earlier stages of capitalist competition led to centralization and concentration of capital in the form of monopolies and finance capital. The fundamental economic need of the higher monopoly stage of capitalism to continuously export capital to stay profitable pushed the capitalists to conquer and divide up the world, which also ratcheted up tensions over time as acute rivalries intensified over who would accumulate the most colonies, markets, and outlets for investment. Lenin aimed for his pamphlet to help his audience understand "the fundamental economic question, that of the economic essence of imperialism, for unless this is studied, it will be impossible to understand and appraise modern war and modern politics." The truth of this argument—which Harrison also made during the war—applied to not just European but also US imperialism. As we have seen, the behavior of robber barons like Morgan and Rockefeller exemplified the rise of monopolies, finance capital, and the export of capital leading to division and competition for world markets.

Yet Hubert Harrison had an analytical component that the leading Socialist theoreticians in the United States and Europe lacked: race consciousness.

Of course, Lenin's Bolsheviks and some other left-wing European Marxists did support self-determination for oppressed nations. However, they did not theorize anti-imperialist politics with an explicitly *racial* lens.[36] Harrison himself noted this, remarking in 1919 how although some minimal signs of racial awareness could be seen in a recent Bolshevik declaration, nevertheless "eyes which for centuries have been behind the blinders of Race Prejudice cannot but blink and water when compelled to face the full sunlight."[37] Europeans had a long way to go in terms of developing race consciousness. By contrast, Harrison's racial analysis went beyond something of secondary or incidental relevance to the class question, as white Socialists in the United States treated it. As early as 1915, Black thinkers like Locke, Du Bois, and Harrison had pointed out that "the racial aspect of the war in Europe was easily the most important" because of the implications of "democracy" and "self-determination" for the colonized and "colored" majority of the world's population, despite the fact that so few white publications—Socialist or otherwise—commented on the racial dimension of the war.[38]

In a Black Marxist fashion, Harrison argued for a dialectical view of the relationship between race and class consciousness. For example, he pointed out that when British workers insisted that "no one will maintain that the Africans are fit for self-government," it represented the same elitist principle whereby the British ruling class told those same workers, "No one maintains that the laboring classes of Britain are fit for self-government." Both positions sprang from a superiority complex, one racial and the other based on class. The "selfish and ignorant" white worker with such a superiority complex thus failed to realize that his destiny was inseparably bound up with "the hundreds of millions of those whom he calls 'niggers.'" Working-class "self-government"—that is, workers' control of the means of production—formed the cornerstone of revolutionary Socialism. If white workers maintained such elitist attitudes toward African workers, they clearly lacked the respect and humility toward racially oppressed people necessary for a truly "proletarian internationalism" of the kind that so many white Socialists claimed to profess. For example, the Communist Party of South Africa, in its early days, even went so far as to raise the slogan "White workers of the world unite"![39]

Wartime Propaganda, "Disloyal" Speech, and State Repression

You ask me why the [Industrial Workers of the World] is not patriotic to the United States. If you were a bum without a blanket; if you had left your wife and kids when you went west for a job, and had never located them since; if your job had never kept you long enough in a place to qualify you to vote; if you slept in a lousy, sour bunkhouse, and ate food just as rotten as they could give you and get by with it; if deputy sheriffs shot your cooking cans full of holes and spilled your grub on the ground; if your wages were lowered on you when the bosses thought they had you down . . . if every person who represented law and order and the nation beat you up, railroaded you to jail, and the good Christian people cheered and told them to go to it, how in hell do you expect a man to be patriotic? This war is a business man's war and we don't see why we should go out and get shot in order to save the lovely state of affairs which we now enjoy.

—Anonymous statement on why the IWW is not patriotic (1918)

For Hubert Harrison, the "Wobblies" in the IWW, and anyone else who wanted to publicly express opposition to the war, the threat of state repression loomed large. On September 5, 1917, the Department of Justice descended on the headquarters of the Industrial Workers of the World in fifteen cities from Los Angeles to New York, arresting people and confiscating literature and organizational documents. A total of 162 leading Wobblies, including "Big Bill" Haywood, were indicted, and 93 were convicted. Sentences ranged from ninety days to twenty years, and the organization was fined some $2.3 million in total. According to historian Sidney Lens, 2,000 more IWW members were rounded up in the first two months of 1918, and innumerable foreign-born radicals, including Emma Goldman and her partner Alexander Berkman, were arrested and deported. "Socialist Kate Richards O'Hare got five years in prison for an antiwar speech in North Dakota," wrote Lens. "Rose Pastor Stokes got [sentenced to] ten years in prison. Five members of the Socialist executive committee got sentences of up to twenty years from a federal judge." As noted earlier, the government arrested Socialists A. Philip Randolph and Chandler Owen and imprisoned Eugene Debs for giving antiwar speeches.[40]

Because of the threat of state repression, Hubert Harrison took care to speak in language compatible with the official war aims. He spoke in these terms not because he supported the war but because the Espionage Act of 1917 and the Sedition Act of 1918 prohibited wartime dissent and "disloyal, profane, scurrilous, or abusive language" about the government. By framing the struggle to end lynching, segregation, and disenfranchisement as aligned with Wilson's war aims, Harrison managed to avoid imprisonment and deportation as a noncitizen. As one federal agent tasked with monitoring the radical Black press in this period put it, "These colored editors have a certain talent for spreading a seditious feeling without uttering any actually seditious words." Harrison's editorship of *The Voice* demonstrated this quality, and his successful avoidance of prison and deportation allowed him to continue spearheading Black wartime dissent in and beyond Harlem.[41] How did he do it?

Harrison fashioned his political criticisms with language that the federal censors in the post office could not single out as seditious. For example, in one speech he criticized the mayor of New York City for his "wartime jackass patriotism" rather than any federal government officials or politicians. Mayor John Purroy Mitchel got the nickname of the "fighting Mayor" for challenging the Democrats' Tammany Hall political machine successfully on an anticorruption platform.[42] But as Harrison put it, "They call Mitchel our fighting Mayor . . . but who the hell did he ever fight? Who ever heard of Mitchel being where bullets were flying thick? When it comes to a showdown, we are Negroes first, last, and all the time and to hell with. . . ."[43] Whatever Harrison said next was drowned out by wild cheering. By attacking the local mayor rather than Woodrow Wilson, Harrison could get across dissident opinions that were not technically seditious but could catch in the crossfire those more powerful individuals who spoke or acted like his local target.

He also deployed a pseudo-patriotic framework to attack lynching during the war, writing that "no man who loves America . . . or who is truly loyal to her institutions, can justify mob action while the courts of justice are open." Whites who roasted Negroes alive disrespected the laws of the country they claimed to love. "We are at the very moment fighting lawless passion. Germany has outlawed herself among the nations because she has disregarded the sacred obligations of law and has made lynchers of her armies. Lynchers emulate her disgraceful example." Here, Harrison sought to stoke white American opposition to lynching by placing lynchers in the same camp as the German government, upon which the United States had declared war. Simultaneously, he urged pro-war people what a real war for democracy might mean: "America is in this war to win. The nation will brook no attempt to compromise its declared principles. The world—the whole world, Tennessee as well as Turkey—must be made safe for democracy; and we must fight on until this end is accomplished." Here again, Harrison cleverly aligns the fight against lynching, segregation, and disenfranchisement with President Wilson's official war aim of "democracy."[44]

In addition to selecting ostensibly nonseditious targets and frameworks for his *Voice* editorials during the war, Harrison became adept at communicating subtle messages between the lines that would prompt discerning readers to think critically about something without Harrison referring directly to it. For example, he argued that it was silly for people to dismiss calls for democracy in the Black community as "disloyalty" because such calls expressed "fullest loyalty to the letter and spirit of the President's war aims," and "to say that it isn't is to presume to accuse the President of having war-aims other than those which he set forth in the face of Europe."[45] In other words, if democracy for Black people clashed with the official war aims, then the president lied whenever he cast it as a war for democracy. With statements like these, Harrison managed to cleverly express opposition to the war without triggering federal censorship, arrest, or deportation.[46]

After the cessation of the war, Harrison changed his tune and became much more outspoken. During the war, Harrison expressed dissent with statements like, "As for Wilson, I love Wilson as much as I love—well, it would be treason to say it."[47] Apparently, he could not resist trolling the censors once in a while as he went about avoiding their repression of free speech. With the postwar evaporation of state censorship of free speech, Harrison excoriated Wilson very explicitly for his doublespeak: "This man who prated of 'the rights of small nationalities,' of 'self-determination,' of 'the right of all those who submit to authority to have a voice in their own government'—it was this greatest of all hypocrites who suppressed freedom of speech and of the press in these United States, let loose upon Hayti and Santo Domingo the awful horrors of unlicensed butchery, and sold out the hopes of all the world for peace and democracy at the Congress of Versailles."[48]

Lest anyone think Harrison actually took Wilson at his word during the war, he explained clearly how he "was well aware that Woodrow Wilson's protestations of democracy were lying protestations, consciously and deliberately designed to deceive." But because of the consequences of voicing dissent during the war, "I chose to pretend that Woodrow Wilson meant what he said, because by so doing I could safely hold up to contempt and ridicule the undemocratic practices of his administration and the actions of his white countrymen in regard to the Negro." Harrison called this political method a "camouflage" approach that allowed him to tell the truth in a way that proved "safer and more effective" given the threat of state repression during the war.[49]

By carefully navigating the propaganda war, Harrison discovered the psychology of repetition behind war propaganda. During his days in the Socialist Party, Harrison had already concluded that "capitalist newspapers are published to suppress news, not to issue news."[50] However, during the war, Harrison made an even more perceptive exposure of the selling of government policy and its basis in repeating the same lie over and over. He pointed to the example of an advertisement that appeared in magazines and on billboards in the streets that presented a "masterly illustration of the principle of repetition." The National Biscuit Company had an ad campaign called "U-Need-A Biscuit" that had been running since 1902. Harrison noted that when one first saw a sign with the message, one could ignore the appeal, "but as the days go by the constant insistence reaches our inner consciousness and we decide that perhaps after all we do need a biscuit." He raised this example as a case study precisely analogous to the war propaganda for "democracy," which, according to Harrison, "was the U-need-a Biscuit advertised by Messrs. Woodrow Wilson, [David] Lloyd George, Georges Clemenceau and thousands of perspiring publicists, preachers and thinkers" who guided the ship of state in government and by way of the columns of white newspapers.[51]

Historically, the 1910s represented a time when mass propaganda was just emerging as a conscious technique of social control by way of the Committee on Public Information and the Creel Commission, which coordinated public relations for the Wilson administration. Early propaganda theorists like Edward Bernays, the "father of public relations," pointed out, approvingly, that "the conscious and intelligent manipulation of the organized habits and opinions of the masses is an important element in democratic society. Those who manipulate this unseen mechanism of society constitute an invisible government which is the true ruling power of our country."[52] Bernays believed that if the public thought for themselves, society would break down. Therefore, the strategic use of propaganda, the "engineering of consent," was essential in order to manipulate the masses.[53] As Bernays put it, "Good government can be sold to a community just as any other commodity can be sold."[54] He spoke from experience as a member of the Committee on Public Information, a government propaganda agency that "sold" White House policy to the public during the war in precisely this way.[55]

Another authoritative voice of elite opinion extolling the benefits of propaganda, Walter Lippmann established the theoretical foundations for manipulation and control of the public through the news media. His 1922 book *Public Opinion*, a foundational text for modern American journalism, stated bluntly that "the public must be put in its place, so that each of us may live free of the trampling and roar of a bewildered herd." Lippmann argued that the techniques for what he called the "manufacture of consent" had improved enormously as a result of psychological research coupled with the modern means of communication. In Lippmann's view, "a revolution is taking place, infinitely more significant than any shifting of economic power. Within the life of the generation now in control of affairs, persuasion has become a self-conscious art and a regular organ of popular government." In the era of propaganda, he felt it was no longer possible to believe in "the original dogma of democracy" because "the common interests very largely elude public opinion entirely, and can be managed only by a specialized class whose personal interests reach beyond the locality." Only the specialized few can define the "common interests," and they can use psychology-informed propaganda and the mass media communications system to "manufacture the consent" of the public.[56] As the famous linguist and forensic media critic Noam Chomsky put it, ever since the English Civil War of the 1600s, "there has been a deepening recognition among elites in the West that as you begin to lose the power to control people by force, you have to start to control what they think."⁵⁷

Harrison pointed out these dynamics of consent manufacturing through the repetitive drumbeat of propaganda. In his words, "You cannot get men to go out and get killed by telling them plainly that you who are sending them to get the other fellow's land, trade and wealth, and you are too cowardly or too intelligent to go yourself and risk getting shot over the acquisition." That would not work, he reasoned, "so you whoop it up with any catch word which will serve as sufficient bait for the silly fools whom you keep silly in order that you may always use them in this way." Rather than tell people that they had to kill and die in order to enrich the American oligarchs of finance capital, the government instead cast the war as a fight to safeguard "democracy." In other words, the rhetoric of "democracy" was used "mainly as a convenient camouflage behind which competing imperialists masked their sordid aims."⁵⁸ Apparently, old habits die hard.

Harrison analyzed acutely the public relations method by which President Wilson's propagandists engineered consent. And how it backfired. As Harrison saw it, "democracy" served as the key buzzword. The forces who trumpeted it fostered in people of color "a democratic complex which in its turbulent insistence is apt to trouble" the powers that cooked up the "democracy" mantra. Harrison lampooned the hypocrisy of the propaganda peddlers "because they haven't any of the goods which they advertised in the first place," and even if they did, they had no intention of passing any of it on to the non-white peoples of the world whose appetite for democracy they had unintentionally stimulated. In other words, "democracy" offered a nice-sounding platitude that marshaled support for the war among white workers but on the other side of the color line would ultimately prove contrary to the interests of the war makers when the "darker races" would seek a measure of real democracy instead of endless colonial domination.⁵⁹

Later Harrison would expand and generalize his critique of the corporate media even further. In a fictional short story he worked on titled "Land of the Living Lie," he depicted a quasi-imaginary world in which "if a writer wished to 'succeed' he had to avoid telling 'the plain un-varnished truth' [or] else his book was boycotted or damned by all the review-writers whose salaries were paid by the editors of the large newspapers and magazines which were 'supported' by the rich business men's advertisements and by the credit which was necessary to carry on their business and which could be withheld by the great banking houses owned by these same business men." In this world, "the printed lie" supplied "an element of social control, enabling the people who were on top to maintain their position by feeding the minds of the people at the bottom with such information and ideas as would induce them to pursue courses of conduct destructive of their own interests, but conducive to the ode of their overlords." Though ostensibly a dystopian future, the short story clearly drew upon Harrison's astute observations of the psychological use of the mass media for political manipulation in a "democracy."[60]

The Liberty Congress of Negro-Americans

In April of 1918, Harrison received a letter from Adam Clayton Powell Sr. and William Monroe Trotter inviting him to a meeting "to help arrange for a great liberty Convention" to be held in Washington, DC.[61] As noted previously, Harrison and the Liberty League had already developed a plan the previous year for taking the grievances of the Black community to the United States Congress. This made him a natural candidate for co-organizing a conference for that purpose with Powell and Trotter. The purpose of the national gathering was to extend democracy (for which the United States was supposedly fighting in Europe) to African Americans and "to take positive measures to secure from the Government guarantee of the abolition of disfranchisement and of all caste discriminations, civil and political."[62] Trotter's call for delegates went out to a vast network of Black churches, business, civic, literary and fraternal orders and social organizations.

Upon learning of these plans, the US Military Intelligence Bureau (MIB) called Trotter into their office to interview him about the purpose of his upcoming Liberty Congress in the nation's capital. Trotter explained that the Congress would protest racial oppression and press the case for the government to extend to Black people at home the democracy for which African American soldiers were fighting and dying in France. After failing to convince Trotter to abandon or postpone the congress or to seek the counsel of NAACP board chairman Joel Spingarn, who was also working for US military intelligence, the MIB spoke with Trotter a second time over the phone. The agent on the other end of the line attempted to impress upon Trotter "the danger of such a convention if it should get out of control of the sane and sensible leaders, and how the airing of the grievance of the colored people and their publication, possibly exaggerated, throughout the country would greatly assist the German propagandist." Trotter remained unmoved. The military intelligence agent concluded privately afterward that "arrangements, however, can undoubtedly be made through the proper colored leaders to emphasize a strong direction and control over the convention if it is held."[63] Simply put, the federal government saw the Liberty Congress of Negro Americans as a threat.[64]

Though they were not able to prevent or even temporarily forestall the Liberty Congress, the Wilson administration and US military intelligence managed to organize a competing conference for Black newspaper editors in the same month of June 1918 in order to steal the thunder from the Liberty Congress and rally the biggest opinion shapers in the Black press around a pro-war editorial policy. The government-sponsored gathering included the editors of major African American newspapers such as the *Chicago Defender,* the *New York Age, Amsterdam News,* and the *St. Louis Argus.* It included notable pro-war Black leaders such as W. E. B. Du Bois and Archibald Grimké of the NAACP, as well as stalwart protégés of Booker T. Washington such as Robert Moton of Tuskegee, Charles W. Anderson, and Emmett J. Scott, the special advisor on Black affairs to the secretary of war. Government records show some thirty-one colored editors present, from all parts of the country except the far west.

Major Joel E. Spingarn took the reins as a key conference organizer. Maj. Spingarn at the time served as both chairman of the board of the NAACP and an agent of US military intelligence in the antiradical branch focused on "Negro subversion." Emmett Scott, the special assistant to the secretary of war for Negro affairs and former personal secretary of Booker T. Washington, presided over the conference. George Creel of the Committee on Public Information (the federal government's war propaganda department) addressed the conference on the first day. Representatives of the Shipping Board and Food Administration addressed the conference the second day, and on the third day representatives of the French army addressed the Black editors. The conference also heard from such champions of Black progress as Secretary of War Newton Baker and Assistant Secretary of the Navy Franklin D. Roosevelt, who would later gloat about writing the constitution of Haiti while he was ruling over the island as its de facto governor.[65] The government officials made clear that the Black editors had been called to Washington to assist the government in winning the war and to offer input about how to "keep up the morale of the colored people" toward this end.[66]

The Liberty Congress of Negro-Americans also took place in June of 1918, and Harrison played a key role in the event, thanks in part to Liberty League alumna, Brooklyn real estate broker, and newspaper seller Irena Moorman-Blackston, who paid for him to travel from New York to DC that summer and joined him as one of the few Black women delegates at the congress.[67] In his diary, Harrison remarked about the congress proceedings that when his turn came to moderate the gathering, his conduct of the business at hand appeared such a clear improvement upon what went before that the delegates unanimously elected him chairman of the congress. As Harrison recorded in his private diary, "I had been presiding hardly an hour before enthusiastic commendations were expressed from the floor. If I were given much to meg-

Figure 4.2 Photograph of delegates to the national Liberty Congress of Negro-Americans of June 24–29, 1918, in Washington, DC. Hubert Harrison, who was elected chairman of the Liberty Congress, is in the front row, the second person from the right. William Monroe Trotter, the other leading organizer of the conference, is seated on Harrison's right side.

alomania my head would have grown as big as the church."[68] Harrison here offers a glimpse into the emotional excitement that marked perhaps his first real taste of collective recognition by fellow Black dissidents and activists from all across the country.

Harrison noted that the Liberty Congress had delegates from thirty-three states, from as far away as Oklahoma, and that the delegates included many Black people of respect and distinction such as doctors, lawyers, ministers, editors, and teachers. Being chairman in this setting was not an easy task. For example, to Harrison's dismay, "many of the delegates were bent upon interminable wrangling and disputation of a childish sort, and it was only by the most skillful combination of tact and repression that they were constrained to do practical work." Yet overall Harrison had positive reflections about the experience, concluding that "on the whole, this was the most notable gathering of Negro Americans in a generation—and most of the delegates felt this."[69]

The congress seemed historic not only for its size and representation but also for its impact.

Harrison marvelled at all the speakers he witnessed at the congress. On July 1, the Liberty Congress heard a speech from US congressman Leonidas Dyer of Illinois, who had presented an antilynching bill to Congress in the aftermath of the East St. Louis anti-Black pogrom of 1917. After the congressman came a stirring speech from Allen Whaley, William Monroe Trotter's assistant. Building on Dyer and Whaley, West Indian–born Dr. M. A. N. Shaw of Boston was the next to take the podium. About Dr. Shaw's speech Harrison noted, "I have never heard that speech surpassed. I could have listened all night." Dr. Shaw was a hard act to follow. Harrison begged the audience to adjourn and hear him speak on the following night instead because it was getting late. In response there were cries from all over the church for "Harrison! Harrison!" The audience took a vote to decide the matter, and four-fifths of the audience stood to indicate their support for Harrison speaking. He unleashed the Harlem Hellfighter within. One military intelligence file reported him declaring, "They take our brothers and lynch them and then expect us to go to war as loyal citizens. They say that the federal Government cannot protect us here, but they can go over to Serbia ... and reestablish government." He held their rapt attention until 12:35 A.M.[70]

The Liberty Congress took aim at federal government policy. Harrison reported they organized subcommittees on resolutions, voting rights, and a petition to the federal government. The Liberty Congress asked for a joint session of the two houses of Congress to consider the grievances of the 12 million "people of the Negro race and their demand for democracy at home" from the nation spending billions of dollars on a war to "make the world safe for democracy." The MIB monitored the proceedings, took note of the participants and Harrison's leading role, suspected the gathering of promoting "pro-German propaganda and activities." The MIB also made use of African American school teachers from Washington, DC, as informants.[71]

The MIB recorded that a Mrs. Simpson from Boston denounced the way "Emmett Scott had a number of the colored editors come to Washington to be wined and dined at the Government's expense for the sole purpose of muzzling them." She also spoke of how "Emmett Scott and all of his constituents should be in a city of their own and that is the city of the dead, where they can remain silent. I am sorry that he is not here tonight to hear this for himself, but ... I came here for the express purpose of fighting him. I feel for you people here under the dome of the capital. Your hands are tied. We people in Massachusetts can say just what we think and we have come here to say it for you, for you are not able to say it for yourselves."[72]

Maj. Walter Loving's assessment for the MIB concluded that the secrecy of the proceedings of the government's editors conference added to popular suspicions that the gathering looked like a "hand picked, star chamber affair, where certain Negro editors and others had met with officials of the War Department to compromise race issues." Loving determined that the leaders of the "radical [Liberty Congress] outgeneraled the leaders of the editors' conference" by giving the fullest publicity to their proceedings and thereby gaining immediate popular approval and support for their platform.

At least two things make the Liberty Congress historically significant. Above all, it cohered the only organizationally independent national gathering of dissident African Americans during the war. Though the Liberty Congress chose not to openly and explicitly oppose the war itself on account of the Sedition and Espionage Acts, it did create space for Black leaders across the country to convene and express a national New Negro consciousness and protest movement out of the militant sentiment that pervaded the younger and more forward-thinking people of African descent across the country. Second, it set a precedent for independent national Black gatherings in Washington, DC. In the short term, a gathering similar to the Liberty Congress took place in Washington in December 1918, followed by the National Equal Rights League's Liberty Conference in June of 1919.[73] In a longer-term sense, the Liberty Congress must be counted as a political forerunner and ancestor of A. Philip Randolph's March on Washington Movement in 1941, Randolph and Bayard Rustin's actual March on Washington in 1963, and Dr. King's Poor People's Campaign in 1968.

A Clash of the Titans: Du Bois and Harrison in the Crucible of War

By the time of the white world war, W. E. B. Du Bois had become a national Black political influencer as editor of the NAACP's *Crisis* magazine. In the immediate months following US entry into the war, Du Bois stayed true to form and denounced incidents of anti-Black violence like the East St. Louis pogrom and the execution of the thirteen Black soldiers in Houston who revolted against racial oppression in the summer of 1917.[74] However, Du Bois changed his tone once the Bureau of Investigation started complaining to the NAACP board about the content of his editorials in *The Crisis*.

As the US war effort proceeded, Du Bois continued toning down his criticisms of racial oppression. This culminated in his July 1918 editorial, wherein he wrote perhaps the single most regrettable editorial sentence of his whole life: "Let us, while this war lasts, forget our special grievances and close our ranks shoulder to shoulder with our own white fellow citizens and the allied nations that are fighting for democracy."[75] Du Bois, with all his prestige and political authority, openly called on Black people to "forget" about lynching, segregation, disenfranchisement, the epidemic of anti-Black massacres—grievances he himself had spent so many years exposing and denouncing—in order to fight, kill, and even die for a brand of "democracy" in Europe that African Americans could not access at home.

Harrison responded in a devastating and fearless manner in a *Voice* editorial titled "The Descent of Dr. Du Bois." He first pointed out that Du Bois, of all people, knew better than anyone that African Americans could not "preserve either their lives, their manhood or their vote (which is their political life and liberties)" while lynching and Jim Crow reigned supreme. Evoking the Declaration of Independence by referring to "life" and "liberty," Harrison subtly reminded his readers that the United States itself had always denied to Black people the "freedom" it claimed as its defining value. Using the logic of the government's own stated framework, he concluded that "instead of the war for democracy making these [rights] less necessary, it makes them more so."[76] In other words, a war for democracy required redressing Black grievances even sooner—if people of African descent in the United States were to remain patriotic and loyal Americans.

Harrison blasted Du Bois for selling out. The "people whom our white masters have 'recognized' as our leaders (without taking the trouble to consult us)" decried Harrison, "have already established an unsavory reputation by advocating this same surrender of life, liberty and manhood, masking their cowardice behind the pillars of war-time sacrifice." But why and how could a stalwart race man like Du Bois make such a cardinal blunder?

Harrison pointed out a crucial fact: Du Bois advanced his call to close ranks and forget about racial grievances shortly after he had applied for a captaincy in the War Department. The government had investigated *The Crisis* for sedition and had convened a national conference of Black newspaper editors whose secret proceedings none of the editors would discuss afterward, including Du Bois. In Harrison's view, "The responsibility, therefore, for a course of counsel which stresses the servile virtues of acquiescence and subservience falls squarely on his shoulders." By using words like *subservience*, Harrison placed Du Bois in the same league as Booker T. Washington. Moreover, the succession of events appeared "too clear to admit of any interpretation other than that of deliberate, cold-blooded, purposive planning," in Harrison's estimation.

Although NAACP board chairman and army major Joel Spingarn shaped the overall strategy of US military intelligence regarding "Negro subversion" in 1918, Du Bois was no mindless pawn in the game. In fact, some months before applying for his own commission, Du Bois had referred a young Black graduate of Harvard to the director of military intelligence for an army commission.[77] In June of 1918, *The Crisis* editor worked closely with Major Spingarn in setting up the pro-war editors' conference to undermine the Liberty Congress. He went along with the censorship of *The Crisis* and worked with Spingarn to recruit Black agents for military intelligence. Du Bois hoped that creating a Black presence within the US Army intelligence apparatus would mean "that when the question of unrest among Negroes arises, these men would be able to point out to the government why the unrest existed and offer a remedy."[78] On the other hand, opposing the war would have meant leaving the NAACP and *The Crisis* entirely, not to mention possible imprisonment under the Espionage Act.[79]

Historical scholarship has confirmed Harrison's assessment. Major Spingarn was not only a personal friend of Du Bois's but also, as chairman of the NAACP board, Du Bois's boss and employer. Spingarn had recently become a field-grade officer in the antiradical branch of US military intelligence that specialized in "Negro subversion." His new task would be to set up a "counter espionage system among colored people themselves."[80] As a military intelligence officer, Spingarn undertook various methods by which to suppress "Negro subversion." He ordered an internal audit of the NAACP's leaders, branches, and members. He tasked white NAACP board member Charles H. Studin with censoring *The Crisis*. Studin, acting on the direct urging of the director of military intelligence, General Marlborough Churchill, assured the general that that no pains would be spared to make every issue of the magazine "comply with the wishes of the Government" because helping to win the war was now *The Crisis*'s "paramount purpose."[81]

Spingarn's attempt to recruit Du Bois to spy on Black radicals during the war formed a key part of the War Department's strategy, leading to Du Bois's infamous "Close Ranks" editorial. In a memorandum to his superior officer, Spingarn mentioned *The Crisis* editorial as indicative of a "gradual change of tone" in the Black press and an "effect of the M.I.B. policy." The director of the MIB, Colonel Marlborough Churchill, responded with a handwritten note at the bottom: "Very satisfactory." The "Close Ranks" editorial, according to historian Mark Ellis, thus crucially influenced the decision of the War Department to offer Du Bois the captaincy in military intelligence. As Harrison rightly suspected, some deliberate, cold-blooded, and purposive planning was afoot. The capitulation of *The Crisis* editor marked the "descent of Du Bois" and his authority as a Black leader not just among New Negro militants, but also among some NAACP members.[82]

Du Bois's behavior offers a case study of abandoning one's original convictions under the high-pressure government coercion of wartime loyalty. In

1915, Du Bois had declared that "lying treaties, rivers of rum, murder, assassination, rape, and torture have marked the progress of Englishman, German, Frenchman, and Belgian on the dark continent."[83] But in his infamous "Close Ranks" editorial of 1918, he now proclaimed, "That which the German power represents today spells death to the aspiration of Negroes and all the darker races for equality, freedom and democracy." The idea that only *German* power was the greatest evil in the world would have been news to the "darker races" in their millions living under British, French, and Belgian colonial rule—as Du Bois himself had so eloquently argued three years earlier. (Not to mention Native Americans, African Americans, Mexican Americans, Hawaiians, Puerto Ricans, Cubans, Filipinos, Haitians, Dominicans, Alaskan Inuits, Virgin Islanders, and other peoples living under US colonial rule before, during, and after President Wilson's supposed fight for "democracy.")

After the war concluded, Du Bois attempted to recover from his catastrophic fall from grace as a Black leader by writing a postwar editorial about how Black people must "return fighting," but for many New Negro militants, the damage had already been done.[84]

After the war, Harrison took Du Bois to task like a Harlem Hellfighter determined to "return fighting." "The Negro leaders of the future will be expected not only to begin straight, take a moral vacation, and then go straight again. They will be expected to go straight all the time; to stand by us in war as well as in peace; not to blow hot and cold with the same mouth, but 'to stand four-square to *all* the winds that blow.'"[85] For Harrison, Black leadership in the age of the New Negro had to rest on political principle and moral consistency. Written in Marcus Garvey's *Negro World*, Harrison's critique of Du Bois also constituted a kind of shot across the bow of the Garvey movement, a theme we will engage more fully in chapter 8.

While Du Bois made a critical error in attempting to join the government, Harrison made some moves during the "Close Ranks" affair that also merit criticism. Harrison's decision to expose Du Bois originally grew out of a request by Maj. Loving for information from a "radical" perspective on the debate in Black communities about the significance of Du Bois' army commission. Loving met with Harrison, who wrote out his perspective for the army man, who then gave the information to his superiors in military intelligence. Loving noted that if Du Bois "continues as editor of *The Crisis* I believe that the storm of popular resentment among the colored people will gradually die out, whereas his appointment to a commission in the army would give the radicals... opportunity to implicate the government in this affair.... A man cannot desert overnight the principles he has followed for twenty-five years without incurring the suspicion and mistrust of his people." The MIB likewise concluded that Du Bois would lose his credibility and effectiveness as a pro-war propagandist if he became an agent of the government and so they chose to abort Du Bois's application for the army commission.[86]

Harrison's decision to supply information to the MIB apparently rested on the same mistaken assumption Du Bois had made: that a clever Black person working with the government could somehow influence its policies in a pro-Black direction. He imagined that other radicals like him might be willing to cooperate "in allaying friction and promoting goodwill" in exchange for the government "dumping once and for all" Black collaborators like George Haynes and Emmett Scott. In this case, Harrison's rage clouded his judgment. After one conversation with Maj. Loving, Harrison noted to himself, "I shall live to see Emmett Scott paid off for what was done to me in 1911 and Geo. Haynes for—other things." Harrison apparently wanted revenge on Scott for his role—as a zealous assistant to Booker T. Washington and the "Tuskegee Machine"—in effectuating Harrison's firing from the postal office.[87]

Curiously, before the "Close Ranks" affair, Harrison himself briefly toyed with the idea of joining the army. In his diary entry for March 27, 1918, Harrison recorded how he went to the local exemption board's office "to find out whether it was possible to enter an officers' training camp and so prepare for ultimate service in the Army in the event that the war comes over here." Even though he saw the conflict as a "white war" and a product of the capitalist system, the possibility of the war coming home to the United States tempted him to join the military. However, he quickly abandoned his momentary impulse to join the army later that same day. In his diary, he described how "reading a malignant article in this evening's *Sun* from its 'cracker' correspondents in France insulting our Negro soldiers in France . . . has cleared the air for me." The article triggered a revulsion at his temptation to become a US soldier by reminding him that white racists maligned Black troops not only abroad but at home too. "Until the white men of this country can put patriotism ahead of race I shall not," noted Harrison. "So long as they will treat us as 'niggers' rather than as fellow citizens will those of us who respect themselves keep from fighting for a damned 'Jim Crow' democracy who's tangled threads of hypocrisy, cant and cruelty will weave their dangerous web across the nation's path to self-respect."[88]

Harrison wrote to Emmett Scott to inquire whether and how he might join the army, but he never got a reply. He did, however, register for the draft, most likely in response to the "slacker raids" conducted by the Justice Department in which local police, sailors, soldiers, and vigilante "patriots" of the American Protective League worked together to apprehend more than 50,000 men, many at the point of a bayonet, forcing them to show their Selective Service papers. Harrison registered in September of 1918, just two months before the armistice that brought an end to hostilities. He would find out years later that he had been put in the first-class category (i.e., eligible for conscription) despite being the supporter of a family with four children, which should have exempted him. About this bureaucratic injustice Harrison remarked that "such was the malignancy of the Scott-Haynes gang," referring to his Black federal government archenemies Emmett Scott and George Haynes.[89]

The Colored International

The white world war sparked a wave of revolutionary stirrings not just in the minds of New Negro radicals but throughout the colonized world. For example, the armed Irish Easter Rising exploded in Dublin in 1916, followed by guerrilla war throughout Ireland from 1918 to 1921. An upsurge of demonstrations and strikes exploded against British rule in India, including Britain's infamous Jallianwala Bagh massacre of pro-independence protesters in 1919, the same year as the Egyptian Revolution of 1919 against British domination of the nation which hosted the supremely geostrategic Suez canal. These postwar rebellions emerged concurrent with nationalist agitation in China by student protests in 1919, part of a larger political awakening that culminated in civil war and the Shanghai general strike of 1926–27. Before his capture and execution in Haiti in 1919, Charlemagne Péralte led a guerrilla war against the US occupation of Haiti. The same year also saw a general strike and revolutionary upheaval in Trinidad, led by Black workers in Port-of-Spain. Clements Kadalie, a migrant worker from Nyasaland, founded the Industrial and Commercial Workers' Union of Africa in 1919, which became a major "center of African industrial and political struggle for the next decade," according to historian David Seddon.[90] Charlotte Maxeke founded the Bantu Women's League in South Africa (1918); Mekatilili Wa Menza led the Giriama people's anticolonial struggle in Kenya (1910s); and John Chilembwe led an anticolonial uprising in Nyasaland (1915). Not to mention the emergence of figures like Emiliano Zapata, who led a revolution in Mexico throughout the 1910s. The first two decades of the twentieth century witnessed stirrings of anticolonial and pan-Islamic social movements from Morocco to Iraq to Siberia. This global "rising tide of color against white world supremacy" terrified white supremacist intellectuals like Lothrop Stoddard. He represented a 1920s forerunner of those who promote the so-called Great Replacement theory and the upholding of global white supremacy today.

This "rising tide of color" around the world also stimulated Harrison's groundbreaking political theory of colored internationalism.[91] It received its most sweeping, comprehensive, and politically advanced expression in a call to action that Harrison wrote in 1921 for Marcus Garvey's *Negro World* titled "Wanted—A Colored International." Harrison based his case on both the domestic racial oppression in the United States and the situation beyond US borders: "When we look upon the Negro republics of Haiti and Santo Domingo where American marines murder and rape at their pleasure while the financial vultures of Wall Street scream with joy over the bloody execution which brings the wealth of those countries under their control; when we see the Virgin Islanders in the deadly coils of American capitalism gasping for a breath of liberty, and Mexico menaced by the same monster, we begin to realize that we must organize our forces to save ourselves from further degradation and ultimate extinction." The same US government that oppressed African Americans at home committed atrocities against nonwhite peoples across the Caribbean and Latin America.[92]

As we have seen, for Harrison the capital accumulated from the exploitation of white workers in Europe and America eventually sought outlets for investment outside its national boundaries and thereby become the reason for the exploitation of workers abroad in Africa and Asia. Therefore, Harrison argued, the purpose of treaties and agreements between capitalist powers was to unify and standardize the exploitation of "black and brown and yellow" peoples so that "the danger to the exploiting groups of cutting each other's throats over the spoils may be reduced to a minimum. . . . Hence the League of Nations, which is notoriously not a league of the white masses, but of their gold-brained governors." Here one catches a glimpse into Harrison's view of what he called the "capitalist internationalism" of Woodrow Wilson's vaunted League of Nations as an institution of domination over working-class people, both white and nonwhite, which Lenin derided as the "League of Imperialist Bandits."[93]

After dominating within their "home" territory, the capitalist countries had united internationally to harmonize their domination of the nonwhite world such that, as Harrison put it, "the subject races and the subject classes are tied to each other like Kilkenny cats in a conundrum of conflict which they cannot escape until the system which so binds them both is smashed beyond possibility of 'reconstruction.' And thus it becomes the duty of the darker races to fight against the continuance of this system from without and within." Here was the crux of his call to action: linking working people and people of color all over the world in a race-conscious, anticapitalist, anti-imperialist struggle to smash the reigning system beyond any possibility of reconstruction.

Because white domination and imperialism were an international problem, it would require an international solution. For starters, "a call should be issued for a congress of the darker races which should be frankly anti-imperialistic and should serve as an international center of cooperation from which strength may be drawn for the several sections of the world of color." Harrison argued that this congress should include the voices of oppressed people from places like India, Egypt, China, West and South Africa, the West Indies, Hawaii, the Philippines, Afghanistan, Algeria, and Morocco. The congress "should be made up of those who realize that capitalist imperialism which mercilessly exploits the darker races for its own financial purposes is the enemy which we must combine to fight with arms as varied as those by which it is fighting to destroy our manhood, independence and self-respect." In short, the congress would forge a global weapon for the "world of color," that is, a *Colored* International. And by his inclusion of armed struggle in the vision, Harrison here made clear that his was no halfway vision of revolution.[94]

Interestingly, despite his difficult experience in the Socialist Party, Harrison did not rule out working with white radicals who were genuine in their commitment to overturning systems of domination: "The international of the darker races must avail itself of whatever help it can get from those groups within the white race which are seeking to destroy the capitalist international of race prejudice and exploitation which is known as bourgeois 'democracy' at home and colonial imperialism abroad." White workers who genuinely wanted to fight the system could become allies in the struggle.

However, whatever alliances were possible with white political forces had to be on Black-emancipatory terms. African Americans could not allow white leftists to break down Black racial solidarity, and "until we can co-operate with them on our own terms we choose not to co-operate at all, but to pursue our own way of salvation." Harrison remained hard as a crystalline touchstone about the need for radical humility on the part of European Socialists and Communists: "Sauce for the black goose ought to be sauce for the white gander, and the temporary revolutionists of today should show their sincerity by first breaking down the exclusion walls of white workingmen before they ask us to demolish our own defensive structures of racial self-protection." In other words, African Americans had every right to put "race first"—and the white left had no business complaining about the nationalist sentiments of an oppressed nationality—as long as the root problem of structural white supremacy remained intact. White radicals seeking collaboration across the color line could demonstrate sincerity by first breaking down the racial superiority complex of white workers: "Those who will meet us on our own ground will find that we recognize a common enemy in the present world order and are willing to advance to attack it in our joint behalf." In other words, white radicals who demonstrated *in practice* their opposition to white supremacy could join forces with the Colored International for a common purpose.[95]

Harrison's vision for the "Colored International" comprised a race-conscious internationalism that developed, in part, out of the Marxist tradition of radical working-class internationalism. Following the decline of the

International Workingmen's Association, which constituted the First International, a global federation of Socialist and social-democratic parties came together to form the Second International.[96] At the outbreak of World War I, however, most of the European parties of the Second International capitulated to the pressures of patriotism and national chauvinism, siding with their own respective ruling classes rather than the proletarian internationalism that they had espoused on paper before the outbreak of war. Not all the socialists capitulated. But European Socialist delegates to the antiwar Zimmerwald Conference joked in a self-deprecating fashion about how a half century after the founding of the First International, all the principled internationalists could still fit onto four horse-drawn coaches.[97] It proved a formative moment for delegates like Lenin and Trotsky.

Four years later, the Bolsheviks in power had made Trotsky commander in chief of the Red Army while Lenin focused on launching a third, Moscow-based Communist International or "Comintern." Before its degeneration and eventual dismantling under Stalin, the Comintern formed a new, Bolshevik-inflected global "school" for developing the most advanced strategies and tactics for political parties fighting for the liberation of the workers of the world. As an international gathering of various Communist parties all over the world, the Comintern sought to refocus and coordinate the global struggle for working-class revolution. Though space does not permit a deeper dive here, the record of its early Congresses remains one of the most potent bodies of proletarian revolutionary strategy, tactics, and experience ever assembled, including for the political struggle against fascism, liberalism, petit-bourgeois social democrats, and the kind of ultra-leftism that Lenin saw as "infantile." As a product of the Russian Revolution and the pro-war capitulations and betrayals of the Second International, the Comintern's early congress took a strong stand not only against capitalist imperialism but also for the right of oppressed nations to self-determination.[98]

Harrison's vision for how the Colored International would relate to white people proved analogous in some respects with Lenin's vision of how the Communist International should relate to nationalist movements in the colonial world. Lenin's draft theses on the national and colonial questions for the second congress of the Comintern spoke, among other things, about "the need for a determined struggle against attempts to give a communist coloring to bourgeois-democratic liberation trends" in the colonized world. Not pretending that any struggle against imperialism among oppressed nationalities was naturally or automatically Communist was akin to not pretending that any struggle against capitalism was naturally or automatically antiracist, let alone pro-Black. Similarly, Lenin spoke of how "the Communist International must enter into a temporary alliance with bourgeois democracy in the colonial and backward countries, but should not merge with it, and should under all circumstances uphold the independence of the proletarian movement even if it is in its most embryonic form." This idea forms a corollary to Harrison's suggestion that the Colored International could enter into an alliance with the white radical movement in imperialist countries on its own terms but should not necessarily merge with it or subordinate its race consciousness and instead should uphold an independent and anti-racist politics of internationalism.

The African Blood Brotherhood (ABB) originally advanced a revolutionary and class-conscious Black (inter)nationalist politics that dovetailed with that of Harrison's Colored International. Grace P. Campbell constituted the backbone of the ABB, whose parent branch met in her apartment. Harrison first met Campbell through his work with Frances Reynolds Keyser and the Empire State Federation of Women's Clubs, with which both Harrison and Campbell had been active. Like Cyril Briggs and Richard B. Moore, Grace P. Campbell joined the Socialist Party in the late 1910s on the crest of the New Negro radicalization and Black Socialist tradition that Harrison had inaugurated in Harlem. When white Socialist Party spokesman Algernon Lee lectured at the Harlem People's Educational Forum and reiterated Eugene Debs's argument that the party had nothing special to offer Black people, members like Campbell and Moore resigned from the party, joining with Cyril Briggs to form the ABB.[99] In its drive to maintain a working relationship with revolutionary Marxist white radicals, the ABB would end up testing Harrison's insistence that Black internationalists should not downplay Black independence or dilute their anti-racism in such coalitions.

As for the difference between Harrison's versus the ABB's relationship to the Communist Party, one particular story paints a telling picture. In 1921, Communist Party leader and founding member Rose Pastor Stokes convened a meeting of Black radicals in her home.[100] Attendees included Claude McKay, W. A. Domingo, Hubert Harrison, Edgar M. Grey, and Cyril Briggs. Stokes made an offer to finance Harrison's Liberty League of Negro-Americans in exchange for his help with recruiting Black people into the Communist Party. Much like how Harrison had groundings with Black Communists to discuss making the Garvey movement more class conscious, the white Communists were attempting to get Harrison to help them in the same task. He rejected the Stokes' proposition on the grounds that "we will not allow either Communists or Quakers to break down our developing racial solidarity, and we shall denounce every attempt to stampede us into their camps on their terms until they shall have first succeeded in breaking down the opposing racial solidarity of the ranks of white labor."[101] Harrison chose to keep the Liberty League Black-led, Black-funded, and focused on autonomous Black struggles, "thus foiling any plan that the communists might have entertained of using him as their stalking-horse against Garvey," as Garvey movement historian Robert Hill puts it.[102] After all, the Communist Party emerged from a split within the Socialist Party, whose limitations Harrison knew all too well from his own experience. "Once bitten" by the white left, Harrison remained "twice shy" toward its overtures.

Cyril Briggs, a key leader and cofounder of the ABB, chose to accept Stokes's offer. Although founded as an independent revolutionary Black internationalist organization in 1919, by 1921 the ABB chose to unite with white radicals, this time in the Communist rather than the Socialist Party. This development in some ways tethered the ABB's foreign policy to the internationalism of the Comintern, which in its early years betrayed a highly Eurocentric brand of internationalism. For example, the third congress of the Comintern took place in Moscow in July of 1921, just a few weeks after Harrison's call for a "Colored International." Out of the forty-one unanimously passed "Theses on the International Situation," thirty-six of them (87.8 percent) concerned Europe or the United States, as opposed to Africa, Asia, or Latin America.[103] Only 291 words out of 8,318 (3.5 percent) were devoted to colonized peoples anywhere. The first three congresses of the Comintern thus represented an anticapitalist and anti-imperialist internationalism without a clear understanding of white racial domination or Eurocentrism. This fact dovetailed with the more general neglect of Black and African communities by the Communist parties, much like their Socialist predecessors had demonstrated.

Scholars like Minkah Makalani and Winston James have shown that Briggs's decision and that of other Black Socialists at the time to join the Communist Party emerged not because of white US Communists' wonderful record of serious antiracist politics but because of the Comintern's principled stand—following Lenin—on the right of oppressed nations to self-determination. In effect, Briggs, Campbell, and McKay thus opted to push the white Communists for greater attention to the "Negro question" from within the party. Their tireless efforts to shift Comintern policy would bear more and more fruit as the 1920s unfolded. In response to arguments leveled by Black Communists like McKay and Otto Huiswoud, the Comintern adopted a whole set of theses on the so-called Negro question in its fourth congress in 1922. By the time of its sixth congress in 1928, and in response to arguments from Black Communists like Harry Haywood, the Comintern would go even further and adopt the famous "Black belt thesis," which used a Leninist formulation—theorizing African Americans as an oppressed nation with the right of self-determination in the Southern United States—to trigger the Comintern, particularly the Communist Party of the United States, to take the Negro question more seriously by linking it to their own principled Leninist commitment to the right of nations to self-determination.

In this manner, the coherence of this first generation of Black Communists also emerged in the context of the failure of the ABB and other Harlem radicals, including Harrison, to push the Garvey movement in a more class-conscious direction at the Universal Negro Improvement Association's 1921 annual convention. As Jeff Perry has pointed out, Harrison articulated the call for a "Colored International" not only in the context of turning down an offer from the Eurocentric Communist Party but also while he was in the process of distancing himself from the imperial ambitions of Marcus Garvey, who spoke of going "back to Africa" in connection with the founding of a "Racial Empire upon which 'the sun shall never set.'"[104]

To make even clearer the distinctiveness of Harrison's "colored" internationalism, we must consider the other internationalist politics on offer at the time. Tuskegee Institute foreign policy in this period represented what historian Angela Zimmerman has aptly called the "Segregationist International."[105] As essentially a program for the "globalization of the new South," it proved neither anticapitalist nor anti-imperialist nor opposed to global white supremacy.[106] W. E. B. Du Bois's pan-African congresses of 1919–27 did much to promote independence in sub-Saharan Africa and the Caribbean, fighting both imperialism and white supremacy.[107] While antiracist and somewhat anti-imperialist, these congresses gave expression to a mostly Black elite and elite-aspiring politics dominated by pro-capitalist figures like Blaise Diagne and other representatives of the "talented tenth" of Black and African communities. Marcus Garvey's global Black nationalist movement, which we explore in much greater depth in chapters 7 and 8, was surely anti-racist in the early 1920s but neither anti-capitalist nor anti-imperialist, given Garvey's determination to build an African empire based on the accumulation of Black capital.

To be fair, the aforementioned individuals and organizations did not remain static. Tuskegee did not remain committed to segregation forever. W.E.B. Du Bois became a Communist in the 1930s, integrating a revolutionary Marxist class consciousness to his anti-imperialist and antiracist politics. His pan-African congress movement likewise stopped being purely an elite affair, as its fifth congress in 1945 featured for the first time figures like George Padmore and others representing African trade unions, as well as Socialist and Communist forces in the pan-African world. As we have seen, Black Communists like Otto Huiswoud and Claude McKay set in motion a process of pushing the Comintern in a more race-conscious direction culminating in the party taking a stand for self-determination of African Americans in the South. In the 1930s, the US Communist Party went further in its antiracist politics: it fought to free the Scottsboro Boys and Angelo Herndon; built the multiracial Southern Tenants Farmers Union; ran African American James Ford as their vice presidential candidate in 1932 and 1936;

organized the American Negro Labor Congress to empower Black workers in the labor movement; and even mounted an explicit internal campaign against "white chauvinism" within the party. Garveyism, though never abandoning its commitment to capitalism, did develop an increasingly anti-imperialist politics as Garvey's dreams of a Black empire on which the sun would never set got overtaken by African and Afro-Caribbean mass movements for national independence against the European imperialist powers. Nevertheless, Harrison's call for a Colored International—as early as 1921—crystallized the seed form of a radically anticapitalist, anti-imperialist, and colored internationalist politics to which few other figures or organizations could lay claim, except the ABB and the anti-imperialist elements within the Garvey movement to which Harrison's call in the *Negro World* gave voice. What about the longer term trajectory of Harrison's vision?

Indeed, something akin to Harrison's vision of a Colored International did eventually take shape in the form of the 1927 League Against Imperialism conference in Brussels. Conceived as a kind of radical alternative to the League of Nations, it gathered Communist, Socialist, and nationalist leaders from places like South Africa, Algeria, Indonesia, Palestine, Iran, India, China, Afro-America, Peru and Puerto Rico.[108] Though Harrison did not make it to the conference, his Liberty League alumnus and race-conscious Communist protégé Richard B. Moore drafted the final "Resolution on the Negro Question" which the Brussels conference adopted.[109] The League's call for the rights of darker nations to rule themselves in turn laid the ground work for various subsequent regional pan-American, pan-African, and pan-Asian conferences culminating in the Bandung conference of 1955.[110]

Meanwhile, the Leninist contribution to the Communist International— the European counterpart to the Colored International—would live on in the Fourth International. As Trotsky argued, the struggle of the oppressed nations for national unification and national independence is doubly progressive because, on the one side, this prepares more favorable conditions for their own development, while on the other side, this deals blows to imperialism. That, he argued, is the reason why in the struggle between a "civilized," imperialist, "democratic" republic and a backward, barbaric monarchy in a colonial country, Socialists must stand completely on the side of the oppressed country notwithstanding its monarchy and against the oppressor country notwithstanding its "democracy."

Nowadays, precious lessons like those from the Third, Colored, and Fourth Internationals appear on the verge of extinction. Fortunately, Harrison was crystallizing an even more lasting breakthrough in relation to the Motherland of his ancestors.

Chapter 5

The Untamed, Untamable African

> **HERITAGE**
>
> By Countee Cullen
>
> What is Africa to me:
> Copper sun or scarlet sea,
> Jungle star or jungle track,
> Strong bronzed men, or regal black
> Women from whose loins I sprang
> When the birds of Eden sang?
> One three centuries removed
> From the scenes his fathers loved,
> Spicy grove, cinnamon tree,
> What is Africa to me?

In his poem "Heritage," Harlem Renaissance poet Countee Cullen engaged a haunting and inexorable question for people of African descent in the diaspora: What is Africa to me? Most Black people on the western banks of the Atlantic Ocean are descendants of a centuries-long history of war, conquest, kidnapping, and enslavement. For that reason, the question of what Africa means to most people racialized as Black in the Western Hemisphere presents an inherently uncomfortable reckoning with ancestral trauma. How does one deal with the world-historic and unspeakable destruction of one's cultural, linguistic, spiritual, and ancestral heritage?

As early as 1907, Hubert Harrison provided an unequivocal response to this question in his diary:

> Poor heart-sore and soul-starved Mother Race, who shall minister to thy deep desires, who shall bind up thy wounds and raise thee up again if these and such as these are to be thy prophets and thy priests? Oh Africa! When shall be the term of thy long degradation? Behold here, even now, I pledge thee, O my Mother, that I shall devote my years to thee, shall work for thy redemption even in the land of thine exile and set before mine eyes an ideal of service to thee inextricably blent with service for myself; shall love thee and be proud of thee and glory in thy power now lying dormant and shall strive to bring it to the light. Take my youth, my

labors, my love, my life, my all and do thou when I shall have died for thee, take me to thy bosom, an untamed, untamable African.

This "Pledge to the Mother Race from an Untamed African" expressed a profound inner striving, an oath both spiritual and prophetic.[1] Written in his private diary at the tender age of twenty-four, before he began his career as a public figure, Harrison's intimate and moving pledge revealed an extraordinary devotion to Africa and Africana peoples that would guide him for the rest of his life.

Harrison could identify proudly as an "untamed and untamable" African from such an early stage of his life thanks first and foremost to the vestiges of African cultural heritage that survived trans-Atlantic enslavement and passed from one generation to the next right down to his childhood in St. Croix. Noting that the people of the Virgin Islands were "almost entirely of African extraction," Harrison explained how the social characteristics of the Black population of the islands could only be fully understood and appreciated "by reference to similar characteristics to be found in the West African Negroes from among whom the slaves for the Danish Islands were mainly drawn—the locale extending from the Upper Gold Coast to the south-eastern limits of Nigeria." He described these social customs of St. Croix as being "rooted in the African communal system," aspects of which the African-descended peoples of the island had kept alive.[2]

Although the African-descended people of St. Croix had survived the gratuitous violence of slavery (like their Caribbean and mainland North and South American relatives), Black life on St. Croix offered more than simply endless doom and gloom. Harrison recounted his childhood memories of open and easily accessible gardens on every plantation, which were stocked with trees bearing "mangoes, mammy-apples, sour-sops, avocado-pears, sugar-apples, and bananas." The fruits could be freely picked by anyone, even passers-by. In addition, every family of agricultural laborers—like the one he grew up in—had a "half-acre of provision land on which yams, tannias, okra, sago and potatoes" were grown for family consumption, "the surplus being regularly disposed of in the towns on Saturday . . . in markets that exactly reproduced those to be found in the hinterlands of Sierra Leone, Liberia, the Cameroons, and Yoruba."[3] These childhood memories of communal agricultural cultivation showed Harrison's historical consciousness of the African and land-based wisdom and roots of Black culture in the Virgin Islands, the cradle of his deep-seated African identity.

Unfortunately, the image of Africans in US popular culture at the time did not help Harrison or anyone else view Africa in a positive light. For example, African travelogues like Henry Stanley's *How I Found Livingstone* (1890) and

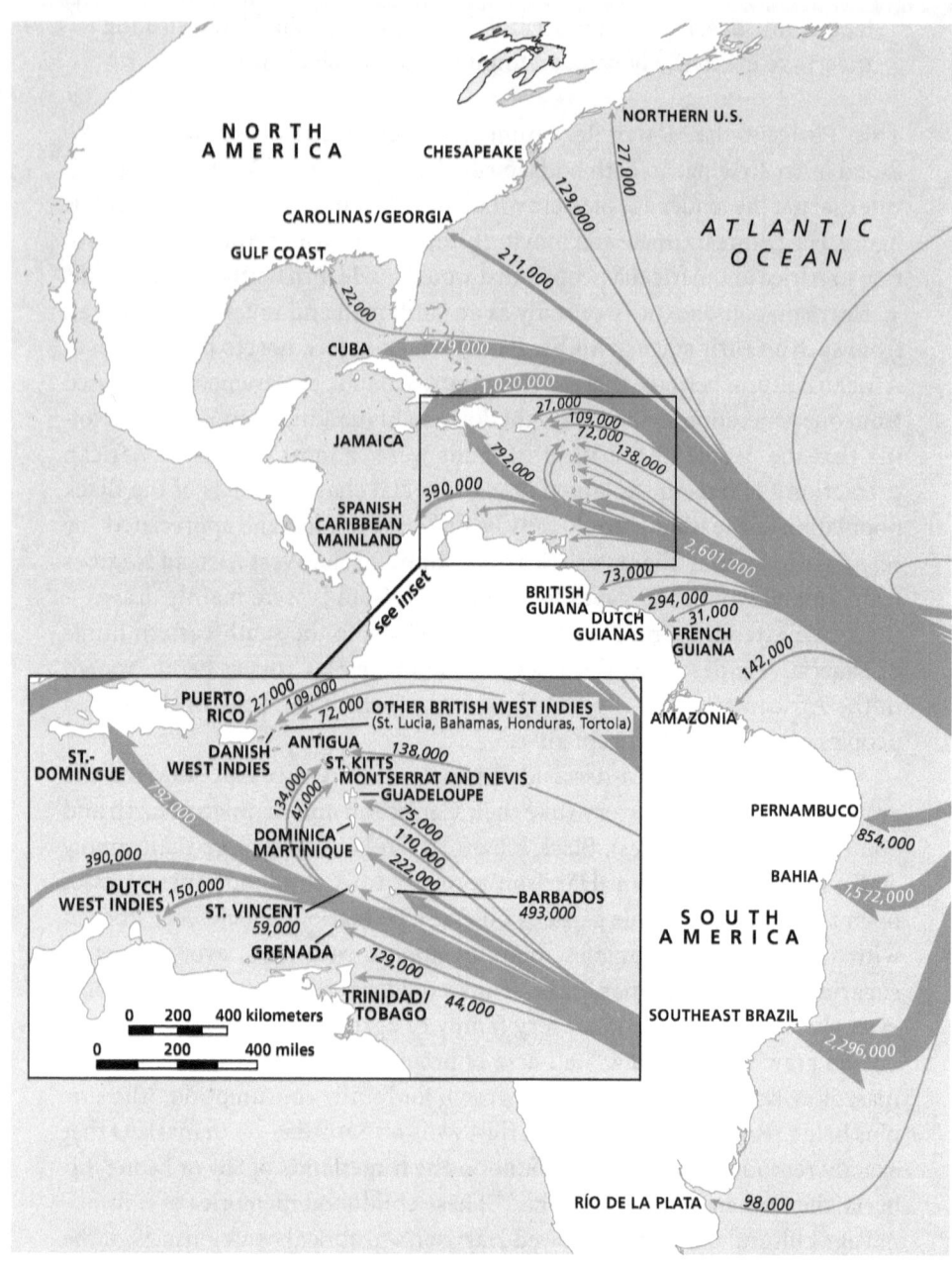

Map 5.1 This map shows the scale and direction of the enslaved human beings who Europeans took out of Africa. Reprinted by permission from Yale University Press.

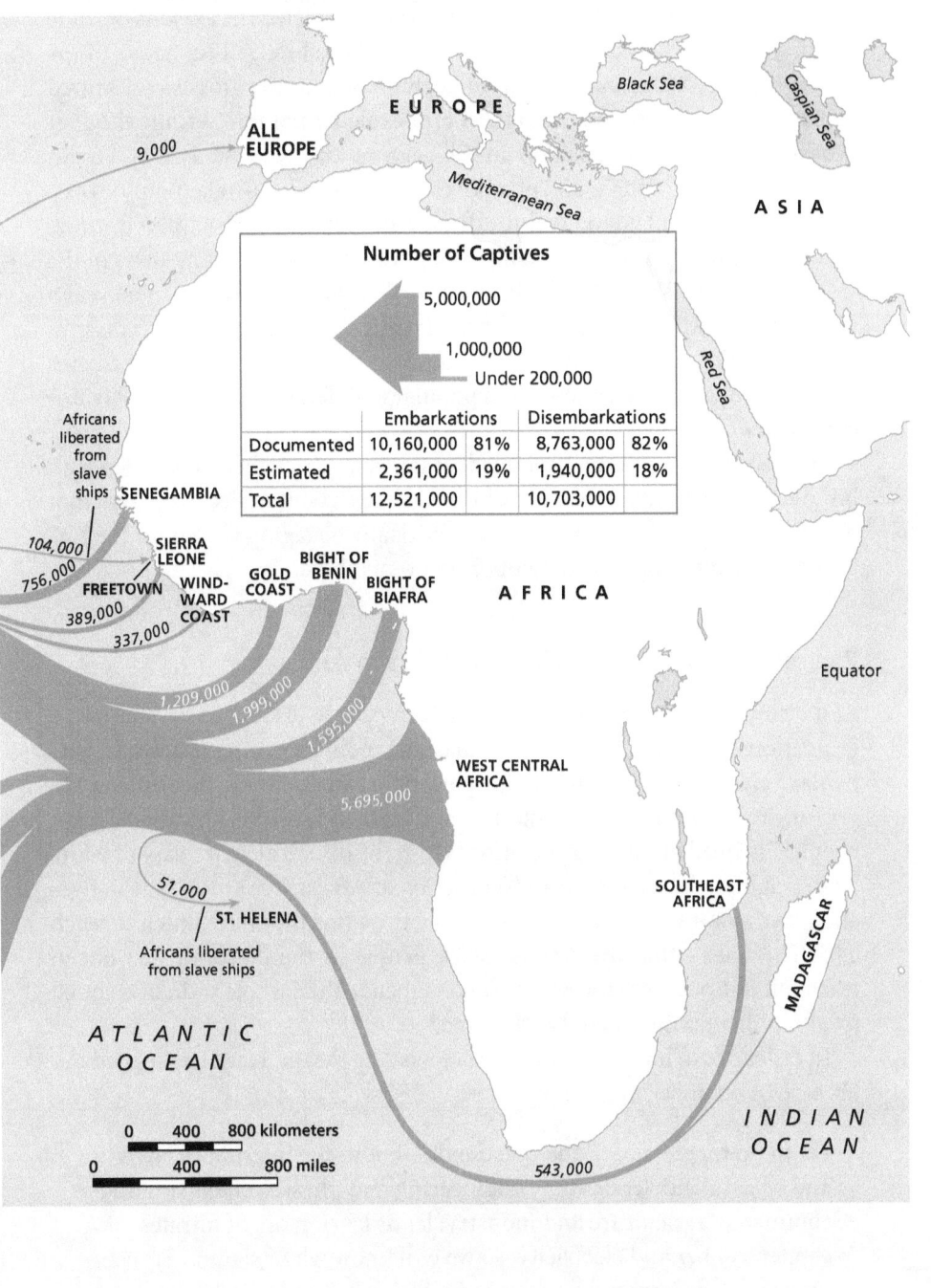

Joseph Conrad's *Heart of Darkness* (1899), which depicted the exploits of white explorers on the "dark" continent, constituted the best-selling books of the day, saturating Western audiences with dehumanizing and grossly caricatured depictions of the African "savage." Large-scale exhibitions—from the 1893 World's Colombian Exposition in Chicago to the 1904 St. Louis World's Fair—featured exhibits with "primitives" and "cannibals" taken out of their African context and put on real-life display. In 1906, one such exhibit featured a Congolese man named Ota Benga alongside chimps and orangutans in the "Monkey House" section of the Bronx Zoo.[4] The fact that the very next year a young, Black, working-class Caribbean immigrant living right next door in Harlem could so forcefully assert a positive African identity underscores Harrison's uncanny rejection of the popular and dehumanizing anti-African caricatures of the day.

Harrison's identity as an "untamed, untamable African" corresponded with his untamed and untamable thirst for knowledge about Africa, which set him down a path of reading, studying, and critically engaging with both the history of the continent and contemporary events there.

Radical Humility: Harrison's Relationship to Africa

As a result of his rigorous studies of African peoples, Harrison crystallized a generational paradigm shift in Afro-diasporic political consciousness. In particular, Harrison broke with the paternalist attitude of the nineteenth century to express a most profound and radical humility toward African people: "Instead of futile expectations from the doubtful generosity of white land-grabbing, let us American Negroes go to Africa, live among the natives and LEARN WHAT THEY HAVE TO TEACH US (for they have much to teach us)." This idea—that the task of Black people in the diaspora was not to teach but to *learn from* the Motherland—upended the whole train of colonial thinking that predominated at the time.[5]

In order not to leave any doubt about what he meant, Harrison spelled out his case in no uncertain terms:

> Let us go there—not in the coastlands—but in the interior, in Nigeria and Nyassaland; let us study engineering and physics, chemistry and commerce, agriculture and industry; let us learn more of nitrates, of copper, rubber and electricity; so we will know why Belgium, France, England and Germany want to be in Africa. Let us begin by studying the scientific world of the African explorers and stop reading and believing the silly slush which ignorant missionaries put into our heads about the alleged degradation of our people in Africa. Let us learn to know Africa

and Africans so well that every educated Negro will be able at a glance to put his hands on the map of Africa and tell where to find the Jolofs, Ekois, Mandigos, Yorubas, Bechuanas, or Basutos and can tell something of their marriage customs, their property laws, their agriculture and systems of worship. For not until we can do this will it be seemly for us to pretend to be anxious about their political welfare.[6]

Harrison's call for humility toward African people rested on a number of cold hard facts that so-called Western civilization had completely disavowed. Africans had sciences and industry of their own. They had their own cultural traditions, agricultural and legal systems, and cosmologies. It was folly for anyone to claim to care about Africans' welfare without first studying African societies on their own terms, rather than through the superiority complex of a "civilizing" mission. Winston James has identified this approach as among "the most distinctive features of Harrison's political thought" for the way it contrasted with the dominant perspective within the mainstream of US intellectual culture, both white and Black as we will soon see.[7]

Harrison did not merely study African peoples but also taught about them. In 1921, for example, Harrison gave a weekly lecture series devoted to African life and customs, African kinship relations, African spirituality, African secret societies, and African systems of government. A concurrent Sunday series featured talks on the "Black Man in History and Civilization," "Egypt and Ethiopia," "The Cradles of Civilization," "One Thousand Years of West African History," "The War of Races in Africa" (on early colonization and the slave trade), and "The Partition of Africa."[8] According to the *Howard University Record*, he gave an inspirational talk at the historically Black institution that "will no doubt lead to much Pan-African thought at the University."[9]

Harrison's emphasis on studying Africa with respect and humility helped spark a wider change in Harlem's African consciousness. Harlem activists like Richard B. Moore recalled how the cultivation of a positive identification with Africa among Black people was commonplace in Harlem because it had been fostered and continuously stimulated by the outdoor soapbox speakers. Because of where he locates Harrison in the wider community of Africa-conscious orators, his account is worth quoting in full. Writing in the Harlem-based *Freedomways* magazine in 1963 at the request of John Henrik Clarke, Moore wistfully recounted how

> freelance advocates such as William Bridges, Strathcona R. Williams, Alexander Rahming, Edgar M. Grey, Arthur Reid, and the Basuto "Prince" Mokete M. Manoedi held forth constantly on African history and stressed unity with the African people. Militant socialists like Chandler Owen, A. Philip Randolph, Rev. George Frazier Miller, Grace P.

Campbell, Anna Brown, Elizabeth Hendrickson, Frank Poree, Otto Huiswoud, W.A. Domingo, Tom Potter, Frank D. Crosswaith, Rudolph Smith, Herman S. Whaley, John Patterson, Victor C. Gaspar, Ramsay, Ross D. Brown, and the writer of this account—all steadily emphasized the liberation of the oppressed African and other colonial peoples as a vital aim of their world view. Above all Hubert H. Harrison gave forth from his encyclopedic store, a wealth of knowledge of African history and culture which brought this consciousness to a very great height.[10]

Moore's account, as a firsthand observer and practitioner of the tradition he describes, remains notable for its authenticity regarding the most memorable Africa-conscious orators in the Harlem of the 1910s and '20s. Moore's reservation of Hubert Harrison for the final and most salutary mention—with an impact "above all" the others—speaks to Harrison's central role in modeling African consciousness and identity for Black people in the diaspora.

In this chapter, we investigate how Harrison turned the mainstream "common sense" about Africa on its head and inspired an extraordinary sense of strength, pride, and world-historic achievement for African people. We also explore Harrison's engagement with some of his contemporaries while contrasting his ideas with the civilizationist assumptions they harbored. We close by exploring Harrison's International Colored Unity League as a grassroots pan-African organization that sought, among other things, a Black nationalist resolution of the land question for African Americans.

Harrison's Case against the "Civilizing" Mission in Africa

> Not only white Westerners, but Black ones also seem to think that Africa is a land of jungles and swamps and that African "natives" wear rings in their noses and cook and eat each other. . . . Yet these misconceptions hurt both the African and the Western Negro, effectively preventing that active goodwill and mutual help which grows out of mutual understanding of each other.
>
> —Itambo Asong [Hubert Harrison], "The West African Woman"

Harrison called on Black people to stop "believing the silly slush which ignorant missionaries put into our heads about the alleged degradation of our people in Africa," an argument that constituted a paradigm shift in consciousness from the paternalism of the civilizationists. According to historian Ibrahim Sundiata, nineteenth-century figures like Martin Delany, Bishop Henry Turner, Booker T. Washington, Alexander Crummell, and Edward Blyden all saw slavery as "providential, even if highly painful."[11] Harrison came to a rather different conclusion: that Euro-Christianity provided a cover for the unspeakable violence of capitalist slavery and colonization. There was nothing superior about European civilization over African civilization and consequently nothing superior about Westernized Africans in the diaspora over Africans on the continent. In this way, he turned on its head the central assumption of most political thinkers—Black and white—who thought that Africans somehow lacked "civilization."

Harrison exposed this civilizationist mindset by demonstrating its utter falsity. If "civilization" meant a stable society with a system of government, laws, industry, and commerce "then the Hausas and Mandingoes, the people of the Ashanti and Dahomey, and the Yorubas of the Gold Coast had and have all these, and they are consequently civilized," wrote Harrison. "So were the Zulus and Bechuanas, the Swazis and Mashonas of South Africa, as well as the Baganda people of Uganda." He pointed out that if civilization means medical knowledge, then groups like the Yoruba and numerous southern African peoples "possess an intelligent knowledge of the pathology of . . . disease and use a variety of efficacious medicines" to treat it. And on the religious test, "not only do Africans believe in Gods, but . . . from the Bobowisi of the Ashanti, the Mawa of Dahomey, the Olorun of the Yoruba, down to the Umkulunkulu of the Zulus, most of them have a more or less clear perception of . . . God." Even by Eurocentric standards of measurement—government, laws, commerce, medicine, religion—continental Africans had their own civilizations.[12]

This raised a simple question: If many civilizations already existed in Africa, then how and why would outsiders attempt to "civilize" Africa? Harrison answered this question by calling the colonizer's bluff: "The real civilization meant by most whites who talk of civilizing Africa is the system which produces profits by taking the land from under the feet of the workers, producing a propertyless, landless proletarian class which must either work (for wages) or starve. Such a class doesn't exist anywhere among black Africans except where white peoples have robbed them of their lands by force."[13] Harrison's description recalls Langston Hughes's poem "Johannesburg Mines":

In the Johannesburg mines
There are 240,000
Native Africans working.
What kind of poem
Would you
Make out of that?
240,000 natives
Working in the
Johannesburg mines.

As we saw in chapter 4 on the white world war, Harrison understood that colonialism was not rooted in European benevolence but the drive of monopoly capital to exploit Black, white, and "colored" labor for profit. For him, the "civilizing" of Africa meant "the establishment of the European system, of 'concessions' for rubber, railroads, factories and mines, whereby the labor of the native population and the new tastes developed in their minds yield enormous revenues to the white people who rule these lands." In other words, *civilization* formed a euphemism for racial capitalism.[14]

This brings us to Harrison's analysis of the role of missionaries in Africa, which offered quite the contrast to the religious zeal that often saturated African American views of Africa. First, Harrison offered some deliciously sardonic questions about why white missionaries didn't work harder to spread Christian values in their own countries, where alcoholism, homelessness, and so many other evils were widespread: "Isn't there still a large jail population in every Christian country? And do not the atheists and agnostics and rationalists exist by the millions at home?" asked the Black freethinker, tongue in cheek. "The legislators like Lloyd George . . . who plunged millions of British Christians into a bath of blood—have the missionaries yet succeeded in teaching them 'the love of Christ, who died to save all men'?" In other words, white Christian missionaries ought to "civilize" their own countries first before worrying about Africans.[15]

Second, Harrison argued that the work of the missionary abroad related that of a soldier—they were both part of a larger institutional machinery: "In the modern European state every institution is used by the dominant class to some end which contributes to the general social purpose of that class." Whether they understood it or not, missionaries played the role of pawns in a larger geopolitical game. In fact, for the missionary to be most effective, "it is better for his masters that he should not see them as his masters. Then he can be quite 'sincere,' earnest and spiritually-minded." Capitalist and imperialist interests lurked behind missionary work, regardless of whether its ground-level functionaries were conscious of it and regardless of their good intentions: "The white missionary's function is to spread that form of religion which will soft-soap the soul of black Africa so that the business of robbing and ruling it shall become less costly and less dangerous to those who do the robbing and the ruling." Missionaries functioned as handmaidens of colonial domination.[16]

Harrison did not directly address the question of Black missionaries. And to their credit, some missionaries did oppose and expose colonial atrocities. For example, the white rulers of South Africa imposed restrictions on the operations of the African Methodist Episcopal Zion Church on the grounds that it threatened colonial stability by fomenting Black nationalism in the country.[17] However, examples like this were the exception to the rule.

Harrison took these ideas—that Africans already had "civilization" before Europeans came, that Western talk of "civilizing" formed an ideological element in the machinery of imperialism, and that Black people in the diaspora would benefit far more from an attitude of humility toward Africans—to their logical political conclusion: African self-determination. In Harrison's words, "The present Negro population of Africa is quite able to work out its own salvation on the spot."[18] This idea represented a conception of "Africa for the Africans"—not as an imperative for Black diasporic emigration or African American "development" or "civilizing" of Africans—but as the idea that continental Africans themselves would be the driving force of their own liberation.

Harrison's stance of respect and humility for Africans marked a position that other Harlem radicals, including Black Marxists and Black (inter)nationalists, shared and would develop even further. Harrison's protégé Cyril Briggs, for example, declared that his *Crusader* magazine stood "for a free Africa, and that without any frills of international control" on the grounds that Africans had governed themselves without white tutelage for millennia since the time of ancient Egypt and Ethiopia.[19] W. A. Domingo would evince a similar commitment to African redemption from within, rather than something "forced upon the Africans from outside."[20]

Arturo Schomburg: A "Unique Negro" Mentor

One of Harrison's key mentors and friends was Arturo Alfonso Schomburg (1874–1938), who he first encountered in spaces like St. Benedict's Church lyceum. Schomburg was born on January 24, 1874, in Puerto Rico to a Black mother from St. Croix and a white immigrant father from Germany. After his studies in Black literature at St. Thomas College, Schomburg's politicization began as an activist in the struggle for Cuban and Puerto Rican independence. He served, for example, as the secretary of Cuban independence fighter Jose Martí's newspaper *Patria*. In 1898, Schomburg left the Cuban and Puerto Rican independence movements due to sectarian infighting and came to identify more strongly with the Black struggle in the Americas and his own African ancestry.

The erudite journalist John E. Bruce (1856–1924) became a kind of surrogate father figure and journalistic influence on Hubert Harrison. Bruce, born enslaved in Maryland, grew up during the Civil War and Reconstruction. He took courses at Howard University, worked with T. Thomas Fortune in the

Afro American League, and founded or edited multiple Black newspapers. He also had African artifacts in his house, including a picture of Afro-Russian national poet Alexander Pushkin, an African spear and battle shield, African masks, and so on. Bruce and Schomburg founded the Negro Society for Historical Research (NSHR) in 1911, bringing African, Caribbean, and African American history buffs into a common research organization for the first time.[21]

Both Schomburg and Bruce were part of masonic fraternal orders, which afforded them greater social networks for developing Africa-centered scholarship. As scholar John S. Wright puts it, "Free African societies and fraternal orders like the Prince Hall Masons . . . provided a counter-conventional intellectual matrix for mastering the secular and sacred freethought traditions of the Radical Enlightenment," offering Black men "secret access to a 'perennial philosophy' that hypothesized an unbroken continuity with, and reverential attitude toward, the esoteric symbol systems and pagan wisdom literatures of ancient North Africa and the Orient."[22] Even Harrison would join the Grand United Order of Odd Fellows and San Manuel Lodge in 1914, perhaps in part due to his intellectual curiosity about Black fraternal orders and their relationship to ancient Kemetic (Egyptian), Islamic, and other African traditions.

Harrison served as the founding secretary of the NSHR, under the tutelage of Schomburg and Bruce.[23] In Harrison's words, they formed the NSHR "to collect and preserve the memorials of Negro achievement, and to diffuse among the descendants of the Africans in this land of their dispersion some knowledge of their nobler past."[24] Above all, Harrison's tenure in the NSHR provided an opportunity for him to get intellectual guidance from his elders regarding the independent study of Black history.[25] The NSHR boasted an impressive roster of corresponding members, including Alain Locke, William Ferris, and W. E. B. Du Bois. It drew the participation of honorary members from places like Barotseland, Liberia, Sierra Leone, Barbados, Cuba, South Africa, Panama, and England. It counted within its ranks various women such as Emma Brown Philly, Marie Du Chatellier, Mary Butler, Florence Bruce, Lillian Urquhart, and Veronica Nickelson.[26]

During the first few years of the NSHR's existence, Harrison had to balance his time there with that he spent on other pursuits, including his work as a full-time organizer in the Socialist Party, but he grew closer to Schomburg as he moved toward a "race first" and "Africa first" political outlook after his departure from the Socialists in 1914. In 1918, for example, Harrison recorded in his diary that he met up with Schomburg at 135th Street and Lenox Avenue and that they "had a long talk on books relating to the Negro and African affairs, lasting till one o'clock. He has a private library which has become famous as the best public or private collection of books on the Negro that there is in the United States. And he has read more widely on Negro History than any man whom I have met."[27]

Indeed, Schomburg developed an unparalleled knowledge of Black history. For example, Schomburg knew that the fables of Aesop were "originally related as folk-lore by a Negro from Aethiopia to the Greeks, who in turn published them."[28] He knew of the pre-Columbian African presence in Panama and Mexico, anticipating the groundbreaking scholarship of Ivan Van Sertima's *They Came before Columbus* (1976).[29] Van Sertima's book combined botanical, metallurgical, linguistic, artistic, cosmological, nautical, archaeological, and European eyewitness evidence to illuminate the extensive African presence in the Americas before Columbus. Yet Schomburg knew of the pre-Columbian Africans in the Western Hemisphere over half a century before Van Sertima's book. Schomburg knew that in North Carolina there were many enslaved Black people who could read and write Arabic. He knew that Black men like Juan Latino, Anton Wilhelm Amo, Jacobus Elisa Johannes Capitein, Francis Williams, and James William Charles Pennington had received degrees in European universities in the sixteenth through nineteenth centuries.

Schomburg wrote passionately about the rich tradition of Black abolitionism as lived through figures like Gustavus Vassa, Julien Raymond, Baron de Vastey, Prince Saunders, Peter Williams, Absalom Jones, Nathaniel Paul, James Varick, Richard Allen, Frederick Douglass, James McCune Smith, William Wells Brown, Martin Delany, and Alexander Crummell.[30] In a *Negro World* piece titled "A Unique Negro," Harrison declared of Schomburg that "for sheer erudition on Negro history and literature he is unrivalled."[31]

Schomburg had a profound critique of mainstream US history's omission of Black people. Part of his argument for having a "chair of Negro history" was that "the white institutions have their chair of history," which grounded them in "the history of their people and whenever the Negro is mentioned in the textbooks it dwindles down to a foot note." Speaking at a summertime class for teachers, Schomburg gave examples from the American Revolution: "The white scholar's mind and heart is fired, because in the temple of learning he is told how on the 5th of March, 1770, the Americans were able to beat the English; but to find Crispus [Attucks], it is necessary to go deep into special books." Attucks, a man of mixed African and Wampanoag descent, became the "first American" to die for the American Revolution. "In the orations delivered at Bunker Hill, Daniel Webster never mentioned the Negroes having done anything, and is silent about Peter Salem," lamented Schomburg. Salem became a hero at the Battle of Bunker Hill, fighting the British with some twelve other Black troops in that iconic battle of the American Revolution. "In the account of the battle of Long Island City and around

New York under Major-General Nathaniel Greene," he continued, "no mention is made of the 800 Negro soldiers who periled their lives in the Revolutionary war." As Schomburg put it, "cases can be shown right and left of the palpable omissions" of Black people from white historical narratives.

Schomburg wondered aloud, "Where is our history . . . and our chair of Negro History to teach our people our own history? We are at the mercy of the 'flotsam and jetsam' of the white writers." As he saw it, "we need in the coming dawn the man, who will give us the background for our future, it matters not whether he comes from the cloisters of the university or from the rank and file of the fields." Though cast in masculinist language, his explicit openness to a scholar "from the rank and file of the fields" revealed a striking reflection of his own independent and self-taught intellectual attainments. In Schomburg's words, "We need the historian and philosopher to give us, with trenchant pen, the story of our forefathers and let our shoulder and body, with phosphorescent light, brighten the chasm that separates us. And we should cling to them just as 'blood is thicker than water.'" Thanks to the urging of Harrison and others, Schomburg wrote a powerful article, "The Negro Digs Up His Past," which had a profound influence on a young John Henrik Clarke's decision to move from his humble roots in Union Springs, Alabama, to Harlem in order to study and eventually master African world history, effectively answering Schomburg's wistful incantation.[32]

Schomburg advocated for the study of Black history as part of racial pride and self-love, self-determination, and affirmation, not to mention as an antidote to noxious notions of European superiority. Therefore, he wrote, "we must research diligently the annals of time and bring back from obscurity the dormant examples of [our] agriculture, industry and commerce, upon these the arts and sciences and make common the battle ground of our heritage."[33]

Harrison's estimation of Schomburg's intellectual prowess only grew as the two became closer. Apportioning humility where humility was due, Harrison admitted frankly, "I pride myself on knowing something of Negro history and literature and of the books treating of those subjects; but I unhesitatingly declare that Schomburg's knowledge on these points must be at least eight or ten times as extensive as my own." Such a declaration meant a lot coming from Hubert Harrison, given his own addiction to reading and learning about African peoples. Yet whereas Harrison read widely in an eclectic range of subjects like English literature, sexology, geopolitics, sociology, theological criticism, and economics, Schomburg maintained a singular, laser-like focus on books and knowledge by and about people of African descent.[34]

Schomburg harbored an aversion to writing, apparently because of his self-consciousness about lacking the fluency of a native English speaker.

Harrison, himself no stranger to the pen, strongly encouraged Schomburg to write, declaring in Marcus Garvey's *Negro World* that if Schomburg "would but write as he reads" then "when the sun of the New Negro shall be shining in the zenith of its glory yet to come, [Schomburg's] name would be hailed with acclaim as that of the first great historiographer of the Africans of the dispersion."[35]

Harrison's closeness to Schomburg positioned him for the momentous project of moving Schomburg's personal library from Brooklyn to Harlem. In 1924–25, Harrison served on the committee (alongside the NAACP organizer James Weldon Johnson and Black businessman and NAACP officer John E. Nail) that planned and oversaw the transfer of Schomburg's vast collection into the holdings of the 135th Street Harlem branch of the New York Public Library. Since then, the collection has grown into an international pan-African research mecca of its own. Indeed, the Schomburg Centre for Research in Black Culture remains to this day one of the top research institutions in the world for Black and Africana studies.[36]

Harrison's friendship and association with figures like Schomburg and the NSHR offers a glimpse into the intellectual world that shaped his cultivation of an Africana epistemology. He engaged with the work of the wider community of Black and Africa-conscious scholars like W. E. B. Du Bois, George Wells Parker (author of *The African Origin of the Grecian Civilization* and *Children of the Sun*), Benjamin Brawley of Morehouse College, William Leo Hansberry of Howard University, Carter G. Woodson (founder of the groundbreaking *Journal of Negro History* and the Association for the Study of Negro Life and History), independent journalist and historian J. A. Rogers, Drusilla Dunjee Houston (Oklahoma-based author of *Wonderful Ethiopians of the Ancient Cushite Empire*), the pioneering Black biologist Ernest Just, and Monroe Work (author of the *Negro Year Book* at the Tuskegee Institute).[37] Engaging with figures such as these placed Harrison in a community of cutting-edge Black scholars who, like him, sought to restore African history and elaborate a body of knowledge and information empowering to Black people beyond the limits of what the white academy would allow.

Whitewashing Civilization's Black Beginnings

> History is a clock that people use to tell their political and cultural time of day. It is also a compass that people use to find themselves on the map of human geography. History tells a people where they've been and what they've been, where they are and what they are. Most important, it tells a people where they still must go, what they still must be.
>
> —John Henrik Clarke, "A Great and Mighty Walk"

> To control a people you must first control what they think about themselves and how they regard their history and culture. And when your conqueror makes you ashamed of your history and your culture, he needs no prison walls and no chains to hold you.
>
> —John Henrik Clarke, "Why Africana History?"

John Henrik Clarke emerged as one of the finest examples of the Africa-centered Black scholarly tradition in Harlem. It emerged from figures like Schomburg, J. A. Rogers, and Hubert Harrison's studies of ancient African history. Harrison, for example, talks on what he called "civilization's Black beginnings." Following a tradition of Black scholarship going back at least to the nineteenth century, Harrison pointed to European sources regarding the Egyptian influence on ancient Greece, which had been taken to represent the origin of so-called Western civilization. For example, he advocated reading the second book of Herodotus, the so-called father of history. For Harrison, the significance of the Greek historian's book was that Herodotus reported "that many of the Egyptians were black and all of them were dark; that the Greeks derived their art and science and religion from them; that the black Ethiopians gave civilization to Egypt and often reigned and ruled over them." Harrison pointed out other Greeks who acknowledged ancient Greece's debt to Egypt, including Plato, Aristotle, Pythagoras, and Diodorus. Furthermore, because Egypt influenced the Greeks, the Greeks influenced the Romans, and the Romans influenced European civilizations writ large, the origin of Western civilization was not European but African, not "white" but "Black."[38]

Harrison distilled this argument about the African origins of Western civilization into concise language:

> Down the dim dusk of the ages the man from Africa appears as the burden-bearer of Western civilization. Long ago, while yet the world was wrapped in ignorance and savagery, he laid in ancient Ethiopia the sure foundations of Egyptian culture, as Egypt's own sons have confessed; and later, by the lotus-laden waters of old Nile, he mingled his blood and brain in the mightiest edifice of social craftsmanship and culture that the world has seen for six thousand years. There, as the Father of History [Herodotus] has told us, did white Greece come to learn letters and law, religion and art, science and philosophy; to light her torch of culture at the resplendent blaze built by the black and brown children of the land of Kham, and from this torch to kindle the fire of civilization upon the altars of barbarian Rome, whence sottish Saxon and brute German, wild Celt and wandering Goth have taken tribute of light and heat to warm themselves and enlighten the world of the present.[39]

In other words, ancient Ethiopia and Kemet formed the foundations of Greek, and by extension Roman, and by extension so-called Western "civilization." His mention of the land of "Kham" refers to the biblical myth about the Africans as the cursed "sons of Ham," and his inversion of Rome as a "barbarian" influence on the sottish/brute/wild/wandering Europeans conveys a deliciously anti-imperialist assault on the white supremacist notion of civilization beginning with "white" or European people.

Harrison's juxtaposition of African achievements with European deficiencies revealed his biting and comical wit in making historical arguments with earth-shattering implications for white supremacist ideology. "From the days before Christ walked in Galilee," wrote Harrison, Black people "within the lordly sweep of the Niger were building city-states in Benin and Yoruba, in Sokoto, Kanem and Timbuktu."[40]

Harrison's mention of Timbuktu evokes the grandeur of ancient Mali. In the fourteenth century, the city of Timbuktu had 115,000 people, with some 25,000 in the Sankore university, where Islamic scholars from all over Africa went to study. (London, at that time had a total population of 20,000 people.) One of Mali's rulers, the Muslim king Mansa Musa, had amassed some $400 billion (in modern US dollars) worth of gold, making him the richest person in the world. When the massive caravan for his pilgrimage to Mecca (*hajj*) arrived in Cairo, the Islamic scholar Ibn Fadl Allah al-Omari famously described how Mansa Musa spent and gave away so much gold that it sparked an inflation that destabilized the city's economy for over a decade following the historic visit.[41]

These West African city-state formations, "expanded by conquest, commerce, and culture, developed into the twofold empire of the Mellestine Songhay and Ghana, which from the sixth to the sixteenth century, over a territory as vast as two-thirds of the present United States, maintained agriculture and the industrial arts, commerce and science, while semi-savage Europe was burning witches, eating food with its fingers, and touching for the King's evil." In short, prior to the sixteenth century, West African civilization, scholarly knowledge, and technological development had progressed far in advance of Europe.

As a reflection of white supremacy, the mainstream intellectual consensus in the West held that historically Europeans were always and already more advanced and developed than Africans. "But there is Egypt," countered Harrison. "And in the presence of her mighty pyramids and temples that have outstared the suns of sixty centuries we may reject with cold contempt the prejudiced conjectures of a race whose religion is a lie, whose democracy is a sham and whose accomplishments have all been made in the latest half-hour registered upon the face of the great clock of time." Pointing out the relatively

Figure 5.1 The Egyptian pyramids at Giza. Wikimedia Commons.

recent emergence of European civilization (as compared to African civilization) stood the mainstream white consensus on its head.

Like Africa-conscious thinkers before and after him, Harrison thus challenged the dominant Eurocentric view of history, according to which stale pale males like Socrates, Plato, and Aristotle constituted the "founding fathers" of Western philosophy—and by extension "civilization" itself.⁴² Harrison argued that modern global power relations created the motive for rewriting history in a Eurocentric manner. In his words, "The white race has lied and strutted its way to greatness and prominence over the corpses of other peoples. It has capitalized, Christianized, and made respectable, 'scientific,' and 'natural,' the fact of its dominion." "It has read back into history the race relations of today," he declaimed, "striving to make the point that previous to its advent on the stage of human history, there was no civilization or culture worthy of the name."⁴³

In this way, Harrison stood in a longer tradition of Black thinkers who rejected European arguments that ancient Kemet/Egypt was not a Black or African civilization. In 1887 Frederick Douglass, for example, observed how "it has been the fashion of [white] American writers to deny that Egyptians were Negroes and claim that they are of the same race as themselves. This has, I have no doubt, been largely due to a wish to deprive the Negro of the moral support of ancient greatness and to appropriate the same to the White race."⁴⁴ Forty years later, Harrison could make the same observation, noting that "today it is necessary to pretend that the ancient Ethiopians (whose very name means 'black-faced') and Egyptians were 'white' as well as the black Fulani, since otherwise geometry, architecture, astronomy, medicine, iron-smelting and religion would have to be credited to people who would be forced in our country to ride in 'Jim Crow' cars."[45] Anti-Black racism, thanks to centuries of racial slavery, formed a foundational element of the modern world. Therefore, Europeans had to distort and falsify the historical record to make it appear that the ancient Egyptians were not Black or even African people.[46]

Besides Egypt, Harrison offered various other ancient African civilizations to obliterate the commonplace notion of Black racial inferiority and supposed lack of any meaningful history. For example, he spoke about Carthage, the ancient North African metropolis with "seven-story houses, central heating systems, electors, theatre programs, sports, cheer-leaders, marbles, checkers, eye-glasses, bills of exchange, bankers and a banking system, and cross-word puzzles."[47] He spoke about Great Zimbabwe and how the structures, ruined temples, and residences there testified to the existence of a Black African people who lived in a highly sophisticated society.[48] By unearthing African civilizations that exceeded their contemporary European counterparts in sophistication, he turned the tables on the dominant Eurocentric view of African history. And, as was his wont, he backed up his claims with evidence culled from European explorers, historians, and archaeologists like Constantin-François de Chassebœuf, the comte de Volney; Heinrich Schliemann; Albert Felix Dubois; Dr. Heinrich Barth; Byron Khun de Prorok; and Flora "Lady Lugard" Shaw.[49]

Harrison's talks on Africa blew people's minds. A report on his 1920 speech at the Women's Christian Alliance Hall in Philadelphia, for example, noted how Harrison "showed his exhaustive knowledge of his race's history, and the relation in which Egypt stood to Greece in the days of Aeschylus and Herodotus, the father of history. . . . These lectures are intended to dispel the delusion and darkness from the minds of our people regarding Africa and the Africans."[50]

Harrison's Contemporary African Studies

Harrison studied not only African history but also contemporary African life and politics. He did not simply preach about learning from Africans. He actively sought out African thinkers and ideas. For example, he went to hear Sierra Leonean educational reformer Adelaide Smith Casely-Hayford lecture on the subject of women in West Africa.[51] He read African newspapers like *The Lagos Weekly Record* of Nigeria, *The Gold Coast Independent* of the Gold Coast, and *The African Telegraph* of South Africa.

As editor of *The New Negro* in 1919, Harrison had reprinted articles from the likes of Kobina Sekyi, the Gold Coast nationalist lawyer and leader of the National Congress of British West Africa. In one such article titled

"Education in West Africa," Sekyi excoriated the impact of Westernized education on Indigenous Africans. In Sekyi's view, the colonizer designed mission and trade "education" to produce clerks, many of whom grew up to be wealthy traders. Wealthy native traders then sent their children to Europe to be trained on European lines, a few of the latter embracing European professions such as law, medicine, and engineering. "Missionaries and traders worked in concert to establish 'education,'" decried Sekyi, "and this in the end almost succeeded in breaking up the social life of the people among whom they moved: the former destroyed the ultimate religious sanctions which regulated their civil life, and the latter opened up new vistas and afforded new examples of duplicity and cunning."

Sekyi decried the role of Western education and indoctrination in destroying Indigenous African knowledge. The formation of a new "educated" class of Africans led to further agreements and treaties with European mercantile and government officials. Sekyi noted how when "education" flourished there were some splendid intellectual men, "the equals, and often the superiors, of those who taught them." But he lamented how at the same time, "the native point of view was ceasing to be. Things native began to be regarded as savage by the natives themselves. The Mission Schools, now subsidized by the Government, together with the newer Government schools, disseminated 'education.' All classes sent their children to the schools to be 'educated.' The insignia of 'education,' European clothing, European habits of life and thought, began to settle in the land, each succeeding generation being more Europeanized than the preceding." Sekyi thus analyzed how Western education buttressed the colonization of Africa, laying the basis for the neocolonialism of postindependence African leaders by training a class of thoroughly Europeanized Africans.[52]

Harrison regarded activists and thinkers from the Gold Coast (modern Ghana) like Kobina Sekyi, J. E. Casely Hayford, and John Mensah Sarbah as the "tiptop of Negro intellect, enterprise, and achievement." They founded the protonationalist Aborigines' Rights Protection Society to challenge the British colonial government in the Gold Coast.[53] He subscribed to and reprinted articles from publications like Dusé Mohamed Ali's London-based *African Times and Orient Review*, for which Harrison's "father in journalism" John E. Bruce had served as a distributor. Harrison also greatly respected the work of political and intellectual figures like John Tengo Jabavu, editor of the first Xhosa-language newspaper, and Solomon Tshekisho Plaatje, the first general secretary of the South African Native National Congress (which would become the ANC) in South Africa. Not to mention Ernest Samuel Beoku-Betts, a popular jurist and politician in Sierra Leone.[54]

Harrison did not merely read books about Africa but also wrote reviews of them. As we noted in chapter 3 on Harrison's outdoor speaking, his regular book review column in Garvey's *Negro World* broke ground as the first of its kind for a Black newspaper. For example, Harrison noted that George W. Ellis's book *Negro Culture in West Africa* detailed the lives of the Vai people of Liberia and their "domestic industries and arts, successful social institutions and a system of writing—the Vai syllabic system—invented by themselves." He commented on *In the Shadow of the Bush* by P. A. Talbot, about the Ekoi people of northern Nigeria, and how the book documented their religion, agriculture, industrial arts, science, law, philosophy, and culture, "their method of telling news by drum-tap code, [and] their secret hieroglyphic language called Nsibidi." Harrison spoke of *A Transformed Colony* by T. J. Alldridge about Sierra Leone, "which includes Sherbro island in which are found the curious soap-stone images called *nomolis* carved by the hands of black sculptors thousands of years ago." For understanding the Congo, Harrison recommended fellow freethinker Sir Arthur Conan Doyle's *Crime of the Congo* and E. D. Morel's books *King Leopold's Rule in the Congo* and *The Black Man's Burden*.[55]

Harrison's book reviews engaged critically with the content and perspective of the books he read. A case study and clear example of this can be seen in his review of *The Black Man's Burden* by E. D. Morel, the British journalist who founded the Congo Reform Association to publicize the atrocities in King Leopold's Congo Free State. In one of the most savage bouts of wanton colonial destruction of human life in modern history, the Belgian monarchy of King Leopold II presided over the mass murder of some 10 million Congolese people.[56]

Harrison appreciated how Morel's books spoke plainly about the brutal facts of colonial rule because Harrison himself did not mince words when attacking colonial violence. Analyzing Morel's treatment of the British acquisition of Rhodesia, the "atrocious butcheries" of Queen Victoria's "responsible" government, Lothar von Trotha's German conquest of the Herero people in Namibia, the Belgian king Leopold II's mass slaughter in the Congo, France's taking of Morocco and the French Congo, Italy's attack on Tripoli, and the Portuguese raids on Angola and the Cocoa Islands, Harrison asked poignantly, "What then, must black people conclude, is the collective character of white Christians? The facts here given as a small slice of their imperialistic record show them to be crooked and contemptible liars, cold-blooded bandits and canting, psalm-singing hypocrites."[57]

Harrison also endorsed Morel's analysis of the propaganda dimension of inter-imperialist rivalry among the colonial powers in Africa: "If the

English-speaking public still thinks of Belgium's Congo as the supreme atrocity, it must be remembered . . . that England [with] its cable monopoly, controlled the news of the world and Belgium did not. The English (and Americans) could, therefore, 'play up' the Congo atrocities to a gasping world while the Belgians couldn't 'play up' [the atrocities of Britain]." The propaganda battle for "hearts and minds" represented an important factor in the ability of a given imperial power to advance its interests against its rivals. He quoted approvingly Morel's contention that "each one of the imperialist groups can be perfectly trusted to tell the full and complete *truth about the other*" and therefore only "by collating these several national truths we can get the entire international story."[58]

While approving of Morel's honesty about colonial atrocities and propaganda, Harrison criticized Morel's white liberal framework. Morel denounced colonial atrocities not to hasten the end of colonialism but to advocate a more "humane and practical" version of white rule over Black Africans: "As long as the African can furnish fit scope for Mr. Morel's sympathies as an object of compassion so long and so far is Mr. Morel his champion and defender. But he refuses to rise above that philanthropic role and consider the black race as humanly the equal of his race in rights or as an independent shaper of its own destiny."[59] Despite this critique of Morel's white-saviorist assumptions, Harrison suggested that Black people seek out the book anyway because it supplied so many of "the facts on which we rest our case against the white man's domination of our motherland."[60]

African American Views of Africa in Harrison's Day

> The intellectual pursuits of white men on the whole are limited by their racial interests [such that] most of them . . . know next to nothing of Africa except in the popular sense of its being a "dark" continent whose only worthwhile affairs are sufficiently comprehended in the missionary and commercial exploits of white intruders. But this is just as true of the vast majority of Negroes on this side—even the intelligent and well-informed ones, and until Negro editors, lawyers, ministers, and teachers know the facts, at least, about Africa and the Africans we should not expect white editors, lawyers, ministers and teachers to know them.
>
> —Hubert Harrison, "Books about Africa"

Unfortunately, Harrison was right. As the "scramble for Africa" unfolded in the late nineteenth century, the overwhelming consensus among white people was that Africans (and other nonwhite peoples) were backward savages who needed to be Christianized and "civilized" by colonial rule. Rudyard Kipling's famous 1899 poem "The White Man's Burden" gave expression to this sentiment by referring to colonized peoples as "half-devil and half-child."⁶¹ As the white British arch-colonialist Cecil Rhodes put it in his *Confession of Faith*, "I contend that we are the finest race in the world and that the more of the world we inhabit the better it is for the human race."⁶² These racial views of European superiority were legitimized by the white science of the academy, especially in disciplines like anthropology and ethnology, which were intimately connected with the colonial project.⁶³

While white people generally thought Africans to be inferior beings, many of the leading African American figures in the late nineteenth and early twentieth centuries also held problematic views regarding Africa and European colonialism. Often, the most prominent African American opinion shapers maintained a superiority complex of their own, following the nineteenth-century Black nationalists and emigrationists who felt that Africans needed to be "civilized" and Christianized from without.⁶⁴ In so doing they demonstrated a contradictory relationship with Western imperialism: even when they cast Africa in a positive light or criticized white domination, they simultaneously maintained a superiority complex regarding the "uncivilized" natives of Africa.⁶⁵ As historian Kevin Gaines has suggested, middle-class preoccupations with racial uplift ideology—as a strategy for achieving Black respectability and worthiness of full citizenship—ultimately hampered consistent African American criticism of colonial domination by reenforcing the civilizationist ideological framework of the colonizer.⁶⁶ The distinctiveness of Harrison's contrasting position of radical humility, with which we began this chapter, radiates most clearly in light of the views on Africa of his most prominent African Americans contemporaries.

The emigrationist tendency among Black nationalists of the nineteenth century rested on an identification with the African continent in order to teach rather than learn from Africans. The great abolitionist minister Alexander Crummell, for example, wrote that the continent had "millions of torpid and benighted souls" representing "the power of the devil in his strongholds," and therefore the task of the "sons of Africa" in the United States was to "usher therein light, knowledge, [and] blessedness" because "the Gospel *must* be preached in all the world. The Master commands it . . . and that man must be demented who cannot see God's beneficent providence in colonization."⁶⁷

Even Martin Delany, though freed somewhat from the evangelical zeal of a missionary like Crummell, still saw Christianity as "the most advanced civilization that man ever attained" and spoke of "Africa for the African race, and Black men to rule them" on the assumption that only a "new element" (i.e., advanced and intelligent African Americans) could foster industrial development in Africa and other such "well-regulated pursuits of civilized life" that "the natives" lacked.⁶⁸ Therefore, although Delany ranked among the most advanced of the nineteenth-century Black nationalist thinkers, he and his generation still largely maintained a superiority complex toward continental Africans.

The trailblazing journalist and "race man" T. Thomas Fortune wrote several fiery editorials in the 1880s denouncing European imperialism in Africa. On the other hand, Fortune based his opposition to emigration on the notion that "Africa is a country without an organized government, an accepted religion, and a uniform language," and at the end of the day, "civilized men don't abandon organized government for chaos."⁶⁹

In a similarly contradictory manner, the great antilynching crusader Ida B. Wells spoke, on the one hand, about Africa's relationship to African Americans as the "the land of their forefathers, the most fertile of its kind, and the only one which the rapacious and ubiquitous Anglo-Saxon has not entirely gobbled." Yet, in the very same breath, she also spoke of Africans as "simple natives" and enthused about the possibility that enterprising middle-class Black Americans could bring "capital, skilled labor, and intelligent direction" to Liberia, much like the "Romans who invaded Britain" or the "Puritans who came over in the 'Mayflower'" and gave the world "the greatest country of the age."⁷⁰ Wells thus likened the potential role African Americans could play in Africa to that which the British colonists had played in Massachusetts—without apparently recognizing the rapaciousness of the colonial unsettlers' destruction of the *Massachusett* people, among so many other Indigenous peoples destroyed by the consolidation and expansion of the white unsettler colony. Views about Africa and Western colonialism professed by other notable Black women activists like Nannie Burroughs, Frances Ellen Watkins Harper, and Pauline Hopkins revealed similar contradictions to those of Fortune and Wells.⁷¹

The most prominent African American at the turn of the twentieth century, Booker T. Washington, proved utterly reactionary on African affairs. For example, Washington collaborated in Togoland with German colonizers who saw his brand of industrial education as well suited to stabilize white rule over African cotton plantations on the model of the Jim Crow South. Predictably, this colonial project distorted local ethnic identities by racializing all Togolese as *negre* (Black), imposed forced taxation, destroyed local industries, introduced pass laws, and wrought severe economic and land dispossession. When the Togolese resisted forcefully in the southern city of Tove in 1895, military officers led by Hans Gruner undertook a scorched-earth campaign that included cutting off heads of the Ewe people and sending such battlefield "trophies" back home to anthropologists in Germany. Upon their arrival, Booker T. Washington's subordinates worked diligently under the very same Hans Gruner and were housed in the very huts that the Ewe left vacant after fleeing the German reign of terror.[72]

In their South West African colony, the Germans built concentration camps and labor camps in order to torture Africans, perform eugenics experiments on them, and work them to death for the benefit of German capital.[73] Even after the Germans committed the "first genocide of the twentieth century" against the Herero and Nama peoples in what is now Namibia,[74] Booker T. Washington went so far as to declare, "I have followed with great care the policies and plans according to which the German officials have dealt with the natives of Africa. Their work succeeds by these means in a wholesome and constructive manner. They do not seek to repress the Africans, but rather to help them that they may be more useful to themselves and to the German people. Their manner of handling Negroes in Africa might be taken as a pattern for other nations." By such shameless celebration of colonial genocide, it is perhaps no wonder that Tuskegee Institute representatives collaborated with European colonizers in other places like Sudan and South Africa on the grounds that they were helping to "civilize" backward Africans with Christian uplift, hard work, and Western consumerism.[75]

Some scholars have argued that Washington's approach to Africans offered something different to (and more positive than) his accommodationist approach to African Americans. Manning Marable, for example, argued that Washington's philosophy "helped to create a nationalistic, proud and dynamic elite" in South Africa.[76] Indeed, Washington's approach resonated with some of his counterparts among the enterprising, Western-educated, middle-class Black people who chafed at their exclusion from the colonial state apparatus following the unification of the Republic of South Africa. And Washington did receive words of praise from pan-African nationalists like Edward Wilmot Blyden, J. E. Casely Hayford, and Dusé Mohamed Ali.[77]

However, the notion of Booker Washington as a secret or closeted African nationalist overlooks the enthusiasm for his project from colonial powers like Germany and Britain, who both saw the utility of the Tuskegee model of industrial education for stabilizing white rule over Black Africans.[78] True, Washington did join E. D. Morel's Congo Reform Association and lobby the US government against Belgian atrocities in the Congo. But he also collaborated with the German and British colonialisms that sought out and deployed the Tuskegee model of industrial education as a stabilizer of colonial rule. In other words, he criticized colonialism not just selectively but in a way that targeted the colonial power (Belgium) that formed an imperial rival to Britain and Germany in Africa. Washington thus dutifully adapted his global political outlook to fit in line with that of his white capitalist financial sponsors. In the realm of foreign policy, Washington thus appeared "as in a tailor's mirror, from new angles but in the usual posture," as his biographer Louis Harlan put it.[79]

W. E. B. Du Bois initially revealed an attitude toward continental Africans that sprang from similarly civilizationist assumptions. Although he incisively analyzed the racial politics of imperialism before the World War I and called for extending democracy to the "yellow, brown, and black peoples" of the world, he also maintained that "we must train the native races in modern civilization." To his credit, Du Bois played a key role as an architect of the Pan-African Congress movement that had been gathering steam since the nineteenth century. However, during the Paris Peace Conference in 1919, Du Bois still pushed for Belgian, German, and Portuguese colonies to be administered by an international governing commission, which "must represent not simply the white world, but the civilized Negro world." Certainly his call on the imperial powers to draw up a code of law for the protection of educational, economic, and political rights of the "natives of Africa" was well-intentioned. But by implying that African people were "uncivilized," Du Bois reinforced the same framework propagated by white colonizers to justify and perpetuate their domination. Implicit in his attitude was the elitist notion that the same "talented tenth" that was fit to lead Black Americans was, by extension, fit to lead Black Africans. Du Bois, in other words, aimed for a kinder, gentler, and African American–inclusive civilizing mission for the African "natives" in the period following the end of the white world war.[80]

Harrison, by contrast, maintained a more sober view about the powerlessness of Western Black people like Du Bois to administer African territories: "We may read in headlines the startling item 'Negroes Ask for German Colonies,' but Negroes of sense should not be deluded. They will not get them because they have no battleships, no guns, no force, military or financial. They are not a Power." Asking for Black participation in the running of African colonies was utopian, given that they had no force with which to claim or maintain them: "The King-word of modern nations is POWER.... The secret of England's greatness (as well as of any other great nation's) is not Bibles but bayonets—bayonets, business and brains.... So long as the lands of Africa can yield billions of business, so long will white brains use bayonets to keep them." Control of Africa rested not on morality but on militarism.[81]

To his credit, Du Bois evolved in his views over time. In retrospect, he acknowledged his naivete when recalling how at the Pan-African Congress of 1919, "we were ... weak and ineffective amateurs chipping at a hard conglomeration of problems."[82] In 1922, three years after he first began his work to organize pan-African congresses, Du Bois wrote that he no longer thought "that Africa should be administered by West Indians or American Negroes." In fact, "they have no more right to administer Africa for the native Africans than native Africans have to administer America."[83] In this way he came to evolve from his civilizationist position toward a more Harrison-like humility toward African people. Indeed, Du Bois became increasingly radical over time, eventually repudiating the focus on a "talented tenth" in favor of leadership by working-class people as he came to identify more strongly with the ideas of Karl Marx and the Communist commitment to the emancipation of labor from capitalism.

Even Africa-centered leaders in Marcus Garvey's Universal Negro Improvement Association and African Communities League (UNIA) demonstrated quite paternalistic attitudes toward African peoples, at least initially. For example, Garvey adopted Martin Delany's slogan of "Africa for the Africans!" which in Garvey's vision, just like Delany's, implied sovereign rule or administration of a continental African territory by more "advanced" Black people of the diaspora. Similarly, the fourth item in the list of the UNIA's official objectives was "to assist in civilizing the backward tribes of Africa." This call to "civilize the backward tribes" simply echoed the rhetoric that white imperialists used to conquer and dominate Africa. That the UNIA also officially sought "to promote a conscientious spiritual worship among the native tribes of Africa" implied that Indigenous Africans had no worthwhile conscientious spiritual traditions of their own. Much like Du Bois, Garvey cabled British foreign secretary Lord Balfour in 1918 to communicate the UNIA's postwar peace demand that "the captured German colonies in Africa be turned over to the natives with educated Western and Eastern Negroes as their leaders."[84]

Meanwhile, Garvey's declaration of himself as the "Provisional President of Africa" rankled some continental Africans who, like Harrison, chafed at this reductionist and monolithic conception of "Africa as a country" wherein the agency and authority of elders, chiefs, and leaders of the Akan, Yoruba, Zulu, Kikuyu, Luhya, and all other African peoples were to be superseded by a Jamaican who had never set foot on the continent.[85] Garvey once asked, "Why should not Africa give to the world its black Rockefeller, Rothschild, and Henry Ford?"[86] In response to Garvey's aspiration to build a Black empire of capital in the African world, class-conscious Black Harlem Socialists like Frank Crosswaith foresaw how "with Africa as our Empire, there will still be ragged, underfed, and poverty-stricken Negroes. All that we will have done will be to have exchanged our white parasites and profiteers for black parasites and black profiteers."[87] Sound familiar? It would prove an astute prediction for 1920 in light of the Black neocolonial parasites and profiteers that would come to replace the white colonizers in Africa a half century later.

Marcus Garvey's second wife, Amy Jacques Garvey, offers another example of the problematic orientation of some Africa-centered Black leaders towards African people. To her credit, Amy Jacques played a key role in the Garvey movement by working as Marcus Garvey's secretary, compiling and publishing *The Philosophy and Opinions of Marcus Garvey*, serving as an associate editor of the *Negro World*, establishing the paper's "Our Women and What They Think" column, and laboring tirelessly to get her husband released from prison.[88] According to historian Tony Martin, she "ran the organization almost single-handedly when Garvey was either imprisoned or otherwise unavailable."[89] Regarding Africa, however, her views did not—initially at least—go beyond "commonsense" colonial paternalism. In 1924, for example, she argued that because white missionaries were hypocritical, Africa needed Black missionaries who could teach Africans "how to live progressive lives on earth" and transmit to them "a Christianity that will satisfy their spiritual wants."[90] This view implied that Africans on the continent did not know how to "live progressive lives" and suffered from a lack of sufficiently satisfying Indigenous spiritual traditions of their own.

Amy Jacques also evinced the Islamophobic mindset of a chauvinist Christian missionary: "Mohammedanism will triumph in Africa if Negro Christians are so selfish as to allow it," she warned. "We [therefore] appeal to the Negro churches of all denominations to unite in this work of helping the African in Africa to know Christ and to know his own possibilities as a man. If we fail to heed the cry of awakened Africa, Mohammedanism will conquer, and a further breach will be created between Africans at home and Africans abroad."[91] To be sure, Arab and Muslim civilizations had their own share of atrocities to answer for, including the enslavement of Black Africans for many more centuries than the capitalist slavery that Euro-Christians had perpetrated on Africans. But claiming Islam as a bigger barrier to pan-African unity than Christianity demonstrated a glaring absolution of Christianity's role in justifying the enslavement and colonization of African peoples.

Hubert Harrison viewed Islam as a more favorable religion than Christianity for Africans. Though a fundamentally antireligious freethinker, he argued that under Islam all true believers belonged to a common community (the *Ummah*) and that Muslims were equal "not only 'in the sight of God,' but in the sight of the magistrate, and in every civil right." Christianity, on the other hand, "as organized and made effective in all her institutions, from the church to the jail, insists that only white men are men and that Negroes especially must be treated like dogs." Harrison also appreciated Islam for the way it strove to promote knowledge and free inquiry, including in its universities where algebra, the astrolabe, and so much of the knowledge of the ancient world was developed (and later seeded Europe's "Enlightenment").

With Christian dogma in charge of Europe's education system, by contrast, "the Inquisition . . . sat cross-legged at the birth of every scientific idea to ensure that it would be stillborn."[92]

In this way, Harrison affirmed the argument of his fellow Virgin Islander Edward Wilmot Blyden's book *Christianity, Islam, and the Negro Race*, which also saw Islam as a positively unifying force for Africans. Unlike Amy Jacques Garvey, Harrison took great inspiration from pan-Islamic movements among the "hundreds of millions of black, brown and yellow peoples from the Senegal [in west Africa] to the shores of the Yellow Sea [in east Asia]" because he saw it as part and parcel of the general post-war mass movement of the "darker races" internationally against white arrogance, racial prejudice, and imperialism.[93] In terms of journalism, he greatly respected the work of figures like Dusé Mohamed Ali and reprinted articles from Ali's *African Times and Orient Review* in *The New Negro* and *The Negro World*. Ali's London-based magazine expressed pan-African, pan-Islamic, and pan-Asian perspectives on current events.

Recent work by scholars like Robert Vinson has uncovered the positive and liberatory impact of Garveyism on the continent, particularly on Black nationalism in South Africa.[94] In many ways, the Garvey movement brought a pan-African identity and ethos down from the Mount Sinai of the "talented tenth" to the level of ordinary people. Yet Marcus Garvey himself initially betrayed a civilizationist attitude toward Africans, even when extolling their agency. In 1923, for example, he declared "Africa will redeem herself, not so much from without as from within. What we want is to implant the right kind of education in the minds of the natives, to let them realize that they are entitled to freedom like the other races of the world, and see to it that they push forward until they have succeeded in dislodging the alien enemy."[95] While envisioning African redemption coming from within, the notion of implanting the "right" education in the natives remained a far cry from Harrison's injunction to "LEARN WHAT THEY HAVE TO TEACH US (for they have much to teach us)." Here, again, Harrison's radical humility proved a solid touchstone.

One need not doubt the sincerity of Garvey's commitment to make Africa the "land of Black peoples of the world" in order to see that some of the views with which he attempted to achieve that objective did not, at least in the first decade of the UNIA's existence, fundamentally break with the paternalist mindset of the nineteenth century. To their credit, both Marcus and Amy Jacques Garvey would eventually move in the direction of Harrisonian humility and full self-determination for Africa by the end of the 1920s, which paved the way for the Garvey movement to inspire multiple different African leaders in nationalist struggles against European colonialism, as we will see in the chapter 7.[96]

The International Colored Unity League: Harrison's Grassroots Pan-Africanist Organization

Following his break with Marcus Garvey in 1922, Harrison's subsequent major Black movement-building project emerged in the International Colored Unity League (ICUL), an organization he founded in 1924. The ICUL's significance lies in the fact of it being Harrison's last major independent organizational undertaking. Harrison advanced an unmistakably pan-African vision for the ICUL. As one newspaper reported, "The word 'international' in the title of the league means... that all Negroes in America, no matter what part of the world they originally came from, were eligible for membership in the new organization."[97] The league made a deliberate and explicit appeal to continental Africans, West Indians, and African Americans.

Because of its pan-African orientation, the ICUL represents a notable local and grassroots model of pan-Africanism, as compared to the elite-oriented pan-African congresses that Du Bois organized in Europe. In that sense it reprised and extended the model of the Liberty League of Negro-Americans, "under whose banner the West Indian and American Negroes first cooperated on anything like a large scale."[98] The ICUL launched a campaign to establish branches across the country, raise money, and publish a magazine, *The Voice of the Negro*, in which Harrison articulated the purpose, program, and objectives of the organization. By the end of 1925, the ICUL had some 550–600 members.[99]

Fundamentally, the purpose of the ICUL was the construction of collective Black economic, political, and social power. It explicitly sought

> to stop Negros from hating one another and Negro leaders from attacking each other; to mobilize all that energy against lynching, disfranchisement and Jim Crow; to use the ballot of the Northern Negro to secure such enforcement of the Constitution as will put the ballot into the hands of the Southern Negro . . . to encourage our people to buy, to own and to use property in town and country, building up by cooperative action such economic structures as will enable them to stand on their own legs and keep the dollars of the race; to co-operate with the Negro church, lodge and other organizations that are already doing good work and to help them to do better.[100]

In other words, the ICUL represented a kind of second incarnation of the Liberty League of Negro-Americans but with a cooperative economic program and an eye toward more intentional collaboration with fraternal and faith-based organizations.

As for its motivating ethos, the ICUL sought to organize Black communities on the basis of love. Although racial oppression arose from the white man's making, Black people needed to do the work to overcome it. How? "First, by organizing—and that involves cohesion solidarity of which binding force the great name is LOVE: love of race, love for one another, a blood-is-thicker-than-water policy, racial support and self-support, racial respect and self-respect." This emphasis on love of Black people and self-respect is at the core of what Cornel West has called the tradition of "Black prophetic fire," and the deep and abiding love for Black people manifested in so many of that tradition, from Nat Turner and Bishop Henry McNeil Turner to Laura Adorkor Kofi, Mekatilili Wa Menza, and Noble Drew Ali.[101]

Harrison explained why this unifying force of Black love was necessary: "Every lynching-bee and Jim Crow car is teaching us that we must stand by each other; one for all and all for one, in matters of money, mind, politics and religion, if we wish to survive and succeed. But since there is work to do, we must organize to do that work. And that work is always where we are. In Boston or Bridgetown, Jamaica or Georgia, the old advice is still valuable: 'Cast down your buckets where you are!'" Here, Harrison riffed on a theme that Booker T. Washington sounded regarding the need for Black people to build where they were and to take active ownership over their own collective destiny. It also constituted a rejection of the Garveyist and emigrationist notion that Black Americans had to physically return to Africa in order to get free.[102]

In the interest of racial unity, the ICUL seemed designed to accommodate Black business owners. Harrison argued that because Black money did not stay in Black communities but instead got siphoned off by spending on white-owned businesses, Black people needed to keep Black money in the Black community. The ICUL's economic program advocated buying agricultural land in areas where Black people were concentrated and raising farm produce cooperatively for direct sale to the Black community in order to eliminate white middlemen. The idea was to establish cooperative groceries served by Black farms, and Black ownership of apartment houses, halls, and suburban households, which would offer employment to Black architects, engineers, and artists, generally "keeping the cycle of Negro industry and commerce as far as possible within the Negro's control."[103] This idea built upon his experience observing the UNIA's array of Black-owned businesses in Harlem.[104]

This pro-business articulation of the ICUL's economic program also suggests a possible conservative turn in Harrison's economic thought. In particular, the question of *how* Black people should own and manage the means of economic production—under workers' collective control or as profit-maximizing capitalists—is not clear. This did not necessarily mean that Harrison had abandoned Socialism as a long-term goal. For example, the ICUL's stated purpose of encouraging Black people "to buy, to own and to use property in town and country, building up by cooperative action such economic structures as will enable them to stand on their own legs" allows for a Socialist-minded interpretation on account of the emphasis on cooperative economics, for which there already existed a rich tradition in African American communities.[105] However, without any explicit reference to Socialism, the emancipation of Black labor, workers' control of industry, or a concrete ICUL cooperative enterprise to examine, it remains unclear whether and to what extent Harrison conceived his vision of cooperative economics in the ICUL as a replacement or alternative to capitalist economic relations.[106]

In any case, Harrison's call for Black ownership of the means of production led to one of the most distinguishing features of the ICUL program, the demand for a separate Black state: "We urge as a final solution of the graver aspects of the American race-problem the setting up of a state or states, in the Union as a homeland for the American Negro, where we can work out the ultimate economic and racial salvation as a part of the American people." In Harrison's vision, no one would be forced to live in the Black state, but Black aspirations there could flourish and bear fruit such that Black people could become governors, generals, judges, congressmen, and whatever else they wanted without the handicap of white supremacy and the racial proscriptions on Black achievement endemic to the rest of the country.

On the grounds that "America is ours and we are hers," Harrison conceived of the Black state as another one of the United States of America rather than a separate country.[107] Harrison's idea took inspiration from the Garvey movement's attempt to forge an independent Black sovereign authority, as did Cyril Briggs's call in 1919 for a separate Black state. Proposals like those of Garvey, Briggs, and Harrison influenced the slogan "Self-determination for the Black Belt" raised by the Communist Party in the late 1920s, as well as a similar demand in the 1960s by a broad range of Black political leaders and organizations like the Republic of New Africa, which called for a territorial state for African Americans in South Carolina, Georgia, Alabama, Mississippi, and Louisiana. The Louisiana-born Black nationalist matriarch Queen Audley "Mother" Moore embodied this trajectory by her participation in the Garvey movement in the 1920s and the Communist Party in the 1930s before becoming an elder and mentor to Malcolm X's generation of Black nationalists, including by stepping forward as the first signatory on the Republic of New Afrika's Declaration of Independence in 1968.[108]

Harrison's advancing of his own version of the larger separatist tradition in US Black political thought is significant because it invites us to rethink the land question for African Americans. Simply put, Black people in the United States have never truly had any rights to land (or anything else) that the white masters of the country were willing to respect. Yet according to the UN Declaration on the Rights of Indigenous Peoples, Indigenous peoples have a right to land and territory. Indigenous wisdom holds that Mother Earth does not belong to humans but that humans belong to Mother Earth. However, if we accept the Euro-capitalist or so-called Enlightenment-era notion of "rights," then African Americans, much like Native Americans and other Indigenous peoples, were dispossessed of their "right" to territory. For African Americans, this dispossession took place when they were kidnapped as enslaved people and taken from their Indigenous lands on the African continent. Though nominally citizens, African Americans occupy a position neither settler nor Indigenous in the traditional sense. The land claim evolved to encompass the historic "Black belt" in the South because the westward-expanding unsettler colony forced high concentrations of African people to live and toil on plantations there. The land claim is complicated by the fact Uncle Sam "cleared" that land by committing multiple genocides, including against Choctaw, Chickasaw, Cherokee, Creek, and Seminole peoples.

The idea of "40 acres and a mule" that emerged after the Civil War would have, at least to some degree, redressed the forced landlessness and political nonsovereignty that resulted from enslavement. Yet it was quickly aborted by the federal government. All subsequent efforts to subsume African Americans under the capitalist framework and political parameters internal to the white (un)settler colony of the United States—including Marxist analyses positioning "New Afrikans" as exploited workers but *not* as an internally colonized and landless people—have overlooked this fundamental fact. The emergence of separatist and land-based appeals, including during the historic moments when the national struggle for Black freedom has crested (the Civil War and Black Reconstruction, the Interwar period, the 1960s), demonstrates that the problem facing African Americans is deeper than just class exploitation and racial oppression upon US territory. It is also a problem of lacking any sovereign territory of their own. Although Harrison did not apparently devote much time or energy to explicitly unpacking the meaning of (un)settler colonialism in the United States for Indigenous Native Americans, his adoption of a position in favor of a separate state for Black people constituted a political reckoning with the traumatic impact of landlessness, collective territorial non-sovereignty, and statelessness that continue to haunt the descendants of enslaved Africans inside the United States.

Alongside advocating a Black nationalist resolution of the land question for African Americans, the ICUL's goals and objectives included friendly and active cooperation with fraternal organizations, Black newspapers, Black school teachers, and even the Black church, "which has done more for the education and spiritual uplift of the masses than any other agency in the race."[109] This last point speaks to Harrison's growth into greater spiritual tolerance as compared to his reputation for militant agnosticism and decades of anti-Christian agitation as the leading Black freethinker.

Harrison did not suddenly become religious, but he did support the Black radical theology of Rev. Ethelred Brown's Unitarian Church. In *The Voice of the Negro*, he wrote, "All our readers who have intellectually and ethically outgrown the fundamental doctrines of orthodox churches but who still believe in the religious value of a modern liberal church are invited to attend The Harlem Community Church."[110] At the very least, Harrison had come to the conclusion that different spiritual beliefs and religious faiths must not divide Black communities in their collective struggle for liberation. Given that Garvey grew successful in part thanks to his nondenominational but faith-positive orientation, Harrison apparently took a cue from the UNIA on this score. After Harrison's death, Rev. Brown would rename his Harlem Community Church the Hubert Harrison Memorial Church, signaling how Unitarian churchgoers could recognize Harrison's immensely spiritual force in the Harlem community despite his agnostic freethinking.

While documentation is scarce, the ICUL clearly represented Harrison's last major innovative organizational project. He died suddenly and mysteriously following an appendicitis operation in December of 1927, a mere eight months after the ICUL published its first issue of *The Voice of the Negro*. The Educational Forum of the ICUL met at the 135th Street Harlem branch of the New York Public Library. But as an organization conceived, founded, and headed by Hubert Harrison, it does not appear that the ICUL survived for very long beyond his passing. However, its program demonstrated new strains of thought in Harrison's evolution, such as collaboration with Black people of faith and the call for a separate Black state. The ICUL differed from Garveyism in many ways, such as by its emphasis on a domestic political struggle for Black rights. By combining elements from both the Liberty League of Negro-Americans and the Garvey movement's striving for global Black nationality and collective political sovereignty, the ICUL may have grown into a larger and more significant political force during the heady years of the 1930s if not for Harrison's untimely death.

In the end, Harrison's pan-African studies, identity, and work for Africa-conscious organizations like NSHR, the Liberty League, the UNIA, and the ICUL, not to mention the Outdoor Grioversity of Harlem's intellectual street culture, planted seeds for the future, particularly the kinds of African consciousness and pride that would reemerge in the 1960s and '70s. In that period, Black folks: fashioned new ideas of "Black Power," "Black Is Beautiful," and pan-Africanism for anticolonial liberation; claimed for themselves meaningful African names, cultural rites, and rituals; adopted new holiday ceremonies like Kwanzaa; sought out African spiritual practices like Ifá, Voodoo, rootwork, and conjure; learned the pan-African language of KiSwahili; established the field of Black and Africana Studies; and celebrated African artists from Miriam Makeba to Fela Kuti—all of these things gave expression to this consciousness. People of the African diaspora sought to reconnect and heal the damage done to their ancestral inheritance, almost as if they had taken up the younger Harrison's humble pledge from 1907:

> *Oh Africa! . . . I pledge thee, O my Mother, that I shall devote my years to thee, shall work for thy redemption even in the land of thine exile . . .*
>
> *. . . when i shall have died for thee, take me to thy bosom, an untamed, untamable African . . .*

Chapter 6

Black Free Love Politics and the Queer New Negro

> What happens if we imagine Black subjects as desiring and desirous? How can we carefully theorize Black pleasures and Black longings? What happens if we work to unleash Black sexual imaginations, to cultivate Black erotic longings and to advocate for Black sexual freedoms? . . . Ultimately, this work reminds us again and again that sexual world-making and political world-making go hand in hand, that Black political and Black sexual freedom are one and the same.
>
> —Jennifer C. Nash, "Black Sexualities"

> The reason given for the black band across the pelvic region of these female figures involved an attitude of the American mind towards matters of sex, which may well be described as erotic bashfulness.
>
> —Hubert Harrison, "Three Black Bands"

Hubert Henry Harrison broke new ground for the Black radical tradition in relationship to the most personal, sensitive, and controversial of topics: sex. The revolutionary Jamaican Socialist poet Claude McKay maintained a close friendship with Harrison. McKay said of him that "erotically he was very indiscriminate." This makes for an interesting comment given McKay's own sexual fluidity. Meanwhile, in a time before the development of mass media technologies like television and the internet, and when the federal government had criminalized erotica writ large, Harrison built his own illegal archive of arousal. The openly gay writer and painter Richard Bruce Nugent spoke of Hubert Harrison's "superlative collection of erotic literature," which according to Nugent was "second to none in New York." As literary scholar Saidiya Hartman notes, the collection "filled [Harrison's] head with a range of lovely variations and offered diverse blueprints of the possible."[1]

Over the course of his adulthood Harrison had a complex roller coaster of a love life. In 1907, at the age of twenty-four, he recorded his first love interest in his diary, one Williana Jones (Burroughs). When Harrison discovered that she was already engaged to his close friend Charles Burroughs, he responded not with jealousy but its opposite, compersion or sympathetic joy for another's happiness. The next year, Harrison met Irene Louise "Lin" Horton, and the following year they got pregnant and then married. Harrison's warmth, compersion, and respect for Williana kept them on such good terms that she ended up serving as an official witness to his marriage.[2]

After getting married, Hubert continued to engage in romantic dalliances outside the home. The tensions this created with his wife Lin would eventually boil over and lead him to move out in 1914 (the same year he started speaking on free love). He then lived on his own while coparenting their four daughters (Frances Marion, Alice, Aida, and Ilva Henrietta). In subsequent years, he would alternate between moving in to live with his wife and children and moving out to have more independence. Hubert and Lin would have a fifth child, William, in 1920, and during their eighteen years of marriage before he died, Hubert and Lin never divorced.

As a wider Black erotic awakening caught on in Harlem in the 1920s, Hubert Harrison would encounter perhaps the most passionate lover of his life, Elsie Dearborn. He would also cultivate romance with high-profile women including Amy Ashwood Garvey and the famous sculptress Augusta Savage.[3]

In 1926, Harrison attended his first drag ball in Harlem—and loved it. Some 1,500 people packed the Renaissance Casino for an annual dance sponsored by the Hamilton Lodge of the Odd Fellows, complete with prizes awarded for the best "masquerades," or what we would today call drag queens. "The floor was so full of homosexual men," noted Harrison in his diary, "white and Negro, gorgeously disguised as women, that, of ten dances I had, only two were with real women. . . . It was glorious, intoxicating! It was hard to believe that some of them were not really women."

Whether or not all the queens identified as "homosexual" in the way Harrison assumed, he clearly felt stimulated and intrigued by what he saw. He even got up the nerve to try dancing with one (*"Don't fuck it up!"*). As he later recounted, "One young temptress was said to be a male but I can't believe it. She was ravishing! I tried to get dances with her and failed." Though he did not get the dance he wanted, he was still so jazzed that he ended up volunteering as one of the judges tasked with selecting the top three most dazzling contestants for cash prizes. "Altogether," said the forty-two-year-old free-loving veteran of New York City night life, "it was one of the most delightful evenings I have ever spent." By the late 1920s, Harlem had developed into a dynamic space for expressing and engaging a wide range of nonmainstream sexualities, including for Hubert Harrison. But we are getting ahead of the story.[4]

Crystallizing a Black Free Love Politics

Sex has long been a forbidden subject in polite and "respectable" conversation, at best confined to the shadows of a passing mention or faint whisper. But not for Hubert Harrison. In fact, his radicalism in relation to erotic energy presents one of the most potent and generative dimensions of his political legacy. As we saw in chapter 3 on the Outdoor Grioversity, Harrison demonstrated what we might call a kind of *intellectual* nonmonogamy by refusing to confine himself to one theoretical framework or scholarly discipline and instead loving many simultaneously. As a result, his thinking on the subject of sex reveals a startlingly eclectic range of insights. Especially in relation to compulsory monogamy and its social, economic, and political implications. By *compulsory monogamy* we refer to the cultural paradigm and legal framework that coercively enforces *one* as the only moral and socially acceptable maximum number of sexual partners a person can have in any given period of time. The most "Godly" Christian behavior was abstinence-until-marital-monogamy.

Harrison was not a sex radical simply because he rejected compulsory monogamy or because he could (and often did) have more than one lover. Various contemporaries of his, including W. E. B. Du Bois, Amy Ashwood Garvey, Alain Locke, Gladys Bentley, Claude McKay, Zora Neale Hurston, Langston Hughes, and Paul Robeson, did not limit their intimate erotic lives to just one partner at a time. Meanwhile, blues women like Lucille Bogan, Bessie Smith, Rosa Henderson, Gertrude "Ma" Rainey, Ida Cox, Alberta Hunter, and Ethel Waters gave artistic expression in their lyrics to themes like women's erotic pleasure, financial independence, bodily autonomy, homoerotic desire, and sexual nonmonogamy. Not to mention the countless and nameless other men, women, and nonbinary people of African descent who also cultivated variety and freedom in their sexual and romantic lives, whether they went to Church and loved Jesus or not. Literary scholar Thomas Wirth has noted how in the Harlem of the 1920s one could move around in a "social matrix in which the existence of extramarital sexual relationships of all kinds—homosexual and heterosexual—was taken for granted."[5]

Harrison distinguished himself in this "matrix" by articulating a revolutionary and multifaceted political perspective on sex. He spoke publicly on free love and legalizing access to contraception as early as 1914. In 1915, he began to denounce both church- and state-based forms of sexual repression. In 1917, he offered quite possibly the very first public-facing lecture series of sex education in African American history (see figure 6.1). In 1921, Harrison gave another set of lectures for a chiropractic college on "Sex and Sex Problems."

Unfortunately, no transcript or notes for these sex talks appear in Harrison's papers. However, we can reconstruct the basic contours of his perspective by mining his intellectual influences on the subjects featured in his lectures. Drawing on a range of influences including Socialism, freethought, social science, anticolonial politics, European American sex radicalism, and African culture, Harrison (once again) crystallized something quite distinctive, what I call a Black free love politics. This raises a number of questions: What happens if we read Harrison not simply as a "philanderer" but as the

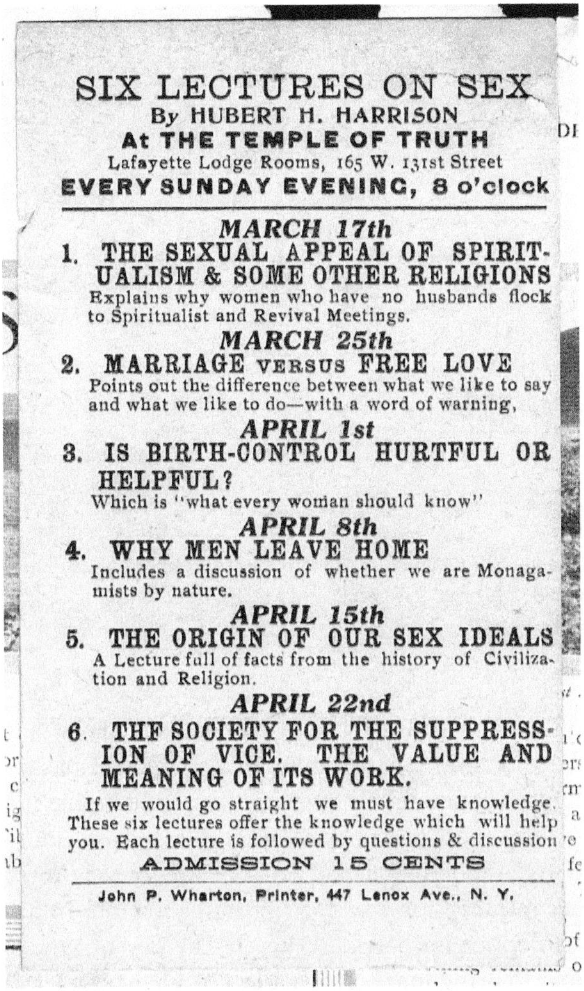

> **SIX LECTURES ON SEX**
> By HUBERT H. HARRISON
> At **THE TEMPLE OF TRUTH**
> Lafayette Lodge Rooms, 165 W. 131st Street
> **EVERY SUNDAY EVENING, 8 o'clock**
>
> **MARCH 17th**
> 1. **THE SEXUAL APPEAL OF SPIRITUALISM & SOME OTHER RELIGIONS**
> Explains why women who have no husbands flock to Spiritualist and Revival Meetings.
>
> **MARCH 25th**
> 2. **MARRIAGE** VERSUS **FREE LOVE**
> Points out the difference between what we like to say and what we like to do—with a word of warning.
>
> **APRIL 1st**
> 3. **IS BIRTH-CONTROL HURTFUL OR HELPFUL?**
> Which is "what every woman should know"
>
> **APRIL 8th**
> 4. **WHY MEN LEAVE HOME**
> Includes a discussion of whether we are Monagamists by nature.
>
> **APRIL 15th**
> 5. **THE ORIGIN OF OUR SEX IDEALS**
> A Lecture full of facts from the history of Civilization and Religion.
>
> **APRIL 22nd**
> 6. **THE SOCIETY FOR THE SUPPRESSION OF VICE. THE VALUE AND MEANING OF ITS WORK.**
> If we would go straight we must have knowledge. These six lectures offer the knowledge which will help you. Each lecture is followed by questions & discussion
> **ADMISSION 15 CENTS**
> John P. Wharton, Printer, 447 Lenox Ave., N. Y.

Figure 6.1
Hubert Harrison's sex lectures in the spring of 1917. Hubert H. Harrison Papers, flat box 740, Rare Book and Manuscript Library, Columbia University, New York.

crystallizer of a Black free love politics? On what intellectual grounds did he conclude that we are not monogamists by nature? How did Harrison's sex radicalism connect with his other projects, like building momentum for Socialism, freethought, women's rights, and Black/pan-African liberation?

"Is Birth-Control Hurtful or Helpful?—Which Is What Every Woman Should Know"

Harrison's birth control advocacy constitutes one of the first Black political voices on record in the United States agitating publicly in favor of legalizing access to contraception. It was a lonely position to take at that time for a

> # Six Lectures on Sex and Sex Problems
> *by*
> ## HUBERT H. HARRISON, Instructor in Embryology
> ### AT THE COSMOPOLITAN COLLEGE OF CHIROPRACTIC
> In the College Building, 240 West 138th Street
>
> Saturday, May 14—The Nature and Origin of Sex
> Saturday, May 21—The Origins of Our Sex Ideals
> Saturday, May 28—The Mechanics of Sex
> Saturday, June 4—Analysis of the Sex Impulse
> Saturday, June 11—Sex and Race
> Saturday, June 18—Marriage and Free Love
>
> Lectures are limited to students of the college and their friends. This ticket entitles holder to admission to the entire series. Price $3.00.
> Lectures begin promptly at 8 P. M.   Questions and answers.
> Without this ticket the price of admission to any lecture will be $1.00

Figure 6.2 Hubert Harrison's sex education course as an instructor of embryology in 1921. Hubert H. Harrison Papers, box 16, folder 39, Rare Book and Manuscript Library, Columbia University, New York.

number of reasons. For one, it was against both federal and state laws that had banned and criminalized not only contraception but all manner of sex-related speech. As a result, Black communities often lacked awareness and information about modern methods of contraception. Meanwhile, most churches preached against it. Catholic archbishop Patrick Hayes of New York, for example, pronounced contraception a worse sin than abortion. In his words, "to take life after its inception is a horrible crime; but to prevent human life that the Creator is about to bring into being is satanic." Orthodox Jews, conservative Protestants, the Greek Orthodox Church, and many Black churches concurred with the Roman Catholics about the "un-Godly" nature of contraception.[6]

Along with figures like Emma Goldman, Elizabeth Gurley Flynn, and Mary Ware Dennett, a young woman named Margaret Sanger blazed a trail in the modern movement for "birth control," a phrase that she, perhaps more than any other person, helped popularize in the early twentieth century. Sanger courageously defied postal censorship, multiple arrests, and government harassment and persecution of her efforts. Yet Sanger's generation of white women's rights advocates was not the first to practice women's autonomy in relationship to reproduction.

Women of African descent, for example, have a "rich and complex legacy of activism in the struggle to control their own bodies and reproductive lives," as reproductive justice scholar-activist Loretta Ross has pointed out. For example, "slave women drew on African folk knowledge about contraception and abortion as forms of resistance to the oppressive conditions of slavery. They were so successful that entire plantations of slaves failed to have children, frustrating slave owners' plans for profit." Black women in the rural South, as well as on the African continent, had taken care of conception and reproduction for millennia with their own spiritual rituals and practices, intuitive feminine bodily self-awareness, and a vibrant tradition of natural medicine that included knowledge of herbal abortifacients. What the white women of Sanger's generation did was to blaze a trail for waging an open political struggle in the public square to decriminalize access to sex education and contraception.[7]

Margaret Sanger also exerted a direct influence on Hubert Harrison's birth control advocacy. During his tenure in the Socialist Party (1911–14), Harrison organized as a member of the same Branch 5 as Sanger. Although we have no a transcript of exactly what he said about birth control, he most likely based his 1917 lecture "Is Birth-Control Hurtful or Helpful?"—much like he based his subtitle ("Which Is What Every Woman Should Know")—on a series of articles titled "What Every Girl Should Know" that Sanger wrote for the Socialist Party's *New York Call* in 1912–13, the publication of which was initially censored by the government.

Dedicated in proud Socialist fashion to "the working girls of the world," Sanger's series presented a range of themes relating to sex education, including the physical and mental aspects of sexual health, sexual development during adolescence, puberty, the female sex organs, ovulation, menstruation, sexual desire and attraction, masturbation, love, reproduction, abortion, miscarriage, sexually transmitted infections, and menopause. As a devoted party member, paid organizer, and voracious reader, Harrison read, absorbed, and discussed Sanger's writings with his party comrades. He then began speaking publicly, both about birth control and free love, in 1914, the year after Sanger's series concluded.[8]

Though mentioned earlier, it bears repeating: Harrison's presentations on these subjects establish him as one of the first documented public-facing voices of modern sex education in African American history. We cannot know exactly who attended Harlem's Temple of Truth (later renamed the Lafayette Theater) on 131st Street between Lenox and Seventh Avenue to hear him speak on this subject. But for a talk there in 1917 aimed at "what every woman should know," most likely his audience would have included some segment of the suffragist, Socialist, activist, and otherwise politically conscious "race women" with whom he had worked in other settings, such as Williana Burroughs, Grace P. Campbell, Eslanda Cardozo Goode, Irena

Moorman-Blackston, Helen Holman, Gertrude Miller-Faide, Madam C. J. Walker, A'Lelia Walker, Elizabeth Anna Hendrickson, Lucille Randolph, and Bernia Smith Austin. Sex education and contraception advocacy were both illegal. So Harrison undertook great risk in coming out publicly for the cause that had landed Margaret Sanger in jail the previous year for attempting to open in Brooklyn the first clinic in the United States to offer means of contraception. But it was not in vain.

Harrison's birth control advocacy from 1914 to 1917 crystallized a generational shift of attitudes as other Black voices began to take up the cause. In 1918, A. Philip Randolph's Socialist *Messenger* magazine announced a lecture series by an organization called the Women's Political Association that included birth control as a topic for discussion. The Socialist-oriented Women's Political Association in Harlem emerged thanks to the leadership of women like Grace P. Campbell and Eslanda Cardozo Goode's Negro Women's Campaign Committee, which helped win the struggle for a Black woman's right to vote in New York in 1917. In 1919, Black voices like Chandler Owen and lesbian playwright Mary Burrill first appeared in the pages of Margaret Sanger's *Birth Control Review*, advocating access to birth control as a means to alleviate the hardships afflicting economically impoverished Black families whose numerical size outstripped their financial means.

In the wake of the white world war, Sanger increasingly drifted away from the radical, working-class, and Socialist politics of her prewar years. Her decision to seek funding from more well-to-do sponsors like John D. Rockefeller coincided with her adoption of increasingly elitist and eugenicist views. Writings of hers like "Birth Control and Racial Betterment" (1919), for example, made a case for birth control as a way to sterilize and thereby limit the population of the "unfit." Given the presence of these eugenicist elements within the history of birth control advocacy, some Black folks have regarded *birth control* as little more than a euphemism for racist Black population control and limitation.

Unfortunately, some early Black advocates of birth control access followed the eugenics-infused approach of Sanger. For example, W. E. B. Du Bois spoke in 1930 of how "the mass of ignorant Negroes still breed carelessly and disastrously, so that the increase among Negroes, even more than the increase among whites, is from that part of the population least intelligent and fit, and least able to rear their children properly." This argument assumed the Black masses to be less intelligent, less "fit," and less able to rear children properly than the so-called talented tenth of the race.[9]

Harrison's support for legalizing contraception did not emerge from the elitist attitudes that resonated with white eugenics-supporting robber barons like Rockefeller and Carnegie. On the contrary, Harrison had by 1920 already demonstrated his opposition to this reactionary basis on which to make the case for birth control. "We breed so fast," he noted, "that the white doctors in their hospitals from the South to Harlem are driven to perform operations upon colored women—unbeknown to them—to be sure that they will not be breeders of men. But we will survive, although some of us who study too hard and drink too hard and do some other things too hard may go crazy once in a while." In addition to his opposition to the forced sterilization of Black women, the dark humor in Harrison's self-deprecating and irreverent identification with the masses—and the things they did that lost them "respectability" in the eyes of the "talented tenth"—rejected the elitist logic of eugenicist elements within birth control advocacy.[10]

Sexuality historians John D'Emilio and Estelle Freedman have argued that it would be hard to overstate the importance of the liberalizing impact of the birth control movement on US sexual culture. In their words, "It signaled a profound shift in the sexual norms that had reigned supreme among the middle classes for half a century. To advocate fertility control for women though access to contraceptive devices rather than through abstinence implied an unequivocal acceptance of female sexual expression. It weakened the link between sexual activity and procreation, altered the meaning of the marriage bond, and opened the way for more extensive premarital sexual behavior among women." Harrison's risky decision to engage (as a noncitizen!) in illegal progressive birth control agitation in Black communities in the 1910s was extraordinary. But it was by no means the only element of his sexual radicalism.[11]

"The Origin of Our Sex Ideals—A Lecture Full of Facts Drawn from the History of Civilization and Religion"

Harrison's 1917 series included a talk on "The Origin of Our Sex Ideals." In this talk he outlined what he called the "materialistic interpretation of morals," locating the European cultural hegemony of monogamy and women's oppression in historical changes to the economic mode of production. He leaned on works like Socialist Clarence Meily's book *Puritanism*, which made a Marxist argument: that the rise of male-owned private property led to the rise of a moral system requiring sexual monogamy (for married women) as a mechanism for ensuring the male proprietor could know which children are his so that he could hand down his property to his descendants. This also entailed a shift from matrilineal to patrilineal (and patriarchal) culture thanks to the tremendous importance that inheritance gave to female chastity under feudal conditions of property.[12] In short, monogamy and women's chastity facilitated the transferability of a propertied man's wealth to his heirs.

Harrison concurred with Meily's analysis of sex-negative religious morality as an "instrument fashioned by the bourgeoisie to affect its own class dominance by preaching as [moral] 'virtues' those lines of social action which conserved its own class interests." In this view, the "custodians" of morality such as intellectuals and priests did not contribute directly toward economic production and therefore their existence depended to a large degree on the good will and economic support of the ruling, property-owning class. This inexorably led intellectuals and priests to define laws and preach as "moral" the patterns of sexual behavior that served the interests of their ruling-class sponsors. The law, in Harrison's view, functioned to "crystallize into formal statement the dominance of the masters, and to adjust their private differences peacefully between themselves so that their position may not be imperiled by internal strife." In a nutshell, laws and morals regarding sex arose not as something fixed by biology or ordained by God but instead emerged as historically contingent products of class struggle. In particular, the hegemonic influence of ruling-class interests on the sociocultural naturalization over time of what *they* wanted to define and standardize as "moral" and "legal" sexual behavior for the society over which they ruled.[13]

Because of the predominance of Puritan unsettlers in the founding of the Massachusetts Bay Colony and colonial New England, a distinctly prudish strain of Christianity shaped the sexual norms that became standardized in US culture. In Meily's words, "The ascetic discipline so eagerly welcomed by Puritanism, and which had for its most important object the utter eradication of the sexual impulse, finding itself measurably justified by the economic needs of the bourgeoisie, flamed into the most lurid, fantastic, and absurd excesses in the matter of sex repression. Not content with condemning sexual irregularities, all natural and perfectly normal sex instincts and desires were placed under ban. Sex itself became evil. Anything which suggested sex was of the devil." It was an apt description of the extreme sex negativity of US white middle-class Christian culture.[14]

While they allowed for an active sex life between husband and wife, the Puritans abhorred things like homosexuality, masturbation, and sex between unmarried people. Meily jokingly dedicated his book to "that sorely betrayed and somewhat bedraggled goddess, 'Liberty,' with whom, however, Puritanism has prevented the author's personal acquaintance." Harrison similarly saw Puritanism as "that coercive moral code which has plagued the world for nearly 400 years by sticking its inquisitive nose into everybody's business."[15]

In Harrison's view, Meily had made clear "how the moral 'virtues' changed their form and character as the changing economic substrat[a] made new lines of action necessary to the stability of each new order. The sheer force of society is, of course, exerted on behalf of the moral system so evolved—

'society'—being the formal disguise under which each new proprietary class masked its own class interests." Meanwhile, the workers toiled and suffered as "the learning of the lawyer and the piety of the priest would be thrown into the scale against them: the State would bind their bodies while the Church would bind their souls: law, morality and religion would link themselves together in one tyrannic[al] trinity for the exploitation of the proletariat."[16]

Implicit within this class-conscious diagnosis of the problem lay the solution of Socialism/Communism. If the feudal and capitalist stages of class society required the sexually repressive moral code of compulsory monogamy, then a classless society would remove the root cause of that legal and moral expectation. In such a society, wrote Meily, "no longer will the desire of transmitting private wealth and aristocratic position to a restricted and definitely ascertained progeny actuate the man in enforcing monogamy and female chastity, since neither private wealth nor aristocratic position will longer exist for transmission." In addition, "no longer will the woman's economic dependence constrain her to submit to masculine rule in the regulation of the supremely important function of reproduction."[17]

The Socialist in Harrison could see that the struggle for a romantic culture beyond compulsory monogamy went hand in hand with the working-class struggle against capitalism. He encountered this radical argument for free love not only among bohemians, anarchists, and Socialist radicals but also by reading books like German sexologist Iwan Bloch's *The Sexual Life of Our Time in Its Relations to Modern Civilization* (1908). In this encyclopedic work covering dozens of topics, Bloch argued that capitalism wages war on love, because the rule of capital subjects the whole of sexual life, like everything else, to its own laws and commodifications. Conversely, free love was love liberated from the domination of the state and of capital.

For its fullest realization, free love required an economic revolution that would bring about the equality of man and woman in a society without property and wages—and without women or sex possessing a commercial value. According to Bloch, many working-class people for a long time had already realized the idea of free love, in part because they had no need to base their sexual morality on bequeathing private property to "legitimate" heirs. By definition, they had no property to bequeath. Considerations truer to authentic feelings of love drew working-class men and women together, without requiring the blessing of a priest to legitimize erotic intimacy. In short, free love was part and parcel of a larger social revolution against the church, the state, and capitalism.

This theory of Bloch's got tested in practice through the steps toward human sexual liberation accomplished, however briefly, by the Bolshevik-led revolution in Russia. Bolshevik legislation established the right of divorce, decriminalized homosexuality, sex work, and abortion, granted women the vote, and socialized housework with free nurseries, laundries, and dining halls under the direction of Alexandra Kollontai's national women's department. In 1923, Dr. Gregory Batkis, who worked in the field of public health at the University of Moscow, explained the Bolshevik government's policy in *The Sexual Revolution in Russia*. In writing about the Bolsheviks' policy, he described the most groundbreaking sex laws the modern world has ever seen. They had passed legislation that

> does not intervene in any sexual relationship between two adult individuals that is not forced and which is free from pressure. Sexual intercourse of that kind is treated as a matter of private concern of the persons involved. The question of public morality is thus irrelevant for legislation. Acts of homosexuality, sodomy and *any other forms of sexual pleasure* have the same legal status as the above mentioned. Whilst European legislation defines all this as a breach of public morality, Soviet legislation makes no difference between homosexuality and so-called "natural" intercourse. *All forms of intercourse are treated as a personal matter.* Criminal prosecution is only implemented in cases of violence, abuse or a violation of the interests of others. . . .
>
> This revolutionary legislation reflects the sexual revolution as it proceeded in real life. The enemies of this new society invent myths and lies about wild free love, the socialization of women and similar nonsense and spread it throughout the whole world. . . . Observation of real life teaches us the exact opposite. . . . Today, we have already seen the liberation of love from all political and economic constraints. Free love in Russia is not some kind of rampant and wild self-realization but rather a relation between two free and independent human beings.[18]

While it is not clear how much Harrison knew about the sexual revolution underway in Russia, he had begun speaking on free love at least three years *before* the revolution that brought the likes of Lenin, Trotsky, Kollontai, and the free love legislation into power. But what kind of case did Harrison himself make for free love?

"Marriage versus Free Love" and "The Difference between What We Like to Say and What We Like to Do"

As we noted earlier, Harrison and monogamous marriage did not mix. In a satirical piece written under a pseudonym, he revealed his thoughts about marriage, after some fifteen years of experiencing it. In the piece, the author suggests marriage was instituted to give women a "good grip" on men, an arrangement whereby the woman tags the man as her "meal ticket for life," forming a financial burden on the man who, willingly if gullibly, falls prey to her deadly charms. He concluded the piece with a poetic verse from Rudyard Kipling's poem "The Winners" and the refrain, "He travels the fastest who travels alone."[19] Harrison, of course, was not the only person who reacted against monogamous marriage in this period.

In the New York City of the early twentieth century, a free love politics re-emerged among white radicals who chafed at the strictures of traditional marriage and the rigid policing of sexuality by church and state, much like their nineteenth-century antecedents had. At the center of this story one finds the Socialists, anarchists, and free-spirited bohemians of various stripes who lived and congregated in the downtown neighborhood of Greenwich Village. Sex parties flourished alongside experimental and sex-positive theater groups in the Village. Some of the ideas and writings of these radicals radiated outward from the pages of the *Masses* newspaper, edited by Max Eastman. This left-wing publication featured articles, essays, poems, and short stories on a wide range of subjects from Socialist economics and imperialism to women's rights.

During his time in the Socialist Party, Hubert Harrison had in 1910–11 worked in the offices of *The Masses* and got acquainted with the white radicals of the Village, who "dispensed with the sanctity of marriage and the ideal of lifelong monogamy." According to D'Emilio and Freedman, "Like earlier free lovers, they termed the marriage-based family a shackle that bound women to men in a property relationship. Unions based on sexual attraction and emotional compatibility, they argued, did not need the approval of church or state, and ought to be [able to be] dissolved at the will of either member."[20]

Edwin C. Walker (1849–1931), a European American freethinker and sex radical, exerted a direct influence on Harrison. Walker worked with anarchist freethinking women's rights and free love advocates like Moses Harman and his daughter Lillian Harman in the 1880s. Sometime in the 1890s, Walker moved to New York City and founded an organization called "the Propaganda of Free Discussion," which had among its objectives to "systematically increase the circulation of the periodical publications devoted to the cause of sex rationalism and freedom" and also "to oppose further invasive 'moral' and sexual, and press-censoring legislation, and . . . to agitate for the repeal or the judicial nullification of existing archaic and reactionary statutes." In defiance of the federal Comstock laws that criminalized all manner of sex-related publications, Walker published multiple pamphlets—most of which would have been considered "obscene" and therefore illegal—on subjects such as sex education, variety versus monogamy, sex morality, Puritanism, the sexual enslavement of women, love and the law, what young people need to know about sex, shame and love, the future of secularism, and the ethics of freedom.²¹

Walker founded the Sunrise Club in 1889, which Harrison joined sometime around 1908. The Sunrise Club convened a progressive forum promoting critical intellectual engagement with a wide range of subjects and ideas. It met biweekly over dinner and counted Harrison as not just as a regular member but also as a featured speaker on numerous occasions. He helped stimulate Black participation in the Sunrise Club, for example attracting 37 Black folks (out of some 200 audience members) to his talk on comparative theology in 1924, "the largest number according to Walker, that the club has ever had at a function." The week after the event, Walker demonstrated his respect and gratitude by chairing a special dinner in Harrison's honor.

Harrison not only befriended Walker but also read the writings of this veteran freethinker, free speech advocate, and free lover who was thirty-four years his elder. He greatly respected Walker, whose arguments—based on his decades of experience not just theorizing but also practicing romantic variety and freedom—offer a glimpse into some of the arguments for free love that Harrison took in.²² Walker's pamphlet on "Variety vs. Monogamy," for example, offered a concise but profound meditation on this "explosive question."

Walker maintained that humans had an inborn need for variety in their sexual relationships. He argued the more complex the organism, the more complex its sexual patterns. The wide diversity in human cultures caused by geography, climate, race, education, and many other factors made it as impossible to create uniformity in the relations of the sexes as it would be to secure uniformity in religious belief. Therefore it made sense to expect a similarly wide diversity in modes of sexual expression. As a one-size-fits-all notion, compulsory monogamy made no sense in the face of so much sexual variation across time and space and across diverse individuals and cultures. Not to mention the fact that "no rule is applicable . . . to the same individuals for life," as Walker put it. Said differently, an individual person's sexual needs and desires often change over the course of their lifetimes, posing a fundamental question for the cultural expectation of lifelong monogamy.²³

Monogamy for Walker meant exclusive possession of a lover, which implied a lack of legal, social, or cultural freedom. He argued that we are not happy when we feel jealous, and we are sure to feel jealous if we believe in a zero-sum conception of love based on exclusive possession of a lover. Simply put, jealousy emerges, at least in part, as a function of perceived scarcity. Just like no one gets jealous at another's plate of food at the family holiday dinner table if the *food* is free and in plentiful abundance, people would not be likely to get so jealous over another's lover(s) if *love* was free and in plentiful abundance. Instead of the obsession with possession, by honestly accepting freedom of the affections and variety in romantic life, "we realize that . . . we can hold all that is ours and no more" and will "cease to rave and murder" out of jealousy. Walker's point offered an answer to those who argued against free love on the grounds that it encouraged "limitless" promiscuity, which he implicitly argued was not possible given the natural limits of our finite time and energy as humans.

In addition to releasing humanity from possessiveness and jealousy, variety and freedom in romance also exerted a moderating and comforting influence on one's emotional life in Walker's view. For example, if two partners' paths were to diverge (or even if a lover died), the "blade of grief [would be] dulled" because peace and healing and joy could be restored through the embrace and support of lovers "old or new, one or many" rather than the overwhelming grief and existential devastation that often accompanies the end of a monogamous relationship. Here free love offered a pathway toward additional forms of emotional support, resilience, and potential for human development. On a lighter note, the antireligious freethinker in Walker joked about how most Protestants acknowledged the morality of remarriage after the death of a spouse, "thus practically announcing themselves in favor of monogamy here but of polygamy . . . in heaven."[24]

In the final analysis, the cultural coercion of compulsory monogamy inhibited human development. Walker believed that no single romantic partner was likely to be able to fulfill all of another person's emotional, intellectual, spiritual, financial, romantic, social, political, *and* sexual needs. And if humans have a variety of needs, then in order to fully meet those needs we need some degree of variety in our relationships. This revealed compulsory monogamy not to be an advanced or more highly evolved form of relationship (as white anthropologists argued) but one that was constraining and backward. For instance, a "highly developed woman or man" might require many individuals to be fully complemented and supported in their own development. His argument conjured a vision of nonmonogamy with the potential for collective harmonization of masculine and feminine energies throughout society by way of an expansive conception of love that could bring the inherent social interdependence of human connection and community to a higher level of development. "The conclusion therefore," wrote Walker, "must be that monogamy represents a comparatively undeveloped physical, emotional, intellectual, and social state." Compulsory monogamy effectively shackles our potential for higher human evolutionary development.[25]

Unfortunately, we may never know exactly what Hubert Harrison said about free love. But if his good friend and veteran freethinking mentor Edwin C. Walker is any indication, free love defenders, including Harrison, had clear reasons for the supporting the kind of monogamy-optional government legislation established by the Bolshevik revolution. Difficult as it might seem to imagine now, the Russian government was crafting laws aimed at facilitating sexual freedom (as part of a revolutionary Socialist step forward for human evolution). They were about as close as one could get to the polar opposite of the prevailing sex laws in the United States.

"Sex Control and the Price We Pay for It": Church, State, and Anti-Black Sexual Repression

In 1915, Harrison gave a talk entitled "Our Puritanic Prudes: Sex Control and the Price We Pay For It." What he said about this is not difficult to imagine, given the political forces arrayed against him. In the late nineteenth century, the US government deployed a national policy of extreme Puritanical sexual repression in reaction to a battle with one Socialist and free-loving woman. Speaking from the radical wing of the white women's movement, Victoria Claflin Woodhull (1838–1927) declared publicly, "Yes, I am a Free Lover. I have an inalienable, constitutional and natural right to love whom I may, to love as long or as short a period as I can; to change that love every day if I please, and with that right neither you nor any law you can frame have any right to interfere." Woodhull's free love politics stood in a European American tradition of sex radicalism that rejected government regulation of sexuality. Dating back to at least the 1820s, "free love referred not to promiscuity—sex with multiple partners—but to the belief that love, not marriage, should be the precondition for sexual relations."[26]

Woodhull emerged as a leading suffragette and spiritualist and the first woman to run for president in the United States. She attacked the institution of monogamous marriage as a sexist mechanism for making white women into property and for stifling sexual and romantic freedom. As a Socialist, she emerged as a leader of the US section of the First International Workingmen's Association until it expelled her in 1872—in part for her free love politics—with the approval of Karl Marx himself.[27]

Even worse, the conservative Christian moral crusader Anthony Comstock attempted to prosecute Woodhull for her "obscene" views. Although Comstock failed to convict Woodhull, his defeat gave him the impetus to lobby Congress to pass what became known as the Comstock laws of 1873. Criminalizing use of the federal postal service to send anything "obscene," including contraceptives, sex toys, personal letters with sexual contents, and publications containing sex-related information, the Comstock laws affected a sea change in the repression of sexuality in the United States. The Comstock laws became the legal apparatus through which the federal government began policing, censoring, and banning anything to do with sex under the cover of safeguarding the society from "obscenity." Around the same time, Comstock founded the New York Society for the Suppression of Vice (NYSSV) and was anointed with special government powers by the New York state legislature to search, seize, arrest, and collect a portion of the fines levied in resulting court cases.

With the support of wealthy backers like J. P. Morgan, Comstock would go on to persecute not only free lovers but also erotic literature distributors, sexual education and birth control advocates, artists whose paintings depicted too much bare skin, and anything else he personally deemed "obscene." This included the banning of books by notable writers like Theodore Dreiser and James Joyce. From 1873 to 1915, Comstock made over 3,000 arrests and destroyed over 3 million pictures, postcards, and books he had declared "obscene." He boasted shamelessly of how Madame Restell, a British-born midwife and abortion provider who slit her own wrists after he arrested her, was the *fifteenth* person he had driven to commit suicide.[28] Comstock's strategies and tactics would inspire a young law student by the name of J. Edgar Hoover, who would become the notorious founding father and director of the Federal Bureau of Investigation (FBI).[29]

Comstock's reactionary Christian-inflected crusade drew the resistance of various progressives and free speech advocates. In the era before the advent of the American Civil Liberties Union, Edwin C. Walker, friend and mentor to Hubert Harrison, wrote a pamphlet in 1903 excoriating Comstock's campaign of censorship and eviscerating the arguments defending "Comstockery," as its critics had derisively branded the terrorizing regime of antisexual state repression.[30]

Traversing a similar path years later, Harrison also spoke out against Comstockery. In 1915, he gave a talk exposing the "works and ways" of "St. Anthony Comstock" and the aforementioned "Our Puritanic Prudes: Sex Control and the Price We Pay for It." Though there is no transcript of these talks, Harrison likely spoke about Stanisław Przybyszewski's book *Homo Sapiens*, which was banned that same year. The Polish writer's novel featured various instances of nonmonogamous sexuality, so when Alfred Knopf tried to publish it, the NYSSV succeeded in getting it legally designated as "obscene" in a New York court, forcing it off the market in one of the society's many successful "antivice" operations. In 1917, Harrison devoted the final installment in his series of lectures on sex to the NYSSV and the impact of its operations. By taking up the cudgel against state censorship of the "obscene" and its destructive impact on sexual freedom and artistic/literary expression, he lent an early Black voice to the larger movement of free lovers, freethinkers, and free speech defenders who fought tooth and nail against Comstockery.

Much like the federal Comstock laws, laws relating to sexual morality in New York state were extremely restrictive in the early twentieth century. For example, a pregnant woman "who takes any medicine, drug, or substance, or uses or submits to the use of any instrument or other means, with intent thereby to produce her own miscarriage" could get up to four years in prison. Furthermore, any person who "provides, supplies, or administers to a woman... or who prescribes for, or advises or procures a woman to take any medicine, drug, or substance,... with intent thereby to procure the miscarriage of a woman" could be found guilty of manslaughter in the first degree! Adultery was not just seen as immoral but was also criminalized as a misdemeanor. New York State lawmakers had placed both anal and oral sex in the same category as bestiality and necrophilia, thereby making them punishable by up to twenty years in prison. In addition, "any person who sells, lends, gives away, or in any manner [offers]... for distribution... any recipe, drug or medicine for the prevention of conception" could be found guilty of a misdemeanor. Anyone with the intention to lend, give, sell, or distribute "any obscene, lewd, lascivious, filthy, indecent or disgusting book, magazine, newspaper, story paper, writing, paper, picture, drawing, photograph, figure or image... or mechanical contrivance with moving pictures of nude or partly [nude] female figures" could be imprisoned for up to a year and/or fined $1,000.[31]

Meanwhile, medical schools were recommending surgical removal or cauterization of the clitoris as a cure for masturbation in girls. Best-selling doctors advocated vindictive circumcision without anesthetics or else sewing the foreskin shut with a silver wire as a cure for the same in boys. If all of that weren't enough, the government could also permanently obliterate a person's sexual-reproductive capacity as it was legal for state-appointed boards to *sterilize* "the feeble-minded, epileptic, criminal and other defective inmates" in prisons, mental hospitals, reformatories, and other state institutions. Such sterilization reared its ugly head not only in New York but in numerous other US jurisdictions like Indiana, Virginia, and North Carolina. The Western medical industrial complex sterilized countless Black, Puerto Rican, and Native American women. California's "Asexualization Acts" led to the sterilization of some 20,000 disproportionately African American and Mexican people who were deemed to be mentally ill or "sex delinquents." In 1927 even the Supreme Court decided it was perfectly legal and constitutional for a state to forcibly sterilize people, on the grounds that "three generations of imbeciles are enough."[32]

As Harrison argued, laws were historically used "to crystallize into formal statement the dominance of the masters, and to adjust their private differences peacefully between themselves." Clearly, the state and federal "masters" of the United States wanted a machinery of sex laws affirming a white, heteronormative, sex-negative, middle-class, vanilla, and monogamous pretense of propriety. As we have seen already, Harrison maintained that racism was not inborn in humans because if it were natural it would not need so many legislative enactments to bolster it up. In similar fashion, he could see how if the moral code of the Puritans were natural then it would not need such a fierce machinery of Puritanical state repression to bolster it up. On the contrary, as psychiatrist Mary Jane Sherfey has argued, "The strength of the drive determines the force required to suppress it."[33]

Comstock's NYSSV was not the only "antivice" (i.e., sex-negative) squad on the scene. In New York City, a private organization called the Committee of Fourteen (COF) "monitored and investigated neighborhood vice conditions, prostitution, and interracial leisure establishments, and lobbied for municipal governments to regulate illegal and unrespectable urban amusements," in the words of historian LaShawn Harris. The COF, in turn, created a model that would inspire antivice committees all across the country, supported by wealthy white donors like John D. Rockefeller, Julius Rosenwald, George Foster Peabody, and various lesser-known corporate executives. Fred R. Moore, who in 1907 had become owner and editor of the conservative *New York Age* newspaper with Booker T. Washington's blessing, served as an advisory board member of the COF. In that capacity, he worked to recruit Black COF undercover agents to conduct surveillance and gather intelligence of the kind that could be used to shut down Black-owned establishments that catered to interracial socializing, sex work, and other forms of "vice."

Conservative Black businessmen like Moore supported the COF in order to promote "respectable" and "moral" behavior in the community and to reduce "crime," but the COF faced criticism from some African Americans for working with the New York Police Department and elitist urban reformers to shutter certain Black-owned businesses (a lot more than white-owned ones doing the same thing). The COF also harassed and disparaged Black women wearing short or bobbed hair in public, and constrained underground economic activity of the kind that some working-class Black people in New York depended on due to the racially exclusionary hiring practices in so many aboveground occupations and industries. At the same time, according to historian Kevin Mumford, Black women "reformers like Nannie Helen Burroughs and Mary Church Terrell railed against '[B]lack flappers' for their immoral style and leisure habits, suggesting the extent to which sexual conservatism pervaded the [B]lack middle class."[34]

Comstock's zeal as the national censor and persecutor flowed in part from religious dogma, which exerted a sex-negative influence throughout society. In Harrison's home neighborhood of Harlem, Rev. Adam Clayton Powell Sr., pastor of the famous Abyssinian Baptist Church, offered a prime example. On the subject of sex, Powell declared, "I have as much sympathy as anyone for a liar, thief, sex pervert or libertine, and I would do anything I could to save them from these sins." The reverend thus saw "libertines" or free lovers as morally degenerate. Like so many other Christian pastors, Rev. Powell also preached against "homosexuality and all manner of sex perversions." Meanwhile, Moore's *New York Age* amplified Powell's conservative moral tirades well beyond the confines of the church's walls by publishing his sermons.[35]

Like many white sex radicals, Harrison's freethinking orientation made it easier for him to reject reactionary church doctrines about sex as part of his rejection of religious dogma more generally. As we saw in chapter 3, he decried the "dubious blessing" of the church on Black people, lamenting the way in which Christianity "still enslaves the minds of those whose bodies it has long held bound."[36] He argued that the influence of the church explained why Black people were largely absent from all the streams of radicalism on the white side of the color line, including theological criticism and freethought, as well as radical economic ideas like single tax, Socialism, and anarchism. Not to mention free love!

In addition to rampant church and state repression of sex, people of African descent also had to contend with the sexual dimensions of anti-Black racism. More than half of the state governments in the country, including all the Southern states, had laws making interracial marriage (and its attendant interracial "miscegenation") illegal. As part of the racial ideology of Jim Crow segregation, white people created a new conception of the free Black male as a sexual threat to the purity of white womanhood, who had to be protected by slaying the "beast." Best-selling books like Thomas Dixon's *The Clansmen*, and the infamous movie *Birth of a Nation* that it spawned, depicted the Black man as an inherent rapist. This derogatory image of Black men became a mainstream cultural concept during the Jim Crow era and became a common justification for lynching.

A "scientific" account of the supposed hypersexuality of African Americans appeared in the respected journal *Medicine* in 1903. "In the increase of rape on white women," wrote Dr. William Lee Howard, "we see the explosion of a long train of antecedent preparation. The attacks on defenseless white women are evidence of racial instincts that are about as amenable to ethical culture as is the inherent odor of the race." The anatomical root of the problem, in Dr. Howard's expert white medical opinion, was "the large size of the Negro's penis." This signaled that "the African's birthright" was "sexual madness and excess." Dr. Howard offers a striking example of using the cloak of science to mask the sexual prejudices and insecurity of white men—and to justify castration when they lynched Black men.[37]

These racist notions became commonplace due to the way in which "miscegenation"—especially the taboo on Black men having sexual contact with white women—formed a keystone in the ideological architecture of Jim Crow segregation. However, Ida B. Wells's painstaking investigative research—which proved so decisive in the crystallization of the antilynching movement—showed that "only one-third of the 728 victims [lynched in the past eight years] have been charged with rape, to say nothing of those of that one-third who were innocent of the charge." Instead of a legitimate response to the "innate bestiality" of Black men, Wells argued that lynching in reality comprised "an excuse to get rid of Negroes who were acquiring wealth and property and thus keep the race terrorized and 'keep the nigger down.'" Indeed, lynching formed a mechanism of racial discipline and punishment for the purpose of social control, white racial bonding, community renewal, and libidinal satisfaction.[38]

The ritual of taking body parts from the mutilated victim, and the Black penis as the most highly prized souvenir, affected a violent and systematic disciplining of Black manhood, sexual dignity, erotic vitality, and paternal coherence, as philosopher and literary theorist David Marriott has pointed out. "Under lynch law the reproductive capacity and sexual activity of the black penis are subject not only to racial prohibitions but are also inscribed in a legalized violation of kinship structures and arbitrary communal will. Furthermore, this forcible interruption of [B]lack patrilineal succession—excluding Black men and boys from 'the Father's name, the Father's law'—constantly renews itself through an initiatory economy of legalized castration and communal ritual." Lynching a Black man supplied white people with a mechanism for repressing not only his sexuality but also his ability to produce and support his ideas, dreams, ambitions, children and family life, Black-owned institutions political protest movements, or anything else that appeared threatening to white society.[39]

Meanwhile, white men created racist images of Black women—like the hypersexual and promiscuous "Jezebel"—to justify their rape and sexual abuse of Black women. In this way, the sexual oppression of Black women—especially being raped by white mobs and individuals—went hand in hand with the castration and lynching of Black men by white men, women, and even children. The psychological toll on Black men and boys—of knowing his wife, sister, mother, or daughter has been raped—represented the other side of the coin for the toll taken on Black women and girls by the lynching and castration of a husband, brother, father, or son.[40]

Audre Lorde, in her famous meditation "The Uses of the Erotic: The Erotic as Power," pointed out how "in order to perpetuate itself, every oppression must corrupt or distort those various sources of power within the culture of the oppressed that can provide energy for change. For women, this has meant a suppression of the erotic as a considered source of power and information within our lives." According to evolutionary anthropologist Eric Michael Johnson, "Judaism, Christianity, Islam and Hinduism each share a fundamental concern over the punishment for a woman's sexual freedom." Sexuality scholars Christopher Ryan and Cacilda Jethá also exemplify Lorde's point perfectly, writing that "despite repeated assurances that women aren't particularly sexual creatures, in cultures around the world men have gone to extraordinary lengths to control female libido: female genital mutilation, head-to-toe chadors, medieval witch burnings, chastity belts, suffocating corsets, muttered insults about 'insatiable' whores, pathologizing, paternalistic medical diagnoses of nymphomania or hysteria, the debilitating scorn heaped on any female who chooses to be generous with her sexuality . . . all parts of a worldwide campaign to keep the supposedly low-key female libido under control. Why the electrified high-security razor-wire fence to contain a kitty-cat?"[41]

The suppression of the erotic as a source of power has been central to the oppression not just of women but also of Black men. Indeed, the suppression of Black men's erotic power—both real and imagined—had become a sadistic and ritualized national sport in the United States. According to data from the NAACP for the years 1890–1927, white people made a ritualized human sacrifice every eighty-six hours—roughly twice per week—in Harrison's lifetime. This was inevitably a gross underestimate, constituting only those lynchings that made their way into the printed record. Lynching and castration not only disciplined Black masculine and erotic-generative power, but also—like the widespread rape and sexual assaults against Black women domestic workers in white homes—violently distorted how Black people saw themselves and their own erotic energies. White society casted Black sexuality as deviant, bestial, and hyperpromiscuous. With the additional burden of the sex-negative morality of church and state, the pressure to assimilate and strictly adhere—to the "good, Christian, middle-class respectability" of sexual chastity-until-monogamous-marriage—was even more acute in Black communities.[42]

In a context where contraceptives, abortion, anal sex, oral sex, extramarital sex, polygamy, sex toys, sex work, and erotica were all illegal; where Uncle Sam hounded sex educators, free lovers, and birth control advocates with suicide-inducing levels of persecution; where the church policed sexual morality with relentless sex-negative tirades and injunctions; and where the "unsexing" of Black men had become a weekly ritual human sacrifice for white supremacy arousal and community building, Hubert Harrison's open advocacy of free love, access to contraception and sex education, and public lectures arguing that we are not monogamists by nature appear almost unspeakably radiant, risky, and revolutionary. Did his claim that we are not naturally monogamous have merit?

"Why Men Leave Home—A Discussion of Whether We Are Monogamists by Nature"

> I think the darkest part of [marriage] is that we insist we're something we are not. We insist we are monogamous, but we are not. And the dangerous thing is that we build our social structure upon this false base, and so we have confusion, the double standard, resentment, and dishonesty between the sexes. I think it absolutely essential for women as well as men, to be able to find interest, companionship, and joy in other human beings. Very few individuals are many faceted enough, complete enough, to satisfy all the needs of another individual.
>
> —Eslanda Robeson, "Children and Education"

Hubert and Irene Harrison's marriage, like that of Black Communists Paul and Eslanda Robeson, underwent extreme tensions as a result of his extramarital affairs and surely set the stage for Eslanda to draw the same conclusion as Harrison—that we are not monogamists by nature. Harrison's perspective on this question emerged from a wide array of influences. While we don't have a transcript of his lecture on the subject, Harrison himself "left home" and stopped cohabiting with his wife in part because he knew that he himself was not a "monogamist by nature." But he didn't think he was unique and had a number of reasons for making the much broader claim that *we*—humans—are not monogamists by nature.

Some people might think that the desire for sexual variety is natural for men but not for women. An unforgettable response to this idea emerged from the pen of Mark Twain, who Harrison greatly respected as an anti-imperialist, world-traveling, freethinking humorist and satirical writer. In his talks on English literature, Harrison used to give an entire lecture on the now-canonical American author and placed Twain in the category of "literary greatness" for writing about universal qualities that transcend their time and place of origin. In response to the "commonsense"—and highly sexist—notion that the desire for sexual variety is natural for men but not for women, Twain offered an irreverant, sex-positive, and downright hilarious response: "Now [here] you have a sample of man's 'reasoning powers,' as he calls them. He observes certain facts. For instance, that in all his life he never sees the day that he can satisfy one woman; also, that no woman ever sees the day that she can't overwork, and defeat, and put out of commission any ten masculine plants that can be put to bed to her. He puts those strikingly suggestive and luminous facts together, and from them draws this astonishing conclusion: The Creator intended the woman to be restricted to one man."[43]

In addition to white sex-radical influences, the untamed, untamable African in Harrison took a cue about the question of monogamy from Indigenous African cultures. In particular, he studied deeply and lectured explicitly on the nineteenth-century pan-African intellectual and fellow Virgin Islander Edward Wilmot Blyden's *African Life and Customs* (1908). For a society in which people worked and shared the land in common and which developed over centuries in harmony and interdependence with nature, Blyden spoke of how African economic life was naturally "co-operative not egoistic or individualistic." As Blyden put it, "*We*, and not *I*, is the law of African life." On the question of marriage, Blyden articulated an unequivocal defense of one of the many valences of nonmonogamy in the African context: "The foundation of the African family," he wrote, "is plural marriage." Moreover, "contrary to the general opinion, this marriage rests upon the will of the woman" because it lightens her workload in the home, allowing for collective cooperation with regard to the reproductive labor of cooking, cleaning, and child-rearing.[44] As the Haitian proverb goes, *Men anpil chay pa lou* (Many hands make the work lighter).

"European writers generally assume that where polygamy exists women are mere serfs," Blyden observed. "However this may be elsewhere, it is not so in Nigeria. There a man's first wife is the head of the house. The younger wives obey her as such, and they generally get on peacefully together." According to this system, "the first wife, far from objecting to her husband's marrying other wives, insists on his doing so, because it lightens her household duties, some of which she can delegate to the others. In many cases, wives bring their husbands before the Native Court on charges of cruelty for refusing to get other wives." As the African proverb goes, it takes a village to raise a child.

Blyden made the case that this form of plural marriage not only empowered to women but also better for children: "When a child is born the system of polygamy affords protection to the mother according to native custom which frees her from marital duties for a period which ranges from two to three years [thanks to the labor of the other wife or wives]. This ensures that there are no sickly bottle-fed babies among them. The child gets the full care of the mother during the period when it needs it most and grows up strong and sturdy, while the mother avoids the strain of too frequent child-bearing. This . . . is the main reason why they can rear large families of healthy children."

On the question of monogamy, Blyden spoke wryly of how the Westernized woman, "beguiled by the unnatural monopoly given to her by the Marriage Ceremony of the Church . . . has come to believe that she needs no rest, that the cruel imposition upon her energies is a part of the order of Nature and so clings to a state of things which she knows is fraught with evil for herself and her children—so strong is the love of power and the charm of monopoly in the human heart." Blyden further extolled African plural marriage over Euro-Christian monogamy on the grounds that it worked against prostitution, that it accorded with "Nature" rather than "the dictum of any ecclesiastical hierarchy," and that it also accorded with the collectivist culture of Africans. He argued that plural marriage also mitigated against the situation obtaining in places like England, which had over 5 million unmarried women.[45]

Harrison's Caribbean birth and upbringing on St. Croix undoubtedly informed his endorsement of Blyden's ideas and rejection of monogamy as the only valid standard for sex, love, and marriage. He was the only child of his biological mother and father. However, his mother, Cecilia Elizabeth Haynes, had children by more than one father. His father, William Adolphus Harrison, had children by more than one mother. As a result, Hubert had numerous layers of siblings and extended family on all sides growing up on. Here we take note that many Indigenous African languages don't have a word for *cousin* because people in that category are all culturally and kinship-wise considered brothers or sisters. In any case, from a very young age, Harrison had been raised in the African tradition of "It takes a village to raise a child."

He explicitly endorsed Blyden's arguments about prostitution. "Another advantage of African polygamy," he wrote, "is the absence of the surplus woman, and, consequently, of 'the social evil' of western countries." Harrison also concurred with German philosopher Arthur Schopenhauer's argument, nearly identical to Blyden's, that in comparison to a society that allows for plural marriage, compulsory monogamy created a larger class of women without the financial support of a husband, thereby forcing more of them into hard and menial work or else prostitution. On the grounds that in London alone there were 80,000 prostituted women, Schopenhauer wondered provocatively, "What are they but the women, who, under the institution of monogamy have come off worse? Theirs is a dreadful fate: they are human sacrifices offered up on the altar of monogamy."[46] Harrison noted his response to this argument in the margins of his book of Schopenhauer essays: "Good point."

From an African angle of vision, Harrison made another radical argument about the roots of prostitution, namely that it represented the "seamy side of White Christian Civilization." He noted how prostitution never became established among Indigenous or so-called primitive peoples, and "if educated white men were not so distressingly ignorant of comparative racial facts, they would know that this is the converging testimony of all the anthropologists and sociologists." As we saw in chapter 5, Harrison's analysis of colonialism emphasized that a propertyless proletarian class—people forced to work or starve—only existed among Black Africans where white colonizers had robbed them of their ancestral lands by force to impose capitalism. Regarding prostitution, he observed similarly that "the prostitute in Africa exists only in the coast regions where the African tribal system has been disrupted and supplanted by the invading capitalistic system of white Christian civilization."

This point of Harrison's raises an even bigger one: Indigenous peoples more generally—including those living in a state of egalitarian, hunter-gatherer, "primitive communist" societies or the so-called savagery that white archaeologists say defined the overwhelming majority of human existence and evolution—have rarely, if ever made monogamy compulsory in their cultural approach toward sex or love.

The social sciences of the white imperial powers created a derogatory view of the various peoples of Africa, Asia, and the Americas as subhuman "savage races" to justify their colonization. In this process, ethnologists, anthropologists, and evolutionary biologists studied a wide range of non-European peoples, including the Australian Aboriginal peoples, Malays, Tahitians, and Polynesians in the Pacific, the Lisu peoples of Myanmar and China, the Iroquois and Pueblo Indians of North American, the Mayan, Quechua, and Selk'nam peoples of Central and South America, the Yorubas of West Africa, the Yakuts of northern Siberia, and so on.

None of them had historically made sexual monogamy compulsory. On the contrary, they often featured explicitly and intentionally nonmonogamous erotic energy exchange traditions. For example: the wedding-night gangbang rituals of the Marind-anim people of Indonesia; the rampant sexual promiscuity without jealousy of the matrilineal Mosuo women of China; the post-hunting extramarital sex rituals of the Kulina people of Brazil; the conception of shared or *multimale* biological paternity (and the collective fathering that results) in the South American Indigenous cultures of the Ache, Arawete, Bari, Canela, Cashinahua, Curripaco, Ese Eja, Kayapo, Kulina, Matis, Mehinaku, Piaroa, Piraha, Secoya, Siona, Warao, Yanomami, and Ye'kwana peoples.[47]

Dr. Patricia Dixon-Spear, who wrote a book-length work on African American women who have embraced plural (polygynous) marriage, makes a simple yet profound observation that Hubert Harrison may well have also made. In her words, "It was not until after the 15th century, with European world conquest and domination, that the idea of polygyny as an inferior marriage practice and monogamy as the superior marriage practice came to dominate the world."[48] This fact alone suggests that human beings are not monogamists by nature.

In one of the pioneering works of sexology that Harrison studied carefully called *Psychopathia Sexualis* (1886), German psychiatrist Richard von Krafft-Ebing maintained that the historical emergence of monogamy as the legal, religious, and moral standard marked the "Christian nations'... mental and material superiority over the polygamic races, and especially over Islam." The non-Christian world (and especially Muslims) thus represented the backward inferiority of shameless nonmonogamy that European Bible holders eventually overcame due to their being a smarter and more advanced race. But by the early twentieth century, the newly emerging "social sciences" like ethnology, anthropology, and evolutionary biology—and the Eurocentric knowledge regime they elaborated—had increasingly superseded the biblical justification of marital monogamy as the only God-fearing sexual relationship. Although they may have harbored a range of different intellectual, ideological, and political investments, the European social scientists advanced a new "scientific" idea that as humans evolved toward "higher" stages of development, marriage practices evolved from "inferior" and plural forms like polygyny to the "superior" and singular form of monogamy.[49]

Harrison studied, for example, the work of American anthropologist Lewis H. Morgan, who in *Ancient Society* (1877) famously advanced a three-stage theory of progressive human development from "savagery" to "barbarism" to "civilization" with a corresponding progression within the family structure toward monogamy. Friedrich Engels borrowed heavily and openly from Morgan's telos, as demonstrated in his book *The Origin of the Family, Private Property, and the State* (1884), which argued that group marriage characterized of savagery, the pairing family characterized of barbarism, and monogamy characterized civilization. As feminist monogamy critic Angela Willey argues, "The geographically distanced Other—specifically through anthropological accounts of marriage and sexual practices—comes to stand in for the imagined *evolutionary past* in (Western European) sexological discourse on monogamy."[50]

In his reading of European thinkers, Harrison saw clearly how the most vaunted white scientists elaborated a Eurocentric and colonial worldview, regardless of whether their "science" gave off a more popular or scholarly or Christianity-inflected vibe. "The social and psychological sciences can be 'worked' to produce results according to the prejudices of the scientist," observed Harrison. "A scientist is, after all, not an angel but a human being—subject as much to the pressure of his environment, educational, social, racial and others. Yet... the Birmingham police seem to think that when they put on the cloak of 'science' the thing under that cloak becomes at once insulated from the human currents of prejudice and error. This is sheer nonsense. In reality they assume the cloak in order to 'put over' their prejudices with greater authority and effect." By rationalizing compulsory sexual monogamy as a "higher" stage of human development, white intellectuals threw a cloak of science over the sex-negative religious morality of the church to "put over" their racist and Puritanical prejudices (and impose them on the rest of the world) with greater authority and effect. In Harrison's words, "The white race has ... capitalized, Christianized, and made respectable, 'scientific,' and 'natural,' the fact of its dominion."[51]

Some of the elements of Harrison's analysis—that we are not monogamists by nature and that our historically and culturally contingent sex ideals originate from private property, class society, colonialism, white supremacy, and Puritanical morality—have returned in updated form with the publication of books like *The Myth of Monogamy* and *Sex at Dawn*. Like Harrison did, these works draw on a wide array of evidence from sociological, biological, archaeological, and historical studies to add even more evidence to the case that humans are not naturally monogamous. *Sex at Dawn* points out, for example, that

- Only 3 percent of mammals and *1 in 10,000* invertebrate species can be considered sexually monogamous.
- Neither chimpanzees, gorillas, bonobos, *nor any other* social primate (the mammals biologically closest to humans) exhibit sexual monogamy.
- Male and female human sexual anatomy bears various physiological traits geared for nonmonogamous sexuality.
- Historically, women's sexual capacity has been hypocritically disavowed and repressed *precisely because* women have a greater sexual capacity than men, which threatens men in power.[52]

Suppose Harrison was right and we are not monogamists by nature but by compulsion. Then are we heteronormative by nature? Or by compulsion?

The African Roots of the Queer New Negro in Harlem

As the 1920s unfolded, Harrison's home neighborhood developed into a mecca not just for Black people generally but also for various nonmainstream sexualities that found expression and affirmation amid a proliferation of creative, artistic, and erotic flowerings of the so-called Harlem Renaissance.[53] Among African American artists, blues women played an exceptional role in breaking mainstream cultural and sexual taboos to express an African American, working-class, Southern-born, and plantation-inflected way of being, knowing, living, loving, suffering, thriving, and surviving in this world.

Lucille Bogan sang the following in "Shave 'Em Dry" (1935), for example:

> I got nipples on my titties
> Big as the end of my thumb
> I got somethin' between my legs
> That'll make a dead man cum
> Baby won't you shave 'em dry...
> Now if fuckin' was a thing that would take me to heaven
> I'd be fuckin' in the studio til the clock strikes eleven . . .

In "Till the Cows Come Home" (1934), Bogan sings:

> You know both a my mens
> They are tight like that
> They got a great big dick just like a baseball bat
> Oooooh, fuck me
> Do it to me all night long
> I want you to do it to me baby
> Honey, till the cows come home.

Meanwhile, Bessie Smith sang in "The Boy in the Boat" (1930) of how

> When you see two women walking hand in hand,
> just look 'em over and try to understand:
> They'll go to those parties—have the lights down low
> only those parties where women can go.

Bessie, speaking from experience, gives voice to women who choose to not only connect sexually with other women but also to do so in party and group-play settings.

In 1925, Bessie Smith and Clara Smith (no blood relation) sang "My Man Blues," which tells their story of discovering that Clara's "smooth Black daddy" happens to be the same man, Charlie Gray, who Bessie thinks is her man. Apparently, Gray had cultivated separate relationships with both Clara and Bessie without either's knowledge of the other. But after Bessie sings,

> Don't you know that's my man?
> Yes, that's a fact.

Clara replies,

> I ain't seen your name printed up and down his back.

Clara's reply is a challenge to the possessive attitude that Bessie is expressing. Upon realizing that both Clara and Bessie had bought him clothes in the past and also that both women had helped each other, Bessie eventually accepts Clara's suggestion that they "get it fixed." She relents, singing,

> Well, then
> I guess we got to have him on cooperation plan
> I guess we got to have him on cooperation plan.

They then sing together of how "ain't nothin' different 'bout that rotten two-time man." Nevertheless, the song ends with their resolve to work together in order to share him.

In a context marked by derogatory cultural stereotypes of curvy and dark-skinned Black woman as a desexualized "Mammy," the blues women reclaimed their erotic power from the Puritanical policeman within the church, the state, and white supremacy. Unfortunately, as Angela Davis has pointed out, "because [blues] women like Bessie Smith and Ida Cox presented and embodied sexualities associated with working-class black life—which, fatally, was seen by some Renaissance strategists as antithetical to the aims of their cultural movement—their music was designated as 'low' culture, in contrast, for example, to endeavors such as sculpture, painting, literature, and classical music."[54] Northern elite, elite-aspiring, and wannabe-white Black people perceived the "promiscuity" of Southern migrants as backward, developmentally deficient, and in need of "uplift" and moral reform.

But blues music is not "low culture." On the contrary, as Clyde Woods has argued in his groundbreaking study of the relationship between the blues and plantation power in the Mississippi delta, "the blues offers a multiethnic working-class vision of a flawed United States haunted by its own practices of ethnic oppression and enforced poverty. In the face of this reality, the blues and its extensions offer an unapologetic celebration of life, resistance, spiritual affirmation, community, social[ity] and humanity, and the highest levels, the 'upper rooms,' of African American culture and philosophy." The blues, in other words, expresses what Memphis-born multi-instrumental pan-African blues and jazz musician Baba Ekpe calls *Black-on-Black love*.[55]

Not just the blues but also jazz, vaudeville, theater, novels, poetry, and fashion all gave expression to a wider range of Black sexual, artistic, and creative energies, as did various physical spaces for exploring unorthodox sexualities. Alexander Gumby's studio "bookstore" on Fifth Avenue, for example, became a popular gathering spot for literary gay men.[56] Then there were the notorious parties of A'Lelia Walker, the heiress to Madam C. J. Walker who became a millionaire by building a hair treatment products empire. A'Lelia hosted massive parties at both the "Dark Tower" residence at 136th Street and her inherited upstate Hudson River estate mansion called Villa Lewaro. Lesbian dancer Mabel Hampton recalled a time she entered the Dark Tower and "there were some fourteen or fifteen men and women, black and white, none of whom were wearing any clothes, lounging about on oversized pillows." She noted that the men had paired with men and the women with women.[57]

Various kinds of queer-friendly parties took root in Harlem and for different reasons. Among the most common (on account of the pervasiveness of economic hardships for Black people) were the rent parties, which were organized by financially precarious Harlem tenants to help raise money to pay the rent. Rent parties featured music, food, bootleg liquor, and participation by sexually exploratory Harlemites. There were also the "buffet flats," or private parties offering a buffet-style variety of sexual choices in addition to music, food, reefer, and liquor. Some were racy establishments that flaunted the law by openly accommodating gambling and sex workers. Others were more like brothels, with patrons paying to witness or experience gourmet sexual novelties and pleasures. Hazel Valentine ran a "sex circus" on 140th Street. "Called 'The Daisy Chain' or the '101 Ranch,' it catered to all varieties of sexual tastes, and featured entertainers such as 'Sewing Machine Bertha,' who would eat up all the women, and an enormous transvestite named 'Clarenz.'"[58] Not to mention the annual drag ball sponsored by the Hamilton Lodge of the Odd Fellows that Harrison attended in 1926.

In a time before the hardening of rigid and categorical sociopolitical identities regarding sexual orientation, the erotic explorations of these awakening "New Negroes" remained fluid and dynamic. Richard Bruce Nugent emerged as a notable member of this community for being one of the first to be "out," that is, an openly gay Black man. Nugent was born in Washington, DC, in 1906, and after attending Dunbar High School he moved to Harlem, where he found his artistic voice as a young painter and part of the journal *FIRE!!* along a range of colorful figures including Wallace Thurman, Zora Neale Hurston, Gwendolyn Bennett, Countee Cullen, and Langston Hughes. According to Nugent, "Harlem was very much like the Village. People did what they wanted to do with whom they wanted to do it. You didn't get on the rooftops and shout, 'I fucked my wife last night.' So why would you get on the roof and say 'I loved prick.' You didn't. You just did what you wanted to do. Nobody was in the closet. There wasn't any closet."[59]

In other words, specific sexual acts or scenes based on same-sex attraction did not necessarily involve the adoption of the rigid or categorical sexual identities that we have today like "gay" or "lesbian" or "polyamorous." Interested parties exchanged erotic energy pragmatically without necessarily attaching a specific label or political identity to it. As Thomas Wirth noted, many Harlemites in the 1920s moved in a social matrix in which not only were extramarital sexual relationships of all kinds (including homosexual and heterosexual ones) taken for granted but also done in a manner "defined by sophisticated, 'modern' attitudes and a general rejection of conventional sexual mores, not by sexual orientation. Both extramarital dalliances and same-sex interests were effectively 'open secrets'—acceptable in private, gossiped about, but not publicly acknowledged."[60]

On some level, the queer New Negro of Harlem had African roots. In a loving critique of Carter G. Woodson's *The History of the Negro Church*, Harrison argued that the Europeans' enslavement of Africans in the Western world uprooted them from their Indigenous spiritual traditions. White nations imposed a Euro-Christian power structure on top of that spiritual foundation, a foundation that continues to shape the form that Black religiosity takes. "But no attempt is made by Dr. Woodson even to sketch these African foundations of his theme, consequently no one will learn from his work how differently Negroes worship God, or anything of their emotionalism, or of their age-long divorce of practical ethics from religious preachments under Christian teaching and example."[61] The African roots of Black spirituality explained the propensity of people of African descent in the diaspora to "divorce" their practical ethics from what most Christians preach.

Though he may not have realized it, Harrison's point applies quite profoundly to the vast and diverse range of African sexualities before colonization. In ancient Kemet (Egypt) goddesses such as Mut (goddess of motherhood) and Sekmeht (goddess of war) were often depicted as women with erect penises. In the sixteenth century, the Imbangala people of Angola had men in women's apparel who husbands kept among their wives and also a group of cross-dressing male diviners known as *chibados*. King Mwanga II of Buganda (present-day Uganda) ruled as an openly gay monarch who resisted Christianity and colonialism. In the royal palaces of Northern Sudan, daughters were sometimes given enslaved girls for sex. In the Congo, Azande warrior men could marry boys who operated as temporary wives, who could in turn become warrior men and marry "boy wives" of their own. In what is now Angola, Queen Njinga of the Mbundu people, who rose to power and fought against the Portuguese in the seventeenth century, often dressed as a man, had multiple wives, and also had a harem of male concubines who she made to dress as women.[62]

The Dagara people of Burkina Faso do not have words for *gay* or *lesbian* or *bisexual* or *transgender* but instead call queer folks "gatekeepers," who are respected in the community as having the ability to bridge the material and spirit worlds, to unlock the "gates" between them. They are seen by the Dagara culture as possessing a sacred sexuality that elevates their spirituality and positions them to mediate conflicts in the community as masculine-feminine energy balancers. Oyèrónkẹ́ Oyěwùmí has shown how the Igbo and Yoruba peoples of Nigeria did not have a gender binary, nor did they assign a gender to babies when they were born, instead waiting until later life.[63]

According to Nigerian scholar Bright Alozie, the cultivation of same-sex relationships was common among "the Siwa people of Egypt, Benin people of Nigeria, Nzima people of Ghana, San people of Zimbabwe and Pangwe people of present-day Gabon and Cameroon." Not to mention the special forms of same-sex companionship that enslaved Africans forged on the slave ships—in the traumatic experience of the trans-Atlantic *Maangamizi*—and that continued in the "New World," including the *malungo* in Brazil, the *malongue* in Trinidad, the *batiment* in Haiti, and the *sippi* and *mati* in Surinam.[64]

And yet, some people still believe that "homosexuality is un-African"!

The African continent—especially before colonization—featured a near-boundless diversity of regions, climate zones, rare earth minerals, animals, plants, ethnic groups, languages, cultures, cosmologies, *and sexualities*. The vast array of Indigenous, nonhetero, nonmonogamous, and often spiritually significant multitudes of erotic energy circuitry was precisely what European colonizers sought to destroy or suppress by imposing upon Africans their sex-negative religious morality. Colonizers inscribed laws based on homophobic theologies into the machinery of state in Africa. In short, Indigenous African erotic multiplicity was itself a vast and dynamic source of power. This exemplifies perfectly Audre Lorde's point that every oppression must necessarily corrode and disrupt the sources of power—including erotic power—within the cultures of oppressed people that can provide life-force energy for fighting against oppression.[65] No wonder the energies of Black erotic multiplicity reemerged from the political awakening of Africa-conscious Harlem! This also underscored Harrison's point that the African roots of Black culture explain the tendency of Black folks to "divorce" their practical ethics from the hypocritical Euro-Christian teachings imposed by slavery and colonization.

In light of the wide range of Indigenous sexualities in Africa, Asia, and Latin America—before the white colonizer "civilized" them—Langston Hughes's poem "Lament for Darker Peoples" hits even harder:

I was a red man one time,
But the white men came.
I was a black man, too,
But the white men came.
They drove me out of the forest.
They took me away from the jungles.
I lost my trees.
I lost my silver moons.

Now they've caged me
In the circus of civilization.
Now I herd with the many—
Caged in the circus of civilization.[66]

Like their ancestors, African-descended workers caged in the circus of "civilization" in the United States, did not—and could not—place lifelong monogamy at the center of their universe in matters of sex, love, or marriage. Although enslaved people did "jump the broom" and enact wedding rituals for themselves, enslavers could rip apart romantic partners and entire families at any time as enslaved people had no custody over their own bodies, let alone their children. As a result, enslaved people—in defiance of hypocritical injunctions from the church—maintained a more flexible and dynamic relationship to love, marriage, and family that extended into the Jim Crow era. As Du Bois observed, "While to some extent European family morals were taught [to] the small select body of house servants and artisans, both by precept and example, the great body of field hands were raped of their own sex customs and provided with no binding new ones." In his 1915 statistical study of Black families, Du Bois reported that nine-tenths of the general population in the United States were "observing the monogamic sex mores," whereas only one-half of the Black population were doing so.[67] They could neither practice their own sex customs, nor those of the Christian enslaver. They were "caged in the circus of civilization." Sigmund Freud made a similar point. "Though he was wrong about a lot, it appears Sigmund Freud got it right when he observed that 'civilization' is built largely on erotic energy that has been blocked, concentrated, accumulated, and redirected."[68]

Conclusion

Some nine months after the 1926 drag ball, Harrison recorded revealing diary reflections on another queer-friendly event at the Renaissance Casino. He spoke on behalf of the Harlem-based Virgin Islands Congressional Council, which was hosting its annual dance after a round of lobbying politicians on behalf of Virgin Islanders. Harrison regretted that "this dance is degenerating more and more into a tribade's annual; for about a third or more of the dancers on the floor are made up of female couples. This homo-sexual tendency is very strongly pronounced among Virgin Islands' women." While apparently a homophobic comment, Harrison did not oppose same-gender love on principle. After all, he maintained close friendships with people like Claude McKay, Langston Hughes, and Richard Bruce Nugent and had the night of his life at the first drag ball he attended. That Harrison found the drag queens he encountered less than a year before so attractive, and even tried to dance with someone he could hardly believe was a man, speaks to his open-mindedness about sex. As a masculine and heterosexual man, Harrison's comment may have reflected his self-interested desire for a larger pool of potential dance partners at one of the biggest events of the year for his fellow Virgin Islanders.[69] Or perhaps his comment reflected a sexist double standard of disdain for lesbian women but not for his gay and bisexual male friends.

The seeming incongruence of Harrison's homophobic comment compared with his general sexual radicalism exemplifies the way in which his striving for sexual liberation unfolded over many years of trials, tribulations, social/cultural/political contestations, and new realizations. For example, the context of church and state repression of sex writ large—mixed with the hypersexualized racial stereotypes deployed to justify the widespread rape of Black women (and men) and lynching of Black men (and women)—makes Harrison's sex radicalism all the more striking: it was not only illegal, "obscene," culturally taboo, and blasphemous to the church, but for a sexually "deviant" Black man also punishable by lawless white mob ritual torture, castration, and execution. As we saw in chapter 3 on Harrison's Outdoor Grioversity, he survived an attempt on his life on at least one occasion by a white lynch mob of Irish Catholics, the spiritual heirs of those who perpetrated the anti-Black massacre during the "draft riots" in New York during the Civil War. Harrison had hella courage. For a Black working-class immigrant to speak publicly about free love, to say out loud that we are not monogamists by nature, and to agitate for access to contraception (in the 1910s!) demonstrated a distinctive shamelessness about sex, not to mention an unusual ethic of radical sexual honesty and vulnerability.

Harrison's sex radicalism came at considerable cost to his social standing, given that coming out publicly as a free lover did not win him any points in "respectable" social circles. According to historian Winston James, "Harrison seemed to have developed a certain notoriety as a philanderer and this diminished his standing and popularity."[70] US military intelligence noted similarly that "one of the chief reasons why Harrison, who is really a very intelligent and highly educated man and scholar, has failed in nearly all his undertakings is said to be his abnormal sexualism, in spite of the fact that he is the father of several children."[71]

On the other hand, Harrison also understood how embracing his own erotic energy gave additional vitality to his thinking, speaking, and writing, much like the way in which the erotic awakening energized so many other Black creatives of the so-called Harlem Renaissance. In that frame, the federal agents surveilling Harrison overlooked the way he tapped into his erotic power as a wellspring of life-force energy to do extraordinary things like read up to five books a day, crystallize radical new ideas and organizations, and speak on street corners to a mass audience multiple nights a week.

At the end of the day, Harrison stood in his truth and offered his masculine erotic energy to multiple women, including romantic connections that brought about moments of deep healing and wild pleasures in a world that systematically denied both to Black people. His Black free love politics gave expression to the larger sexual awakening that would unfold in Harlem. This awakening in turn created spaces for more expansive forms of Black love and erotically liberating intimacies, including some that made even the sex-radical Harrison uncomfortable. And, despite all their struggles, he never stopped loving Lin.

What do we make of these contradictions? We all have our spots and wrinkles. And hurt people hurt other people. Thanks to things like the church, the state, slavery, hate, lynching, and rape, modern society as a whole remains sexually traumatized. Healing those wounds requires a radical love that addresses itself toward repairing the damage—damage done to our masculinity and femininity, damage done to our families and bonds of kinship, damage done to our conceptions about love and marriage, to our level of sexual satisfaction, and the damaging aspects of how we must navigate our naturally vast and many-splendored erotic potential in a hostile and sex-negative society.

Harrison's Black free love politics highlights the manner in which so many of the traumas, trials, and tribulations we grapple with in our sexual and romantic lives have larger structural causes: the oppression of compulsory monogamy as a mechanism for preserving the private property and private-family ideology of the ruling class; the world-historic patriarchal subordination of women within class-divided societies; the Puritanical morality and relentless sexual shaming and policing from the churches, mosques, and synagogues; the legacy of Comstockian sexual repression by the government; capitalism's creation of an immense majority class of those who must work for a wage or starve, including those for whom the so-called choice to do sex work imposes itself quasi-coercively as the only apparent means of economic survival; the traumatization of Black sexual vitality and the relentless oppression of its sacred, erotic, and life-generative power by rape and lynching; and the role of imperialism in violently imposing all of the above on African people and other colonized peoples all over the world.

Harrison's Black free love politics also suggests a way out: namely, that the struggle for a love that is radical, healing, and as limitless as Blackness itself is part and parcel of the struggle for Black and pan-African liberation, women's liberation, spiritual decolonization, and the emancipation of labor *and love* from capitalism. Black free love politics invites us to decenter monogamy as the be-all and end-all for sexual and romantic connection. To be clear: the implicit argument here is not that plural marriage or free love or same-sex intimacy must become the new compulsory standards, the things to which all forward-thinking people should aspire. The point is that *no* particular sex, love, or marriage configuration should be compulsory. If the vast size of his erotica collection is any indicator, Harrison apparently concluded that we have a world to win if we can learn to embrace the wide and non-binary spectrum of natural, beautiful, and life-giving erotic energies that we are capable of as human beings. Apart from the studies of "settler sexuality" that Indigenous scholars like Kim Tallbear have undertaken, the predominant frameworks of political radicalism today have largely failed to interrogate compulsory monogamy and its implications. But how can we honestly imagine political liberation without sexual liberation too? Black free love politics presents a critical and sorely neglected variable in the algebraic equations for revolution. As the late, great Maya Angelou put it, "Love liberates. It doesn't just hold; that's ego. *Love* liberates."[72]

Chapter 7

Hubert Harrison: Global Mass Movement Catalyst

> What do I care about death in the cause of the redemption of Africa? . . . Life is not worth its salt except [if] you can live it for some purpose. And the noblest purpose for which to live is the emancipation of a race and the emancipation of posterity.
>
> —Marcus Garvey, *Negro World*, April 28, 1923

> Perhaps no phrase has done more to consolidate the sentiment of the Negroes of the world than that summed up in the two words: "Negro First." If we remember correctly, the slogan was coined by the well-known lecturer and scholar, Hubert Harrison.
>
> —*Negro World*, "Race First!" July 26, 1919

Hubert Henry Harrison and his Liberty League of Negro-Americans catalyzed emergence of the largest international organization of Black people in modern history: the Universal Negro Improvement Association and African (Imperial) Communities League (UNIA). Founded in 1914 by Marcus Garvey and Amy Ashwood, the UNIA originally sought to establish a Tuskegee-style school for industrial education in Jamaica. Ashwood and Garvey's encounter with Harrison and the Liberty League in Harlem gave them a practical model for convening an organization that combined African Americans and African Caribbeans of various national origins with a "race first" ideology, social movement building orientation, and internationalist vision of collective self-determination. As we will see, Marcus Garvey might never have become the namesake of Garvey*ism*—as a global mass movement for pan-African nationality—without the decisive influence of Hubert Harrison.

During its heyday, the Garvey movement represented an attempt to forge and sustain what Charles Carnegie has called a "transcendent and transterritorial notion of sovereignty" for the Black world.[1] As Robbie Shilliam has pointed out, the UNIA developed a range of state-like features including paramilitary units, a civil service, a youth cadet program, a travel passport, a court system, its own flag and national anthem, a semiofficial church, an auxiliary health service, a shipping line, and a range of industrial enterprises that sought to carve out an exclusively Black-owned economy. Not to mention its formal bureaucracy, complete with potentates, dukes, presidents, and other governmental titles. During his travels Garvey acted like a head of state, garnering an audience with figures like the governor of British Honduras and the president of Costa Rica.² Pointing additionally to the fact of its semiofficial recognition by the League of Nations in 1922 and 1928, Shilliam argues that the Garvey movement "managed to coalesce, however briefly and imperfectly, an extra-territorial Pan-African sovereign authority."³ Yet global Black nation building was not the only dimension of Garveyism.

With tens of thousands of members spread across hundreds of Black communities along both shores of the Atlantic Ocean, the ground-level substance of the Garvey movement inevitably went beyond the lofty ideals of its Harlem-based officialdom. Various racially awakened elements of the African diaspora joined the Garvey movement, "from dockworkers in South Africa to sharecroppers in the United States, from cocoa farmers in Ghana to intellectuals in Nigeria, from ethnic mobilizers in Zimbabwe to activists in Cuba."⁴ Garvey's Harlem-based *Negro World* newspaper published in English, French, and Spanish editions to give voice to the movement's multiple and sometimes contradictory tendencies, both "individualist and collectivist, nationalist and internationalist, working-class and bourgeois."⁵

Whereas in Trinidad UNIA members led some of the spectacular labor struggles of the postwar period, the organization's leading Black women in New Orleans spoke of Garveyism as "our church, our clubhouse, our theatre, our fraternal order and our school, and we will never forsake it while we live."⁶ Beneath the nation building aspect, the Garvey movement comprised a kind of "pan-African potter's clay," an inspiring source of global race pride that captured the transnational Black imagination largely thanks to its malleability and adaptability to different local and national contexts.⁷ As the eminent Garvey movement scholar and archivist Robert Hill put it, "The Garvey movement . . . was not a single movement; it was several movements that faced in multiple directions."⁸

While partisans of the Garvey movement have often overestimated its size (as we will see in chapter 8), the movement's critics have often underestimated its political significance. Yet no history of pan-Africanism could be taken seriously without engaging with the titanic historical influence of Marcus Garvey and Garveyism. The Garvey movement's call for pan-African national sovereignty influenced African nationalist movements in such diverse places as Canada, Nigeria, Sierra Leone, the Gold Coast, South Africa, Trinidad, Cuba, Honduras, Guyana, Barbados, Bermuda, Jamaica, Panama, Senegal, and Cameroon. Kwame Nkrumah proudly and openly acknowledged Garvey as a significant influence on his pan-Africanism. As the first prime minister of an independent Ghana, Nkrumah placed a black star in the center of Ghana's flag as an homage to the UNIA's Black Star Line shipping company. Figures like Nnamdi Azikiwe and Jomo Kenyatta, the first independent heads of state of Nigeria and Kenya respectively, claimed a deep influence from Garveyism in their youth. Both of Malcolm X's parents were UNIA members: his father was a Garveyist preacher, and his mother had written for Garvey's *Negro World*. Even the Vietnamese anticolonial revolutionary Ho Chi Minh took in Garvey's influence during his time in New York.[9]

Simultaneously, the UNIA attracted an array of extraordinary women like Amy Ashwood Garvey, Amy Jacques Garvey, Henrietta Vinton Davis, Maymie de Mena, Adelaide Casely-Hayford, Maude Lena Gordon, Charlotta Bass, "Queen Mother" Audley Moore, and Ethel Collins, all of whom would play important roles in carrying forward Garveyism's message about Black pride, pan-African nationalism, and racial self-empowerment into the second half of the twentieth century, well beyond Garvey's death in 1940.[10] As Garvey scholar Barbara Bair puts it, "For each of these... [better-known] UNIA women, there are hundreds of others that would aptly illustrate the spectrum of roles, self-images, class affiliations, marital status, routes to power, and philosophies of leadership represented by women in the Garvey movement.... Garveyism was not only a 'new manhood movement' but a new womanhood movement as well." Their experience and contributions comprised an "efficient womanhood," as the scholar of women in the Garvey movement Natanya Duncan has uncovered.[11] How did Garvey develop this mass movement strategy?

Hubert Harrison offers a key missing piece of the puzzle regarding how and what and why Garveyism ultimately came to be. By analyzing Garvey's politics before and after his encounter with Harrison, we can uncover a decisive influence on the meteoric rise to prominence of Garvey and Garveyism.

Garveyism before Garvey

Garvey like the rest of us all followed Hubert Harrison.

—W. A. Domingo, interview with Theodore Draper, January 18, 1958

Radical Jamaican-born activist Wilfred Adolphus Domingo got elected president of an elevator operators trade union and later a West Indian food import merchant in Harlem. He knew Marcus Garvey from their boyhood days in Jamaica and did a great deal to help Garvey get settled when he first moved to New York City. Domingo showed Garvey around, introducing him to various Harlem activists like Hubert Harrison, whose Liberty League they would both join in 1917. In the summer of 1918, following the fracture and splitting of the Liberty League, Domingo helped Garvey start the UNIA's *Negro World* newspaper by finding him a sympathetic printer, the same one who produced the Socialist Party's *New York Call*. Domingo became the *Negro World*'s first editor and taught Garvey how to chair meetings using parliamentary procedures.[12]

Eventually, Garvey put Domingo "on trial" before the executive committee of the UNIA for writing openly Socialist editorials for the *Negro World*. Domingo won his "case" but resigned in the summer of 1919 on the grounds that Garvey's methods were "medieval, obscure, and dishonest," especially the Black Star Line shipping venture, which he believed to be "bordering on a huge swindle." According to his Socialist comrade Richard B. Moore, Domingo "broke with Garvey because nobody with any sense of dignity, human dignity, could stand Garvey for very long, that is in the position of a subordinate, because Garvey didn't reason. He ... treated you as if you just didn't exist as a human being with any dignity in your own right. So Domingo broke with Garvey and then became his most active opponent." And in Domingo's war against Garvey, Hubert Harrison would defend the UNIA as Domingo's main intellectual antagonist. Domingo would not be the only Caribbean-born Black Socialist to introduce Garvey to Harlem, edit his newspaper, teach him new things, and welcome him to the city that the UNIA now called home. But we are getting ahead of ourselves.[13]

On August 17, 1887, Marcus Garvey was born in the rural peasant community of St. Anne's Bay, Jamaica. He trained as a printer's apprentice and led a strike of print workers in 1907. He traveled extensively in Central America observing the poor working conditions and treatment of Caribbean migrants. Experiences like this provided stimulus for his emerging racial consciousness regarding the subordinate position of Black people throughout the region. By 1912 he made his way to London, where he would work for Dusé Mohamed Ali's *African Times and Orient Review*. Reading Booker T. Washington's autobiography *Up from Slavery* inspired Garvey to duplicate Washington's example. "In a word," said Garvey of the UNIA in 1915, "our society desires to establish a Tuskegee in Jamaica." However, the organization initially struggled to fundraise, prompting Garvey to set sail for the United States and visit Washington's Tuskegee Institute in Alabama for financial support.[14]

Garvey did not merely seek funding from Booker T. Washington but also endorsed Washington's Institute as a model for what he wanted to achieve in his home country. For example, in 1915 the UNIA advertised its intention to establish an "Industrial Farm and Institute" that would provide training in agriculture and the trades and train "our young women to be good and efficient domestics."[15] Unfortunately for Garvey, the "Wizard" of Tuskegee passed away in 1915 before Garvey reached Alabama, prompting Garvey to eulogize him as "the greatest hero sprung from the stock of scattered Ethiopia."[16] Hubert Harrison, by contrast, got fired from his postal job by Washington's dastardly "Tuskegee Machine" as punishment for his published criticisms of Booker T. Washington.

Following in Washington's footsteps, Garvey embraced an explicitly white-friendly orientation in the first three years of the UNIA's existence. For example, in his speech to the first annual meeting of the UNIA in Jamaica in August of 1915, Garvey emphasized that because so many Black Jamaicans were engaged in "villainy and vice of the worst kind, immorality, Obeah and all kinds of dirty things," the UNIA's task was to "go among the people and help them up to a better state of appreciation among the cultured classes and raise them to the standard of civilized approval. To do this we must get the co-operation and sympathy of our white brothers."[17] Black people, being uncivilized, needed to be raised up to a higher standard if they were ever to receive the "civilized approval" of white people.

As startling as this white-positive sentiment may sound—in light of the militant Black nationalism for which Garvey would later become legendary—it was no slip of the tongue. When the new Tuskegee president Robert Moton came to Jamaica for a visit in early 1916, Garvey prepared a detailed memorandum about how he wanted to solve the race problem "on the broadest humanitarian lines," by which he meant "on the platform of Dr. Booker T. Washington. . . . Hence you will find that up to now my one true friend as far as you can rely on his friendship is the white man." Garvey then boasted of how the white colonial establishment, including "his Excellency the Governor, the Colonial Secretary, Hon. H. Bryan, C.M.G. Sir John Pringle, Hon. Brigadier-General, L.S. Blackden, [and] all members of the Privy Council, have been our patrons on several occasions and they are still friends of the Association." Not only that, but "the Brigadier-General has lectured to us, also His Lordship Bishop J.J. Collins, S.J., His Worship the Mayor of Kingston, Hon. H.A.L. Simpson, M.L.C., Mr. R.W. Bryant, J.P., ex-Mayor of Kingston who has visited us more than a dozen times, and many other prominent dignitaries of the country" offered their "civilized" approval of Garvey's fledgling organization.[18]

The notion of multiple white colonial officials lecturing UNIA gatherings would have been almost unthinkable after 1917, but Garvey's white-positive and civilizationist orientation fitted with his fixation on Booker T. Washington's model of industrial education, which derived its financial support from rich white sponsors like Andrew Carnegie, John D. Rockefeller, and J. P. Morgan.[19] Not to mention Garvey's early exposure to—and emulation of—the Brotherhood movement in England, as Robert Hill has detailed.[20] As late as June of 1917, shortly before his address at the inauguration of Harrison's Liberty League, Garvey was still seeking financial support for his organization from Tuskegee.[21]

By contrast, Hubert Harrison already adopted a politics based on Black financial and organizational independence from white people. Harrison's approach emerged from his bitter experience with the white-funded accommodationism of Booker T. Washington's Republican-aligned "Tuskegee Machine," the white racist "Southernism" of the Socialist Party, the openly white-supremacist and Ku Klux Klan-friendly Democratic Party of Woodrow Wilson, and the white "professional friends of the Negro" who founded and funded the National Association for the Advancement of Colored People (NAACP). Harrison concluded on the basis of his own experience that the political interests of Black working people like himself could not be advanced through the Democrats, Republicans, Socialists, or any other white-controlled political formation. He turned toward agitation primarily in his home neighborhood of Harlem precisely because he had come to the conclusion that in order to make any real progress, Black folks "must depend upon ourselves and not upon white people."[22] Harrison thus placed a premium on Black self-reliance and racial solidarity before Garvey ever set foot in the United States.

This white approval-seeking, Tuskegee-based approach to domestic Black uplift at home dovetailed with Garvey's conservative views on global affairs. In the realm of foreign policy, Garvey took a position of loyalty and support for the British and French in the "Great War" raging in Europe, declaring, "Thrice we hail: 'God save the King! Long live the British Empire'" and "may continuous victory follow the French army against the foe, and France once more resume her peaceful and civilizing influence on the world."[23] Garvey's statements at this point reflected his admiration of European empires. Harrison, by contrast, did not attribute any "civilizing influence" to Britain or France but instead spoke as early as 1915 of how the white imperialist nations were fighting over who would control the "colored" majority of humanity who lived in Asia and Africa, as we saw in chapter 4.[24]

Garvey arrived in New York City in 1916, but his first attempt at public speaking there ended in him fainting and falling off the stage.[25] Not to be deterred, Garvey toured the country, speaking in numerous cities and continuing to attempt to raise money to set up an industrial trade school in Jamaica. During this tour, Garvey inevitably came face to face with the grim realities of racial oppression in the United States and numerous Black voices who discouraged the idea of building a Tuskegee-style institution in Jamaica.[26] By the time he returned to New York in the spring of 1917, he had run out of money and strained his relationship with his partner Amy Ashwood such that he seriously considered returning to his home country. As summer approached, he found himself in anything but an auspicious situation in the city that would later house the UNIA headquarters. Luckily for Garvey, he would soon encounter a unique opportunity for redemption thanks to the man who A. Philip Randolph called the "father of Harlem radicalism."[27]

Whereas Marcus Garvey found himself down and out in the spring of 1917, Hubert Harrison and the "New Negro Manhood Movement" were on the rise, as we discussed in chapter 2.[28] When Harrison put out a call for the formation of the Liberty League of Negro-Americans on June 12 to protest against lynching and racial oppression, 2,000 people packed the Bethel African Methodist Episcopal Church in Harlem to support the new organization. Because Harrison wanted to collaborate with Black people of the "New Negro" type who were similarly interested in self-help and racial progress, he welcomed the little-known but energetic younger Jamaican called Marcus Garvey and gave him a platform at the Liberty League's inaugural mass meeting. By all accounts, Garvey shined in his speech before Harrison's audience. Garvey's oratorical skills had apparently grown tremendously during his cross-country tour. Multiple observers of Garvey noted that he eulogized Harrison, offered an impassioned endorsement of the Liberty League, and joined it.[29]

Thus, by the time Garvey returned to Harlem in 1917, he had not only improved his public speaking skills; he also saw by comparison how deeply Harrison's approach to organizing the Liberty League had resonated in the Black mecca of Harlem, whose racial consciousness and political awareness Harrison had worked so hard to cultivate. Garvey himself reportedly acknowledged the challenges he had encountered while trying to gain a foothold in the United States, explaining that he "had made up his mind to return to Jamaica in the spring of 1917, when he became associated with Mr. W.A. Domingo and Mr. Hubert Harrison."[30] By Harrison's recollection, when Garvey arrived in Harlem "he was so poor that some of us had to give him food and clothes."[31] The hospitality from other, better-established Caribbean migrants like Domingo and Harrison gave Garvey a new lease on life in Harlem at a critical moment of need. The model and inspiration of Harrison's Liberty League convinced Garvey not only to stay in the United States but also to make Harlem his new base of operations.[32]

Richard B. Moore, a Caribbean-born activist in Harlem, witnessed up close the relationship between Harrison's Liberty League and the emergence of Garvey's movement. According to Moore, Garvey "emerged as a leader in the Liberty League of Afro-Americans which had been launched and guided forward by Hubert H. Harrison, the man whom I think more than any other man in Harlem, the cultural renaissance of that period was chiefly stimulated. It was Harrison, also, who introduced Garvey to his first great audience in Bethel church and gave him his start. . . . Garvey came into the light of public leadership as a result of that introduction by Hubert H. Harrison in the mass meeting [of the Liberty League] at Bethel church." In other words, the Harlem UNIA division emerged out of the proverbial womb of the Liberty League.

Despite its initial successes, the Liberty League eventually developed internal divisions over who would control its newspaper (*The Voice*), divisions that would prove fatal to the league but decisive in the rise of the future flagship UNIA division. Moore offered a firsthand account of what happened: "Despite the welcome and favorable introduction accorded to him by Harrison, Garvey was not slow to take advantage of the schism that developed in the Liberty League. This dissension arose over the ownership of *The Voice*, which Harrison insisted was his own while several members held that this newspaper, which was supported by the League, should belong to the organization. In the split which ensued, Garvey influenced a number of assenters to join with him to launch in New York [a new branch of] the Universal Negro Improvement Association and African Communities League."[33] While other historical sources about the cause and substance of this factionalism in the Liberty League are scarce, a government informant corroborated Moore's account.[34] Once again, the Harlem UNIA branch was formed from a factional splintering of Harrison's organization.

Harrison influenced the Garvey movement in more subtle and indirect ways, such as through his inspiring example of New Negro journalism in *The Voice*. As Harlem activist Hodge Kirnon said, *The Voice* "really crystallized the radicalism of the Negro in New York and its environs."[35] As we saw in chapter 2, *The Voice* sparked a genre of World War I–era New Negro journalism that would find expression in subsequent publications like A. Philip Randolph and Chandler Owen's Socialist *Messenger* in the fall of 1917, Garvey's *Negro World* in 1918, Cyril Briggs's *Crusader* in 1919, and W. A. Domingo's *Emancipator* in 1920. Each of these papers followed in the wake of Harrison's *Voice*, which had set an example of how a Black newspaper did not "need to bite its tongue, to 'sell out' to white politicians, nor to hold back from 'showing up' the highly placed Judases who are selling the race and its future for a mess of pottage."[36]

The league ran into other difficulties in the months and years following its inception. Space prohibits a full telling of that story here, but Harrison's biographer Jeffrey Perry has recounted in great detail the shifts in personnel from the Liberty League and *The Voice* toward the UNIA, the *Negro World*, Domingo's *Emancipator*, August Bernier's *Clarion*, and other formations between 1917 and 1920.[37] Critical founders of the New York UNIA division like Issac Allen, John E. Bruce, Gertrude Miller-Faide, Marcus Garvey, Anselmo Jackson, Irena Moorman-Blackston, Charles Seifert, and Orlando Thompson all came from the Liberty League. As Perry demonstrates, the shifts of personnel came about not in a rapid, sweeping, or clear-cut fashion but as the result of various ideological, political, and financial struggles between numerous individuals and political currents that competed for influence within the dynamic and vibrant wartime New Negro moment in Harlem. In the final analysis, multiple observers, including Harrison himself, agreed that the success of the UNIA emerged out of the ruins of the Liberty League's failure.[38]

Garvey would eventually deploy his masterful skills as an orator, organizer, and propagandist in order to build an unprecedented following far beyond just Harlem and Jamaica. What is notable for our purposes here is that Marcus Garvey built the Harlem UNIA alongside a group of dissatisfied fellow members in Harrison's Liberty League.[39] The Liberty League thus gave rise to not just to any old UNIA formation but the New York division that would constitute the international headquarters of the Garvey movement.

"Race First!": Harrison's Influence on the Ideology of Garveyism

Although Harrison and his Liberty League redeemed Garvey's fortunes at a critical juncture, Harrison's influence on Garveyism did not end there. He also "had a profound influence on the thinking of Marcus Garvey during the formative years of his movement in America," according to Harlem-based historian John Henrik Clarke.[40] We have mentioned some of the objective factors that created the conditions for the rise of Garveyism in the United States—Caribbean and Southern African American migration, the racial and political awakening detonated by World War I, the rich tapestry of Black cultures and traditions that came together in Harlem. Alongside these objective factors, a closer look at Harrison reveals his role as a key subjective influence on Garvey's ideology and strategic vision for the UNIA, which copied and adapted various features from Harrison's Liberty League.

Harrison's years of work agitating for Black racial and political consciousness in Harlem, including his role as a key architect of the street-corner speaking tradition there, present another dimension of his influence on Garveyism. As the St. Croix–born *Voice* and *Negro World* writer Anselmo Jackson put it, prior to Garvey's arrival, Harrison "was preaching an advanced type of radicalism with a view to impressing race-consciousness and effecting racial solidarity among Negroes. . . . The very atmosphe[re] was charged with Harrison's propaganda. . . . He was the forerunner of Garvey and contributed largely to the success of the latter by preparing the minds of Negroes through his lectures, thereby molding and developing a new temper among Negroes."[41] Although difficult to measure, this aspect of Harrison's influence on Garveyism cannot be underestimated, given the many years of work that Harrison put in to establish the Outdoor Grioversity and the larger public oral knowledge-building practice that would become a cultural fixture in the Black "Mecca" of Harlem—likewise with Harrison's *Voice* newspaper, which stimulated a range of different New Negro forays into journalism, including the *Negro World*.

The Garvey movement would eventually popularize its brand of Black nationalism with the slogan "race first," but the genealogy of this doctrine reveals Hubert Harrison as the key influence and link to an older tradition of Black racial pride. In the late nineteenth and early twentieth centuries, figures like T. Thomas Fortune, Ida B. Wells-Barnett, and William Monroe Trotter chafed at the political limitations of the two-party system, developing a practical politics of "race first, then party" that forged a path for the World War I–era New Negro movement to follow.[42] Then in 1915 President Woodrow Wilson's speeches employed the slogan of "America First" as his position on the outbreak of the war in Europe. Wilson solemnly declared his intention to stand for "America first, last, and all the time."[43] Harrison remixed and repurposed these themes, declaring shortly after founding the Liberty League in 1917 that "any man today who aspires to lead the Negro race must set squarely before his face the idea of 'Africa First,'" because "when it comes to a showdown, we are Negroes first, last, and all the time."[44]

As he would later make clear, Harrison used the term *Africa* "in its racial rather than geographical sense,"[45] and when his attempt to establish "Africa First" as the guiding doctrine of the New Negro movement failed to stick, he amended the slogan to "Negro First" or "Race First."[46] The latter variation proved more tangible to African American and Caribbean communities who lived under racial oppression on a daily basis but did not necessarily identify positively with Africa, particularly given the demeaning mainstream cultural depictions of Africa as little more than a jungle full of savages. While still in his role as original editor of the *Negro World*, W. A. Domingo confirmed the Harrisonian genealogy of "Race First" with a *Negro World* editorial in July of 1919 titled "Race First!" which noted that "perhaps no phrase has done more to consolidate the sentiment of the Negroes of the world than that summed up in the two words: 'Negro First.' If we remember correctly, the slogan was coined by the well-known lecturer and scholar, Hubert Harrison."[47]

As we saw in chapter 1, Harrison reached the "race first" position in part as a response to his political battles with the "class first" position of the Socialist Party, from which Harrison ultimately resigned on account of his observation that in practice the party prioritized the interests of the white race first and then class solidarity with Black workers as an afterthought.[48] Said differently, had the Socialists been serious about a "class first" politics, they would have had much more concern about Black people, a group *more thoroughly proletarian* than any other element in the country, as Harrison had tried and failed to convince them.

A further example of Harrison's "race first" doctrinal influence on Garvey can be seen in the changed tone of Garvey's speeches. For example, Harrison's articulation of "race first" in 1917 noted how "just as the white men of these and other lands are white men before they are Christians, Anglo-Saxons or Republicans; so the Negroes of this and other lands are intent upon being Negroes before they are Christians, Englishmen, or Republicans. . . . Our first duty [as Negroes] is to ourselves."[49] In other words, European Americans generally acted in accordance with their privileged white racial position first, before their religious or political beliefs entered the picture. To counter this racial oppression, Black people also had to recognize and unite to collectively counter their experience of racial oppression within a white-dominated country. Hence the need to put "race first."

Garvey took Harrison's lesson to heart. Whereas before his tenure in the Liberty League Garvey had boasted about white colonial support for the UNIA in Jamaica, by 1919 he maintained that "we are neither Democrats nor Republicans nor Socialists nor Bolshevists nor I.W.W. [Industrial Workers of the World], all of them are white men, and when they were robbing us from Africa, they robbed us with all parties. . . . Therefore, we are not going to waste time over the white man's politics. All the time we have to waste is with pro-Negro politics."[50] Black people needed a pro-Black orientation to push back against the predominance of anti-Black oppression.

At a popular level, the Garvey movement also came to be associated with the notion of going "back to Africa." However, "Africa for the Africans!" was a far cry from the Tuskegee model of industrial education that Garvey originally set out to emulate. As Caribbean-born Harlem activist Hodge Kirnon noted in the *Negro World*, "an association of Negro peoples with the redemption of Africa as its ideal . . . seemed entirely foreign to Garvey's mind" when he first got to Harlem. Yet, as Kirnon also observed firsthand, the themes surrounding African redemption would "become the cardinal and distinctive features of the movement; also the shaping and inspiring forces to both its numerical and spiritual growth."[51]

In this process, Harrison helped catalyze Garvey's pivot from white-sponsored industrial education to a global movement for pan-African nationality. As we saw in chapter 5 on Harrison's African consciousness, Richard B. Moore insisted that more than any other individual in Harlem, Harrison "gave forth from his encyclopedic store, a wealth of knowledge of African history and culture which brought [African] consciousness to a very great height" in the community.[52] A commitment to the politics of "Africa first" literally

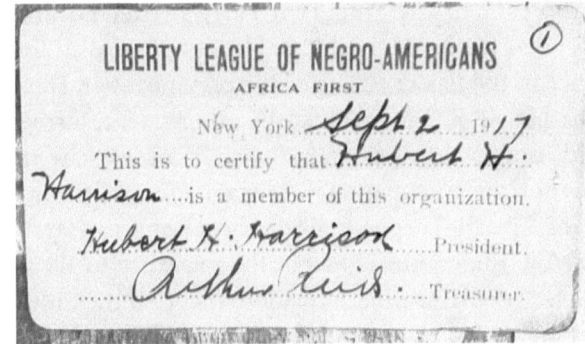

Figure 7.1
"Africa First" on Hubert Harrison's Liberty League membership card. Hubert H. Harrison Papers, flat box 740, Rare Book and Manuscript Library, Columbia University, New York.

inscribed one's membership in the Liberty League (see figure 7.1). The official Liberty League principles declared that "with the 250 millions of our brethren in Africa we feel a special sympathy, and we will work for the ultimate realization of democracy in Africa—for the right of these darker millions to rule their own ancestral lands."[53] The theme of solidarity with millions of Black people in Africa emerged as a cornerstone of Garvey speeches not when he was seeking white elite support to build a trade school in Jamaica but after his tenure in the Liberty League. As Kirnon observed, "An interest in Africa and matters of culture relating to Africa and the Africans . . . [was] being shaped and brought to a near maturity by Harrison before Mr. Garvey came upon the scene."[54] Garvey studied closely the untamed, untamable African.

Harrison influenced not only Marcus Garvey's domestic ideology of "race first" but also his internationalism, as in the case of Ireland. Robert Hill has argued, convincingly, that the Irish struggle "assisted in focusing Garvey's political perspective" far more than any other foreign nationalist movement.[55] For example, in 1919 Garvey insisted that "the time [had] come for the Negro race to offer up its martyrs upon the altar of liberty even as the Irish [had] given a long list from Robert Emmet to Roger Casement."[56] Yet one searches in vain to find a single mention of Ireland or the Irish in the voluminous *Marcus Garvey Papers* before Garvey's tenure in Harrison's Liberty League. On the contrary, the UNIA declared at the start of the white world war, "Thrice we hail: 'God save the King! Long live the British Empire.'" Not to mention Garvey's explicit reverence, as late as 1916, for what he called the "protecting and civilizing influence of the English nation and people."[57] These were not the positions of a staunch supporter of Irish liberation.

By contrast, Harrison's editorials in *The Voice*—the best source available for surmising the content of Liberty League meetings and discussions—contain numerous explicit references to what Black people could learn from the Irish struggle. For example, in 1917 Harrison explicitly argued that African

Americans must follow the path of the Sinn Fein Party in Ireland and organize their vote independently like the Irish republicans who called for "Home Rule."[58] In reference to the Easter Rising of the previous year, Harrison likewise urged Black people to "rise against the government, just as the Irish against England, unless they get their rights."[59] As we saw in chapter 2, explicit support for the Irish national struggle appeared in the inaugural resolutions of the Liberty League.[60] These facts point to Harrison's role in teaching Garvey, among others, about the relevance to Black people of the Irish struggle for self-determination, not to mention the influence of Harrison's radical politics of "colored internationalism" in expanding Garvey and other Liberty League members' global range of vision.

Perhaps most importantly of all, Harrison's Liberty League catalyzed the strategic transition in Garvey's vision for the UNIA, from a vehicle for Tuskegee Institute emulation to a mass movement-building organization. During Garvey's tour of the United States in 1916, he often ran into Afro-Caribbeans who discouraged him from the idea of building an industrial school in Jamaica.[61] Yet he did not have a clear alternative project in mind and nearly returned to Jamaica in the spring of 1917. Right at that moment, he encountered Hubert Harrison and joined the Liberty League, which held out a model not for building a white-funded, brick-and-mortar industrial school but a mass *movement*, with a "race first," *Black*-funded, and internationalist orientation to secure life, liberty, economic advancement, education, and self-empowerment for Black people. Garvey, to his credit, had the brilliance and marketing savvy to take this idea and scale it up into a global Black nation building project. But the practical model and racial ideology for creating a mass movement organization that combined for the first time African Americans and African Caribbeans of various national origins on a large scale with a program of collective Black self-help—this came from the Liberty League.[62]

Harrison knew the league had a seminal influence on the rise of the Garvey movement. The book of essays he published—in response to the occasion of the UNIA's first annual international convention in 1920—begins with an account of the birth of the Liberty League. He did this because, in his words, "*that meeting at historic Bethel on June 12, 1917, and the labors of tongue and pen out of which that meeting emerged were the foundation for the mighty structures of racial propaganda which have been raised since then. This is a fact not generally known because I have not hankered after newspaper publicity.*"[63] Harrison's reference to "mighty structures of racial propaganda" pertained to the massively popular *Negro World* under his editorship, the Black Star Line corporation, and the UNIA's electrifying impact on the racial pride and self-esteem of the global African diaspora. Harrison was generally humble to a fault and viscerally averse to lavish praise, which is one reason he has been so underappreciated historically. Therefore, it appears all the more striking for him to say openly and self-consciously that the UNIA had grown into a gigantic international mass movement of Black people thanks to the foundation laid by his years of work to inaugurate the Liberty League of Negro Americans.

In the realm of visual culture, the UNIA took yet another idea from the Liberty League: a three-colored flag for Black liberation. In 1920, Garvey's UNIA adopted a tricolor to symbolize the blood that must be shed for liberty (red), the racial color of people of African descent (black), and the rich and fertile land of Africa (green).[64] Given the popularity in the 1900s of such anti-Black songs as "Every Race Has a Flag but the Coon" and the feeling of statelessness that drove the nation building aspect of the Garvey movement, a flag that symbolized Black nationality was no minor matter. For example, when the *Negro World* ran a "Why I am a Garveyite" competition in 1927, multiple winning entries submitted by UNIA members referenced the organization's flag in particular as having attracted them to Garveyism. Although the red, black, and green remains a pan-African symbol to this day, informing the flag colors of multiple African countries, the idea of a *tricolor* design for Black liberation came directly from the flag design of the Liberty League. According to Harrison, the UNIA's red, black, and green represented an adaptation of the Liberty League's tricolor of black, brown, and yellow, originally designed to symbolize both the "three colors of the Negro race in America" and "our dual relationship to our own and other peoples" of color around the world.[65]

The parent body of the UNIA held its main meetings at a venue called Liberty Hall in Harlem. Liberty Halls popped up across the country as the standard name given to all UNIA meeting halls, following that of the Harlem-based New York division. According to Harrison's son William, his father had given the name "Liberty Hall" to the venue at 114 West 138th Street to mark where the Liberty League meetings took place. When Garvey first started the UNIA chapter in Harlem, they met at the Palace Casino and only later moved into Liberty Hall sometime in 1919 or 1920, after Harrison's Liberty League had ceased regular meetings.[66]

Harrison's influence on the Garvey movement became even more acute when at the end of 1919, with *The Voice* having gone bankrupt, Harrison accepted an invitation from Marcus Garvey to edit Garvey's *Negro World* newspaper. Garvey initially sought out Harrison to lead a UNIA university (a project that would come to fruition in the form of a Booker T. Washington University at 3–13 West 136th Street in Harlem on the eve of Harrison's departure from the *Negro World*). But apparently they settled on Harrison as a

Negro World editor instead. At the time, Garvey had Yale graduate William H. Ferris as editor. Ordained as an African Methodist Episcopal Church minister, Ferris had worked with "race first" figures like William and Geraldine Trotter and T. Thomas Fortune. He had also published a two-volume interdisciplinary book, *The African Abroad: Or, His Evolution In Western Civilization: Tracing His Development Under Caucasian Milieu*. In accepting Garvey's offer to take the helm of the paper in January of 1920, Harrison brought valuable experience from his tenure editing publications like *St. Mark's Mirror* (c. 1905), *The Masses* (1910–11), *The Voice* (1917–18), and *The New Negro* (1919). In a diary entry, Harrison recounted how his first order of business was to radically transform the appearance and layout of the paper.

Assuming the position of de facto managing editor, he moved all the poetry submissions onto one page under the heading "Poetry for the People," much like the poetry section he had previously made in *The Voice*. According to eminent Garveyism scholar Tony Martin, "There exists no greater demonstration of the massive interest in poetry of which Black communities are capable, than that to be found within the pages of the *Negro World*." Martin points to the fact of UNIA members and leaders at all levels of the organization writing poems. He argues that this poetry archive presents an area in which the "Garvey era" surpassed the Black Arts Movement of the 1960s, on the grounds that the *Negro World* poetical outpourings came from North, Central, and South America, the Caribbean, and the African continent. According to Martin, the greatest number of poems appeared in 1920 and 1921, the same years that Harrison worked as *Negro World* editor and inaugurated the "Poetry for the People" section. Harrison's editorship gave voice to young and little-known writers like Ethel Trew Dunlap, Augusta Savage, Zora Neale Hurston, Eric Walrond, Claude McKay, and Lucian B. Watkins.[67] In addition, Harrison also created new sections for "West Indian News Notes," to centralize all the stories about current events of interest in the Caribbean, and a section for responses to readers' questions.

Most significantly according to his own estimation, Harrison also created the first regular book reviews section in a Black newspaper. As he noted in March of 1922, "It is now two years since I inaugurated in this newspaper the first (and up to now the only) regular book-review section known to Negro newspaperdom. Since that time I have observed that the magazine called *The Crisis* has been attempting to follow my footsteps in the trail—with such success as was achievable by youth and inexperience." His derisive comment apparently referred to Jessie Fauset, who had published some book reviews under W. E. B. Du Bois's editorship of the NAACP's magazine.[68] Harrison's book review column would inspire numerous other *Negro World* book reviewers to follow in his footsteps, including William Ferris, John E. Bruce, Eric

Walrond, Arthur Schomburg, J. A. Rogers, Dusé Mohamed Ali, and Robert L. Poston. Harrison even included the occasional review from white Socialists like Mary White Ovington.[69]

Harrison redesigned the layout of the lead articles and inner pages of the *Negro World*. He shortened the editorials so that they did not "run to literary essays" and led by example with op-ed pieces of his own in order to demonstrate to Ferris and Garvey that the editorials needed to have "terseness, point, pungency and force." In addition to widening the scope of the paper to include more poetry, news, and literary criticism from across the Black world, Harrison also helped organize the *Negro World* production process by introducing a filing system for the office and another filing system for letters from readers.[70]

Harrison sought to raise the quality of the paper's content, which he felt would languish due to the shoddy work of Ferris, who in Harrison's opinion "ha[d]n't the slightest idea of newspaper work." Through his hard work and showing where Ferris had fallen down on the job, Harrison convinced Garvey to promote him to the position of having sole and final authority on matters relating to the admission of copy and to the design of the paper. Of this step, Harrison remarked, "I had to do this for the salvation of the paper," but he lamented the increase of work that came with the new responsibility, particularly once Ferris "shirked" his work as associate editor even further in order to focus on raising money for the first international convention that the UNIA was preparing for in August.[71]

Ultimately, Harrison had a momentous impact on the national and international profile of the paper. According to Jeffrey Perry, "Before Harrison's editorship [the *Negro World*] had a circulation of about ten thousand. On May 1, 1920 [four months after Harrison took over], it went from six to ten pages per issue, and in June it reached a circulation of fifty thousand as it swept the globe with its race-conscious message."[72] Of course, the paper traveled so far not only due to Harrison's reboot of the layout and editorial acumen but also as a result of the rise in Garvey's popularity, including among Black dockworkers and longshoremen who clandestinely smuggled the *Negro World* into British colonies in Africa and the Caribbean to evade postal censorship by colonial authorities.[73] Nevertheless, the paper saw a five-fold increase in its circulation on Harrison's watch. According to Tony Martin, "The *Negro World* penetrated every area where Black folk lived and had regular readers as far away as Australia. British military intelligence cited it as a factor in uprisings and unrest in such diverse places as Dahomey, British Honduras, Kenya, Trinidad, South Africa, and Cuba."[74]

Another telling example of Harrison's influence on the UNIA emerged in the process of drafting the Declaration of the Rights of the Negro Peoples of the World at the famous First International UNIA Convention in 1920. According to special government agent P-138 (Herbert Boulin), during the drafting of the declaration, Harrison "insisted that the majority of the bills were not strong and outspoken enough; that the white man must be denounced in the strongest of language in the Bill of Rights." The undercover government informant went on to say about the declaration's line-item grievances that, on Harrison's suggestion, "a number of them were sent back to the framers, (he offering his help), to put the necessary 'kick' in them." Harrison thus played a key role in shaping the document that UNIA members would call their "Magna Carta" for the Black race.

Harrison versus the "Subsidized Sixth":
Race First or Class First?

In addition to priming the pump for Black and African consciousness in Harlem, founding the Liberty League incubator, and transforming the *Negro World*, Harrison performed an invaluable service for the Garvey movement by his defense of the "race first" doctrine from attack by Black Socialists. By 1917 the New York Socialist Party local had begun to regain an interest in African Americans, in part as a result of the emergence of the New Negro movement in Harlem that Harrison, among others, had worked so hard to crystallize.[75] Two youths named A. Philip Randolph and Chandler Owen had started their own magazine and eventually ended up joining the New York local that Harrison had formally left in 1914. They had become radicalized by factors like the white world war, Harrison's street-speaking Black Socialist example in Harlem, and their radical political discussions with college students and other young people in the Independent Political Club. By 1919, Randolph and Owen's revolutionary Socialist *Messenger* achieved the unique distinction of being "the most able and the most dangerous of all the negro publications," according to the US Justice Department.[76] The Black Socialists would clash swords with Harrison over a simple yet provocative question:

Should a Black radical put "race first" or "class first"?

This question has vexed Black progressive thinkers down to the present day because of the peculiar and complex historical relationship between racial oppression and class exploitation in the United States. Because race versus class would become such a durable—and fundamental—theoretical and organizational challenge for Black radicals, it is instructive to return to the arguments that came up in Harrison's day, when the question got crystallized in such explicit terms. While the tension between "class first" advocates like Randolph and Owen and "race first" advocates like Harrison and the UNIA had been building for some years prior, the debate emerged most forcefully just two months after Harrison joined the Garvey movement and assumed the managing editorship of the *Negro World*.[77]

In March of 1920, Harrison wrote a *Negro World* editorial titled "Race First versus Class First." He argued that historically white people had derived their knowledge of what Black communities were thinking and doing from their own white vantage point, or from the "selected exponents of Negro activity" who were closest to them. The Socialist Party did the same. He charged that "the Socialist party of America has secretly subsidized both a magazine [*The Messenger*] and a newspaper [*The Emancipator*] to attempt to cut into the splendid solidarity which Negroes are achieving in response to the call of racial necessity." The "class first" argument of the Black Socialists drove a wedge into the racial solidarity that had emerged with the New Negro movement. As a result, "'radical' young Negroes may betray the interests of the race into alien hands just as surely as 'the old crowd.' For, after all, the essence of both betrayals consists in making the racial requirements play second fiddle to the requirements dictated as best for it by other groups with other interests to serve." Harrison added, "The fact that one group of alien interests is described as 'radical' and the other as 'reactionary' is of very slight value to us." Randolph and Owen were reproducing the "Old Crowd Negro" tradition of token Black figures working for white political interests.[78]

Harrison marshaled various examples to demonstrate the anti-Black racial prejudice of the Socialist Party. He recalled how the party had failed to condemn the Southern Socialists who had prevented Black audiences from attending Jewish Socialist Theresa Malkiel's Southern speaking tour events, how they had refused to allow their own presidential candidate to tour the South because they knew that Eugene Debs would not remain silent on race prejudice, how they had accommodated Jim Crow segregation in their Southern branches, and how their lust for the votes of white Southerners made them "willing to betray by silence the principles of inter-racial solidarity which they espoused on paper."[79] Harrison quoted from the party's 1912 national convention majority report, which held that racial matters were a "product of biology" that did not change essentially with economic systems and would outlast the capitalist system because "race consciousness is inborn and cannot be wholly unlearned." As we saw in chapter 1, this document expressed a grotesque racial essentialism, solemnly declaring that ultimately "economic and political considerations lead to racial fights and to legislation restricting the invasion of the white man's domain by other races."[80]

On this basis, Harrison rejected the newfound interest in the "Negro question" by the Socialist Party, whose fortunes and popularity had shrunk significantly since its 1912 heyday when Eugene Debs won 6 percent of the vote, the highest ever for a Socialist presidential candidate. The war that divided and redivided the white world also split the party right before the Russian Revolution helped spark its left wing to break off in a move that would lay the foundations for the Communist Party. But for now, Harrison argued that the Socialist Party's message of class solidarity had come "too late," as race solidarity was now the sentiment that Black people had come to see as the best method for advancing the Black community: "We say Race First, because you have all along insisted on Race First and class after when you didn't need our help." In other words, the "race first" theory and practice of the New Negro radicals represented, among other things, a response to the de facto and unspoken "race first" theory and practice of white radicals in the Socialist Party. Anticipating the charge that he had become anti-Socialist, Harrison emphasized that "the writer of these lines is also a Socialist; but he refuses in this crisis of the world's history to put either Socialism or your party above the call of his race." If white radicals (much like white liberals and conservatives) insisted on putting white people first, then self-respecting Black people, including Black radicals, had no choice but to put Black people first too.[81]

Randolph and Owen initially offered a curt response: "So far as the attacks on Socialism are concerned," they wrote, "no answer is necessary because of the weakness and superficiality of the arguments presented. Some editor of the Negro World, who signs his name 'H. H.,' wrote an article in last week's issue which was too shoddy in logic, too fragile in facts, and too forceless in presentation to be entitled to a decorous answer." Thus the editors of *The Messenger*, either unwilling or unable to answer Harrison's arguments, at first ignored them.[82]

By contrast, Black Socialist W. A. Domingo took Harrison on directly in the pages of his *Emancipator*. Domingo agreed with Harrison regarding the defensive nature of "race first." He argued that "race first is forced upon oppressed peoples as a weapon of defense. This is inescapable as the prejudice exerted against a group makes no discrimination between the members of the group," and therefore "in fighting that discrimination all Negroes must unite." However, Domingo argued, though a Black landlord and Black tenant may both face discrimination in public and should unite against it, how they chose to respond to housing issues would inevitably differ based on their class position. So while "the Negro landlord and tenant will both unite as to the necessity of fighting discrimination in places of public accommodation," at other times, "the black tenant will unite with white tenants to fight their landlord without regard to his race color, creed or sex," and "black landlords will support white landlords who go to [lobby the state legislature in] Albany to see that rents are not reduced." In situations like these, he argued, "the race interests of Negroes and Caucasians become confused and class interests appear."

And because economic conditions and class position shaped one's access to the "sustenance of life" such as food, clothing, and shelter, they "cannot be ignored."[83]

Domingo went on to argue that "race first implies biological self-preservation. It does not mean the right of the shrewd and unscrupulous ones of a race to plunder their fellows." In the hands of the UNIA, "race first" had been taken beyond a sound defensive posture into Garvey's project of duping and defrauding fellow Black people in Domingo's view. As the original *Negro World* editor, Domingo's thinly veiled attack on Garveyism flowed from his own first experience working for Garvey—and having to part ways with the UNIA for his Socialist politics. In Domingo's words, "A race must preserve itself, but it can best do so by seeking to abolish the economic conditions which make biological continuity difficult." "Race first" should be reserved for the defensive task of ensuring physical survival, while also fighting for a classless society not based on racial oppression. The capitalist economic system produced racism, which led to unique existential threats against Black people (e.g., lynching and pogroms). Therefore, while "race first" constituted a sound response to these threats to Black people's general survival, the surest way to preserve Black life was to address the root cause of the problem, namely the class-based rule of capital, which stoked anti-Black racism in order to keep the working class divided along the lines of race.[84]

Responding directly to the internal Socialist Party document that Harrison quoted, Domingo wrote, "If 'economic and political considerations lead to racial fights and to legislation restricting the invasion of the white man's domain by other races,' then the only sensible thing for a weak people (not biologically, of course) to do is to fight as a race to save themselves from extinction while assisting groups inside the ranks of their oppressors which are striving to abolish these same 'economic and political considerations.'" Black people should employ "race first" as a defensive move while supporting white "class first" radicals who were fighting the capitalist system from within the ranks of white communities. Domingo likened this approach to the military strategy of dividing the ranks of the enemy while maintaining one's own ranks intact.[85]

Domingo finished his case by arguing that Harrison's brand of "race first" politics would ultimately weaken the class struggle: "In the present crisis in world history when plans for a League of Nations to enslave the darker races are being discussed, it is crass folly for anyone to do anything that will break down class lines among the whites by sending out challenges on behalf of the black race. If he does that, mark him down as less than a fool." Making Black demands would cause white workers to unite with white capital and weaken class consciousness, which in turn would weaken the class struggle against the very system at the root of anti-Black racial oppression. "Race first," Domingo concluded, "is, therefore, justifiable for defensive purposes only, while class first is essential to the rendering of 'race first' unnecessary."[86]

Not surprisingly, Harrison came in for criticism from the Socialists for working with Marcus Garvey. Domingo made some thinly veiled ad hominem attacks on Harrison, raising questions about whether certain individuals "who are today condemning the Socialist Party" could "explain scientifically the matter of the magnetism that inheres in 35 pieces of green paper." This comment referred to Harrison's weekly salary as *Negro World* editor, as if to suggest that Harrison defended "race first" only because Garvey was paying him to do so.

Harrison responded with a piece called "Just Crabs," an allegory that he described later as "a delightful inspiration in the course of defending, not Mr. Garvey personally, but the principles of the New Negro Manhood Movement," which Harrison had helped to crystallize in formations like the Liberty League, *The Voice*, and the Liberty Congress. Harrison likened Black Socialists in New York to a "barrel of crabs" in which as soon as one crab begins crawling up the side of the barrel to escape captivity, the others get together to pull it down. In his view, this behavior didn't "seem to get them or us anywhere" because the day had dawned for Black people in Harlem to make strides by going into business, saving their money, and collectively investing in enterprises that would mean roofs over their heads and an economic future for themselves and their families.

"But," Harrison interrupted, "the Subsidized Sixth are sure that this is all wrong and that we have no right to move an inch until the Socialist millennium dawns, when we will all get 'out of the barrel' together." The "Subsidized Sixth" phrase evoked the "talented tenth" but refashioned it to emphasize white Socialist Party financial backing for the six Black Socialist contributing editors of *The Emancipator*: W. A. Domingo, Richard B. Moore, A. Philip Randolph, Chandler Owen, Cyril Briggs, and Anselmo Jackson. As Harrison argued, "it does not seem to have occurred to them that making an imperfect heaven now does not unfit any one for enjoying the perfect paradise which they promise us—if it ever comes."[87] If cooperatively owned Black businesses could improve the quality of life for some Black communities in the short term, this would not foreclose a transition to socialist relations of production in the future, but Harrison seemed doubtful that white radicals would ever develop the political vision and power to bring about such a transition.

Unfortunately, Harrison attacked a straw man in suggesting that the Black Socialists did not want Black people to "move an inch" until the dawning of a Socialist America. To their credit, Black Socialists were fighting to bring Black workers into labor unions and to oppose capitalism in solidarity with all the workers of the world, much like Harrison had been attempting to do in the party a decade prior. For that reason that Harrison's grew tired not so much with the idea of Socialism but rather the way the Socialist Party had ensnared young Black radicals within a disingenuously "class first" white political framework. Speaking of the "Subsidized Sixth," he said, "Truly, it is said of them that 'the power over a man's subsistence is the power over his will'—and over his 'scientific radicalism,' too." Harrison thus saw his interlocutors' acceptance of financial backing from white Socialists as a factor that distorted their politics by inducing them to take positions (consciously or unconsciously) that would not offend their financial sponsors.

In the heat of the battle, Harrison responded to the ad hominem attacks with some disparaging remarks of his own: "When the reek of the poison gas propaganda has cleared away and the smoke of the barrage has lifted it will be found that 'White Men's Nigger' is a phrase that need not be restricted to old-line politicians and editors." Meanwhile, in a naked attack on Harrison's reputation as a free lover, Randolph and Owen called him a "licentious, lecherous, and libidinous prevaricator." Harrison in turn referred to Randolph and Owen as the "sexless twins in the barrel of crabs" who had fooled white Socialists into thinking they were graduates of Columbia University. Harrison accused them of only joining the party after being rejected by Democrats and Republicans, implying that they became Socialists "overnight" and only as a last resort to secure financial backing for their magazine. They, in turn, accused him of praising war veteran Guy Empey's pro-war autobiography *Over the Top* as a book of high literary quality. Harrison eventually went so far as to write a long-form, serialized, cryptic, allegorical, and polemical poem titled "The Crab Barrel" about the folly of his Black Socialist antagonists.[88]

In May of 1920, roughly a month after the air had cleared somewhat from the petty, personalistic, and perverse exchange of blows, Harrison returned to a more sober register of communication in order to advance one of his most direct and cogent statements on the subject of Socialism in Black communities. His decision to write "An Open Letter to the Socialist Party of New York City" in the *Negro World* demonstrated that he still respected the Socialists—Black and white—enough to try one last time to reach them with his message.

He rearticulated the argument that the "New Negro" came to be as a result of the war rather than anything Socialists or Bolsheviks had done: "During the recent world war the Negro in America was taught that while white people spoke of patriotism, religion, democracy and other sounding themes, they remained loyal to one concept above all others, and that was the concept of race. Even in the throes of war, and on the battle fields of France it was 'race first' with them. Out of this relation was born the new Negro ideal of 'race first' for us. And today, whether Negroes be Catholics or Protestants, capitalists or wage workers, Republicans or Democrats, native or foreign-born, they begin life anew on this basis."

Harrison observed that, despite all the slings and arrows exchanged, his antagonists had said nothing about the biological essentialism of the official Socialist Party position on race. Speaking past the Black Socialists directly to the white party leaders, he offered that "some day, perhaps you will know enough to put Socialism's cause in the hands of those who will refrain from using your party's organ for purposes of personal pique, spite and venom. When that day dawns Socialism will have a chance to be heard by Negroes on its merits." Harrison felt that the Black Socialists had abused their support from the white Socialists by using their magazine and paper to cast aspersions on "race first" advocates: "Even now, if you should send anyone up here (black or white) to put the cause of Karl Marx, freed from admixture of rancor and hatred for the Negro's own defensive racial propaganda, you may find that it will have as good a chance of gaining adherents as any other political creed. But until you change your tactics . . . your case among us will be hopeless indeed."[89] Despite their betrayals, Harrison held out the possibility that the majority-white party could still get a fair hearing if it would approach Black communities with more respect and humility.

He also took some of the Socialists' criticisms to heart. For example, the UNIA's Negro Factories Corporation set up a number of Black-owned businesses in Harlem, including laundries, restaurants, a doll factory, tailoring and millinery establishments, and a printing press. While sympathetic to Socialism in theory, Harrison also supported the principle of Black consumers supporting Black-owned businesses (especially Black cooperatives) as a natural extension of "race first" in relation to economic life. He saw it as a policy that held the potential to keep Black dollars in the Black community to the mutual benefit of Black consumers and businesses. Yet he also lamented how "race first" was "subject to the risk of being exploited dishonestly," particularly by businessmen who "seem to want other black people to pay them for being black" regardless of the quality of the goods or services they provided their customers. He gave the example of so-called factories for brown-skinned dolls in which "most of the factoring consist[s] of receiving these dolls from white factories and either stuffing them with saw dust, excelsior or other filling, or merely changing them from one wrapper to another" and then selling them at inflated prices that made it harder for Black mothers to buy them and teach race pride to their children.[90]

Responding to the notion that the whole UNIA represented an inherently conservative politics, Harrison wrote, "Just as the Socialist Party officially declares that it exercises no control or veto power over the religious beliefs of its individual members, so the U.N.I.A does not dictate to any member what his economic or political beliefs shall be." Harrison here gave voice—and validation—to those elements of the UNIA who were not necessarily in agreement with Garvey's capitalistic economic orientation. For example, Harrison penned a passionate *Negro World* editorial on improving the working conditions of Black postal workers, whose situation he knew from his own experience as a postal worker. The workers wrote him a letter of thanks in response and felt validated as workers by the UNIA as a result.[91] In this way, Harrison's ideological warfare with the Black Socialists afforded him some opportunities to make space in the pages of the *Negro World* for expressing a class consciousness and solidarity with labor that contrasted with the more capitalistic and tendencies in the UNIA leadership.

According to Perry, Harrison's robust defense of "race first" temporarily silenced criticism from the Black Socialists. But Black Socialist and Communist attacks on Garvey and Garveyism would only grow stronger as the 1920s unfolded. At the same time, Harrison would himself soon grow weary of Marcus Garvey, as we will see in chapter 8. The anti-Garvey crusade of Domingo's *Emancipator*, Randolph and Owen's *Messenger*, and also Cyril Briggs's *Crusader*, which all devoted a lot of energy to exposing corruption in Garvey's Black Star Line steamship corporation, attacked Garveyism directly in its home fortress of Harlem. According to Moore, in the last analysis Domingo "was able to bring out only ten issues, but those ten issues really made a dent in the confidence of the people in respect to the Garvey movement."[92] Therefore, as damaging as the Black Socialists' attacks ultimately were to Garvey's cause, one can only imagine how much bigger and deeper the damage to the UNIA would have been had Garvey *not* had the brilliant crystallizer touchstone of Black socialist politics spearheading the defense of "race first" from the helm of the *Negro World* in the lead up to the very first annual International UNIA Convention.

Nobody in the country knew the Socialist Party and its internal racial politics better than Hubert Harrison, the party's first secular Black historical materialist theoretician and organizer. Marcus Garvey, by contrast, openly admitted about himself that "he could not explain Socialism if he was called upon to do so." For a battle that threatened to destroy the interest of rank-and-file Harlemites in the Garvey movement, the UNIA could not have hoped for a better polemicist than Harrison.[93]

Meanwhile, Harrison's open letter revealed something of the reluctant and reactive nature of his "race first" position, in that he might have been more comfortable in a radical "class first" organization like the Socialist Party if not for its now hidden, now open anti-Black racism and tokenistic approach to what it called, quite whitely, the "Negro problem."[94] As historian Winston James puts it, "Harrison's [B]lack nationalism was the last resort of a [B]lack socialist in a racist land."[95]

If the Black Socialist arguments to Harrison found confirmation in his eventual departure from the Garvey movement, Harrison's arguments to his Black Socialist protégés would find confirmation in the fact that most of them would eventually leave the Socialist Party, in part due to their collective failure to defeat its anti-Black racism. This is made clearer by the fact that most of them would subsequently devote their energies to more explicitly Black-led formations. A. Philip Randolph became founder and president of the Brotherhood of Sleeping Car Porters, the first Black labor union to receive a charter in the American Federation of Labor.[96] Domingo, Moore, and Grace P. Campbell would join Cyril Briggs to build the African Blood Brotherhood (ABB), a revolutionary Black internationalist organization.[97]

In 1922, Chandler Owen's brother Toussaint moved to New York City from the south, following the decline of a large tailoring establishment in which he worked as a highly skilled tailor. Chandler mistakenly thought that the Socialist-led needle trades unions would help his brother find work in the city. But Toussaint died "poverty-stricken" the very next year. George Schulyer's remark that the unions in the needle trades were "Jewish and Italian unions rather than labor unions" suggests that Socialist and white working class racism formed a key factor in Toussaint's dispossession, if not of his life, then his livelihood. His brother's death made Chandler feel so "embarrassed, disillusioned, and bereaved" at the behavior of his white socialist 'friends of labor' that he left New York and the Socialist Party never to return. That all these Black radicals left the Socialist Party, usually for more racially affirming organizations, vindicated Harrison's criticisms about the anti-Black racism of the white "radicals."[98]

In light of their initial enthusiasm about the Socialist cause—and their vociferous attacks on "race first"—the resignations of Harrison's Black Socialist successors from the party offered a damning indictment not of the "class first" Marxist doctrine in theory but of the Socialist Party's anti-Black *version* of the "class first" doctrine in practice. It reinforced the idea that "race first" made sense for Black people in an anti-Black world. Winston James writes, "It is as if there is a hidden and unwritten law of tendency in the United States which states that because of the racism of the labor movement and its organizations, black socialists are almost inexorably pushed to a black nationalist position."[99] Meanwhile, the class-radical politics they learned in the Socialist Party would inform the decisions of working-class Socialists like Domingo, Harrison, and Jackson to eventually leave the UNIA in disgust on account of

Garvey's conservative politics and problematic behavior, which we explore more fully in chapter 8.

Other Influences on Garveyism

Unearthing the decisive influence of Hubert Harrison and the Liberty League on the rise and shape of Garveyism does not require a disavowal of the UNIA's various other influences. Given its transnational scope, the UNIA contained within it a multiplicity of Black cultural, ideological, and political tendencies. For example, the Garvey movement drew from the rich history of the Black nationalist tradition of the nineteenth century. Wilson Moses has noted how in the decades before Garvey's rise, patterns of "authoritarian collectivism, separatism, mysticism, and civilizationism [had already] appeared in black bourgeois cultural and institutional life." Garvey would manifest all of these tendencies and more according to Moses, including the patriarchal, disciplinary, and uniformed "pseudomilitarism" of the Hampton–Tuskegee model, the "back-to-Africa" emigrationism of Bishop Henry McNeal Turner and Chief Alfred Sam, the "lodge hall gentility" of the Black Greek letter and fraternal order traditions, and the entrepreneurial ethos of Booker T. Washington's National Negro Business League. In this sense, much of the substance of Marcus Garvey's vision represented the culmination—and recombination—of its nineteenth-century influences.[100]

Harrison's Liberty League also built upon this heritage. For example, Harrison had served as a secretary of the Negro Society for Historical Research under the tutelage of Arturo Schomburg and John E. Bruce, who inherited the legacy of nineteenth-century thinkers like Alexander Crummell, Edward Wilmot Blyden, and Henry McNeal Turner. Not to mention the nineteenth-century journalistic exponents of "race first" like T. Thomas Fortune, Ida B. Wells-Barnett, and William Monroe Trotter. Indeed, Fortune and Wells both joined the Garvey movement in the 1920s. The impetus toward Black nationalism, racial solidarity, and group consciousness is a tendency with deep roots in the United States and emerged in African American political thought long before Caribbean immigrants like Harrison or Garvey came to adopt it. In this regard, both Harrison and Garvey were shaped by African American traditions of Black nationalism.

Restoring Harrison to the origin story of Garveyism does not require a denial of Marcus Garvey's own unique abilities as a publicist, organizer, and popularizer of Black racial pride. Style-wise, Garvey emphasized the glittery drama of performance, often sporting a Napoleonic hat festooned with white feathers and a flashy military general's uniform with gold epaulets. A certificate of membership in the UNIA described it as an organization "striving for the FREEDOM, MANHOOD, and NATIONALISM of the Negro, and to hand down to posterity a FLAG OF EMPIRE—to restore to the world an Ethiopian Nation one and Indivisible out of which shall come our princes and rulers." This majestic aesthetic added to the UNIA's mass appeal as an organization grounded in the pride of Black nationality—especially for fellow Caribbeans who bore the rich cultural tradition of the island carnival celebration in their bones. Not to mention Anglophone Caribbean migrants who grew up under the British cultural influence of reverence for royal regalia. According to Garvey, "To organize Negroes we have got to demonstrate: you cannot tell them anything; you have got to show them; and that is why we have got to spend seven years making noise; we had to beat the drum; we had to do all we did; otherwise there would have been no organization."[101]

As many of his harshest critics conceded, Garvey did more to raise the self-esteem and racial consciousness of Black people internationally than perhaps any other single Black personality in modern history. Joyce Moore Turner, a historian and daughter of Harrison protégé Richard B. Moore, has drawn out some important contrasts between Garvey and Harrison. She observed that Garvey proved astute in adopting Harrison's ideas but that he also took care to eschew the radical political traditions that Harrison embodied. This undoubtedly broadened Garvey's appeal.

In addition, Garvey proved "clever enough to provide religious sentiment and ritual while maintaining a nondenominational base; flamboyant enough to create a world of fantasy—a royal court where the individual's self-esteem was elevated . . . and visionary enough to paint a picture of a glorious past and future."[102] Indeed, Garvey has been called a "Black Moses" for adroitly cultivating a religious and messianic leadership style to which Black churchgoers could relate.[103] Harrison, on the other hand, generally favored an intellectually rigorous, freethinking/antireligious, and scientific worldview, which probably limited his appeal to the large faith-oriented segment of Black communities. He was referred to by Harlem residents not as a Black Moses but as the "Black Socrates" for his intellectual curiosity and wide-ranging breadth of knowledge.

At the end of the day, social movements are founded and built collectively and cannot be reduced to the singular, often male individuals who are often seen as The Leader. As we have noted, Black women usually form the backbone of Black movements (and of the most visible male "leaders"), leading with their own agency in myriad ways even when they do not receive the recognition or visibility that is their due. Garvey's wives, Amy Ashwood and Amy Jacques, both gave life and decisive support and inspiration to Garvey and Garveyism in the most critical of ways. Instead of simply replacing one

Great Man (or Great Woman) theory of Garveyism with another, the aim is to build on the recent historiographical trend of decentering Marcus Garvey from the history of Garvey*ism* by showing that Harrison offers a unique angle of vision with which to take into account individuals whose contributions to the movement further illustrate its richly textured social history. It just so happens that Harrison was a major political and intellectual crystallizer in his own right whose numerous contributions to Black life—including those he made to the Garvey movement—have been thoroughly marginalized, ignored, and written out of history.

In conclusion, Hubert Harrison and his Liberty League of Negro-Americans crystallized the key elements that one of its alumni, Marcus Garvey, adopted to build the largest international organization of Black people in modern history: settling in the United States and Harlem in particular (rather than returning to Jamaica) for a base of operations, the numerous Liberty League alumni (including Garvey) who founded what became the parent body UNIA division, the "race first" ideology and African consciousness (rather than seeking white funding and approval), a model for an organization that combined African Americans, Africans, and African Caribbeans, the mass movement orientation, the colored internationalism and support for the Irish and other nationalist struggles, and the idea of a tricolor flag for pan-African nationality. Not to mention Harrison's transformation of the *Negro World* into the premier paper of the international African diaspora, and his polemical defense of "race first" from vociferous attacks by Black Socialists. Without Harrison and the Liberty League, Marcus Garvey might never have transcended his fixation on Tuskegee-style industrial education to build the largest mass movement for pan-African nationality the world had ever seen. So why in the world did the Garveyists write this untamed, untamable African out of their own history and origin story? And why, if it had amplified his Liberty League template so spectacularly, did Harrison leave the UNIA?

Chapter 8

A Garvey Critic like No Other

> Garvey . . . personified the qualities that the good leader should possess.
> —Tony Martin, *African Fundamentalism*

> He has plastered the air with lies.
> —Hubert Harrison, August 28, 1920

Hubert Henry Harrison was far more than just a footnote in the origin story of Garveyism. On the contrary, he played a decisive role in the Garvey movement's very existence and ascension to prominence, as we have seen in chapter 7. By founding the Liberty League of Negro-Americans, he managed to recruit Marcus Garvey into an organization building a "race first," tricolor-flag-bearing, Harlem-based, African American and African Caribbean, pan-Africanist mass movement in solidarity with oppressed people all over the world. Marcus Garvey—alongside other Liberty League alumni—adopted these elements to reimagine and transform the Universal Negro Improvement Association and African Communities League (UNIA) from a fundraiser for a Jamaican Tuskegee Institute into the largest international organization of Black people in modern history. But this is not why Garvey and his partisans have largely excluded Hubert Harrison from their origin story.

In addition to his multidimensional and decisive contributions to the rise of Garvey and Garveyism, Harrison's firsthand observations of Garvey's leadership and behavior did not endear him to the self-declared "Provisional President of Africa." As a result of working full-time in the UNIA headquarters, editing the *Negro World*, attending the first annual UNIA convention, and observing Garvey up close in other settings, Harrison came to conclude that Garvey was egomaniacal, financially corrupt, imperialistic, dictatorial, and a liar. The descriptor that Harrison uses multiple times in his notes for Garvey is "mountebank," which the dictionary defines as "a person who sells quack medicines, as from a platform in public places, attracting and influencing an audience by tricks, storytelling, etc." In Harrison's view, the emperor had no clothes.

Of course, Hubert Harrison had no monopoly on criticism of Marcus Garvey. W. A. Domingo had concluded by the end of 1919 that Garvey's methods were "medieval, obscure, and dishonest."[1] Ida B. Wells-Barnett, while initially a Garvey supporter and featured speaker at UNIA events, also later lamented how Garvey became "drunk with power."[2] Around the same time, Domingo's *Emancipator* and the Black Communist-oriented *Crusader* under Cyril Briggs led a crusade against the Black Star Line (BSL) and Marcus Garvey. W.E.B. Du Bois, after showing some initial interest in the UNIA, soon became a major enemy of the Garvey movement. In 1922–23, Socialists A. Philip Randolph and Chandler Owen worked with Robert Bagnall and various National Association for the Advancement of Colored People (NAACP) leaders to launch the "Garvey Must Go!" campaign, which openly called on the federal government to deport Garvey. Garvey had many critics and hardcore antagonists in the Black community.

However, Harrison's criticisms of Garvey remain unique for a number of reasons. The first concerns Harrison's authoritative stature as the "father of Harlem radicalism" and a key crystallizer of the New Negro movement before Garvey's arrival in the same Black "Mecca" where Garvey would relocate the UNIA headquarters. The second concerns the ways in which Harrison and the Liberty League crystallized the seed form of the Garvey movement and greatly influenced much of its content, ideology, and strategic orientation. Finally, the third reason is that Harrison's criticisms, unlike those of Briggs, Randolph, or Du Bois, did not stem from a place of opposition to the doctrine of "race first" but from Harrison's intimate firsthand experience as a high-level UNIA leader and insider.

While the Garvey movement's critics have often minimized or underestimated its world-historic importance, its champions have often vastly overestimated its numerical size and integrity. Although Harrison played an enormous role as a catalyst for the rise of Garveyism, his scathing criticisms of Marcus Garvey obliterate some of the Garvey movement's biggest claims to fame. As a result, Harrison's restoration to the history of Garveyism reveals him to be, in key respects, a touchstone-like test for the quality and purity of the Garveyist project, much as he had been a touchstone for the Socialist Party's claim to stand for the emancipation of the whole working class.

Because Harrison's relationship to Garveyism shifted over time—from crystallizer/catalyst to UNIA leader, and then from to internal critic to external critic—his angle of vision creates a uniquely intimate, candid, and multidimensional picture of the movement's weaknesses as well as its real, rather than imagined, strengths. Given Harrison's role in having seeding and catalyzing Garvey's capacity to build the largest international organization of Black people in modern history, the political stakes and possibilities for the UNIA's ultimate trajectory could scarcely have been higher for the fate of the pan-African world. With this in mind, we can better appreciate both Harrison's problems with Marcus Garvey and also his efforts—including as editor of the *Negro World*—to push the UNIA in a class-conscious, anti-imperialist, and political party-building direction.

Harrison's Assessment of Marcus Garvey

In May of 1920, just a few months after starting his job as editor of the *Negro World*, Harrison had already developed such strong misgivings about his new employer that he decided to record them in his private diary. He noted first his problem with Garvey's penchant for saying too much in public, regardless of the consequences. He gave the example of the Liberia commission, Garvey's plan to send a team of official UNIA representatives to secure land for a UNIA-owned colony in West Africa. Although Garvey had initially selected him to lead the delegation, Harrison was ultimately unable to head the first UNIA Liberia commission because of Garvey's insistence on premature publicity.

According to Harrison, the trouble began when some "pin-headed preachers and other ignorant howlers" of the UNIA offered an "insane collection of bombastic rantings as to what the 'Commission' would do" at a public meeting in Liberty Hall. This happened before Harrison and John E. Bruce's replacement on the commission, Rev. James Eason, got their passports. Then, Hudson Pryce (a newly hired *Negro World* associate editor) called Garvey and explained to him that if the information about what the commission would do in Liberia appeared publicly in the *Negro World*, the State Department would almost surely decline the commissioners' pending requests for passports. Garvey insisted the plans for the Liberian commission constituted "good propaganda" and ordered that they go into the paper anyway. "So, there will be no passports for us," Harrison concluded, "and it is mainly due to Marcus Garvey's prime defect, bombastic blabbing. He talks too much and too foolishly."[3]

In the same diary entry, Harrison then proceeded to articulate his "general estimate of Mr. Garvey's character and abilities." His first problem was Garvey's obsessive egotism. After recounting how he had given Garvey a platform at the historic Liberty League inauguration in June of 1917 and subsequently encouraged his audiences to attend Garvey's speeches, Harrison lamented how Garvey refused to return the favor once he began achieving fame and political fortune of his own. Then when UNIA members would ask Garvey to call in Harrison and make use of his ideas and abilities, Garvey would say that "Harrison [had] his own propaganda" and was "dangerous," even though Harrison's main message at that time was "Race First!" Harrison concluded that "the first big defect, then, in Mr. Garvey's make-up is a defect in the size of his soul. He is spiritually as well as intellectually a little man. That is why he doesn't want around him men who are of larger girth either way." Harrison felt that when Garvey did find someone in his organization who loomed larger, "he does not utilize them in any way which would aid, amplify, or modify his chaotic plans and notions. [But] if he can use them as hired bravos, then so far, so good."

Before he joined forces with Garvey in 1920, Harrison warned Garvey that he would not be a "yes man" for any leader or organization. But he saw this as precisely what Garvey demanded from UNIA leaders and members. As Harrison put it, Garvey "quarreled with every person he ever worked with unless they were willing boot-lickers and glorifiers of himself. His insane egotism and jealousy were boundless." Unfiltered estimates like this, appearing in a private diary, offer a window into Harrison's most candid feelings and observations. His concern about Garvey's jealousy towards—and mistreatment of—his presumptive "subordinates," including Harrison, set the stage for trouble.[4]

Like many others both within and outside the UNIA, Harrison expressed vehement criticism regarding Garvey's handling of the BSL shipping company. The BSL, incorporated in 1919, formed a central economic enterprise of the UNIA and an attempt to create a Black-owned shipping company that could facilitate direct trade between African, African American, and Caribbean markets and also transport Black passengers who otherwise had to face Jim Crow segregation on white-owned shipping lines.[5] Harrison initially campaigned with UNIA members to raise money for the BSL but very soon grew wary of its financial management. He cited Garvey's inability to account for moneys that he collected before incorporating the BSL as evidence that the whole operation comprised little more than a "money getter" from the start.

Apparently it turned into a rather leaky "money getter," because according to Harrison, Garvey's "ignorance of ships and shipping matters has resulted in his paying out tens of thousands of dollars unnecessarily and he has been victimized again and again by the white men from whom ships and ship accessories were bought." He further regretted the way Garvey "lies to the people magniloquently, bragging about impossible things while not owning the ships outright." Harrison felt that the BSL fired the imagination of UNIA supporters primarily because "Garvey has a great talent for lying."[6]

Harrison's earliest misgivings about Garvey grew into full-blown revulsion during the first UNIA convention in August 1920, on account of Garvey's dishonesty. For example, Harrison remarked about the opening fanfare of the convention that it constituted a "splendid success" overall because Madison Square Garden looked "packed from top to bottom" with some 15,000 attendees. Yet Garvey seized on the event to claim that 25,000 *delegates* were present.[7] Not only did Garvey inflate the attendance figure but he also implied every attendee at the rally was an elected representative of a Black community with voting rights in the convention. But how many such delegates were actually present?

During the convention elections, Harrison noted how the official balloting showed that Francis Ellegor, the sole nominee for the office of commissioner-general, got 103 votes, "the highest number cast for any office." Garvey himself, the sole nominee for president general, received 92 votes. Although not all the voting delegates signed it, a count of the signatories to the UNIA Declaration of Rights reveals 123 "duly elected representatives" of the African diaspora. Robert A. Hill, the dean of Garvey movement scholarship and editor of the multivolume published archive of the *Marcus Garvey Papers*, compiled a list of names based on accounts printed in the *Negro World*, the *Negro World Convention Bulletin*, and the records of the Bureau of Investigation. His count for convention delegates came to 144. "Yet," lamented Harrison, "despite such facts, [Garvey] is again declaring in circulars out today that there will be 20,000 delegates in the parade on Tuesday."[8]

Harrison criticized Garvey for the falsehoods propagated at the convention not just about the number but also the nature of the so-called delegates and the extent to which the "international" convention genuinely represented the Black communities for whom it claimed to speak. According to Harrison, not only were most of the delegates from the West Indies but also "many of them were simply residents of New York whom [Garvey] called in to pose as delegates *sent* from the West Indies and Africa." For example, Rev. George Alexander McGuire "represented" Antigua despite having lived mostly in the United States since 1894. Prince Madarikan Deniyi of Nigeria was cast as a "delegate" even though he had been "in America for more than six years studying." Harrison offered his own case as an example, recalling how "Garvey insisted on recognizing me when I rose to speak as 'the gentleman from the Virgin Islands,'" even though Harrison had been living in the United States for twenty years and the Virgin Islands had not actually elected or sent any delegates to the convention. Examples like this suggest the convention's "delegates" did not necessarily represent their countries of origin, let alone the whole African diaspora, as Garvey claimed.[9]

His disgust with Garvey's behavior at the convention led him to eventually boycott its proceedings in protest. As we noted in chapter 7, Harrison played a key role in "adding the necessary kick" to the UNIA's Declaration of the Rights of the Negro Peoples of the World. But according to Harrison, "One would have thought that the best brains would have been brought together in a committee to elaborate such a document. But this would not have suited Garvey's book. He is afraid of brains." Instead of letting a subcommittee draft the document, Garvey "put forth the silly proposal that each delegate should present resolutions from the floor.... Meanwhile he had prepared his own [Declaration of Rights] and presented it from the chair." Harrison then noted how the other delegates' resolutions were brought forward as amendments and extensions of Garvey's document, but whenever anything came up that Garvey didn't approve of, "he ruled it 'out of order.'" Undercover federal agent P-138 (Herbert S. Boulin) corroborated this assessment, noting that Garvey ruled over the process "with an iron hand." Although Harrison apparently convinced the iron hand of the need to add the "necessary kick" to its declarations, he did not ultimately put his signature to the document, a telling indicator of his disgust with Garvey's behavior.[10]

When the convention turned to elect UNIA officers, Harrison remarked that "Garvey shamelessly electioneered for the candidates whose names he had 'suggested' to the Convention while condemning canvassing and electioneering for others." Harrison noted, for example, that Garvey sent his nondelegate office workers like Harry Watkis, Henry Plummer, and Arden Bryan to vote for his chosen candidates as though they were delegates. According to Harrison, Garvey even tried to send his secretary (and side lover) Amy Jacques (who was not a delegate) to vote, only to be stopped by Arnold Ford, the sergeant at arms, who forced Garvey to rule against allowing Ms. Jacques a ballot. Where Garvey could not get extra votes with loyal nondelegates, he resorted to other antidemocratic means: "Several of his candidates were defeated on Thurs 26th and [Garvey] ruled, therefore, that no one was elected who didn't have 'a two-thirds majority.'" Then when someone pointed out that John Gordon, "his personal flunkey and not three weeks in the Association, was not elected either," Garvey protested fiercely but eventually had to yield.[11]

The next day saw a new election for Gordon's office, which ended in a tie. Garvey had already voted but then insisted that he had the right to cast another vote as the president general of the UNIA. Harrison reported that Garvey did just that "and thus elected his henchman." Though Garvey ultimately got his way in many such "elections," his antidemocratic behavior "revealed Garvey to the delegates and lined up much sentiment against him." When delegates nominated Harrison to be the official "Speaker In Convention," Harrison got thirty-nine votes, Frederick Toote got thirty, and Garvey's designee Rev. B. F. Smith got only seventeen votes. Harrison subsequently withdrew from the ballot and called on his supporters to vote for Toote, which they did, electing Toote to the position. Though he clearly could have held the position, Harrison withdrew in protest, to the confusion and dismay of his supporters.[12]

Harrison's dissatisfaction with Garvey's behavior during the convention did not go unnoticed among UNIA officials. Rev. James Eason revealed to

Harrison that the UNIA's international organizer, Henrietta Vinton Davis, had begun intriguing against him in an effort to get Garvey to dismiss Harrison from the editorship of the *Negro World*. Davis had given up a career in vaudeville stage performance to devote herself to building the UNIA, spoke in favor of reparations for slavery, and regarded Garvey as "a man chosen by God to lead his people." According to Eason, when William Ferris (the other *Negro World* editor, who Garvey had made the chancellor of convention) refused to sign the Declaration of Rights, Garvey allegedly "turned to Miss Davis who was seated by his side on the platform and said: Now, you see? If I had taken your advice and removed Harrison from the paper I wouldn't have had anybody left." Harrison said of this story that "Eason didn't care who he repeated it to."[13] Hodge Kirnon corroborated the story, telling Harrison that according to UNIA Philadelphia division president Fred Toote, Davis and UNIA office worker Harry Watkis had asked Toote to use his influence with Garvey to have Harrison removed from the paper on the grounds that Harrison was "an enemy of the movement." When Toote asked them for specific examples or evidence to support that claim, they couldn't produce any "but insisted on the general blanket-assertion" anyway. Apparently an anti-Harrison faction had emerged within the UNIA leadership.[14]

By the end of the convention, Harrison felt Garvey had become an embarrassment and noted in his diary the reason for his decision to distance himself from its proceedings. "In plain English," noted Harrison, Garvey "has made an ass of himself and has made the movement a matter of ridicule." Although he had already recorded some private reservations about Garvey a few months before the convention, Harrison relinquished whatever respect he had left in Garvey's leadership by the convention's end. After the closing reception, Harrison concluded, "Thus ends the most colossal joke in Negrodom, engineered and staged by its chief mountebank." Thus while the first UNIA convention may have helped catapult and consolidate the profile of Garvey's movement and organization to the outside world, for Harrison it comprised a decisive hammer blow to his interest in Marcus Garvey.[15]

However disillusioned he felt, Harrison did not resign himself to acquiescence in the face of Garvey's problematic behavior during the convention. Instead, he made moves to confer and dialogue with other UNIA members who felt similarly. For example, on September 4, Harrison had a meeting with Mr. Clifford Bourne, "an intelligent delegate to the Convention who is in revolt. He hails from Puerto Barrios, Guatemala." A few months later, Harrison had a positive meeting with Rev. James David Brooks, the secretary-general of the UNIA, and other disaffected UNIA members: "Both [Secretary-General] Dr. Brooks and [Assistant President General] Dr. [John Dawson] Gordon are evincing an outspoken listing for me which seems to indicate that, in their minds, Garvey's star is setting. [Chaplain-General Rev. George Alexander] McGuire too is making approaches. I shall watch and wait." This comment suggests that Harrison and other disaffected UNIA members had serious concerns about Garvey's hegemonic power in the organization following the convention.[16]

Days after the close of the convention, Garvey's *Negro World* described Harrison as "the most scholarly and learned member of the convention." It went so far as to declare that "there is scarcely a man in all the race whose knowledge of economics, religion, sociology, politics, and literature is so nearly inexhaustible." It made for an ironic statement, given Harrison's private postconvention opinion of Garvey as a liar, an autocrat, and a fraud.[17]

Alongside the vastly inflated claim of having 20,000 delegates at the 1920 convention, Harrison also took issue with Garvey's claim about the size of the UNIA membership. In his list of Garvey's "lies," Harrison recorded a note that read, "4,000,000 members vs. 73,000 Off Rep 4/8/21." This suggests that not only did Garvey not have the 4 million members that he claimed but that the actual UNIA membership numbered 73,000 in 1921. Was this accurate? According to historian Lerone Bennett, Garvey had sold 40,000 BSL shares.[18] Robert Hill wrote of the BSL that it had some 35,000 shareholders.[19] In their introduction to *Marcus Garvey: Life and Lessons*, Garvey movement historians Robert A. Hill and Barbara Bair say that by 1925, the movement had "tens of thousands" of members.[20] Whether UNIA membership stood at 35,000 or 40,000 or 73,000 or some other figure in the "tens of thousands," Garvey inflated the UNIA membership astronomically with his claim to 4 million members.[21]

How did Garvey arrive at such a vast overestimate for the size of his organization? Amy Jacques Garvey, who replaced Amy Ashwood Garvey to become Garvey's second wife and a key UNIA leader and organizer in her own right, offered an explanation. Besides the formal UNIA branches and divisions, there were "chapters of Garveyites under different names in fraternities, and 'pockets' of Garveyism as a philosophy among study groups etc." In her words, "Garveyism is a COMMON FAITH" such that "the man, woman or child who has heard Garvey speak, or has read his writings becomes inspired, and if converted to Garveyism is a changed person in outlook; however, most of them will not give him credit for the change."[22] Counting UNIA members based on arbitrarily estimating the number of people who had ever come into contact with Garvey—in person or in print—bore an eerie similarity to the method used for calculating the number of "delegates" at the 1920 convention: anyone and everyone who showed up to the opening parade was counted as a delegate. Harrison had a much simpler explanation than Amy Jacques, namely that Garvey had "plastered the air with lies."[23]

Harrison also recoiled at Garvey's misappropriation of funds. In the months before UNIA conventions Garvey would advertise a Convention Fund in the *Negro World*, which frequently ran to tens of thousands of dollars. "Yet," Harrison remarked, "no visiting delegate ever got even a glass of lemonade that that delegate didn't pay for. What [Garvey] did with the Convention funds is as much a mystery today as the Liberian Loan fund, the fund for 'Certificates of Race Loyalty,' the 'African Redemption Fund,' the money collected in 1918 to send delegates to the Peace Congress and the other ballyhoo devices by which money was extracted from his dupes while he prated of 'dying for his race.'" Here one gets a sense of the emotional bitterness Harrison felt toward the corruption he witnessed in Garvey's financial operations. Others, like Madarikan Deniyi, made a similar criticism that Garvey's African Redemption Fund and Liberian Loan Fund were "fraudulent schemes" to pay the salaries of Garvey and his officials.[24]

During the convention, Harrison learned from Cyril Crichlow, a UNIA reporter and Garvey's speech stenographer, that for the entire month-long convention Garvey "had paid them *one hundred dollars a day* to report the Convention proceedings" (emphasis in original). Harrison—privately in his diary—reacted viscerally to Critchlow's disclosure: "Good Lord! Think of the way this insane ass, Garvey, wasted thirty one hundred dollars of the people's money!" By contrast, Garvey paid Harrison only thirty five dollars a week for editing the *Negro World*.[25]

Speaking of financial wastefulness, Harrison also detested Garvey's lavish lifestyle. According to Harrison, when Garvey first arrived in the United States, "he was so poor that some of us had to give him food and clothes. He wouldn't work, not he. He had discovered a method of living without working. Today, he is well-fed, well-groomed, and well-off. In his flat for which he pays rent of $150 a month, there are splendid couches swinging by chains from the ceiling." Harrison went further, noting that "Garvey is a worshipper of Garvey. On the [BSL ship] 'Yarmouth' he had two life-sized oil-paintings of himself. His office and his apartment contain dozens of such paintings." Given Harrison's lifelong economic hardships and financial struggles as the primary breadwinner for his five children, these comments reveal a distinct element of working-class anger toward Garvey's use of UNIA finances for personal and narcissistic ends.[26]

His dismay at Garvey's luxuries found no comfort in the glaring contrast between the grandiose salaries that Garvey allocated for UNIA officers and the actual funds available. Harrison reported that the third week of the convention "was taken up with aimless talks and the 'election' of a 'Provisional President of Africa,'" namely Garvey himself, drawing a $25,000 per year salary. The Leader of African Americans, Rev. James Eason, would dwell in a "Black House" in

Washington, DC, "to hob-nob with 'the other ambassadors'" for $10,000 a year. Two leaders of the West Indian Black population were also elected, as well as a leader "for the Negroes of the world." Then during the fourth week of the convention they elected other high positions including a potentate at $12,000 a year, a high commissioner general, an international organizer at $6,000 a year, a chaplain general, a minister of legions at $3,000, a surgeon general "and other such high-sounding magnificos." These positions added up to over $55,000 in annual salaries. Yet, according to Harrison, the chancellor's report showed that the organization had only $2,000 in its coffers.[27]

Not surprisingly, Harrison chafed at what he called Garvey's "cowardly evasions on lynching." Recall that Harrison's pre-UNIA work in the Liberty League had been oriented primarily on the domestic struggle against lynching, Jim Crow segregation, and disenfranchisement rather than on the shipping lines and other business ventures that Garvey championed. In that context, the comment suggests that Harrison began to feel that going from the Liberty League and Liberty Congress to Garvey's financially dubious stock-selling schemes now looked like a step backward. Although he did occasionally issue flashy rhetorical threats that the UNIA would "lynch a white man for every lynched Black person," Garvey did not make agitation against lynching a consistent part of the official UNIA program or objectives. In fact, to the chagrin of the NAACP (and to the favor of white Southerners), Garvey denounced the effort to pass federal antilynching legislation on the grounds that it was just an attempt by white Republicans to appease Black people and would be unenforceable in practice. He reportedly even once thanked white Southerners for "lynching race consciousness into Black people."[28]

Harrison took issue with another aspect of Garvey's behavior that many others would also find objectionable, namely Garvey's relationship to the Ku Klux Klan. After Garvey praised President Warren G. Harding's statement in 1921 on the importance of "recognizing a fundamental, eternal, and inescapable difference" between the races, Richard B. Moore recounted how the People's Educational Forum in Harlem adopted a resolution condemning Garvey.[29] Around the same time, Harrison made a comparison between Marcus Garvey and the Ku Klux Klan's Imperial Wizard "Colonel" William Simmons.[30] It would prove a prophetic observation because Garvey would meet directly with the Ku Klux Klan the following summer, on account of a shared interest in complete racial purity and separation.[31]

These criticisms seemed warranted by Garvey's own words. He once declared, for example, "I regard the Klan, the Anglo-Saxon clubs and White American societies, as far as the Negro is concerned, as better friends of the race than all other groups of hypocritical whites put together. I like honesty and fair play. You may call me a Klansman if you will, but, potentially, every white man is a Klansman, as far as the Negro in competition with whites socially, economically and politically is concerned, and there is no use lying." In New Orleans, Garvey declared, "This is a white man's country. He found it, he conquered it, and we can't blame him if he wants to keep it. I am not vexed with the white man of the South for Jim Crowing me because I'm Black. I never built any street cars or railroads. The white man built them for your own convenience. And if I don't want to ride where he's willing to let me then I'd better walk."[32]

Garvey's appreciation of the white nationalist Klan, complete racial separation, and racial purity in the 1920s dovetailed with similar ideas he would adopt in the 1930s, namely that Black people needed "extreme nationalism" of the kind demonstrated by fascist leaders in Europe. In 1937, Garvey cast Adolf Hitler as "dominant ... of the true-man type." He even boasted wistfully of how "we were the first Fascists" at a time when Italian dictator "Mussolini was still an unknown." Garvey went so far as to claim that "Mussolini copied our Fascism."[33] Herein lies one of Garvey's central contradictions. On the one hand, he famously spoke of how "we are going to emancipate ourselves from mental slavery, for though others may free the body, none but ourselves can free the mind." A noble idea, this line would later be memorialized forever by Bob Marley's "Redemption Song." On the other hand, as French scholar Jérémie Kroubo Dagnini has noted, Garvey also "tended to put Western culture/civilization on a pedestal. For example ... he tended to idolize Western leaders such as Napoleon and Hitler—though they were extremely racist."[34]

Garvey's statements of accommodation toward Jim Crow segregation and his meeting with the Ku Klux Klan sparked vehement opposition among some African Americans. In 1923, the nativist "Garvey Must Go!" campaign emerged in which members of the NAACP and the Urban League, the Black socialist *Messenger* magazine, and other opponents of Garvey openly called for the deportation of the Jamaican UNIA president and for increased state repression against the Garvey movement. This campaign took place in a context in which Garvey and his movement were already having to deal with domestic opposition and state repression on a vast scale, including harassment by New York District Attorney Edwin Kilroe, George Tyler's attempted assassination of Garvey, infiltration of the UNIA by J. Edgar Hoover's Bureau of Investigation, and constant surveillance from US military intelligence, naval intelligence, the postal service, the State Department, and British intelligence, to name a few. Garvey, the leo, proved a lion-hearted fighter.

Another thing that vexed Harrison about Garvey concerned the latter's embrace of Zionist ideology. When Garvey tapped Harrison to lead the UNIA's first Liberia delegation, he did so on the political grounds of a Black Zionism modeled on the Jewish colonization of Palestine. At Liberty Hall in 1922, for example, Garvey asked, "If the Jews can have Palestine, why not the Negroes another Palestine in Africa?" Then again in 1924 Garvey declared, "We are asking the world for a fair chance to assist the people of Liberia in developing that country, as the world is giving the Jew a fair chance to develop Palestine." This argument by analogy demonstrated why the Yiddish press saw the Garvey movement as "Black Zionism" and Garvey as a kind of "Black [Theodor] Herzl."[35]

According to Hill, the model for the UNIA's paramilitary Universal African Legion may have taken inspiration directly from the Jewish Legion, the military formation of Jewish volunteers in the white world war that fought as part of the British army to drive the Ottomans out of Palestine. "The Jewish Legion was the brainchild of militant Zionist Vladimir Jabotinsky," noted Hill, "to whom Garvey bears more than a passing ideological resemblance."[36] Jabotinsky spoke with brutal candor about the fundamental nature of Jewish Zionism as a colonizing project that would have to proceed "in defiance of the will of the native Arab population of Palestine," just like every other historical instance of colonization had proceeded in defiance of the will of the Indigenous people being colonized.[37]

By contrast, Harrison did not look to any form of Zionism as a political template for African redemption. Although we have seen no direct statements from Harrison on Jewish Zionism, the Balfour Declaration, or Palestine, he openly supported the anticolonial movements of the Arab and Islamic worlds, including figures like Mohammad Farid in Egypt and King Faisal I of Iraq. As we saw in chapter 4, Harrison's call for a "Colored International" envisaged an alliance of the "darker races" *against* capitalism, white domination, and colonialism. In spelling out his vision, he explicitly included Algeria, Morocco, and Afghanistan, and he also noted approvingly Islam's unifying role as "the religion which linked together and still links the souls of hundreds of millions of black, brown and yellow peoples from the Senegal to the shores of the Yellow Sea." He enthused about how "it is this multitudinous mass which is now on the move, struggling upward to their 'place in the sun,' under the impact of white arrogance, greed and race-prejudice which call to their aid the forces of religion, business, imperialism and war." Harrison did eventually make explicit his rejection of Garvey's Black Zionism, arguing that "the destiny of the American Negro lies in the future of America and no one need think that he will mortgage that future for the sake of a barbaric dream of African Empire with Dukes of Uganda and Ladies of the Nile."[38]

Indeed, the anti-imperialist in Harrison saw through Garvey's colonial designs on the African continent. One of the items on the list of Harrison's explicit grievances about Garvey reads, "Changed policy from Negro self-help to Invasion of Africa."[39] The Liberian government came to the same conclusion in 1924, when it summarily expelled the UNIA from Liberia.[40] Elie Garcia, the official UNIA commissioner to Liberia, had tried to warn Garvey that the "degenerated," "morally weak," and "tyrannical" Americo-Liberian ruling elites did not want any "enlightening of the native tribes" by outsiders and that the Liberians regarded the notion of a ruler for all Black people in the world as a "troublesome nightmare."[41] Harrison's opposition to a policy of "invasion of Africa" reflected his opposition to the way Garvey envisioned going "back to Africa" as a project to establish a Black empire "on which the sun shall shine as ceaselessly as it shines on the Empire of the North today," as Garvey put it. Garvey took inspiration not only from Jewish Zionism but also from Caesar's Rome and the British Empire as models for his imperial vision of African redemption.[42]

Harrison also recorded Garvey's "ignorance" as a distinctive grievance, which included a note suggesting that Garvey too often spoke about Africa "as a country." We can surmise the substance of this criticism from some of the continental Africans who also seemed to find this aspect of Garvey's approach problematic. The Basutoland-born Garvey critic M. Mokete Manoedi, for example, maintained that "it is about as sensible and logical to speak about a president of Africa as it is to speak of a president or king of Europe or of all the Americas." The Nigerian student Madarikan Deniyi raised a similar concern, asking, "How can Marcus Garvey and the U.N.I.A. redeem Africa without the consent and cooperation of the black kings, chiefs, and presidents who were born and elected to rule the natives in Africa?" As we saw in chapter 5 on Harrison's African consciousness, contrary to the UNIA's official stated commitment to "civilizing the backward tribes of Africa," Harrison maintained that the responsibility of Black people in the diaspora was to study African civilizations, sciences, social customs, agriculture, and systems of worship not to colonize them but to "LEARN WHAT THEY HAVE TO TEACH US (for they have much to teach us)."[43]

In sum, Harrison objected to Garvey's "bombastic blabbing," "insane egotism," "jealousy of successful subordinates," "plastering the air with lies" about the number of convention delegates and the size of the UNIA, financial corruption of the BSL, "shameless electioneering" at the convention, numerous "ballyhoo devices" for getting money from UNIA members, lavish lifestyle, "cowardly evasions on lynching," dalliance with the Ku Klux Klan, "invasion of Africa," colonial Zionism, and ignorance for viewing Africa "as a country." Other than that, Garvey was surely a perfect leader in Harrison's eyes!

The Liberty Party and New Negro Political Independence

Harrison did not resign himself to acquiescence nor bolt for the exit in the face of his disillusionment with Garvey. Instead, he took steps to push UNIA members to develop a "race first" formation that would bypass Garvey's official abstention from politics. In this regard, Harrison did something relatively small and short-lived but historically significant: founding the Liberty Party as an all-Black political party to challenge Republicans, Democrats, and Socialists in the 1920 elections.[44] While archival sources on it are scarce, the story of the Liberty Party sheds further light on Harrison's effort to build Black unity around "race first" candidates who would run for office on a platform that would benefit Black people both inside and outside of the UNIA.

The fact that Harrison worked full time as editor of the *Negro World* and a dues-paying member of the politically nonpartisan UNIA at the time of the Liberty Party's formation demonstrates his determination, as Jeff Perry put it, "to draw followers from the Garvey movement and the broader 'New Negro' movement into political action."[45] If, as Garvey preached, Black people need their own organizations, economic ventures, newspapers, churches, and lands, then one might think having their own political party would be a natural extension of the same "race first" logic. Clearly, Harrison's efforts to encourage UNIA members to build a political party of their own only chafed against Garvey's aversion to party politics and rankled the faction of UNIA leaders that began intriguing against Harrison at the 1920 convention.

Harrison's Liberty Party, much like the Liberty League and Liberty Congress, presented a new political vehicle for a historic trend that he elaborated: the "race first" approach to politics. It conjured the late nineteenth-century "negrowump" politics of figures like T. Thomas Fortune, who argued that Black people should appraise their political interests according to "race first, then party."[46] The Liberty Party seemed deliberately designed to break the white monopoly on political parties under which Black people had been forced. According to Harrison, the emergence of the New Negro in politics signaled the realization among African Americans "that they were sold out by the Republican party in 1876" when the party sold out Southern Blacks in their abandonment of Reconstruction. Not to mention the fact that lynching and disenfranchisement had only increased in the late nineteenth and early twentieth centuries "with the continuing consent of a Republican Congress, a Republican Supreme Court and Republican President."[47] He understood that even after Reconstruction, African Americans had remained loyal to the Republican Party because it touted itself as the party of Abraham Lincoln, Frederick Douglass, and emancipation.

For that reason, Harrison sought to dispel Black illusions in the Republican Party by turning a critical eye toward Lincoln's actual track record, developing a critique that crystallized a radical reappraisal of the dominant Lincoln narrative in US memory and historiography at that time. He began lecturing on "Lincoln vs. Liberty: Fact vs. Fiction" as early as 1911 and by 1920 he began lecturing on the subject at Liberty Hall in Harlem before UNIA audiences. His basic argument was that the "burden of gratitude" Black people had toward the Republican Party of Lincoln is what "keeps us from using our political power solely on our own behalf," and therefore Black people had a duty to investigate and rethink the grounds of that gratitude. Most Black people saw Lincoln as the greatest president in history, but for Harrison this notion of Lincoln as a God-like "Great Emancipator" did not align with the facts of history. Harrison saw the popular narrative about Lincoln as one of the "historical myths of America," which propagated widespread misconceptions about Lincoln's relationship to slavery and emancipation. As against the mainstream Lincoln mythology, the notes for Harrison's talks indicate that his touchstone for Lincoln had developed many sides:

1. That Lincoln was not an abolitionist
2. That he had no special love for Negroes
3. That he opposed citizenship for Negroes
4. That he favored making slavery perpetual in 1861
5. That he denied officially that the war was fought to free the slaves
6. That he refused to pay Negro soldiers the same wages that he paid the white soldiers
7. That the Emancipation Proclamation was signed not for the slave's sake but as an act to cripple the armies of the South
8. That it did not abolish slavery and was not intended to

Harrison had documentary evidence for each point, noting that Lincoln's own words often formed the evidence most damaging to the Lincoln mythology. Harrison's trailblazing historical reappraisal of Lincoln would be elaborated decades later, when historians like Lerone Bennett would prove Harrison's conclusions and obliterate the Lincoln mythology even more comprehensively.[48]

Alongside a radical break from the Republican Party of Lincoln, the creation of a Black political party emerged as a logical outgrowth of the postwar New Negro political awakening. In the context of the corrupting influence of the Republicans and Democrats and Socialists, who at best only countenanced Black representatives who towed their party's line, African American voters needed to "be concentrated for the realization of racial demands for justice and equality of opportunity and treatment" by carrying the doctrine of "Race First" into the arena of electoral politics.⁴⁹ Yet domestic political experience was not the only impetus for forming an all-Black party.

The Liberty Party also emerged, in part, from a specific political lesson that Harrison drew from international freedom struggles like that of the Sinn Fein ("We Ourselves") movement of Ireland. He argued that "In the British Parliament the Irish Home Rule party clubbed its full strength and devoted itself so exclusively to the cause of Free Ireland that it virtually dictated for a time the policies of Liberals and Conservatives alike. *The new Negro race in America will not achieve political self-respect until it is in a position to organize itself as a politically independent party and follow the example of the Irish Home Rulers.*"⁵⁰ If the Irish were able to influence British politics by banding together despite being a colonized minority, then Black people could do the same to influence US politics despite being a colonized minority. "Sinn Fein" in the Irish context was analogous to "Race First" in the African American context of New Negro politics. It was an argument that he likely learned from William Monroe Trotter, who had made the same case in the early 1900s.⁵¹ In short, the Negro was a colonized subject.

For this reason, Harrison urging Black people to vote only for Black candidates in the 1920 elections had a simple logic.⁵² Given the structure of US politics, the only mainstream Black candidates one could vote for would have had to be white-funded Republicans, Democrats, or Socialists. Having Black electoral candidates who were not beholden to white masters would therefore require forming a new party.

William Bridges first put out an explicit call for a Black political party in his *Challenge* magazine, one of the many Black radical broadsheets in Harlem that had taken inspiration from Harrison's *Voice*. Bridges's springtime call for a Black party was then reproduced in the Harrison-edited *Negro World* in June of 1920.⁵³ In August, Bridges, Harrison, and Edgar Grey founded the Liberty Party. The Liberty Party held street meetings in various Northern cities, including Philadelphia, Milwaukee, and Harlem.⁵⁴ By September, Bridges wrote to Harrison of Liberty Party meetings he had organized in Milwaukee. He gushed about the tremendous potential of the party to grow in the Midwest. However, few if any prominent Black people supported the Liberty Party, a situation underscored by the fact that, despite his enthusiasm, Bridges reported that the meetings he organized in Wisconsin drew fewer than twenty people.⁵⁵

Harrison, as chairman of the New York section of the party, quickly grew dissatisfied with Bridges's flailing efforts to build the Liberty party and offered to "repair the damage" by campaigning for the party in Philadelphia.⁵⁶ In October 1920, the Liberty Party held a meeting of about 150 people, in which those assembled nominated a range of prominent Black leaders including W. E. B. Du Bois, James Weldon Johnson, Kelly Miller, William Pickens, William Monroe Trotter, and Rev. James Eason. In a telling political measurement of the times, the Philadelphia-based African American minister and Garvey movement leader Rev. James Eason got the most votes and became the party's candidate for president. Rev. Easton, one of the most popular of UNIA leaders, had just been elected to the position of "Leader of American Negroes" at the UNIA's first annual convention.[57]

The Liberty Party seems to have broken down following Bridges's visit to Wisconsin. Ostensibly, he went there to convince the Industrial Workers of the World and Victor Berger of the Socialist Party to support the Liberty Party. However, upon Bridges's return to Harlem, he called on Black people to support the Socialists. Apparently, instead of Bridges winning the hearts and minds of the white radicals he encountered, they won his. This led to infighting between Harrison and Bridges, and the collapse of the Liberty Party.[58] Bridges' politics apparently continued to wander. A postelection article in the *Negro World* reported that the Liberty Party was set to expel him for secretly working for the Democratic Party as a Tammany Hall district captain.[59]

Though ultimately not successful, the Liberty Party nevertheless has historical significance. For one thing, it built on George Edwin Taylor's 1904 candidacy by running—for only the second time in US history—a Black presidential candidate.[60] For another, by constituting the second formation in US history of a Black political party, it became a forerunner of related efforts at Black party building that would take shape in the 1960s including the Mississippi Freedom Democratic Party, the Black Panther Party, and the "Freedom Now" Party.[61]

A Radical Voice within the Garvey Movement

Perhaps the most lasting way that Harrison tried to shift the course of the Garvey movement was by compiling his writings into a second book, *When Africa Awakes: The "Inside Story" of the Stirrings and Strivings of the New Negro in the Western World*. With essays culled mostly from his editorials in *The Voice*, the *Negro World*, and the *New Negro* magazine, it offered Harrison's radical analysis of a wide range of subjects, from the program of the Liberty League, to lynching, to arguments for armed self-defense and against the "white world war" to reflections on the perils and pitfalls of white "friends of the negro." Harrison completed it during the first international UNIA convention in August and had it published by December. Eventually, Harrison's book would find a place among the handful of books explicitly recommended for study in the "Cadets" class for the youth sections of the UNIA, representing another significant yet subtle example of Harrison's influence on the Garvey movement.[62] Publishing a book after the convention would prove to be only the first among many major efforts he would undertake to push the Garvey movement in a more radical direction.

Another step Harrison took in this direction was to make explicit and consistent calls for mass political action in solidarity with the African-descended peoples of the Caribbean. Echoing Black Socialist W. A. Domingo's call for mass protest against US imperialism in Haiti, Harrison made use of his position at the helm of the *Negro World* to cast a similar spotlight on Haiti during the first UNIA international convention.[63] He denounced the fact that white American "cracker marines" installed a president of their choosing in Haiti, subverted the legislative bodies of the Haitian republic, butchered Haitian citizens in cold blood, and forced "peoples of African descent" there into slavery, building roads without pay. "What boots it that we strike heroic attitudes and talk grandiloquently of Ethiopia stretching forth her hands when we Africans of the dispersion can let the land of [Toussaint] L'Overture lie like a fallen flower beneath the feet of swine?" In tones imbued with the UNIA's pan-African mythopoetics, he was asking the whole organization what the UNIA would do for Haiti.[64]

Harrison did not merely ask the hard questions but gave clear answers by calling for the political mobilization of African Americans to put pressure on the US government on behalf of the "peoples of African descent" in Haiti. In the *Negro World*, he proposed organizing large-scale propaganda meetings in such places as Faneuil Hall, Madison Square Garden, and Black churches, adding that "we could in our newspapers and magazines agitate for the withdrawal of the forces of the American occupation, as the Irish did on behalf of Ireland; we could, at least, get up a gigantic petition with a million signatures and carry it to Congress. Even a 'silent protest parade' would become us better than this slavish apathy and servile acquiescence in which we are now sunk."[65] By referencing the NAACP's silent protest parade following the East St. Louis pogrom, he advanced a case for analogous political action in solidarity with the Haitian people.[66] Black people in the United States needed to protest on behalf of Black people in the Caribbean, not only because the US military occupation had outlawed civil protest in Haiti but also because the US government—which African Americans could theoretically influence—that refused to stop committing atrocities against the Haitians.[67]

After the 1920 convention, Harrison also began working with dissident UNIA members in Philadelphia during their internal revolt against the local division president Fred A. Toote. The trouble in Philly seems to have started when some UNIA members there discovered that Toote had been misappropriating funds from the local division's treasury and siphoning off them to the parent body—for the purchase of a church building they never saw, for the payment of crew members of the Yarmouth like Captain Joshua Cockburn while it docked in Philly, for a $1,500 "loan" to the African Legion, and for other expenses—without the consent of the membership. Joseph St. Prix, owner of a shoe repair business and chairman of the board of trustees for the Philly UNIA division, got together with some BSL stockholders and members of the division to protest the disappearance of their moneys. Toote failed to provide documentation or explanation for where the moneys went, attempted to forbid St. Prix and other dissenters from holding meetings, and at one point called openly on the local division to "go hunt [UNIA officer Edward D.] Smith-Green and murder him for a traitor."[68] St. Prix's group became so disgusted that they began pooling resources to create a fund for taking legal action against Toote, "having lost complete confidence in his integrity." They also leveled a protest and formal request to the UNIA parent body for his removal as president.

Marcus Garvey himself eventually traveled to Philly to quell the rebellion, but it backfired. As one nameless Philly UNIA member noted privately, "It is a sad reminiscence when we look back upon the beautiful words of Marcus Garvey, 'The Man who fools with the Negro's money is skylarking with his life,' and compare them with his conduct in adjusting the Philadelphia misunderstanding. Words are really meaningless when they are uttered with no intent to application. On the night of October 8 at a specially called meeting over which the Honorable gentleman presided, the veneer under which he has masqueraded for upward of two and a half years was completely torn from his face. In grief we witnessed his adroit performance." It is not clear exactly what Garvey did, but the Philly dissident (possibly St. Prix) noted that Garvey had threatened him with "trouble if I persisted in my attitude toward this hireling puppet Toote. . . . [Garvey's] conduct in Philadelphia was altogether out of harmony with his pretended racialism. For instance, he evinced utter disregard for those who dared to oppose his nefarious will. Departing from his teachings of establishing a government whose justice will be exemplary to the other nations and people, by consigning all who pointed to misconduct to the gallery of traitors."[69] Things were getting hot in Philly!

During this internal conflict, St. Prix became Harrison's point of contact for a series of Harrison's speaking engagements in Philly, and he sought St. Prix's opinion about the prospect of giving educational classes twice a week in Philly and possibly organizing "either a local committee or a branch of the Liberty League" with those who resonated with his message.[70] The UNIA parent body in New York responded by sending E. L. Gaines, the head of Garvey's paramilitary Universal African Legion, to quell the Philly local division's turmoil—and slander Harrison. St. Prix reported that, "Mr. Gain[e]s (of the UNIA) arrived here with a propaganda that British gold is being circulated to frustrate the plans of the UNIA by a certain N.Y. Gentleman. You may draw your own conclusion."[71] After the Liberty Congress, the United States branded him a pro-German figure. (Much like Lenin and Trotsky got branded as German agents.) And now, Marcus Garvey had branded Harrison a British agent to slander him in the eyes of the Philly division.

Harrison's response articulated a strategy based on continuing to build and do positive work without worrying about or responding to such baseless attacks. "As to Mr. Gain[e]s," he wrote, "he seems to be a great, big joke. He must have 'British gold' on the brain. Don't mind the old f—t, but go right ahead. Our motto is 'Not Busting, But Building,' and we can afford to stick to that. If we do good work and neither attack anyone or notice any attacks made on us, the Liberty League will attract hosts of friends in the City of Brotherly Love."[72] Harrison thus sought not to "bust" the UNIA but rather to "build" the Liberty League. By taking a positive and proactive approach that neither attacked the UNIA or its leader openly nor responded to divisive or sectarian attacks from similar quarters, Harrison sought the high road, avoiding petty squabbles that would inevitably weaken both the UNIA and his attempt to revive the Liberty League.

It is difficult not to notice here how Garvey's attempts to crush dissent and monopolize power within the UNIA dovetailed with his admiration of the robber barons, who had themselves crushed their rivals in order to achieve monopoly power in the capitalist economy. "If the oil of Africa is good for Rockefeller's interest," opined Garvey, "if the iron ore is good for the Carnegie Trust; then surely these minerals are good for us. Why should we allow Wall Street and the capitalist group of America and other countries to exploit our country when they refuse to give us a fair chance in the countries of our adoption? Why should not Africa give to the world its black Rockefeller, Rothschild and Henry Ford? Now is the opportunity."[73]

Garvey's aspiration to become a Black capitalist on the scale of the largest white capitalists in the world drew sharp and poignant criticism from the Black left. For example, the St. Croix–born Socialist and labor organizer Frank Crosswaith predicted that "with Africa as our Empire, there will still be ragged, underfed, and poverty-stricken Negroes. All that we will have done will be to have exchanged our white parasites and profiteers for black parasites and black profiteers. Such a change will not help the race to any extent; it will certainly benefit the Emperor and his henchmen!"[74] By making this argument in 1920—while the vast majority of Africans still suffered under white European colonial rule—Crosswaith employed class consciousness to make a keen and prophetic observation that would find confirmation in the neocolonialism that followed the struggles for African independence over half a century later, as we mentioned in chapter 7.

In the spring of 1921, Harrison and a group of Black Communists in Harlem explored the possibility of pushing the Garvey movement in a more anti-capitalist direction. According to Claude McKay, the Jamaican-born revolutionary Communist poet and novelist, Harrison suggested having a meeting for this purpose with the "Black Reds." The meeting took take place at the office of the left-wing *Liberator* magazine, where McKay had recently become an editor. In addition to Harrison and McKay, Grace Campbell (a Black Communist and leading organizer of the African Blood Brotherhood), Richard B. Moore, W. A. Domingo, Cyril Briggs, Joseph Fanning (another African Blood Brotherhood member who owned the only Black cigar store in Harlem), and Otto Huiswoud (the first Black member of the Communist Party) were present. According to McKay, "The real object of the meeting . . . was to discuss the possibility of making the Garvey Back-to-Africa Movement more class-conscious."[75]

One of the most notable things about McKay's account is that Hubert Harrison instigated the meeting in the first place. As Jeffrey Perry so aptly put it, Harrison gave voice not only to "the most race-conscious of the class radicals" in the Socialist Party but also to "the most class-conscious of the race radicals" in the Garvey movement. In 1920, Harrison had vociferously defended the "race first" position from attacks by his "class first" Black Socialist protégés, and in 1921 he refused a funding offer from the Communist Party to become the party's "stalking horse" against Garvey. Yet Harrison clearly sympathized enough with their Socialist critique—of Garvey's quest for a Black capitalist empire—to initiate a discussion with the key Black Socialists in Harlem about building class consciousness within the Garvey movement. Harrison's discussions with the "Black Reds" would prove a catalyst for the attempt by Cyril Briggs and the African Blood Brotherhood in August of 1921 to push the second international UNIA convention in a class-conscious direction, an attempt which failed miserably when Garvey decided to summarily expel them from the convention.[76]

After his meeting with McKay and the Black Communists, Harrison undertook to build a radical and colored internationalist politics within the Garvey movement. In May of 1921, for example, the *Negro World* published Harrison's call to action titled "Wanted—A Colored International," as noted in chapter 4. It constituted the most compelling and sophisticated articulation of his call for an alliance among the "darker races" against the "white capitalist internationalism" of "race prejudice and exploitation which is known as bourgeois 'democracy' at home and colonial imperialism abroad."[77] Then, during the UNIA's second international convention that year, the August 14 issue of the *Negro World* carried William Ferris's editorial in defense of Black empire building as well as a piece by Harrison called "A New International," which repeated more concisely his earlier argument for a "Colored International." That a single issue of the paper contained pieces both for and against Black imperialism exemplified some of the contradictions in the soul of UNIA during that convention and Harrison's unique position as a voice of radicalism in the pages of the *Negro World* in this period.

Harrison undertook other steps to shift the course of the UNIA away from Garvey's intended line of march. For example, when Garvey left the country to tour the Caribbean in the spring of 1921, Harrison took advantage of his absence and tried to shift the ideological direction of the UNIA by expounding on his own ideas, including some pointed criticisms of Garvey, in the Outdoor Grioversity. According to Garvey scholar Robert Hill, the increasing friction between Harrison and Garvey is what made Garvey demote Harrison's position on the *Negro World* staff as Harrison became more outspoken about his differences with Garvey. According to a US military intelligence report from September 1921, he was "conducting meetings nightly and attacking the great leader, Garvey, without using his name." Harrison remained on the *Negro World* editorial staff because Garvey was apparently "afraid" to dismiss him entirely, but still downgraded his influence on the paper by a demotion to the position of contributing editor.[78] After his departure from the paper altogether in 1922, Harrison's wildly popular "Poetry for the People" section of the *Negro World* would likewise be retired, though poetry would still make a "scattered" appearance throughout the paper in the ensuing years after Harrison's editorship.[79]

Though we have found no written transcripts of Harrison's speeches "attacking the great leader," one can glean clues as to how he attacked Garvey without naming him by his review of white American playwright Eugene O'Neill's play *Emperor Jones*. *Emperor Jones* parodied the life of Marcus Garvey, featuring Charles Gilpin in the role of Brutus Jones, an African American who commits murder and then escapes from jail to a small Caribbean island where he becomes "a successful faker lording it over a group of his people in the style of emperor." By his critical descriptions of the main character, Harrison's review of the play advanced a barely veiled critique of Garvey—and right in the pages of the *Negro World*! Here we recall how Harrison cleverly managed to evade censorship and deportation during the white world war while still catching the Wilson administration in the crossfire of his attack on local pro-war exponents of "democracy" hypocrisy. In Harrison's words, the emperor "by superior cunning, chicanery . . . [and] appeals to the supernatural and the far away... manages to fool and cow the people while he sucks up every dollar in sight." Many *Negro World* writers reviewed Emperor Jones unfavorably on the grounds that it "does not elevate the Negro," and at least one *Negro World* reader suggested Harrison was an Uncle Tom for reviewing the play favorably. Yet Harrison felt that the play was meant to be a realistic depiction of "the soul of an ignorant and superstitious person" and that in that respect it was "genius."[80]

In stark contrast to Garvey's majestic pomp and flair, replete with fancy military uniforms and grandiose titles, Harrison the "Black Socrates" modeled a humbler disposition. In fact, Harrison saw Garvey's showmanship as a reflection of the inferiority complex of internalized oppression "which needs the aid of garish uniforms, swords, struttings, and 'big talk'" in order to suppress the feelings of unimportance that slavery had produced in Black people. Harlem activist Hodge Kirnon felt similarly that Garvey's aesthetic "seemed rather a childish imitation of European royalty and aristocracy... which is now relegated to the scrap-heap of worn-out ideas, forms and customs of the past." He added that there was very little in the UNIA constitution, bylaws, or activities that savored of real internal democracy.[81] Garvey's veneration and emulation of European empires, dictators, titles, and aesthetics in a militant Black nationalist movement brings to mind Langston Hughes's poem "House in the World":

> I'm looking for a house
> In the world
> Where the white shadows
> Will not fall.
>
> *There is no such house,*
> *Dark brothers,*
> *No such house*
> *At all.*[82]

After the expulsion of the Black Communists from the second UNIA convention, Harrison emerged as one of the first Black voices to criticize an aspect of Garvey's outlook that Black Marxists would also find objectionable: the eerie resemblance of Garvey's approach to that of the Ku Klux Klan. As early as November 1921, Harrison contacted the *Sunday World* to try to publish a piece titled "Inside the Garvey Movement" to expose what he felt were the most disturbing aspects of Garvey's behavior. In his pitch to the editor, Harrison spoke of certain tendencies in the movement he had observed, which paralleled those of the Ku Klux Klan "both in method and essential purpose." This statement proved prophetic because Garvey did indeed end up meeting with the Ku Klux Klan the following year in June of 1922, apparently because of their common interest in racial separation and maintaining the "purity" of the races. Harrison thought that the publication of his insider's view would be a "minor journalistic feat" given how "some other papers ... have gullibly swallowed what Garvey had to say of himself," instead of investigating the truth of the matter for themselves. Garvey's statements of accommodation toward the Klan and Jim Crow would eventually spark vehement opposition among many African Americans, including the famous "Garvey Must Go!" campaign mentioned earlier.[83]

Harrison believed that he had a wealth of material and sought to convince the *Sunday World* editor of "the bombshell nature of it," but he expressly stipulated that if they did publish his exposé on Garvey, his name should not appear in any connection with it. Fearing reprisals, Harrison knew that he dared not reveal himself in print as such a sharp Garvey critic, in part because his job as a contributing editor for the *Negro World* would be placed in jeopardy. Indeed, Garveyites would end up physically attacking or threatening various Garvey critics including W. A. Domingo, Rev. Ethelred Brown, Mokete Manoedi, E. D. Smith-Green, and Rev. George Alexander McGuire. At the UNIA's 1922 convention, Garvey advised Chandler Owen and others who disagreed with him to "get themselves another job" because he, Garvey, "could not be responsible for anything that might happen to them because they might come up with a hand off or a leg off or a broken head." Shortly after that convention, A. Philip Randolph received a severed human hand in the mail. Garvey denied any involvement in the threatening provocation, calling it a "publicity stunt" on the part of Black Socialists to get them more attention and sympathy.[84]

Whether or not the hand came from a UNIA member (or someone in the Klan, or J. Edgar Hoover), three months later Garvey loyalists assassinated dissenting ex-UNIA member Rev. James Eason right before he was due to testify in Garvey's mail fraud trial. While we have seen no archival evidence that this act followed from an explicit order from on high, Marcus Garvey and his lieutenants like Fred Toote certainly nurtured a murderous attitude toward "traitors" in their speeches at UNIA events. Years later in 1928, for example, a UNIA member murdered the Garveyist prophetess Laura Adorkor Kofi in Florida. In the 1930s, same fate would also meet Black Communist Alfred Levy. Therefore, while it does not appear that Harrison's exposé was ultimately published, he certainly had good reason to be cautious.[85]

Although Harrison generally kept his candid opinions of Garvey private, in part for fear of the consequences, he did relax his caution about denouncing Garvey in print following the conclusion of Garvey's federal trial and conviction for mail fraud in June of 1923. Space does not permit a recounting of all the details of that long and acrimonious trial. But to make a long story short, the US government convicted Garvey of "using the mails to defraud" ordinary people of monies they had sent to buy shares in BSL ships that the UNIA aspired to buy but did not yet actually own. The fact the BSL advertised the ships *as though* they owned them is how the government made their case for mail fraud. Garvey's defenders can reasonably argue that he was basically convicted of fundraising (while Black).

Like Domingo's *Emancipator*, Black revolutionary Communist Cyril Briggs had worked hard to expose the BSL's financial mismanagement and Garvey's alleged financial misappropriations and fraudulent operations in his *Crusader* magazine. And it was Briggs who had initially suggested to the US government that they investigate Garvey for mail fraud, which became precisely the charge that they would ultimately use to arrest, try, convict, and deport Garvey. Regardless of the political and ideological differences he had with the Garvey movement, Briggs played a shameful role by helping the Feds in this way. By offering J. Edgar Hoover and the Bureau of Investigation not only support but an actual strategy for the persecution and ultimate deportation of Garvey, Briggs became an enabling factor in the state repression that dealt a devastating hammer blow to the largest international organization of Black people in modern history. Like the "Garvey Must Go!" campaign, it became yet another shameful lesson in the pitfalls of Black community infighting that holds back racial progress.

To his credit, Harrison did not join these campaigns, and we have found no evidence that he called for the deportation of Garvey. Much like W. A. Domingo, Harrison knew better—as a Caribbean immigrant himself—than to call for Garvey's deportation. There existed another reason he did not join the chorus of Black liberals, Socialists, and Communists who called openly for increased state repression of the UNIA: Harrison believed that Garvey was destined to end up in "a room where he can't hurt his head when he hits it against the walls—because those walls will be padded."[86]

Harrison thought the trial fair probably because of his own negative opinion of Garvey, but such a highly political trial could never have been fair in any objective sense. During the Jim Crow era of segregation and disenfranchisement, the white American ruling class witnessed the rise on its "own" soil of a "Black messiah" at the head of the largest international organization of Black people in modern history with a "race first" and pan-African nationalist program. This at a time when Uncle Sam enacted the ritual of white mob lynching and castration—on far less threatening Black men than Marcus Garvey—twice a week. In the final analysis, the Garvey trial emerged from the work of a young J. Edgar Hoover's federal bureau of state repression, and one would be hard pressed to find an instance where Hoover attempted to give one of his Black targets a "fair trial."[87]

In any event, Harrison expressed a mixed and telling verdict of his own. On the one hand, he lamented how even after the trial Garvey loyalists "still believed that Garvey never did a crooked thing in his life." He felt that Garvey's guilty verdict represented a "colossal collapse" demonstrating that "wind, noise, and bluster are not the foundations for anything permanent." On the other hand, Harrison defended what he saw as the core positive contribution that Garvey had made. In Harrison's words, "The original program of the Universal Negro Improvement Association was a good one, and is still good. That program was based on the belief that Negroes should finance the foundations of their future and not go begging to the white race either for help, leadership or a program."

"But," he noted, "this was not a novel contribution by Garvey. It had been the program of the Liberty League of which Garvey was a member in 1917 in New York. From that League Garvey appropriated every feature that was worthwhile in his movement. His notion of a racial flag was one. . . . Outdoor and indoor lectures, a newspaper, protests in terms of democracy—all these were adopted from the Liberty League. . . . Then came the Black Star Line—an idea which Garvey took bodily from [Charles] Seifert, one of the original members of the Liberty League." Given that none of these elements belonged to Garvey's original dream of building a Tuskegee Institute in Jamaica, Harrison's emphasis here revealed both his pride in the Liberty League's decisive influence on the transformation of the UNIA and also his anger, frustration, and disappointment with the organization's trajectory under Garvey's dictatorial control.[88]

Harrison's interest in exposing Garvey eventually crossed paths with a unique collaborator: Garvey's first wife and UNIA cofounder Amy Ashwood Garvey. Amy Ashwood and Harrison had a torrid romantic affair in 1925, a fact that became public when the court subpoenaed Harrison to testify in her divorce trial with Marcus Garvey. However, Amy Ashwood and Harrison's interest in one another was not only sexual. Amy Ashwood had enlisted Harrison as the ghostwriter of a book she wanted to write called "The Rise and Fall of Marcus Garvey." Sharing and comparing their experiences with Marcus Garvey confirmed and deepened Harrison's apprehensions toward the UNIA leader. As Harrison noted in his diary, "I am learning a great deal of this magnificent and mendacious mountebank, Garvey. He was, evidently, the dirtiest robber that ever rose to prominence."[89] Yet the book never saw the light of day. Amy Ashwood's first biographer, Lionel Yard, speculated that "perhaps this manuscript would have given us information about the inner workings of the UNIA that never received public exposure. . . . It must have been such an important, and possibly debunking document, that the staunch Garveyites organized a committee to destroy it."[90]

Conclusion

Harrison left the Garvey movement decisively in 1922, two years after he first became editor of the *Negro World*. Although Harrison ultimately failed to shift the trajectory of Garvey and the official Harlem-based UNIA leadership in all the ways he wanted, it was certainly not for lack of trying. He had published a UNIA-directed book (*When Africa Awakes*), called for political solidarity with Haitians, Crucians, and Afro-Caribbeans living under US military occupation, founded the all-Black Liberty Party that ran UNIA leader Rev. James Eason for president, worked with Black Communists in an attempt to make the Garvey movement more class-conscious, validated and supported the concerns of UNIA members who chafed at Garvey's authoritarian rule, agitated *Negro World* readers against imperialism and for a Colored International, and voiced public criticisms of "His Supreme Highness, the Potentate" in order to open people's eyes to the dangers of authoritarian forms of leadership. Harrison did not always express his dissent openly and forthrightly in the way that he did toward Booker T. Washington or the Socialist Party, in part for fear of reprisals and at least in part because the Garvey movement represented, on some level, a spectacular "race first" descendant of his own Liberty League and Harlem New Negro movement that he had worked so hard to cultivate. But by his efforts to influence the UNIA from within and amplify its Africa-conscious, colored internationalist, antilynching, anti-imperialist, anticapitalist, and political party-building tendencies, Harrison symbolized and gave voice to the most radical and transformative potential of the Garvey movement.

At the end of the day, Harrison's commitment to Black people lay not with an individual leader or organization but with, as he put it retrospectively, "the principles of the New Negro Manhood Movement, a portion of which had been incorporated by [Garvey] and his followers of the UNIA and ACL."[91] If Garvey's organization represented the business-oriented or "(in)corporate(d) sector" of the New Negro movement, then Garvey represented its CEO. This characterization offers a telling indicator of Harrison's vantage point and conjures the Socialist critique of Garvey's vision for a Black empire based on the accumulation of capital. While a highly dynamic organization in some respects, the UNIA also lost a whole number of potential leaders and supporters due to Garvey's egotism. Even Garvey loyalists like William Ferris could lament how Garvey lost "brilliant scholars, writers, orators, preachers, and lawyers" because he wouldn't listen to their ideas or criticisms.[92] Harrison's criticisms of Garvey—as egomaniacal, corrupt, dictatorial, imperialistic, ignorant, and an egregious liar—reflect Harrison's role as a proverbial touchstone that put Garvey's leadership to the test and revealed a number of its impurities.

To be fair, Marcus Garvey did work with Socialists in the early years of his sojourn in New York. For example, Domingo and Harrison were both early *Negro World* editors; the UNIA endorsed A. Philip Randolph, Chandler Owen, and George F. Miller in the 1918 local New York elections; and Garvey had even allowed white leftists like Eugene Debs and Rose Pastor Stokes to speak at UNIA events. Garvey even sang the praises of Vladimir Lenin and Leon Trotsky, appreciating their efforts to establish a Russia free of czarist despotism.[93] Yet during the course of Harrison's tenure at the *Negro World*, Marcus Garvey increasingly turned away from the Socialist and Communist left and came to believe that, in his words, "capitalism is necessary to the progress of the world, and those who unreasonably and wantonly oppose or fight against it are enemies to human advancement."[94]

As an anticapitalist and radical internationalist, Hubert Harrison naturally had a very different conception of New Negro politics and the meaning of "race first." Nevertheless, after the decline of his Liberty League and the rise of the UNIA, he climbed aboard Garvey's ship and did his best to influence it from within. In that capacity, Harrison watched in real time how Garveyism grew into a broad church representing various influences. Eventually, once the wave of political radicalism from the immediate postwar period ebbed, the messianic and commercially oriented Black nationalist tradition of figures like Paul Cuffe, Martin Delany, Chief Alfred Sam, and Booker T. Washington ultimately took center stage in Garvey's vision for the UNIA.[95] According to Robert Hill, Garvey abandoned whatever radicalism he had in 1921, quite possibly as part of a back-room agreement with the State Department that he made in order to get back into the United States after his tour of Central America that year.[96]

Restoring Harrison to the history of Garveyism reveals the decisive impact of the Black radical tradition that he symbolized, as Marcus Garvey's greatest catalyst and gravest critic.

This raises a number of questions. What if the UNIA had gone in a more class-conscious, anti-imperialist, and political party-building direction, much like the trajectory that Du Bois's pan-African congresses took? What if both formations had found means to link up with forces like the African Blood Brotherhood, the Comintern, and the Colored International? Was that even possible? Unfortunately, there was a bigger problem brewing. One that threatened to completely wash away the Black Socialists, Communists, and Garveyists altogether. And, of course, Hubert Henry Harrison.

Chapter 9

The Renaissance School of Negro History

HARLEM NIGHT CLUB

By Langston Hughes

Sleek black boys in a cabaret.
Jazz-band, jazz-band,—
Play, pLAY, PLAY!
Tomorrow.... who knows?
Dance today!

White girls' eyes
Call gay black boys.
Black boys' lips
Grin jungle joys.

Dark brown girls
In blond men's arms.
Jazz-band, jazz-band,—
Sing Eve's charms!

White ones, brown ones,
What do you know
About tomorrow
Where all paths go?

Jazz-boys, jazz-boys,—
Play, pLAY, PLAY!
Tomorrow.... is darkness.
Joy today!

The standard narrative about the significance of Harlem between World War I and the mid-1930s is that a renaissance took place there consisting of a unique flowering of Black literary, visual, and performing arts.[1] In high school history textbooks, for example, the so-called Harlem Renaissance remains one of the most common stories told about African American history and collective achievement in the early twentieth century. In the words of historian Nathan Huggins, "The Harlem Renaissance has become a phenomenon marking something more than the fact that Afro-Americans wrote poems and

Figure 9.1 Legendary jazz singer Ella Fitzgerald performing with Chick Webb at the Savoy Ballroom. Located on Lenox Avenue between 140th and 141st Street, the Savoy Ballroom was one of the most popular in Harlem. A *New York Age* headline on March 20, 1926, noted, "Savoy Turns 2,000 Away on Opening Night—Crowds Pack Ball Room All Week." Photograph by Otto F. Hess, 1940, New York Public Library, New York.

stories, painted and sculpted, and infused new life into the American theatre. Rather, it symbolizes [B]lack liberation and sophistication—the final shaking off of the residues of slavery, in the mind, spirit, and character." Renaissance liberation sounded great. But how could this widely accepted "renaissance" narrative symbolize a breakthrough for Black liberation if Hubert Harrison rejected it whole stock? This is a complex question, which once again conjures Harrison's touchstone-like quality. Because of its deliberate emphasis on white-marketable art instead of Black political agitation—and the way it has dominated popular conceptions of Harlem's significance in the early twentieth century—the standard "renaissance" narrative has played a unique role in writing Hubert Harrison out of history.[2]

Harrison crystallized multiple new—and radical—dimensions of the "New Negro" idea, which had been around since the late nineteenth century. He spoke, for example, of a "New Negro Manhood Movement" in 1916 and a "New Negro Womanhood" in 1917. He wrote of a "New Negro politics" in his *Voice* editorials of 1917–18 and edited the *New Negro* magazine in 1919. As we have seen from his relationship to the Socialist Party and Industrial Workers of the World, the freethought movement, the Liberty League and Liberty Congress, the Outdoor Grioversity, the rise of Garvey and Garveyism, Black free love politics, and the Colored International, Harrison's crystallizations of New Negro politics sparked a range of momentous intellectual and political breakthroughs within and beyond Harlem.

The postwar economic empowerment of Black communities in the South—from Tulsa and Memphis to Durham and Atlanta—created much anxiety and mouth-watering grist for the butcheries of Uncle Sam's white lynch mobs and pogromists. In the Northern cosmopolis of New York City, the postwar Black political awakening caused alarm not only to US military intelligence but also to middle-class liberals, both Black and white. They would ultimately settle on the promotion of a trendy new market for "high art" as a strategy for effacing Black militancy.[3] And sure enough, after 1925 the meaning of "New Negro" would never be the same.

That year saw the appearance of Alain Locke's anthology titled *The New Negro: An Interpretation*. Locke's book aimed to illuminate "the Negro in his essential traits" as demonstrated by the contemporary short stories, poetry, and interpretive essays on Black literature and culture that Locke compiled. "We speak," he wrote in the foreword, "of the offerings of this book embodying these ripening forces as culled from the first fruits of the Negro Renaissance." The idea was that if Black people could produce and show off their sophisticated artistic capabilities, it would raise their esteem in the eyes of white people, which would in turn stimulate a broader social equality and racial acceptance.[4]

Harrison's role, as one of the earliest and most forceful critics of the "renaissance" trope, exposes from within the way in which this trope comprised a conscious distortion, co-optation, and depoliticization of the "New Negro." Like a touchstone, the story of Harrison's critical assessment and rejection of the renaissance craze—combined with his deliberate erasure by its architects—reveals the contradictory and problematic role of the renaissance narrative, which has dominated our conception of the significance of early twentieth-century Harlem history since Locke.[5]

While Harrison's historical erasure has had many factors, the construction of what I call the "Renaissance School of Negro History" ranks among the most complex and illuminating among them. After all, while Harrison's tenure in the Socialist and Garvey movements may seem relatively short-lived, his tenure as a well-known educator and highly regarded intellectual in Harlem was not. For twenty years, Harrison shared his knowledge in a wide range of fields (labor economics, global geopolitics, evolutionary biology, African history, English literature, and so on) with the people of his beloved home neighborhood. In that sense, he typifies the "renaissance man" who, like Leonardo Da Vinci, had wide-ranging interests and expert knowledge in multiple disciplines. This raises a simple question: How and why would the emergence of a "Harlem Renaissance" exclude and erase a Harlem renaissance man *par excellence* like Hubert Harrison?

Eclipsing the "Old Protest Psychology": A *New Negro* for White Liberals

Born into the "smug gentility" of middle-class Black Philadelphia in 1885, Alain LeRoy Locke had an upbringing marked by what Locke called the "frantic respectability of the free, educated Negro tradition" that marked his parents' "bulwark against proscription and prejudice."[6] After attending Philly's Central High School, one of the top secondary schools in the country, he earned a degree in philosophy from Harvard University in 1907. After spending three years at the University of Oxford as the first African American Rhodes scholar, he undertook graduate studies at the University of Berlin. According to his biographers, "As far as the 'talented tenth' was concerned, Locke was exponentially more elite and educated." He would make a career as a philosophy professor at Howard University after earning the nickname of the "Proust of Lenox Avenue" for his "effete European academic quality" and the "refined egotism at the heart of his endeavors."[7] As the postwar militancy of the radical New Negro movement subsided, Locke would emerge as a kind of national curator—for the white publishing industry at least—of Black artistic culture.

In the spring of 1924, Gwendolyn Bennett, Regina Anderson of the 135th Street New York Public Library, and Charles Johnson of the National Urban League's *Opportunity* magazine put together a very special dinner. The purpose was to celebrate the publication of Jessie Fauset's new novel (*There Is Confusion*) and to encourage the work of up-and-coming young Black artists like Eric Walrond, Countee Cullen, and Langston Hughes. Invitees for the dinner included some major intellectual and literary figures like Horace Liveright, H. L. Mencken, W. E. B. Du Bois, Georgia Douglas Johnson, Oswald Garrison Villard, James Weldon Johnson, and Thomas Montgomery Gregory. Some 125 guests came out for the Civic Club event. Charles Johnson invited Hubert Harrison, but it does not appear that he attended. According to historian Jeffrey Stewart, the event represented the "first of its kind—an interracial communion between Black writers and white custodians of American culture to break bread and try to find a common language to talk about a literary awakening in America built around Negroes writing poems, short stories, and novels about the Black experience in America."[8]

The dinner precipitated a number of interracial literary connections and networking opportunities. Luckily for him, Alain Locke's performance as master of ceremonies for the evening caught the attention of dinner attendee Paul Kellogg, the white editor of the philanthropic and social-reform-minded *Survey Graphic* magazine.[9] Kellogg left the dinner so impressed by the "coming out" party for young Black writers that he subsequently convinced Locke to edit a special Harlem number of the *Survey Graphic*, which they would publish the following year under the title "Harlem: Mecca of the New Negro."[10]

In the months before its publication, Kellogg made clear the ethos that animated his vision of the special issue: "We are striking out along new lines in this Harlem number; offering a new approach—different from the economic-educational approach of Hampton and Tuskegee on the one hand; and on the other hand, different from the political approach of the Negro rights, lynching, discrimination, and so forth." The goal was to advance a new framework for racial progress based neither on industrial education nor on political resistance to oppression but instead on sophisticated cultural representation through the medium of the arts. As Kellogg put it, he wanted to interpret "the affirmative genius of writers, thinkers, poets, artists, singers and musicians, which make for a new rapprochement between the races at the same time that they contribute to the common pot of civilization." The task at hand was to present a "racial and cultural frontage" that was "affirmative, and nascent, *different from the old protest psychology* [emphasis added]." Kellogg's idea—of a handpicked group of Black artists constituting the face of a new solution to the race problem—was indeed quite different from "the old protest psychology."[11]

Alain Locke, the academic philosopher and connoisseur of high art, concurred with Kellogg's vision of a culturalist approach to racial problems. In Locke's words, "The days of obstruction and oppression exist only in the reactionary minds and fevered imagination of political demagogues. The young Negro of today is interested not in race problems and race controversy, but in self-development and in releasing those latent spiritual gifts of art, of literature, music or whatnot which are in him."[12]

Harlem's postwar rise in Black trade unionists, Socialists, Communists, Garveyists, and sexual libertines suggests that Locke's insistence that young Black people had no interest in "race problems" articulated a projection of his own personal disinterest. His biographers spoke of Locke's "strong sense of elitism," a quality that fitted, for example, with his "respectable," refined, and gentlemanly disinclination toward calling attention to racial oppression in ways that might make white people uncomfortable.[13] As Locke put it, "I would much prefer to see the black masses going gradually forward under the leadership of a recognized and representative and responsible elite than see a frustrated group of malcontents later hurl these masses at society in desperate strife."[14] Thus, as a member of the "recognized and representative and responsible elite" himself, Locke's interest in deploying Kellogg's "new racial and cultural frontage" as against the "old protest psychology" flowed from his own privileged class position.

The mainstream distribution that Kellogg's Harlem *Survey Graphic* received demonstrated that Kellogg and Locke were not alone in their desire to advance a "new frontage" in the face of the radical Black awakenings of the postwar period. For example, white philanthro-capitalists such as George Foster Peabody bought 1,000 copies of Kellogg's magazine to send to people "interested in the Negro problem," including to Christian missionaries in Africa. Joel and Amy Spingarn of the National Association for the Advancement of Colored People (NAACP) paid the cost of 1,000 copies for sending to students. James Weldon Johnson promoted the anthology throughout his upwardly mobile literary and social network. Almost immediately after it came out, white publishing mogul Albert Boni signed a contract with Locke to make the Harlem number into a book with the hope—which would prove successful—that it would be sent to every college and library in the country.[15]

Albert Boni and Horace Liveright's publishing company treated Hubert Harrison very differently from Alain Locke. In a two-part series for the *Negro World* called "On a Certain Condescension in White Publishers," Harrison recounted, "I recall my humorous amazement when, after writing to Boni & Liveright for a review copy of a book dealing with the anthropology of colored peoples, I received and read their reply. The supercilious magnificence of that reply was regal in its sweep. They wanted me to supply them with back numbers of the journal—and even then they simply subsided into silence. What could Negroes know of anthropology, whether as critics or simple readers?"[16] By contrast, the well-connected and elite support for Locke's work amounted to the anointment and ascension of not just a new hand-picked dean of Black art critics but liberal white America's official New Negro. As Kellogg said in a letter to Locke on the eve of publication, "With Alain Locke spread all over the contents page I guess there will be no uncertainty in people's minds as to who is our star."[17]

In the pantheon of Locke, Kellogg, and Boni's handpicked voices in *The New Negro*, Hubert Harrison bears the unique distinction of being deliberately edited out of the picture not once but twice. To his credit, one of Locke's original outlines included a piece by Harrison, titled "The White Man's War." Locke's description of this piece noted that it dealt with "the effect of the war upon the Negro, and the analysis of the disillusionment of the treatment inconsistent with the principles of democracy and self-determination, reaction among the generation that took part in it toward the church, the state, and capitalism."[18] The piece did not make it into the *Survey Graphic*'s Harlem number, nor into the *New Negro* anthology. Kellogg claimed that Harrison's piece had generated concerns at a staff meeting because it was "disproportionately long." If true, surely Locke or Kellogg or Boni (or Harrison) could have edited it down to a more concise version. But in fact, as Barbara Foley has pointed out, Harrison's contribution had been accorded one of the shortest word limits (2,200 words) of all the pieces under consideration. As Foley has argued, they cut Harrison's piece because his radical indictment of such forces as the church, the state, and capitalism "was too much for Kellogg." Not to mention Harrison's explicit linking of white people with the world war.[19]

In the place of "The White Man's War," another of Locke's draft outlines included an article by Hubert Harrison called "The Negro and Radicalism," a piece slated to cover "the normal Negro social temperament, the normal Negro social attitude, the reactions of protest, the points of radical indictment, the reaction of those masses to the radical, the attitude of radical organizations toward the Negro, Garveyism as race radicalism, [and a] forecast of the forces of agitation and protest." Once again, Harrison's essay never made it into Locke's collections. That not one but two pieces of Harrison's writings were considered and then discarded shows that his omission—and the historical erasure it portended—was no accident.

Harrison's elimination represented a larger neutering of key radical New Negro voices so that Kellogg's "philanthropic" transcendence of the "old protest psychology" could present to the world a "new racial and cultural frontage." In the book version, the white corporate publisher did worse than simply cut Harrison from the literary selections (despite the inclusion of pieces by Kellogg himself and "Old Crowd Negro" Tuskegee president Robert Moton). A key crystallizer of the original New Negro movement in Harlem—and author of two different books about it—is nowhere to be found *even in the extensive bibliography* that concludes the anthology![20]

While Kellogg or Boni may bear the ultimate responsibility for not publishing Harrison's writings, Locke clearly acquiesced in this process, as demonstrated by his exclusion of Harrison's works from the bibliography. These editorial decisions reflected the larger socioeconomic forces that sought to channel the New Negro movement energies away from subversive outlets like Garveyism or Socialism/Communism and toward politically nonthreatening expressions of Black art and culture. In the 1924 dinner party for Jessie Fauset and her peers, white literature professor and critic Carl Van Doren had spelled out quite bluntly what the white literary press wanted from young Black writers, namely "art rather than anger." This dovetailed with Johnson and Locke's message that night to the young Black writers about how they were going to have to avoid the racial harangue of earlier Negro creative writers if they wanted to get published.[21]

Thus, in addition to omitting Harrison, Locke's *New Negro* contained no selections from other militant New Negro voices such as Marcus Garvey, A. Philip Randolph, Chandler Owen, Cyril Briggs, or Richard B. Moore. The anthology excluded activist women like Grace P. Campbell, Williana Burroughs, Amy Ashwood Garvey, Amy Jacques Garvey, Henrietta Vinton Davis, and Eslanda Cardozo Goode. It excluded poems from the militant pen of a Lucian B. Watkins, Walter Everette Hawkins, Ethel Trew Dunlap, or Andy Razaf. Meanwhile, the selections from potentially hard-hitting artists like Langston Hughes and Claude McKay were decidedly nonthreatening at best and editorially neutralized at worst. And, of course, no Blues women.

Locke's treatment of Claude McKay is illuminating, given McKay's position as a Jamaica-born "Black Bolshevik" who had penned the poetic anthem of the radical New Negro movement ("If We Must Die"). McKay was a close friend of Hubert Harrison, who did not mince words in praising McKay as the "greatest living poet of Negro blood in America today." Consider, for example, McKay's poem "The White House," which Locke saw fit to include in both the *Survey Graphic* and *New Negro* anthologies:

> Your door is shut against my tightened face,
> And I am sharp as steel with discontent;
> But I possess the courage and the grace
> To bear my anger proudly and unbent.
> The pavement slabs burn loose beneath my feet,
> And passion rends my vitals as I pass,
> A chafing savage, down the decent street;
> Where boldly shines your shuttered door of glass.
> Oh, I must search for wisdom every hour,
> Deep in my wrathful bosom sore and raw,
> And find in it the superhuman power
> To hold me to the letter of your law!
> Oh, I must keep my heart inviolate
> Against the potent poison of your hate.

Without asking or even notifying McKay, Locke changed the title of the poem from "The White House" to "White Houses," utterly neutralizing McKay's scathing and pointed attack on the United States presidency as a symbol of potent and poisonous anti-Black hate. McKay had told Locke to correct the title after the *Survey Graphic* edition came out, yet Locke ignored McKay and neutered the radical poem's title again in the *New Negro* anthology. As McKay wrote in a frustrated letter to Locke, "What does a man [like me] care about entering a lot of uninteresting white houses?" With palpable exasperation, McKay wrote emphatically, "I cannot understand why you have done it. You knew my address. You might easily have contacted me. What is the very ordinary and usual procedure among literary people?" McKay pointed out that he took the poem "Negro Dancers" out of his own book *Harlem Shadows* (which Locke insisted on including in *The New Negro*) because "[he] did not consider the poem up to the level of [his] other work." This echoed Harrison's critique of James Weldon Johnson's poetry anthology three years prior, which also featured pieces that Harrison felt were far beneath the standard of the best work of the poets that Johnson included.[22]

The consciously and treacherously antiradical politics of Locke's volume explains why his *New Negro*—that had been officially announced, funded, and promoted by white publishing capital—generated so much enthusiasm with liberal white influencers of the day. Prominent journalist and social critic H. L. Mencken, for example, gushed that Locke's book symbolized "a phenomenon of immense significance" because "what it represents is the American Negro's final emancipation from his inferiority complex.... That inferiority complex, until very recently, conditioned all his thinking, even (and perhaps especially) when he was bellowing most vociferously for his God-given rights."[23] At long last, the Negroes are no longer bellowing for their rights. Hallelujah! Similarly, the *New York Times* noted how in Locke's volume "the negro ... is finding a new dignity in success that does not interfere with that of the whites, and is far more of an asset to the country than when he was a slave."[24] Here the *Times* let slip an embarrassing but revealing assessment: Locke managed to showcase the Black people who were doing even more for the country than their enslaved ancestors. How wonderful!

In the debate that emerged in the 1920s about the proper relationship between art and "propaganda"—then defined simply as information designed to influence public opinion—Locke articulated a position against propaganda. He felt Black art should be free of explicit messaging that drew attention to racial oppression, a practice he saw as tainted by the "besetting sin of monotony and disproportion" that inevitably "perpetuates the position of the group inferiority even in crying out against it." He disapproved of the way journals like *The Crisis* and *Opportunity*, which had been leading vehicles for Black artistic expression, were also "avowed organs of social movements and organized social programs." Like his white publishers, Locke also had grown weary of the "old protest psychology" and wanted to see Black people produce only "pure" art or art free of social or political messages.[25]

On the other side of the debate spectrum, W. E. B. Du Bois argued that "*all* art is propaganda and ever must be, despite the wailing of the purists."[26] In his view, if art is not propaganda for positive social change, then it becomes (by default) a kind of passive propaganda for the status quo. For propaganda advocates like Du Bois, "pure" or "neutral" art—that is, art without social or political implications—was not possible in an era when lynching, sexual violence, pogroms, and Jim Crow racial oppression reigned supreme. As historian Howard Zinn put it, "you can't be neutral on a moving train."[27]

Locke's "antipropaganda" view reflected, in part, the distance between Locke's social set and that of Black poor and working people. He lamented, for example, to the fact of Harlem being "swept by revolutionary oratory" as among those features that made the neighborhood "grotesque with the distortions of journalism."[28] This was not how everyday community members saw things. As we noted in chapter 3, the Harlemites not educated at Harvard and Oxford but who regularly partook of the "revolutionary oratory" and wide-ranging intellectual culture of the cost-free Outdoor Grioversity certainly did not congregate in masses large enough to block traffic because they regarded the radical stepladder speakers as "grotesque."

Ultimately, Northern white capital empowered Locke precisely for his ability to cast a reactionary hostility to political protest in wistful and romantic tones. For example, Locke wondered, "Is this more the generation of the prophet or that of the poet; shall our intellectual and cultural leadership preach and exhort or sing? I believe we are at that interesting moment when the prophet becomes the poet and when prophecy becomes the expressive song." The notion of "the prophet" becoming an artist sounds alluring. However, Locke sought to avoid propaganda, feeling it to be self-defeating. He ultimately sought to replace "one-sided" propaganda with "Truth." And, in his words, "If we can accomplish that, instead of having to hang our prophets, we can silence them or change their lamentations to song."[29] Locke here wrongly assumed that community prophets were not interested in truth and that their truth-telling somehow did not offer a necessary corrective to a society based on lies.

Even worse, the fact that the thought of "having to hang" the Hubert Harrisons of the world would even cross Locke's mind—let alone come out of his pen—says much about his political and social distance from those who did not share his qualms about making a "one-sided" case, for example, against the practice of "having to hang" Black bodies like strange fruit. This kind of mentality and behavior helps explain McKay's disdainful remark about Locke, namely that McKay "couldn't imagine such a man as the leader of a renaissance, when his artistic outlook was so reactionary."[30]

From *New Negro* to *Nigger Heaven*

The year after Locke's *New Negro*, in 1926, Carl Van Vechten, one of the most prominent white writers and celebrity cultural promoters of New York City, published a novel called *Nigger Heaven*. Thanks in part to its controversial title, the book set off a larger debate about artistic depictions of Black life. Apart from fierce debate, the stir surrounding Van Vechten's book ultimately helped to stimulate a new literary trend that would come to be closely associated with the "Negro Renaissance" that Locke's *New Negro* had proclaimed. The sharp controversy that erupted between critics and admirers of the book reflected the larger debate about the politics of Black art. As we will see, it also helped set the stage for Harrison's wholesale rejection of the "renaissance."

In his review of the book for Harlem's *Amsterdam News*, Harrison criticized *Nigger Heaven* on the grounds that he felt it constituted a "viciously false" depiction of the Harlem nightlife that the author sought to portray. Harrison noted that Van Vechten "was well and favorably known to Harlem's new and nocturnal aristocracy" and had been "wined and dined by the seekers after salvation by publicity, by the pundits of 'advancement' and by the white pen-pushers who manufacture retail prominence for the smart snotties of the New Renaissance—Negro type, model 1926." Harrison's reference to the "New Renaissance—Negro type, model 1926" and the manufacture of "retail prominence" offers in a nutshell his whole critique of the "renaissance" phenomenon as a commodification of Black culture created for a primarily white market.[31]

But his main problem with the book, apart from its offensive title and "faked nigger dialect," was its "cheap shoddy" quality with "neither atmosphere, depth nor character" whose "poor putty figures . . . are jerked by visible wires that are visibly rusty—and they creak so!" Though he believed the book to be a poor specimen of literary craftsmanship, Harrison did think Van Vechten had the capacity for better writing, as demonstrated by his previous works *Peter Whiffle*, *The Tattooed Countess*, and *The Blind Bow Boy*. And despite his criticisms of *Nigger Heaven*, Harrison hoped the book would spur Black writers to write "of the actual lives of actual Negroes in this Harlem, which has been suffering for six years from blasé neurotics whose Caucasian culture has petered out and who come to this corner of Manhattan for pungent doses of unreality, such as we get in *Nigger Heaven*." The book clearly demonstrated for the aspiring Black novelist how *not* to write about Harlem and thereby sounding a call to action for more authentic artistic depictions of the community. Harrison's review emerged alongside other negative reviews in Black papers like the *Chicago Defender* and the *Pittsburgh Courier*.[32]

According to historian Emily Bernard, Van Vechten felt "crushed by the wave of denunciation" from Black critics and "was pained by the suggestion that he had betrayed the people he loved—Black people." Van Vechten described Harrison's review in particular as an "attack" that caused him to have nightmares about being "a Negro chased in riots." Given the history of slavery, lynching, and the epidemic of actual Black individuals and communities chased by white rioters, one wonders if Van Vechten ever stopped to ponder the irony of his dream and how it must feel for his nightmare to be other people's lived reality.

The negative reviews also set off a flurry of defensive moves from Van Vechten's supporters. Many Black voices of the "renaissance" persuasion raved about the book. Charles Johnson of *Opportunity* called the book "the first achievement of a novel of Negro life." Nella Larsen of *The Crisis* wondered aloud, "Why, oh why, couldn't we have done something as big for ourselves?" James Weldon Johnson of the NAACP claimed that the author of *Nigger Heaven* had "achieved the most revealing significant and powerful novel based exclusively on Negro life yet written." Johnson even went so far as to defend the use of the N-word in the title, something that even Van Vechten admitted was a terrible insult when used by a white man. There were exceptions to this trend. Du Bois, for example, called the book "a blow in the face." Both Du Bois and Black poet laureate Countee Cullen broke off personal relations with Van Vechten for a time out of disgust. But overall, the privileged social circles in which Van Vechten had ensconced himself gave it a positive reception.[33]

Two years before publishing *Nigger Heaven*, Van Vechten had taken to meeting Black artists and intellectuals and inviting them to interracial parties where they could interact with white New York socialites. He had written articles in *Vanity Fair* and other publications extolling the virtues of his newest "discoveries" like Negro spirituals and poetry, the blues, and the Black theater. He promoted the work of Black artists like Langston Hughes, Aaron Douglas, Bessie Smith, Countee Cullen, Ethel Waters, and Paul Robeson. This earned him credibility as a booster of the "Negro Renaissance," whose arrival Locke's *New Negro* had announced. When it came time for Van Vechten to publish a book about Black Harlem, he not only tapped people like Walter White and the NAACP to publicize it in advance. He also sent out a questionnaire about Black literary representation and authenticity, reprinted in *The Crisis*, stimulating a discussion that ensured his book a receptive and sympathetic audience. Even the Van Vechten–sympathetic historian Emily Bernard admitted that literary reviewers like Walter White, Eric Walrond, Charles Johnson, and James Weldon Johnson "praised the novel as accurate and honest. Of course, they were all members of the Negro Renaissance."[34]

In fact, so many glowing reviews and defenses of *Nigger Heaven* followed after the criticisms that Harrison felt moved to expand his attack to include the positive reviewers too. Harry Hansen of the *New York World* and Mary White Ovington of the Socialist Party and NAACP, for example, both produced positive reviews that also candidly admitted that they were unacquainted with the book's actual subject matter. Harrison's response was devastating: "Some white critics are not above surrendering themselves to 'the emotions of a cult' and endorsing something bizarre and 'exotic' just because it falls in with the present ephemeral jazz idea of what 'the Negro' is. That idea . . . is largely a conventionalized expression of their own inner need for a new evocation." A kind of white liberal solidarity among these critics led them to review the novel favorably because of the way it titillated their racial preconceptions about a community they knew nothing about.[35]

Harrison made clear that he did not base his negative review of the book "on the popular ground that it doesn't present the Negro in favorable light" because "it is no part of the critic's right to dictate to the creative artist what aspects of life he should select for representation." By his own admission, his criteria for reviewing books were based on literary merit, artistic excellence, and "sociologic truth, or lack of it."

On these grounds, Harrison also criticized James Weldon Johnson for his fulsome praise of the book. Johnson claimed that "the story comprehends nearly every phase of life in the Negro metropolis." Harrison contradicted this brazen overstatement, noting that the story "doesn't even touch such vital and obtrusive 'phases of life' in the Negro metropolis as the churches and their influence, politics, the labor movement, the lodges and fraternalism, economic penetration by whites . . . prostitution, organized superstition, or the newspapers."[36] He also suggested that Johnson's glowing review of *Nigger Heaven* flowed from his personal friendship with Van Vechten.

Because of its commercial success as a novel based on Harlem nightlife, Van Vechten's book, like his *Vanity Fair* articles before it, fueled a certain mania among white people by whetting their appetite for more literature about "the Negro." For that reason, it has been hailed as a book that, like Locke's *New Negro*, helped open the door to a new mass market for literature about Black life, stimulating a "renaissance" wherein artists like Arna Bontemps, Countee Cullen, Rudolph Fisher, Langston Hughes, Zora Neale Hurston, Nella Larsen, Claude McKay, Jean Toomer, and others were able, with the help of publicity gurus like Van Vechten, to gain a wider audience. Claude McKay went so far as to speak of the NAACP and their ilk as setting up a "Ministry of Culture" for Afro-America.[37]

As historian Nathan Huggins has argued, Black people in the 1920s were self-consciously new to the commercialized arts and needed supporters, guides, and patrons from among those who knew how to navigate the white-dominated industry. In that sense, and to the extent that it led to wider awareness of African Americans' humanity, Van Vechten's stimulation of white interest in Black life seemed a positive step forward.

At the same time, the newfound interest in Black art was not without its contradictory effects. Eventually, one had to ask the fateful question, "Whose sensibilities, tastes, and interests were being served by such art, the patron or the patronized?"[38] Hubert Harrison shined a bright light on this question by analyzing the new genre of literature that *Nigger Heaven* stimulated. In so doing he raised an even deeper question about the meaning of this "Negro Renaissance," which would, over time, become canonized as the "Harlem Renaissance."

The Cabaret School of Negro Literature: Harrison's Case against "Renaissance"

Hubert Harrison emerged as one of the first voices in Harlem to radically critique the way in which white people "discovered" and exploited Black arts for their own financial gain, while enlisting Black gatekeepers to help them sell it as a "renaissance." With great verve and candor, Harrison offered an analysis of the economic and social forces behind the emergence of the renaissance narrative. Alongside his critique, he also expressed his hopes and dreams that a more authentic flowering of Black arts would eventually emerge from the younger generation.

Harrison's analysis started with the context in which the so-called renaissance phenomenon arose. The second decade of the twentieth century began with a deep sense of crisis in the world following the wanton destruction and instability detonated by the white world war. Books like Oswald Spengler's *The Decline of the West* (1918) articulated the same crisis, which reflected itself in the new art forms. As Harrison put it, "Art as related to life is dying down among the white race.... Pictorially, they have been seeking salvation among 'primitives,' from the South seas to the Congo forests, as witness Picasso, Matisse, Gauguin, van Gogh.... They go to China for card games, to Old Egypt for dress designs, to the orient for their 'new' religions and to the Negro 'down South' or in Harlem cabarets for the zip, pep and verve needed to make their literature and art stand up."[39] Western "civilization" had lost its luster, so white artists and cultural producers looked to nonwhite peoples for inspiration, leading to a spike of white interest in Black culture during the 1920s.

Harrison analyzed the Harlem experience in terms of the American tradition of minstrelsy and Black people as objects of entertainment: "When these whites, seeking local (and other) color, first 'discovered' the Negro they came to Harlem ... with certain 'fixations' about the Negro in their minds, the most basic of which was the characteristic American one that he existed to furnish entertainment to others." He also pointed out the essentializing nature of the white gaze: "Whatever about [the Negro] was quaint, queer, odd, bizarre, and different was seized upon as the essential he, the 'real' Negro, the thing for which white editors, publishers and readers had been waiting all these years." Harrison located the site of this "discovering" in the cabaret, and if the cabaret or Harlem dive bar offered the "easiest point of contact for these discoverers of 'The New Negro,'" then the whole conception of white writers and tourists in Harlem would tend to result in a narrow, distorted, and fetishized relationship to Black people.[40]

Indeed, white cultural producers did write books (like *Nigger Heaven*) that propagated reductive caricatures of Harlem life. In turn, the interests of white publishers and the audience they catered to led Black artists to exploit negative stereotypes of their own community for commercial gain. And, explained Harrison, "as soon as the resultant 'stuff' began to sell, the colored cognoscenti, Harlem's high intelligentsia, flocked to the new centers of cultural exposition like a swarm of bees, and, in order that they might 'get in on the graft' and sell their 'stuff' downtown, they laid themselves out to attain the imitation which is the most fruitful form of flattery." Black artists had started producing paintings, novels, magazine illustrations, poems, and plays that catered to the white tourist experience and preconceptions of cabaret life in Harlem. Ironically, the Black artist who reproduced distorted white cultural stereotypes remained "unconscious of the fact that he is giving creative inspiration to the whites when he starts . . . to imitate from them their imitation of him." Here Harrison suggests that some Black artists ended up becoming disingenuous caricatures of themselves as they were drawn into the process of catering to the exotic fetishism of white audiences. As Paul Laurence Dunbar put it in a famous poem that speaks to this dynamic, "We wear the mask."[41]

As a result of this curiously contrived new market for the arts and culture industry, the Black intelligentsia became a contractor and conduit for white exploitation of Harlem nightlife. According to Harrison, they opened up Harlem to "the official expositors" and even "competed for the honor of entertaining them and shepherded their guests about Harlem with the air of exclusive proprietors." Soon enough "cabaret parties became the order of the night, and at the cabarets the colored cognoscenti soon learned to see with the eyes of the angels whom they were entertaining." Thus, the prejudiced white gaze elicited a kind of evil twin in its middle-class Black caretakers who judged their own legitimacy under the rubric of white approval and therefore came to see Harlem in the refracted white light of their paymasters.[42]

Harrison felt that these "grotesque antics" of inebriated white tourists ushered around Harlem by the "colored cognoscenti" are what ultimately "furnished the aesthetic principles upon which a 'new' art of the New Negro was predicated." This took many forms, ranging from portrait painting and magazine illustrations to fiction and poetry. "Oddly enough," he remarked, the new trend did not catch on in the Black press but instead within "race" magazines like *The Crisis* and *Opportunity*, which derived their prestige "wholly or in part from the white world" and therefore "cheerfully transformed themselves into official vehicles for the exposition of these new principles."

Harrison decried how "young 'poets'—extremely young—were seduced by the opportunity for self-advertising into contributing alleged poems in which many lines consisted of one word each, and rhythm, cadence and idea were conspicuous by their absence." Harrison may have been justifiably concerned by the way young poets like Langston Hughes and Countee Cullen were "seduced"—perhaps in more ways than one—by older figures like Alain Locke and Carl Van Vechten. But his comment also revealed a pedantic disdain for new poetic forms that did not adhere to the "rhythm and cadence" of previous generations of poets, which Harrison preferred.[43]

While Harrison clearly found this situation objectionable, he perceived an even deeper problem in the way in which the "new art" propagated a negative view not only of Harlem but of Black people as a whole. What Harrison dubbed the "Cabaret School of Negro Literature" became known for its coarse vulgarity and foul language, a characteristic he felt was "imitated from its Greenwich Village godfathers." The result? Both white audiences and Black intellectuals mistook "the language of the gutter for the language of the common people," which Harrison felt exacerbated the popular tendency to "identify Negro-ness with nastiness" and ultimately gave the whole race a bad name.[44]

Some defenders of this "Cabaret School" genuinely believed that their cultural and artistic output expressed the lived reality of poor and working-class Black Harlemites. Harrison responded to this claim directly: "It is a poor defense to hide behind the claim of representing the humbler elements of society. For, in the first place, the real representation of these elements among us is still left to white writers who attempt it with artistic seriousness—like [Thomas] Stribling, [Eugene] O'Neill, Paul Green, Mrs. [Julia] Peterkin and DuBose Hayward." Moreover, argued Harrison, exemplary Black and white writers of humble origin like John Bunyan, Robert Burns, Gerald Massey, Paul Laurence Dunbar, and Claude McKay "have not been notorious for vulgarity." The idea that crass vulgarity necessarily corresponded to Black working-class life was inaccurate and furthered harmful stereotypes.[45]

Harrison's disdain for the corrupting influence of the "midnight maniacs from downtown" and their "colored Brahmins" led him to reject the notion that the Cabaret School of Negro Literature and the fanfare surrounding it represented a genuine renaissance. For starters, he argued that the existence of a "renaissance" would imply that the second decade of the twentieth century had produced more or better Black literature than the decades preceding it, which he could not permit. In Harrison's words, "Those who think that there is [a Negro literary renaissance] are usually people who are blissfully ignorant of the stream of literary and artistic products which have flowed uninterruptedly from Negro writers from 1850 to the present."[46]

As against the "blissfully ignorant," he offered examples of notable Black literary works that had escaped the "renaissance" trumpeters, including *The American Cavalryman* by Henry Francis Downing (1917), *The Leopard's Claw* by George Ellis (1917), *Veiled Aristocrats* by Gertrude Sanborn (1923), *The Vengeance of the Gods* by William Pickens (1922), *Sidelights on Negro Soldiers* by Charles Williams (1923), and *Two Colored Women with the American Expeditionary Forces* by Addie Hunton and Kathryn Johnson (1920). Harrison also mentioned Black authors Joseph T. Wilson, George Williams, William C. Neill, William Wells Brown, Rufus L. Perry, Atticus G. Haygood, the essays of T. Thomas Fortune, and the fictional writings of Francis Ellen Watkins Harper, Pauline Hopkins, Paul Laurence Dunbar, and Charles Chesnutt, not to mention his celebration of books by J. A. Rogers. Harrison joked that if you asked the "renaissance" peddlers what they know of these authors, they would "stammer and evade to cover up their confusion."

To emphasize that it wasn't just white readers who were ignorant of the vast range of pre-1920s Black literature, he cited Du Bois's 1905 *A Select Bibliography of the Negro American*, which made no mention of Charles Chesnutt, despite Chesnutt having already published four novels at that time. This exemplified a larger behavioral pattern of what Harrison called the "guardians of the gate," who he felt were not independent minded enough to recognize brilliant Black artists without those artists first being recognized by cultured white opinion. As Harrison put it, "From Dunbar to Countee Cullen, from James Edwin Campbell to Claude McKay, [Langston] Hughes and [Jean] Toomer . . . every Negro of real or alleged merit in literature or any other art has had to be first pointed out by white critical opinion before these hounds of spring could bay upon the trail."[47] As a result, the "casual discoverer thinks that the stream of Negro literary production bubbled up at the precise point that he discovered it."[48] Because Black "guardians of the gate" like Du Bois depended on white approval and funding for their prominence, they acted as a rubber stamp by validating only those artists who white "discoverers" had first deemed worthy of promotion.

So confident was Harrison in his claim that there was no real renaissance underway that he threw down a challenge to the general public: "If anyone . . .

should care to pick any decade between 1850 and 1910, I will undertake to present from among the Negroes of that decade as many writers and (with Schomburg to back me) as many lines of literary and artistic endeavor as he can show for this decade. And I go further! I will also undertake to show (with perhaps three exceptions) more able Negro writers for any decade in that period than can be found today." Considering that Harrison was a voracious consumer of Black literature, that he initiated the first regular book review column in a Black newspaper, and that (according to Harrison) Schomburg knew eight or ten times more about the history of Black literature than Harrison, it presented a mighty dare.[49]

Only one person responded, a John P. Davis of Cambridge, Massachusetts. Davis was a journalism and law student at Harvard who would later become a coeditor of the journal *FIRE!!* with other "Harlem Renaissance" artists.[50] Davis called Harrison's case "dogmatic" and "so cantankerous, so perfectly ridiculous," stating that Harrison "seemed to be suffering from that dreadful malady; a little learning." He argued that the presence of a continuous stream of African American literature from 1850 to present was "irrelevant" because "the publication of novels, books of poetry, plays, historical treatises, and books on Negro folk songs—written by Negroes [today] is unparalleled by any previous decade in American Life." He acknowledged that "of course, it need not follow that the quantity of these productions increases their quality. But I think it does." Davis explained that he would "rather have [Phillis Wheatley's] complete works irretrievably lost than almost any sonnet that Countee Cullen has written."[51]

For reasons we can only imagine, Harrison did not respond to Davis. Having lived in Harlem for twenty years, as far as Harrison could see, "the matter of a Negro literary renaissance is like that of the snakes of Ireland—there isn't any." The whole notion of a Black "renaissance" was a concoction produced by an unholy alliance between white people—who Zora Neale Hurston called "Negrotarians" for specializing in patronizing "the Negro artist"—and their Black intellectual "Niggerati" collaborators. Historian David Levering Lewis has identified various personalities who fit Hurston's description, including James Weldon Johnson, Jessie Fauset, Charles Johnson, Walter White, and Alain Locke.[52]

Although Harrison explicitly argued against the existence of a "Negro Renaissance," he simultaneously and prophetically foreshadowed the growth of higher-quality Black arts in the years to come. "Within the next ten years," he ventured in 1926, "the froth will be blown off the tankard and we will lift to our lips the real beer of literature with life in it, with snap and tang and color, brewed by Negro writers freed from the leading-strings of Greenwich Village neurotics, who like Van Vechten, mistake near-beer for the genuine lager." His optimism for the future led him to support and promote artists like Walter E. Hawkins, Andy Razaf, Lucian Watkins, Augusta Savage, Charles Gilpin, Angelina W. Grimké, Claude McKay, and Eubie Blake. According to Harlem resident Oscar Benson, Harrison "was always willing to help or encourage a young writer or speaker." Harrison prophesized that "some time soon there will be a genuine literary renaissance" because the opportunity to represent the "nine-tenths" of Black life left out by the Cabaret School was "still open for true creative artists from the younger generation of Negroes."[53]

The Renaissance Industry and the Black Working Class

Harrison's critique of the "Negro renaissance" may have been among the first of its kind, but certainly not the last. Langston Hughes, for example, joked in his autobiography about how some Black people thought the race problem had at last been solved through the tolerance created by the artistry of people like Cullen, McKay, Locke, and Gladys Bentley. "I don't know what made any Negroes think that," wrote Hughes, "except that they were mostly intellectuals doing the thinking."[54] Folklorist, poet, English professor, and "renaissance" contemporary Sterling Brown hesitated to use the term *renaissance* on the grounds that the "five or eight years generally allotted are short for the lifespan of any 'renaissance,'" and Harlem formed a "cashier's till" that did not represent the rest of Black America.[55]

Young writer and "renaissance" participant Wallace Thurman eventually wrote a novel criticizing the white "Negrotarians," thrill-seeking tourists, the "Niggerati," and self-interested Black artists who sold themselves and the respect of their race for the "renaissance" fad. Thurman pointed out that the focus of the "renaissance" on a narrow slice of Black Harlem artists may have increased their own visibility and prestige, but in so doing it left behind the rest of the community. He pointed out that there were tens of thousands of Black people in Harlem, yet "it is fashionable only to take notice of a bare thousand ... the cabaret entertainers, the actors, the musicians, the artists, and the colorful minority who drift from rent party to speakeasy to side-street dives. The rest are ignored ... because we live in an age when only the abnormal is interesting."[56]

Young Harlem resident Arthur Davis, who was a university student in the 1920s, sounded a similar criticism of the "renaissance" architects: the way they overlooked the role of local institutions in Harlem's rich cultural life. For example, the 135th Street branch of the New York Public Library, under the direction of Ernestine Rose, featured "an intelligent and efficient group of young Negro and white librarians [that] made the branch a cultural center for the Harlem Community."[57] Then, as now, one could find exhibitions of African art alongside the work of young Black painters and sculptors. Moreover, as Davis recalled, "attached to the branch as a kind of unofficial lecturer-in-residence was Hubert Harrison, the Dean of the Harlem Street Orators. A rather formal black man with a broad West Indian accent . . . he was a fascinating and versatile speaker, taking all subjects for his province—politics, religion, the race problem, colonialism, literature—and handling them all with equal facility and ease."[58]

The decision of the "renaissance" boosters to disavow local fixtures of Harlem's intellectual culture like the 135th Street library and the Outdoor Grioversity underscores that they only cared about what could be profitably sold to white audiences. Black Harlem community residents, on the other hand, often had a less transactional and more organic relationship to the Black arts. Davis reminisced, for example, about how "the jazz musician and the blues singer, blowing and singing their respective 'racial' hearts out, became popular symbols in New Negro poetry, but as I recall the twenties, I realize that we didn't talk in daily conversation about these performers in that light. For one thing, we hadn't then 'intellectualized' jazz and the blues. . . . We enjoyed them and took them in our stride."[59]

Took them in our stride. For the bellhops, porters, domestics, cooks, messengers, and elevator operators, the creative expression of Black musicians, painters, sculptors, actors, playwrights, singers, poets, dancers, novelists, and street-corner orators presented their creative offerings to be enjoyed as part of affirming one's own being in community: *living Blackness* from the inside, rather than commercializing it for the outside. For ordinary people, recalled Davis, Harlem "was not the phony exotic primitivism which the white folks came uptown nightly to find in cabarets and other hot spots. Our enjoyment was in part the pride of having a city of our very own—a city of black intellectuals and artists, of peasants just up from the South, of West Indians and Africans, of Negroes of all kinds and classes."[60]

Speaking of classes, Langston Hughes went to the root of the economic contradictions of the "renaissance" and its relationship to working-class Harlemites: "The ordinary Negroes hadn't heard of the Negro Renaissance. And if they had, it hadn't raised their wages any." Hughes noted, for example, how Black Harlemites didn't like certain places like the Cotton Club that had a "Jim Crow" policy of excluding Black patrons in order to maintain a white bourgeois clientele. "Nor did ordinary Negroes like the growing influx of whites toward Harlem after sundown," recalled Hughes, "flooding the little cabarets and bars where formerly only colored people laughed and sang, and where now the strangers were given the best ringside tables to sit and stare at the Negro customers—like amusing animals in a zoo." Here Hughes points to the distorted picture of the community that he felt many outsiders experienced.

Of course, African Americans could not even patronize white clubs downtown, let alone sit and gawk at the European-descended people in them.[61]

Over time, those who lived in Harlem got tired of "all those white folks in the speakeasies and night clubs" and started to see if they "could find some place to have a drink that the tourists hadn't yet discovered." This led to the rise of house parties, which offered a more affordable nighttime social space free from the gaze of outsiders. Given that some 48 percent of Harlem renters spent more than twice as much of their income on rent as their white counterparts did, the phenomenon of rent parties emerged to offer a chance for tenants to socialize and pay the bills at the same time. Not to mention that in these settings you could drink, laugh, and "do the black-bottom with no stranger behind you trying to do it, too."[62]

Hughes witnessed firsthand the tension between ordinary Harlemites and the commercial market that sprung up from the sudden white interest in the "Negro Renaissance." In his words, "Non-theatrical, non-intellectual Harlem was an unwilling victim of its own vogue. It didn't like to be stared at by white folks. But perhaps the downtowners never knew this—for the cabaret owners, the entertainers, and the speakeasy proprietors treated them fine—as long as they paid."[63]

This observation speaks to the financial flows of the "two Harlems." As a keen observer who lived right in the center of the neighborhood (134th Street between Seventh and Lenox Avenues), Hubert Harrison noted how on weekdays a tide of Black folks went out of Harlem to work while a "thin stream" of white immigration flowed in to manage their daytime businesses. Then on Saturday nights the "returning colored flood" swept back into Harlem with its wages, but most of that money would also flow out with another "thin white tide" on account of who owned the businesses. He deplored how none of the outgoing money developed the local economy in Harlem that would encourage the ambitions of Black youth because it all ended up in white pockets.[64]

Meanwhile, he noted, "the bank that collects our savings lends them out to white men to fertilize white business in our midst and will not lend them to Negroes to fertilize Negro business."[65] To make matters worse, while Black-owned businesses struggled, Harrison observed, "the business that panders to ephemeral pleasure flourishes in our faces. They are the poolrooms, the night clubs and cabarets, the dance halls, the numbers, the Italian rum shops," which all made money for their owners.[66] Claude McKay made a similar observation when he noted that "the saloons were run by the Irish, the restaurants by the Greeks, the ice and fruit stands by the Italians, the grocery and haberdashery stores by the Jews." The only viable Black businesses he saw, besides barbershops, were the churches and the cabarets.[67] So while there were some Black entrepreneurs who benefited economically from the nighttime exploits of white visitors and the "Negro Renaissance" they conjured, it was not enough of an economic base to drive empowering or sustainable development.

The exploitation of Black Harlem by white capital formed the structural backdrop to the "renaissance" phenomenon. In this context, it was not difficult to see that the buyers, sellers, and product—the "Negro Renaissance" industry—like so many other white-owned industries—was not designed and deployed to materially benefit the Black community. As Harrison put it, "This 'Negro literary renaissance' has its existence at present only in the noxious night life of Greenwich Village neurotics who invented it, not for the black brothers' profit but for their own."[68]

To his credit, even Alain Locke soon developed a critical appraisal of the phenomenon launched, in part, by his own *New Negro* anthology. Reflecting in the January 1929 issue of *Opportunity* magazine, Locke no longer spoke of a "Negro Renaissance" but instead wrote of a "Negrophile movement" whose "proportions show the typical curve of a major American fad, and to a certain extent, this indeed it is." Even worse, he explained, "there is inevitable distortion under the hectic interest and forcing of the present vogue for Negro idioms . . . to get above ground, much forcing has had to be endured; to win a hearing, much exploitation has had to be tolerated. There is as much spiritual bondage in these things as there ever was material bondage in slavery." Locke's contention that slavery formed the best standard of comparison for what the "American fad" symbolized presented a uniquely damning indictment of the "present vogue" that he helped set in motion and initially championed so enthusiastically.[69]

Like Harrison, Locke eventually concluded that the future held better prospects for Black literature. Writing of the thousands of people who were "under the spell" of a "Negrophile movement," he argued that the trendy "American fad" would not be recognized as such until a clearing away of the inauthentic could take place, a process that was necessary, however painful it might be: "In this, as with many another boom, the water will need to be squeezed out of much inflated stock and many bubbles must burst." Although he used a different metaphor, Locke's desire to see the vacuous artistic elements replaced by more authentic ones recalled Harrison's concern: "The real significance and potential power of the Negro renaissance may not reveal itself until after this reaction, and the entire topsoil of contemporary Negro expression may need to be ploughed completely under for a second hardier and richer crop."[70]

The Renaissance School of Negro History and the Erasure of Hubert Harrison

Harrison made the bold proclamation that there was no literary renaissance in Harlem. He contended, against the stream of the "renaissance" vogue, that the increase in literary quantity did not correspond with an increase in quality. Too often it actually brought about a *decrease* in quality thanks to the corrupting prejudices of the white consumer market, as demonstrated by the "Cabaret School" that caricatured and prostituted Black culture for financial gain in such way that even Alain Locke would eventually liken to slavery.

In the final analysis, the argument was not a question of the merits of "pure" art versus "propaganda" art. Locke's *New Negro*—and the larger Harlem Renaissance Industry that descended from it—did not marginalize Black Socialist, Communist, free loving, freethinking, anarchist, and Garveyist voices by way of state repression or lawless mob murder. Instead of "having to hang the prophets" of these social movements, Locke and the white literary gatekeepers that anointed him managed to exclude the politically threatening artistic expression to which the radical postwar "New Negro" moment gave rise by advancing in its place a one-sided artistic propaganda campaign of their own with the goal of eclipsing the "old protest psychology."

As Black studies scholar Perry A. Hall has pointed out, the privileging of literary works over other forms (e.g., the libertine lyricism of the blues women) implied a white and masculinist standard against which to measure racial advancement, which assumed that Black people must attain such narrow standards in order to be considered equal to white people.[71] Moreover, the cultural framework of racial progress was already elitist, because the focus on arts, especially the "high art" of literary production, tended to privilege those with university-level education and/or white liberal boosters like Paul Kellogg, Albert Boni, Carl Van Vechten, and Charlotte Mason, to which the majority of African American artists did not have access. Elite white sponsorship of the "renaissance" peddlers, including the queer and free-loving figure of Alain Locke, led them to downplay the erotic awakening of the times in favor of a more US-patriotic and sexually "respectable" narrative.

The drive to disavow and disremember the radical Black awakening of the postwar era—in order to justify a more moderate and patriotic ethos—did not happen in a vacuum. The international economic and social order underwent a deep crisis of legitimacy in the aftermath and convulsions of the "white world war," including the global reverberations of the Russian Revolution. In the US context, a generation of African Americans not only took up arms to defend themselves from lynching and the epidemic of pogroms before, during, and after the "Red Summer" of 1919 but also underwent world-historic changes in social organization, intellectual development, and political militancy. Despite unprecedented labor battles like the Seattle general strike or the Green Corn Rebellion, and despite the birth of the Communist Party, the US working class did not manage to take power in a Bolshevik-style revolution (like in Russia) feared so much by the American ruling elite. Instead, the postwar radicalization eventually receded with a corresponding ebb in African Americans' class consciousness and race activism. This opened a political space during the Roaring Twenties that the Renaissance School of Negro History would step forward to fill, with fateful consequences for Harrison and other radical voices of New Negro politics.

Of course, the United States was not the only place where the radical fervor of the immediate postwar period eventually waned, opening the door to forces hostile to any further progressive social or political transformation. In this regard, another critic of historical revision appears eerily and startlingly relevant. Consider the keen observer who once decried how

> in encyclopedias and other reference books, the biographies were made over ... and events were delineated in a new manner—for the sake of exalting some while demoting others.... Professors in universities and school teachers are compelled to change written textbooks in a hurry in order to accommodate themselves to the successive stage[s] of the official lie.... The epochs of ideological reaction which, more than once in history, have run parallel with economic successes, engender the need for revising revolutionary ideas and methods; and create their own conventional lie.... In point of fact, the lie in politics, as in daily life, serves as a function of the class structure of society. The oppressors erect the lie into a system of befuddling the masses in order to maintain their rule.

This is not a quote about the way encyclopedias and other reference books delineated events in a new manner for the sake of exalting one or another Negro "renaissance" artist while demoting Hubert Harrison, even though J. A. Rogers did once lament how "others, unquestionably his inferiors, received the recognition that was [Harrison's] due." It is not a quote about the "renaissance" narrative becoming an "official lie" enshrined in the written textbooks of professors in universities or school teachers. Nor is it about the "economic successes" of the Renaissance Industry as a factor in its own reactionary ideological need to completely usurp the militant ethos of the radical New Negro movement that seeded and preceded it, that is, to create their own new "conventional lie."

The quote comes from Leon Trotsky's book *The Stalin School of Falsification* (1937). Trotsky analyzed, among other things, the way in which the Soviet Union under the rule of Joseph Stalin had rewritten the official history of the Russian Revolution to reflect the interests of a new bureaucratic ruling caste. The Stalinist regime not only banished Trotskyists and other dissenters from the Russian Communist Party and the Soviet Union. In addition to assassinating him, Stalinism also erased Trotsky's name from books and airbrushed him out of archival photographs.[72] Yet the language of Trotsky's quote could just as easily be used to indict the Renaissance School of Negro History that airbrushed our crystalline touchstone out of Harlem history in the interest of the American ruling class and its demand for "good" and patriotic Negro heroes.

The class and race radicalism of the "New Negro" of 1917–21 lost a lot of ground as the 1920s unfolded in the face of the Palmer Raids and "Red Scare"; the resurgence of the Ku Klux Klan; Uncle Sam's undying worship of monopoly capital and women's oppression; the continuance of anti-Black massacres, lynchings, disenfranchisement, and segregation even after the war for "democracy"; and the rise of a politically patriotic and culturalist revision of the New Negro movement.

Halfway around the world, revolutionary workers' power in Russia also underwent a general decline as the 1920s unfolded as a result of: the attack on the Russian Revolution by twelve different invading armies; the sharp decline of the Russian working class in terms of its overall health, productivity, numerical size, morale, and political weight due to the Russian Civil War (1918–22); and the increasingly tenuous coalition between the socialist workers and capitalist peasantry, which was further strained by the Civil War. Most importantly, the failure of the German revolution—and a broader revolutionary overthrow of capitalism and bourgeois governments across Europe—left the fledgling workers' state in Russia isolated, effectively forcing it to devote all its resources to military defense and competition with the West, which required a rampant exploitation of working people for the (re)accumulation of capital.[73]

As a result, following the radically democratic Russian Revolution of 1917, an antidemocratic Stalinist bureaucracy eventually came to prominence by the end of the 1920s and imposed a counterrevolution in the name of the same Socialist revolution that it was strangling. The new ruling caste of the USSR could not have attained hegemony without obliterating Leon Trotsky's Left Opposition and a whole generation of "Old Bolsheviks" and genuine revolutionaries from its official history and memory.[74]

In a similar way, following the radical New Negro movement of the 1910s, the antiradical Renaissance Industry that came to prominence in the 1920s imposed a counterrevolutionary "New Negro renaissance" narrative in the name of the same "New Negro" movement that it was consciously and deliberately aiming to eclipse from prominence. It scarcely could have attained hegemony as a new racial frontage against the old protest psychology without eliminating Hubert Harrison and a whole generation of radical New Negroes from its official history and memory.

Of course, analogies like these are imperfect. The trajectory of a workers' and peasants' social revolution that would shape the fate of 130 million people in the Russian-speaking world presented quite a different set of challenges compared with the situation facing 12 million Black people in the United States. But the radical New Negro movement and the Russian Revolution were both part of the same world-historic moment of international political radicalization detonated by the white world war. And they were also both victims of the defeat and degeneration of the transformative potential of that postwar awakening as workers failed to take power outside Russia and ruling elites around the world recovered from the crisis, finding new ways and means to continue their system based on the exploitation of working people, competitive capital accumulation, and international military rivalry.

In this context, the construction of a "renaissance" paradigm reflected an elite strategy to divert attention from racial oppression, class inequality, and imperialist militarism after the white world war.

Yet all hope was not lost. Black Socialist, Communist, sex-radical, Garveyist, and otherwise visionary writers continued to produce their own short stories, plays, poems, songs, and other works of art into the 1930s—and beyond. And some of the most vaunted "renaissance" artists like Langston Hughes became even more radical in that decade.

By 1937, Claude McKay could already reflect on how "the Harlem Renaissance movement of the antic nineteen twenties was really inspired and kept alive by the interest and presence of white bohemians. It faded out when they became tired of the new plaything."[75] Over time, McKay was proved wrong, because after fading out, the plaything would continue to be faded back in. Beginning with John Hope Franklin's discussion of a "Harlem Renaissance" in his textbook *From Slavery to Freedom* in 1947, a vast literature has emerged to entrench and elaborate the "renaissance" interpretation of the postwar New Negro movement.

The Black awakening of the 1960s, like Harrison's radical New Negro movement(s) half a century prior, was largely driven by a militant reaction to racial oppression, class exploitation, and imperialist domination (in Cuba, Algeria, Vietnam, and so on). Among other things, the epoch of civil rights and Black Power generated renewed interest in the New Negro movement of the early twentieth century, with many following Locke's renaissance-based interpretation. By the 1970s, interest in this narrative became apparent among the same kinds of elite intellectuals to whom Locke's notion of a "Negro Renaissance" originally appealed—and for the same reason: as a convenient political escape hatch from the militant Black social struggles of the preceding years. Works like Harvard historian Nathan Huggins's 1971 book *Harlem Renaissance* rebirthed interest in this narrative, effectively reinitializing it for the post–civil rights generation. A decade later, David Levering Lewis's magisterial book *When Harlem Was in Vogue* offered yet another proverbial down payment on the construction of this Renaissance School of Harlem history. Building on this tradition, Henry Louis Gates and Gene Andrew Jarrett published another *New Negro* anthology by that same name in 2007, essentially an updated variation on the theme of Locke's *New Negro* of 1925.

Meanwhile, various scholars have broadened the range of artists and geographic regions legible under the rubric of the Harlem Renaissance, adding further depth and nuance to the narrative framework that Locke's anthology set in motion. On the positive side, this work has made it clear how the Harlem-centered focus of the renaissance narrative has often obscured the other centers of Black economic, intellectual, and cultural life. The interwar years actually saw a national renaissance *season* that characterized numerous cities, including Memphis, New Orleans, Washington, DC, Durham, Atlanta, Chicago, and the American West, not to mention Black communities across the world in places like London, Paris, and Havana.[76]

Nevertheless, the Renaissance School of Negro History has dominated the conceptualization, marketing, and consumption of early twentieth-century Harlem since 1925 and still, a century later, remains the "proving ground" for reinterpretations of New Negro movement history.[77] The mainstream consensus has canonized a dozen or two artists, including those like Hughes, Hurston, and McKay who came to severely criticize or renounce entirely the very forces—from Black elites like Alain Locke to white liberal Negrotarians—that created this "American fad" in the first place. To be more precise: the "renaissance" consensus has canonized the *politically nonthreatening* works of a select group of artists, as Langston Hughes's incendiary Communist writings of the 1930s, "Always the Same" (1932) for example, have been sorely neglected by scholarly studies and popular memorialization.[78]

Ironically, even the scholars who worked to further entrench Locke's renaissance framework have agreed with the criticisms of it as an antiradical contrivance. Huggins acknowledged that "of course, like other historical 'watersheds,' the Harlem Renaissance is merely a convenient fiction." Lewis, reflecting some years after the original publication of his book, admitted that at the end of the day, "the Harlem Renaissance reveals itself to be an elitist response on the part of a tiny group of mostly second-generation, college-educated, and generally affluent Afro-Americans—a response, first to the increasingly raw racism of the times, second to the frightening Black Zionism of the Garveyites, and, finally, to the remote, but no less frightening, appeal of Marxism." Gates and Jarrett similarly admitted that "Locke's appropriation of the ['New Negro'] name in 1925 for his literary movement represented a measured co-opting of the term from its fairly radical political connotations."[79]

On the one hand, multiple artists, critics, and scholars have criticized or renounced the contrived nature of the renaissance narrative, including central figures who initiated or elaborated it to their own direct benefit. On the other hand, a century after Locke first "broke ground" for its foundation, the Renaissance School of Negro History remains the standard-bearing interpretation of the "New Negro movement" and the dominant paradigm for interpreting the significance of Black Harlem in the early twentieth century.

This intellectual contradiction reflects the contentious struggle over the substance and meaning of Black liberation. Literary scholar Anthony Dawahare has aptly noted about this tension that "at stake was whether the Black masses—many of whom were radicalized by the failed promises of World War I, the racist backlash of the Red Summer, and the political reverberations of the Bolshevik Revolution—would continue to support American capitalism or, conversely, embrace Black nationalism or socialism as solutions to racism and class inequality in America."[80]

This explains why the synthetic Renaissance "fad" continues to exert such paradigmatic hegemony over our conception of Harlem history in Harrison's day. The Harlem Renaissance Industry continues to benefit from the way the renaissance framework keeps doing what it was originally designed for, namely, to foreclose—in a most sophisticated, nuanced, and white-marketable fashion—any serious recollection (let alone extension) of the radical New Negro movement. Especially the Black socialist, Black nationalist, Outdoor Grioversity-grounded, freethinking, queer and free-loving artistic output that the postwar New Negro movement had crystallized. Alain Locke articulated the ethos of what would emerge over time as the Renaissance School of Negro History: "Instead of having to hang our prophets, we can silence them or change their lamentations to song."

In effect, they assassinated Hubert Henry Harrison from memory.

Conclusion: The Forbidden Legacy of Hubert Harrison

Hubert Henry Harrison was struck by a bout of appendicitis on December 7, 1927. He had Dr. Leo Fitz Nearon, a race-conscious Black doctor in Harlem and specialist on gastrointestinal problems, as his private physician.[1] Dr. Nearon had diagnosed Harrison's condition as chronic appendicitis and recommended an operation to remove his appendix. Harrison checked himself into Bellevue Hospital for the appendectomy on Tuesday, December 13, performed by a surgeon named Dr. Maurice E. Marlow during the morning of Thursday, December 15. According to newspaper reports, after the operation Harrison was "doing so well that several of his close friends and his wife were permitted by Dr. Marlow . . . to visit him." On Friday, he continued to improve, "but during the night he took a turn for the worse and, on Saturday, had sunk rapidly until he died at 5 p.m. on Saturday evening."[2] According to Harrison's biographer Jeffrey Perry, "On Saturday complications arose that produced paralysis of the intestines, and death followed. What probably happened was that his appendix had ruptured, causing widespread infection." Meanwhile, writes Perry, "Hubert's daughter Aida said that the family was told that their father had died of peritonitis, which she suspects may have been tuberculosis related."[3] Peritonitis is a potentially fatal infection or inflammation of the tissue lining the abdomen, which can be caused by any number of things, including a ruptured appendix or even a surgical wound. Strangely enough, some years later in 1934 Dr. Marlow allegedly committed suicide by poisoning himself with a morphine overdose.[4]

This account of Harrison's death raises some thorny questions. Wouldn't it have been obvious to Dr. Marlow if Harrison's appendix had already ruptured and caused a widespread infection prior to the surgery? Given that Harrison was doing well enough to see visitors on Thursday after the surgery and apparently continued to improve on Friday, what explains his sudden and fateful "turn for the worse" on Friday night? Was there any foul play involved in Harrison's death? Is it possible that he was, for example, injected with a fatal poison (or morphine overdose) on Friday night to make his death *appear* like the result of a complication that arose after the surgery? According to Harrison's daughter Aida, her mother always thought there was something suspicious about her father's death. In an interview decades later, Aida said that for herself, his death was "totally unexpected" because her last memory of her dad was him telling her that he would be going into the hospital for a "brief stay."⁵

In any case, on December 17, 1927, at the age of forty-four, Hubert Harrison transitioned to join the ancestors. He was scheduled to speak on "Soviet Russia and the Darker Races" at the 135th Street YMCA on Christmas Day but died the previous weekend.⁶

Numerous obituaries spoke to the significance of Harrison's life. The *Pittsburgh Courier* remarked that "to those who have little faith in the ability of the common man and woman on the street to appreciate 'deep' subjects of philosophic or scientific interest, it was a revelation to see Hubert Harrison, mounted on his street-corner ladder and surrounded by a crowd of several hundred Negroes, discussing philosophy, psychology, economics, literature, astronomy or the drama, and holding his audience spellbound." In addition,

> While intelligent white people throughout the country have just recently awakened to the necessity of adult education, it has been going on for over fifteen years among the Negroes in New York, and in that work Dr. Harrison more than played his part. . . . His achievements should prove an inspiration to many young Negroes, for, despite the handicap of poverty, he became one of the most learned men of his day and was able to teach the wide masses of his race how to appreciate and enjoy all of the finer things of life, to glance back over the whole history of mankind, and to look forward "as far as thought can reach."⁷

The *New York Times* declared, "Tens of thousands of New Yorkers will miss the philosophy of the most brilliant street orator that this Metropolis has produced in the last generation."⁸ The *New York News* called Harrison the "father of the Harlem intellectual."⁹

Harlem resident Oscar Benson's eulogy hit the nail on the head about Harrison, noting how "he was original . . . he instituted a new school of social thought, packed a new forum, dignified the soap-box orator; blocked Lenox and Seventh Avenue traffic; sent humble men to libraries and book stores; sent them about to day and night schools; taught Negroes to think for themselves; taught them that in spite of all the handicaps of slavery and propaganda of anthropologists and sociologists, who said that the Negro was an imitator, that no one knew what the Negro could do until he tried."¹⁰

(Un)Silencing the Past: The Politics of Harrison's Erasure

Harrison's death set off a struggle, not over *how* he would be remembered but over *whether* he would be remembered at all. A foreboding silence from

Figure C.1 Harrison pictured with a cane as part of an obituary in the *New York News* of December 31, 1927. Hubert H. Harrison Papers, box 18, folder 8, Rare Book and Manuscript Library, Columbia University, New York.

certain key periodicals signaled that those with the power to ignore and forget Harrison would do just that. Harlem activist Hodge Kirnon, writing two months after Harrison's death, noted how the prominent race magazines—*The Messenger*, *The Crisis*, and *Opportunity*—all failed to run obituaries. "This concerted silence is ominous," wrote Kirnon; "It does appear that there is something wrong somewhere."[11] Something wrong indeed. Kirnon also noted how the absence of any mention of Harrison in these journals had become a subject of popular discussion in the community.

Edgar Grey, a Liberty League and UNIA alumnus, sometime government informant, and ex-comrade of Harrison's, offered a eulogy after Harrison's passing: "Your big Negro newspapers and business houses, schools and other organizations who had positions allowed themselves to be so hateful that they would not hire [Harrison]."[12] Clearly Harrison had a number of powerful enemies. In addition to the repressive power of prominent institutions, Grey believed that Harrison "died for his convictions," another example of the suspicions surrounding the circumstance of his death.

Without waiting for those who "had positions," Harlem community members took it upon themselves to memorialize their beloved Black Socrates. His death was the front-page story in Harlem's standard-bearing newspaper the *Amsterdam News*.[13] Over 1,000 people attended his funeral, including various Socialists, Communists, artists, working people, freethinkers, free lovers, youth, elders, masons, and ex-Garveyists who respected him.[14] A Hubert Harrison Memorial Committee of the 135th Street public library presented the library with a lifelike portrait of the late Harrison as a gift in 1930, which was mounted for some time on the first floor of the building.[15] Rev. Ethelred Brown changed the name of his Harlem Community Church to the Hubert Harrison Memorial Church. A small group of individual scholars and community members intermittently tried to document and memorialize Harrison's legacy in print from the 1940s onward, but these efforts largely failed to keep his memory alive as the years and decades went by, as we noted in the introduction.

Various personal factors contributed to Harrison's erasure. His humble racial and economic background and social class made it harder for him to get recognition and respect from influential individuals and institutions that revered academic titles and degrees. (At times he adopted the title "Dr.," but this was an honorary title.) As Harrison once observed, "Prejudice plays as great a part in history as in life."[16] To make matters worse, he died young at age forty-four.

Structurally speaking, the biggest reason for Harrison's erasure concerns the politics of history itself.[17] As he himself once put it, "I know the tremendous weight of the social proscription which it is possible to bring to bear upon those who dare defy the idols of our tribe," and therefore "those who live by the people must . . . be careful of the people's gods." At the same time, his critical mind and commitment to speaking hard truths did not allow him to remain silent when he had a criticism to make. As a result, institutions like the Tuskegee Institute, the Socialist and Communist Parties, the NAACP, the Garvey movement, the Christian church, and the Harlem Renaissance Industry disavowed Harrison's significance and influence during his life. In this way, one could argue that Harrison's historical erasure began *before* he died. The individuals and organizations he criticized not only felt stung by his criticisms but also harbored disdain for his advocacy and practice of free love in the sex-negative age of Comstockery. Those who ignored or marginalized him during his life in turn did nothing to acknowledge or remember his contributions after his death.

Another reason why Harrison has been accorded no place of prominence in history is that he did not like to boast or brag about himself. For example, he claimed (quite accurately) that he was not widely known as a major influence on the emergence of Garveyism because he did not "hanker after newspaper publicity."[18] In fact, he maintained an explicit aversion to praise. Harrison once said that "if there is one thing which I hate next to lying and hypocrisy in human beings, it's praise. . . . Through most of life it has been a hard medicine to swallow. The first dose bewilders, the next annoys, the third irritates, and the added installments make me feel murderous."[19] In line with his Socratic demeanor and disposition, glory and accolades were the furthest thing from his mind. Although Harrison's humble disposition likely contributed to his reduced visibility in history, it also fit with his ability to listen to and learn from striking workers, the "plain people of Negro ancestry," and continental Africans. By maintaining an ethos of humility he ended up sacrificing public recognition for his political principles, much like Ella Baker and so many other grassroots and self-effacing leaders have done historically.[20]

In addition to not tooting his own horn, another factor in Harrison's disremembrance emerges from the pattern among Black people of not giving credit to each other where credit is due. W. E. B. Du Bois, for example, attempted to push Ida B. Wells-Barnett off the list of the "founding 40" of the NAACP.[21] Carter G. Woodson failed to give credit to Arturo Schomburg's work in his book *The Negro in Our History*.[22] Marcus Garvey failed to give any credit to Harrison, whose Liberty League had catalyzed his meteoric rise by transforming the horizons of his vision for the UNIA. As J. A. Rogers said of Harrison, "No one worked more seriously and indefatigably to enlighten his fellowmen; none of the Afro-American leaders of his time had a saner and more effective program but others, unquestionably his inferiors, received the recognition that was his due."[23]

Harrison himself offered a salient explanation of this missing Black credit problem as a function of racial oppression. In his article explaining how prominent African American intellectuals in the universities marginalized and neglected J. A. Rogers's classic book *From "Superman" to Man*, Harrison observed, "The Negroes whom Christian slavery reduced to the social level of brutes still have today some of the traits of the slave. And one of these finds continuous expression in our 'big Negroes,' namely, 'Don't help to push any other Negro into notice if you have won notice yourself. Notice for them detracts from your notice.'"[24] Black people often seek to counter their oppression by "being somebody" and therefore feel, even if only subconsciously, that by giving credit where credit is due to other Black people their own "somebodiness" will diminish.

Alongside personal and Black-community-specific factors, the obliteration of Harrison's example from common knowledge also speaks to the larger problem of who has the power to control mainstream history. As Harrison himself put it, "The dominant ideas of any society which is already divided into classes are as a rule the ideas preservative of existing arrangements. But since those arrangements include a class on top, the dominant ideas will generally coincide with the interests of that class. The ethics of its own advantage, then, will be diffused by that class throughout that society—will be, if need arise, imposed upon the other classes, since every ruling class has always controlled the public instruments for the diffusion of ideas." As Karl Marx and Friedrich Engels put it in *The Communist Manifesto*, "The ruling ideas of each age have ever been the ideas of its ruling class." The history Harrison's radicalism presents a range of ideas that represent a mortal threat to the American ruling class.[25]

Sustaining the ideas that buttress the ruling class requires manufacturing and propagating a view of history that accords with their interests. As George Orwell said in his famous book *1984*, "Who[ever] controls the past controls the future. Who[ever] controls the present controls the past." History and memory constitute critical components of the ruling ideas in society, and therefore the general public's understanding of US history has to be carefully managed. This is critically important in relation to African Americans, whose collective lived experience reveals, like a touchstone, the falsity of the ruling mythology about freedom, democracy, the American dream, and so on. In order to maintain domination and control in the present, the powers that be must shape the society's relationship to (and understanding of) the past so that hard-won economic and political lessons of previous generations of fighters for liberation do not gain more and more recognition or traction cumulatively over time.[26]

In this case, the American ruling class that owns the means of production—including the publishing industries that produce US history textbooks, the corporate news media, the corporate donors for most history museums, the boards of trustees for the universities, the social media and Big Tech companies, Hollywood, and so on—overwhelmingly shapes what shall be the ruling or "commonsense" ideas about history. In light of the aforementioned industries, it becomes clear how ruling-class ideology has at its disposal immeasurably more means of dissemination than anything that dares to challenge it. The same American ruling class that sought to suppress the history of Black radicalism (among other things) during and before Harrison's day has continuously fought to do so ever since. This project of collective social memory management—by way of continuous disavowal and erasure of entire bodies of knowledge deemed subversive to the status quo—has been fundamental to the US government's ideological self-justification and consent manufacturing process.[27] Harrison helps us to see how the historical erasure of revolutionary thinkers forms an indispensable part of limiting the horizon of public knowledge. His case also speaks to the necessity of intentionally reclaiming and recovering the visionary figures who remain at risk of erasure from memory.

Nikola Tesla: Forbidden Genius of Clean Energy

This study of Harrison and his erasure raises a question: How many other crystallizer touchstone radical visionaries have been written out of history? In the course of studying Harrison's example, I naturally stumbled upon others. The most illuminating of all—whose example and legacy can literally save the world—emerged in the figure of Nikola Tesla (1856–1943). Although they both lived in Manhattan in the opening decades of the twentieth century, I have seen no evidence that Hubert Harrison and Nikola Tesla ever met or interacted face to face. However, among the many scrapbooks he created for various topics, Harrison devoted one whole scrapbook to clippings of articles about science, and the scientific and technological genius of Tesla was no stranger to the New York newspapers.

Much like the radical political insights of Hubert Harrison, the implications of Tesla's work are astounding—and profoundly threatening to the status quo. As a result, Nikola Tesla—like Harrison—has been scandalously marginalized in history, excluded from view seemingly in direct proportion to the revolutionary implications of his legacy. As with the challenge of unearthing Harrison's significance, it took me a great deal of research (while fighting an uphill battle with my own initial and quite formidable skepticism) to reach the extraordinary vistas that Tesla's story has to offer to the open-minded, particularly in the light of Harrison's critique of capitalism's corrupting influence on science. Tesla's legacy not only further illuminates Harrison's ideas but can also liberate humanity by the most extraordinary leaps and bounds and in ways difficult to even fully imagine.

Born in Serbia in 1856 and trained in Prague and Budapest, Nikola Tesla had intellectual gifts that defy language. He had a rare, almost spiritual gift for technological innovation. Meanwhile, his eidetic memory allowed him to recall images with vivid and photographic clarity of detail at will. He could reportedly engineer entire prototypes of new inventions *in his mind*. As a result, Tesla ended up developing multiple groundbreaking technologies: fluorescent lights, radio wave technology, bladeless turbines, robotics, particle beam weaponry, remote control, ozone therapy, electric bio-healing, and wireless communication (to name a few!). Not to mention the alternating current (AC) electricity system we're still using, which has dominated the world for the last century. He accumulated some 300 patents in twenty-six different countries!

Nikola Tesla moved to New York City in 1884 and spent his first year there working for the famed inventor Thomas Edison. By the end of the 1880s, Tesla had his own electrical engineering laboratory. In 1901, Tesla started building his technological *magnum opus*, the Wardenclyffe Tower, just an hour-and-a-half train ride away from Manhattan on Long Island. The enormous mushroom-shaped structure stood 187 feet (57 meters) high. Meanwhile, the tower columns plunged 120 feet (36.5 meters) into the ground, while sixteen iron pipes reached down yet another 300 feet (91.4 meters), gripping the depths of the Earth like the subterranean root system of a tree.

Tesla initially pitched the project to his chief financial backer, J. P. Morgan, as a wireless communication system. Morgan had signed an agreement to grant Tesla $150,000 in exchange for a 51 percent stake in the commercial applications of his wireless technology patents. In reality, Tesla began building the Wardenclyffe in order to create a new kind of energy circuit between the ionosphere and the electromagnetic conductivity of the Earth itself to transmit limitless and free wireless electricity for industry, transportation, and instantaneous communication anywhere in the world.[28]

It is difficult to overemphasize how profound Tesla's technological achievement appeared and the size of the threat it posed to global capitalism. For starters, Tesla's free wireless energy and communications system would have rendered John D. Rockefeller's multimillion-dollar Standard Oil empire worthless. It would have made obsolete all of the capital already invested in coal mines, coal-based power plants, steam engines, fossil-fueled maritime ships and automobiles. It would have ended the need for both Tesla's own alternating current (AC) and Edison's direct current (DC) electrical power systems, plus all the telegraph and telephone lines. After taking hold in the United States, Tesla's energy system paradigm shift would have obliterated all the aforementioned industries in Britain, France, Germany, Italy, Japan, and every other industrializing capitalist country.

Perhaps most importantly, by making things like oil, gas, and coal (not to mention nuclear power) completely unnecessary, Tesla's clean energy revolution would have spared the world from the negative impacts of dirty energy: air and water pollution, oil spills, acid rain, ocean acidification, deforestation, soil erosion, strip mining, and nuclear disasters, as well as the ominous fossil-fueled warming of global temperatures and the unthinkable climate catastrophe it now portends.

By its impact on the supply and demand of energy sector raw materials alone, Tesla's free wireless energy paradigm would have fundamentally disrupted and transformed global commodities prices, world trade balances, and stock market valuations. It also would have rendered negligible the energy cost of producing and distributing food, clothing, housing, and electricity, thus contributing to the abolition of world poverty. Indeed, Tesla's vision of a global free wireless energy system implied not only a world-historic revolution in the world economy but an evolutionary leap forward for the whole of human existence.

Tesla did not initially tell Morgan that he erected the Earth-resonant Wardenclyffe Tower for free wireless *power* transmission because he understood that his technology constituted what he himself called a "radical departure" from the fossil fuel-based energy system. He understood that his extraordinary feat of scientific engineering would inexorably render worthless all the existing engines and machinery in the world, "on which billions of dollars have been spent," as Tesla put it. So when Tesla ran into financial shortfalls, Morgan refused to advance him any further funding.[29]

Out of desperation, Tesla eventually opened up about his real objective of free wireless power generation and transmission. He tried to convince Morgan to send him more funding on the grounds that the project would bring about "a revolution so great that almost all value and all human relations will be profoundly [upended]," pointing out the fact that "these new developments do not concern any country in particular, but the whole world." As Tesla pleaded, "I have perfected the greatest invention of all time—the transmission of electrical energy without wires to any distance, a work which has consumed ten years of my life." If only Morgan would finance his life's greatest work to completion, then "in one bound, humanity will advance centuries." Yet Morgan remained cold as ice to Tesla's increasingly desperate and emotional pleas. To make matters worse, not only did Morgan deny Tesla any further funding but also refused to relinquish his 51 percent ownership stake in Tesla's wireless patents, effectively holding Tesla in a position where he could never achieve a controlling stake for the development of his own technology even if he could have raised enough money from other financial sponsors. Tesla suffered a devastating nervous breakdown as a result.[30]

The mind-bending implications of Tesla's technology explain why J. P. Morgan—decisively and irrevocably—moved to block Tesla's vision from reaching fruition. After all, Morgan owned General Electric and Western Union, as well as numerous lucrative copper and coal mines which all stood to go the way of the dinosaur in the face of Tesla's proposition. Morgan's US Steel controlled 60 percent of the steel industry and also encompassed everything from Andrew Carnegie's gargantuan steelworks to Rockefeller's iron ore and shipping interests. Morgan had over a billion dollars' worth of capital investments in not just retaining but *further expanding* the wired, for-profit, fossil-fueled energy infrastructure and telegraph lines. Nikola Tesla's incalculably revolutionary threat to capitalist society explains why, much like Hubert Harrison, his political significance has been scandalously marginalized in popular memory and academic scholarship alike.

Unfortunately, the abortion of Tesla's technological masterpiece would become just one example in a longer history of corporate and state suppression of energy technologies that threaten the paradigm of capitalist scarcity and endless fossil fuel extraction. Clean energy systems like Tesla's have appeared like a specter haunting the fossil fuel industry, and the powers that be have entered into an unholy alliance to exorcise it. A long history of brilliant clean energy inventors, from Thomas Henry Moray in the 1920s to Stan Meyer in the 1990s, for example, have had their technologies—and their existence in popular awareness—suppressed.

According to the Federation of American Scientists, the US government has sequestered *over 6,000 patented inventions*, including energy technologies, on the grounds of "national security." A declassified 1971 US government document revealed, for example, that solar panels with greater than 20 percent energy conversion efficiency were on the "patent security" list. Considerations of space prohibit a full discussion of this issue here. But the long and hidden history of energy technology suppression explains, for example, the startling fact that while information technology has gone from room-sized computers to wristwatch-sized smartphones in just a few decades, our transportation technologies remain largely chained to the fossil-fueled internal combustion engine of the nineteenth century![31]

Hubert Harrison made a startlingly durable critique of science that—whether he deliberately intended it to or not—spoke directly to the fate of Tesla's revolutionary legacy:

> Let us try to imagine a world without telegraph or telephone, a world in which we wouldn't know in New York what had happened in London until six weeks later; without railroads or steamships or automobiles; where diphtheria choked its tens of thousands of helpless infants to death each year for lack of our present anti-toxin and no man who worked for a boss could ever own a book because of its price; a world without newspapers, magazines or movies.
>
> Yet our ancestors lived in such a world, and their world has been transformed into the one about us in the last hundred and fifty years. The magician responsible for this change—we call him Science. . . . Engineering, chemistry, biology, astronomy, physics—all these are divisions of that science which has transformed the world in less than

two centuries. And it is a singular fact that those people who have most of it are able to impose their will on those who have less or none at all.

Not only were the worlds of science and technology in a period of extraordinary transformation but the powerful forces who had captured the magician we call Science had imposed their will on those who had no independent, let alone equivalent, relationship to the magician. Harrison's argument about science reveals an even more unsettling insight: the financial ruling class could bend the boundaries and theoretical paradigms of science to their own interests.[32]

In other words, capitalism not only bent the horizons of energy technology to its benefit by suppressing Tesla but also managed to take control of the direction, parameters, and permissible limits of scientific inquiry itself. For example, Tesla once called Albert Einstein's theory of relativity "a beggar wrapped in purple whom ignorant people take for a king." Ouch. In the early twentieth century, there weren't many people in a position to make that claim and be taken seriously. Besides Nikola Tesla. Yet while the scientific establishment recognizes a distinctive *Newtonian* physics (e.g., an apple falling from a tree) and *Einsteinian* physics (e.g., the theory of relativity), it effectively denies the very existence of a distinctive *Teslan* physics. As a result, Tesla emerges not only as an incomparable crystallizer of clean energy technology but also as a Harrison-like touchstone for the quality and purity of science and the ruling paradigms—both theoretical and technological—of the scientific establishment.[33]

Harrison's critique of science, as a weapon of the powerful over the powerless under capitalism, perfectly explains the abortion—and subsequent suppression—of Tesla's offering: a world with free, clean, and abundant energy for anyone on Earth. As if commenting on Tesla's example, Harrison went further, arguing that "science and scientific things are not merely matters of book-learning and colleges and high collars; but matters that concern you and me and the other 1700 million humans down to the very roots of our everyday lives. We cannot think ourselves out of their control since they are responsible for the food we eat and the water we drink, the clothes we wear, the places we live in, the work we do, and even the ideas we have inside our heads."[34] Those with the power to impose their particular economic and political paradigms on society have done likewise to our very conception of what is "scientifically" possible. In short, only the permissible is possible. Nothing else.

Here Harrison's argument implies a profound critique of the non-neutrality of science under capitalism. Not only social and psychological sciences but the "hard" sciences can also be worked to produce results according to the prejudices of the scientist, for reasons Harrison explained perfectly. "A scientist is, after all, not an angel but a human being—subject as much to the pressure of his environment, educational, social, racial and others." Moreover, "even savants are prone to forget that they do most of their thinking with their desires, beliefs, prejudices and subconscious urges, which they then proceed to rationalize."[35]

As a result, scientists and electrical engineers can claim "objective" authority on the grounds of theoretical paradigms that have been historically constrained by the dictates and requirements of capitalism, without even realizing how poisonous and corrupting this reality is for the vaunted "objectivity" and authority of their science. As Noam Chomsky once argued, paraphrasing Henry Kissinger, "experts" are those who articulate the needs of the people in power.

In Harrison's day, science no longer existed as an objective method of knowledge creation based on reasoned hypotheses followed by experimentation, observation, gathering empirical evidence, and drawing rational conclusions. Instead, Uncle Sam had captured the magician of Science in order to impose his will, Tesla and his ilk be damned!

Lessons, Legacies, and Limitations

Harlem resident Oscar Benson, in a tribute following Harrison's death, remarked that "nearly every genius whether he be writer or speaker is accused by critics of following some certain school of thought. Of Shakespeare they say Bacon; of Emerson, Plato; of Nietzsche they say Schopenhauer. . . . Therefore they strip most men of the reputation of being original and no man is genuine or a genius without being original. [But] Hubert Harrison . . . instituted a new school of thought."[36] "A new school of thought" perfectly describes the generative power of his integration of multiple radical traditions. In Harrison's words, the task was to get education "not only in school and college, but in books and newspapers, in market-places, institutions, and movement. Prepare by knowing; and never think you know until you have listened to ten others who know differently—and have survived the shock."[37] It would be hard to find a more concise articulation of the *Harrisonian* methodology.

This methodology offers a number of enduring lessons. For example, it invites us not to make one singular radical perspective hegemonic but instead to weigh and appreciate its particular insights in relationship to multiple other critical vantage points. What gives a political framework its coherence—as with Marxism, pan-African (inter)nationalism, decolonization, feminism, freethought, sexual liberation, and so on—is its ability to illuminate a system of oppression or political antagonism in society. At the same time, no single one of them has proven multidimensional enough to adequately encompass the larger complex of mutually reinforcing systems of domination. The roots of injustice are many, and no individual paradigm is an island but is instead part of a larger totality. Apprehending and accounting for the full complexity of social and political life requires more than just one frame of reference. Harrison employed what we might call an open-source epistemology, for which knowledge and wisdom can come from any direction and the more directions, the better. Both for uncovering new possibilities and for crystallizing new ideas and organizations.

Harrison's prismatic crystallography invites us to see multiple radical frameworks in light of their own event horizons, or boundaries beyond which events have no effect on the observer. For example, as much as the Socialist Party espoused a commitment to working-class emancipation on paper, the specific oppression of lynching, segregation, anti-Black pogroms, and disenfranchisement faced by Black workers proved an event horizon of the party, having little to no transformative impact on their "class first" politics. Black liberation, much like free love, proved an event horizon, even for the left-wing or "revolutionary" Socialists like Eugene Debs. The white question proved a fatal flaw their quest to achieve the totalizing social revolution that they professed. Harrison's story, in other words, suggests that no class-radical, or race-radical, or faith-radical, or sex-radical movement can ultimately succeed without interrogating and transcending its own event horizons. Each of these radicalisms connects directly with other structural forces (outside of its particular frame) that undergird the social order. As Fannie Lou Hamer used to say, "No one is free until everybody's free." By crystallizing multiple radical political gemstones in a single kaleidoscope, the *Harrisonian* method opens a line of flight for transcending the event horizons of multiple liberatory traditions by seeing each one of them as inextricably linked to all *the others*.

One of the main barriers in the way of reaching this destination remains the arrogance of expertise and authority, which the mastery of any single framework, whether radical or mainstream, too often entails. Harrison invites us to check this brand of egotism that is so prevalent within Western individualism and single-issue thinking. For example, Harrison appreciated J. A. Rogers' book *As Nature Leads*, for pointing out that

> the white man in America really desires the presence of the Negro as a setting for the white man's egotism, and [Rogers] goes on to tell of a little white girl in the South who was asked why she objected to the removal of the Negroes and replied, "Cause then Ah would have nobody to be better than." Isn't that so deliciously human? The great majority of us who prate of "democracy," "liberty," "equality," black as well as white, when put to

the test, want to have something "to be better than" and until we breed that strain of the ancestral pig out of human nature our democracy and our religion will be just gilded shams.[38]

One glimpses Harrison's invitation to humility in his whimsical rendition of the egotism at the heart of the white world (war):

> Let's say we are white Anglo-Saxons. We find ourselves top-dog on the heap and thereupon we proceed to write social science and re-write history to prove that we are on top because we are Anglo-Saxons; that . . . no other were ever intended to be on top . . . that top-ness (superiority) is Anglo-Saxon-ness (racial) and that's that. Then along come some other Nordics, blow up the same bladder of belief and worship it so much more successfully than we do that, whereas we are ahead of the Zulu with his assegai [wooden spear], they are ahead of us with poison-gas and submarine. What's our next turn? We proceed to scream for help as loudly as we can and to call upon non-Nordics to help save—civilization. . . . Such are the absurdities of that modern form of an ancient disease—Egotism—which we miscall "superiority"!

Harrisons delicious lampooning of "Anglo-Saxon superiority" and "egotism" articulates a critique that also applies to counterhegemonic frameworks, like those of the Socialist Party, the Garvey movement, the freethinkers and free lovers of Harrison's day.[39] In order for Frederick Douglass to fully come into his own as an independent and leading Black abolitionist of the nineteenth century, he had to break with the white political framework of William Lloyd Garrison. Similarly, in order for Harrison to fully come into his own as an independent and leading exponent of radical New Negro politics, he had to break with the white radicalism of the Socialist Party.

Besides crystallizing innovative and groundbreaking political paradigms, Harrison's legacy formed a key link in the arc of Black radicalism that bridged the post-Reconstruction era and that of the generations that came after him. A. Philip Randolph captured the meaning of this arc in profound tones when he said in 1972, "We are creatures of history, for every historical epoch has its roots in a preceding epoch. The black militants of today are standing upon the shoulders of the New Negro radicals of my day, the twenties, thirties, and forties. We stood upon the shoulders of the civil rights fighters of the Reconstruction era, and they stood upon the shoulders of the black abolitionists. These are the interconnections of history, and they play their role in the course of development."[40]

Harrison created a legacy that would become a tributary to the Black awakening of the 1960s. As noted in chapter 4, Harrison's work with William

Monroe Trotter and others at the Liberty Congress of Negro-Americans in 1918 set a precedent for A. Philip Randolph's March on Washington Movement in 1941, which in turn paved the way for Bayard Rustin's March on Washington in 1963. Harrison greatly influenced Randolph, who in turn exerted a great influence on Rustin. Both Randolph and Rustin in turn greatly influenced Martin Luther King Jr.

At the same time, Harrison's seminal influence on the rise and shape of Garveyism as a mass-based Black nationalist movement would find another valence of expression in the Nation of Islam (NOI). One can scarcely imagine Malcolm X rising to the stature he did, including through his prodigious work to grow the NOI, without the childhood influence of his mother and father, who were both active in the Garvey movement in Michigan. As Jeffrey Perry argued, "Harrison is the key link in the ideological unity of the two great trends of the Black Liberation Movement—the labor and civil rights trend associated with Martin Luther King Jr., and the race and nationalist trend associated with Malcolm X."[41]

We could take Perry's argument about Harrison as a "unifying link" even further. Harrison's electoral project of the Liberty Party anticipated political formations like the Mississippi Freedom Democratic Party, the Black Panther Party, and the Freedom Now Party, which represented the largest efforts to build a Black political party in the 1960s. Harrison crystallized a secular Black radical class-conscious politics in the Socialist Party, paving the way for the first generation of Black Communists. He practiced and advocated armed self-defense and developed a "colored internationalist" solidarity with the struggles of oppressed and colonized peoples around the world. These positions further mark him as a political forerunner of the Black Panther Party for Self-Defense. Not to mention his—and Harlem's—experiments with Black free love many decades before the sexual liberation politics of the 1960s.[42]

Now more than ever, the genealogy of the pan-African and African independence movements can claim a piece of Harrisonian ancestry too. Kwame Nkrumah, for example, revealed that "long before many of us were even conscious of our own degradation, Marcus Garvey fought for African national and racial equality" and that Garvey's writings "fired his enthusiasm" more than any other thinker.[43] Harrison's Liberty League crystallized the model—especially in terms of "race first" and mass movement building—without which Garvey's name might never have grown large enough to touch Nkrumah and so many others with the fire of Black pride and pan-African nationalism. Not to mention the oratorical and Black street scholarly tradition that have endured far beyond Harrison's years in institutions like the Schomburg Center for Research in Black Culture at the 135th Street public library in Harlem.[44]

Like all human beings, Harrison had many flaws.

For example, Harrison showed highly contradictory positions in his gender politics. As historian Winston James puts it, "Black socialist men seemed to have held a position on the woman question similar to that held by the white socialists on the Negro Question: they had nothing special to offer Black women; socialism would solve the problem of Black women as it would that of Black men."[45] Harrison's commitments to the politics of "race first" and the "Colored International" followed a default male-dominant orientation. Some of his articulations of the "New Negro Manhood Movement" likewise revealed a male-dominated conception of politics, even though the publicity materials for the launching of the Liberty League also called explicitly for a "New Negro Womanhood." In Harrison's landmark book of New Negro political thought, *When Africa Awakes*, only *one* out of its fifty-one articles is about women, and the article ("The Women of Our Race") describes how much charm, grace, and aesthetic beauty Black women have compared to other women, as opposed to anything about their role as intellectual or political leaders and innovators.

On the other hand, Harrison also could speak of how "the female element in life conserves and protects. The restless masculine element . . . fertilizes it is true, but it also destroys. It is the symbol of aggression, conquest, conflict and destruction by all of which it works changes." This sounds like a critique of patriarchal power. He went on to insist that "the female principle is the more important. . . . It is like capital and labor. Before capital came into existence labor was: I have seen labor functioning without capital, but never capital without labor. Before maleness came femaleness." Thus Harrison could also speak of the feminine element as more primary and essential to life than the masculine.[46]

While his gender politics were at times problematic and contradictory, it would be a mistake to read Harrison as an unreconstructed sexist and misogynist. After all, he was eternally grateful for his mentorship by women like Frances Reynolds Keyser, under whose strategic direction and spiritual guidance he had worked in the White Rose Home for Colored Girls. After attending the sixth biennial convention of the National Association of Colored Women (NACW), he noted in his diary that "these women of the association have been a great inspiration to me." In his view, the NACW's work was "great and noble." He also demonstrated great respect for—and often fruitful collaboration with—various artistic, activist, and intellectual women like Williana Jones (Burroughs), Emma Goldman, Grace P. Campbell, Elizabeth Gurley Flynn, Eslanda Cardozo Goode, Margaret Sanger, Irena Moorman-Blackston, Ida B. Wells-Barnett, Amy Ashwood Garvey, Augusta Savage, Ernestine Rose, and Drusillla Dunjee Houston. Not to mention countless other lesser-known women that he worked with in formations like the movements for pan-African and Black racial empowerment, Black women's suffrage, access to birth control and free love, freethought, the Virgin Islands Association, the Negro Society for Historical Research, and the Socialist Party. Alongside his mistakes and faults as a parent, he also deeply loved all of his five children, four of whom were girls. And he loved Lin till his last breath.

For whatever reason, Harrison seems to have retreated somewhat from his political radicalism in the last few years of his life. From around 1923 to 1927, Harrison sometimes made patriotic arguments, expressing more faith in the country's claim to "democracy" than he had ever done previously. In 1927 his notes for a talk on "The Red Record of Radicalism" not only critiqued the white racial politics of the Socialists but went so far as to ask, "What has revolution ever done for the common man?" This suggests he had abandoned or lost faith in the revolutionary hopes and dreams of his youth. In a talk on "Rockefeller and the Reds," he claimed that "the world grows better bit by bit" and "receives more genuine help in that process from John D. Rockefeller than from all the reds in America." He even claimed that "the professional 'red' is generally a parasite upon the process of production," someone who "doesn't do anything himself and won't let anyone else do anything," because "the bent of his genius is generally along the lines of obstruction and destruction." The idea that white capitalists had done more to help along social progress in the world than white Communists suggests a significant retreat from the class radicalism of his younger days when he shared the platform with Wobblies like "Big Bill" Haywood and Elizabeth Gurley Flynn (who both later became Communists) in defense of the massive strike of 25,000 Paterson silk workers.[47]

Perhaps in part as a result of his poverty and economic precarity, Harrison also seems to have become more unscrupulous in his political dealings. For example, he served as a member of the speakers committee of Tammany Hall, New York City's Democratic Party machine, which in the nineteenth century had opposed Abraham Lincoln and supported slavery. In March 1924 he made a veiled criticism of how in the 1910s, Democratic president Woodrow Wilson had been "making the world safe for Something." Yet during election season later that year, while Harrison campaigned for the Democrats in Indiana, the *Evansville Courier* quoted him as saying, "I challenge you to find one suspicious incident of fraud or corruption in a Democratic administration from Thomas Jefferson to Woodrow Wilson." This is a laughable statement given Harrison's deep familiarity with the arch-racism and political oppression of Black people by the Jeffersons and Wilsons of the world. But in a context where he had been denied jobs and publishing outlets so often, the Democratic Party at least offered a paycheck to promising campaign speakers. Of course, if Harrison shifted by his early forties and "warmed up" to the Democratic Party or the capitalist Rockefellers of the world, it would not be the first or last case of a youthful radical becoming more conservative with age.[48]

Hubert Harrison's Relevance Today

> Had the generation of African Americans who knew him listened to what he was saying, many of the tragic dilemmas in the African world probably would not exist. He was a man for the seasons of his lifetime and for all seasons.
>
> —John Henrik Clarke, "Introduction to *When Africa Awakes*"

As John Henrik Clarke has suggested, Harrison still has much to teach and communicate to the modern world. Arturo Schomburg, an old friend and mentor who also served as one of the pallbearers at his funeral, eulogized Harrison as being "ahead of his time."[49] When considering Harrison's relevance today, it is hard not to notice that in some ways Harrison remains ahead of *our* time. For example, given the history of Western media portrayals of Africa as a backward continent full of AIDS, blood diamonds, Ebola, poverty, "tribal" conflict, and other negative associations, the notion that we must look to Africans in order to, as Harrison suggested, "LEARN WHAT THEY HAVE TO TEACH US (for they have much to teach us)" is still far in advance of how many people—both within and outside of Africa—view the continental birthplace of language, civilization, and humanity itself. As the groundbreaking Senegalese scholar of African history Dr. Cheikh Anta Diop said,

> Insofar as Egypt is the distant mother of Western Cultures and sciences . . . Most of the ideas that we call foreign are often times nothing but mixed up, reversed, modified, elaborated images of the creations of our African ancestors, [including] Judaism, Christianity, Islam, Dialectics, Mechanical Engineering, Astronomy, Medicine, Literature (Novel, Poetry, Drama), Architecture, the Arts, etc. . . . Just as modern technologies and sciences came from Europe, so did, in antiquity, universal knowledge stream from the Nile valley to the rest of the world, particularly to Greece, which would serve as a link. Consequently, no thought, no ideology is . . . foreign to Africa, which was their birthplace.[50]

It would appear Harrison's injunction to learn what Africans and African history have to teach us remains just as relevant today as it was a century ago.

Fortunately, Harrison is beginning to gain a wider hearing, thereby joining the ranks of a number of other notable Virgin Islanders in history like Edward Wilmot Blyden, Rothschild Francis, D. Hamilton Jackson, Queen

Mary, Buddhoe, Elizabeth Hendrickson, Ashley Totten, Casper Holstein, Anselmo Jackson, Frank Crosswaith, and James C. Canegata. Harrison's resurgence, including his own untamed and untamable African identity, evokes an African proverb: "Those who have died have never, never left. The dead are not under the earth, they are in the rustling trees, they are in the groaning woods. . . .'Tis the Ancestors' words when the fire's voice is heard, 'tis the Ancestors' words in the voice of the water."[51]

In evoking ancestral spirits, we close with a return to Ossie Davis's eulogy of Malcolm X, which speaks uncannily to the story told in this book of Hubert Henry Harrison:

> Here—at this final hour, in this quiet place—Harlem has come to bid farewell to one of its brightest hopes—extinguished now, and gone from us forever. For Harlem is where he worked and where he struggled and fought—his home of homes, where his heart was, and where his people are—and it is, therefore, most fitting that we meet once again—in Harlem—to share these last moments with him.
>
> For Harlem has ever been gracious to those who have loved her, have fought for her and have defended her honor even to the death. It is not in the memory of man that this beleaguered, unfortunate, but nonetheless proud community has found a braver, more gallant young champion than this Afro-American who lies before us—unconquered still. . . .
>
> Many will ask what Harlem finds to honor in this stormy, controversial and bold young captain—and we will smile. Many will say turn away—away from this man; for he is not a man but a demon, a monster, a subverter and an enemy of the Black man—and we will smile. . . .
>
> Consigning these mortal remains to earth, the common mother of all, secure in the knowledge that what we place in the ground is no more now a man—but a seed—which, after the winter of our discontent, will come forth again to meet us.[52]

May we meet
with his timeless and revolutionary spirit
that crystalline onyx
again and again
and keep listening
for what the many stories of that
untamed, untamable African touchstone
still have to teach us

Notes

Introduction

1. Hubert Harrison, "The Feet of the Young Men," Trend of the Times, *Boston Chronicle*, March 22, 1924, Hubert H. Harrison Papers, Rare Book and Manuscript Library, Columbia University, New York (hereafter cited as HHP), box 6, folder 43.

2. Hubert Harrison, "The Common People," Trend of the Times, *Boston Chronicle*, April 17, 1925, HHP, box 6, folder 43.

3. Harrison, "The Common People."

4. Ella Baker quoted in Grant, *Ella Baker*, 230.

5. Sheldrake, *New Science of Life*, 131.

6. Anderson, *A. Philip Randolph*, 77.

7. Hubert Harrison, "Pledge to the Mother Race from an Untamed African" (diary entry), November 11, 1907, HHP, box 9.

8. Kirnon, "Contemporary Comment."

9. Kirnon, "Hubert Harrison: An Appreciation."

10. Rogers, *World's Great Men of Color*, 2:611.

11. Hubert Harrison, "'No Negro Literary Renaissance' Says Well-Known Writer," *Pittsburgh Courier*, March 12, 1927.

12. Gould, *Panda's Thumb*, 151.

13. Finkelman, *African American History*.

14. Rogers, *World's Great Men of Color*, 2:432–33.

15. Perry, *Hubert Harrison*, 1:13–14.

16. Harrison, "The Negro and Socialism," 28.

17. Harrison, "No Negro Literary Renaissance."

18. This quote is often misattributed to Frantz Fanon but does not appear in any of his written works. The first instance I could find was Pam Atherton, "Why Some Smart Women Think Palin Is a Good Choice," *Huffington Post*, November 24, 2008, www.huffpost.com/entry/why-some-smart-women-thin_b_137416.

19. Clarke, "Introduction," in Harrison, *When Africa Awakes*, vi.

20. Harrison, *Negro and the Nation*, 41–47.

21. Hubert Harrison, "Politics and Personality," *The Voice*, August 28, 1917, HHP, box 4, folder 72.

22. Edgar M. Grey, "Why Great Negroes Die Young," *New York News*, December 31, 1927.

23. Hubert Harrison, review of *The Negro in American Life*, by Jerome Dowd, *Pittsburgh Courier*, December 2, 1927, HHP, box 4, folder 18.

24. The Hubert Harrison Memorial Church hosted guest lectures by various Black Harlem radicals and freethinkers as a fitting tribute to the life and legacy of its namesake.

"Hubert Harrison Memorial Church," *Amsterdam News*, December 26, 1928, HHP, box 16, folder 21. According to Wikipedia, the historical St. Hubert was the patron saint of hunters, mathematicians, opticians, and metalworkers. Due in part to pressure from atheistic radicals on the left and anti-Harrison conservatives on the right, the Hubert Harrison Memorial Church lasted only nine years. Wikipedia, s.v. "Hubert of Liège," last modified November 5, 2024, https://en.wikipedia.org/wiki/Hubert_of_Li%C3%A8ge. Rev. Ethelred Brown, "A Brief History of the Harlem Unitarian Church," September 11, 1949, Egbert Ethelred Brown Papers, Unitarian Universalist Association Archives, Boston, box 1, folder 8.

25. Rogers, *World's Great Men of Color*; Moore, "Africa Conscious Harlem," 315–34; Cruse, *Crisis of the Negro Intellectual*; Foner, *American Socialism and Black Americans*; Samuels, "Hubert H. Harrison"; James, "Hubert Harrison"; Perry, "Hubert Henry Harrison"; Allen, "New Negro"; Watkins-Owens, *Blood Relations*; Clarke, "Introduction," in Harrison, *When Africa Awakes*; James, *Holding Aloft*; Turner, *Caribbean Crusaders*.

26. Power-Greene, "No Negro Renaissance," 28; Asukile, "Harlem Friendship"; Streeby, *Radical Sensations*.

27. Perry, *Hubert Harrison*, vols. 1 and 2; Perry, *Reader*.

28. Harrison, *When African Awakes*, 64.

29. Perry, *Hubert Harrison*, 1:39–46.

30. Perry, *Hubert Harrison*, 1:46, 50–51; Perry, *Reader*, 240.

31. In the United States, poor and working-class white people formed a social control buffer between Black labor and white capital. In the Anglophone Caribbean, by contrast, a middle-class Black or Brown social layer performed this function. There, white people were a tiny minority and therefore relied upon socioeconomic promotion of nonwhite people into positions of social management and administrative control. For this reason, the construction and function of race, though based on white superiority in both cases, remained fundamentally different. For more on this, see Allen, *Invention of the White Race*, vol. 2.

32. For more on Caribbean migration and the racial aspect of the radicalization of Caribbean migrants in this period, see James, *Holding Aloft*, chaps. 1–3.

33. Harrison, *Negro and the Nation*, 4.

34. Harrison, *Negro and the Nation*, 5–6.

35. Harrison, *Negro and the Nation*, 15.

36. Harrison, *Negro and the Nation*, 17–18.

37. Harrison, *Negro and the Nation*, 18.

38. Young, *Robert R. Church*, 253; White, *Judge Lynch*, 304.

39. Davis, *Women*, 175.

40. Jaspin, *Bitter Waters*; Loewen, *Sundown Towns*.

41. White mobs attacked Black communities in East St. Louis in 1917, in Philadelphia in 1918, and in Knoxville, Tennessee; Washington, DC; Chicago, Illinois; Charleston, South Carolina; Longview, Texas; Omaha, Nebraska; San Francisco, California; Bisbee, Arizona; El Dorado and Elaine, Arkansas; Bogalusa, Louisiana; Montgomery, Alabama; Pickens, Vicksburg, and Ellisville, Mississippi; Lake City, Florida; Gary, Indiana; at least seven cities in Georgia; Corbin, Kentucky; Norfolk, Virginia; and New London, Connecticut, in 1919. McWhirter, *Red Summer*; Krugler, *1919*; Voogd, *Race Riots*; Woodward, *Origins of the New South*, 351. For more on this, see also chapter 2, p. 69.

42. Spivey, *Schooling for the New Slavery*.

43. Harrison, *Negro and the Nation*, 12–15.
44. Harrison, *Negro and the Nation*, 15.
45. Spivey, *Schooling for the New Slavery*, xv.
46. Thornbrough, *T. Thomas Fortune*.
47. Giddings, *When and Where I Enter*.
48. Hine, "Rape and the Inner Lives of Black Women," 917.
49. Fox, *Guardian of Boston*; Greenidge, *Black Radical*.
50. Hunter, *To 'Joy My Freedom*.
51. Heller and Rudnick, *1915, The Cultural Moment*.
52. Wilson, *New Freedom*.
53. Harrison, *When Africa Awakes*, 76.
54. As his biographer put it, Harrison's life "truly [moved] from the nineteenth century to the twentieth." Perry, *Hubert Harrison*, 1:52.
55. Perry, *Hubert Harrison*, 1:54–55.
56. Parascandola, *"Look for Me,"* 9.
57. Perry, *Hubert Harrison*, 1:87.
58. Watkins-Owens, *Blood Relations*, 44, 49, 42–43, 57.
59. Turner, *Caribbean Crusaders*, 28.
60. Harris, *Sex Workers*.
61. Trotter, "African American Fraternal Associations."
62. Johnson, *Black Manhattan*, 3.
63. Crowder, "Harlem's Street Scholar Community," 45.
64. "Hubert H. Harrison!," *Pittsburgh Courier*, December 31, 1927.
65. Harrison, *When Africa Awakes*, 93.

Chapter 1

1. Zinn, *People's History*, 253–70.
2. "Socialists Were Shy," *Auburn Advertiser*, October 14, 1912, HHP, flat box 740.
3. Hubert Harrison to Lothrop Stoddard, July 1, 1921, HHP, box 2, folder 19.
4. Zinn, *People's History*, 270–93; Lens, *Labor Wars*; Smith, *Subterranean Fire*.
5. Lens, *Labor Wars*, 8.
6. Hunter, *To 'Joy My Freedom*; Cole, *Ben Fletcher*; Kelly, *Race, Class, and Power*; Harold, *New Negro Politics*.
7. Arnesen, *Encyclopedia of U.S. Labor*, 248.
8. Foner, *Industrial Workers of the World*, 127; Loewen, *Sundown Towns*.
9. Hubert Harrison, diary entry, September 28, 1914, HHP, box 9, diary 1; Perry, *Hubert Harrison*, 1:56.
10. Perry, *Hubert Harrison*, 1:83, 86.
11. Jones, *American Work*, 303, 306.
12. Spivey, *Schooling for the New Slavery*, 8–10; Washington, *Up From Slavery*, 32.
13. Perry, *Reader*, 164.
14. Hubert Harrison, "Insistence upon Its Real Grievances the Only Course for the Race," *New York Sun*, December 8, 1910.
15. Foner, *American Socialism and Black Americans*, 209–12.
16. Harlan, *Booker T. Washington: The Making of a Black Leader, 1856–1901*, 254.

17. Perry, *Hubert Harrison*, 1:132–34.

18. Dewey, *Later Works*, 163.

19. Sheppard, *Inefficiency of Capitalism*.

20. Karl Marx, "Theses on Feuerbach," Marx/Engels Internet Archive, accessed November 14, 2024, www.marxists.org/archive/marx/works/1845/theses/theses.htm.

21. Frederick Engels, Preface to the 1883 German edition of the *Communist Manifesto*, accessed December 11, 2024, https://www.marxists.org/archive/marx/works/1848/communist-manifesto/preface.htm.

22. Fried, *Socialism in America*, 12–15, 382, 387.

23. Debs, "Capitalism and Socialism."

24. Debs, "Capitalism and Socialism."

25. Debs, "Capitalism and Socialism."

26. Perry, *Hubert Harrison*, 2:189, 192.

27. Selfa, *Democrats*.

28. Hubert Harrison, "The Coming Election," *The Voice*, October 18, 1917, HHP, box 4, folder 35.

29. Kipnis, *American Socialist Movement*, 130; Moore, "Flawed Fraternity."

30. Shannon, *Socialist Party of America*, 43–49.

31. Holm, "To Be Free."

32. Greene, *Grassroots Socialism*, 99; Vidrine, "Negro Locals," 389. For the Oklahoma party's work against disenfranchisement, see Foner, *American Socialism and Black Americans*, chap. 10.

33. Raymond, "A Southern Socialist on the Negro Question," quoted in Perry, *Hubert Harrison*, 1:214.

34. Though the editors of *The New Review* had previously published Harrison's and Du Bois's articles on the topic of "Socialism and the Negro," they refused to publish Harrison's response to Raymond. After pointing out her factual error—that the Klan was founded in 1865, three years *before* Black people in the South got voting rights—Harrison highlighted that as long as Southern white Socialists maintained their racial superiority complex, "we shall have to keep from saying that Socialism stands for the full civic and political equality of all workers." The editor's refusal to print such a sentiment spoke to the difficulty of having a free and open debate about race, even in the pages of a left-leaning Socialist journal. Hubert Harrison, "Southern Socialists and the Ku Klux Klan," letter to the editor, *The New Review* (unpublished). The letter was published years later in the *Negro World*, January 8, 1921. See Perry, *Reader*, 76.

35. Foner, *American Socialism and Black Americans*, 103.

36. Kipnis, *American Socialist Movement*, 132.

37. Honn, "Coming to Consciousness."

38. As early as 1904, Rubinow had written to Du Bois after seeing a report of a speech Du Bois gave regarding the economic side of the "Negro question." Rubinow argued that the foundation of race prejudice was to be found in economic exploitation and that the emancipation of Black people was inseparable from the emancipation of the "whole working class." Isaac Rubinow to W. E. B. Du Bois, November 10, 1904, W. E. B. Du Bois Papers (MS 312). Special Collections and University Archives, University of Massachusetts Amherst Libraries.

39. Foner, *American Socialism and Black Americans*, 204.

40. Debs, "The Negro in the Class Struggle."
41. Debs, "The Negro in the Class Struggle," 133–34. See Honn, "Coming to Consciousness," 60.
42. Perry, *Reader*, 51–52.
43. "Socialist Party Platform of 1912," reprinted in Fried, *Socialism in America*, 391.
44. Harrison, "Socialism and the Negro."
45. Harrison, *The Negro and the Nation*, 52.
46. Interestingly, Harrison even pointed out that "the Indians of Florida and California had been enslaved and under English rule white men, women and children from Ireland had been sold into American slavery" and that "many of the English working class condemned to penal servitude shared the same fate." "The Negro and Socialism: I—The Negro Problem Stated," *New York Call*, November 28, 1911. This would become a crucial piece of Eric Williams's argument that it was the cheapness of the labor rather than the color of the laborer that drove Europeans to enslave Africans. Williams, *Capitalism and Slavery*.
47. Harrison, "Socialism and the Negro."
48. Hubert Harrison, "Race Prejudice–II," *New York Call*, December 4, 1911.
49. Lowie, "Inferior Races."
50. Harrison, "Race Prejudice–II."
51. Hubert Harrison, "Summary and Conclusion," *New York Call*, December 26, 1911.
52. Harrison, "The Negro and Socialism."
53. Harrison, *The Negro and the Nation*, 21–29.
54. Harrison, "How to Do It—And How Not," *New York Call*, December 16, 1911.
55. Harrison, "Socialism and the Negro."
56. Foner, *American Socialism and Black Americans*, 208.
57. Harrison, "How to Do It."
58. One major weakness of color blindness is its failure to acknowledge and address the systematic unearned social privileges afforded to people racialized as white. See, for example, Monnica T. Williams, "Colorblind Ideology Is a Form of Racism," *Psychology Today* (blog), December 27, 2011, www.psychologytoday.com/blog/culturally-speaking/201112/colorblind-ideology-is-form-racism.
59. Harrison, "How to Do It."
60. Harrison, "How to Do It."
61. Samuel Romansky to Julius Gerber, October 12, 1911, The Socialist Party Papers of Local New York, New York University, New York, reel 6.
62. Julius Gerber to Local New York, December 21, 1911, The Socialist Party Papers of Local New York, reel 6.
63. Harrison, "Summary and Conclusion."
64. Perry, *Hubert Harrison*, 1:175, 172.
65. Foner, *American Socialism and Black Americans*, 212.
66. Foner, *American Socialism and Black Americans*, 207–15; Perry, *Hubert Harrison*, 1:170.
67. Foner, *American Socialism and Black Americans*, 215.
68. Though Du Bois and Miller sustained a decades-long familiarity, it does not appear that any letters of correspondence between them in this period survive in the Du Bois Papers.

69. Foner, *American Socialism and Black Americans*, 250.

70. W. E. McDermut, assisted by C. W. Phillips, *National Convention of the Socialist Party Held at Indianapolis, Ind., May 12 to May 18, 1912*, ed. J. Spargo (Chicago, 1912), 209–10, quoted in Harrison, *When Africa Awakes*, 81–82.

71. Carlson, *Roughneck*, 198.

72. Foner, *History of the Labor Movement*, 399, 199; Miller, *Other Socialists*, 100.

73. "Harrison Lecture" (speech, Elizabeth, NJ, December 7, 1912), HHP, flat box 740.

74. Golin, *Fragile Bridge*.

75. Emphasis added. "Sabotage Coming in Silk Mills if Boyd Is Jailed: Negro Agitator Shouts That If Paterson Owners Want to Lose $200,000, Let Them Go Ahead," *New York World*, December 1, 1913, HHP, flat box 740.

76. Flynn, *Sabotage*.

77. "Sabotage Coming in Silk Mills."

78. Golin, *Fragile Bridge*, 145–46.

79. *New York Call*, c. January 29, 1914, HHP, flat box 740.

80. Perry, *Hubert Harrison*, 1:190, 209, 212, 216–18.

81. Hubert Harrison, "Southern Socialists and the Ku Klux Klan," unpublished letter to the editor, *The New Review*, 1914. The letter was published years later in the *Negro World* of January 8, 1921. See Perry, *Reader*, 76–78.

82. Foner, *History of the Labor Movement*, 127.

83. Hubert Harrison, "The Coming Election," *The Voice*, October 18, 1917, HHP, box 4, folder 35.

84. Perry, *Hubert Harrison*, 1:218.

85. Hubert Harrison, "The Duty of the Socialist Party," *New York Call*, December 13, 1911.

86. Clarke, "Introduction," in Harrison, *When Africa Awakes*, vi.

87. Hubert Harrison, "Our Civic Corner," *New York News*, February 9, 1915, HHP, box 13, folder 2.

Chapter 2

1. Perry, *Hubert Harrison*, 1:315–17, 331–32.

2. J. E. Cutler to the Director of Military Intelligence, "Attachment," Washington, DC, August 15, 1919, memorandum for the Director of Military Intelligence, National Archives, Washington, DC, 10218-361, reprinted in Hill, *Marcus Garvey Papers*, 1:491. This multi-volume collection of Marcus Garvey papers is hereafter referred to as *MGP*.

3. Marlborough Churchill, "Memorandum for the Chief of Staff: Subject, the Negro Situation," August 20, 1919, National Archives, Record Group (RG) 65, 10218-361; Maj. Walter Loving, "Final Report on Negro Subversion," August 6, 1919, Major Walter Loving Papers, Howard University, Washington, DC, box 113-1, folder 12, 11.

4. Giddings, *Ida*; Bay, *To Tell the Truth Freely*, 45, 103.

5. Brown, *Upbuilding Black Durham*; Gilmore, *Gender and Jim Crow*.

6. Bay, *To Tell the Truth Freely*, 100–103.

7. Bay, *To Tell the Truth Freely*, 108.

8. Silkey, *Black Woman Reformer*.

9. Giddings, *Ida*, 474.

10. Kellogg, *NAACP*, 231–32; Zangrando, *NAACP Crusade against Lynching*, 43–46.

11. Harrison, *When Africa Awakes*, 12–13.
12. Giddings, *When and Where I Enter*, 30.
13. Hubert Harrison, diary entry, October 1907, HHP, box 9.
14. For more see Perry, *Hubert Harrison*, 1:100.
15. Hubert Harrison, diary entry, January 1, 1909, HHP, box 9.
16. Hubert Harrison, diary entry, April 27, 1908, HHP, box 9.
17. Harrison, diary entry September 3, 1908, HHP, box 9.
18. "A Notable Social Event," *New York Age*, March 25, 1909.
19. J. E. Robinson, "St. Mark's Lyceum," *New York Times*, February 22, 1907.
20. *New York Age*, April 15, 1909, 3.
21. *New York Age*, July 22, 1909, 2.
22. Perry, *Hubert Harrison*, 1:75, 77.
23. Perry, *Hubert Harrison*, 1:350–51.
24. "Campaign for Women Nearing Its Close," *New York Age*, November 1, 1917.
25. Lindsey, "Gendering the Black Radical Tradition," 106.
26. Hubert Harrison, "Election Results," *The Voice* (November 14, 1917), HHP, box 4, folder 55.
27. For a biographical overview of Campbell's political trajectory, see Lindsey, "Gendering the Black Radical Tradition."
28. Hicks, *Talk with You Like a Woman*, 167.
29. Hill, *MGP*, 2:271.
30. Greenidge, *Black Radical*; Edwards, "William Monroe Trotter."
31. Perry, *Hubert Harrison*, 1:272.
32. Hubert Harrison, "Resolutions," *The Voice*, September 19, 1917, reprinted as "Resolutions Passed at the Liberty League Meeting," in *When Africa Awakes*, 11–12.
33. Harrison, *When Africa Awakes*, 11–12; Getachew, *Worldmaking after Empire*.
34. Hubert Harrison, "Declaration of Principles," *Clarion*, September 1, 1917, reprinted in Perry, *Reader*, 89–92.
35. Hubert Harrison, "Prejudice Growing Less and Co-Operation More, Says Student of Question: Writer of Special Article for Courier Readers Says Immigrants Are Becoming Americanized and Naturalized—Garveyism Has Had Little Effect on Mental Outlook," *Pittsburgh Courier*, January 29, 1927.
36. McLaughlin, *Power, Community, and Racial Killing*, 2.
37. McLaughlin, *Power, Community, and Racial Killing*, 171.
38. Meier, *Negro Thought in America*, 137.
39. Meier, *Negro Thought in America*, 167.
40. Lumpkins, *American Pogrom*, 1.
41. McWhirter, *Red Summer*.
42. Johnson, *Black Manhattan*, 26.
43. Woodward, *Origins of the New South*, 351.
44. Krugler, *1919, The Year of Racial Violence*, 13.
45. Loewen, *Sundown Towns*, 36.
46. Cary Bradburn, "Argenta Race Riot of 1906," in *Encyclopedia of Arkansas* (Central Arkansas Library System, 2006–), March 19, 2015, www.encyclopediaofarkansas.net/encyclopedia/entry-detail.aspx?entryID=2415.
47. Williams, "Long Hot Summers," 14.

48. McWhirter, *Red Summer*, 13; Voogd, *Race Riots and Resistance*; Hobbs, *Democracy Abroad*.

49. Loewen, *Sundown Towns*; Dunbar-Ortiz, *An Indigenous People's History*; Carrigan, *Making of a Lynching Culture*.

50. Jaspin, *Buried in the Bitter Waters*.

51. While "Great Retreat" constitutes a notable attempt to conceptually distinguish the phenomenon in question from the "Great Migration," it remains problematic for at least two reasons. First, it implies that Black people fleeing the Jim Crow South were somehow *not* "in retreat." Second, "Great Retreat" (like its migration-focused counterpart) comes across as a rather grandiose and almost celebratory phrase to describe the massive and desperate scattering of African American refugees fleeing a decades-long, nationwide epidemic of white terrorism and racial "cleansing." See Loewen, *Sundown Towns*; Jaspin, *Buried in the Bitter Waters*; and Lumpkins, *American Pogrom*.

52. Hubert Harrison, "Make a Drive for Liberty" (leaflet), HHP, flat box 740; A. Jackson, "Analysis of the Black Star Line," reprinted in Hill, *MGP*, 2:271.

53. Emphasis in original. John E. Bruce to Hubert Harrison, July 8, 1917, HHP, box 1, folder 18.

54. William Monroe Trotter to Hubert Harrison, November 17, 1917, HHP, box 3, folder 45.

55. Makalani, *In the Cause of Freedom*, 35; "William Harrison's Research Notes on Life of Hubert Harrison," February 23, 1951, Jeffrey Perry Collection of Harrison Materials, box 8, folder 12.

56. Kornweibel, *No Crystal Stair*, 44.

57. Snyder, *120 Years of American Education*, 21.

58. Harlan, *Booker T. Washington: The Making of a Black Leader*, 254.

59. Hubert Harrison, "A Difference of Opinion," *Negro World*, July 8, 1920.

60. *The Voice*, July 4, 1917, HHP, box 6, folder 25; Harrison, *When Africa Awakes*, 8.

61. I sometimes say "so-called Middle Passage" because this phrase remains an abominable euphemism that whitewashes the process wherein Europeans and their African collaborators kidnapped, shipped, and enslaved some 15 million African human beings, precipitating millions of deaths between the wars they sparked between Africans on the continent and those whose lives ended on the Atlantic Ocean. The phrase *slave trade* is similarly objectionable for its reduction of unspeakable horror to an economic transaction. I prefer the term *Maangamizi*. For deeper analysis, see Williams, "Naming the Unspeakable."

62. Hubert Harrison, "Untitled, 1st Issue," *The Voice*, July 4, 1917, HHP, box 6, folder 25.

63. Hubert Harrison, "Owing to the High Cost of Manhood *The Voice* Has Gone Up to 5 Cents," *The Voice*, date unknown, HHP, box 13, folder 2; Hubert Harrison, "Affidavit of Circulation," August 21, 1917, HHP, box 4, folder 5.

64. Harrison, "Owing to the High Cost of Manhood."

65. Hubert Harrison, "Send Us the News," *The Voice*, September 4, 1917, HHP, box 6, folder 18.

66. Hubert Harrison, "Announcement: *The Voice* for Sale," *The Voice*, date unknown, HHP, box 6, folder 50.

67. Hubert Harrison, "Selling Space vs. Selling Self," *The Voice*, July 10, 1917, HHP, box 4, folder 73.

68. Perry, *Hubert Harrison*, 1:305.

69. Randolph and Owen originally edited the *Hotel Messenger* for the Headwaiters and Sidewaiters Society of Greater New York, but the union bureaucracy fired them for publishing an article exposing corruption inside their union. Bynum, *A. Philip Randolph*, 86–87.

70. Rogers, *World's Great Men of Color*, 2:438.

71. Perry, *Hubert Harrison*, 1:56.

72. W. Harrison, "William Monroe Trotter—Fighter," 240.

73. Kersten, *Reframing Randolph*, 75n62.

74. Bundles, *On Her Own Ground*, 261; Giddings, *Ida*, 587; Martin, *Amy Ashwood Garvey*, 37.

75. Turner, *Caribbean Crusaders*, 37.

76. See Perry, *Hubert Harrison*, 1: chap. 11 for more on the financial challenges facing *The Voice* under Harrison's editorship.

77. Hubert Harrison, "The New Negro," *The New Negro* 3, no. 7, August 1919, HHP, box 17, folder 8.

78. Hubert Harrison, "The Need for It," *The New Negro* 4, no. 1, September 1919, HHP, box 17, folder 8.

79. Harrison, "The Need for It."

80. Federal Surveillance of Afro Americans report, Jeff Perry Collection of Harrison Materials, box 22, 29–30.

81. Putnam, *Radical Moves*, 123–24, 151.

82. "Exchange List," HHP, box 4, folder 55.

83. Hollingsworth Wood, "Urban League Movement," 119.

84. Hubert Harrison, diary entry, June 2, 1915, HHP, box 9.

85. Lindsey, "Gendering the Black Radical Tradition," 103–4.

86. Ovington, *National Association for the Advancement of Colored People*.

87. W. E. B. Du Bois, "The Talented Tenth," in Washington, *The Negro Problem*.

88. Higginbotham, *Righteous Discontent*, chap. 2; James, *Transcending the Talented Tenth*, 16–17; Spivey, *Schooling for the New Slavery*.

89. Harrison, "The Right Way to Unity," *Boston Chronicle*, May 10, 1924.

90. Harrison, "The Common People," *Boston Chronicle*, April 17, 1925.

91. Robinson, *Black Marxism*, 193.

92. Harrison, *When Africa Awakes*, 58.

93. Hubert Harrison, "The Line-Up on the Color Line," *Negro World*, December 4, 1920, reprinted in Perry, *Reader*, 216.

94. Harrison, *When Africa Awakes*, 58.

95. Ovington, *Black and White Sat Down Together*, 87.

96. Harrison, "Our Professional Friends," in *When Africa Awakes*, 55–60.

97. Francis Dearborn [Hubert Harrison], "The Black Tide Turns in Politics," c. December 1921, HHP, box 8, folder 6; Harrison, *When Africa Awakes*, 56.

98. Harrison, "Our Professional Friends."

99. Harrison, "Our Professional Friends."

100. Harrison, "Our Professional Friends."

101. Hubert Harrison, "Why Is the Red Cross?," *The Voice*, July 18, 1918, HHP, box 4, folder 41.

102. Trotsky, *History of the Russian Revolution*; Cliff, *Lenin*; Rabinowitch, *Bolsheviks Come to Power*.

103. Reed, *Ten Days That Shook the World*, 14.

104. Maj. Walter H. Loving to the Director of Military Intelligence, "Report of Mass Meeting during January, 1919," February 17, 1919, in Hill, *MGP*, 1:363; Harding, *Lenin's Political Thought*; Lih, *Lenin Rediscovered*.

105. Harman, *Lost Revolution*; Broué, *The German Revolution*.

106. Nigel Anthony Sellars, "Green Corn Rebellion," in *The Encylopedia of Oklahoma History and Culture* (Oklahoma Historical Society, 2007–), accessed October 31, 2024, www.okhistory.org/publications/enc/entry?entry=GR022.

107. Foner, *History of the Labor Movement*, 8:1.

108. O'Connor, *Revolution in Seattle*, 132–33.

Chapter 3

1. William Pickens, "Evolution Discussed on Harlem Streets," *The Associated Negro Press*, August 23, 1926, HHP, box 8, folder 19.

2. Crowder, "Harlem's Street Scholar Community," 56.

3. Vincent, *Black Power and the Garvey Movement*, 40.

4. "Call Harrison's [illegible] Celebrated Harlem Mass Leader Dies after Operation," *New York News*, December 24, 1927, HHP, box 18, folder 8; Asukile, "Harlem Friendship," 59.

5. Hale, "Griot."

6. Hale, *Griots and Griottes*.

7. Ethelred Brown, "A Brief History of the Harlem Unitarian Church," September 11, 1949, Egbert Ethelred Brown Papers.

8. Johnson, *Black Manhattan*, 162–63.

9. Harris, *Sex Workers*, locs. 725–28, Kindle.

10. Barlow, *Voice Over*, 8–9. Radio remained dominated by white ownership and programming until the 1970s. Williams, *Legendary Pioneers of Black Radio*.

11. Crowder, "Harlem's Street Scholar Community," 42.

12. Crowder, "Harlem's Street Scholar Community," 41; Watkins-Owens, *Blood Relations*, 57.

13. Moore, *Caribbean Militant in Harlem*, 30.

14. On the weekends, indoor forums at places like the New Harlem (formerly Lenox) Casino, the 135th Street library, and Lafayette Hall offered further educational lectures. Harrison, *When Africa Awakes*, 96; Perry, *Hubert Harrison*, 1:227.

15. Davis, "Growing Up in the New Negro Renaissance," 429.

16. Lynette Holloway, "Show Time for Sad Time at Apollo," *New York Times*, August 7, 1992.

17. Crowder, "Harlem's Street Scholar Community," 45.

18. Harrison, *When Africa Awakes*, 85.

19. Turner, *Caribbean Crusaders*, 58.

20. "Topics in Wall Street," *New York Times*, September 14, 1912.

21. Perry, *Hubert Harrison*, 1:225.

22. Jackson, *Black Socrates*, 5.

23. Moore, *Caribbean Militant in Harlem*, 31.

24. Foner, *History of the Labor Movement*, vol. 4; Perry, *Hubert Harrison*, 1:207, 223. Fights like this to defend Harlem soapbox speaking spaces continued well into the 1930s.

Crowder, "Harlem's Street Scholar Community," 46; "Dr. Hubert Harrison Fined Five Dollars," *Amsterdam News*, August 8, 1923.

25. "Negro Speaker Turns on Mob in the Subway Fells Man with Iron Bar—Angry Crowd Had Followed Him from Street Lecture," *NY World*, August 12, 1914, HHP, flat box 740.

26. Bayor and Meagher, *New York Irish*, 401.

27. Perry, *Hubert Harrison*, 1:224.

28. *Truth Seeker* 50, no. 35 (September 1, 1923): 567, HHP, flat box 740.

29. Quoted in Logan and Winston, *Dictionary of American Negro Biography*, 293.

30. Miller, *Rosy Crucifixion*, 560–61.

31. McKay, *Long Way from Home*, 92.

32. "The Death of Hubert Harrison," *New York Times*, December 31, 1927.

33. Maj. Walter H. Loving to the Director of Military Intelligence, February 17, 1919, quoted in Hill, *MGP*, 1:363.

34. William Pickens, "Evolution Discussed on Harlem Streets," *The Associated Negro Press*, August 23, 1926, HHP, box 8, folder 19.

35. Freire, *Pedagogy of the Oppressed*.

36. Hodge Kirnon, "Hubert Harrison: An Appreciation," *Amsterdam News*, January 4, 1928.

37. "Lament Death of Dr. Hubert Harrison: Eulogized by Several Who Knew His Life and Worth," *Amsterdam News*, December 28, 1927.

38. Anderson, *A. Philip Randolph*, 77.

39. Hubert Harrison, diary entry, August 27 and 28, 1924, HHP, box 9; email communication with Dr. Bracey in possession of author (October 15, 2019). For more on Chicago's "Bughouse Square" in Washington Park, see Higbie, *Labor's Mind*, chapter 2.

40. Trotsky, *My Life*, 295.

41. Hubert Harrison, "Humorous Phrases," *The Voice*, December 14, 1917; Harrison, *Negro and the Nation*, 13.

42. Harrison, *When Africa Awakes*, 128.

43. Hubert Harrison, "How to Do It—And How Not," *New York Call*, December 16, 1911.

44. Benson, "Literary Genius of Hubert Harrison."

45. Hodge Kirnon, "Hubert Harrison: An Appreciation," *Amsterdam News*, January 4, 1928.

46. Hubert Harrison, diary entry, March 7, 1908, HHP, box 9, folder 4.

47. *Amsterdam News*, December 21, 1927, HHP, box 18, folder 8.

48. Harrison, *When Africa Awakes*, 8; Hubert Harrison, "On Praise" (autograph manuscript), April 8, 1920, HHP, box 5, folder 46.

49. Benson, "Literary Genius of Hubert Harrison."

50. Perry, *Hubert Harrison*, 1:58.

51. Perry, *Hubert Harrison*, 1:85.

52. Harrison, *When Africa Awakes*, 129, 123; Hubert Harrison, "Dr. Harrison's Last Article: 'World Problems of Race': Writer Said Both Science and History Try to Rob Negro of Past Heritage, 'Ancient Ethiopians' Called White Lest Negroes Get Credit for Medicine, Geometry, Religion and Architecture," *Pittsburgh Courier*, December 31, 1927.

53. Perry, *Reader*, 291.

54. Jackson, *Black Socrates*, 4.

55. Hubert Harrison, "The Living Lie," undated, HHP, box 5, folder 7.

56. Harrison, *When Africa Awakes*, 129–31.

57. Rojas, *From Black Power to Black Studies*, 128.

58. Hubert Harrison, "Education out of School," *Boston Chronicle*, February 23, 1924.

59. Harrison, *When Africa Awakes*, 93.

60. Hubert Harrison, "Letter to Miss Frances Reynolds Keyser" (diary entry), May 20, 1908, HHP, box 9, folder 1.

61. Harrison, "Letter to Miss Frances Reynolds Keyser."

62. For more on Harrison's freethought and relationship to *The Truth Seeker*, see Perry, *Hubert Harrison*, 1: chap. 4.

63. "Hubert Harrison Dies," *Amsterdam News*, December 21, 1927.

64. *Amsterdam News*, December 21, 1927, HHP, box 18, folder 8.

65. Avrich, *Modern School Movement*.

66. "The Modern School, Francisco Ferrer Association, Hubert Harrison" (advertisement c. 1914), HHP, flat box 740.

67. "'How God Grew, The Evolution of the Idea of God' by Hubert Harrison at the Radical Forum," *New York Call*, November 29, 1914; "'Jesus Christ and the Working Man: A Challenge to the Christian Socialists,' Hubert Harrison at the Harlem Casino for the Radical Forum," *New York Call*, October 4, 1914, HHP, flat box 740.

68. Jackson, "Black Atheists."

69. Hubert Harrison, diary entry, May 20, 1908, HHP, box 9.

70. Jackson, "Black Atheists."

71. Hubert Harrison, "Paine's Place in the Deistical Movement," *Truth Seeker* 38, no. 6 (February 11, 1911): 87–88, reprinted in Perry, *Reader*, 40–42.

72. Joseph Silver (secretary, Secular Society of New York), letter to the editor, *Truth Seeker*, December 30, 1916.

73. Hubert Harrison, "The Negro a Conservative: Christianity Still Enslaves the Minds of Those Whose Bodies It Has Long Held Bound," *Truth Seeker* 41 (September 12, 1914): 583, reprinted in Harrison, *Negro and the Nation*, 41–47.

74. John G. Jackson, "The Black Atheists of the Harlem Renaissance" (lecture, American Atheists Convention, 1984), Nation of Atheism, https://nationofatheism.tripod.com/cgi-bin/the_black_atheist.html; Cameron, *Black Freethinkers*.

75. Jackson, *Black Socrates*, 2.

76. Jackson, *Black Socrates*, 5.

77. Hubert Harrison, "First Principles," publication unknown (*Negro World*?), July 16, 1921, HHP, box 13, folder 7.

78. Perry, *Hubert Harrison*, 1:43, 397.

79. Hubert Harrison, diary entry, March 7, 1908, HHP, box 9.

80. Perry, *Hubert Harrison*, 1:15.

81. Perry, *Hubert Harrison*, 1:56.

82. Perry, *Hubert Harrison*, 1:70–78.

83. Perry, *Hubert Harrison*, 1:208–9.

84. Perry, *Hubert Harrison*, 467n27.

85. Hubert Harrison, "Just Suppose: A Riddle for 'Scientific Radical' Liars, with Apologies to C. OW," *Negro World*, April 10, 1920.

86. Sinclair Wilberforce [Hubert Harrison?], "Harrison Delivers Inspiring Lecture," *The Voice*, July 1, 1918, HHP, box 18, folder 7.

87. Hubert Harrison, "Public Notices, Record, and References" (scrapbook), HHP, box 13, folder 5. Hubert Harrison, "A Reply to *Nigger Heaven*," c. 1926, HHP, box 16, folder 38; "135th St. (Harlem) Library Notes," *Negro World*, February 3, 1923.

88. Harrison, "Just Suppose."

89. "Hubert Harrison to Lecture at N.Y.U.," *Amsterdam News*, October 13, 1926.

90. "Negro Scholar Receives Remarkable Tribute at New York University," *Amsterdam News*, July 4, 1926.

91. "Negro Scholar Receives Remarkable Tribute"; "Hubert Harrison to Lecture at N.Y.U."

92. Hubert Harrison, "The Summer College Course," *The Voice of the Negro* 1, no. 4 (May 1927), HHP, box 17, folder 10.

93. "World Problems of Race: Course Syllabus," The Institute for Social Study, 1926, HHP, box 13, folder 5.

94. Hubert Harrison, diary entry, April 6, 1921, HHP, box 9; Hubert Harrison, "Frightful Friendship vs. Self-Defense," HHP, box 13, folder 7.

95. Hubert Harrison, "Negro Society and the Negro Stage, Preamble [Part 1]," *The Voice*, September 19, 1917, reprinted in Perry, *Reader*, 371.

96. Perry, *Hubert Harrison*, 1:194–95.

97. Perry, *Hubert Harrison*, 1:7, 406.

98. William Pickens, "Hubert Harrison: Philosopher of Harlem," *Amsterdam News*, February 7, 1923.

99. Hubert Harrison, *The Embryo of The Voice of the Negro* 1, no. 1 (February 1927), HHP, box 17, folder 10.

100. "World Problems of Race: Syllabus," The Institute for Social Study broadside, HHP, box 16, folder 46.

101. Crowder, "Willis Nathaniel Huggins."

102. Carruthers, "John Henrik Clarke."

103. Huggins and Jackson, *A Guide to Studies in African History*; Huggins and Jackson, *Introduction to African Civilizations*; Jackson, *Christianity before Christ*; Jackson, *Pagan Origins of the Christ Myth*; Jackson, *Ethiopia and the Origin of Civilization*.

104. Sinnette, *Arthur Alfonso Schomburg*, 86.

105. Kelley, *Freedom Dreams*, xi.

Chapter 4

1. Hubert Harrison, "Africa Here and There," *Negro World*, November 12, 1921, HHP, box 13, folder 7.

2. Lens, *Forging of the American Empire*, 246.

3. Lens, *Forging of the American Empire*, 247–48.

4. Lenin, *Imperialism*, chap. 5.

5. Lenin, *Imperialism*, chap. 5.

6. Butler, "America's Armed Forces."

7. Wilson, *New Freedom*.

8. McWhirter, *Red Summer*, 107.

9. Hubert Harrison, "Wanted—A Colored International," *Negro World*, May 28, 1921.

10. Lens, *Forging of the American Empire*, 195.

11. Lens, *Forging of the American Empire*, 222–25; Schmidt, *Occupation of Haiti*, 85.

12. Perry, *Hubert Harrison*, 1:260; James, *The Black Jacobins*.

13. Lens, *Forging of the American Empire*, 226.

14. Lens, *Forging of the American Empire*, 221, 272.

15. Butler, *War Is A Racket*, chap. 1; Hugh Rockoff, "Until It's Over, Over There: The U.S. Economy in World War I?" (working paper no. 10580, The National Bureau of Economic Research, June 2004), www.nber.org/digest/jan05/w10580.html.

16. Butler, *War Is A Racket*, chap. 1.

17. Hubert Harrison, "Some Reasons Why Such a Collection Is Necessary," c. 1925, HHP, box 6, folder 28.

18. Hubert Harrison, "The White War and the Colored World," *The Voice*, August 14, 1917.

19. *Encyclopaedia Britannica Online*, s.v. "Sir Harry Hamilton Johnston," accessed May 19, 2016, www.britannica.com/biography/Harry-Hamilton-Johnston.

20. Harry Johnston, "The Future of Africa," reprinted in *The Crisis* 17 (June 1919): 75; Harrison, *When Africa Awakes*, 116.

21. Marx and Engels, *Manifesto*, 13.

22. Harrison, *When Africa Awakes*, 96–98.

23. Harrison, *When Africa Awakes*, 116.

24. Harrison, "Soft Pedaling for Peace," publication unknown (*Negro World*?), January 21, 1922, HHP, box 13, folder 7.

25. Harrison, *When Africa Awakes*, 120.

26. Harrison, *When Africa Awakes*, 121.

27. Locke and Stewart, *Race Contacts and Interracial Relations*, xl.

28. Locke and Stewart, *Race Contacts and Interracial Relations*, 110.

29. Perry, *Hubert Harrison*, 1:157.

30. Brawley, *Africa and the War*, 30–38.

31. Du Bois, "African Roots of War."

32. Randolph and Owen, *Terms of Peace*; Hubert Harrison, "Some of Our Friends," *The Voice*, September 19, 1917.

33. Zinn and Arnove, *Voices of a People's History of the United States*, chap. 14.

34. Helen Keller, "Strike against War," reprinted in Arnove and Zinn, *Voices of a People's History*, 284–88.

35. Lenin, *Imperialism*.

36. Lenin, "The Socialist Revolution," 143–56.

37. Harrison, *When Africa Awakes*, 116.

38. Harrison, *When Africa Awakes*, 113–14.

39. Harrison, *When Africa Awakes*, 119, 121; Jackie Shandu, "Battle for the Soul of the Economic Freedom Fighters: Race First or Class First?," *Daily Maverick*, December 18, 2014.

40. Lens, *Forging of the American Empire*, 262; Kornweibel, *Investigate Everything*, 183; "Harding Frees Debs and 23 Others Held for War Violations," *New York Times*, December 24, 1921.

41. Hill, *Crusader*, 1:xvi.

42. Augustus Cerillo, "Mitchel, John Purroy," in *American National Biography Online* (Oxford University Press, 2000–), February 2000, www.anb.org/articles/06/06-00440.html.

43. Hubert Harrison, article, *NY World*, October 17, 1917, HHP, flat box 740.
44. Hubert Harrison, editorial, *The Voice*, August 1, 1918, HHP, box 4, folder 8.
45. Hubert Harrison, editorial, *The Voice*, July 11, 1918. Quoted in Hill, *Crusader*, 1:15.
46. Harrison did not officially become a US citizen until 1922. Perry, *Hubert Harrison*, 1:411.
47. Hubert Harrison, article, *NY World*, October 17, 1917, HHP, flat box 740.
48. Hubert Harrison, "The Real Woodrow Wilson," *Negro World*, April 9, 1921.
49. Hubert Harrison, "The Negro and the War," in *When Africa Awakes*, 25.
50. Quoted in a letter from W. A. Moss of Brooklyn regarding a lecture Harrison gave there on May 24, 1912, HHP, box 13, folder 1.
51. Hubert Harrison, "U-Need-A Biscuit," *Negro World*, July 17, 1920, reprinted in *When Africa Awakes*, 98–100.
52. Bernays, *Propaganda*, 37.
53. Bernays, "Engineering of Consent."
54. Bernays, *Propaganda*, 120.
55. Manning and Romerstein, *Historical Dictionary of American Propaganda*, 24.
56. Rossiter and Lare, *Essential Lippmann*, 91–92.
57. Chomsky, *Understanding Power*, 16.
58. Harrison, *When Africa Awakes*, 5.
59. Harrison, "U-Need-A Biscuit."
60. Harrison, "Land of the Living Lie," HHP, box 5, folder 7.
61. Adam Clayton Powell Sr. and William Monroe Trotter to Hubert Harrison, April 3, 1918, HHP, box 3, folder 13.
62. "Liberty Congress Plans Indorsed [sic]," *St. Louis Argus*, May 17, 1918.
63. Fred W. Moore (intelligence officer, Northeastern Department) to Chief, Military Intelligence Branch, Washington, "Subject: Proposed Convention of Negroes," National Archives, RG 165, case file 10218–153 MI 4–41, June 19, 1918.
64. Perry, *Hubert Harrison*, 1:373–78.
65. "Colored Editors and Leaders in Conference," *St. Louis Argus*, July 5, 1918. On Roosevelt writing Haiti's constitution, see Schmidt, *Occupation of Haiti*, 111.
66. Talbert, *Negative Intelligence*, 119.
67. Perry, *Hubert Harrison*, 1:380.
68. Hubert Harrison, diary entry, July 1, 1918, HHP, box 9, folder 4.
69. Harrison, diary entry, July 1, 1918.
70. "Excerpts from Addresses at Colored Liberty Congress: June 24-25-26-27, 1918," July 2, 1918, War Department MIB files, Washington, DC, 2; Hubert Harrison, diary entry, July 1, 1918, HHP, box 9.
71. "Federal Surveillance of Afro-Americans (1917–1925): The First World War, the Red Scare, and the Garvey Movement" (Frederick, MD: University Publications of America, 1986), Jeffrey B. Perry Collection, box 22, 4, 9.
72. "Excerpts from Addresses," 2.
73. Hill, *MGP*, 1:318n1.
74. Haynes, "Houston Mutiny and Riot"; Smith, "Houston Riot of 1917."
75. Du Bois, "Close Ranks," 111.
76. Hubert Harrison, "The Descent of Du Bois," *The Voice*, July 25, 1918.

77. Talbert, *Negative Intelligence*, 118–19.
78. Talbert, *Negative Intelligence*, 121.
79. Lewis, *Du Bois: The Fight for Equality*, 573.
80. Talbert, *Negative Intelligence*, 119.
81. Jordan, *Black Newspapers*, 114.
82. Major J. E. Spingarn to Colonel Marlborough Churchill, "Memorandum for Colonel Churchill, Subject: Changed Attitude of Colored Press," July 6, 1918, MID 10218-154-MI4-41 DNA, FSAA, reel 19, reprinted in Jeffrey B. Perry Research Files, Federal Surveillance of Afro-Americans, box 22, 4; Ellis, "'Closing Ranks' and 'Seeking Honors.'"
83. Du Bois, "African Roots of War."
84. Du Bois, "Returning Soldiers," 13.
85. Harrison, *When Africa Awakes*, 70–73.
86. Maj. Walter H. Loving to Nicholas Biddle, "Subject: Conditions among Negroes in the United States," July 22, 1918, Major Walter Loving Papers, box 113-1, Military Intelligence Correspondence 1905–1917, folder 10.
87. Hubert Harrison, diary entries, March 22, April 25, November 3, 1919, HHP, box 9. See also Perry, *Hubert Harrison*, 1: chap. 12.
88. Harrison, diary entry, March 27, 1918, HHP, box 9.
89. Perry, *Hubert Harrison*, 1:371, 514n16; Harrison, diary entry, March 27, 1918, HHP, box 9.
90. Seddon, "Popular Protest and Class Struggle," 71.
91. Stoddard, *Rising Tide of Color*.
92. Harrison, "Wanted—A Colored International."
93. Harrison, "Wanted—A Colored International."
94. Harrison, "Wanted—A Colored International."
95. Harrison, "Wanted—A Colored International."
96. Katz, *Emancipation of Labor*; Hallas, *The Comintern*.
97. Nation, *War on War*.
98. Trotsky, *First Five Years of the Communist International*; Hallas, *The Comintern*.
99. Samuels, "Five Afro-Caribbean Voices," 85–86.
100. For more on Stokes, see Tamarkin, *Rose Pastor Stokes*; Zipser and Zipser, *Fire and Grace*.
101. Harrison, "Wanted—A Colored International."
102. Hill, *MGP*, 2:681–82n1; Hill, *Crusader*, 1:xi; Kornweibel, *Seeing Red*, 141–42.
103. Trotsky, "Theses of the Third World Congress."
104. Marcus Garvey, "African Fundamentalism," reprinted in Martin, *African Fundamentalism*, 5.
105. Zimmerman, *Alabama in Africa*.
106. See chapter 5 on Harrison's African politics for further discussion of Tuskegee Institute foreign policy under Booker T. Washington.
107. See, for example, Provenzo and Abaka, *W. E. B. Du Bois on Africa*.
108. Prashad, *Darker Nations*, 20, 286n8.
109. Turner and Turner, *Richard B. Moore*, 189.
110. Prashad, *Darker Nations*, 21–22.

Chapter 5

1. Hubert Harrison, "Pledge to the Mother Race from an Untamed African" (diary entry), November 11, 1907, HHP, box 9.
2. Hubert Harrison, "The Virgin Islands," November 1923, HHP, box 6, folder 48.
3. Harrison, "Virgin Islands."
4. Campbell, *Middle Passages*, 138–41.
5. Hubert Harrison, "Africa and the Peace," in *When Africa Awakes*, 33–35.
6. Harrison, "Africa and the Peace."
7. James, *Holding Aloft*, 129.
8. Hubert Harrison, "Know Thyself!," *Negro World*, April 16, 1921, HHP, box 13, folder 7.
9. *Howard University Record*, vol. 8, March 3, 1919, 144, HHP, flat box 740.
10. Moore, "Africa Conscious Harlem."
11. Sundiata, *Brothers and Strangers*, 7.
12. Hubert Harrison, "On Civilizing Africa," *Negro World*, December 18, 1920, HHP, box 13, folder 7.
13. Harrison, "On Civilizing Africa."
14. Harrison, "On Civilizing Africa."
15. Harrison, "Africa as She Is," *Negro World*, February 19, 1921, HHP, box 13, folder 7.
16. Harrison, "Africa as She Is."
17. See Skinner, *African Americans and U.S. Policy toward Africa*, chap. 5, and Campbell, *Songs of Zion*.
18. Hubert Harrison, "The Negro and the Nation," Radio Broadcasting of American Telephone and Telegraphic Co., June 21, 1923, reprinted in Perry, *Reader*, 290.
19. Hill, *Crusader*, 1:114.
20. Wilfred A. Domingo, "Africa's Redemption," *The Emancipator*, March 27, 1920.
21. For biographical treatments of Schomburg, see Sinnette, *Arthur Alfonso Schomburg*; Valdés, *Diasporic Blackness*.
22. Carr, "African Philosophy of History," 219.
23. Perry, *Reader*, 325.
24. Hubert Harrison, "A Unique Negro," *Negro World*, July 5, 1921, HHP, box 4, folder 66.
25. Crowder has made the point that members of Carter G. Woodson's Association for the Study of Negro Life and History were mostly university-educated African Americans, whereas Bruce's NSHR had mostly Africans, West Indians, and African Americans from outside the academy. Crowder, "Harlem's Street Scholar Community," 54.
26. Cromwell, *Apropos of Africa*, 176.
27. Hubert Harrison, diary entry, March 28, 1918, HHP, box 9.
28. Schomburg, *Racial Integrity* (1913), 6.
29. Sinnette, *Arthur Alfonso Schomburg*, 54–55, 156; Van Sertima, *They Came before Columbus*.
30. Arthur Alfonso Schomburg, "The Negro Digs Up His Past," in Locke, *New Negro*, 231–37.
31. Harrison, "A Unique Negro."
32. Clarke, "Influence of Arthur A. Schomburg," 5.
33. Schomburg, *Racial Integrity* (1913), 18–19.
34. Harrison, "A Unique Negro."

35. Harrison, "A Unique Negro."

36. Sinnette, *Arthur Alfonso Schomburg*, 134.

37. William Leo Hansberry, "Negro People in the Civilization of the Prehistoric and Early Ancient World" (syllabus), Howard University, 1923, HHP, box 8, folder 8; Carter G. Woodson to Harrison, May 6, 1927, HHP, box 3, folder 55; Perry, *Reader*, 322–23, 339–40; Asukile, "Harlem Friendship"; Monroe Work to Harrison, July 20, 1922, HHP, box 3, folder 56. Drusilla Houston to Harrison, Oct 3, 1927, HHP box 2, folder 44.

38. "Dr. Hubert Harrison Opens Lecture Series," *Amsterdam News*, October 6, 1926; Carr, "African Philosophy of History"; Bruce, "Early Black American Historians"; Harrison, "In the Melting Pot," 8; Hubert Harrison, "Dr. Harrison's [illegible] . . . Writer Said Both Science and History Try to Rob Negro of Past Heritage," *Pittsburgh Courier*, December 31, 1927.

39. Hubert Harrison, "The Black Man's Burden II," *Negro World*, July 11, 1920, HHP, box 4, folder 15.

40. Harrison, "Black Man's Burden II."

41. Clark, *Through African Eyes*, 39–41.

42. See Moses, *Afrotopia*, especially chap. 3.

43. Harrison, *When Africa Awakes*, 114.

44. McFeely, *Frederick Douglass*, 332.

45. Harrison, "Dr. Harrison's [illegible]."

46. As the twentieth century unfolded, scholarship on the African influence on Western "civilization" would extend even further in the work of scholars like John G. Jackson, Willis N. Huggins, George M. James, John Henrik Clarke, Cheikh Anta Diop, Marimba Ani, Yosef Ben-Jochannan, Jacob Carruthers, Chancellor Williams, Martin Bernal, and Anthony Browder.

47. Hubert Harrison, "Digging for Lost African Gods," *Opportunity*, August 1926, HHP, box 4, folder 42.

48. Hubert Harrison, "Who Built the Great Zimbabwe?" (review of work by John H. Harris), undated autograph manuscript, HHP, box 6, folder 63.

49. Harrison, "Black Man's Burden II."

50. Report on Hubert Harrison's 1920 speech at the Women's Christian Alliance Hall in Philadelphia, UNIA Papers, Philadelphia Division records, Schomburg Center for Research in Black Culture, New York, box 1.

51. Hubert Harrison, diary entry, March 19, 1921, HHP, box 9; Cromwell, *African Victorian Feminist*.

52. Sekyi, "Education in West Africa," 11–12.

53. Hubert Harrison, "A Difference of Opinion," *Negro World*, August 7, 1920.

54. Hubert Harrison, "Education Out of School," *Boston Chronicle*, 1924, HHP, box 6, folder 43; Hubert Harrison, notes on a book review of *The Negro in American Life* by Willis J. King, *Opportunity*, October 1926, Jeff Perry Collection of Harrison Materials, box 23.

55. Hubert Harrison, "Books about Africa," *Negro World*, December 11, 1920.

56. Hochschild, *King Leopold's Ghost*.

57. Harrison, "Books about Africa."

58. Harrison, "Books about Africa."

59. Hubert Harrison, "The Black Man's Burden," *Negro World*, December 11, 1920.

60. Harrison, "Black Man's Burden."

61. Rudyard Kipling, "The White Man's Burden," 1899, Internet Modern History Sourcebook, Fordham University, accessed November 1, 2024, https://origin.web.fordham.edu/halsall/mod/Kipling.asp.

62. Cecil Rhodes, "Confession of Faith," 1877, Kimball Files, accessed July 30, 2015, http://pages.uoregon.edu/kimball/Rhodes-Confession.htm.

63. Asad, *Anthropology and the Colonial Encounter*; Lewis, "Anthropology and Colonialism"; Baker, *From Savage to Negro*, 14–16.

64. Moses, *Golden Age of Black Nationalism*, chap. 2.

65. See, for example, Mitchell's discussion of the "Black Man's Burden" in *Righteous Propagation*, chap. 2.

66. Gaines, "Black Americans' Uplift Ideology," 450.

67. Emphasis in original. Alexander Crummell, "The Relations and Duties of Free Colored Men in America to Africa," reprinted in Uya, *Black Brotherhood*, 63–71.

68. Martin Delany, "A Project for an Expedition of Adventure," reprinted in Uya, *Black Brotherhood*, 71–82.

69. Quoted in Alexander, *T. Thomas Fortune*, 267.

70. Ida B. Wells, "Afro-Americans and Africa," *The A.M.E. Church Review* 9, no. 1 (July 1892): 40–44, Ida B. Wells Papers, University of Chicago, Chicago, box 8, folder 9.

71. Mitchell, *Righteous Propagation*, 62; Gaines, "Black Americans' Uplift Ideology," 435.

72. Zimmerman, *Alabama in Africa*, chap. 3.

73. Erichsen, *Angel of Death*.

74. Olusoga and Erichsen, *Kaiser's Holocaust*.

75. Harlan, "Booker T. Washington and the White Man's Burden," 446, 442; Zimmerman, *Alabama in Africa*, 147.

76. Marable, "Booker T. Washington and African Nationalism."

77. Zimmerman, *Alabama in Africa*, 184–85.

78. Spivey, *Schooling for the New Slavery*, 113.

79. Harlan, "Booker T. Washington and the White Man's Burden," 441–42.

80. Du Bois, "African Roots of War"; Du Bois, *World and Africa*, 9, 11.

81. Harrison, "Africa and the Peace."

82. Du Bois, *World and Africa*, 12.

83. W. E. B. Du Bois, "Africa for the Africans," in Provenzo and Abaka, *W. E. B. Du Bois on Africa*, 101.

84. Adi and Sherwood, *Pan-African History*, viii; A. Garvey, *Garvey and Garveyism*, 11; Hill, *MGP*, 1:288.

85. See Sundiata, "Garvey Aftermath," 83.

86. Garvey, *Philosophy and Opinions* (1923), 67–68.

87. Frank Crosswaith, "Building a Negro Empire," *The Emancipator*, April 10, 1920.

88. See Taylor, *Veiled Garvey*, chaps. 3–4.

89. Martin, "Women in the Garvey Movement," 72.

90. Amy J. Garvey, "Christianity in Africa," *Negro World*, November 15, 1924, reprinted in Vincent, *Voices of a Black Nation*, 365.

91. A. Garvey, "Christianity in Africa."

92. Harrison, "Africa as She Is."

93. Hubert Harrison, "The Brown Man Leads the Way, Part 1, review of *The New World of Islam* by Lothrop Stoddard," *Negro World*, October 29, 1921.

94. Vinson and Schwartz, *The Americans Are Coming!*

95. Marcus Garvey, "Editorial," *Negro World*, April 14, 1923.

96. A. Garvey, *Black Power in America*, 33.

97. "Negroes Plan New American State," *Monitor*, June 7, 1924, HHP, box 13, folder 5.

98. Hubert Harrison, "Prejudice Growing Less and Co-Operation More, Says Student of Question: Writer of Special Article for Courier Readers Says Immigrants Are Becoming Americanized and Naturalized—Garveyism Has Had Little Effect on Mental Outlook," *Pittsburgh Courier*, January 29, 1927.

99. Hubert Harrison to Arthur Hillard, December 27, 1925, HHP, box 2, folder 2.

100. Hubert Harrison, "The I.C.U.L.," c. 1924 HHP, box 17, folder 10.

101. West and Buschendorf, *Black Prophetic Fire*.

102. Harrison, "The I.C.U.L."

103. Harrison, "Program and Principles of the International Colored Unity League."

104. Martin, *Race First*, 13.

105. For a history of Black cooperatives, see Nembhard, *Collective Courage*.

106. Hubert Harrison, "The Roots of Power," *Boston Chronicle*, June 21, 1924, HHP, box 6, folder 43.

107. Harrison, "Program and Principles of the International Colored Unity League."

108. Hill, *Crusader*; Davenport, *How Social Movements Die*; Onaci, *Free the Land*.

109. Harrison, "Program and Principles of the International Colored Unity League."

110. Hubert Harrison, "On Religion," *The Embryo of The Voice of the Negro* 1, no. 1 (February 1927), HHP, box 17, folder 10.

Chapter 6

1. Nugent, *Gay Rebel of the Harlem Renaissance*, 149; Hartman, *Wayward Lives*, 292–93; McKay, *Long Way from Home*, 96.

2. Marriage certificate of Mr. Hubert H. Harrison and Miss Irene L. Horton, HHP, box 14, folder 11.

3. For more on these love affairs, see Perry, *Hubert Harrison*, 2: chaps 12, 16.

4. "Hamilton Lodge Ball an Unusual Spectacle," *New York Age*, March 6, 1926; Hubert Harrison, diary entry, February 26, 1926, HHP, box 9, folder 2.

5. Davis, *Blues Legacies and Black Feminism*; Hartman, *Wayward Lives*; Woolner, *Famous Lady Lovers*; Nugent, *Gay Rebel of the Harlem Renaissance*, 21.

6. Weisbord, *Genocide? Birth Control and the Black American*, 5.

7. See chapter 3 in Silliman et al., *Undivided Rights*, p. 57.

8. Perry, *Hubert Harrison*, 1:222.

9. Du Bois, "Black Folks and Birth Control," 166.

10. Hubert Harrison, "The Line-Up on the Color Line," *Negro World*, December 4, 1920; Perry, *Reader*, 219.

11. D'Emilio and Freedman, *Intimate Matters*, 233.

12. Hubert Harrison, "The Materialistic Interpretation of Morals," *New York Call Sunday Magazine*, November 3, 1912, HHP, box 13, folder 2; Perry, *Hubert Harrison*, 1:222; Scrapbook, HHP, flat box 740.

13. Harrison, "Materialistic Interpretation of Morals."

14. Meily, *Puritanism*, 103.

15. Meily, *Puritanism*, 6; Harrison, "Materialistic Interpretation of Morals."

16. Harrison, "Materialistic Interpretation of Morals."

17. Meily, *Puritanism*, 136–37.

18. Grigory Batkis, *Sexual Revolution in Russia* (1925), *In Defence of Marxism* (website), https://marxist.com/the-sexual-revolution-in-russia.htm.

19. Alcofribas [Hubert Harrison], "Flappers vs. Bachelors," *The Tattler*, January 27, 1924, HHP, box 13.

20. D'Emilio and Freedman, *Intimate Matters*, 230.

21. West, "Moses Harman Story"; Stoehr, *Free Love in America*, 286; Walker, *Who Is the Enemy?*; Walker, "Variety vs. Monogamy," 2.

22. Hubert Harrison, diary entry, May 26, 1924, HHP, box 9, folder 2.

23. Walker, "Variety vs. Monogamy," 2, 4.

24. Walker, "Variety vs. Monogamy," 5, 2.

25. Walker, "Variety vs. Monogamy," 3.

26. Stoehr, *Free Love in America*, 39–40; D'Emilio and Freedman, *Intimate Matters*, 113.

27. "Notes on the 'American Split,'" The International Working Men's Association, 1872, Marxists Internet Archive, accessed November 1, 2024, www.marxists.org/archive/marx/works/1872/09/splits.htm.

28. Broun and Leech, *Roundsman of the Lord*, 193.

29. De Grazia, *Girls Lean Back Everywhere*; Werbel, *Lust on Trial*.

30. Walker, *Who Is the Enemy?*

31. Spingarn, *Laws Relating to Sex Morality in New York City*, 6, 7, 10, 31.

32. Ryan and Jethá, *Sex at Dawn*, 251, 286; Weisbord, *Genocide? Birth Control and the Black American*, 31–34; Sanjana Manjeshwar, "America's Forgotten History of Forced Sterilization," *Berkeley Political Review*, November 4, 2020, https://bpr.studentorg.berkeley.edu/2020/11/04/americas-forgotten-history-of-forced-sterilization; Alonso, "Autonomy Revoked."

33. Ryan and Jethá, *Sex at Dawn*, 254.

34. Harris, *Sex Workers*, 125–28; Mumford, *Interzones*, 47.

35. Powell, *Against the Tide*, 216–17, 57–59.

36. Hubert Harrison, "The Negro a Conservative: Christianity Still Enslaves the Minds of Those Whose Bodies It Has Long Held Bound," *Truth Seeker*, September 12, 1914, reprinted in Perry, *Reader*, 42.

37. Frederickson, *Black Image in the White Mind*, 279.

38. Wells-Barnett, *Crusade for Justice*, 64.

39. Marriott, "Bordering On," 15.

40. Curry, *Man-Not*, 4; White, *Ar'n't I a Woman?*; Collins, *Black Feminist Thought*.

41. Lorde, *Uses of the Erotic*; Ryan and Jethá, *Sex at Dawn*, 97, 39.

42. NAACP data showed a yearly average of 101 recorded lynchings in the period between 1890 and 1927. White, *Judge Lynch*, 19, 304.

43. Twain, *Letters from the Earth*.

44. Blyden, *African Life and Customs*, 11.

45. Blyden, *African Life and Customs*, 16–24.

46. Schopenhauer, *Essays of Arthur Schopenhauer*, 84–86.

47. Ryan and Jethá, *Sex at Dawn*, 90, 137.

48. Dixon-Spear, *We Want for Our Sisters What We Want for Ourselves*, 1.

49. Willey, *Undoing Monogamy*, 28–30.

50. See Dixon-Spear, *We Want for Our Sisters What We Want for Ourselves*, chap. 1; Willey [emphasis in original], *Undoing Monogamy*, 28–30.

51. Hubert Harrison, "Science and Race Prejudice," *Boston Chronicle*, February 2, 1924, HHP, box 13, folder 4; Harrison, *When Africa Awakes*, 114.

52. Ryan and Jethá, *Sex at Dawn*, 97, 106, 59, 39.

53. I say "so-called" here because of how the renaissance framework has worked to erase Harrison and the radical New Negro movement he symbolized, as recounted in chapter 9.

54. Davis, *Blues Legacies and Black Feminism*, xiii.

55. Woods, *Development Arrested*, 20.

56. Garber, "A Spectacle in Color."

57. Wilson, *Bulldaggers, Pansies, and Chocolate Babies*, 13.

58. Garber, "A Spectacle in Color."

59. Nugent, *Gay Rebel of the Harlem Renaissance*, 21.

60. Nugent, *Gay Rebel of the Harlem Renaissance*, 21.

61. Hubert Harrison, "Negro Church History: A Book of It Badly Marred by Neglect of the Race Foundation," *New York World*, July 23, 1922, HHP, box 5, folder 29. Woodson, to his credit, would eventually assert the importance of African inheritances in African American culture in *The African Background Outlined* (1936).

62. Leah Buckle, "African Sexuality and the Legacy of Imported Homophobia," Stonewall, October 1, 2020, www.stonewall.org.uk/about-us/news/african-sexuality-and-legacy-imported-homophobia.

63. Somé, *Spirit of Intimacy*, chap. 9; Oyěwùmí, *Invention of Women*.

64. Bright Alozie, "Did Europe Bring Homophobia to Africa?" *Black Perspectives*, October 21, 2021, www.aaihs.org/did-europe-bring-homophobia-to-africa; Wekker, *Ik ben een gouden munt*, 145, cited in Tinsley, "Black Atlantic, Queer Atlantic," 198; Wekker, *Politics of Passion*. On the Maangamizi, see Williams, "Naming the Unspeakable."

65. Lorde, *Uses of the Erotic*.

66. Hughes, *Collected Poems*, 39.

67. Du Bois, *American Negro Family*, 21, 152.

68. Ryan and Jethá, *Sex at Dawn*, 28.

69. Hubert Harrison, diary entry, November 16, 1926, HHP, box 9.

70. James, *Holding Aloft*, 129.

71. Hill, *Crusader*, 1:xi.

72. Maya Angelou, "Love Liberates," accessed December 17, 2024, https://www.youtube.com/watch?v=qULRYgAphjc.

Chapter 7

1. Carnegie, "Garvey and the Black Transnation," 51.

2. Martin, *Race First*, 44.

3. Shilliam, "What About Marcus Garvey?"

4. West and Martin, *From Toussaint to Tupac*, 11. See also Lewis and Warner-Lewis, *Garvey: Africa, Europe, and the Americas*.

5. Younis, "With Drops of Ink We Make Millions Think," 45.

6. Harold, *Rise and Fall of the Garvey Movement*, 45.

7. West and Martin, *From Toussaint to Tupac*, 11.
8. Hill, *MGP*, 11:lxxxix.
9. Quinn-Judge, *Ho Chi Minh*, 19.
10. Bair, "True Women, Real Men"; Blain, *Set the World on Fire*; Duncan, *An Efficient Womanhood*.
11. Bair, "True Women, Real Men," 166; Duncan, *An Efficient Womanhood*.
12. Hill, *MGP*, 1:528.
13. W. A. Domingo to Alain Locke, September 21, 1925, Alain Locke Papers, Howard University, Washington, DC, box 164-25, folder 28; Hill, *MGP*, 1:528; Richard B. Moore (speech from December 7, 1970), Richard B. Moore Papers, box 11, folder 13; Yard, *Amy Ashwood Garvey*, 44; Perry, *Hubert Harrison*, 1:315, 331–32.
14. Martin, *Amy Ashwood*, 24; Edwards, "Garveyism," 218.
15. Hill, *MGP*, 1:165.
16. "UNIA Memorial Meeting for Booker T. Washington," *Daily Chronicle*, November 24, 1915, reprinted in Hill, *MGP*, 1:166.
17. Hill, "First England Years and After," 59.
18. Hill, "First England Years and After," 63.
19. Spivey, *Schooling for the New Slavery*, ix; Kelly, "No Easy Way Through," 84.
20. Hill, "Comradeship of the More Advanced Races."
21. Hill, *MGP*, 1:203, 207.
22. Hubert Harrison, "Our Civic Corner," *NY News*, February 9, 1915, HHP, box 13, folder 2.
23. Hill, *MGP*, 1:194, 203; "Resolution Adopted by Negro Improvement Association," *Gleaner*, September 17, 1914, reprinted in Hill, *MGP*, 1:70.
24. Harrison, *When Africa Awakes*, 96, 113.
25. Anselmo Jackson, "Analysis of the Black Star Line," *The Emancipator*, March 27, 1920.
26. "Garvey's Speech," Collegiate Hall, March 25, 1921, Correspondence with Robert Hill folder, John Henrik Clarke Papers, Schomburg Center for Research in Black Culture, New York.
27. "Reporter Sues Garvey," *Chicago Defender*, September 28, 1918, reprinted in Hill, *MGP*, 1: 282; Jackson, "Analysis of the Black Star Line"; Grant, *Negro with a Hat*, 95; Anderson, *A. Philip Randolph*, 80.
28. Perry, *Hubert Harrison*, 1:272, 406n27.
29. Johnson, *Black Manhattan*, 253; Jackson, "Analysis of the Black Star Line."
30. *Negro World*, September 10, 1921, 5.
31. Hubert Harrison, "Marcus Garvey at the Bar of United States Justice," *Associated Negro Press*, c. early July 1923, reprinted in Perry, *Reader*, 194–99.
32. Robert A. Hill, "Convention Reports," August 29, 1921, in *MGP*, 3:709; Jackson, "Analysis of the Black Star Line"; Johnson, *Black Manhattan*, 253.
33. Richard B. Moore, "Marcus Garvey and His Critics," in Clarke, *Marcus Garvey and the Vision of Africa*.
34. Robert A. Hill, "Introduction," in *The Crusader*, 1:xi.
35. Hodge Kirnon, "Contemporary Comment as to H.H.," *Negro World*, August 21, 1920.
36. Hubert Harrison, "Owing to the High Cost of Manhood *The Voice* Has Gone Up to 5 Cents," *The Voice*, date unknown, HHP, box 13, folder 2.
37. Perry, *Hubert Harrison*, 2:332–39.

38. Hill, *MGP*, 2:271; Turner, *Caribbean Crusaders*, 61–62; Hubert Harrison, "On Garvey's Character and Abilities" (diary entry), May 24, 1920, HHP, box 9, reprinted in Perry, *Reader*, 188–90; Hill, *MGP*, 3:709. For the Liberty League to UNIA personnel shifts, see Perry, *Hubert Harrison*, 1: chap. 11.

39. Perry, *Hubert Harrison*, 2:334.

40. Clarke, *Marcus Garvey and the Vision of Africa*, 197.

41. Jackson, "An Analysis of the Black Star Line."

42. Alexander, *T. Thomas Fortune*, xviii.

43. A. S. Henning, "Wilson for America First; Cry for 1916 Is Announced by President," *Chicago Tribune*, October 12, 1915.

44. Hubert Harrison, article, *NY World*, October 17, 1917, HHP, flat box 740; Hubert Harrison, "New Policies for the New Negro," *The Voice*, September 4, 1917.

45. Harrison, *When Africa Awakes*, 8.

46. In the original 1917 version of "New Policies for the New Negro," Harrison wrote "Africa First," and then in the 1920 reprint he changed it to "Race First." Harrison, "New Policies for the New Negro" (1917); Harrison, *When Africa Awakes*, 39–40.

47. Wilfred A. Domingo, "Race First!," *Negro World*, July 26, 1919, reprinted in Hill, *MGP*, 1:468–70.

48. Harrison, *When Africa Awakes*, 79–86.

49. Harrison, "New Policies for the New Negro" (1920).

50. Marcus Garvey, "UNIA Meeting at Carnegie Hall," New York City, August 25, 1919, reprinted in Hill, *MGP*, 1:506.

51. A. Garvey, *Garvey and Garveyism*, 11; Hodge Kirnon quoted in Hill, "Introduction," in *MGP*, 1:lxviii.

52. Moore, "Africa Conscious Harlem."

53. Hubert Harrison, "Declaration of Principles," *Clarion*, September 1, 1917, reprinted in Perry, *Reader*, 89.

54. Hill, *MGP*, 1:lxxn111.

55. Hill, *MGP*, 1:lx–lxxviii.

56. Hill, *MGP*, 1:lx–lxxviii, lxxii.

57. Hill, *MGP*, 1:194, 203; "Resolution Adopted by Negro Improvement Association," *Gleaner*, September 17, 1914, reprinted in Hill, *MGP*, 1:70; Hill, "The First England Years and After," 64.

58. Hill, *Crusader*, 1:xii–xiii. Harrison, "New Policies for the New Negro" (1920).

59. Hill, *Crusader*, 1:xii–xiii.

60. Harrison, *When Africa Awakes*, 11; Harrison, "Declaration of Principles."

61. "Garvey's Speech," Collegiate Hall, March 25, 1921, Correspondence with Robert Hill folder, John Henrik Clarke Papers; "Reception Given Marcus Garvey," *Gleaner*, March 24, 1921, reprinted in Hill, *MGP*, 3:275.

62. African Caribbeans and African Americans had collaborated before the Liberty League on a small scale, for example in the church lyceums and in the Negro Society for Historical Research. Hubert Harrison, "Prejudice Growing Less and Co-Operation More, Says Student of Question: Writer of Special Article for Courier Readers Says Immigrants Are Becoming Americanized and Naturalized—Garveyism Has Had Little Effect on Mental Outlook," *Pittsburgh Courier*, January 29, 1927.

63. Harrison, *When Africa Awakes*, 8, emphasis in original.

64. Martin, *Race First*, 44.

65. Perry, *Reader*, 90, 197.

66. Burkett, *Black Redemption*, 5; Yard, *Amy Ashwood Garvey*, 43; "William Harrison's Research Notes on Life of Hubert Harrison," HHP, box 8, folder 12.

67. For an excellent overview of *Negro World* poetry, see Martin, *Literary Garveyism*, chap. 4.

68. Hubert Harrison, "On a Certain Condescension in White Publishers [Part I]," *Negro World*, March 4, 1922.

69. Martin, *Literary Garveyism*, 91.

70. Hubert Harrison, "Re: Garvey and U.N.I.A," (c. 1922) HHP, box 4, folder 61; Hubert Harrison, "Connections with the Garvey Movement" (diary entry), March 17–18, 1920, HHP, box 9, reprinted in Perry, *Reader*, 182.

71. Harrison, "Re: Garvey and U.N.I.A."; Harrison, "Connections with the Garvey Movement."

72. Hubert Harrison, "Wednesday March 17, 1920" (diary entry), March 17, 1920, HHP, box 9, reprinted in Perry, *Reader*, 183.

73. Martin, *Race First*, 93–99.

74. Martin, *Race First*, 193.

75. Perry, *Reader*, 176.

76. Kornweibel, *Seeing Red*, 91.

77. The first major public clash was a debate that the Socialists organized titled "Race First or Class First?" at the Palace Casino in December 1918 between Harrison and Owen. Harrison, *When Africa Awakes*, 87–89.

78. Hubert Harrison, "Race First versus Class First," *Negro World*, March 27, 1920, reprinted in *When Africa Awakes*, 79–82.

79. Harrison, "Race First versus Class First."

80. Harrison, "Race First versus Class First."

81. Harrison, "Race First versus Class First."

82. Chandler Owen and A. Philip Randolph, "Opinion of Owen & Randolph Editors of the 'Messenger,'" *The Emancipator*, April 3, 1920.

83. W. A. Domingo, "Race First versus Class First," *The Emancipator*, April 3, 1920.

84. Domingo, "Race First versus Class First."

85. Domingo, "Race First versus Class First."

86. Domingo, "Race First versus Class First."

87. Turner, *Caribbean Crusaders*, 78.

88. Hubert Harrison, "'Just Suppose,' A Riddle for 'Scientific Radical' Liars, with Apologies to C[handler]. OW[en]," *Negro World*, April 10, 1920; A. Philip Randolph and Chandler Owen, "Opinion of Randolph & Owen Editors of the 'Messenger,'" *The Emancipator*, April 17, 1920; Hubert Harrison, "The Crab Barrel," *Negro World*, April 3, April 10, April 17, 1920.

89. Hubert Harrison, "An Open Letter to the Socialist Party of New York City," *Negro World*, May 8, 1920, reprinted in *When Africa Awakes*, 82–86.

90. Hubert Harrison, "Patronize Your Own," *Negro World*, May 1, 1920.

91. Postal workers to Hubert Harrison (1920), HHP, box 3, folder 2.

92. Richard B. Moore, "Garvey's Opposition," Richard B. Moore Papers, Schomburg Center for Research in Black Culture, New York, box 11, folder 13.

93. Hill, *MGP*, 3:174.

94. Harrison, "An Open Letter to the Socialist Party."

95. James, *Holding Aloft*, 128.

96. For more on the Brotherhood, see Anderson, *A. Philip Randolph*; Arnesen, *Brotherhoods of Color*; Bates, *Pullman Porters and the Rise of Protest Politics in Black America*; Harris, *Keeping the Faith*.

97. After just two years of independence, the ABB had dissolved into the Communist Party by 1921. This demonstrated once again the precarity and difficulties of holding together an independent Black Marxist organization. The move into the Communist Party set the stage for a third generation of Black efforts to fight racism inside a white "class-conscious" organization. For more on the ABB, see Hill's introduction to *Crusader*, vol. 1, and Makalani, *In the Cause of Freedom*, especially chap. 1.

98. Foner, *American Socialism and Black Americans*, 335–36; Hill, *MGP*, 1:221n2; James, "Being Red and Black in Jim Crow America," 373; Anderson, *A. Philip Randolph*, 142–43.

99. James, *Holding Aloft*, 186.

100. Moses, *Golden Age of Black Nationalism*, 197–98.

101. Certificate of membership for the Universal Negro Improvement Association and African Communities (Imperial) League, J. R. Casimir Papers, Schomburg Center for Research in Black Culture, New York, folder 2. Garvey quoted in Carnegie, "Garvey and the Black Transnation."

102. Turner, *Caribbean Crusaders*, 62.

103. Burkett, *Garveyism as a Religious Movement*.

Chapter 8

1. Wilfred Domingo to Alain Locke, September 21, 1925, Alain Locke Papers, box 164-25, folder 28; Hill, *MGP*, 1:528.

2. Wells-Barnett, *Crusade for Justice*, 381.

3. Hubert Harrison, diary entry, May 24, 1920, HHP, box 9, folder 1, reprinted in Perry, *Reader*, 191–93.

4. Harrison, diary entry, May 24, 1920; Hubert Harrison, "re: Garvey and U.N.I.A.," c. 1922, HHP, box 4, folder 61.

5. Martin, *Race First*, 152.

6. Harrison, diary entry, May 24, 1920. Historian Judith Stein concurred with the claim made by Harrison and others that the BSL did not technically own all the ships it claimed to own. For more on the mismanagement of the BSL and its critics, see Stein, *World of Marcus Garvey*, chaps. 4, 5, and 10, and also Perry, *Hubert Harrison*, 2: chap. 12; Hubert Harrison, "Convention Bill of Rights and Elections" (diary entry), August 31, 1920, HHP, box 9, folder 1; Hubert Harrison, "Marcus Garvey at the Bar of United States Justice," *Associated Negro Press*, c. early July 1923, reprinted in Perry, *Reader*, 194–99.

7. Hill, *MGP*, 2:499.

8. Hill, *MGP*, 2:577–78, 682–83; Perry, *Reader*, 191.

9. Hubert Harrison, diary entry, August 28, 1920, HHP, box 9, folder 1. Biographical information on McGuire taken from Hill, *MGP*, 2:508n1.

10. Report by Special Agent P-138 8-14-20, DNA RG 65, file OG 329359, TD; Harrison, "Convention Bill of Rights and Elections."

11. Harrison, "Convention Bill of Rights and Elections."
12. Harrison, "Convention Bill of Rights and Elections."
13. Harrison, "Convention Bill of Rights and Elections."
14. Harrison, "Convention Bill of Rights and Elections." On her advocacy of reparations, see *Negro World*, July 17, 1920, 9; Seraile, "Henrietta Vinton Davis and the Garvey Movement."
15. Harrison, "Convention Bill of Rights and Elections."
16. Hubert Harrison, diary entry, September 4, 1920; Hubert Harrison, diary entry, April 7, 1921, HHP, box 9.
17. "A Walking Encyclopedia," *Negro World*, September 4, 1920, UNIA Papers, miscellaneous box.
18. Bennett, *Wade in the Water*, 210.
19. Hill, *MGP*, 1:xlviii.
20. Hill and Bair, *Marcus Garvey*, xv.
21. Hill, *MGP*, 1:9. In 1920, the NAACP had 91,203 members. This suggests it was larger than the UNIA, though of course without the international spread of Garvey's organization. Kellogg, *NAACP*, 137. For statistics on UNIA branches outside the United States, see Martin, *Race First*, 16.
22. Garvey, *Garvey and Garveyism*, 265.
23. Harrison, diary entry, August 28, 1920.
24. Harrison, "Marcus Garvey at the Bar of United States Justice"; Madarikan Deniyi, "African Redemption Fund Is Fraud: Negroes in America Are Warned to Beware of Fakers," September 1, 1921, reprinted in Hill, *MGP*, 4:1–2.
25. Hubert Harrison, diary entry, December 11, 1920, HHP, box 9.
26. Harrison, diary entry, December 11, 1920. Garvey movement historian Tony Martin concurred with this picture of Garvey's early years in the United States as making do with meager rations. Martin, *Amy Ashwood*, 51.
27. Harrison, "Convention Bill of Rights and Elections."
28. Harrison, "re Garvey and U.N.I.A."; Rolinson, *Grassroots Garveyism*, 69, 141.
29. Richard B. Moore, untitled, Richard B. Moore Papers, box 11, folder 13.
30. Hubert Harrison, "Mr. J.O.H. Cosgrave, Sunday World," letter, November 13, 1921, HHP, box 2, folder 16.
31. Stein's chapter "The UNIA Goes South: Garvey and the Ku Klux Klan" in *The World of Marcus Garvey* gives an overview of this episode.
32. Stein, *World of Marcus Garvey*, 154.
33. Garvey, *Philosophy and Opinions* (1977), 71; Bair, "True Women, Real Men," 158.
34. Dagnini, "Marcus Garvey: A Controversial Figure."
35. Garvey quote from *Negro World*, August 8, 1922, reprinted in Hill, *MGP*, 6:41n1; also *Negro World*, June 14, 1924, quoted in Hill and Bair, *Marcus Garvey*, liv; Diner, "Draw Together by Self-Interest," 33.
36. Hill, "Black Zionism," 49.
37. Vladimir Jabotinsky, "O Zheleznoi Stene" [The iron wall], *Rassvyet* (November 1923), quoted in Moshé Machover, "Israelis and Palestinians: Conflict and Resolution" (Barry Amiel and Norman Melburn Trust Annual Lecture (London), November 30, 2006).
38. Hubert Harrison, "The Brown Man Leads the Way, Part 1, Review of *The New World of Islam* by Lothrop Stoddard," *Negro World*, October 29, 1921; Perry, *Reader*, 290.
39. Harrison, "re Garvey and U.N.I.A."

40. For more, see Sundiata, *Brothers and Strangers*.

41. Hill, *MGP*, 2:667.

42. Harrison, "re Garvey and U.N.I.A"; Hill, *MGP*, 1:lx.

43. Manoedi, *Garvey and Africa*, reprinted in Hill, *MGP*, 9:651; Harrison, "re Garvey and U.N.I.A."; Sundiata, "Garvey Aftermath," 83; UNIA program reproduced in A. Garvey, *Garvey and Garveyism*, 11; Harrison, *When Africa Awakes*, 33–35.

44. Hill, *MGP*, 1:210–11n1. In 1904, the National Negro Liberty Party (NNLP), which ran George Edwin Taylor as its candidate for president, emerged out of "at least a decade of efforts at state and regional levels across the south to secure pensions for ex-slaves" and general Black dissatisfaction with the Democrats and Republicans. It was the first all-Black political party in US history. Though the NNLP did not last long, it certainly paved the way for the similar effort by Harrison some sixteen years later. For a history of Taylor and the NNLP, see Mouser, *For Labor, Race, and Liberty*, 108.

45. Perry, *Reader*, 148.

46. Alexander, *T. Thomas Fortune*, xviii.

47. Harrison here was speaking in 1912, before Woodrow Wilson had been elected. Harrison, *When Africa Awakes*, 42.

48. Harrison, "Notes on Lincoln and Liberty: Fact vs. Fiction," February 10, 1920, HHP, box 13, folder 3; Hubert Harrison, "Lincoln and Liberty: Fact versus Fiction; Chapter Two. Lincoln Not an Abolitionist, Republicans Opposed Abolitionist Doctrine," *Negro World*, March 12, 1921; Hubert Harrison, "Lincoln and Liberty: Fact versus Fiction; Chapter Three. Lincoln and Republican Party Favor Perpetual Slavery," *Negro World*, March 19, 1921, reprinted in Perry, *Reader*, 130; Bennett, *Forced into Glory*.

49. Harrison, *When Africa Awakes*, 45.

50. Hubert Harrison, "The New Policies for the New Negro," *The Voice*, September 4, 1917, HHP, box 5, folder 35, reprinted in *When Africa Awakes*, 40, emphasis in original.

51. Fox, *Guardian of Boston*, 36–37.

52. Hill, *MGP*, 2:254n2.

53. Hubert Harrison, "A Negro for President," *Negro World*, June 19, 1920, reprinted in *When Africa Awakes*, 44.

54. Hill, *MGP*, 2:254n2.

55. William Bridges to Hubert Harrison, September 3, 1920, HHP, box 1, folder 9.

56. Hubert Harrison to T. W. Swann, September 11, 1920, HHP, box 2, folder 24.

57. Hill, *MGP*, 1:l.

58. Hill, *MGP*, 2:254n2.

59. "Negro Party Brands Bridges as a Faker," *Negro World*, November 6, 1920, HHP, box 13, folder 7.

60. Taylor ran unsuccessfully as the presidential candidate for the short-lived National Negro Civil Liberty Party. Mouser, *For Labor, Race, and Liberty*.

61. Of course, various other efforts at building Black political power took place in the 1960s, like the Mississippi Freedom Democratic Party and the Black Panther Party. Ali, *In the Balance of Power*, 141; Walton, *Black Political Parties*, 199.

62. Burkett, *Garveyism as a Religious Movement*, 31.

63. Wilfred A. Domingo, "In the Claws of the American Eagle," *The Emancipator*, March 27, 1920; Hubert Harrison, "Help Wanted for Hayti" and "The Cracker in the Caribbean," *Negro World*, 1920, reprinted in *When Africa Awakes*.

64. Harrison, "Cracker in the Caribbean," in *When Africa Awakes*, 105–8; Hubert Harrison, "Hands across the Sea," *Negro World*, September 10, 1921, reprinted in Perry, *Reader*, 238.

65. Harrison, "Hands across the Sea."

66. Lewis, *W. E. B. Du Bois: Biography of a Race*, 352.

67. Harrison, "Cracker in the Caribbean."

68. UNIA Philadelphia Division Records, Schomburg Center for Research in Black Culture, box 1, Letters folder.

69. [Joseph St. Prix?], untitled notebook page, November 9, 1920, UNIA Philadelphia Division Papers, Letters folder; Handwritten note, UNIA Philadelphia Division Records, box 1.

70. Hubert Harrison, letter, December 1, 1920, UNIA Philadelphia Division Records, box 1.

71. Joseph St. Prix to Hubert Harrison, November 29, 1920, UNIA Philadelphia Division Records, box 1.

72. Hubert Harrison to Joseph St. Prix, December 1, 1920, UNIA Philadelphia Division Records, box 1.

73. Garvey, *Philosophy and Opinions* (1923), 67–68.

74. Frank R. Crosswaith, "Building a Negro Empire," *The Emancipator*, April 10, 1920.

75. "Claude M'Kay, African Poet, Made Co-Editor," *Chicago Defender*, April 2, 1921; McKay, *A Long Way from Home*, 89.

76. Hill, *MGP*, 2:681–82n1; Hill, *Crusader*, 1:xli. For a detailed account of this conjuncture of Harrison and the Black Reds' relationship to Garvey, see Hill's introduction to *The Crusader*, and Perry, *Hubert Harrison*, 2: chap 10. For Briggs's account of the ABB experience at the 1921 UNIA convention, see Briggs, "Negro Convention."

77. Hubert Harrison, "Wanted—A Colored International," *Negro World*, May 28, 1921.

78. Harrison, diary entry, September 4, 1920; Harrison, diary entry, April 7, 1921; Hill, *MGP*, 4:13, 14n3.

79. Martin, *Literary Garveyism*, 43.

80. Martin, *Literary Garveyism*, 93; Hubert Harrison, "The Emperor Jones," *Negro World*, June 4, 1921.

81. Hodge Kirnon, article, *The Promoter*, September 1920, 8.

82. Emphasis in original, Hughes, *Collected Poems*, 138.

83. Stein, *World of Marcus Garvey*, 154; Harrison, "Mr. J.O.H. Cosgrave, Sunday World"; New Orleans Garvey quote taken from Stein, *World of Marcus Garvey*, 154; Stein's chapter "The UNIA Goes South: Garvey and the Ku Klux Klan" gives an overview of this subject. Randolph, "U.N.I.A.," reprinted in Cronon, *Marcus Garvey*, 117.

84. Hill, *MGP*, 5:7–8.

85. Moore, "Critics and Opponents of Marcus Garvey," 230–31; Garvey quoted in Hill, *MGP*, 5:8. Eason's murder is covered in Hill, *MGP*, vol. 5. Kofey's murder is covered in vol. 7. Joseph St. Prix, UNIA Philadelphia Division Records, scrapbook. On Alfred Levy's murder, see Hill, *MGP*, 7:406–9.

86. Martin, *Race First*, 315–20; Harrison, "Marcus Garvey at the Bar of United States Justice."

87. For more on the trial, see Stein, *World of Marcus Garvey*, chap. 10; Harrison, "Marcus Garvey at the Bar of United States Justice"; Perry, *Hubert Harrison*, 2: chap. 14.

88. Harrison, "Marcus Garvey at the Bar of United States Justice."

89. Hubert Harrison, diary entries for March 1925, HHP, box 9.

90. Hubert Harrison, diary entry, March 2, 1925, HHP, box 9; Yard, *Amy Ashwood Garvey*, 75. For more detail on Harrison's relationship with Amy Ashwood and his role in the Garvey's divorce trial see Perry, *Hubert Harrison*, 2: chaps. 16 and 18.

91. Harrison, *When Africa Awakes*, 55.

92. Ferris, "UNIA," 9.

93. Hill, *MGP*, 1:284, 287, 305, 527–28.

94. Garvey, *Philosophy and Opinions* (1923), 72.

95. Moses, *Classical Black Nationalism*, 31–34.

96. Hill, *MGP*, 1:lxxix–lxxx.

Chapter 9

1. David Levering Lewis offers 1919 to 1934. Lewis, *When Harlem Was in Vogue*, xvi. For Nathaniel Huggins it was "between World War I and the Great Depression." Huggins, *Voices from the Harlem Renaissance*, 3. George Hutchinson periodizes it from 1918 to 1937. Hutchinson, *Cambridge Companion to the Harlem Renaissance*, 7.

2. Huggins, *Voices from the Harlem Renaissance*, 3–4.

3. Jimoh, "Mapping the Terrain of Black Writing."

4. Locke, *New Negro*, xxvii.

5. Martin, *Literary Garveyism*; Martin, *African Fundamentalism*; Dawahare, *Nationalism, Marxism, and African American Literature*; Maxwell, *New Negro, Old Left*; Foley, *Spectres of 1919*, 198–99. In an otherwise excellent book, Foley erroneously claims Harrison believed that race "does not change essentially with changes of economic system. It is deeper than any class feeling and will outlast the capitalist system." This was in fact not a quote from Harrison but from the Majority Report of the Committee on Immigration from the Socialist Party's 1912 national convention. Foley, *Spectres of 1919*, 103. See Harrison, "Race First versus Class First," in *When Africa Awakes*, 79–82.

6. Harris and Molesworth, *Alain L. Locke*, 12.

7. Harris and Molesworth, *Alain L. Locke*, 295, 2.

8. Charles Johnson to Hubert Harrison, March 13, 1924, HHP, box 2, folder 53; Stewart, *New Negro*, 409.

9. Foley, *Spectres of 1919*, 205.

10. Kellogg, "Harlem: Mecca of the New Negro."

11. Paul Kellogg to Alain Locke, February 5, 1925, Alain Locke Papers (hereafter ALP), box 164-88, folder 6.

12. Alain Locke, "Correspondence with Publisher," ALP, box 164-122, folder 12.

13. Harris and Molesworth, *Alain L. Locke*, 11.

14. Locke, "High Cost of Prejudice," 501.

15. Paul Kellogg to Alain Locke, March 20, 1925, ALP, box 164-88, folder 6.

16. Hubert Harrison, "On a Certain Condescension in White Publishers [Part I]," *Negro World*, March 4, 1922.

17. Paul Kellogg to Alain Locke, February 20, 1925, ALP, box 164-88, folder 6.

18. Alain Locke, "The *Survey Graphic* Harlem Issue Prospectus," c. 1924, ALP, box 164-115, folder 9.

19. Foley, *Spectres of 1919*, 225.

20. Alain Locke, notes on the *Survey Graphic* Harlem number, ALP, box 164-115, folder 10.

21. Stewart, *New Negro*, 412, 414.

22. Claude McKay to Alain Locke, August 1, 1926, ALP, box 164, Correspondence.

23. H. L. Mencken, "The New Negro," *American Mercury* (February 1926), ALP, box 164-122, folder 19, Reviews of *New Negro*.

24. "Book Review," *New York Times*, December 20, 1925, ALP, box 164-122, folder 19.

25. Locke, "Art or Propaganda?," 12.

26. Du Bois, "Criteria of Negro Art."

27. Zinn, *You Can't Be Neutral on a Moving Train*.

28. Locke, "Harlem."

29. Locke, "Art or Propaganda?"

30. McKay, *A Long Way from Home*, 241.

31. Hubert Harrison, "'Homo Africanus Harlemi,' a Review of *Nigger Heaven* by Carl Van Vechten," *Amsterdam News*, September 1, 1926.

32. Harrison, "Homo Africanus Harlemi."

33. Bernard, *Carl Van Vechten and the Harlem Renaissance*, 136, 146–47; Coleman, *Carl Van Vechten and the Harlem Renaissance*, 111, 149, 129.

34. Bernard, *Carl Van Vechten and the Harlem Renaissance*, 83–103, 119.

35. Hubert Harrison, "*Nigger Heaven*—A Review of the Reviews," *Amsterdam News*, November 13, 1926.

36. Harrison, "*Nigger Heaven*—A Review of the Reviews."

37. Lewis, *When Harlem Was in Vogue*, 179.

38. Huggins, *Harlem Renaissance*, 128.

39. Hubert Harrison, "Cabaret School of Negro Writers Does Not Represent One-Tenth of Race: Dr. Hubert H. Harrison Takes Shot at 'Midnight Maniacs from Greenwich Village' in Article," *Pittsburgh Courier*, May 28, 1927.

40. Harrison, "Cabaret School of Negro Writers."

41. Harrison, "Cabaret School of Negro Writers."

42. Harrison, "Cabaret School of Negro Writers."

43. Harrison, "Cabaret School of Negro Writers."

44. Harrison, "Cabaret School of Negro Writers."

45. Harrison, "Cabaret School of Negro Writers."

46. Hubert Harrison, "'No Negro Literary Renaissance' Says Well-Known Writer," *Pittsburgh Courier*, March 12, 1927.

47. Harrison, "*Nigger Heaven*—A Review of the Reviews."

48. Harrison, "No Negro Literary Renaissance."

49. Harrison, "No Negro Literary Renaissance"; Perry, *Reader*, 291.

50. Hughes, *Big Sea*, 236.

51. John P. Davis, "No Negro Renaissance?," *Pittsburgh Courier*, April 2, 1927.

52. Harrison, "No Negro Literary Renaissance"; Thurman, *Infants of the Spring*, 85; Lewis, *When Harlem Was in Vogue*, 175, 179.

53. Harrison, "*Nigger Heaven*—A Review of the Reviews"; Perry, *Hubert Harrison*, 1:6; Benson, "Literary Genius of Hubert Harrison"; Harrison, "No Negro Literary Renaissance"; Harrison, "Cabaret School of Negro Writers."

54. Hughes, *Big Sea*, 228.

55. Brown, "New Negro in Literature," 57.

56. Thurman, *Infants of the Spring*, 137.

57. Davis, "Growing Up in the New Negro Renaissance," 435.

58. Davis, "Growing Up in the New Negro Renaissance."

59. Davis, "Growing Up in the New Negro Renaissance."

60. Davis, "Growing Up in the New Negro Renaissance," 432.

61. Hughes, *Big Sea*, 228, 225.

62. Hughes, *Big Sea*, 228, 229; Lewis, *When Harlem Was in Vogue*, 108.

63. Hughes, *Big Sea*, 229.

64. Perry, *Hubert Harrison*, 1:88; Turner, *Caribbean Crusaders*, 28.

65. Hubert Harrison, "The Roots of Power," *Boston Chronicle*, June 21, 1924.

66. Hubert Harrison, "Harlem's Neglected Opportunities: Twin Source of Gin and Genius, Poetry and Pajama Parties," *Amsterdam News*, November 30, 1927.

67. McKay, *A Long Way from Home*, 43.

68. Harrison, "No Negro Literary Renaissance."

69. Locke, "1928: A Retrospective Review," reprinted in Vincent, *Voices of a Black Nation*, 353–56.

70. Locke, "1928: A Retrospective Review."

71. Hall, "Perspectives on Interwar Culture."

72. Trotsky, *Stalin School of Falsification*, 16–17.

73. For a concise overview of this process, see Chris Harman, "How the Revolution Was Lost," International Socialism (1st series), no. 30 (Autumn 1967), https://www.marxists.org/archive/harman/1967/xx/revlost.htm.

74. In the 1920s and 1930s, Trotsky analyzed the material conditions underlying the degeneration of the Russian Revolution and the emergence of the Stalinist bureaucracy in terms of a number of factors. See, for example, Trotsky, *Revolution Betrayed*; Hallas, *Trotsky's Marxism*.

75. McKay, *Harlem: Negro Metropolis*, 248.

76. Chinitz, "New Harlem Renaissance Studies"; Hatch, *Lost Plays of the Harlem Renaissance*; Lamothe, *Inventing the New Negro*; Watts, *Hearing the Hurt*; Glasrud and Wintz, *The Harlem Renaissance in the American West*; Briggs, *The New Negro in the Old South*; Makalani and Baldwin, *Escape from New York*.

77. Maxwell, *New Negro, Old Left*.

78. Smethurst, "Langston Hughes in the 1930s," in *The New Red Negro*.

79. Huggins, *Voices from the Harlem Renaissance*, 5; Lewis, *When Harlem Was in Vogue*, xv; Gates and Jarrett, *The New Negro*, 6.

80. Dawahare, "Spectre of Radicalism," 68.

Conclusion

1. "Some Facts on Race Business," *New York Age*, August 17, 1916.

2. "Celebrated Harlem Mass Leader Dies after Operation," *Amsterdam [News (?)]*, (microfilm) vertical file, Schomburg Center for Research in Black Culture, New York.

3. Perry, *Hubert Harrison*, 2:749.

4. "Doctor Kills Self by Poison after a Bridge Game Row," *Chicago Tribune*, November 19, 1934.

5. Jeffrey Perry interview with Aida Richardson (question #66), August 4, 1983, Jeffrey B. Perry Collection of Hubert Harrison Research Materials, box 13.

6. "Hubert Harrison Dies: Harlem Scholar Succumbs after 'Minor' Operation," *Amsterdam News*, December 21, 1927.

7. "Hubert H. Harrison," *Pittsburgh Courier*, December 31, 1927.

8. "The Death of Hubert Harrison," *New York Times*, December 31, 1927.

9. "Celebrated Harlem Mass Leader Dies after Operation," *New York News*, December 24, 1927.

10. Benson, "Literary Genius of Hubert Harrison."

11. Hodge Kirnon, "Kirnon Flays Monthly Race Magazines," *New York News*, February 28, 1928.

12. Edgar M. Grey, "Why Great Negroes Die Young," *New York News*, December 31, 1927.

13. "Hubert Harrison Dies."

14. "Lament Death of Dr. Hubert Harrison: Eulogized by Several Who Knew His Life and Worth," *Amsterdam News*, December 28, 1927.

15. "Hang Hubert Harrison's Portrait in Library," *Amsterdam News*, September 10, 1930.

16. Hubert Harrison, "Plan to Write a 'History of the Negro in America'" (diary entry), November 25, 1907, HHP, box 9, folder 1.

17. Trouillot, *Silencing the Past*, 28–29.

18. Harrison, *When Africa Awakes*, 8.

19. Hubert Harrison, "On Praise" (autograph manuscript), April 8, 1920, HHP, box 5, folder 46.

20. Ransby, *Ella Baker and the Black Freedom Movement*.

21. West, *Black Prophetic Fire*, 216n21.

22. Des Verney, *Arthur Alfonso Schomburg*, 127.

23. Rogers, *World's Great Men of Color*, 2:611.

24. Hubert Harrison, "White People versus Negroes: Being the Story of a Great Book," *Negro World*, January 7, 1922.

25. Harrison, "The Real Negro Problem," HHP, box 6, folder 5; Marx and Engels, *Marx/Engels Selected Works, Vol. One*, chap. 2.

26. Orwell, *1984*, 88.

27. Chomsky and Herman, *Manufacturing Consent*.

28. Jonnes, *Empires of Light*, chap. 13.

29. Tesla, *My Inventions*, chap. 5.

30. Seifer, *Tesla: Wizard at War*, chap. 6; Carlson, *Tesla*, 358, 360; Seifer, *Tesla: Wizard at War*, 63.

31. Steven Aftergood, "Invention Secrecy Hits Recent High," Federation of American Scientists, October 31, 2018, https://fas.org/publication/invention-secrecy-2018; H. L. Mourning, J. C. Morris, and Bert Convey, "Armed Services Patent Advisory Board 'ASPAB' Patent Security Category Review List [Originally Classified Confidential—Now Unclassified]," January 1971, Project on Government Secrecy, https://sgp.fas.org/othergov/invention/pscrl.pdf. For more on the history of energy suppression, see Gary Vesperman, "95 Cases of Energy Suppression," in *Energy Invention Suppression Cases*, September 3, 2007, www.padrak.com/vesperman/Vesperman_2.doc.

32. Hubert Harrison, "The World We Live In," *Boston Chronicle*, December 1, 1924, HHP, box 13, folder 4.

33. Another example: Maxwell's equations form the core scientific theory behind the electrical engineering (EE) principles taught in universities. In other words, they have excluded from the curriculum a priori the kind of science and mathematics that undergirded the greatest technological achievements of Nikola Tesla. This ensured that no plucky young EE major would be taught the scientific, theoretical, or technical means by which one could dream of engineering new energy technologies. And then if such a technology *is* stumbled upon—in spite of the official ban imposed by the scientific establishment—it gets bought out and "blackshelved" by industry or sequestered under the government's prohibited "patent security list." For more on Tesla's physics in relation to Maxwell, Einstein, electromagnetism, and gravity, see Seifer, *Tesla: Wizard at War*, chaps. 17 and 18.

34. Harrison, "The World We Live In."

35. Hubert Harrison, "Science and Race Prejudice," *Boston Chronicle*, February 2, 1924, HHP, box 13, folder 4; Hubert Harrison, review of *The Negro in American Life*, by Jerome Dowd, *Pittsburgh Courier*, December 2, 1927, HHP, box 4, folder 18.

36. Oscar Benson, "Literary Genius of Hubert Harrison," *New York News*, December 24, 1927.

37. Harrison, *When Africa Awakes*, 93.

38. Hubert Harrison, "'Superior'—To Whom?," *Boston Chronicle*, March 5, 1924.

39. Harrison, "'Superior'—To Whom?"

40. Anderson, *A. Philip Randolph*, 21.

41. Vincent, "Garveyite Parents of Malcolm X"; Perry, *Hubert Harrison*, 1:5.

42. Ali, *In the Balance of Power*, 141; Walton, *Black Political Parties*, 199.

43. Garvey, *Black Power in America*, 33.

44. Stevens, "Early Political History of Wilfred A. Domingo."

45. James, "Being Red and Black in Jim Crow America," 382.

46. Hubert Harrison to Lothrop Stoddard, July 21, 1921, HHP, box 2, folder 19.

47. Hubert Harrison, "The Red Record of Radicalism," c. 1927, HHP, box 6, folder 7; Harrison, "Rockefeller and the 'Reds,'" 3; Hubert Harrison, advertisement for upcoming talks, April 1927, HHP, box 16, folder 14.

48. "Two Colored Men Speak at Court House," *The Vincennes* (Indianapolis), October 16, 1924, HHP, box 13, folder 5.

49. "Lament Death of Dr. Hubert Harrison."

50. Diop, *Civilization or Barbarism*, 3–4.

51. Proverb taken from "In Memoriam: Dr. Ivan Van Sertima (1935–2009)," Rutgers University Africana Studies, last accessed November 4, 2024, https://africanastudies.rutgers.edu/people/core-faculty/faculty/90-ivan-van-sertima-in-memoriam-1935-2009.

52. Davis, "Eulogy for Malcolm X."

Bibliography

Primary Sources
Manuscript and Archival Sources

Boston, MA
  Egbert Ethelred Brown Papers, Unitarian Universalist Association Archives
New York, NY
  Hubert H. Harrison Papers, Rare Book and Manuscript Library, Columbia University
  Jeffrey B. Perry Collection of Hubert Harrison Research Materials, Rare Book and Manuscript Library, Columbia University
  John Henrik Clarke Papers, Schomburg Center for Research in Black Culture
  J. R. Casimir Papers, Schomburg Center for Research in Black Culture
  New York Call Archives, New York Public Library
  Richard B. Moore Papers, Schomburg Center for Research in Black Culture
  Socialist Party Papers of Local New York, New York University
  Universal Negro Improvement Association (UNIA) Papers, Schomburg Center for Research in Black Culture
Washington, DC
  Alain Locke Papers, Howard University
  Major Walter Loving Papers, Howard University
  National Archives

Books and Book Chapters

Butler, Smedley D. *War Is a Racket*. New York: Round Table Press, 1935.
Debs, Eugene V. "Capitalism and Socialism." In *Labor & Freedom*. St. Louis: Phil Wagner, 1916. www.marxists.org/archive/debs/works/1912/1912-capsoc.htm.
———. *Writings and Speeches of Eugene V. Debs*. New York: Hermitage Press, 1948.
Flynn, Elizabeth Gurley. *Sabotage: The Conscious Withdrawal of the Workers' Industrial Efficiency*. Chicago: IWW Publishing Bureau, 1917.
Harrison, Hubert. *When Africa Awakes*. 1920; Baltimore: Black Classics Press, 1997.
Hill, Robert A., ed. *The Marcus Garvey and Universal Negro Improvement Association Papers* (13 vols). Berkeley: University of California Press, 1983.
Huggins, Willis N., and John G. Jackson. *A Guide to Studies in African History: Directive Lists for Schools and Clubs*. New York: Federation of History Clubs, 1934.
Lenin, V. I. *Imperialism, the Highest Stage of Capitalism*. Petrograd, 1917.
Locke, Alain. *The New Negro: An Interpretation*. New York: Boni, 1925.
Locke, Alain, and Jeffrey C. Stewart, eds. *The Critical Temper of Alain Locke: A Selection of His Essays on Art and Culture*. New York: Garland Publishing, 1983.

Moore, Richard B. "The Critics and Opponents of Marcus Garvey." In *Marcus Garvey and the Vision of Africa*, edited by John Henrik Clarke. New York: Vintage Books, 1974.

Scarborough, William Sanders, with Michele V. Ronnick, eds. *The Works of William Sanders Scarborough: Black Classicist and Race Leader*. Oxford: Oxford University Press, 2006.

Schomburg, Arthur Alfonso. *Racial Integrity: A Plea for the Establishment of a Chair of Negro History in Our Schools and Colleges, Etc.* New York: August Bernier, 1913.

———. *Racial Integrity: A Plea for the Establishment of a Chair of Negro History in Our Schools and Colleges, Etc.* Baltimore: Black Classics Press, 1979.

Schopenhauer, Arthur. *The Essays of Arthur Schopenhauer*. Translated by T. Bailey Saunders. Brooklyn: Neidorf Book Company, 1914.

Trotsky, Leon. *The Bolsheviki and World Peace*. New York: Boni and Liveright, 1918.

———. *First Five Years of the Communist International Vol. 1*. New York: Monad Press, 1972.

———. *History of the Russian Revolution*. Chicago: Haymarket Books, 2008.

———. *My Life: An Attempt at an Autobiography*. New York: C. Scribner and Sons, 1930.

———. *The Revolution Betrayed: What Is the Soviet Union and Where Is It Going?* Detroit: Labor Publications, 1991.

———. *The Stalin School of Falsification*. New York: Pathfinder Press, 1937.

———. "Theses of the Third World Congress on the International Situation and the Tasks of the Comintern." In *First Five Years of the Communist International*, vol. 1. London: New Park, 1973.

Walker, Edwin C. *Who Is the Enemy: Anthony Comstock or You?* New York: E. C. Walker, 1903.

Washington, Booker T. *The Negro Problem: A Series of Articles by Representative American Negroes of Today*. Los Angeles: Hard Press, 2012.

———. *A New Negro for a New Century*. Chicago: American Publishing House, 1900.

———. *Up from Slavery*. New York: Limited Editions Club, 1970.

Wells-Barnett, Ida B. *The Reason Why the Colored American Is Not in the World's Columbian Exposition*. 1893; Champaign: University of Illinois Press, 1999.

———. *Crusade for Justice: The Autobiography of Ida B. Wells*. Edited by Alfreda Duster. Chicago: University of Chicago Press, 1970.

Wilson, Woodrow. *The New Freedom: A Call for the Emancipation of the Generous Energies of a People*. New York: Doubleday, 1913.

Periodicals

African American Review
AME Church Review
American Historical Review
American National Biography
Amsterdam News
Atlantic Monthly
Birth Control Review
Boston Chronicle
Challenge
Chicago Defender
Clarion
Crisis
Crusader
Emancipator
Historian
Houston Review
International Socialist Review
Journal of World History
Kansas History: A Journal of the Central Plains
Messenger
Modern Quarterly
Nation
Negro World

New Review
New York Call
Pittsburgh Courier

Southwestern Historical
Quarterly
Voice

Western Journal of Black
Studies

Periodical Articles

Asong, Itambo [Hubert Harrison]. "The West African Woman." *New Negro* 4, no. 1 (September 1919).
Benson, Oscar. "Literary Genius of Hubert Harrison," *New York News*, December 24, 1927.
Briggs, Cyril. "The Negro Convention." *Toiler* 4 (October 1, 1921).
Butler, Smedley D. "America's Armed Forces." *Common Sense* 4, no. 11 (November 1935).
Davis, Ossie. "Eulogy for Malcolm X." Faith Temple Church of God In Christ, New York City (February 27, 1965). https://americanradioworks.publicradio.org/features/blackspeech/odavis.html.
Du Bois, W. E. B. "The African Roots of War." *Atlantic Monthly* 115, no. 5 (May 1915).
———. "Black Folks and Birth Control." *Birth Control Review* 16, no. 6 (June 1932).
———. "Close Ranks." *Crisis* 16, no. 3 (July 1918).
———. "Criteria of Negro Art." *Crisis* 32 (October 1926).
———. "Returning Soldiers." *Crisis* 18 (May 1919).
Ferris, William. "The UNIA." *Spokesman* 2 (March 1926).
Harrison, Hubert. "In the Melting Pot (re Herodotus)." *New Negro* 4, no. 2 (October 1919).
———. "The Negro and Socialism: I—The Negro Problem Stated." *New York Call* (November 28, 1911).
———. "Program and Principles of the International Colored Unity League." *Voice of the Negro* 1, no. 1 (April 1927).
———. "Rockefeller and the 'Reds.'" *Voice of the Negro* 1, no. 1 (April 1927).
———. "Socialism and the Negro." *International Socialist Review* 13 (July 1912).
Hine, Darlene Clark. "Rape and the Inner Lives of Black Women in the Middle West." *Signs* 14, no. 4 (Summer 1989).
Hollingsworth Wood, L. "The Urban League Movement." *Journal of Negro History* 9, no. 2 (April 1924).
Kellogg, Paul. "Harlem: Mecca of the New Negro." *Survey Graphic* 53, no. 11 (March 1, 1925).
Kirnon, Hodge. "Contemporary Comment as to H.H." *Negro World*, August 21, 1920.
Kirnon, Hodge. "Hubert Harrison: An Appreciation." *Amsterdam News*, January 4, 1928.
Locke, Alan. "Art or Propaganda?" *Harlem* 1 (November 1928).
———. "Harlem." *Survey Graphic* 53, no. 11 (March 1, 1925).
———. "The High Cost of Prejudice." *Forum* 78 (December 1927).
———. "1928: A Retrospective Review." *Opportunity* (January 1929).
Lowie, Robert. "The Inferior Races." *New Review* (December 1913).
Randolph, Asa Philip. "The U.N.I.A." *Messenger* 5 (August 1923).
Raymond, Ida M. "A Southern Socialist on the Negro Question." *New Review*, no. 12 (December 1913).

Sekyi, Kobina. "Education in West Africa." *New Negro* (October 1919).
Vidrine, Eraste. "Negro Locals." *International Socialist Review* 5, no. 7 (January 1905).
Walker, Edwin C. "Variety vs. Monogamy: An Address before the Ladies' Liberal League of Philadelphia." *Light Bearer Library* 1, no. 1 (December 1897).

Secondary Sources
Books and Book Chapters

Adi, Hakim. *Pan-Africanism and Communism: The Communist International, Africa, and the Diaspora, 1919–1939.* Trenton, NJ: Africa World Press, 2013.

Adi, Hakim, and Marika Sherwood. *Pan-African History: Political Figures from Africa and the Diaspora since 1787.* London: Taylor & Francis, 2003.

Alexander, Shawn Leigh. *T. Thomas Fortune: The Afro American Agitator.* Gainesville: University Press of Florida, 2008.

Ali, Omar. *In the Balance of Power: Independent Black Politics and Third-Party Movements in the United States.* Athens: Ohio University Press, 2020.

Allen, Ernie, Jr. "The New Negro: Explorations in Identity and Social Consciousness." In *1915: The Cultural Moment: The New Politics, the New Woman, the New Psychology, the New Art, and the New Theatre in America*, edited by A. Heller and L. Rudnick. New Brunswick, NJ: Rutgers University Press, 1991.

Allen, Theodore W. *The Invention of the White Race, Volume 2: The Origin of Racial Oppression in Anglo-America.* New York: Verso Press, 2012.

Anderson, Jervis. *A. Philip Randolph: A Biographical Portrait.* New York: Harcourt Brace Jovanovich, 1972.

———. *This Was Harlem: A Cultural Portrait, 1900–1950.* New York: Farrar, Straus and Giroux, 1982.

Anderson, S. E. *The Black Holocaust for Beginners.* Danbury, CT: For Beginners, 1995.

Andrews, William L., Frances Smith Foster, and Trudier Harris. *The Oxford Companion to African American Literature.* New York: Oxford University Press, 1997.

Arnesen, Eric. *Brotherhoods of Color: Black Railroad Workers and the Struggle for Equality.* Cambridge: Harvard University Press, 2001.

———. *Encyclopedia of U.S. Labor and Working-Class History.* New York: Routledge, 2007.

Asad, Talal. *Anthropology and the Colonial Encounter.* New York: Humanities Press, 1973.

Avrich, Paul. *The Modern School Movement.* Princeton, NJ: Princeton University Press, 1980.

Bair, Barbara. "True Women, Real Men: Gender, Ideology, and Social Roles in the Garvey Movement." In *Gendered Domains: Rethinking Public and Private in Women's History*, edited by Dorothy O. Helly and Susan M. Reverby. New York: Cornell University Press, 2018.

Baker, Lee D. *From Savage to Negro: Anthropology and the Construction of Race, 1896–1954.* Berkeley: University of California Press, 1998.

Baldwin, Davarian L., and Minkah Makalani. *Escape from New York: The New Negro Renaissance.* Minneapolis: University of Minnesota Press, 2013.

Banks, William M. *Black Intellectuals: Race and Responsibility in American Life*. New York: W. W. Norton, 1998.
Barash, David P., and Judith Eve Lipton. *The Myth of Monogamy: Fidelity and Infidelity in Animals and People*. New York: Henry Holt and Company, 2002.
Barlow, William. *Voice Over: The Making of Black Radio*. Philadelphia: Temple University Press, 1999.
Bates, Thompkins Beth. *Pullman Porters and the Rise of Protest Politics in Black America, 1925–1945*. Chapel Hill: The University of North Carolina Press, 2001.
Bay, Mia. *To Tell the Truth Freely: The Life of Ida B. Wells*. New York: Hill and Wang, 2009.
Bayor, Ronald H., and Timothy J. Meagher. *The New York Irish*. Baltimore: Johns Hopkins University Press, 1997.
Bennett, Lerone. *Forced into Glory: Abraham Lincoln's White Dream*. Chicago: Johnson Publishing Company, 2000.
———. *Wade in the Water: Great Moments in Black History*. Chicago: Johnson Publishing Company, 1992.
Bernard, Emily. *Carl Van Vechten and the Harlem Renaissance: A Portrait in Black and White*. New Haven, CT: Yale University Press, 2013.
Bernays, Edward L. *Propaganda*. New York: Liveright Publishing Corporation, 1928.
Blain, Keisha N. *Set the World on Fire: Black Nationalist Women and the Global Struggle for Freedom*. Philadelphia: University of Pennsylvania Press, 2018.
Blyden, Edward W. *African Life and Customs*. Baltimore: Black Classic Press, 1994.
Bogues, Anthony. *Black Heretics, Black Prophets: Radical Political Intellectuals*. London: Routledge, 2003.
Brawley, Benjamin. *Africa and the War*. New York: Duffield & Company, 1918.
Briggs, Gabriel A. *The New Negro in the Old South*. New Brunswick, 2015.
Broué, Pierre. *The German Revolution, 1917–1923*. Chicago: Haymarket Books, 2006.
Broun, Heywood, and Margaret Leech. *Anthony Comstock, Roundsman of the Lord*. New York: A. & C. Boni, 1927.
Brown, Leslie. *Upbuilding Black Durham: Gender, Class, and Black Community Development in the Jim Crow South*. Chapel Hill: The University of North Carolina Press, 2009.
Brown, Sterling A. "The New Negro in Literature (1925–1955)." In *The New Negro Thirty Years Afterward: Papers Contributed to the Sixteenth Annual Spring Conference of the Division of the Social Sciences*. Washington, DC: Howard University Press, 1956.
———. *A Son's Return: Selected Essays of Sterling A. Brown*. Boston: Northeastern University Press, 1996.
Bundles, A'Lelia. *On Her Own Ground: The Life and Times of Madam C. J. Walker*. New York: Scribner, 2001.
Burden-Stelly, Charisse. *Black Scare/Red Scare: Theorizing Capitalist Racism in the United States*. Chicago: University of Chicago Press, 2023.
———. *Organize, Fight, Win: Black Communist Women's Political Writings*. New York: Verso, 2022.
Burkett, Randall K. *Black Redemption: Churchmen Speak for the Garvey Movement*. Philadelphia: Temple University Press, 1978.
———. *Garveyism as a Religious Movement: The Institutionalization of Black Civil Religion*. Chicago: American Theological Library Association, 1978.

Bush, Roderick D. *We Are Not What We Seem: Black Nationalism and Class Struggle in the American Century.* New York: New York University Press, 1999.

Bynum, Cornelius L. *A. Philip Randolph and the Struggle for Civil Rights.* Champaign: University of Illinois Press, 2010.

Cameron, Christopher. *Black Freethinkers: A History of African American Secularism.* Evanston: Northwestern University Press, 2019.

Campbell, James T. *Middle Passages: African American Journeys to Africa, 1787-2005.* New York: Penguin Press, 2006.

———. *Songs of Zion: The African Methodist Episcopal Church in the United States and South Africa.* Oxford: Oxford University Press, 1995.

Carlson, Peter. *Roughneck: The Life and Times of Big Bill Haywood.* New York: W. W. Norton, 1983.

Carlson, W. Bernard. *Tesla: Inventor of the Electrical Age.* Princeton, NJ: Princeton University Press, 2015.

Carrigan, William D. *The Making of a Lynching Culture: Violence and Vigilantism in Central Texas, 1836-1916.* Champaign: University of Illinois Press, 2006.

Carroll, Rebecca. *Uncle Tom, or New Negro? African Americans Reflect on Booker T. Washington and "Up from Slavery" One Hundred Years Later,* 1st ed. New York: Broadway Books/Harlem Moon, 2006.

Chomsky, Noam. *Understanding Power: The Indispensable Chomsky.* New York: New Press, 2002.

Chomsky, Noam, and Edward Herman. *Manufacturing Consent: The Political Economy of the Mass Media.* New York: Pantheon Books, 1988.

Clark, Leon E. *Through African Eyes Vol. 1: The Past, The Road to Independence.* New York: Apex Press, 1988.

Clarke, John Henrik. "Introduction." In *When Africa Awakes,* by Hubert Harrison. Baltimore: Black Classics Press, 1997.

———, ed. *Marcus Garvey and the Vision of Africa.* New York: Vintage Books, 1974.

Cliff, Tony. *Lenin,* 4 vols. London: Bookmarks, 1985.

Cole, Peter. *Ben Fletcher: The Life and Times of a Black Wobbly.* Chicago: Charles H. Kerr, 2007.

Coleman, Leon. *Carl Van Vechten and the Harlem Renaissance: A Critical Assessment.* New York: Garland, 1998.

Collins, Patricia Hill. *Black Feminist Thought: Knowledge, Consciousness, and the Politics of Empowerment.* New York: Routledge, 2000.

Cooper, Anna J. *The Voice of Anna Julia Cooper: Including "A Voice from the South" and Other Important Essays, Papers, and Letters.* Lanham: Rowman & Littlefield, 1998.

Cromwell, Adelaide M. *An African Victorian Feminist: The Life and Times of Adelaide Smith Casely Hayford 1848-1960.* Oxford: Taylor & Francis, 2014.

———. *Apropos of Africa: Sentiments of Negro American Leaders on Africa from the 1800s to the 1950s.* London: Cass, 1969.

Cronon, E. David. *Black Moses: The Story of Marcus Garvey and the Universal Negro Improvement Association.* Madison: University of Wisconsin Press, 1955.

Crowder, Ralph L. *John Edward Bruce: Politician, Journalist, and Self-Trained Historian of the African Diaspora.* New York: New York University Press, 2004.

Cruse, Harold. *The Crisis of the Negro Intellectual: A Historical Analysis of the Failure of Black Leadership.* New York: Morrow, 1967; New York: New York Review Books, 2005.

Curry, Tommy J. *The Man-Not: Race, Class, Genre, and the Dilemmas of Black Manhood.* Philadelphia: Temple University Press, 2017.

Davenport, Christian. *How Social Movements Die: Repression and Demobilization of the Republic of New Africa.* New York: Cambridge University Press, 2015.

Davies, Carole Boyce. *Left of Karl Marx: The Political Life of Black Communist Claudia Jones.* Durham, NC: Duke University Press, 2008.

Davis, Angela Y. *Blues Legacies and Black Feminism: Gertrude "Ma" Rainey, Bessie Smith, and Billie Holiday.* New York: Pantheon Books, 1998.

———. *Women, Race, and Class.* New York: Vintage Books, 1983.

Davis, Arthur Paul. "Growing Up in the New Negro Renaissance." In *Cavalcade: Negro American Writing from 1760 to the Present*, edited by A. P. Davis and J. S. Redding. Boston: Houghton Mifflin, 1971.

Davis, John P. *The American Negro Reference Book.* Englewood Cliffs, NJ: Prentice-Hall, 1966.

Dawahare, Anthony. *Nationalism, Marxism, and African American Literature between the Wars: A New Pandora's Box.* Jackson: University Press of Mississippi, 2003.

———. "The Spectre of Radicalism in Alain Locke's New Negro." In *Left of the Color Line*, edited by Bill Mullen and James E. Smethurst. Chapel Hill: The University of North Carolina Press, 2003.

De Grazia, Edward. *Girls Lean Back Everywhere: The Law of Obscenity and the Assault on Genius.* New York: Random House, 1992.

D'Emilio, John, and Estelle B. Freedman. *Intimate Matters: A History of Sexuality in America.* Chicago: University of Chicago Press, 1998.

Dewey, John. *John Dewey: The Later Works, Volume 6:1931–1932.* Carbondale: Southern Illinois Press, 1985.

Diner, Hasia R. "Draw Together by Self-Interest: Jewish Representation of Race and Race Relations in the Early Twentieth Century." In *African Americans and Jews in the Twentieth Century: Studies in Convergence and Conflict*, edited by V. P. Franklin, Nancy Grant, Harold Kletnick, and Genna McNeil. Columbia: University of Missouri Press, 1998.

Diop, Cheikh Anta. *Civilization or Barbarism: An Authentic Anthropology.* Brooklyn: Lawrence Hill Books, 1991.

Dixon-Spear, Patricia. *We Want for Our Sisters What We Want for Ourselves: African American Women Who Practice Polygyny by Consent.* Baltimore: Black Classics Press, 2009.

Du Bois, W. E. B. *The American Negro Family.* Atlanta: Atlanta University Press, 1908.

———. *Black Reconstruction in America.* New York: Atheneum, 1992.

———. *The World and Africa: An Inquiry into the Part Which Africa Has Played in World History.* New York: International Publishers, 1965.

Dunbar-Ortiz, Roxanne. *An Indigenous People's History of the United States.* Boston: Beacon Press, 2014.

Duncan, Natanya. *An Efficient Womanhood: Women and the Making of the Universal Negro Improvement Association.* Champaign: University of Illinois Press, 2025.

Edwards, Adolph. *Marcus Garvey, 1887–1940*. London: New Beacon Publications, 1967.
Edwards, Brent Hayes. *The Practice of Diaspora: Literature, Translation, and the Rise of Black Internationalism*. Cambridge: Harvard University Press, 2003.
Edwards, Linda McMurry. *To Keep the Waters Troubled: The Life of Ida B. Wells*. Oxford: Oxford University Press, 1998.
Edwards, W. A. "Garveyism: Organising the Masses or Mass Organisation?" In *Garvey: His Work and Impact*, edited by Rupert Lewis and Patrick E. Bryan. Trenton, NJ: Africa World Press, 1991.
Erichsen, Casper. *The Angel of Death Has Descended Violently among Them: Concentration Camps and Prisoners-of-War in Namibia 1904–1908*. Leiden: African Studies Center, 2005.
Esedebe, Peter Olisanwuche. *Pan-Africanism: The Idea and Movement, 1776–1963*. Washington, DC: Howard University Press, 1982.
Ewing, Adam. *The Age of Garvey: How a Jamaican Activist Created a Mass Movement and Changed Global Black Politics*. Princeton, NJ: Princeton University Press, 2014.
Factor, Robert L. *The Black Response to America: Men, Ideals, and Organization, from Frederick Douglass to the NAACP*. Reading, MA: Addison-Wesley, 1970.
Fax, Elton C. *Garvey: The Story of a Pioneer Black Nationalist*. New York: Dodd, Mead, 1972.
Finkelman, Paul, ed. *Encyclopedia of African American History—1896 to the Present*, 5 vols. Oxford: Oxford University Press, 2009.
Foley, Barbara. *Spectres of 1919: Class and Nation in the Making of the New Negro*. Urbana: University of Illinois Press, 2003.
Foner, Philip. *American Socialism and Black Americans: From the Age of Jackson to World War II*. Westport, CT: Greenwood Press, 1977.
———. *Black Socialist Preacher: The Teachings of Reverend George Washington Woodbey and His Disciple, Reverend G.W. Slater*. San Francisco: Synthesis Publications, 1983.
———. *History of the Labor Movement of the United States*, 10 vols. New York: International Publishers, 1988.
———. *The Industrial Workers of the World, 1905–1917*. New York: International Publishers, 1947.
Foner, Philip, and James Allen. *American Communism and Black Americans: A Documentary History, 1919–1929*. Philadelphia: Temple University Press, 1987.
Fox, Stephen R. *The Guardian of Boston: William Monroe Trotter*. New York: Atheneum, 1970.
Franklin, V. P., Nancy Grant, Harold Kletnick, and Genna McNeil. *African Americans and Jews in the Twentieth Century: Studies in Convergence and Conflict*. Columbia: University of Missouri Press, 1998.
Fredrickson, George M. *The Black Image in the White Mind: The Debate on Afro-American Character and Destiny, 1817–1914*. Middletown, CT: Wesleyan University Press, 1971.
Freire, Paulo. *Pedagogy of the Oppressed*. London: Penguin Books, 1972.
Fried, Albert. *Socialism in America: From the Shakers to the Third International: A Documentary History*, 1st ed. Garden City, NY: Doubleday, 1970.
Gaines, Kevin. "Black Americans' Uplift Ideology as 'Civilizing Mission': Pauline Hopkins on Race and Imperialism." In *Cultures of United States Imperialism*, edited by Amy Kaplan and Donald Pease. Durham, NC: Duke University Press, 1993.

———. *Uplifting the Race: Black Leadership, Politics, and Culture in the Twentieth Century*. Chapel Hill: The University of North Carolina Press, 1996.

Garber, Eric. "A Spectacle in Color: The Lesbian and Gay Subculture of Jazz Age Harlem." In *Hidden from History: Reclaiming the Gay and Lesbian Past*, edited by Martin Duberman, Martha Vicinus, and George Chauncey. New York: NAL Books, 1989.

Garvey, Amy Jacques. *Black Power in America: Marcus Garvey's Impact on Jamaica and Africa; The Power of the Human Spirit*. Kingston: Miguel Lorne Publishers, 1968.

———. *Garvey and Garveyism*. Kingston: United Printers, 1963.

Garvey, Marcus. *Marcus Garvey: Life and Lessons: A Centennial Companion to the Marcus Garvey and Universal Negro Improvement Association Papers*. Edited by Robert A. Hill and Barbara Bair. Berkeley: University of California Press, 1987.

———. *The Marcus Garvey and Universal Negro Improvement Association Papers*, 13 vols. Edited by Robert A. Hill. Berkeley: University of California Press, 1983–.

———. *Philosophy and Opinions of Marcus Garvey*. Edited by Amy Jacques Garvey. New York: Universal Pub. House, 1923.

———. *Philosophy and Opinions of Marcus Garvey, or Africa for the Africans*. Edited by Amy Jacques Garvey. London: Cass, 1977.

Gates, Henry Louis, Jr., and Gene Andrew Jarrett. *The New Negro: Readings on Race, Representation, and African American Culture, 1892–1938*. Princeton, NJ: Princeton University Press, 2007.

Geiss, Imanuel. *The Pan-African Movement: A History of Pan-Africanism in America, Europe, and Africa*. New York: Africana, 1974.

Getachew, Adom. *Worldmaking after Empire: The Rise and Fall of Self-Determination*. Princeton, NJ: Princeton University Press, 2019.

Giddings, Paula. *Ida: A Sword Among Lions: Ida B. Wells and the Campaign Against Lynching*. New York: Amistad, 2008.

———. *When and Where I Enter: The Impact of Black Women on Race and Sex in America*. New York: Morrow, 1984.

Gilmore, Glenda. *Defying Dixie: The Radical Roots of Civil Rights, 1919–1950*, 1st ed. New York: W. W. Norton & Co., 2008.

———. *Gender and Jim Crow: Women and the Politics of White Supremacy in North Carolina, 1896–1920*. Chapel Hill: The University of North Carolina Press, 1996.

Givens, Jarvis R. *Fugitive Pedagogy: Carter G. Woodson and the Art of Black Teaching*. Cambridge: Harvard University Press, 2021.

Glasrud, Bruce, and Cary D. Wintz, eds. *The Harlem Renaissance in the American West: The New Negro's Western Experience*. New York: Routledge, 2011.

Golin, Steve. *The Fragile Bridge: Paterson Silk Strike, 1913*. Philadelphia: Temple University Press, 1988.

Gould, Stephen Jay. *The Panda's Thumb: More Reflections in Natural History*. New York: W. W. Norton, 1980.

Grant, Colin. *Negro with a Hat: The Rise and Fall of Marcus Garvey and His Dream of Mother Africa*. London: Jonathan Cape, 2008.

Grant, Joanne. *Ella Baker: Freedom Bound*. New York: John Wiley, 1998.

Greene, James R. *Grassroots Socialism: Radical Movements in the Southwest, 1895–1943*. Baton Rouge: Louisiana State University, 1978.

Greenidge, Kerri K. *Black Radical: The Life and Times of William Monroe Trotter.* New York: Liveright, 2020.
Hale, Thomas A. "Griot." In *Oxford Encyclopedia of African Thought*, edited by F. Abiola Irele and Biodun Jeyifo. Oxford: Oxford University Press, 2010.
———. *Griots and Griottes: Masters of Words and Music.* Bloomington: Indiana University Press, 1998.
Hall, Perry A. "Perspectives on Interwar Culture: Remapping the New Negro Era." In *Harlem Renaissance Revisited: Politics, Arts, and Letters*, edited by Jeffrey O. G. Ogbar. Baltimore: Johns Hopkins University Press, 2010.
Hallas, Duncan. *The Comintern.* London: Bookmarks, 1985.
———. *Trotsky's Marxism: And Other Essays.* Chicago: Haymarket Books, 2003.
Harding, Neil. *Lenin's Political Thought: Theory and Practice in the Democratic and Socialist Revolutions.* Chicago: Haymarket Books, 2009.
Harlan, Louis. *Booker T. Washington: The Making of a Black Leader, 1856–1901.* New York: Oxford University Press, 1972.
———. *Booker T. Washington: The Wizard of Tuskegee, 1901–1915.* New York: Oxford University Press, 1983.
Harman, Chris. *The Lost Revolution: Germany 1918–1923.* London: Bookmarks, 1982.
Harold, Claudrena. *New Negro Politics in the Jim Crow South.* Athens: University of Georgia Press, 2016.
———. *The Rise and Fall of the Garvey Movement in the Urban South, 1918–1942.* London: Routledge, 2007.
Harris, Abram L. *Race, Radicalism, and Reform: Selected Papers.* New Brunswick, NJ: Transaction Publishers, 1989.
Harris, Lashawn. *Sex Workers, Psychics, and Numbers Runners.* Champaign: University of Illinois Press, 2016.
Harris, Leonard. *Alain L. Locke: Biography of a Philosopher.* Chicago: University of Chicago Press, 2008.
Harris, Leonard, and Charles Molesworth. *Alain L. Locke: The Biography of a Philosopher.* Chicago: University of Chicago Press, 2010.
Harris, William H. *Keeping The Faith: A. Philip Randolph, Milton P. Webster, and the Brotherhood of Sleeping Car Porters, 1925–37.* Champaign: University of Illinois Press, 1991.
Harrison, Hubert. *The Negro and the Nation.* New York: Cosmo-Advocate, 1917.
———. *When Africa Wakes: The "Inside Story" of the Stirrings and Strivings of the New Negro in the Western World.* New York: Porro Press, 1920.
Hartman, Saidiya V. *Scenes of Subjection: Terror, Slavery, and Self-Making in Nineteenth-Century America.* Oxford: Oxford University Press, 1997.
———. *Wayward Lives, Beautiful Experiments: Intimate Histories of Social Upheaval.* New York: W. W. Norton, 2019.
Hatch, James V., and Leo Hamalian, eds. *Lost Plays of the Harlem Renaissance, 1920–1940.* Detroit: Wayne State University Press, 1996.
Heller, Adele, and Lois Palken Rudnick, eds. *1915, The Cultural Moment: The New Politics, the New Woman, the New Psychology, the New Art & the New Theatre in America.* New Brunswick, NJ: Rutgers University Press, 1991.
Hicks, Cheryl D. *Talk with You Like a Woman: African American Women, Justice, and*

Reform in New York, 1890–1935. Chapel Hill: The University of North Carolina Press, 2010.

Higbie, Tobias. *Labor's Mind: A History of Working-Class Intellectual Life*. Chicago: University of Illinois Press, 2018.

Higginbotham, Evelyn Brooks. *Righteous Discontent: The Women's Movement in the Black Baptist Church, 1880–1920*. Cambridge, MA: Harvard University Press, 1993.

Hill, Robert A. "Black Zionism: Marcus Garvey and the Jewish Question." In *African Americans and Jews in the Twentieth Century: Studies in Convergence and Conflict*, edited by V. P. Franklin, Nancy Grant, Harold Kletnick, and Genna McNeil. Columbia: University of Missouri Press, 1998.

———. *The Crusader*. New York: Garland, 1987.

———. "The First England Years and After, 1912–1916." In *Marcus Garvey and the Vision of Africa*, edited by John Henrik Clarke. New York: Vintage Books, 1974.

Hill, Robert A., and Barbara Bair, eds. *Marcus Garvey: Life and Lessons: A Centennial Companion to the Marcus Garvey and Universal Negro Improvement Association Papers*. Los Angeles: University of California, 1987.

Hobbs, T. B. *Democracy Abroad, Lynching at Home: Racial Violence in Florida*. Gainesville: University Press in Florida, 2016.

Hochschild, Adam. *King Leopold's Ghost: A Story of Greed, Terror, and Heroism in Colonial Africa*. New York: Houghton Mifflin, 1998.

Holcomb, Gary Edwards. *Claude McKay, Code Name Sasha: Queer Black Marxism and the Harlem Renaissance*. Gainesville: University Press of Florida, 2007.

Hooker, James R. *Henry Sylvester Williams: Imperial Pan-Africanist*. London: Collings, 1975.

Hopkins, Pauline. *The Magazine Novels of Pauline Hopkins*. New York: Oxford University Press, 1988.

Horne, Gerald, and Charisse Burden-Stelly. *W. E. B. Du Bois: A Life*. New York: Bloomsbury Publishing, 2019.

Howard University Graduate School Division of the Social Sciences. *The New Negro Thirty Years Afterward: Papers Contributed to the Sixteenth Annual Spring Conference . . . April 20, 21, and 22, 1955*. Washington, DC: Howard University Press, 1956.

Howe, Irving. *Socialism and America*, 1st ed. San Diego: Harcourt Brace Jovanovich, 1985.

Hudson, Peter J. *Bankers and Empire: How Wall Street Colonized the Caribbean*. Chicago: University of Chicago Press, 2017.

Huggins, Nathan Irvin. *Harlem Renaissance*. New York: Oxford University Press, 1971.

———. *Voices from the Harlem Renaissance*. New York: Oxford University Press, 1995.

Huggins, Willis N., and John G. Jackson. *An Introduction to African Civilizations, with Main Currents in Ethiopian History*. New York: Bloomsbury Academic, 1969.

Hughes, Langston. *The Big Sea: An Autobiography*. New York: Farrar, Straus and Giroux, 2015.

———. *The Collected Poems of Langston Hughes*. Edited by Arnold Rampersad and David Roessel. New York: Vintage Books, 1995.

Hunter, Tera. *To 'Joy My Freedom: Black Women's Lives and Labors after the Civil War*. Cambridge, MA: Harvard University Press, 1997.

Hutchinson, George. *The Cambridge Companion to the Harlem Renaissance.* Cambridge: Cambridge University Press, 2007.
Ikonné, Chidi. *From DuBois to Van Vechten: The Early New Negro Literature, 1903–1926.* Westport, CT: Greenwood Press, 1981.
Irele, F. Abiola, and Biodun Jeyifo, eds. *The Oxford Encyclopedia of African Thought.* Oxford: Oxford University Press, 2010.
Jacobs, Sylvia M. *The African Nexus: Black American Perspectives on the European Partitioning of Africa, 1880–1920.* Westport, CT: Greenwood Press, 1981.
Jackson, John. *Christianity before Christ.* Brattleboro, VT: Echo Point Books & Media, 2020.
Jackson, John G. *Ethiopia and the Origin of Civilization.* Baltimore: Black Classic Press, 1985.
———. *Hubert Henry Harrison: The Black Socrates.* Austin: American Atheist Press, 1987.
———. *Pagan Origins of the Christ Myth.* Eastford, CT: Martino Publishing, 2016.
Jackson, Major. *Countee Cullen: Collected Poems.* New York: Library of America, 2013.
James, C. L. R. *The Black Jacobins: Toussaint L'Ouverture and the San Domingo Revolution.* New York: Vintage Books, 1963.
———. *A History of Negro Revolt.* London: Fact, 1938.
James, Joy. *Transcending the Talented Tenth: Black Leaders and American Intellectuals.* New York: Routledge, 1997.
James, Winston. "Being Red and Black in Jim Crow America." In *Time Longer than Rope: A Century of African American Activism, 1850–1950,* edited by Charles M. Payne and Adam Green. New York: NYU Press, 2003.
———. *Holding Aloft the Banner of Ethiopia: Caribbean Radicalism in America, 1900–1932.* London: Verso, 1997.
Jaspin, Elliot. *Buried in the Bitter Waters: The Hidden History of Racial Cleansing in America.* New York: Basic Books, 2007.
Johnson, Cedric, and Ronald W. Walters. *Bibliography of African American Leadership: An Annotated Guide.* Santa Barbara: ABC-CLIO, 2000.
Johnson, James W. *Black Manhattan.* New York: Alfred A. Knopf, 1930.
Johnson, Nicholas. *Negroes and the Gun: The Black Tradition of Arms.* Amherst, NY: Prometheus Books, 2014.
Jones, Jacqueline. *American Work: Four Centuries of Black and White Labour.* New York: W. W. Norton, 1998.
Jones, Thai. *More Powerful Than Dynamite: Radicals, Plutocrats, Progressives, and New York's Year of Anarchy.* New York: Bloomsbury, 2014.
Jonnes, Jill. *Empires of Light: Edison, Tesla, Westinghouse, and the Race to Electrify the World.* New York: Random House, 2003.
Jordan, William G. *Black Newspapers and America's War for Democracy, 1914–1920.* Chapel Hill: The University of North Carolina Press, 2001.
Kaplan, Amy, and Donald Pease, eds. *Cultures of United States Imperialism.* Durham, NC: Duke University Press, 1993.
Katz, Henryk. *The Emancipation of Labor: A History of the First International.* London: Bloomsbury Academic, 1992.
Kelley, Robin D. G. *Freedom Dreams: The Black Radical Imagination.* Boston: Beacon Press, 2002.

———. *Hammer and Hoe: Alabama Communists during the Great Depression*. Chapel Hill: The University of North Carolina Press, 1990.
———. *Race Rebels: Culture, Politics, and the Black Working Class*. New York: Free Press, 1996.
Kellner, Bruce. *The Harlem Renaissance: A Historical Dictionary for the Era*. Westport, CT: Greenwood Press, 1984.
Kellogg, Charles Flint. *NAACP: A History of the National Association for the Advancement of Colored People*. Baltimore: Johns Hopkins Press, 1967.
Kelly, Brian. *Race, Class, and Power in the Alabama Coal Fields, 1908–21*. Urbana: University of Illinois Press, 2001.
Kersten, A. E. *Reframing Randolph: Labor, Black Freedom, and the Legacies of A. Philip Randolph*. New York: New York Press, 2015.
King, Shannon. *Whose Harlem Is This Anyway? Community Politics and Grassroots Activism during the New Negro Era*. New York: NYU Press, 2015.
Kipnis, Ira. *The American Socialist Movement, 1897–1912*. New York: Monthly Review Press, 1972.
Kornweibel, Theodore. *"Investigate Everything": Federal Efforts to Ensure Black Loyalty during World War I*. Bloomington: Indiana University Press, 2002.
———. *No Crystal Stair: Black Life and the Messenger, 1917–1928*. Westport, CT: Bloomsburg Academic, 1975.
———. *Seeing Red: Federal Campaigns against Black Militancy, 1919–1925*. Bloomington: University of Indiana Press, 1998.
Krugler, David F. *1919, The Year of Racial Violence: How African Americans Fought Back*. Cambridge: Cambridge University Press, 2015.
Lamothe, Daphne. *Inventing the New Negro: Narrative, Culture, and Ethnography*. Philadelphia: University of Pennsylvania Press, 2008.
Lee, Christopher J. *Making a World after Empire: The Bandung Moment and Its Political Afterlives*. Athens: Ohio University Press, 2010.
Legum, Colin. *Pan-Africanism: A Short Political Guide*. New York: F. A. Praeger, 1965.
Lens, Sidney. *The Forging of the American Empire: From the Revolution to Vietnam, A History of U.S. Imperialism*. Chicago: Haymarket Books, 2003.
———. *The Labor Wars: From the Molly Maguires to the Sit-Downs*. Chicago: Haymarket Books, 2009.
Lewis, David L. *W. E. B. Du Bois: Biography of a Race, 1868–1919*. New York: Henry Holt, 1993.
———. *W. E. B. DuBois: The Fight for Equality and the American Century, 1919–1963*. New York: Henry Holt, 2000.
———. *When Harlem Was in Vogue*. Oxford: Oxford University Press, 1989.
Lewis, Rupert. *Marcus Garvey: Anti-Colonial Champion*. Trenton, NJ: Africa World Press, 1988.
Lewis, Rupert, and Patrick E. Bryan. *Garvey: His Work and Impact*. Trenton, NJ: Africa World Press, 1991.
Lewis, Rupert, and Maureen Warner-Lewis, eds. *Garvey: Africa, Europe, and the Americas*. Trenton, NJ: Africa World Press, 1994.
Lih, Lars. *Lenin Rediscovered: What Is to Be Done? In Context*. Boston: Brill, 2006.
Lindsey, Lydia. "Gendering the Black Radical Tradition: Grace P. Campbell's Role in the

Formation of a Radical Feminist Tradition in African-American Intellectual Culture." In *Revolutionary Lives of the Red and Black Atlantic since 1917*, edited by David Featherstone, Christian Høgsbjerg, and Alan Rice. Manchester: Manchester University Press, 2022.

Linnemann, Russell J. *Alain Locke: Reflections on a Modern Renaissance Man*. Baton Rouge: Louisiana State University Press, 1982.

———. *Race Contacts and Interracial Relations: Lectures on the Theory and Practice of Race*. Edited by Jeffrey C. Stewart. Washington, DC: Howard University Press, 1992.

Loewen, James. *Sundown Towns: A Hidden Dimension of American Racism*. New York: New Press, 2005.

Logan, Rayford W. *The Negro in American Life and Thought: The Nadir, 1877–1901*. New York: Dial Press, 1954.

Logan, Rayford W., and Michael R. Winston. *Dictionary of American Negro Biography*. 1st ed. New York: Norton, 1982.

Lorde, Audre. *Uses of the Erotic: The Erotic as Power*. Trumansburg, NY: Crossing Press, 1984.

Lumpkins, Charles L. *American Pogrom: The East St. Louis Race Riot and Black Politics*. Athens: Ohio University Press, 2008.

Makalani, Minkah. *In the Cause of Freedom: Radical Black Internationalism from Harlem to London, 1917–1939*. Chapel Hill: The University of North Carolina Press, 2011.

Makonnen, Ras. *Pan-Africanism from Within*. London: Oxford University Press, 1973.

Manning, Martin J., and Herbert Romerstein. *Historical Dictionary of American Propaganda*. New York: Bloomsbury Academic, 2004.

Manoedi, Mokete M. *Garvey and Africa*. New York: New York Age Press, 1922.

Marable, Manning. *Black Leadership*. New York: Columbia University Press, 1998.

———. *W. E. B. Du Bois: Black Radical Democrat*. Boulder: Paradigm Publishers, 2005.

Martin, Tony. *Amy Ashwood Garvey: Pan-Africanist, Feminist, and Mrs. Marcus Garvey No. 1, or, A Tale of Two Amies*. London: Majority Press, 2007.

———. *Literary Garveyism: Garvey, Black Arts and the Harlem Renaissance*. Dover, MA: Majority Press, 1983.

———. *Race First: The Ideological and Organizational Struggles of Marcus Garvey and the Universal Negro Improvement Association*. Westport, CT: Greenwood Press, 1976.

———. "Women in the Garvey Movement." In *Garvey: His Work and Impact*, edited by Rupert Lewis and Patrick E. Bryan. Trenton, NJ: Africa World Press, 1991.

Martin, Tony, ed. *African Fundamentalism: A Literary and Cultural Anthology of Garvey's Harlem Renaissance*. Dover, MA: Majority Press, 1991.

Marx, Karl, and Friedrich Engels. *Manifesto of the Communist Party*. London: Lawrence & Wishart, 1983.

———. *Marx/Engels Selected Works, Vol. One*. Moscow: Progress Publishers, 1969.

Maxwell, William J. *New Negro, Old Left: African-American Writing and Communism between the Wars*. New York: Columbia University Press, 1999.

McDuffie, Erik S. *Sojourning for Freedom: Black Women, American Communism, and the Making of Black Left Feminism*. Durham, NC: Duke University Press, 2011.

McFeely, William S. *Frederick Douglass*. New York: W.W. Norton, 1995.

McKay, Claude. *A Long Way from Home*. New Brunswick, NJ: Rutgers University Press, 2007.

McLaughlin, M. *Power, Community, and Racial Killing in East St. Louis*. New York: Palgrave Macmillan, 2005.
McWhirter, Cameron. *Red Summer: The Summer of 1919 and the Awakening of Black America*. New York: Holt, 2011.
Meier, August. *Negro Thought in America, 1880–1915: Racial Ideologies in the Age of Booker T. Washington*. Ann Arbor: University of Michigan Press, 1963.
Meily, Clarence. *Puritanism*. Chicago: C. H. Kerr Co-operative, 1911.
Miller, Henry. *Plexus: Book Two of the Rosy Crucifixion*. London: Grove Press, 1965.
Miller, Sally M. *Other Socialists: Native-Born and Immigrant Women in the Socialist Party of America, 1901–1917*. New York: Tamiment Institute, 1983.
Mitchell, Michelle. *Righteous Propagation: African Americans and the Politics of Racial Destiny after Reconstruction*. Chapel Hill: The University of North Carolina Press, 2004.
Moore, Richard B. *Richard B. Moore, Caribbean Militant in Harlem: Collected Writings, 1920–1972*. Edited by W. Burghardt Turner and Joyce Moore Turner. Bloomington: Indiana University Press, 1988.
Morgan, H. W. *American Socialism, 1900–1960*. Englewood Cliffs, NJ: Prentice-Hall, 1964.
Moses, Wilson J. *Afrotopia: The Roots of African American Popular History*. Cambridge: Cambridge University Press, 1998.
———. *Alexander Crummell: A Study of Civilization and Discontent*. Oxford: Oxford University Press, 1989.
———. *Black Messiahs and Uncle Toms: Social and Literary Manipulations of a Religious Myth*. University Park: Pennsylvania State University Press, 1982.
———. *Classical Black Nationalism: From the American Revolution to Marcus Garvey*. New York: NYU Press, 1996.
———. *Creative Conflict in American Thought: Frederick Douglass, Alexander Crummell, Booker T. Washington, W. E. B. Du Bois, and Marcus Garvey*. Cambridge: Cambridge University Press, 2004.
———. *The Golden Age of Black Nationalism, 1820–1925*. Oxford: Oxford University Press, 1988.
Moss, Alfred. *The American Negro Academy: Voice of the Talented Tenth*. Baton Rouge: Louisiana State University Press, 1981.
Mouser, Bruce L. *For Labor, Race, and Liberty: George Edwin Taylor, His Historic Run for the White House, and the Making of Independent Black Politics*. Madison: University of Wisconsin Press, 2011.
Mullen, Bill, and James E. Smethurst. *Left of the Color Line: Race, Radicalism, and Twentieth-Century Literature of the United States*. Chapel Hill: The University of North Carolina Press, 2003.
Mumford, Kevin J. *Interzones: Black/White Sex Districts in Chicago and New York in the Early Twentieth Century*. New York: Columbia University Press, 1997.
Myrdal, Gunner. *An American Dilemma: The Negro Problem and Modern Democracy*. New York: Harper and Row, 1962.
Naison, Mark. *Communists in Harlem during the Depression*. Champaign: University of Illinois Press, 1983.
Nation, R. C. *War on War: Lenin, the Zimmerwald Left, and the Origins of Communist Internationalism*. Durham, NC: Duke University Press, 1989.

National Civil Liberties Bureau. *The Truth About the IWW: Facts in Relation to the Trial at Chicago by Competent Industrial Investigators and Noted Economists.* New York: National Civil Liberties Bureau, 1918.

Nelson, Bruce. *Divided We Stand: American Workers and the Struggle for Black Equality.* Princeton, NJ: Princeton University Press, 2001.

Nembhard, Jessica G. *Collective Courage: A History of African American Cooperative Economic Thought and Practice.* University Park: Pennsylvania State University Press, 2014.

Nembhard, Len S. *Trials and Triumphs of Marcus Garvey.* Millwood, NY: Kraus Reprint Co., 1978.

Nichols, John. *The S Word: A Short History of an American Tradition . . . Socialism.* London: Verso, 2011.

Norrell, Robert J. *Up from History: The Life of Booker T. Washington.* Cambridge, MA: Belknap Press of Harvard University Press, 2009.

Nugent, Richard Bruce. *Gay Rebel of the Harlem Renaissance: Selections from the Work of Richard Bruce Nugent.* Durham, NC: Duke University Press, 2002.

O'Connor, Harvey. *Revolution in Seattle.* New York: Monthly Review Press, 1964.

Ogbar, Jeffrey O. G. *The Harlem Renaissance Revisited: Politics, Arts, and Letters.* Baltimore: Johns Hopkins University Press, 2010.

Olusoga, David, and Casper W. Erichsen. *The Kaiser's Holocaust: Germany's Forgotten Genocide and the Colonial Roots of Nazism.* London: Faber & Faber, 2011.

Onaci, Edward. *Free the Land: The Republic of New Afrika and the Pursuit of a Black Nation-State.* Chapel Hill: The University of North Carolina Press, 2020.

Orwell, George. *1984.* 1949; Boston: Beacon Press, 1983.

Oubre, Claude F. *Forty Acres and a Mule: The Freedmen's Bureau and Black Land Ownership.* Baton Rouge: Louisiana State University Press, 1978.

Ovington, Mary White. *How the National Association for the Advancement of Colored People Began.* New York: NAACP, 1914. www.crmvet.org/info/naacp-orig.pdf.

———, with R. E. Luker, ed. *Black and White Sat Down Together: The Reminiscences of an NAACP Founder.* New York: Feminist Press at the City University of New York, 1996.

Oyěwùmí, Oyèrónkẹ́. *Gender Epistemologies in Africa: Gendering Traditions, Spaces, Social Institutions, and Identities.* Basingstoke: Palgrave Macmillan, 2011.

Padmore, George. *Pan-Africanism or Communism? The Coming Struggle for Africa.* London: Dennis Dobson, 1956.

Parascandola, Louis J., ed. *"Look for Me All around You": Anglophone Caribbean Immigrants in the Harlem Renaissance.* Detroit: Wayne State University Press, 2005.

Pauline Gumbs, Alexis. *Dub: Finding Ceremony.* Durham: Duke University Press, 2016.

Payne, Charles M., and Adam Green. *Time Longer than Rope: A Century of African American Activism, 1850–1950.* New York: New York University Press, 2003.

Perry, Jeffrey B. *Hubert Harrison.* Vol. 1, *The Voice of Harlem Radicalism, 1883–1918.* New York: Columbia University Press, 2009.

———. *Hubert Harrison.* Vol. 2, *The Struggle for Equality, 1919–1927.* New York: Columbia University Press, 2020.

———. *A Hubert Harrison Reader.* Middletown, CT: Wesleyan University Press, 2001.

Powell, Adam Clayton. *Against the Tide: An Autobiography.* Staunton, VA: R. R. Smith, 1938.

Power-Greene, Osman. "No Negro Renaissance: Hubert H. Harrison and the Role of the New Negro Literary Critic." In *The Harlem Renaissance Revisited*, edited by Jeffrey O. G. Ogbar. Baltimore: Johns Hopkins University Press, 2010.

Prashad, Vijay. *The Darker Nations: A People's History of the Third World*. New York: New Press, 2007.

Provenzo, Eugene F., and Edmund Abaka, eds. *W. E. B. Du Bois on Africa*. Walnut Creek, CA: Left Coast Press, 2012.

Putnam, Lara. *Radical Moves: Caribbean Migrants and the Politics of Race in the Jazz Age*. Durham: The University of North Carolina Press, 2013.

Quinn-Judge, Sophie. *Ho Chi Minh: The Missing Years 1919–1941*. Berkeley: University of California Press, 2002.

Rabinowitch, Alexander. *The Bolsheviks Come to Power: The Revolution of 1917 in Petrograd*. Chicago: Haymarket Press, 1976.

Randolph, A. Philip, and Chandler Owen. *Terms of Peace and the Darker Races*. Chicago: Poole Press, 1917.

Ransby, Barbara. *Ella Baker and the Black Freedom Movement: A Radical Democratic Vision*. Chapel Hill: The University of North Carolina Press, 2003.

———. *Eslanda: The Large and Unconventional Life of Mrs. Paul Robeson*. New Haven, CT: Yale University Press, 2013.

Redkey, Edwin S. *Black Exodus: Black Nationalist and Back-to-Africa Movements, 1890–1910*. New Haven, CT: Yale University Press, 1969.

Reed, John. *Ten Days That Shook the World*. New York: International Publishers, 1934.

Robinson, Cedric J. *Black Marxism: The Making of the Black Radical Tradition*. London: Zed, 1983.

———. *Black Movements in America*. London: Routledge, 1997.

Rogers, Joel A. *From "Superman" to Man*. St. Petersburg, FL: Helga M. Rogers, 2008.

———. *World's Great Men of Color*, 2 vols. New York: Collier Books, 1972.

Rojas, Fabio. *From Black Power to Black Studies: How a Radical Social Movement Became an Academic Discipline*. Baltimore: Johns Hopkins University Press, 2010.

Rolinson, Mary G. *Grassroots Garveyism: The Universal Negro Improvement Association in the Rural South, 1920–1927*. Chapel Hill: The University of North Carolina Press, 2007.

Ross, Jack. *The Socialist Party of America: A Complete History*. Lincoln, NE: Potomac Books, 2015.

Ross, Marlon B. *Manning the Race: Reforming Black Men in the Jim Crow Era*. New York: New York University Press, 2004.

Rossiter, Clinton, and James Lare. *The Essential Lippmann: A Political Philosophy for Liberal Democracy*. New York: Random House, 1963.

Ryan, Christopher, and Cacilda Jethá. *Sex at Dawn: The Prehistoric Origins of Modern Sexuality*. New York: HarperCollins, 2010.

Samuels, Wilfred D. *Five Afro-Caribbean Voices in American Culture 1917–1929: Hubert H. Harrison, Wilfred A. Domingo, Richard B. Moore, Cyril V. Briggs, and Claude McKay*. Boulder: Belmont Books, 1977.

Schmidt, Hans. *The United States Occupation of Haiti, 1915–1934*. New Brunswick, NJ: Rutgers University Press, 1995.

Seddon, David. "Popular Protest and Class Struggle in Africa: An Historical Overview."

In *Class Struggle and Resistance in Africa*, edited by Leo Zeilig. Chicago: Haymarket Books, 2002.

Segal, Ronald. *Islam's Black Slaves: The Other Black Diaspora*. New York: Farrar, Straus and Giroux, 2002.

Seifer, Marc J. *Tesla: Wizard at War*. New York: Citadel Press, 2022.

Selfa, Lance. *The Democrats: A Critical History*. Chicago: Haymarket Books, 2008.

Seraile, William. *Bruce Grit: The Black Nationalist Writings of John Edward Bruce*, Knoxville: University of Tennessee Press, 2003.

Shannon, D. A. *The Socialist Party of America: A History*. New York: Macmillan, 1955.

Sheldrake, Rupert. *A New Science of Life: The Hypothesis of Formative Causation*. 1981; London: Icon, 2009.

Sheppard, Brian. *The Inefficiency of Capitalism*. Tucson: See Sharp Press, 2003.

Silkey, Sarah L. *Black Woman Reformer: Ida B. Wells, Lynching, and Transatlantic Activism*. Athens: University of Georgia Press, 2015.

Silliman, Jael, Marlene Gerber Fried, Loretta Ross, and Elena Gutiérrez. *Undivided Rights: Women of Color Organizing for Reproductive Justice*. Chicago: Haymarket Books, 2016.

Sinnette, Elinor Des Verney. *Arthur Alfonso Schomburg, Black Bibliophile & Collector: A Biography*. New York: New York Public Library, 1989.

Skinner, E. P. *African Americans and U.S. Policy Toward Africa, 1850–1924: In Defense of Black Nationality*. Washington, DC: Howard University Press, 1992.

Smethurst, J. E. *The African American Roots of Modernism: From Reconstruction to the Harlem Renaissance*. Chapel Hill: The University of North Carolina Press, 2011.

———. "Langston Hughes in the 1930s." *The New Red Negro: The Literary Left and African American Poetry, 1930–1964*. New York: Oxford University Press, 1999.

Smith, Sharon. *Subterranean Fire: A History of Working-Class Radicalism in the United States*. Chicago: Haymarket Books, 2018.

Snyder, Thomas D. *120 Years of American Education: A Statistical Portrait*. Washington, DC: National Center for Education Statistics, 1993.

Solomon, Mark I. *The Cry Was Unity: Communists and African Americans, 1917–36*. Jackson: University Press of Mississippi, 1998.

Somé, Sobonfu. *The Spirit of Intimacy: Ancient African Teachings in the Ways of Relationships*. New York: William Morrow, 2000.

Spiller, Gustav. *Inter-Racial Problems: Papers from the First Universal Races Congress Held in London in 1911*. New York: Citadel Press, 1970.

Spingarn, Arthur Barnett. *Laws Relating to Sex Morality in New York City*. New York: Century Company, 1915.

Spivey, Donald. *Schooling for the New Slavery: Black Industrial Education, 1868–1915*. Westport, CT: Greenwood Press, 1978.

Stansell, Christine. *American Moderns: Bohemian New York and the Creation of a New Century*. New York: Henry Holt, 2000.

Stein, Judith. *The World of Marcus Garvey: Race and Class in Modern Society*. Baton Rouge: Louisiana State University Press, 1986.

Stephens, Michelle. *Black Empire: The Masculine Global Imaginary of Caribbean Intellectuals in the United States*. Durham, NC: Duke University Press, 2005.

Stephens, Ronald, and Adam Ewing. *Global Garveyism*. Gainesville: University Press of Florida, 2019.

Stevens, M. "The Early Political History of Wilfred A. Domingo." In *Caribbean Political Activism: Essays in Honor of Richard Hart*, edited by Rupert Lewis. Kingston: Ian Randle, 2012.

Stevens, Margaret. *Red International and Black Caribbean Communists in New York City, Mexico and the West Indies, 1919–1939*. London: Pluto Press, 2017.

Stewart, Jeffrey C. *The New Negro: The Life of Alain Locke*. New York: Oxford University Press, 2018.

Stoddard, Lothrop. *The Rising Tide of Color against White World-Supremacy*. New York: Scribner, 1920.

Stoehr, Taylor. *Free Love in America: A Documentary History*. New York: AMS Press, 1979.

Streeby, Shelley. *Radical Sensations: World Movements, Violence, and Visual Culture*. Durham, NC: Duke University Press, 2013.

Sundiata, Ibrahim K. *Brothers and Strangers: Black Zion, Black Slavery, 1914–1940*. Durham, NC: Duke University Press, 2003.

———. "The Garvey Aftermath." In *The United States and West Africa*, edited by Alusin Jalloh and Toyin Falola. Rochester: University of Rochester Press, 2008.

Talbert, Roy. *Negative Intelligence: The Army and the American Left, 1917–1941*. Jackson: University Press of Mississippi, 1991.

Taylor, Nikki M. *America's First Black Socialist: The Radical Life of Peter H. Clark*. Lexington: University Press of Kentucky, 2013.

Taylor, Ula Y. *The Veiled Garvey: The Life & Times of Amy Jacques Garvey*. Chapel Hill: The University of North Carolina Press, 2002.

Terborg-Penn, Rosalyn. *African American Women in the Struggle for the Vote*. Bloomington: Indiana University Press, 1998.

Tesla, Nikola. *My Inventions: The Autobiography of Nikola Tesla*. www.tfcbooks.com/special/mi_link.htm.

Thornbrough, Emma L. *T. Thomas Fortune: Militant Journalist*. Chicago: University of Chicago Press, 1972.

Thurman, Wallace. *Infants of the Spring*. Mineola, NY: Dover Publications, 2013.

Trinkaus, George. *Tesla: The Lost Inventions*. Portland: High Voltage Press, 1988.

Trouillot, Michel R. *Silencing the Past: Power and the Production of History*. Boston: Beacon Press, 2015.

Turner, Joyce M. *Caribbean Crusaders and the Harlem Renaissance*. Champaign: University of Illinois Press, 2005.

Turner, Richard B. *Islam in the African-American Experience*. Bloomington: Indiana University Press, 1997.

Twain, Mark. *Letters from the Earth*. New York: Harper & Row, 1962.

Uya, Okon E. *Black Brotherhood: Afro-Americans and Africa*. Lexington: D. C. Heath, 1970.

Valdés, Vanessa. *Diasporic Blackness: The Life and Times of Arturo Alfonso Schomburg*. Albany: State University of New York Press, 2017.

Van Sertima, Ivan. *They Came before Columbus: The African Presence in Ancient America*. New York: Random House, 2003.

Vincent, Theodore. *Black Power and the Garvey Movement*. San Francisco: Ramparts Press, 1971.
Vinson, Robert Trent, and Bernard L. Schwartz. *The Americans Are Coming! Dreams of African American Liberation in Segregationist South Africa*. Athens: Ohio University Press, 2012.
Voogd, Jan. *Race Riots and Resistance: The Red Summer of 1919*. New York: Peter Lang, 2008.
Walton, Hanes. *Black Political Parties: An Historical and Political Analysis*. New York: Free Press, 1972.
Waskow, Arthur O. *From Race Riot to Sit-In, 1919 and the 1960s: A Study in the Connections between Conflict and Violence*. Garden City, NY: Doubleday, 1966.
Watkins-Owens, Irma. *Blood Relations: Caribbean Immigrants and the Harlem Community, 1900–1930*. Bloomington: Indiana University Press, 1996.
Watts, Erica King. *Hearing the Hurt Rhetoric, Aesthetics, and Politics of the New Negro Movement*. Tuscaloosa: University of Alabama Press, 2012.
Weinstein, J. *The Decline of Socialism in America, 1912–1925*. New York: Monthly Review Press, 1967.
Weisbord, Robert G. *Genocide? Birth Control and the Black American*. London: Bloomsbury Academic, 1975.
Wekker, Gloria. *Ik ben een gouden munt*. Amsterdam: Feministische Uitgeverij VITA, 1994.
———. *The Politics of Passion: Women's Sexual Culture in the Afro-Surinamese Diaspora*. New York: Columbia, 2006.
Werbel, Amy. *Lust on Trial: Censorship and the Rise of American Obscenity in the Age of Anthony Comstock*. New York: Columbia University Press, 2018.
West, Cornell. *Black Prophetic Fire*. Edited by Christa Buschendorf. Boston: Beacon Press, 2014.
West, Martin O., William G. Martin, and Fanon C. Wilkins, eds. *From Toussaint to Tupac: The Black International since the Age of Revolution*. Chapel Hill: The University of North Carolina Press, 2009.
Whalan, Mark. *The Great War and the Culture of the New Negro*. Gainesville: University Press of Florida, 2008.
White, Deborah Gray. *Ar'n't I a Woman: Female Slaves in the Plantation South*. New York: W. W. Norton, 1985.
———. *Too Heavy a Load: Black Women in Defense of Themselves, 1894–1994*. New York: W. W. Norton, 1999.
White, Walter. *Rope and Faggot: A Biography of Judge Lynch*. New York: Knopf, 1929.
Willey, Angela. *Undoing Monogamy: The Politics of Science and the Possibilities of Biology*. Durham, NC: Duke University Press, 2016.
Williams, Eric. *Capitalism and Slavery*. Chapel Hill: The University of North Carolina Press, 1944.
Williams, Gilbert A. *Legendary Pioneers of Black Radio*. London: Bloomsbury Academic, 1998.
Wilson, James F. *Bulldaggers, Pansies, and Chocolate Babies: Performance, Race, and Sexuality in the Harlem Renaissance*. Ann Arbor: University of Michigan Press, 2010.
Wintz, Cary D. *Black Culture and the Harlem Renaissance*. Houston: Rice University, 1988.

Woods, Clyde. *Development Arrested: The Blues and Plantation Power in the Mississippi Delta*. New York: Verso, 1998.

———. *Voices of a Black Nation: Political Journalism in the Harlem Renaissance*. San Francisco: Ramparts Press, 1973.

Woodward, C. V. *Origins of the New South, 1877–1913*. Baton Rouge: Louisiana State University Press, 1951.

Woolner, Cookie. *The Famous Lady Lovers: Black Women and Queer Desire before Stonewall*. Chapel Hill: The University of North Carolina Press, 2023.

Yard, Lionel M. *Biography of Amy Ashwood Garvey, 1897–1969: Co-Founder of the Universal Negro Improvement Association*. New York: Associated Publishers, 1988.

Young, Darius J. *Robert R. Church Jr. and the African American Political Struggle*. Gainesville: University Press of Florida, 2022.

Zangrando, Robert L. *The NAACP Crusade against Lynching, 1909–1950*. Philadelphia: Temple University Press, 1980.

Zimmerman, Andrew. *Alabama in Africa: Booker T. Washington, the German Empire, and the Globalization of the New South*. Princeton, NJ: Princeton University Press, 2010.

Zinn, Howard. *A People's History of the United States*. New York: Harper, 2017.

———. *You Can't Be Neutral on a Moving Train: A Personal History of Our Times*. Boston: Beacon Press, 2002.

Zinn, Howard, and Anthony Arnove. *Voices of a People's History of the United States*. New York: Seven Stories Press, 2004.

Zipser, Arthur, and Pearl Zipser. *Fire and Grace: The Life of Rose Pastor Stokes*. Athens: University of Georgia Press, 1989.

Journal Articles

Alonso, Paola. "Autonomy Revoked: The Forced Sterilization of Women of Color in 20th Century America." *Ibid: A Student History Journal* 13 (Spring 2020).

Asukile, Thabiti. "The Harlem Friendship of Joel Augustus Rogers (1880–1966) and Hubert Henry Harrison (1883–1927)." *Afro-Americans in New York Life and History* 34, no. 2 (July 2010): 54–75.

Bernays, Edward. "The Engineering of Consent." *Annals of the American Academy of Political and Social Science* 250, no. 1 (March 1947): 113–20.

Bruce, Dickson D., Jr. "Ancient Africa and the Early Black American Historians, 1883–1915." *American Quarterly* 36, no. 5 (Winter 1984): 684–99.

Carnegie, Charles. "Garvey and the Black Transnation." *Small Axe* 5 (March 1999): 48–71.

Carruthers, Jacob. "John Henrik Clarke: The Harlem Connection to the Founding of Africana Studies." *Afro-Americans in New York Life and History* 30, no. 2 (July 2006): 173–94.

Chinitz, David. "The New Harlem Renaissance Studies." *Modernism/Modernity* 13, no. 2 (April 2006): 375–82.

Clarke, John Henrik. "The Influence of Arthur A. Schomburg on My Concept of Africana Studies." *Phylon* 49, no. 1/2 (Spring–Summer 1992): 4–9.

Cox, LaWanda. "The Promise of Land for the Freedmen." *The Mississippi Valley Historical Review* 45, no. 3 (December 1958): 413–40.

Crowder, Ralph L. "The Historical Context and Political Significance of Harlem's Street Scholar Community." *Afro-Americans in New York Life and History* 34, no. 1 (January 2010): 34–45.

———. "Willis Nathaniel Huggins (1886–1941): Historian, Activist, and Community Mentor." *Afro-Americans in New York Life and History* 30, no. 2 (July 2006): 127–51.

Dagnini, Jérémie Kroubo. "Marcus Garvey: A Controversial Figure in the History of Pan-Africanism." *The Journal of Pan African Studies* 2, no. 3 (March 2008): 198–208.

Debs, Eugene V. "The Negro in the Class Struggle." *International Socialist Review* 5, no. 5 (1903).

Du Bois, W. E. B. "The African Roots of War." *Atlantic Monthly* (May 1915).

Edwards, William A. "William Monroe Trotter: A Twentieth Century Abolitionist." *Trotter Review* 2, no. 1 (1988): article 6.

Ellis, Mark. "'Closing Ranks' and 'Seeking Honors': W. E. B. Du Bois in World War I." *Journal of American History* 79, no. 1 (June 1992): 96–124.

Harlan, Louis. "Booker T. Washington and the White Man's Burden." *The American Historical Review* 71, no. 2 (January 1966): 68–97.

Harrison, Hubert. "The World We Live In." *Boston Chronicle* (December 1, 1924), HHP box 13, folder 4.

Harrison, William. "Phylon Profile IX: William Monroe Trotter—Fighter." *Phylon* 7, no. 3 (1946): 236–45.

Haynes, Robert V. "The Houston Mutiny and Riot of 1917." *The Southwestern Historical Quarterly* 76, no. 4 (April 1973): 418–39.

Hill, Robert A. "'Comradeship of the More Advanced Races': Marcus Garvey and the Brotherhood Movement in Britain, 1913–14." *Small Axe* 17, no. 1 (2013): 50–70.

James, Portia. "Hubert Harrison and the New Negro Movement." *The Western Journal of Black Studies* 13, no. 2 (Summer 1989): 82–91.

Jimoh, A. Yamisi. "Mapping the Terrain of Black Writing during the Early New Negro Era." *College Literature* 42, no. 3 (Summer 2015): 488–524.

Kelly, Brian. "No Easy Way Through: Race Leadership and Black Workers at the Nadir." *Labor: Studies in Working-Class History of the Americas* 7, no. 3 (Fall 2010): 79–93.

Lenin, Vladimir. "The Socialist Revolution and the Rights of Nations to Self-Determination." *Vorbote* 2 (1916).

Lewis, Diane. "Anthropology and Colonialism." *Current Anthropology* 14, no. 5 (December 1973): 581–602.

Marable, Manning. "Booker T. Washington and African Nationalism." *Phylon* 35, no. 4 (1974): 398–406.

Marriott, David. "Bordering On: The Black Penis." *Textual Practice* 10, no. 1 (1996): 9–28.

McInnis, Jarvis C. "A Corporate Plantation Reading Public: Labor, Literacy, and Diaspora in the Global Black South." *American Literature* 91, no. 3 (2019): 523–55.

Moore, Richard B. "Africa Conscious Harlem." *Freedomways* (Summer 1963): 315–34.

Moore, R. L. "Flawed Fraternity–American Socialist Response to the Negro, 1901–1912." *Historian* 32, no. 1 (1969): 1–18.

Nash, Jennifer C. "Black Sexualities." *Feminist Theory* 19, no. 1 (2018): 3–5.

Samuels, Wilfred D. "Hubert H. Harrison and the 'New Negro Manhood Movement.'" *Afro-Americans in New York Life & History* 5, no. 1 (January 1981): 29.

Seraile, William. "Henrietta Vinton Davis and the Garvey Movement." *Afro-Americans in New York Life and History* 7, no. 2 (July 1983): 7–24.

Shilliam, Robbie. "What About Marcus Garvey? Race and the Transformation of Sovereignty Debate." *Review of International Studies* 32 (2006): 379–400.

Smith, C. Calvin. "The Houston Riot of 1917, Revisited." *Houston Review* 13 (1991): 85–95.

Tinsley, Omise'eke Natasha. "Black Atlantic, Queer Atlantic: Queer Imaginings of the Middle Passage." *GLQ: A Journal of Gay and Lesbian Studies* 14, nos. 2–3 (2008): 191–215.

Trotter, Joe W. "African American Fraternal Associations in American History: An Introduction." *Social Science History* 28, no. 3 (Fall 2004): 355–66.

Vincent, Theodore. "The Garveyite Parents of Malcolm X." *Black Scholar* 20, no. 2 (March–April 1989): 10–13.

West, William Lemore. "The Moses Harman Story." *Kansas History: A Journal of the Central Plains* 37, no. 1 (Spring 1971): 41–63.

Williams, J. A. "The Long Hot Summers of Yesteryear." *The History Teacher* 1, no. 3 (March 1968): 9–23.

Williams, Weldon. "Naming the Unspeakable: Breakthroughs in Africological Nomenclature." *Africalogical Perspectives: Historical and Contemporary Analysis of Race and Africana Studies* 3/4, no. 1 (2006/2007): 51–74.

Dissertations

Carr, Greg Kimathi. "African Philosophy of History in the Contemporary Era." PhD diss., Temple University, 1998.

Holm, Charles R. "'To Be Free from the Slavery of Capitalism': David Walker, Peter H. Clark, and George Washington Woodbey's Black Socialist Thought." PhD diss., University of Texas at Austin, 2021.

Honn, Josh. "Coming to Consciousness: Eugene Debs, American Socialism and the 'Negro Question.'" Master's thesis, Lehigh University, 2002.

Perry, Jeffrey B. "Hubert Henry Harrison, 'the Father of Harlem Radicalism': The Early Years, 1883 through the Founding of the Liberty League and *The Voice* in 1917." PhD diss., Columbia University, 1986.

Samuels, Wilfred D. "Five Afro-Caribbean Voices in American Culture, 1917–1929: Hubert H. Harrison, Wilfred A. Domingo, Richard B. Moore, Cyril V. Briggs, and Claude McKay." PhD diss., University of Iowa, 1977. Schomburg Center for Research in Black Culture, microform, Sc Micro F-10718.

Tamarkin, Stanley. "Rose Pastor Stokes: The Portrait of a Radical Woman, 1905–1919." PhD diss., Yale University, 1983.

Younis, Musab. "'With Drops of Ink We Make Millions Think': Interwar African American Nationalism." PhD diss., University of Oxford, 2017.

Index

Italic page numbers refer to illustrations.

abolitionism, 61, 71, 78 177, 268, 323; Black abolitionists, 167
abortion, 24, 194–95, 200, 205–6, 210
accommodationism, 35–36, 49, 179, 231, 264, 277
advertisements: and Black community, 74, 76; for hair straightening, 74, 76; and propaganda, 136–37; in *The Voice*, 73, 76
Aesop, 167
Africa: African American views of, 176–83; ancient civilizations in, 170–73, *172*; civilizationist mindsets in, 163–64; colonization of, 126, 131, 266; communal systems in, 157; contemporary life and politics in, 173–76, 327; and Garveyism, 227–28; and Harrison, 160–65; Indigenous knowledge, 174; missionary-sponsored education in, 173–74; monogamy in culture of, 212–13; racial vs. geographical sense, 235; sexual culture of before colonization, 220–21
"Africa First" principle, 73, 166, 235, 236–37, *237*
"Africa for the Africans!," 165, 177, 181
African Americans: and Africa, 176–83; and African traditions, 113–14; caricatures of, 296; and collective nature of wisdom, 6; legacy and heritage of, 156–57; and love, 4, 185; as objects of entertainment, 295–96; ownership of means of production, 186; pro-Black business, 185–86; resistance and defiance of, 19–20; self-empowerment of, 3–4; separatist traditions of, 187
African Blood Brotherhood (ABB), 22, 65, 88, 96, 118, 152, 250, 274

African consciousness, 4, 161, 162, 189, 236, 242, 253, 266
Afro-American Council, 71
Afro-American League, 71
agnosticism, 4, 62, 106, 108–9, 111, 188
Ali, Dusé Mohamed, 174, 179, 183, 229, 241
Ali, Noble Drew, 211
amendments, Constitutional, 15, 19, 67
American Civil War, 131; draft riots, 223; Reconstruction, 187. *See also* Lincoln, Abraham
American Federation of Labor (AFL), 33–34, 41, 48, 53
American Negro Labor Congress, 155
American Railway Workers Union, 32, 39
Amsterdam News (newspaper), 73; on geopolitics lectures, 115; Harrison's obituary in, 313; and Liberty Congress, 140; *Nigger Heaven* review, 292; on "Science and Race Prejudice" lecture, 114
anarchists, xii, 53, 102, 199, 201; Francisco Ferrer, 108; on Free Speech, 96, 107, 136, 202, 205; Emma Goldman, 134, 194, 325; Edwin C. Walker, 201–3, 205, 222
Anderson, Charles W., 36, 140
Anderson, Regina, 285
Angelou, Maya, 225
Anglo-Saxon peoples, 115, 127, 178, 236, 263, 323
anthropology, and history of racism, 46–47
anti-imperialism, 77, 133, 149, 153–55, 171, 266
antilynching legislation, *18*, 142
Apollo Theater, 95
Arabic language and world, 117, 148, 167, 182, 265
Aristotle, 91, 170, 172

armed self-defense, 3, 68, 71, 97, 270, 324
Armstrong, Samuel Chapman, 35
art: pure vs. propaganda, 290–91, 304; and "renaissance," 295–96
artists, 192, 205, 216, 218, 219, 284–86, 289–301, 304, 305, 307–9, 313, 325
Asia, 126, 129, 130, 149, 231, 265; immigrants, 43; Indigenous sexualities, 221–22; pan-Asian perspectives, 155, 183. *See also* China; India
atheism, 10, 108, 110, 111
Atlanta, GA: Black economic empowerment in, 284; Cotton Expo speech (Booker T. Washington, 1895), 35; laundry workers' strike in, 33; white violence in, 69
Attucks, Crispus, 167
Austin, Bernia Smith, 196
Austro-Hungarian Empire, 85–86
Azikiwe, Nnamdi, 228

"back to Africa" movement, 154, 236, 266
Bacon, Francis, 111
Baker, Ella, 2, 185, 314
banking: and Black communities, 302; monopolies, 29–30, 121, 123, 138; "Morganization," 121
Bantu Women's League, 148
Barbados and Barbadians, 22, 77, 166, 227. *See also* Haynes, Cecilia Elizabeth; Moore, Richard B.; Seifert, Charles
Bass, Charlotta, 228
Batkis, Gregory, 200
Bebel, Ferdinand August, 113
Beecher, Henry Ward, 109
Belgium, 86, 127, 160, 176, 179
Benga, Ota, 4, 160
Bennett, Gwendolyn, 219, 285
Bennett, Lerone, 261, 268
Benson, Oscar, 103, 300, 311, 321
Bentley, Gladys, 192, 300
Beoku-Betts, Ernest Samuel, 174
Berger, Victor, 44, 270
Berkman, Alexander, 134
Bernays, Edward, 137
Bethune, Mary McCleod, 61

Bible, 4, 107, 180; study, 62, 109, 215; as word of God, 109
biology: evolutionary, 111, 116, 117, 215, 284; Harrison as embryology instructor, 116, 194; and racial differences, 47, 53, 243
birth control, 24, 50, 193–97, 205
Birth of a Nation, The (film), 123, 208
"Black belt thesis," 153, 187
Black church lyceums, 9, 63, 113
Black Communists, 65, 118, 152–54, 211, 274, 276, 280, 324. *See also* *Crusader*; *Emancipator*
Black free love politics, xix, 4, 10, 24, 191–93, 195, 210, 223–25, 304, 313
Black history in school curricula, 7, 61, 167, 117, 282, 305, 315
Black and pan-African liberation, xiv, 10, 11, 57, 162, 165, 188–89, 193, 224, 239, 283, 309, 322, 324
Black manhood, 65, 72, 144, 150, 208–9, 228, 246, 280, 283, 325
"Black man's burden," 14, 116, 170, 175, 268
Black nationalism, 281; emigrationism, 177–78; history of, 251
Black-owned businesses, 248, 302–3
Black Panther Party, xiv, 270, 324
Black Reconstruction (Du Bois), 61
Black Star Line (BSL), 227, 229, 237, 249, 257, 354n6. *See also* Universal Negro Improvement Association (UNIA)
Black studies movement, 105, 118
Black women's club movement, 19–20, 61, 62–63
Black Zionism, 264–66
Blake, Eubie, 300
bleaching, of skin, 74, 110
blues (music), 218; women, 192, 218, 304
Blyden, Edward Wilmot, 71, 118, 162, 179, 183, 212–13, 251, 327
Blyden Society, 118
Board of Education (New York City), 114
Bogan, Lucille, 192, 217
Bolshevik Party, 82–85, 125, 133, 151, 199–200, 305. *See also* Russian Revolution
Boni, Albert, 287, 304
Boni & Liveright publishing, 287

Bontemps, Arna, 294
Boulin, Herbert S. (federal agent P-138), 242, 259
bourgeoisie, 38, 128, 150–51
Bracey, John H., 100
Brawley, Benjamin, 131, 169
Bridges, William, 74, 96, 161, 269
Briggs, Cyril V.: African Blood Brotherhood (ABB), 88, 152, 153, 250; Communist Party, 153; *Crusader* (newspaper), 74–75, 96, 165, 233, 255; *as Emancipator* contributing editor, 246, 249; and FBI, 278; and Garvey and Back-to-Africa movement, 274; as immigrant from Caribbean, 21; on separate Black state, 186
Bronx Zoo, 4, 160
Brooklyn (New York): contraceptive clinic, 196; Equal Suffrage League, 61; Lincoln Settlement, 65
Brotherhood of Sleeping Car Porters, 250
Brotherhood of Timber Workers, 33
Brotherhood Workers of America, 33, 88–89
Brown, Egbert Ethelred, 10, 92, 94, 118, 188, 277
Brown, Sterling, 300
Brown, William Wells, 110, 167, 298
Bruce, John Edward, 24, 71, 73, 113, 165, 233, 240, 251, 256
Buchner, Ludwig, 111
Buddhoe, "General Moses," 328
Bunyan, John, 297
Burbank, Luther, 107
Burns, Robert, 297
Burrill, Mary, 196
Burroughs, Charles, 190
Burroughs, Nannie Helen, 178, 207
Burroughs, Williana Jones, 58, 118, 190, 195, 325
Butler, Smedley Darlington, 122–23, 124, 126
Byrd, Mabel, 118

Cabaret School of Negro literature, 284–85, 296–98, 304, 308–9
Campbell, Grace Philomena: and African Blood Brotherhood (ABB), 88, 152, 250, 274; background and education of, 64–65; and Harrison, 96, 195, 325; and Institute for Social Study, 117; and Liberty League of Negro-Americans, 58; and NLPCW, 77–78; and Socialist Party, 57; and Women's Political Association of Harlem, 196
Campbell, James Edwin, 298
Canegata, James C., 328
capitalism: and Black radicals, 246; and colonialism, 163–64; and communism, xii, 79, 90, 199, 208; concentration of capital, 121–22, 122; and corruption of science, 342–47; critique of, 36–37; and exploitation, 139; "free market," 36; and human nature, 37; and labor history, 31–34; and robber barons, 3, 28–31, 30; and war, 130
Caribbean, 160, 275; deportation, 278; emigration from, 14, 21, 103, 213, 229, 232, 234, 251; imperialism in, 149, 154–55, 157, 271; migrants joining organizations, 23, 25, 68, 166, 226, 235, 238, 252, 254, 280; and print culture, 77, 240
Carlyle, Thomas, 5, 114, 115
Carnegie, Andrew, 3, 29, 230, 318
Carnegie, Charles, 226
Carnegie Hall, 132
Carroll, Lewis, 114
Cary, Mary Ann Shadd, 19
Casely-Hayford, Adelaide Smith, 173, 228
caste system: caste discrimination, 18, 139; in Soviet Union, 306
castration, 224, 278; and lynching, 209–10
chattel slavery, 46, 49
Chesnutt, Charles, 61, 298
Chicago, 69, 100; Washington Park Forum, 100
Chicago Defender (newspaper), 73, 77, 140, 292
Chilembwe, John, 148
China: oppression in, 150, 155; post–World War I rebellions, 148; racist attitudes toward Chinese people, 214; religion in, 108; Shanghai strike, 148; US imperialism, 125
Chomsky, Noam, xii, xv, 137–38, 321
Christianity: critique of, 106–7; and Islamophobia, 182; and oppression of Black people, 109–10; rejection of, 4; and sexual repression, 208

Christianity Before Christ (Jackson), 118
churches: Abyssinian Baptist Church, 21, 58, 63, 208; African Methodist Episcopal Zion Church, 21, 71, 164–65; African Orthodox Church, 21; Anglican Church, 4, 14; Baptist Church, 21, 58, 63, 208; Bethel African Methodist Episcopal Church, 21, 58, 66, 73, 232; Catholic Church, 96, 107, 194; Harlem Community Church, 21, 188; Harlem Unitarian Church, 10–11, 188; Hubert Harrison Memorial Church, 10, 188, 313, 329n24; St. John Coltrane Church, 11; St. Mark's Methodist Episcopal Church, 21
civilizationist mindset, 163–64, 180, 215–16
Civil War, (US), 131; draft riots, 223; Reconstruction, 187. *See also* Lincoln, Abraham
Clark, Peter H., 43
Clarke, John Henrik, 8, 57, 105, 118, 161, 168, 169–70, 234, 327
class consciousness, 45, 48, 53, 133, 152, 154, 245, 249, 273–74
class exploitation, 48, 187, 242, 307
"class first" vs. "race first," 235, 242, 251, 274, 322
class radicalism, 12, 242, 274, 326
class solidarity, 56, 235, 244
class struggle, 38, 44, 51, 54, 199, 245
Clemenceau, Georges, 125, 137
climate catastrophe, 26, 317
"Close Ranks" editorial (Du Bois), 145–46, 147
cognitive dissonance, 8
Collins, Ethel, 228
colonialism, 163–64; in Africa, 175; challenges to, 174; justifications for, 214; and propaganda, 175–76; and prostitution, 214; settler colonialism in United States, 187
"Colored International" (Harrison's internationalist politics), 4, 120, 148–55, 265, 274–75
Colored Socialist Club (CSC), 51–52, 56, 120
Colored Women's Progressive Franchise Association, 19
Columbia University, 11, 131, 247
Columbus, Christopher, 46, 167
comedy, Blackface, 93
Comintern. *See* Communist International

Committee of Fourteen (COF), 207
Committee on Public Information, 137, 140
common people, 2, 23, 79, 103, 297
Communist International (Comintern/Third International), 151, 153–55
Communist Manifesto, The (Marx and Engels), 38, 315
Communist Party (US), 8, 10, 22, 88, 95, 117–18, 150–51, 154–55
community-based education, 102. *See also* Outdoor Grioversity
Comstock, Anthony, 204, 207–8
Comstock laws and Comstockery, 201, 204–5, 224, 313
Comte, Auguste, 111Congo, 127, 175–76, 179, 220, 295
Congo Reform Association, 175, 179
Conrad, Joseph, 160
Constitutional amendments, 15, 19, 67
contraception. *See* birth control
convict leasing, 19, 31–32
Conway, Moncure D., 107
Cooper, Anna Julia, 64
Cooper, James Fenimore, 114
cooperative economic programs, 184–86, 248
Cox, Ida, 192, 218
Creel, George, 140
Creel Commission, 137
Crisis (magazine), 52, 73, 297; Du Bois as editor, 82, 143–46, 240; investigation of for sedition, 144–45; and Nella Larsen, 293; Locke's criticism of, 290; and neglect to publish Harrison's obituary, 312; *Nigger Heaven* review, 293; wartime censorship of, 145
Crosswaith, Frank D., 118, 162, 181, 273–74, 328
Crowder, Ralph, 91, 95
Crummell, Alexander, 71, 162, 167, 177, 251
Crusader (newspaper), 74–75, 76, 96, 233, 249
crystallization, 95; Black Socialism, 45, 249; Colored International, 155; concept, 3–4; free love politics, 192–93, 196, 198, 206; Harrison's legacy, 7–8, 10, 224, 246, 253, 283–84, 324; Harrison's oratory, 95; international revolutionary politics, 120, 160;

New Negro movement, 57, 233, 242, 255, 309; Nikola Tesla's legacy, 316, 320
Cuba, xi–xii, 123, 125, 146, 165, 227, 241, 307
Cullen, Countee, 156, 219, 285, 293, 294, 297

Darwin, Charles, 90, 95, 108, 111–12, 114–15
Davis, Angela Y., 17, 218
Davis, Arthur, 300–301
Davis, Henrietta Vinton, 96, 228, 260, 289
Davis, John P., 299
Davis, Ossie, 6, 328
Days of War, Nights of Love (Crimethinc), xii
Daytona Normal and Industrial Institute, 61
Dearborn, Elsie, 191
Debs, Eugene V., 32, 39–40, 44–45, 49, 131–32, 152, 243, 281
debt peonage, 14–15, 19, 67
Declaration of Independence, 7, 48, 144
Declaration of the Rights of the Negro Peoples of the World (UNIA), 241–42, 258, 260
Deism, 108–9
Delany, Martin, 162, 167, 177–78, 281; "Africa for the Africans!" slogan, 181
de Mena, Maymie, 228
D'Emilio, John, 197, 201
Democratic Party, 40, 99, 231, 270, 326–27
Deniyi, Madarikan, 258, 262, 266
Denmark, 125
Dessalines, Jean-Jacques, 11
Dewey, John, 36
D'Holbach, Baron, 111
dialectical relationships, 95, 133, 327
Dickens, Charles, 114
Diop, Cheikh Anta, 327
direct action, 41, 53–54, 69
disenfranchisement, 15, 19, 34, 43, 47, 102, 127, 134–35, 139, 144, 184, 263, 267, 278, 306
Dixon, Thomas, 208
Dixon-Spear, Patricia, 214
dogma, religious, 4, 106, 107, 208
dolls, brown-skinned, 248
domestic workers, 16–17, 21, 32, 229, 301
Domingo, W. A. (Wilfred Adolphus), 274; on African affairs, 165; anti-imperialism, 271; as Caribbean-born immigrant, 21;

and Communist Party, 152; *The Emancipator*, 75, 233; and Garvey, 254, 228–29, 277; and Hubert Harrison Memorial Church, 118; outdoor oratory, 94, 162; on race first vs. class first, 244–46; and Socialist Party, 57
Dominican Republic, 123, 125
Dominican people, 146
Douglas, Aaron, 293
Douglass, Frederick, 105, 110, 167, 172, 185
Doyle, Arthur Conan, 114, 175
draft, military, 147
draft riots, 223
drag balls, 191, 222–23
drama (theater), 20, 116–17, 201, 218, 293
Draper, John William, 108, 109
Dreiser, Theodore, 104, 205
Du Bois, William Edward Burghardt (W. E. B.), 20, 35, 51, 52, 61, 78, 166; Africa and civilizationist attitudes, 180–81; "The African Roots of War," 131; on art vs. propaganda, 290–91; on Du Bois, 82, 298; and Du Bois' criticism of *Nigger Heaven*, 293; on eugenics, 196; extramarital relationships of, 192; on family structures, 222; freethought, 110; on Garveyism, 255; and Harrison, 143–48; and Liberty Party, 270; and pan-African congresses, 154
Dunbar, Paul Laurence, 61, 296, 297, 298
Duncan, Natanya, 228
Dunlap, Ethel Trew, 240, 289
Dyer, Leonidas, 18, 142

Eason, James, 256, 259–60, 262–63, 270, 277, 280
Easter Rising, 148, 238. *See also* Ireland
Eastman, Max, 201
East St. Louis massacre (1917), 68–69, *70*
Edison, Thomas, 317
education: Black emancipatory, 3; funding for, 18, 19; as indoctrination, 104–5; industrial, 17–18, 19, 79, 102, 230; missionary-sponsored in Africa, 173–74; popular and grassroots, 100; street-corner oratory, 90–99, *92*, *98*

Index 391

Egypt: ancient, 161, 165, 170–73, *172*, 220, 327; Egyptian Revolution, 148
Einstein, Albert, 6, 320
Ekpe, Baba, 218
elections: Black vote, 15, 60, 269, 326; Socialist ticket, 40, 269; women's suffrage, 63–64
Elks (fraternal order), 21
Ellis, George W., 175, 298
emancipation: of slaves, 267, 268; of working class, xiv, 3, 8, 56, 181, 186, 255, 322
Emancipator (newspaper), 75, 233, 246; anti-Garveyism, 249
Emerson, Ralph Waldo, 114
emigrationism, 165, 177–78, 185, 251
Emperor Jones (O'Neill), 275–76
Empire State Federation of Women's Clubs (ESFWC), 61, 63, 152
Engels, Friedrich, 38, 47, 128, 215, 315
England, 114, 176, 180, 213, 230; London, 171, 174, 183, 213, 229
Equal Suffrage League, 61
erasure, historical, 7, 8, 25, 283–84, 288, 313, 315–16
erotica, 190, 210
eroticism, 5, 190–91, *192*, 209–11, 214, 216, 218–19, 221–25
Espionage Act, 134, 143, 145
Ethiopia: ancient, 165, 170–71, *172*; in diaspora, 229, 252
eugenics, 111, 179, 196–97
Eurocentric worldviews, 3, 111, 114, 153, 163, *172*, 215–16
evolutionary biology, 111–12, 115, 116, 214, 215

Faneuil Hall (Boston), 271
Fauset, Jessie, 240, 285, 288, 299
Federal Bureau of Investigation, 143, 205, 258, 264, 278
Federation of American Scientists, 319
feminism, 215, 321
Ferrer, Francisco, 108
Ferris, William H., 166, 240, 241, 260, 275, 280
feudalism, 85, 113, 197, 199
Finnish people, 42, 49, 50, 85, 117
FIRE!! (journal), 219, 299
Fireburn rebellion, 14

First International (Workingmen's Association), 151, 204
Fiske, John, 111, 112
Fitzgerald, Ella, *283*
flags: Ghana, 227; Liberty League, 67–68, 239; UNIA, 226, 239, 252
Fletcher, Ben, 33, 41
Flynn, Elizabeth Gurley, 41, 54, *55*, 194, 325, 326
Foner, Philip, 33–34, 44, 87
Ford, James, 154
Fortune, T. Thomas: on European imperialism in Africa, 178; as journalist, 72–73; and National Afro-American League, 19–20, 71, 165–66; political influence of, 60, 80, 235, 240; "race first" views, 240, 251, 267; writings of, 178, 298
fossil fuel industry, 4, 29, 37, 318, 319
Fourth International, 155
France, 114, 125, 127, 130, 147, 175, 231
Franklin, John Hope, 307
Frederick Douglass Book Center, 118
Freedom Now Party, 324
free love: and class consciousness, 198–200; Comstock laws, 204–8; and contraception, 193–97; criticism of Harrison's stance on, 313; defined by Victoria Woodhull, 204; Harrison's experiences with, 190–91, 202–4, 213; Harrison's influence on, 4, 10, 12, 284, 323–24, 326; Harrison's public speeches on, 197–200; and monogamy, 211–16; and queerness in Harlem, 216–22; and religious repression, 197–98; and white radicals' influence, 200–202. *See also* Black free love politics
free speech, xv, 96, 107, 136, 202, 205
freethinking and freethinkers: Black freethinkers, 110–11, 166; Harrison as, 4, 106–12, 182, 188, 205, 208; *Truth Seeker* (magazine), 107; and women's rights, 201
Freikorps (Germany), 86
Freire, Paolo, 100
Freud, Sigmund, 20, 222

Gaines, Kevin, 177
Garnet, Henry Highland, 71
Garrison, William Lloyd, 78, 323

Garvey, Amy Ashwood: exclusion from Locke's *New Negro*, 289; and Garvey, 231, 252, 279; and Harrison, 191, 279, 325; on monogamy, 192; *Negro World*, 74, 75; Universal Negro Improvement Association (UNIA), 88, 226, 228
Garvey, Amy Jacques, 182, 228, 252, 259, 261, 289
Garvey, Marcus, 3–4, 58, 88, 146; background and education of, 229–30; campaign against, 264, 278; civilizationist orientation, 230; exaggerated statistics, 8; and global Black nationalism, 154; Harrison's influence on, 252–53; Harrison's criticism of, 254–66; on international affairs, 231; and KKK, 263–64, 276–77; and Liberty League, 232; and mail fraud trial, 277–79; *Negro World*, 74, 226; and Philadelphia UNIA revolt, 272–73; as Provisional President of Africa, 181; Tuskegee-based approach of, 230–31; and UNIA creation, 226
Garveyism, 25; Black nationalism, 251–52; foundations of, 226–28; Harrison's influence on, 234–42, 254; "race first" vs. "class first," 242–51
Gates, Henry Louis, Jr., 308–9
General Education Board, 18
General Electric, 29, 121
general strikes, 32, 36, 53, 78, 86, 87, 88, 148, 305
George, Lloyd, 86
German revolution (1918–23), 86
Germany: colonization of Togo, 178–79; in World War I, 66
Ghana, 171, 174, 221, 227
Gilpin, Charles, 275, 300
Gold Coast, 157, 163, 173–74, 227
Goldman, Emma, 134, 194, 325
Goode, Eslanda Cardozo, 23, 58, 63–64, 74, 96, 195–96, 289, 325
Gordon, Maude Lena, 228
Gould, Jay, 29
Gould, Stephen Jay, 5–6
Grand United Order of Odd Fellows, 21, 68, 166, 191, 219
"Great Man" theory of history, 26–27, 253
Great Migration, 69–70, 72

Great Replacement theory, 148
Greece (ancient), 91, 170, 173, 327
Green Corn Rebellion, 86–87, 88, 305
Greenwich Village, 201, 297, 299, 303
Grey, Edgar M., 9, 152, 161, 269, 312
Grimké, Angelina W., 300
Grimké, Archibald, 140
griots, 23, 26, 89, 91–93, 99
Grioversity, Outdoor, 23, 90–93, 92, 95, 98, 99–103, 117, 120, 188, 191, 223, 235, 275, 284, 291. *See also* Outdoor Grioversity
Gumby, Alexander, 218

Haeckel, Ernst, 95, 107, 111
Haeckel, Thomas, 111
Haggard, Rider, 114
hair straightening, 74, 76
Haiti and Haitians, xiv, xv, 11, 123–25, 140, 148–49, 212, 221, 271
Hamer, Fannie Lou, 322
Hampton, Mabel, 219
Hampton Institute, 35, 79, 251, 286
Hansberry, William Leo, 169
Harding, Warren G., 263
Harlem: as Black cultural and intellectual center, 5, 100, 118–19, 216–17; Black political organizations' offices in, 96; and "cabaret life," 296–98; community history classes in, 118; and consciousness of Africa, 161–62; educational spaces (indoor), 117; ethnic voluntary associations in, 22; fraternal societies in, 21–22; free love in, 192; Harrison's activism in, 65–66; Institute for Social Study, 116; Lafayette Theater, 195; Lenox Avenue, 74, 94, 166, 195, 302, 311; Liberty Hall, 268; Liberty League, 232; New York Public Library, 169, 188, 300–301; outdoor oral culture in, 90–99, 92, 98; queer-friendly parties in, 218–19; segregation in, 301–2; sexual freedom in, 218–20; *Survey Graphic* special issue on, 286–87; Temple of Truth, 195
Harlem History Club, 118
Harlem People's Educational Forum, 152
Harlem Renaissance, 25, 282–83, 308–9; misleading claims of, 8

Harlem Renaissance Industry, 25, 300, 303–7, 313
Harlem Tenants League, 22
Harman, Moses, 201
Harper, Francis Ellen Watkins, 178, 298
Harris, LaShawn, 21n60, 207
Harrison, Aida, 191, 310–11
Harrison, Alice, 191
Harrison, Frances Marion, 191
Harrison, Hubert Henry: on accommodationism, 35–36; "Africa first" outlook, 166; African life lecture series, 161; attack on by white mobs, 96–97; on birth control, 196–97; and Black independence, 231; on Black literature, 298–99; as "Black Socrates," 91, 252, 313
"Bolshevism" speech (1919), 85; childhood and education of, 14; on Christianity and Islam, 106–12, 182–83; comparative religion course, 107–8; on compulsory monogamy, 215–16; and Du Bois, 143–48; education and self-education of, 103–4, 112–19; and English literature, 114; erasure of from history, 6–10, 283, 284–85, 304–9, 311–16; and erotica collection, 190; extramarital relationships, 191, 200–201, 211, 279; final illness and death, 188, 310–11; as freethinker, 107–8; on formal education systems, 102, 104–6; and Garvey, 252–53, 254–66, 276–77; and Garveyism, 234–42; on gender roles, 325; on geopolitics, 115–16, 116; knowledge of, 3, 23, 27, 100, 103–4, 118, 284; labor economics course, 113; lectures on sex, 192–93, 193, 194, 197–204; legacy and impact of, 5, 9–10, 188–89, 311, 321–24, 327–28; and Liberty League, 58, 65–72, 66; and Liberty Party, 267–70; on "Manhood Movement," 65–66; materialist analysis of race and class, 45–50; as metaphorical touchstone, 7–9, 25, 27, 47, 255, 280, 283–84, 315, 328; as *Negro World* editor, 240; and New Negro Manhood Movement, 283–84; in New York City, 20–21, 34–36; on *Nigger Heaven* (Van Vechten), 294–95; and Paterson Silk Strike, 55; personality and character of, 97; philosophers studied by, 111; and post office job, 35–36; on poverty, 31; and race consciousness, 57, 132–33; "race first" vs. "class first," 242–51; radicalization of, 2–6, 53–54; on "Renaissance," 295–303, 304; and retreat from Socialism, 52–57, 326; and science, 111–12; on sexuality, 204–11, 222–25; Socialist Party involvement, 39–40, 50–52; street-corner oratory, 90–93, 95; on wartime propaganda, 137–39; White Rose Mission, 61–62; on World War I as "white world war," 126–33
Harrison, Ilva Henrietta, 191
Harrison, Irene Louise "Lin" Horton, 75, 190–91, 224, 236
Harrison, William, 191
Harrison, William Adolphus, 213
Harte, Bret, 114
Hartman, Saidiya, 190
Hausa people, 163
Hawkins, Walter Everette, 110, 289, 300
Hayford, J. E. Casely, 174, 179
Haymarket Square martyrs, 32
Haynes, Cecilia Elizabeth, 213
Haynes, George, 78, 147, 148
Hayti. *See* Haiti
Haywood, William "Big Bill," 41, 52, 54, 55, 132, 326
Hendrickson, Elizabeth Anna, 96, 162, 196, 328
Herndon, Angelo, 154
Herzl, Theodor, 265
Higginbotham, Evelyn, 78–79
Hill, Robert A., 153, 227, 230, 237, 258, 261, 265, 275, 281
Hine, Darlene Clark, 20
history: Black history in school curriculum, 61, 117; erasure of Black history, 167–68; Eurocentric biases, 172–73; "Great Man" theory of, 26–27, 252–53; historical materialism, 45, 133, 249; Nikola Tesla's marginalization in, 316–21; revisionist, 306; textbooks, 7, 30, 32, 167, 282, 305, 307, 315
Hitler, Adolf, 264
Holman, Helen, 96, 196

Holstein, Casper, 328
homosexuality, 191–92, 198, 200, 208, 221. *See also* queerness
Hoover, J. Edgar, 205, 277–78
Hopkins, Pauline, 178, 298
Horton, Irene Louise. *See* Harrison, Irene Louise "Lin" Horton
Houston, Drusilla Dunjee, 169, 325
Howard, William Lee, 208
Howard University, 64, 161
Huggins, Nathan, 282–83, 294, 308
Huggins, Willis N., 116
Hughes, Langston, 28, 31, 163, 192, 219, 221–22, 276, 282, 285; on Black art, 300; new poetic forms of, 297; radicalization of, 307; and "renaissance" ideals, 301–2
Hugo, Victor, 114
Huiswoud, Hermie Dumont, 95
Huiswoud, Otto, 153, 154, 162, 274
human nature, 24, 37, 223, 323; and monogamy, 193, 211, 214, 216
Humboldt, Alexander von, 111
humility, 50, 54, 103, 133, 150, 160–65, 168, 177, 183, 248, 314, 323
humor, 5, 95, 110, 197, 211
Hunter College, 61
Hurston, Zora Neale, 110, 192, 219, 240, 294, 299
Huxley, Thomas Henry, 95, 107, 108, 111
hypersexuality myth, 208–10

Illinois: Chicago, 69, 100; Springfield massacre, 78
imperialism, 115, 116, 120–26, 127, 132, 149–51
India, 4, 67, 76, 130, 150, 155; Jallianwala Bagh massacre, 148
Indigenous peoples: in Africa 174, 178, 181, 187, 212; colonization of by United States, 7, 32, 36–37, 46, 69, 178, 265; and language, 213; and sexuality, 214, 221; and spirituality, 163, 220
industrial education, 79, 230; criticism of, 17–18, 19, 102. *See also* Tuskegee Institute
Industrial Workers of the World (IWW) (aka "Wobblies"), xv, 33–34, 41, 133–34;
"Parting of Ways" cartoon, 42; and working-class solidarity, 41
inferiority myth, 44, 46, 92, 104, 173, 177, 290
Ingersoll, Robert, 40, 107, 108
International Colored Unity League (ICUL), 184–89
internationalism, 67, 76, 120, 148, 150–51, 153, 155
International Longshoremen's Association, 33
interracial contact: literary associations, 285; marriage, 76, 124, 208; socializing, 207, 293. *See also* working-class solidarity
Ireland: Easter Rising, 148, 238; freedom movement, 12, 68, 237–38; Irish Home Rule, 269
Islam: African origin of, 327; Islamic world, 4, 111, 116, 117, 148, 215; Islamophobia, 85, 182; Islamic scholarship, 171; as unifying religion for African diaspora, 108, 182–83, 265, 324; and women's sexuality, 210

Jackson, Anselmo, 65, 233, 234, 246, 328
Jackson, D. Hamilton, 327
Jackson, John G., 110–11, 118
Jamaica, 22, 226, 227, 228, 229, 230, 231–32, 237. *See also* Garvey, Marcus; McKay, Claude
James, Winston, 153, 161, 223, 250, 325
Japan, 77, 116, 317
jazz, xi, 21, 71, 218–19, 282–83, 301
Jewish people, 34, 42, 85, 101, 194, 302
"Jezebel" stereotype, 209, 218
Jim Crow segregation, 15, 35, 72, 208, 209, 243, 257, 263; accommodationism, 264; rationales for, 47. *See also* segregation
Johnson, Charles S., 34, 285, 293, 299
Johnson, Georgia Douglas, 285
Johnson, James Weldon: Black cultural richness in Harlem, 22, 93, 285, 299; Liberty Party, 270; *Nigger Heaven* review, 293, 294; poetry anthology, 290; and Schomburg library committee, 169; *Survey Graphic* anthology, 287
Johnston, Harry, 127–28
Jonas, R. D., 99

Jones, Eugene Kinckle, 78
Jones, Mary Harris "Mother," 39, 41
journalism. *See* media
Joyce, James, 205
Just, Ernest, 5, 169
justice, 47; reproductive, 195; social justice activism, 11
Justice Department, 147, 242

Kadalie, Clements, 148
Kaiser Wilhelm II, 86
Kautsky, Karl, 48, 113
Keats, John, 114
Keller, Helen, 39, 132
Kelley, Robin D. G., 118
Kellogg, Paul, 286–87, 304
Kenya, 228, 241; Giriama movement, 148
Kenyatta, Jomo, 227
Kerensky, Alexander, 84
Keyser, Frances Reynolds, 61–62, *62*, 106–7, 108, 152, 325
Kilroe, Edwin P., 264
Kipling, Rudyard, 14, 114, 176–77, 201
Kirnon, Hodge, 2, 4, 5, 100, 104, 233, 236–37, 260, 276, 312
knowledge: about Africa, 160, 162–63, 236; African folk knowledge, 195; creation, 94–95, 235; griots as storehouses of, 91; Harrison's breadth of, 3, 23, 27, 100, 103–4, 118, 284; Indigenous, 174; Islam's promotion of, 182–83
Kofi, Laura Adorkor, 211, 277
Kollontai, Alexandra, 85, 200
Ku Klux Klan, 17, 43, 276–77; Garvey and, 263–64

labor unions: Brotherhood of Sleeping Car Porters, 250; and industrial sabotage, 54; multiracial, 33; racism within, 250; and violent US labor history, 31–34
Lafayette Theater, 195
land rights, 186–87
Larsen, Nella, 110, 293, 294
Latin America, 4, 76, 121, 149, 153, 221
leadership (bottom-up models), 2, 103
League Against Imperialism, 155
League of Nations, 149, 227
Lenin, Vladimir, xii, 82, *83*, 83–84, 85, 132–33, 149, 151, 153, 200, 281
Lens, Sidney, 32–33, 121, 134
Liberator (magazine), 274
Liberia, 157, 166, 175, 178, 256, 265–66
Liberty Congress of Negro-Americans, 120, 139–43, *141*, 324
Liberty League of Negro-Americans, 3–4, 22, 23, 58, 63, 65–72, *66*, 188; and antilynching bill, 60; on armed self-defense, 71; flag, 67–68; foundations of, 88–89; Independence Day mass meeting, 70–71; influence of, 72, 232–33; internationalism of, 67; and pan-Africanism, 68; shifts toward UNIA, 233–34
Liberty Party, 267–70
libraries: personal, 60–61, 166, 169; public (Harlem), 103, 104, 117, 188, 300, 301, 313; St. Mark's Lyceum, 63
Lincoln, Abraham, 105, 267–68
Lindsey, Lydia, 65
Lippmann, Walter, 137
Liveright, Horace, 285, 287
Lloyd George, David, 125, 137
Local New York (Socialist Party), 45, 50, 55, 242
Locke, Alain LeRoy: "antipropaganda," 290–91; background and education of, 285–86; as Harlem Renaissance figure, 76, 299; on monogamy, 192; on "Negro Renaissance," 303; *The New Negro* anthology, 284, 286–90; on New Negro movement, 25; new poetic forms of, 297; NSHR, 166; on World War I and imperialism, 130, 133
London, England, 171, 174, 183, 213, 229
Longfellow, Henry Wadsworth, 114
Lorde, Audre, 209–10, 221
Louisiana: Black Socialist Party, 43; Brotherhood of Timber Workers, 33, 56; Thibodaux, 32
L'Ouverture, Toussaint, 105, 124
Love, J. Robert, 71
love (in ICUL program), 185. *See also* free love

396 Index

Loving, Major Walter, 59, 97–99, 143, 146–47
Lowell, James Russell, 114
Lusk Committee, 42
Luxemburg, Rosa, 86
lyceums, 63, 91, 106, 113, 165
lynching and mob violence, 16, *17*, 59, 69, 135, 208–9; antilynching activism, 59–60, 263; and castration, 209–10; map of incidents, *18*. See also pogroms

Maangamizi, 221, 336n61
Macaulay, Thomas, 114
Makalani, Minkah, 72, 153
Manhattan (New York): San Juan Hill neighborhood, 21; Twenty-First Assembly district, 75
manhood. *See* Black manhood; New Negro Manhood Movement
Manoedi, M. Mokete, 161, 266, 277
Mansa Musa (king), 171
Marable, Manning, 179
March on Washington (1963), 143, 324
March on Washington Movement (1941), 143, 324
Marley, Bob, 264
marriage: interracial, 76, 124, 208; plural, 212–13, 224–25; polygamy and polygyny, 203, 210, 212–15, 224–25; and sexual freedom, 201. *See also* monogamy
Marriott, David, 209
Martí, Jose, 165
Martin, Tony, 182, 240, 241
Marx, Karl, 37, 38, 48, 106, 113, 315
Marxism, 10, 38, 309, 321. *See also* materialist analysis
Mason, Charlotte, 304
masonic fraternal orders, 21, 166
materialist analysis, 45, 111, 133, 197, 249
"materialistic interpretation of morals," 197
Matthews, Victoria Earle, 60–61
Maxeke, Charlotte, 148
McGuire, George Alexander, 258, 260, 277
McKay, Claude: and Back-to-Africa movement, 274; and Black artists and stereotypes, 294, 297, 300, 302; and Communist Party, 152, 153, 154; on Harlem Renaissance, 307; and Harrison, 97, 190, 222; "If We Must Die," 70; on monogamy, 192; "Negro Dancers," 290; in *Negro World*, 240; and "New Negro" generation, 110; "The White House," 289–90
Mecca, pilgrimage to (*Hajj*), 171
media: Black press, 72–73; journalism in Caribbean, 77; muckraking journalism, 39; New Negro journalism, 233; role in racial prejudice, 46
Melville, Herman, 114
Memphis, TN, 218, 308
Mencken, H. L., 104, 285, 290
Messenger (newspaper), 74, 75, 76, 96, 196, 233, 242; and anti-Garveyism, 249
Mexico, 123, 125, 148, 149, 167
Meyer, Stan, 319
Middle Passage, 73, 221, 336n61
militarism, 180, 251, 307
military intelligence, 24, 58–59, 85, 97–99, 139–40, 144–45, 264, 284
Mill, John Stuart, 12
Miller, George Frazier, 51, 70, 99, 161, 281
Miller, Kelly, 270
Minh, Ho Chi, 228
"miscegenation," 208–9
missionaries: and colonial mindsets, 164–65; and education efforts in Africa, 173–74; paternalistic attitudes of, 162–63
Mississippi, 186, 218; Socialist Party, 43
Mississippi Freedom Democratic Party, 270, 324
mob violence, 69. *See also* lynching and pogroms
Modern School Movement, 102, 107
Mohammedanism, 182. *See also* Islam
monogamy, 192, 200, 211–16; vs. freedom, 202–3; and male-owned private property, 197–99; religious enforcement of, 215. *See also* free love; nonmonogamy
monopolization, 28–31, *30*, 36–37, 121–22, *122*, 132
Moore, Fred R., 207–8
Moore, "Queen Mother" Audley, 186, 228

Index 397

Moore, Richard B.: and African consciousness, 161; as Caribbean immigrant, 21; *The Emancipator,* 246; on Garvey's influence, 229, 232, 236, 263, 274; and Harrison, 100, 118; Institute for Social Study, 117; and League Against Imperialism, 155; and Liberty League, 233; and "New Negro" generation, 110; outdoor oratory in Harlem, 94, 96, 97; and Socialist Party, 57, 152; and Joyce Moore Turner (daughter), 252

Moorman-Blackston, Irena L., 58, 63, 74, 140, 195–96, 233, 325

Moray, Thomas Henry, 319

Morehouse College, 131, 169

Morel, E. D., 175–76, 179

Morgan, J. P., 3, 29–30, 121, 205, 230, 317–19

Morgan, Lewis Henry, 113, 114, 215

Moton, Robert, 140, 230, 288

muckraking journalism, 39

music, 286, 301; blues, 192, 218, 304; jazz, 218–19

Muslim people, 85, 171, 182, 215. *See also* Islam

Myers, Gustavus, 39

National Association for the Advancement of Colored People (NAACP), 22, 23, 52, 60, 61, 77–82, 91, 131, 139–40, 143, 145, 169, 210, 231, 240, 255, 263–64, 271, 287, 293–94, 313, 314; Harrison on, 79–80; "National Association for the Advancement of Certain People," 82

National Association of Colored Women (NACW), 19–20, 60, 61, 62–63, 325

National Brotherhood of Workers of America (NBWA), 33, 89

National Equal Rights League Liberty Conference (1919), 143

National Federation of Post Office Clerks, 34

National League for the Protection of Colored Women (NLPCW), 65, 77–78

National Liberty Congress. *See* Liberty Congress of Negro-Americans

National Negro Business League, 251

National Negro Conference (1909), 79

National Negro Liberty Party (NNLP), 356n44

National Urban League, 20, 34, 77–78

Nation of Islam (NOI), 324

natural selection, 111, 115

Negro Factories Corporation (UNIA), 248

"Negro problem," 28, 44, 114–15, 250, 287

"Negro question," 43–45, 52, 153, 155, 243, 325, 332n38

"Negro Renaissance," 292, 293; and Black working class, 300–303; Harrison's case against, 295–303

Negro Society for Historical Research (NSHR), 71, 130, 166, 251, 326

"Negro subversion," 140, 144–145; *Final Report on Negro Subversion,* 59, 98

"Negrotarians," 299, 300

Negro Women's Campaign Committee, 22, 196

Negro World (newspaper), 74, 146, 233; book reviews in, 175, 240–41; circulation of, 241; "Colored International," 274–75; creation of, 228–29; Harrison's editorship of, 240–41; international reach of, 227; "Poetry for the People," 240, 275; "Race First!," 226; "Race First *versus* Class First," 243; "A Unique Negro" (Harrison), 167; "Wanted—A Colored International," 148–49

Negro Year Book (Tuskegee Institute), 169

New Negro, The (Locke), 76–77, 284, 287–88; omission of militant voices and women, 289

New Negro (magazine), 76; reprints of African articles, 173–74

New Negro Manhood Movement, 72, 232, 246, 280, 325

New Negro Mecca (Harlem), 22, 93, 100, 118, 216, 232, 286

New Negro movement, 3, 20, 25, 58–59, 267–70; focus on common people, 79; global scope of, 82–87; and Harrison's rejection of white pressure, 80–82; and parallels with Russian Revolution, 88, 100–102, 306–7

"New Negro Womanhood," 65, 283, 325

newspapers. *See* media; *names of individual newspapers*
New York City: Board of Education, 114; Bronx Zoo, 4, 160; Carnegie Hall, 132; employment for Black community in, 21; Greenwich Village, 201, 297, 299, 303; housing discrimination in, 21; Manhattan, 21, 75; San Juan Hill neighborhood, 20–21; sexual freedom in, 201; Socialist Party, 44; Tammany Hall, 99, 135, 270, 326. *See also* Brooklyn; Harlem
New York Colored Mission, 21
New York Public Library, 169, 188, 285, 300
New York School of Chiropractic, 116
New York Society for the Suppression of Vice (NYSSV), 205, 207
New York Times (newspaper), xxiii, 95, 97, 290, 311
New York University (NYU), 105
Niagara Movement, 20, 52
Nicaragua, 123
Nietzsche, Friedrich, 110, 112, 321
Nigeria, 157, 160, 175, 212, 221, 227–28, 258
"Niggerati," 299, 300
Nigger Heaven (Van Vechten), 291–95
Nkrumah, Kwame, 227, 324
Nobel family, 121
nonmonogamy, 192, 203, 205, 214–16, 221. *See also* polygamy and polygyny
Normal Teachers College (Howard University), 64
Nugent, Richard Bruce, 190, 219, 222

"obscene," criminalization of, 201–2, 204–5, 223
Odd Fellows. *See* Grand United Order of Odd Fellows
O'Hare, Kate Richards, 39, 134
Oklahoma Socialist Party, 43, 86–87
"old protest psychology," 286, 288, 290, 304
135th Street Public Library, 103, 104, 117, 169, 188, 300–301, 324. *See also* Schomburg Center for Research in Black Culture
135th Street YMCA, 118, 311
O'Neill, Eugene, 275, 297
Opportunity (magazine), 285, 293, 303

Orwell, George, 315
Outdoor Grioversity, 3, 92, 100–102; as preparation for UNIA, 234–35
Ovington, Mary White, 39, 78, 80, 241, 293
Owen, Chandler: *Birth Control Review,* 196; *The Emancipator,* 246; on Garvey, 255, 277; and Independent Political Council, 58; *The Messenger,* 74, 96, 233, 242; and "New Negro" generation, 110; outdoor oratory in Harlem, 99; political influence in World War I era, 131, 134; on race first vs. class first, 244; and Socialist Party, 57
Oyěwùmí, Oyèrónké, 221

Padmore, George, 154
Paine, Thomas, 106, 108–9
Pan-African Congress, 180
pan-African movement, 183, 227, 236; and International Colored Unity League (ICUL), 184; and journalism, 77; of Liberty League, 68. *See also* Garveyism
Panama, 77, 125, 166, 167, 227
Paris Peace Conference (1919), 180
Parker, George Wells, 169
Paterson Silk Strike, 54–55, 55
Patria (newspaper), 165
Payton, Philip, 21
Peabody, George Foster, 207, 287
peonage, 14, 19, 67
Péralte, Charlemagne, 148
Perry, Jeffrey Babcock: as Harrison's biographer, 7, 117, 154, 233–34, 241, 267, 310; on Harrison's legacy, 56, 65, 274, 324; and this book, xiii, xvii–xviii, 12–13; work of to recover Harrison, 11
Peschel, Oscar, 114
Pickens, William, 91, 100, 112, 270, 298
Plaatje, Solomon Tshekisho, 174
Plato, 91, 170, 172, 321
Plessy v. Ferguson, 15
plural marriage, 212–13, 224–25. *See also* polygamy and polygyny
Poe, Edgar Allan, 114
poetry, 240, 275, 290

pogroms, 17, 34, 68–71, 76, 85, 87, 142, 291, 305
police brutality, 40, 43, 68
poll taxes, 15. *See also* voting rights
polyamory, 219. *See also* free love
polygamy and polygyny, 203, 210, 212–15, 224–25
Poor People's Campaign, 143
postal work, 34, 229, 249
poverty, 1, 10, 27, 31, 104, 112, 218, 250, 311, 318, 326–27; impact of on Harrison, 103; and working-class white people, 330n31
Powell, Adam Clayton, Sr., 58, 63, 139, 207–8
press. *See* media
Prince Hall Masons, 166
prisons, 87, 131–32, 134, 182, 206; labor in, 31
privilege, 33, 52, 236, 287, 304, 333n58
proletariat: African Americans as, 45–46, 133, 163, 199, 214, 236; Harrison on, 48, 56–57, 129; revolution, 38, 151–52; and religion, 108
propaganda: anti-Communist, 82; and art, 290–91, 304; *Birth of a Nation* (film), 123; in colonial Africa, 175–76; racial, 271, 273; Socialist Party, 50; UNIA, 256; US surveillance of, 58–59, 99; wartime, 136–40, 142
prostitution, 207, 213–14, 294
Przybyszewski, Stanislaw, 205
Puerto Rico, 146, 155, *158*, 165; sterilization of women in, 206
Puritans, 4, 178, 197–98, 201, 204, 224
Pushkin, Alexander, 166

queerness: in Harlem, 216–20; in precolonial Africa, 220–22; same-sex relationships, 216–22

race consciousness, 57, 132–33, 152, 243
"race first" doctrine, 25, 57, 60, 66, 68, 226, 234–42. *See also* Africa First doctrine
"race riots." *See* pogroms
racial hierarchies: anthropological approaches, 46–47; attempted scientific justification for, 114–15, 172, 215–16

racial uplift ideology, 60, 65, 78, 177, 179, 218, 231
racism: debt peonage, 14–15; in early twentieth-century United States, 14; hypersexuality myth, 208–10; political disenfranchisement, 15; racial oppression vs. class exploitation, 242–51; scientific, 104, 114–15. *See also* lynching; pogroms
radicalism, 2, 4–5, 13, 99–100, 233–34, 281, 288, 306, 309; historiographical suppression of, 315; race and class, 12, 65, 323, 326; sexual, 24, 191–93, 204, 208, 223
Rahming, Alexander, 161
railroad construction, 29–30
Rainey, Gertrude "Ma," 192
Randolph, A. Philip: and Brotherhood of Sleeping Car Porters, 250; "class first" vs. "race first," 242–44; *The Emancipator*, 246; on Garvey, 232, 255, 277; on historical perspectives, 323; and March on Washington Movement, 143; *The Messenger*, 74, 96, 196, 233; and "New Negro" generation, 110; and outdoor oratory in Harlem, 3, 58, 59, 99, 100; political influence in World War I era, 75, 131, 134; and Socialist Party, 57
Randolph, Lucille, 58, 75, 96, 196
Rand School of Social Science, 113
rape and sexual assault, 16–17; accusations of, 59–60, 208–10, 223
rationalism (freethought movement), 106–12
Ratzel, Friedrich, 114
Rawlins, Elliot, 118
Razafinkarefo, Andrea (Andy Razaf), 289, 300
Reconstruction (historical era), 15, 43, 61, 187, 267
Red Cross, 82
"Redemption Song" (Marley), 264
Red Summer of 1919, 69, 87, 305, 309
Reed, John, 39, 84–85
religion: African gods, 220; in conflict with science, 109; Deism, 108–9; dogma, 4, 106, 107, 208; and monogamy, 215; and sexual repression and punishment of women, 210. *See also* Christianity; Islam

Renaissance School of Negro History, 284–85, 296–98, 304, 308–9
"renaissance" trope, 284
Republican Party, 267–68
Republic of New Afrika, 186
Restell, Madame, 205
Rhodes, Cecil, 177
robber barons, 28–31, *30*, 121–22, *122*, 132
Roberts, Charles "Luckey," 71
Robeson, Eslanda, 63, 211
Robeson, Paul, 63, 192, 211
Rockefeller, John D., 3, 29, *29*, 77, 196, 207, 230, 317
Rogers, J. A.: *As Nature Leads,* 322–23; Harrison's influence on, 118, 169, 241; on Harrison's legacy, 5, 7, 75, 305, 314; and "New Negro" generation, 110, 298
Rome, 171, 266
Roosevelt, Franklin D., 140
Roosevelt, Theodore, 20
Rose, Ernestine, 300, 325
Rosenwald, Julius, 77, 207
Ross, Loretta, 195
Rousseau, Jean-Jacques, 108
Rubinow, Isaac, 44, 45, 332n38
ruling class, 30, 46–47, 95, 108, 151, 224, 278, 306, 315
Russell, Charles Edward, 39
Russian Revolution, 82–85, 125, 151, 304–5; and Bolshevik Party, 82–85, 125, 133, 151, 199–200, 305; and education, 84–85; and sexuality, 199–200; Trotsky at the modern circus, 100–101; and workers' power, 84
Rustin, Bayard, 324

sabotage, industrial, 41, 53–55, 56
Sam, Alfred Charles "Chief," 251, 281
Sanger, Margaret, 39, 50, 194–95, 196, 325
Santo Domingo, 136, 149
Sarbah, John Mensah, 174
Savage, Augusta, 191, 240, 300, 325
Schomburg, Arturo Alfonso, 24, 71, 113, 165–69, 241, 251, 314, 327; personal library of, 169

Schomburg Center for Research in Black Culture, xix, 169, 324
Schopenhauer, Arthur, 112, 213, 321
Schuyler, George, 110, 250
Schweinfurth, Georg August, 114
science: in conflict with religion, 109; Harrison's critique of, 172, 216, 319–21
scientific racism, 104, 114–15
Scott, Emmett J., 140, 142, 147, 148
Scottsboro boys, 118, 154
Seattle general strike, 87–88
Second International, 151
Sedition Act, 134, 143
segregation, 35, 51–52, 72, 79, 81, 123–24, 154, 208, 306, 322. *See also* Jim Crow segregation
Seifert, Charles, 233, 279
Sekyi, Kobina, 173–74
self-defense, 3, 68, 71, 97, 270, 324
self-determination, 67, 80, 85, 124, 133, 151, 153–54, 165, 186, 287
Senegal, 227, 265
"separate but equal" doctrine, 15
separatism, 251. *See also* land rights
Serge, Victor, 86
Sex at Dawn (Ryan and Jethá), 216
sex education, 4, 192–96; and Margaret Sanger, 50
sexual assault and rape, 16–17, 146, 208–10, 222–24
sexuality: criminalization of, 4; and morality laws, 206–7; repression of, 204–11. *See also* free love; obscenity charges
sexual liberation and freedom, 10, 12, 190, 199, 200, 204–5, 210, 219, 221, 223, 321–22, 324
Shaw, George Bernard, 114
Shaw, M. A. N., 142
Sherfey, Mary Jane, 207
Sierra Leone, 157, 166, 174, 175, 227
Silent Protest Parade (1917), *70*
Simmons, William (KKK), 263
Sinclair, Upton, 39
single tax, 208
Sinn Fein Party, 238, 269. *See also* Ireland

Index   401

"slacker raids," 147
Slater, George, 43, 49
slavery: chattel, 46, 49; and Christianity, 109–10; legacy of, 222; as *Maangamizi*, 221; map of European transatlantic enslavement, *158–59*; and paternalistic attitudes, 162–63; slave trade, *158–59*; slave women and contraception, 195; and so-called Middle Passage, 73, 221, 336n61
soapbox oratory. *See* Outdoor Grioversity
social control, 137, 138, 209, 321, 330n31
Social Democratic Party, 39
socialism, 22, 24, 28, 38–39, 44–45, 48, 51, 72, 80, 82, 95, 113, 120, 133, 186, 192–93, 199, 208, 244, 247–49, 288, 309, 325; and anti-Black racism, 8; vs. Southernism, 43, 49, 56
Socialist Party of America, 38–41; antiracist resolution (1903), 43; and biological arguments for racism, 52–53; Black Socialists in, 242–51; and Black workers, 43, 49–51; "class first" ideology, 235–36; growing conservatism of, 53–54; in Harlem, 22; Harrison's organizational contribution to, 50–52; and "Negro question," 44, 52–53; and race politics, 42–45; on race, 248
Socrates, 91, 172
solidarity: class, 56, 57, 235, 244; racial, 65, 150, 152, 231, 234, 237, 243–44, 271
South Africa, 76, 133, 148, 150, 163, 174, 179, 227
South African Native National Congress, 174
"Southernism," 43, 49, 231
Southern Tenants Farmers Union, 154
soviets (elected workers' councils), 82, 84–86, 200
Soviet Union, 116, 125, 200, 306, 311. *See also* Comintern; Lenin; Russian Revolution
Spanish-American War, 81
Spencer, Herbert, 95, 111, 112, 114
Spengler, Oswald, 295
Spingarn, Joel, 139, 140, 144–45, 287
Stalin, Joseph, 83, 306
Stalinism, 151, 306
Standard Oil, 29, 121, 123, 317

Stanley, Henry, 157
St. Benedict's Lyceum, 9, 113, 165
St. Croix, 14, 20, 125, 157, 213
sterilization, forced, 196–97, 206
Stirner, Max, 112
St. Louis World's Fair (1904), 160
St. Mark's Lyceum, 9, 63, 113
Stoddard, Lothrop, 115, 148
Stokes, Rose Pastor, 134, 152, 281
Storey, Moorfield, 78
St. Prix, Joseph, 272
Stribling, Thomas, 297
strikes, 32, 36, 39, 53, 86–88, 148, 305. *See also* labor unions
St. Thomas, 118, 165
subservience of Black people, 35, 49, 110, 144
"Subsidized Sixth," 246–47
suffrage, women's, 23, 61, 63–64, 67, 106, 142, 146, 204
Sunday, Billy, 108
"sundown towns," 17, 34, 69
Sunrise Club, 104, 202
Survey Graphic (magazine), 286–87, 288
syndicalism, 53

"Talented Tenth," 2, 73, 78–79, 81, 181
Tammany Hall, 99, 135, 270, 326
taxation, 178; of church property, 4, 107; poll taxes, 15; single tax, 208
Taylor, George Edwin, 270, 356n44
Tennessee, 32, 135
Tennyson, Alfred, 114
Terrell, Mary Church, 65, 207
terrorism, 16–17. *See also* lynching; pogroms; trauma
Tesla, Nikola, 25–26, 316–21, 362n33; as touchstone, 316, 320
textbooks, 7, 30, 32, 167, 282, 305, 307, 315
theater, 20, 116–17, 201, 218, 293
Thurman, Wallace, 93, 219, 300
Toomer, Jean, 294
Toote, Frederick A., 259, 260, 271–72, 277
touchstone: Hubert Harrison as metaphorical, 7–9, 25, 27, 47, 255, 280, 283–84, 315, 328; Nikola Tesla as, 316, 320
trauma, 3, 37, 156, 224

Trinidad, 148, 221, 227, 241

Trotsky, Leon, 83, 85, 101, 200, 281, 299, 306

Trotter, William Monroe: on civil rights and equality, 20, 35, 60, 65, 68, 99; *Guardian*, 20; and Harrison, 71–72; and Liberty Congress of Negro-Americans, 323–24; and Liberty Party, 270; and national gathering for civil rights, 139; on "race first" concept, 235, 240, 251, 269

Truth Seeker (magazine), 95, 107, 109

Tubman, Harriet, 11, 61

Turner, Henry McNeal, 162, 185, 211, 251

Turner, Joyce Moore, 21, 75, 94, 252

Turner, Nat, 211

Tuskegee Institute, 3, 35, 49, 154, 169, 229, 236, 238; and imperialism, 179

"Tuskegee Machine," 36, 72, 99, 147, 230, 231

Twain, Mark, 107, 114, 211–12

Uganda, 163, 220, 265

Uncle Sam (character), 31, 86, 122–23, 125, 210, 278, 284, 306

Uncle Tom (character), 43, 276; as "white man's negro," 59, 247

UN Declaration on the Rights of Indigenous Peoples, 187

unemployment, 32–33, 37

United Civic League of Black Harlem, 78

United Mine Workers, 33

United States: imperialism of, 120–26; Justice Department, 147, 242; Marines, 124–25, 149, 271; Military Intelligence Bureau (MIB), 139, 142, 146–47; State Department, 256, 264, 281; War Department, 143, 144, 145. *See also* Uncle Sam (character)

Universal Negro Improvement Association (UNIA), 8, 22, 88, 96, 154, 181, 226; African Communities League, 181; Black liberation flag, 239; Black Star Line, 227, 229, 237, 249, 257, 354n6; civilizationist orientation, 230; convention (1920), 257–58; Domingo's contribution, 228–29; Harrison's influence, 254; Liberty Halls, 239; Liberty League's influence, 232–34; Negro Factories Corporation, 248; Philadelphia internal revolt, 271–73; Universal African Legion, 265; Washington's influence on, 229–30; youth sections, 270–71

US Army, 36, 122; intelligence tests, 104; imperialist occupations, 125; World War I, 119, 145, 146–47

US Marines, 124–25, 149, 271

US State Department, 256, 264, 281

US Supreme Court, 15, 206, 267

US War Department, 143, 144, 145

Vanderbilt, Cornelius, 29

Van Sertima, Ivan, 167

Van Vechten, Carl, 291–95, 304; new poetic forms, 297

Vesey, Denmark, 81

Vienna revolution (Austria), 85–86

Villard, Oswald Garrison, 78, 80–81, 285

violence: attack on Harrison by white mob, 96–97; rape, castration, and sexual assault, 16–17, 24, 59–60, 208–10, 223–24, 278; Springfield, IL massacre (1908), 78. *See also* lynching; pogroms

Virgin Islands, 125, 157, 222, 326–28. *See also* St. Croix

Vodou (Haiti), 11

Voice (newspaper), 58, 64, 73–77; bankruptcy, 239; conflict in leadership of, 233; as New Negro journalism, 233; and New Negro politics, 74–75

Volney, Constantin-François, 108, 173

Voltaire, 108

von Krafft-Ebing, Richard, 215

voting rights. *See* elections

Walker, A'Lelia, 58, 196, 218–19

Walker, Edwin C., 201–3, 205, 222

Walker, Madam C. J., 58, 75, 76, 196, 218

Walrond, Eric, 240–41, 285, 293

Wa Menza, Mekatilili, 148, 211

Wardenclyffe Tower, 317–18

Washington, Booker T., 3, 19, 34–36, 49; and colonizers in Africa, 178–80; and Garvey, 229–30. *See also* Tuskegee Institute

Washington Park Forum (Chicago), 100

Index   403

Watkins, Lucian B., 240, 289, 300
Wells, Herbert George, 114
Wells-Barnett, Ida B.: on Africa, 178; anti-lynching campaign, *18*, 19, 209; background and education, 59–60; and Du Bois, 314; and Garvey, 254–55; Garvey movement, 235, 251; and Harrison, 325;, influence of, 73; legacy of, 185; and women's suffrage, 63
West, Cornel, 185
West Indies, 71, 77, 114, 184, 258
Westinghouse, George, 31
Wheatley, Phillis, 61, 62
White, Andrew Dickson, 108, 109
White, Walter, 293, 299
"The White Man's Burden" (Kipling), 176–77
White Rose Home for Colored Working Girls, 21, 60–62, *62*, 325
white supremacy, 14; and Africa, 177; and erasure of African history, 172–73; intellectuals, 115; and intelligence testing, 104; and resentment of Black success, 284; and white privilege, 236. See also Great Replacement theory
Williams, Fannie Barrier, 65
Wilson, Woodrow, 3, 20, 123–25, 136–37, 231, 326; League of Nations, 149
Wobblies. *See* Industrial Workers of the World (IWW)
Women's Business League of Greater New York, 63
Women's Loyal Union, 60
Women's Political Association, 22, 196
women's suffrage movement, 23, 61, 63–64, 67, 106, 142, 146, 204
Wonderful Ethiopians of the Ancient Cushite Empire (Houston), 169

Woodbe, George Washington and Annie, 43
Woodhull, Victoria Claflin, 204
Woods, Clyde, 218
Woodson, Carter G., 169, 220, 314
Wordsworth, William, 114
Work, Monroe, 169
workers' state and control, 39, 125, 186, 306
working class, 31–34, 41, 44, 48–49, 56, 87, 128; Black, 33–36, 73, 245, 300–303; German, 86; interracial and international solidarity, 33, 41, 48, 56–57, 67, 86, 235, 243–44, 246–47, 271; Russian, 83, 85, 306
World War I, 126–33; and "Negro subversion," 59, 140, 144–45; and New Negro movement, 58–59, 235, 247–48; postwar uprisings, 148; Socialism in United States during, 243–44; propaganda during, 133–39; and US imperialism, 120–26; as "White War," 126, 147, 155, 287–88; and working-class movements, 86–88
World War II, 67, 130

X, Malcolm, 6, 185, 228, 324, 328

Yard, Lionel, 279
Yiddish press, 265
Yoruba, 157, 163, 171, 214, 221
youth, 1–2, 27, 105, 156, 226, 240, 242, 270, 302, 326–27

Zapata, Emiliano, 148
Zimbabwe, 173, 221, 227
Zimmerman, Angela, 154
Zimmerwald Conference, 151
Zinn, Howard, xii, 120, 132, 291
Zionist ideology, 264–66

www.ingramcontent.com/pod-product-compliance
Lightning Source LLC
Chambersburg PA
CBHW020119240426
43673CB00038B/530